THE LAW OF TREES, FORESTS
AND HEDGEROWS

AUSTRALIA
Law Book Co.
Sydney

CANADA and USA
Carswell
Toronto

HONG KONG
Sweet & Maxwell
Asia

NEW ZEALAND
Brookers
Wellington

SINGAPORE and MALAYSIA
Sweet & Maxwell Asia
Singapore and Kuala Lumpur

THE LAW OF TREES, FORESTS AND HEDGEROWS

CHARLES MYNORS
FRTPI, MRICS, IHBC,
of the Middle Temple, Barrister

London • Sweet & Maxwell • 2002

Published in 2002 by
Sweet & Maxwell Limited of
100 Avenue Road, Swiss Cottage,
London NW3 3PF
(http://www.sweetandmaxwell.co.uk)
Typeset by YHT Ltd, London
Printed in Great Britain by MPG Books, Bodmin

Reprinted 2002
Reprinted 2003

No natural forests were destroyed to make this product;
only farmed timber was used and replanted

A CIP catalogue record for this book is available from
the British Library.

ISBN 0-421-590 408

Acknowledgement

The front cover shows two of the four mulberry trees growing around the fountain outside Middle Temple Hall—planted to celebrate the Golden Jubilee of Queen Victoria. The smaller one, on the left, was removed some time after the War; the other is still flourishing, and was retained as part of the recent reordering of Fountain Court to mark the new Millennium.

Cover photograph © Anthony Kersting

Thanks to the Honourable Society of the Middle Temple for supplying the photograph.

To Janet and Elizabeth,
with love
and immense gratitude

Foreword

By Professor Sir Ghillean Prance, FRS, VMH,
Science Director, Eden Project, Cornwall; Visiting Professor, Reading University; formerly Director, Royal Botanic Gardens, Kew

Whether you have a single tree near the boundary of your garden or own a forest or a woodland or even have a hedgerow, you will find this book both useful and interesting.

Trees are an essential element of life on this planet for their environmental role as absorbers and storers of carbon. They are also beautiful and useful in so many ways. But, anyone who has tried to remove a tree from their property is soon made aware of the laws and regulations involved. Parking in a friend's garage in London is most difficult, and requires great skill, because of the plane tree in front on which there is a preservation order. The early chapters of this book show some of the negative aspects and dangers of trees caused by falling branches, wandering roots or even poisonous leaves and fruits. Trees have caused an amazing number of disputes between neighbours when they grow near boundaries.

This most thoroughly researched book cites a huge range of cases involving all aspects of trees. To the non-lawyer, like me, it is amazing to read how trees, the main focus of my scientific research over the last forty years, have led to so much litigation.

Trees can be dangerous things, which is why the Royal Botanic Gardens, Kew, employs two separate tree gangs that constantly monitor the condition of the trees and prune off any branches that are likely to break off and endanger the visitors. Kew is also constantly giving advice about the behaviour of roots which can cause so much damage to buildings and pavements when trees are planted in the wrong place. A lesson from this book is that if you own trees, inspect them rigorously and frequently to see that they are not likely to fall in a storm or shed branches or intrude unduly on a neighbour.

Further, if you want to remove a tree for any reason get the correct permission, to avoid a run in with the authorities or the law. This can be frustrating but it is worthwhile. I knew a tree in my garden, in the conservation area of Lyme Regis, was dangerous and rotten within, but it still took several weeks to obtain the necessary permit to remove it. There are many hints about how to proceed in such cases in this useful book.

In addition to the cautionary tales emerging from the examples cited here, much of this book is good practical advice to tree growers. It is very thorough in its coverage – from forest and forestry law to plant health laws, planning, environmental assessment and preservation orders. Would-be foresters will find the chapter on the financing of woodlands and forests and grant systems most useful.

This is not just a history of cases but a book that is full of good practical advice. I have certainly learned a lot from reading it, and commend Charles Mynors for the extensive research that has gone into its preparation. Read this book and you might avoid a lot of unnecessary litigation.

Ghillean Prance

Preface

"Now what are the grounds for distinction [in law] between a tree and a bit of a house? Is it that a house is used, and a tree is not? Is it because a house is always built, and a tree is not always planted (it would be absurd to distinguish between planted and self-sewn trees). Is it because a tree is uncommonly lovely, and a house is commonly unlovely? Or is it because people are supposed to know about houses and not about trees?"

I was struck some years ago by the above comment, in Tony Weir's admirable *Casebook on Tort*.[1] Trees are unlike anything else in that they take years, sometimes centuries, to create, but only a few minutes to destroy; they are usually beautiful, but at the same time can be a source of major problems; they are stationary, but cause problems by their movement; they are part of the land on which they were planted, and yet can encroach into other land; and they may outlive many generations. In short, to use a phrase that occurs in two separate judgments[2], trees are subject to "a secret and unobservable operation of nature" – in other words, they grow.

All of these features have led to them being subject to a unique legal framework – a wholly uncoordinated mixture of private and public law; of common law and statute. The focus of the common law has gradually shifted, over a number of centuries, from the original concern over who owned the rights to exploit trees, as an economic resource, to the problems of trees (and more recently hedges) on boundaries, hazardous trees and highway trees. Forestry has generated its own statutory code, more or less untouched by the courts, following the two world wars, while the emphasis has shifted to the preservation of trees for amenity (as part of the planning system), and later as a habitat for other forms of wildlife. But this has resulted in a disparate body of law that has not been collected in one place since 1914, when the last comprehensive book was written – and the law has changed quite a bit since then.

I have therefore endeavoured to find and deal with all recent and current legislation, and more or less all the reported judicial decisions since 1900 (as well as some earlier ones that are still relevant, and one or two unreported ones) which deal in any way with trees, and to place them in some form of legal framework. It is important not to place too much emphasis on the decisions of the lower courts, even when they concern similar facts. Thus it has recently been noted in the House of Lords that "precedent is a valuable stabilising influence in our legal system.

---

[1]   8th edn, Sweet & Maxwell, 1996, p. 217.
[2]   *Noble v Harrison* [1926] 2 K.B. 332, and *Wringe v Cohen* [1940] 1 K.B. 229; see **5.5.1**.

But, comparing the facts and outcomes of cases in this branch of the law [negligence] is a misuse of the only proper use of precedent, viz to identify the relevant rule to apply to the facts as found." Nevertheless, I hope that the collection of cases referred to here will be of value, as an illustration of problems which have occurred in the past and to guide those who are faced with new ones in the future.[3]

This book should be of use to all whose work brings them into contact with trees and hedges – including landowners, surveyors, architects, planners, highway engineers, landscape architects, arboricultural consultants and tree contractors – and to barristers, solicitors, citizens' advice bureaux and all who advise on the law. Inevitably, with such a disparate potential audience, some of what follows may seem obscure, some may be blindingly obvious; a lawyer may not need to be told the difference between a settlement and a trust; a surveyor should know the difference between settlement and subsidence. Also, I have attempted to make each chapter more or less self-explanatory, but that is bound to lead to some slight repetition. On both counts, I apologise if I have not got the balance right.

The book generally attempts to state the law as it was at Easter 2002, but looks forward to some future new legislation (notably that relating to high hedges, and how to remove them, and to rural hedgerows, and how to preserve them). I considered waiting until these matters were resolved, but decided that that might result in this book never being finished at all.

In general, the whole book refers to the law as it is in England and Wales. The Forestry Act applies equally to Scotland, so it seemed artificial to exclude references to practice north of the border in Part III. The code on tree preservation orders and related matters, described in Part IV, strictly applies only south of the border, but there is a very similar system in operation in Scotland. There is, on the other hand, as yet no legislation there dealing with hedgerows (equivalent to that described in Part V of this book).

There is probably no lawyer who could with truth claim to be an expert in all the areas of law touched upon in this book; and I certainly make no such claim. Nor do I pretend to be infallible. So I would therefore welcome any suggestions for ways in which this book might be improved in future editions – and extra material that should be included, or existing material that could more helpfully presented in some other way.

Inevitably, in undertaking a work of this kind I have relied heavily on the knowledge and experience of many others far more learned than I in their various fields. I am particularly grateful to Peter Annett, Steve Clark, and Dr Giles Biddle, each of whom read through substantial parts of this work in draft, and made a number of helpful comments; to David Ainger and Adrian Cooper for their comments on Part II, the general law; Mike Ellisson (of Cheshire Woodlands) and Caroline Davis (of the Tree Council), on hazardous trees; Gordon Inglis (of the Forestry Commission), on forestry generally; Tony Court (of Place Campbell), on the taxation of forestry; Paul Hardy, on criminal matters; and Stephen Crane, on hedgerows.

---

[3]   *Jolley v Sutton LBC* [2000] 1 W.L.R. 1082, per Lord Steyn at p. 109E.

My thanks are also due to all the others who in all sorts of ways have assisted in the progress of this work – sadly, I have not kept a complete record of all of them (I did not think it would take so long to complete). But thanks at least to David Harte, at the University of Newcastle, for discussing ideas for this book and general encouragement right at the beginning; to Nigel Macleod QC and Brian Greenwood for sponsoring my application for a grant from the Alexander Maxwell Trust (and of course to the trustees for actually giving me a grant!); and to Andrew Newcombe, Philip Petchey and others in chambers for moral support; to the librarians in the Middle Temple (to whom, incidentally, I owe the photograph on the front cover); to Rebecca Atkins, for a very thorough job of editing the whole text; and, not least to Sir Ghillean Prance, for contributing such a generous foreword.

In addition, I am acutely conscious that I have probably (perhaps sub-consciously) absorbed the ideas of many other authors, commentators and lecturers over recent years; I have undoubtedly learnt a great deal more by writing this book than anyone else will by reading it. As well as those already mentioned, I should perhaps single out NDG James, John Perlin, Oliver Rackham and Christopher Stone; I have enjoyed their work as much as I have admired it, and hope I have absorbed a little of their learning. And I am still nowhere near being an arboriculturist, so I have been fortunate in working, in various capacities, with a number of real tree experts, including many of those named above, Roy Finch, Ted Green, Jim Harrisson, Chris Neilan and Bryan Wilson.

And I am very grateful to almost all of the above, and to many others, for patiently answering telephone queries on all sorts of obscure points over many years; I hope that the appearance of this book (at last!) is some form of reward.

I am grateful too to Lyndsay Walker and her various predecessors and colleagues at Sweet & Maxwell, for their faith in this project at the outset, and their forbearance as the time to completion stretched from months into years. Forbearance was also what I required – and generally, at least, received – from my clerks and clients and from the parishes of Worcestershire, who often had to wait longer, sometimes much longer, than I would have liked. To them, especially, my apologies and many thanks.

But most of all, I am hugely indebted to my family, and especially to Janet and Elizabeth, for having to live with this project for longer than I would have liked, and very much longer than they would have liked. There is no way in which I could have finished it without their support; but I feel that I have been as a result a poor husband and father, and have let it get in the way of normal life far too much. The fact that the result may be of some small use to others will probably be of little consolation, as will the fact that it is dedicated to them, with love and immense gratitude. As for David, I hope that he will one day understand why I have been locked away in my study for so much of the time.

CHARLES MYNORS

2 Harcourt Buildings, Temple, EC4

June 2002

Alexander Maxwell Law Scholarship Trust

Contents

Full Table of Contents

Abbreviations

The following abbreviations have been employed (in addition to those conventionally used to refer to law reports) largely in order to shorten as far as possible the references in the footnotes to statutes, statutory instruments and Government guidance.

Circ	Circular
DEFRA	Department of the Environment, Food and Rural Affairs
DETR	Department of the Environment, Transport, and the Regions
EIA	Environmental Impact Assessment
EIA Regulations	EIA (Forestry) (England and Wales) Regulations
FA	Forestry Act
HA	Highways Act
HR	Hedgerows Regulations
IHT	Inheritance Tax
MAFF	Ministry of Agriculture, Fisheries and Food
OLA	Occupiers' Liability Act
PPG	Planning Policy Guidance Note
SI	Statutory Instrument
TAN	Technical Advice Note (Wales)
TCP	Town and Country Planning
TCPA	Town and Country Planning Act
TCP(T) Regulations	Town and Country Planning (Trees) Regulations
TPO	tree preservation order
WCA	Wildlife and Countryside Act.

References to "Model Orders" are to be interpreted as explained at **16.3**.

Except as noted, references to "the Minister" "the Secretary of State" in **Part III** of the book (forestry) should be interpreted as explained in **11.2.1**; and references to "the Secretary of State" in **Part IV** (trees of particular value) as explained in **16.2.8**.

Table of Cases

Table of Statutes and Measures

Table of Statutory Instruments

Table of International Treaties

Table of European Directives

Table of Government Guidance

Table of Model Orders

Part I

Introduction

"And God said, 'Let the water under the sky be gathered to one place, and let dry ground appear'. And it was so. God called the dry ground 'land', and the gathered waters he called 'seas'. And God saw that it was good.

"Then God said, 'Let the land produce vegetation: seed-bearing plants and trees on the land that bear fruit with seed in it, according to their various kinds'. And it was so. The land produced vegetation: plants bearing seeds according to their kind, and trees bearing fruit with seed in it, according to their kinds. And God saw that it was good."

– Genesis 1, vv 11–12.

Chapter 1

Introduction

1.1 In the beginning . . .

It seems that trees, and the law relating to them, have always caused problems. At the very beginning, the first law concerning trees, indeed at that time the only law concerning anything, led to all kinds of difficulties:

"You are free to eat from any tree in the garden; but you must not eat from the tree of the knowledge of good and evil, for when you eat of it, you will surely die."[1]

At the start of the second millennium BC, the rapid depletion of timber stocks so alarmed government officials in Babylon that Hammurabi issued an edict that "When I see damage done to a single bough, I will not suffer the man charged with that crime to live."[2] Some while later, Tacitus noted that the penalty under the old German laws for someone who dared peel the bark off a standing tree was to have his navel cut out and nailed to the part of the tree which he had peeled and then to be driven round and round the tree until all his guts were wound about its trunk.[3] Nor were the clergy immune from misdemeanours: a statute had to be passed in 1307[4] specifically to prevent rectors from felling trees in graveyards. And even as recently as 1867, the penalty for "breaking a piece of ivy to the value of 1d" was 14 days imprisonment with hard labour.[5]

But not all cultures have been so harsh. In the highlands of Scotland, for example, woodlands were historically to some extent treated as common property, so that the freemen of the district were entitled to take kindling wood and timber to use in making and repairing ploughs and spears – but only so long as this did not lead to uncontrolled depredation.[6] And the authoritative Dr Oliver Rackham, on whom depends much of our understanding of the history of woods and forests in Britain, points out that the well-known "fact" that forests were in the middle

---

[1] Genesis 2 vv 16,17; compare *Mills v Brooker* [1919] 1 K.B. 555.
[2] *A Forest Journey: the Role of Wood in the Development of Civilisation*, John Perlin, Harvard University Press, 1991, p. 46; current legislation, with lower penalties, is in the Forestry Act 1967.
[3] See now Town and Country Planning Act 1990, s. 210.
[4] *Ne rector arbores in cemeterio posternat* (Edward 1. c. 35); see now Care of Churches and Ecclesiastical Jurisdiction Measure 1991, s. 6.
[5] *Labouring Life in the Victorian Countryside*, Horn.
[6] *On the Other Side of Sorrow: Nature and People in the Scottish Highlands*, Hunter 1995.

ages preserved for hunting by severe laws and barbarous penalties is completely unsustainable as truth.[7]

Times have changed. But trees – and hedges – still cause problems, particularly between warring neighbours, and between those who value them as a communal asset to be preserved and those who simply perceive them as a nuisance. As will be seen, both "preservation" and "nuisance" have become terms of art, and the subject of much litigation.

This Chapter accordingly starts with a brief outline of the reasons for the ongoing conflict: the value of trees (see **1.2**) and the problems they cause (**1.3**). In the light of that, it examines (at **1.4**) the way in which successive governments over the years have attempted to intervene to secure what has been seen as the public good – which itself is constantly shifting. It also, incidentally, provides a guide to the remainder of the Book. And, finally, some cautionary tales to discourage those who may be tempted to venture too eagerly into the courts.

1.2 The value and importance of trees and hedges

1.2.1 Amenity value

Perhaps the most obvious value of trees – at least, as seen from the perspective of someone living in the developed world at the start of the third millennium AD – is as a visual amenity.

First and foremost, then, a tree may be, indeed usually is, a thing of great beauty and interest in itself, regardless of its surroundings – as immortalised in sentimental verse[8] and as evidenced by the burgeoning market in "tree books" appearing each year.[9] And the very fact of a tree's longevity, its normal life greatly exceeding that of a human being, means that it is a direct and tangible contact with both the past and the future.

Secondly, trees and hedges are also the key element in many if not almost all rural views, providing their basic skeletal structure – whether it be in the form of hedgerows or as isolated trees in otherwise open agricultural landscapes, in small woodlands or magnificent forests, or in formal parklands. This has long been recognised by artists, as well as by landscape architects such as Capability Brown (who was of course always willing to add to what nature had provided by planting trees in locations chosen so as to maximise aesthetic appeal); and it is additional to the value of belts of trees and woodland as shelter for animals and cover for birds.

But just as significant, perhaps, is the contribution made by trees to urban and suburban landscapes, improving attractive buildings and views, and helping to hide unattractive ones. They are a major component in gardens, parks and other open spaces. They are an important element in some of the most important street

---

[7] *Trees and Woodland in the British Landscape*, Rackham, first revised paperback edition, 1993, Weidenfeld & Nicholson, p. 23.
[8] Including, of course, the couplet "I think that I shall never see a poem lovely as a tree" – a sentiment that is certainly true of the remainder of the poem (by Joyce Kilmer) of which that is the opening.
[9] Of which one of the best remains the *International Book of Trees*, written by Hugh Johnson in 1973; more recent examples include the idiosyncratic but splendid *Meetings with Remarkable Trees* by Pakenham (Weidenfeld, 1996), and the somewhat selective but visually sumptuous *Silva* by Archie Miles (Ebury Press, 1999).

scenes – and in many of the more ordinary ones they are vital. Hence the considerable literature on "amenity trees" that has grown up in the last fifty years or so – including the publications produced by or for central Government, from *Trees in Town & City*, produced by the Ministry of Housing and Local Government in 1958, to the series entitled *Research for Amenity Trees* produced by the Department of the Environment in the 1990s.[10]

A further aspect of the amenity value of trees is their role as reminders of history. The oldest trees known to exist in Britain, principally yews, are over 1,000 years old.[11] But very many trees are older than any people now living, or even their parents; and their age provides a link to past ages that is itself of value.

"Amenity" has been defined in the courts as "pleasant circumstances or features, advantages"[12]; and one of those must surely be trees.

1.2.2 Economic value

Directly related to their amenity value, of course, is the economic value of trees – a house with an attractive garden, enhanced by strategically located trees, or set in a tree-lined boulevard, may be worth considerably more than a similar one with no such assets (although there may also be some reduction due to the cost of upkeep). The value of a hotel or office complex can also in some cases be enhanced by good landscaping, including mature trees, as may that of building land. And it is noteworthy that some of the highest property values in many towns are in what are often called the "leafy suburbs".

But amenity is by no means the only perspective. Trees have in the past been valued primarily as timber – that is, as an economic resource in their own right, not merely as part of the value of property.

A moment's thought will demonstrate that, without timber, civilisation would not have developed at all, let alone in the way it did. In Britain, throughout its history until the nineteenth century, and in many parts of the world even today, wood has been universally employed for building (lintels and beams, floors and ceilings, windows and doors); for furniture; for transport (wheels, carts, early ships and, later, trains); for industry (tools of all kinds, water wheels, windmills, looms and pit props); to facilitate some of the pleasures of life (barrels for beer and wine, musical instruments, printing presses and paper); and, last but not least, to make fire, without which colder climates could not be inhabited or numerous other materials extracted or processed.

It is thus hardly surprising that, over and over again, and in all parts of the world, land has been systematically deforested, from ancient Mesopotamia[13] through to modern Africa.[14] And this relates as much to the underwood that was used for routine requirements as it does to the timber trees whose loss was more visible. Thus, in England, the Romans arrived to find a land that had already been

---

[10]   As well as technical works such as *Trees in the Urban Landscape: Principles and Practice*, Bradshaw *et al.*, Spon, 1995.

[11]   Many are in churchyards; but in a number cases the tree is older than the earliest church on the site, suggesting that it may be a survivor from a pre-Christian antiquity. Compare this with the oldest in the world, a bristlecone pine in the White Mountains of California, which is around 5,000 years old.

[12]   *Re Ellis and Ruislip-Northwood UDC* [1920] 1 K.B. 343, per Scrutton L.J. at p. 370; see also **15.6.2**.

[13]   See, in particular, *A Forest Journey*, Perlin (above), and the sources cited in it.

[14]   See daily papers passim.

stripped of much of the wildwood that once grew there[15]; and the process continued throughout the following two millennia – although, again, Rackham points out that much of the supposed history of the depredation of woodland for industry or ship-building is demonstrably false.[16]

It remains true, however, that trees are still a significant economic resource, of use (at least in Britain) principally in the building and furniture industries, but also for a wide variety of other purposes.

1.2.3 Trees as an ecological resource

In more recent times, trees have begun to be valued not just in economic terms or as an amenity, but as an ecological resource.

All trees, even (or perhaps especially) those in urban centres, help to filter the air we breathe, and are an important part of the bio-chemical cycle of life. And the massive deforestation currently taking place in other parts of the world is often alleged to cause significant changes to global climate patterns.

More immediately, it is being realised that trees provide a valuable habitat for other species: birds, bugs and beetles; other plants, including lichens; and, by no means the least important, fungi. This is true almost as much in the case of dying and dead trees as it is with living ones; and foresters are learning to retain many veteran trees, even though hollow or partially decayed, which would previously have been thought to be of no further value.[17] But even a small suburban tree may be home to a family of rare birds; and trees and hedgerows in agricultural areas provide valuable shelter for livestock.

Trees are thus not just green lumps on sticks, as shown in architects' drawings; whether or not they are attractive in themselves, they are also complex eco-systems in their own right, and part of the larger eco-system of the area in which they are planted or allowed to grow.

Hedgerows, too, are now valued not just as a visual amenity, and part of the traditional appearance of the countryside, but as part of the natural biodiversity; and both the EC and the UK Government is committed to protect them for that reason.[18]

1.2.4 Trees and human activity

Given the variety and extent of man's indebtedness to trees, just touched upon above, it is not surprising that they have been part of the cultural landscape throughout history. As a result, Rackham identifies six principal ways in which trees now interact with human activities.[19]

The first three involve trees growing more or less naturally. Historically, the most significant of these have always been woodland and wood-pasture. Woodland is simply land on which trees have arisen naturally, managed by the art of woodmanship to yield successive crops in perpetual succession – making use

---

[15] Rackham (above), p. 40.
[16] Rackham, pp. 85, 96. Indeed, it is hard to avoid the suspicion that some, at least, of Perlin's work – although informative and eminently readable – is an example of what Rackham contemptuously describes as "pseudo-history".
[17] See, for example, the various publications produced in connection with English Nature's Veteran Trees Initiative, published in 2000.
[18] *Biodiversity: the UK Steering Group Report*, HMSO, 1995; and see **24.3.2**.
[19] Rackham (above), p. 4.

of the facility that most British trees have of growing again after being felled. Wood-pasture involves grazing animals as well as trees. The third category is non-woodland trees in hedgerows and fields.

The other three involve trees growing in circumstances which have been consciously chosen – that is, either the trees have been deliberately planted or they have arisen naturally but been allowed to remain – so as to lead to some form of economic or other advantage. The oldest of these, which has existed for centuries, is the growing of trees on a commercial basis in orchards, as a source of fruit. Orchards are generally outside the scope of this book – although the legal principles within it will, in principle, be as applicable to trees in orchards as to any others.

More recently, and certainly since Jacobean times, trees have been grown in towns as an amenity – lining the squares of Georgian Bath, the streets of Victorian Kensington and the squares and crescents of the garden cities and new towns[20] – as well as the numerous suburban streets that followed them. This has arguably become much more significant in recent decades, particularly in the light of urban sprawl leading to greater appreciation of gardens and open spaces in towns, suburbs and villages, and of the trees within them and adjacent to highways.

And, finally, much the most recent of these traditions is the planting of trees, usually limited to one or two species, on cleared ground. The trees are then tended, and in due course harvested like any other crop; their stumps are left to die, and the land is re-used – either for more trees, or for some other purpose. This is effectively the practice known as "forestry".

1.3 Problems caused by trees

1.3.1 Introduction

In the light of all these positive features of trees, it might be thought that there is unlikely to be any problem with allowing them all to grow for their full natural lifespan – or, in the case of trees grown commercially for timber, until they reach their maturity. Unfortunately, of course, it is not as simple as that. Trees cause, or are perceived to cause, considerable harm – and even where that harm has not yet taken place, there is always the possibility, or at least the fear, that it will happen in the future. And where they do not cause "harm" as such, their very presence may be extremely inconvenient to those on whose land they are growing.

This is a book on the law, not a manual on trees.[21] Nevertheless, in order to consider the legal principles underlying the approach of the courts towards liability for trees, it is necessary to consider briefly some of the reasons why trees cause problems. These are very broadly in three categories:

- problems due to the position of a tree[22];

---

[20] See *Trees in Towns*, Land Use Consultants (Dept of the Environment, Research for Amenity Trees, No. 1, 1993), p. 5.

[21] For that, see (for example) *The Arboriculturalist's Companion*, NDG James, Blackwell, second edn, 1990, reprinted 1998.

[22] See **1.3.3**.

- problems due to the natural characteristics of a healthy tree[23]; and

- problems due to defects in a tree.[24]

It must not be thought that the law will in all cases provide a remedy to those affected; and, even where it does, the availability of that remedy may be countered by the existence of restrictions (such as tree preservation orders[25]).

For further information, appropriate specialist works should be consulted. On harm caused by roots, for example, see *Tree Root Damage to Buildings*, by P G Biddle,[26] and *Tree Roots and Buildings*, by Cutler and Richardson.[27] And on the failure of trees generally, see in particular the three technical manuals published by the Department of the Environment and the Forestry Commission.[28]

1.3.2 Terminology

It is also important to be clear at the outset as to the meaning of terms used – in this book, in reported judgments of the courts, and elsewhere. Unfortunately the relevant words and phrases are not always used consistently or logically; and their usage also seems to have changed over the last two centuries; the older judgments should be read accordingly.

Injury is defined in the *New Oxford Dictionary of English*[29] as "the fact of being injured; harm or damage", *harm* as "physical injury, especially that which is deliberately inflicted", and *damage* as "physical harm caused to something in such a way as to impair its value, usefulness or normal function". The distinction between "injury", "harm" and "damage" is thus not entirely clear or logical, but in practice seems to be – at least in current English usage – that people and animals may be injured, and vehicles and other objects damaged, but all may be harmed. Otherwise the three terms seem to be more or less synonymous.

As to the above definition of "harm", in the context of harm caused by trees, there may be a crucial distinction between that caused deliberately (or, one might add, more likely negligently) and that for which there is no human cause; but both are harm. A child hit by a falling tree is harmed, regardless of whether or not the harm was negligently inflicted. And "damage", in the above sense, should of course be clearly distinguished from "damages", which are "a sum of money claimed or awarded in compensation for a loss or injury" – which is why the word "harm" has generally been used throughout this book in preference to "damage".

Danger is, so far as relevant, defined in the Dictionary as "the possibility of suffering harm or injury" or "a person or thing that causes or is likely to cause harm or injury"; *risk* is "a situation involving exposure to danger" or "the possibility that something unpleasant or unwelcome will happen". *Hazard* is "a danger or risk" and "a potential source of danger" (as in "a fire hazard"). Every tree is thus hazardous, in that it might cause harm – it might fall (for example, in an exceptionally severe gale), and its roots might harm foundations of buildings if they are allowed to be too close. But the risk (or probability) of such harm may be

---

[23] See **1.3.4**.
[24] See **1.3.5**.
[25] See **Chapters 15 to 19**.
[26] Willowmead Publishing, Wantage, first edn, two vols, 1999.
[27] Longman, fourth impression, 1998.
[28] See **5.7.4**.
[29] Clarendon Press, Oxford: first edn, 1998.

small – either because, for example, the tree is young and in good condition, or because it is in the middle of a forest, far from anyone likely to be hit even if it were to fall – and the tree could then not be said to be dangerous. The meaning of "dangerous" is considered further in the context of hazardous trees.[30]

Safety, by contrast, has two meanings: it is defined as "the condition of being protected from or unlikely to cause danger, risk or injury". Thus, to the extent to which a tree is safe, a person walking underneath it is also safe. However, since every tree is hazardous, there is unfortunately no such thing as an entirely safe tree.

Finally, a *target* is used here, as in much of the relevant literature,[31] in the sense of "the person, animal, structure or object that is at risk of being injured, harmed or damaged by a tree" – even though, obviously, neither the tree itself or (usually) its owner has any wish to harm any specific person or object.

1.3.3 Problems due to the position of a tree

Probably the most common type of complaint that arises as a result of the presence of a tree is not that it is in any way dangerous or defective in itself but simply that it is in the "wrong" place – from the point of view of the complainant. Either it has been planted (or has seeded itself) too close to something, such as a road, a neighbour's land or a building, or (more commonly) that it has become too close to it as it has grown. Or of course simply that the tree is growing on land which is "required" for some other purpose.

The first category of problem under this heading is that of branches growing so that they overhang paths and roads. That is, the trees are (or may be) perfectly sound, but they simply get in the way of high vehicles[32] or people.[33] Branches may also block out light and air[34] or a view, and may harm crops growing beneath them.[35] And the mere existence of branches in a particular location may also be inconvenient or a source of irritation – particularly to the owners of neighbouring land[36] – and thus lead to much unpleasantness and, in extreme cases, litigation.

The second principal category of problem that may be caused by trees as they grow is damage by roots to buildings, walls and paths. This is the result of roots causing soil movement, which in turn damages foundations and other structures.[37] This too is highly likely to lead to litigation, or at least the threat of litigation, where a tree is on one plot of land (or on highway land) and the structure that is damaged is on a neighbouring plot.

Where harm is caused to a building or structure that is on the same land (and thus in the same ownership) as the tree itself, however, that will lead to an insurance claim rather than litigation – since the owner of the building obviously cannot sue himself. Such a claim might itself lead to litigation, of course, but that is beyond the scope of this book.

[30] See **5.10.1**.
[31] See, for example, *Principles of Tree Hazard Assessment and Management*, Lonsdale (the Stationery Office, London, first edn, 1999), p. 145.
[32] *Hale v Hants & Dorset Motor Services* [1947] 2 All E.R. 628, 46 L.G.R. 55; *British Road Services v Slater* [1964] 1 W.L.R. 498, E.G. May 30 (oak).
[33] *Westley v Hertfordshire County Council* (1998) unreported.
[34] *Unwin v Hanson* [1891] 2 Q.B. 115.
[35] *Smith v Giddy* [1904] 2 K.B. 448.
[36] *Lemmon v Webb* [1894] A.C. 1.
[37] *Middleton v Humphries* (1913) 47 ILT 160; *Butler v Standard Telephones and Cables Ltd* [1940] 1 All E.R. 121; and many subsequent decisions (see **1.4.3 and 3.5**).

The third type of problem is simply that a tree or hedgerow is not in any way harmful in itself, but is merely growing on land where someone wishes to carry out some activity (normally built development, but possibly clearance for agriculture) that is incompatible with the tree or hedgerow remaining there. That generally leads to disputes and litigation only where the plants affected are of particular value, and protected in some way; in that case, the role of the law is principally to provide a mechanism for the resolution of the competing claims of all concerned.

1.3.4 Problems due to the natural characteristics of a tree

The second principal category of problems caused by trees is that a tree may cause harm by virtue of its natural characteristics.

So, for example, the fall of a tree or a branch may be due not to a defect in the tree but to an entirely natural cause such as, notably, a very severe gale. Trees have an inherent "safety factor", whereby they are usually able to withstand much stronger mechanical loading than occurs under normal conditions – if this were not so, every tree would fall down in a storm. However, in exceptionally severe conditions, the safety factor of a tree may be exceeded, leading to failure[38] – thus the great gale of October 1987, whilst leaving unscathed many trees that were probably extensively decayed, uprooted many that were perfectly healthy.[39]

Less dramatic, but more common than trees falling or shedding branches, will be people (or occasionally animals) tripping, skidding, slipping or falling, as a result of a nearby tree.

This may occur because the ground becomes covered either with actual bits of the tree – such as branches, leaves, soft fruit (particularly berries) or hard fruit (such as cones) – or with things falling from it – such as aphids,[40] and bird lime. Danger may also occur because trees lead to an area of ground being in shade, which may encourage the growth of moss and algae, leading in turn to an increased risk of slipping and falling.

A further cause of harm is tripping over uneven surfaces, caused by distortion of the ground as a result of pressure from growing tree roots or from changes in moisture levels due to the presence of roots. The movement of the ground, or direct pressure from roots, may also cause any walls above or nearby to distort, leading to instability of buildings and structures.[41] And it is possible for a tree that is blown over by a storm to take a wall with it, or for the ground surrounding the base of the trunk to be lifted along with the root plate beneath.

Nor should it be forgotten that any problems resulting either from items that have fallen onto the ground or from unevenness in the ground itself, from whatever cause, are of special concern to those with impaired mobility (including in particular the elderly and very small children) and those with partial or no sight.

Further risks, especially but not exclusively to children, arise when a tree can be climbed. The most obvious is that the climber will fall, and suffer injury or death. Less likely, but not unknown, is that a tree will be used to gain access to

---

[38] *Hudson v Bray* [1916] 1 K.B. 520 (elm; act of God); *Bruce v Caulfield* (1918) 34 T.L.R. 204, CA (poplar)
[39] *Principles of Tree Hazard Assessment and Management*, Lonsdale, 1999, p. 24.
[40] *R v Test Valley BC, ex p. Anne* [2001] EWHC Admin 1019; see **3.9.3**.
[41] *Elliott v Islington LBC* [1991] 1 EGLR 167.

something dangerous, such as, in particular, electricity wires.[42] And, even if a tree is not climbed, if it comes into contact with wires it will conduct electricity, so that anyone touching it is at risk of electrocution – particularly where the tree is wet. All of these risks are also of particular concern to those working in trees.

A further hazard that is widely known, but relatively rarely encountered in practice, is that arising from the fact that many plants and fungi are poisonous, or contain elements that are poisonous, including belladonna,[43] yew,[44] laburnum, cherry laurel, privet and rhododendron.[45] The ingestion of any of these by humans could in theory cause serious stomach disorder and, in extreme cases, death; but the likelihood of that in practice depends on the amount that is swallowed and the general health of the victim. Some parts (for example, the seed in the berry of a yew or the seed pod of a laburnum) are more likely to cause problems than others – but even they may have to be ingested in quantities that are in practice highly unlikely.

Poisonous plants and trees may well cause problems, however, where they are eaten by animals – it is, for example, well known that yews are poisonous to horses, sheep and cattle; although it seems that it is not so much the growing leaves that cause the problems as the wilting foliage after it has been cut. Rhododendrons, too, cause some problems. And acorns are apparently bad for cattle,[46] although a staple diet for pigs.

Less commonly appreciated than the dangers of poisonous plants, but possibly of greater significance in practice (at least in the context of humans), are the problems that may arise as a result of allergic reactions to contact with plants. Pollen, sap, and leaf and fruit hairs may all trigger allergic reactions in those suffering from allergies to the chemicals concerned.

Further, thorns may cause puncture wounds or scratches of more or less severity. Each of these may in certain cases cause discomfort, illness or even death. It is unlikely that harm of this kind will arise by "accident" – at least to any significant extent. That is, it is easy to prick one's finger on a bramble, but to inflict serious harm requires throwing oneself into a thicket of brambles, which is unlikely. There are, however, certain species of plants (such as the yucca) which exhibit very prominent sharp points at the end of rigid leaves, and indeed any trees and shrubs with thorns, which can cause injuries – especially if in unsuitable locations, for example, at eye height next to paths.

Other than in the case of falling trees and branches, the actual danger from the above sources is real, but relatively slight, notably because the harm likely to be suffered is small – the way to stop people slipping on a path is to sweep the leaves, not to go to court. In practice, therefore with the notable exception of a series of cases at the end of the nineteenth century relating to animals being poisoned by

---

[42] *Buckland v Guildford Gas Light & Coke Co* [1948] 2 All E.R. 1086.
[43] *Glasgow Corpn v Taylor* [1922] A.C. 44.
[44] See footnote 48 below.
[45] Other common poisonous plants include black bryony, cowbane, cuckoo pint, foxglove, green hellebore, hemlock, henbane, ivy, larkspur, lily of the valley, mistletoe, monkshood and thorn apple; and, of course, fungi too may be poisonous.
[46] Even elephants may suffer from too many acorns, as has been found at Longleat: see article in *Wiltshire Times*, October 22, 1999.

yews,[47] and the two already noted relating to children being killed,[48] there has not been much litigation under this heading.

1.3.5 Problems due to defects in a tree

The most spectacular type of problem – although by no means the most common in practice – is where a whole tree falls, causing death or injury to humans or animals, or damage to property, either on the way down or as it lands. Less rare, although still not in fact particularly frequent, is where parts of a tree, notably branches or parts of branches or cones, fall to the ground, with similar results on a smaller scale.

There are a number of causes for such falls. A tree (or some of its branches) may fall as a result of wind pressure or snow loading or, indeed, in some cases when there is no wind at all.[49] This may be due to decay either in its root system, which may lead to the whole tree falling,[50] or elsewhere in the tree, causing the loss of branches; and that decay may be visible on external inspection of the tree or it may be entirely hidden.[51] However, both in below-ground and above-ground failures, decay is a less important factor than growth-related defects – such as, in particular, weak forks or junctions, which may lead to branches falling, or insufficiently developed root systems. And of course a tree may fail simply through old age, so that it falls either in a storm[52] or in good weather.[53]

A further cause of failure is as a result of works that were carried out to a tree in the past – either to the tree itself,[54] or to the ground around it,[55] or to other trees nearby.[56]

The failure of a whole tree or of a significant part of it will, in general, only be a problem if it hits someone or something – which is relatively unlikely, unless the fall is onto a much-used area such as a major road; but if the tree or part of it does hit something, it is likely to cause substantial damage, or injury or even death. And, just as frequently in practice, or at least in the reported cases, further problems may arise if the fallen material is not cleared out of the way promptly.[57]

Either situation is likely to give rise to litigation – on the basis that the state of a tree is not in itself the fault of its owner, but the owner, or the person responsible for its maintenance, should be aware of its state and should take action if it is, or seems to be, dangerous.

---

[47] *Wilson v Newberry* (1871) 7 Q.B. 31, *Erskine v Adeane* (1873) 8 Ch. App. 756, *Crowhurst v Amersham Burial Board* (1878) 4 Ex D 5, *Ponting v Noakes* [1894] 2 Q.B. 281, *Lawrence v Jenkins* (1873) 8 Q.B. 274; see **3.4.4**.

[48] *Glasgow Corpn v Taylor* [1922] A.C. 44, and *Buckland v Guildford Gas Light & Coke Co* [1948] 2 All E.R. 1086; see **5.3.3**, **5.6.2**.

[49] *Noble v Harrison* [1926] 2 K.B. 332 (beech).

[50] *Cunliffe v Bankes* [1945] 1 All E.R. 459 (elm); *Caminer v Northern and London Investment Trust* [1951] A.C. 88, H.L. (elm); *Knight v Hext* [1980] 1 EGLR 111, CA (beech).

[51] See **5.7.3**.

[52] *Brown v Harrison* (1947) E.G., 28 June, CA (horse chestnut); *Williams v Devon County Council* (1966) 200 E.G. 943 (species unknown).

[53] *Shirvell v Hackwood Estates* [1938] 2 All E.R. 1, CA (beech).

[54] *Chapman v Barking and Dagenham LBC* [1997] 2 EGLR 141 at p. 146B (horse chestnut).

[55] *Mackie v Dumbartonshire County Council Western District Committee* (1927) 91 J.P. 158 (elm); and *Lambourn v London Brick Co* (1950) E.G. 146 (elm).

[56] *Sheen v Arden* (1945), unreported; see **5.5.2**.

[57] *Hudson v Bray* [1917] 1 K.B. 520, *Williams v Devon County Council* (1966) 200 E.G. 943.

1.4 The role of the law

1.4.1 Introduction

It will be obvious, given their advantages and disadvantages, both of which can be substantial, that trees will inevitably give rise to conflict in certain circumstances. And where there is potential or actual conflict, the law is not far behind – negatively, to enable the parties to resolve a dispute that has arisen; but, more positively, to provide a framework of duties and rights to regulate the conduct of all concerned so as to minimise the possibility of a dispute arising in the first place.

In practice, the focus of attention has shifted with the passage of time, as different issues have come to the top of the list of priorities.[58] Faced with each new issue, the courts have considered what should be the way forward. And, once the principles have been settled, either through decisions of the higher courts which are then binding by virtue of the common law doctrine of precedent, or through the intervention of Parliament in the form of new legislation, those principles are then applied up and down the land in county courts and criminal courts to the new facts of particular disputes.

This section attempts to outline briefly some of the principal issues that have emerged as being of concern.

1.4.2 The ownership of trees and hedges

The first question to be dealt with by the law was who actually owns trees. If they are of value, who should profit? And if they cause problems, who should be liable?

There has been a constant stream of litigation over many centuries dealing with these issues. In earlier times, of course, land ownership was less fragmented than it is now, so that many trees were on large estates; hence the various cases on the ownership of timber[59] and underwood[60] on land subject to various forms of settlements and leasehold interests – and indeed the numerous decisions as to what was properly categorised as timber.[61] Essentially, many of the disputes resolved around the issue of whether the economic benefit of the trees, as timber, shelter or ornament, should go to the owner of the land or to the occupier of it for the time being. And they should be seen in the context of the gradual development of the principles of property law through the nineteenth century prior to their emergence in more or less their current form in 1925.[62]

The general rules as to ownership are considered in **Chapter 2**; those relating to trees on boundaries are at the start of **Chapter 3**; and those relating to highway trees at the start of **Chapter 6**.

1.4.3 The duties of owners

By the start of the twentieth century, the rules as to ownership were more or less clear; and the focus of attention moved to boundary problems, which are the

---

[58] For a snapshot of the position at 1678, see *Sylva, or a Discourse of Forest Trees*, by John Evelyn, and in particular Book III, Chapter VI, *Of the Laws and Statutes for the Preservation, and Improvement of Woods and Forests.*

[59] See in particular *Honywood v Honywood* (1874) L.R. 18 Eq. 306.

[60] *R v Inhabitants of Ferrybridge* (1823) 1 B. & C. 375.

[61] See **2.3.3**.

[62] And see now the Trusts of Land and Appointment of Trustees Act 1996.

subject of **Chapter 3**. There had been such disputes, of course, for many centuries[63]; but with increasing population, and increasing density of development especially in towns, land was divided into ever-smaller parcels with a corresponding increase in the potential for disputes. *Crowhurst v Amersham Burial Board*[64] was the most important of a sequence of cases towards the end of the nineteenth century regarding livestock being poisoned by the branches of overhanging yew trees. *Lemmon v Webb*,[65] also decided over a century ago, remains the leading case, establishing both the basic rules as to the ownership of boundary trees and the entitlement to take action in relation to encroaching roots and overhanging branches.

Lemmon v Webb itself concerned an overhanging branch; surprisingly, the first case relating to encroaching roots was not decided until 1939.[66] After the war, however, there was an increasing flow of such litigation, particularly following the abnormally dry summers of 1976 and 1977; and the stakes had been raised considerably a few years earlier when, in 1971, insurers decided to provide subsidence cover under domestic buildings policies. Before that there had been almost no litigation, but there were 21,400 claims in 1976, rising to a peak of 60,000 claims in 1991; it is not surprising that liability for root damage became a major issue. The law was finally more or less settled in *Solloway v Hampshire*,[67] and although cases continue to be fought, they largely apply established principles to new factual situations.[68]

Litigation in any of the above circumstances generally does not depend on proof of "fault", and is therefore likely to take the form of a claim for nuisance.[69]

A more recent variation of the boundary dispute is that centred on high hedges. This is the subject of **Chapter 4**, which highlights how little help the law can offer at present, and looks at one possible way forward, likely to be promoted by the Government at some suitable opportunity in the next few years.

The next problems to be dealt with were the relatively rare ones of trees causing harm either by virtue of their natural characteristics or because of some defect. As has been noted already,[70] problems in the first category rarely reach the courts as the harm caused is not sufficient to make litigation worthwhile, and to prevent it is usually straightforward. If it were necessary to start an action, however, it could be framed either as a claim in nuisance or under the principle in *Rylands v Fletcher*,[71] or in negligence or under the Occupier's Liability Acts,[72] or both.

Problems caused by defective and hazardous trees,[73] on the other hand, may well lead to litigation, because they are likely to be unexpected, and the results may be catastrophic. An action against the owners in such a case will usually take the form of a claim in negligence or, where the victim is on the same land as the tree, under the Occupiers' Liability Acts. The principles involved are the subject of

---

[63] See **1.5** for an early example.
[64] (1878) IV Ex D 5; see **3.4.5**.
[65] [1895] A.C. 1, H.L., upholding [1894] 3 Ch. 1, CA; see **3.2.1** (ownership) and **3.6** (abatement).
[66] *Butler v Standard Telephone and Cable Co Ltd* [1940] 1 All E.R. 121; the only previous root decision being the Irish case of *Middleton v Humphries* (1912) XLVII ILT 160 (see **3.5.3**).
[67] (1981) 79 L.G.R. 449, [1981] 1 EGLR 129; see **3.5.4**.
[68] One exception to this is *Delaware Mansions v City of Westminster* [2001] 3 W.L.R. 1007, H.L., upholding [2000] B.L.R. 1, [1999] 3 EGLR 68, CA, overturning (1998) 88 B.L.R. 99; see **3.5.6**.
[69] See **3.3**.
[70] See **1.3.4**.
[71] See **3.3**.
[72] See **5.4**.
[73] See **1.3.5**.

Chapter 5. In terms of the historical development of the law relating to trees, the law of negligence is a relative newcomer – the leading case of *Donoghue v Stephenson*[74] not being decided until 1932 (which explains why the only case of any significance to be based on a claim in nuisance, as opposed to negligence, was *Noble v Harrison*,[75] decided six years earlier).

The rule that has emerged is thus simply that owners are liable to take "reasonable" care for the safety of those who may be affected by the results of defects in their trees. Here there has been some confusion in recent years, with cases such as *Chapman v Barking and Dagenham LBC*[76] suggesting a high degree of liability on the part of owners, in contrast to the important decision of the House of Lords in *Stovin v Wise*[77] which tends to imply that owners may properly balance claims on their time and resources.

In practice, those problems arising from defective trees that have resulted in litigation, at least in the higher courts, have almost all concerned highway trees – that is, either trees on highway land or those on land fronting a highway. This is not surprising, given the involvement of insurers in such cases and the potentially serious nature of any resulting harm. In addition, the principles of the common law (which apply to highway trees as to others) have been overlaid over the last century and a half with a surprisingly large, and ill-assorted, collection of statutory rules, now all in the Highways Act 1980. The resulting law, which is not entirely logical, is explained at **Chapter 6**.

It should not be forgotten that the principles discussed in each of these Chapters are derived from the decisions of the courts over many years. Not all of those decisions are consistent; and they have not addressed all of the potential problems. In particular, each decision deals directly only with the particular facts that gave rise to the litigation concerned – although the judgments in the Court of Appeal and the House of Lords in particular do sometimes attempt to grapple with the wider issues at stake. However, some common themes emerge, and the text here seeks to derive from them some sort of coherent pattern.

It should also be borne in mind that they may seem to have been written principally from the perspective of the owner of a tree, to consider what (if any) liability applies in any particular situation. They should, however, be of equal use to those on the receiving end of problems caused by a tree, in order to enable them to decide whether the owner has failed in discharging that liability, and whether as a result there is a possibility of some form of legal action to redress the resulting harm.

1.4.4 The general law: other provisions

There are numerous other provisions of the law which relate indirectly to trees – that is, to all trees, and not just those of particular amenity value.

Thus there have been passed since the middle of the nineteenth century a whole raft of statutory codes regulating the activities of the various statutory undertakers – from the Railway Improvement Act 1871 (still in force) to the Telecommunications Act 1984. Most of these contain some provisions that are relevant to trees, primarily aimed at preventing dangerous trees impeding the

---

[74] [1932] A.C. 562, H.L.; see **5.2.1**.
[75] [1926] 2 K.B. 332; see **5.1.2**.
[76] [1998] 2 EGLR 141, upheld in CA (unreported).
[77] [1996] A.C. 323, H.L, overturning [1994] 1 W.L.R. 1124, CA; see **6.4.6**.

operation of the service concerned. This is the subject of **Chapter 7**.

Problems with trees also arise in connection with other types of litigation, notably as to the liability of professional advisers, contractors carrying out building developments, and insurers. The principles underlying such disputes are the same as those governing negligence actions generally, but, for completeness, the reported decisions of the courts are here brought together in **Chapter 8** – if only by way of illustrating some of the practical problems that can arise in practice.

Chapters 3 to 8 are principally concerned with liabilities relating to trees that are growing, and to which no works are proposed (other than, possibly, works to avoid or minimise those very liabilities). Where works are proposed to existing trees, for whatever reason, all sorts of other issues arise, not least in relation to the need for various consents, and the requirement to ensure the safety of all concerned. And in addition to planning controls, there are a wide variety of general designations and controls which need to be considered by those carrying out works to trees, such as the restrictions – under both European and domestic legislation – on works affecting rare species of plants and, more significantly, the habitats of protected species of animals, birds and insects.[78] The protection afforded to sites of special scientific interest[79] and environmentally sensitive areas[80] may also be relevant to trees and hedgerows. All these matters are considered in **Chapter 9**.

The planting of new trees, on the other hand, gives rise to relatively few legal problems; such as they are, they are the subject of **Chapter 10**.

Each of those two Chapters is largely a miscellany of cross-references to other provisions of the law which do not relate directly to trees, but which impinge indirectly on works to them – including legislation relating to health and safety[81] and criminal damage.[82] For further details, appropriate specialist texts should be consulted.

1.4.5 Forestry

It has already been noted that, throughout recorded history, all the major civilisations have faced the problem of preventing the depletion of tree stocks.[83] The protection of tree cover in Britain has been the subject of laws in earlier times, but this has been of limited value. Until the twentieth century, however, such protection was designed to prevent the excessive felling of naturally occurring woodland rather than to provide for its replacement.

Thus the planting of *areas* of trees, as opposed to individual trees in parkland, was rare up until the sixteenth century; and even in the seventeenth century was principally a gentleman's hobby – not least as a result of the publication in 1664 of John Evelyn's influential work *Sylva*.[84] In Scotland, and probably in Ireland, where planting was enjoined by statute, the area of plantations overtook that of

---

[78] See **9.3**.
[79] Under section 28 of the Wildlife and Countryside Act 1981, and the Conservation (Natural Habitats etc) Regulations 1994. See also PPG 9 (England), Annex A.
[80] Under section 18 of the Agriculture Act 1986.
[81] See **9.5**.
[82] See **9.6**.
[83] See **1.2.2**; and *A Forest Journey*, Perlin (above), and the sources cited in it.
[84] In which he stated that "nothing less than an *universal Plantation of all the sorts of Trees* will supply, and well encounter the defect".

native woods at some time in the eighteenth century; but that did not happen in England until the twentieth century.[85]

England was, after all, lucky in that – unlike previous world powers, which had had to rely on local woodlands, soon exhausted – it had a far-flung empire, from which it could extract timber at will. It also emerged as a dominant economic power sufficiently late that it was able to rely on coal and iron as the supply of timber dwindled. It is thus perhaps unsurprising that it was not until after the First World War that serious attempts were made to ensure the creation and maintenance of a sufficient national stock of timber.

Such concerns led to the passing of the Forestry Act 1919, which set up the Forestry Commission. That led, in due course, to the emergence of hundreds of acres of conifers, which clothed previously bare hillsides (particularly in the upland regions of Britain) and apparently caused the loss of a number of ancient woods. The 1919 Act was amended a number of times[86] before being replaced by the Forestry Act 1967, which was a consolidating measure. The 1967 Act has itself subsequently been amended,[87] but not radically.

This body of legislation, which has been the subject of remarkably little examination or clarification by the courts, is examined in **Chapter 11**. In association with the growth of commercial forestry, there has arisen over the years a statutory code of controls over the import, export and movement of timber, and the health of seeds, cones and cuttings.

A further issue which has always given rise to particular difficulty has been the financing of forestry – an activity which more than almost any other involves the capital expenditure of substantial sums, with no return for many years, possibly decades, and which therefore requires grant schemes and other mechanisms to make it possible. And the other distinctive feature of forestry is its sometimes significant environmental impact, which has not always been for the better and which has led in recent years to a new system of impact assessment. These issues are considered in **Chapters 12 and 13**.

Finally, there is the relatively straightforward system of controls over felling – by way of licences issued by the Forestry Commission. Felling licences are obviously of importance to those in the forestry industry; but it should not be forgotten that they might also be required by those – such as housebuilders and other developers – felling significant quantities of trees for reasons quite unconnected with commercial forestry. Felling licenses may appear in such cases to be a parallel control to tree preservation orders, but their purpose is, or at least was, in origin, somewhat different, arising historically from a need to manage the felling of trees, rather than to protect those of particular value. Felling licences are the subject of **Chapter 14**, the last in **Part III**.

1.4.6 Protection for significant trees

All the provisions of the law discussed so far apply, at least in principle, equally to any tree, whether a magnificent 300-year old oak or a diseased sycamore sapling. However, it is plain that not all trees are of equal worth; and the passing of

---

[85] Rackham (above), p. 93.

[86] Notably by the Forestry (Transfer of Woods) Act 1923, and the Forestry Acts of 1927, 1945, 1947 and 1951.

[87] By the Trees Act 1970, and the Forestry Acts of 1979, 1981, 1986 and 1991.

legislation controlling land use in the 1930s[88] and, somewhat surprisingly, the Town and Country Planning (Control of Interim Development) Act of 1943,[89] brought in a new regime to protect trees of particular value – which is still, more or less, the system which exists today. The various protective measures that are currently in place are described at **Part IV** of this book.

Probably the time when there is the greatest risk of a tree being felled, or being subjected to the carrying out of unsuitable works, is when a property changes hands or is the subject of a development proposal. Not the least significant protective mechanism in practice, therefore, is the general power for local authorities to control proposed development, which enables them to require new buildings to be sensitively sited in relation to trees and hedgerows – particularly in the light of the provisions of the relevant British Standard governing the carrying out of building works close to trees.[90] More generally, planning policy will usually make it increasingly difficult in practice to carry out works that lead to the loss of veteran trees or ancient woodlands. **Chapter 15** considers these provisions, and also introduces the broad range of other, more specific, protective mechanisms available to protect trees of particular value.

The principal mechanism designed to achieve the protection of trees of value is through the making of "tree preservation orders". This has always been particularly cumbersome – and indeed the corresponding system of "building preservation orders" was in due course replaced with the modern system of listing.[91] In the case of trees, however, the system introduced in 1943 has remained in place to this day more or less unaltered, except as to relatively minor details.[92]

Essentially, if a local authority wishes to protect a tree, a group of trees or a woodland in its area, it must make an order (see **Chapter 16**). Thereafter, anyone who wishes to carry out almost any works to a tree or woodland that has thus been protected must first obtain the consent of the authority or, in default, that of the Secretary of State (see **Chapters 17 and 18**). Further, if works are carried out without such consent, the person responsible may be prosecuted (see **Chapter 19**); and in certain circumstances a replacement tree must be planted unless the authority agrees otherwise (**Chapter 20**).

A more recent refinement, introduced in 1974,[93] is that anyone carrying out works to a tree in a conservation area must first notify the authority, so that it has an opportunity to impose a preservation order on the tree if it wishes[94] (see **Chapter 21**). And a somewhat older system, which may have recently been given new life in relation to trees, is the faculty jurisdiction controlling works in Church of England churchyards (**Chapter 22**).

These statutory mechanisms are relatively new compared to many of the other legal principles, largely derived from the common law and under the Forestry Acts, that were in place when the relevant legislation was first passed. It is therefore not surprising that the legislation contains complex provisions to ensure

[88] In particular the TCPA 1932.
[89] See **16.2.2**.
[90] BS 5837:1991.
[91] Introduced for the first time in the Town and Country Planning Act 1968; see Mynors, *Listed Buildings, Conservation Areas and Monuments*, third edn, 1999.
[92] See now Chapter I of Part VIII of Town and Country Planning Act 1990 (ss. 197–210); and note that the relevant secondary legislation was (at last) updated in 2000 – although that too in practice made relatively little impact on the control machinery.
[93] In the Town and Country Amenities Act 1974, ss. 8 and 9.
[94] See now Town and Country Planning Act 1990, ss. 211–214.

that the new machinery does not entirely override the old rights and duties that existed at 1947.[95] Partly as a result, all of this protective legislation is unsatisfactory both in detail and in overall concept; and it is wide open to abuse. It would benefit from a complete review and overhaul. In the meanwhile, however, it is the best we have.

1.4.7 Hedgerows

Finally, the most recent legislation relates to the protection afforded to important hedgerows, under the Environment Act 1995 and the Hedgerows Regulations 1997. This too is cumbersome and unsatisfactory, but it provides at least some measure of protection. It is the subject of **Part V**.

1.4.8 The future

What of the future? Given the extent to which the law has developed since 1914, when the last comprehensive book[96] was written, it would be rash to make any firm prophecies. But in an age that is apparently increasingly prone to litigation, the law in **Part II** of this book seems likely still to be needed, at least in some form, for many years to come.

However, now that the forestry controls are largely exercised in the interests of amenity, there seems little point in having a system distinct from that operating under the planning acts; it might be sensible to consolidate them into one; and it may be fair to note the increasing emphasis on the environment generally, as opposed to trees valued purely as a visual amenity. On the other hand, are trees of amenity value really under such a threat sufficient to justify the hugely cumbersome mechanisms that exist nominally to protect them?

Looking further ahead, it may be of significance that one of the more influential books on environmental law and ethics is entitled *Should Trees have Standing? – Towards Legal Rights for Natural Objects*.[97] Its thesis might be a step too far for British courts, at least for the moment, but who knows?

1.5 Cautionary tales

Finally, although this book is inevitably strewn with references to disagreements that ended up in the courts, it must be remembered that litigation is almost always an unsatisfactory method of resolving disputes; but sometimes it is the least bad method on offer – particularly where civilised relations have altogether broken down.

This is particularly true of disputes between neighbouring landowners; but trees are often on boundaries, and hedges almost always are, and so often form the focus of hotly contested litigation. The current hot topic at the time of writing is concern over boundary hedges, in particular Leyland cypress. Most disputes do not reach the courts; but a typical example of one that did is *Stanton v Jones*, an appeal from the Birmingham County Court to the Court of Appeal. It was described by the latter as:

---

[95] See in particular the interlocking between tree preservation orders and the law of nuisance, discussed at **17.5**.

[96] Adkin, *The Law of Forestry*, 1914, Estates Gazette.

[97] Christopher D Stone, reprinted by Oceana Publications, New York, 1996.

". . . a dispute about the height and nature of a boundary between two neighbouring landowners. It is a dispute which has been conducted with great acrimony between two parties whom the Recorder described as both being 'elderly gentlemen with definite and determined views as to their rights and obligations'."[98]

Another such dispute was *Moloney v Knapton*, which related to an alleged breach of a restrictive covenant preventing the cutting down trees along the boundary between two neighbours. The judge held as follows:

"Mr Knapton then lost his temper and shouted 'I will not be persecuted, I will not consult my neighbours, and I will do what I like with my own property'. . . . If Mr Whitehouse had spoken to Mr Knapton in a different manner, no doubt Mr Knapton would have said what he was proposing to do, and Mr Whitehouse would have seen that there was no question of Mr Knapton threatening to break the covenant. It was a thousand pities the case had ever come to trial. The parties were all eminently respectable and pleasant people, and their relations must now be embittered. However, I must dismiss the case, with costs."[99]

One of the most recent of these cases was *Hamilton v Weston*,[1] a dispute between two neighbours over a row of six *Leylandii* trees on their mutual boundary, in which the defendants (a married couple) trimmed the trees, to be met with a claim for damages for trespass by their neighbour. The Hereford Small Claims Court issued a declaration that the trees belonged to the defendants – in reliance upon which, the defendants then felled ten of the trees. The plaintiff then applied to the Gloucester Small Claims Court, apparently without mentioning the Hereford decision. The Gloucester court decided the issue in his favour; an appeal by the defendants was unsuccessful. The plaintiff then applied for damages, at which point the defendants (by now represented by counsel[2]) raised the earlier decision in Hereford; the Gloucester court accordingly accepted that it was estopped by that first decision, and struck out the claim.

The plaintiff then appealed to the Court of Appeal, by which time the male defendant had died, and his widow had offered to give to the plaintiff the strip of land on which the trees grew, free of charge, simply to be rid of the litigation. The plaintiff, to the surprise of the Court of Appeal, rejected the offer, since by now he was only interested in winning in the courts. That was, as it turned out, a mistake, as the Court of Appeal upheld the (second) Gloucester decision, and rejected the claim; both that court and the House of Lords refused leave to appeal. The plaintiff subsequently claimed that he would have to sell his house, to pay the costs of the litigation all the way up to and including the petition to the Lords.

The decision of the Court of Appeal in *Hamilton v Weston* effectively turned on a point of procedural law entirely unconnected with the subject matter of the dispute, and indicates yet again how unsatisfactory litigation can be as a way of resolving disputes of this kind.

This is nothing new, of course. The report of one seventeenth century decision,[3] for example, reads (in full) as follows:

"Trespass quare clausum fregit & asportavit les Boards, le Defendant justifie pur ceo, que

[98]   (1994), unreported, CA, per Millett L.J.
[99]   (1966) E.G., January 29, per Cross J.
[1]   [1997] E.G.C.S. 10, CA.
[2]   To whom the author is grateful for details of the case.
[3]   *Masters v Pollie* (1620) 2 Roll. 141.

fuit im grand Arbor quel cresce inter le Close del' Plaintiff et del' Defendant, et que part del' Roots de cett Arbor *extend into the Close* del' Defendant, et que le Arbor fuit nouriched per le Soile, et que le Plaintiff succide le Arbor, *and carryed it away into his own Close*, et ceo sawed it into Boards, et le Defendant entered et pritt ascun del' Boards, et carried eur away *prout ei bene licuit*, et sur ceo le Plaintiff demurre, *Harris* le plea ne vault, car coment que ascun del' Roots del' Arbor sont in le Soile le Defendant, unsore [?] le Corps del' maine parte del' Arbor esteant in le Soile del' Plaintiff, pur ceo tout le residue del' Arbor appertaine a luy auri, Et issint Bracton tient, mes si Plaintiff utt planted un Arbor in le Soile le Defendant, donque auterment terra *quod Curia* concessit, mes Mountague Chief Justice dit, que le Plaintiff ne popet limit le Roots del' Arbor, *how far they shall grow and go*, vide 2 E 4. 23."

The language is perhaps not quite that of modern law reports; but the picture that emerges (if only somewhat hazily) has a contemporary feel.

It would be nice to think that Parliament could intervene to resolve such problems; and indeed the Government has recently resolved to introduce new legislation to deal with the problem of boundary hedges – subject, of course, to the availability of parliamentary time.[4] Unfortunately, however, disputes (and thus litigation) are in the final analysis caused by people, not trees or hedges; and the need for the complex legal mechanisms described in the remainder of this book will therefore probably never entirely disappear.

'diligentia maximum etiam mediocris ingeni subsidium'!

D.

---

[4] See **4.5.1**.

Part II

Trees: the General Law

"I hope that I do not misinterpret the significance of this decision if I say that I do not think that it can be the last word on the position or liability of the tree-owner. . . . Anyone can own a tree: there is no qualifying examination; but to how many people in this country can be credited as much general knowledge as will warn them that a tree's top is unusually large, or that it is in fact diseased, dangerously or otherwise?

"My Lords, I have formed no final view on any of these points. I allude to them only because I think that they still await final exposition, and that it would be regrettable if they were regarded as finally determined by the authority of this case."

– Lord Radcliffe, in *Caminer v Northern and London Investment Trust* (1951).

"We are sorry for the substantial delay. This is due to leaves on the line, and further due to those leaves still being attached to the trees . . ."

– Stationmaster (October 2000)

Chapter 2

Ownership of Trees

2.1 Introduction

2.1.1 General principles

The first matter to be determined in connection with any problem relating to a tree is who is responsible for it – or at least, as a start, who owns it.

The basic principle is that any plant – whether a magnificent tree or a dying weed – is part of the land on which it stands. That is, whether it has been deliberately planted or it has merely seeded itself, the plant belongs to the owner of the soil surrounding the base of its stem. A moment's thought is sufficient to make it clear that it would be very difficult if the position were anything else – not least because a substantial (and significant) portion of any plant lies beneath the surface of the soil, and it makes sense for the owner of the roots to be the same as that of the surrounding soil. The only exception to this general rule relates to agricultural crops.[1]

However, the concept of "ownership" of land is, of course, far from straightforward. In theory at least, "land" – that is, the soil (or other substance) of which it is composed, and thus the trees and other plants growing in it – cannot actually be owned in the same way as other inanimate objects. Instead, English law recognises a series of different types of *interests* or *estates* which may exist in land, each carrying with it certain rights and privileges. Thus, what matters is not so much who owns a tree but who has the duty to look after it and the right to carry out works to it and, eventually, to fell it.

2.1.2 Types of ownership

The first and simplest situation is thus where only one person has an interest in a particular piece of land. The owner of such an interest (the *freehold*) has in practice the right to do with the land more or less whatever he or she wishes – subject, obviously, to relevant private law duties and public law restrictions. The implications of this type of ownership, which is the most common in practice, are considered further below (at **2.2**).

In addition, however, a single piece of land may be subject to a number of overlapping interests. Where this is so, the duties and responsibilities of the

---

[1] See **2.1.3**.

various parties concerned in relation to trees are defined according to principles of law going back many centuries, largely framed in relation to the doctrine of *waste*, especially as it related to trees classified as *timber*. The meaning of those two terms, which is far from straightforward, is explained at **2.3**.

The first situation that may give rise to conflicting rights in relation to timber is where land is subject to the terms of a strict settlement or a trust of land. In these cases, those who currently have the benefit of occupying the land must, to a greater or lesser extent, take into account the interests of those who will own it in the future. Such arrangements carry with them strict rules as to what may or may not be done with any timber on the land (see **2.4**). And the ownership of the land may be linked to one or more other trusts.

Secondly, the owner of the freehold interest in a piece of land may grant a lease to another person, which gives the latter a number of rights and responsibilities in respect of it – the extent of which will vary from case to case, in particular according to the terms of the relevant lease (see **2.5**). The owner of such a leasehold interest (the tenant) may go on to grant a further lease (in fact a sub-lease), which will itself lead to a further division of benefits and duties; and that process may continue ad infinitum. A variation of this is where the freeholder – or the leaseholder – grants (or is deemed by the law to have granted) a licence rather than a lease.[2]

And since property can be divided horizontally (below-ground minerals, for example, are frequently in separate ownership to that of the surface of the land), it follows that, in principle, a tree can be owned by one person while the surrounding soil is owned by someone else. This situation is in practice only encountered in the context of trees leased separately to the land on which they are growing, or reserved from a lease of such land.[3]

Thirdly, land may be occupied by a mortgagee in possession (see **2.6**), although this is only very occasionally encountered in practice. And, finally, there are other species of property rights relating to trees and timber – profits, estovers and rights in common – which are also relatively rare, but which for completeness are considered here (at **2.7**).

Generally, however, the normal principles of land law – and the law in general – will operate so as to determine the rights and duties of all concerned in relation to any trees forming part of the land. So, for example, if a leasehold interest in a piece of land is owned by a company which goes into receivership, or if a freehold is held under a tenancy in common by a couple who then divorce, any trees on the land will be dealt with in precisely the same way as the land itself. Relevant general texts on property law should be consulted; this Chapter highlights only those features of property ownership that relate specifically to trees and other plants.

2.1.3 *Categories of plants*

It should be noted that English law makes a distinction between two basic categories of plants, traditionally known as *fructus naturales* and *fructus industriales*.

Fructus naturales are the "natural" products of the soil, such as grass, flowers and fruit from fruit trees, which do not require annual labour to produce a crop.

---

[2] See **2.5.7**.
[3] See **2.5.4**.

As already noted, plants in this category, which includes most if not all trees, are generally deemed to form part of the land.

In principle, a landowner is always entitled to sever his own *fructus naturales* from the soil in which they were growing, so as to sell them as chattels. That general rule is subject, obviously, to many of the qualifications which form the subject matter of the remainder of this book – so, for example, a tenant for life may not always be able to fell timber on his or her land,[4] and the owner of a tree that is subject to a tree preservation order may not be able to fell it without consent from the local planning authority.[5] Normally a contract for the sale of land has to be in writing,[6] and it might be thought that this would therefore apply also to the sale of standing plants. However, in *Marshall v Green*,[7] a contract for the sale of trees to be felled and removed by the purchaser was held not to be void, even though it was oral.

Fructus industriales are commercially growing crops, such as corn and potatoes, requiring annual labour for their production. They generally do not form part of the land.

The distinction is a somewhat artificial and contrived one, since the category of *fructus naturales* undoubtedly includes many plants in domestic gardens, for example, which require annual labour, and commercial timber, which is clearly an industrial crop. And just as it makes little sense conceptually to separate the ownership of a lawn from that of the soil immediately beneath it, so it makes equally little sense to separate the ownership of a potato plant from that of the soil surrounding its roots. However, the classification is important in considering agricultural tenancies, and is similar (but possibly not identical) to the distinction between emblements and other crops.[8]

This book generally deals with plants in the first of these two categories; the legal problems relating to those in the second category are dealt with by texts on the law of agriculture.[9]

2.1.4 Trees on or near property boundaries

Land is, of course, divided into neighbouring parcels, in separate ownership. This will normally be by vertical division; and since the "land" extends to include the air above the surface and the ground below it, as well as the surface of the land itself, this means that the soil containing the roots of a tree, or the above-ground portion of the tree, may be in two or more completely separate ownerships. And even if the tree itself (including all its roots and branches) is in a single ownership, there may be another plot of land in the immediate vicinity of it which is separately owned.

It goes without saying that such situations, which are frequently found in practice, are the origin of much litigation, either between neighbouring landowners or between private owners and those responsible for public land. The problem of who owns boundary trees is thus of particular importance, and is considered in **Chapter 3**, which examines the extent to which the owner is

---

4   See **2.4.4**.
5   See **Part IV**.
6   Law of Property Act 1925, s. 40.
7   (1875) 1 C.P.D. 35.
8   See **2.4.7**.
9   See, for example, Moss, *Muir Watt and Moss: Agricultural Holdings* (Sweet & Maxwell, 1998).

responsible for them – particularly in the context of encroaching roots and branches. The related topic of boundary hedges is the subject of **Chapter 4**.

2.1.5 Highway trees

Trees are frequently found in highway land. The position here is complicated by the fact that, regardless of any theoretical rights of ownership that may vest in the owners of neighbouring land, the highway authority has rights and (at least as important) responsibilities similar to those arising from ownership.

The position regarding trees in and immediately adjacent to highways has thus, not surprisingly, given rise to much litigation over the years. As with boundary trees, therefore, the ownership of such trees is best discussed in the context of general responsibility for them, and is accordingly dealt with at the start of **Chapter 6**.

2.1.6 Trees on Forestry Commission land

The Forestry Commission does not own land or trees as such. Forests and woodlands in public ownership are in fact owned by the Crown,[10] and merely "placed at the disposal of the Commission". However, the Commission may use such land for the purpose of exercising any of its functions under the Forestry Act 1967, and it owns any timber produced there.[11] For all practical purposes, therefore, it may be assumed that the Commission is the owner of trees growing on land in its control.

For further discussion, see **Chapter 11**.

2.1.7 Trees in churchyards

The freehold of a Church of England church and of the churchyard associated with it, is vested in the incumbent (that is, the vicar or rector) for the time being.

However, the care and maintenance of a churchyard, and thus the upkeep of the trees within it, has for many years been the responsibility of the parochial church council (the PCC).[12] This applies equally to churchyards that are in active use and those that have been closed for burials by Order in Council under the Burial Acts.[13] However, where a closed churchyard is transferred to the local authority, under the provisions of the Local Government Act 1972,[14] that authority takes over the functions of the PCC with respect to maintenance and repair.

This means that it is the PCC or the relevant local authority on which falls the duties and responsibilities which are generally those of the "owner" of a tree – such as those arising under the law of negligence and nuisance.

Works to existing trees in churchyards, and the planting of new ones, are also subject to control under the faculty jurisdiction of the Church of England; see **Chapter 22**.

[10] That is, the relevant Government department – see **11.2.1**.
[11] FA 1967, s. 3; see **11.2.3, 11.3.4**.
[12] Parochial Church Councils (Powers) Measure 1956, s. 4(1)(ii)(c); Canon F14; Care of Churches and Ecclesiastical Jurisdiction Measure 1991, s. 6(1), as amended by Church of England (Miscellaneous Provisions) Measure 1995, s. 13.
[13] 1991 Measure, s. 6(5).
[14] Local Government Act 1972, s. 215.

2.2 Trees on freehold land

2.2.1 Ownership

It has already been noted that the owner of a freehold interest in land (the *freeholder*) has in practice the right to do with the land more or less whatever he or she wishes. This means that he or she can in theory plant trees, shrubs, hedges and other plants at any location, suitable or otherwise, without anyone's permission. If a weed or any other plant seeds itself, the freeholder may uproot it or retain it at will. And existing plants on the land, of whatever age, and whether self-sown, planted by the freeholder or planted prior to his or her ownership, may in principle be freely pruned, lopped, topped or felled – although that apparent freedom is severely circumscribed in practice.[15]

One problem that is likely to be of particular significance in the context of trees is the precise location of the boundaries of the land owned. The original conveyance should in theory have made this clear, but in many cases it will have specified the land with only an outline description, such as "all that land and buildings situate at and known as 23 Acacia Avenue". The boundary of the land conveyed will usually be shown on a Land Registry plan, or other copy of an Ordnance Survey plan in the case of unregistered land; but such plan may be said to be "for identification purposes only" – compare the alternative phrase "more particularly delineated", as in *Eastwood v Ashton*,[16] and see also the "mutually stultifying" use of both expressions exemplified in *Neilson v Poole*.[17]

This may be of little consequence in the case of a small urban garden – inspection of the site will often make it perfectly clear where the boundaries are, and which trees are included and excluded; the only problem will be to discover who maintains the fences. In the case of a more spacious suburban property, however, where the boundary is somewhere in the middle of a generous belt of shrubbery, and even more in the case of extensive tracts of rural property, the precise boundary may be far from clear. As already noted, the particular problems relating to trees and hedges on boundaries are considered in greater detail in subsequent chapters.[18]

It may also be noted at this point that, even if a tree is planted entirely on a piece of land in the ownership of A, it may of course subsequently grow so that its roots extend into the soil of a neighbouring piece of land owned by B, and its branches extend into the airspace above that soil. In such a case, the ownership of the tree is unaffected; that is, although B may have rights to take action in relation to those invading roots and branches, they remain A's property (whether still attached to the remainder of the tree or after being severed from it). Conversely, if part of B's tree invades A's soil or airspace, that may give A certain rights, but he acquires no ownership over the tree or any part of it.[19]

2.2.2 Restrictions on rights of the owner

As mentioned above, the freedom of the freeholder to deal freely with his or her trees is in fact subject to a number of private law duties, such as those owed to the

[15] See **2.2.2**.
[16] [1915] A.C. 900.
[17] (1969) 20 P. & C.R. 909.
[18] See **Chapters 3** and **4**.
[19] See **3.2.2**.

owners of neighbouring land, to visitors to the land and to the public at large. These are the subject of the following chapters of this Part of this book. It is also subject to public law restrictions, such as those under planning legislation, considered in **Part IV** of the book.

Further, it should be noted that although the owner of the soil also owns any living vegetable matter arising out of it, including plants growing wild upon the land, it is nevertheless possible for a stranger to pick wild mushrooms, or flowers, fruit or foliage from a wild plant, without being guilty of either theft or criminal damage.[20]

2.3 Trees on land in multiple ownership; the doctrine of "waste"

2.3.1 Introduction

The situation sometimes occurs whereby there is more than one person entitled to at least some interest in a piece of land – and hence in any trees on the land.

First, there are the various conveyancing devices involving different kinds of trusts and other such arrangements. The most common now is a *trust of land*, created under the Trusts of Land and Appointment of Trustees Act 1996 (replacing the *trust for sale*), which is an arrangement whereby the legal ownership of land vests in trustees, whilst the equitable (or beneficial) ownership is in the beneficiaries of the trust.[21] This enables the beneficial ownership, including the right of exclusive possession and occupation, to be shared amongst several people. A common form of this arrangement is where land is to be occupied by more than one person (such as a husband and wife) concurrently. However, it is also possible to find examples of the trust for sale used as a device to create successive interests in land.

An arrangement that is less commonly found now is the *strict settlement*, since 1926 governed by the Settled Land Act 1925, whereby the equitable (and beneficial) ownership vests in a succession of named persons, and the legal interest is vested either in the person who is currently entitled to the equitable interest in possession or in the trustees of the settlement.[22]

Secondly, once it has been established who is the freeholder of a piece of land, or the person entitled to beneficial occupation under a trust, that person may wish not to occupy the land, but instead to allow someone else to do so, no doubt in most cases in exchange for money. Many freeholders (and others entitled to do so) have therefore created out of their interest in the land one or more subsidiary interests. The most common of these is the *leasehold interest* (otherwise known as a tenancy), whereby a second party is given the exclusive right to possess and occupy the land – even to the exclusion of the freeholder. And the leaseholder may in turn grant a sub-lease of some or all of the land held under the head-lease.

A variation of this is the *licence*, whereby the person who has the exclusive possession of the land (by virtue of a freehold or leasehold interest) grants to someone else the right to be on the land, but not necessarily to the exclusion of the owner.

---

[20] See **9.6**.
[21] See **2.4.1**.
[22] See **2.4.3**.

The common feature of all of the above arrangements, by way of distinction from the situation where the freehold is owned by one person without any other interest in existence, is that more than one person has a concern as to what happens to the land. In the case of concurrent interests under a trust of land, each holder of a beneficial interest has a concern to see that the value of that interest is not diminished by the holders of the other such interests. And where either a trust of land or a strict settlement has been used to create successive rights to occupy land, those with future rights (historically known as *remaindermen*) do not want to see the value of those rights diminished by the present occupiers. Similarly, in the case of the land let under a lease, or occupied under a licence, the freeholder will one day regain absolute occupation, and will generally want to find the land more or less in the condition in which he or she saw it when the lease or licence was granted.

This has obvious application to the question of the ownership of trees. The "land" in question may be a country estate, with a handsome cedar tree on the lawn outside the main south elevation of the ancestral castle; it may be a suburban semi-detached house with, at the bottom of the garden, a row of unkempt but dense self-sown sycamores screening the view of the neighbouring waste tip; or it may be several thousand hectares of hillside planted with conifers. In each case, the monetary value of the property, and in the first two cases the enjoyment derived from occupying it, will be significantly diminished if the trees are removed. If, therefore, one or more of the present occupiers are entitled simply to carry out whatever works they wish to trees on the land, those with other present or future rights may justifiably feel aggrieved.

On the other hand, those in occupation of the land – possibly for many years – naturally want to deal with it in practice as if they were the full beneficial owners. They may indeed have to do so for the benefit of the land, by, for example, felling timber that has reached maturity, and removing buildings and trees that may have become damaged by storms. It would clearly not be satisfactory if they were unable to do so.

The law has accordingly developed rules as to what may be done by whom in situations of this kind where land is subject to multiple interests, by reference to what is known as the doctrine of "waste".

2.3.2 Waste

"Waste" is defined as any action or inaction on the part of the owner of an estate in land which permanently alters the physical character of that land – which would include works to any trees already growing on the land, and the planting of any new ones. The unauthorised commission of waste can operate to alter the value of any future interests in land, and thus (generally) to transfer wealth from the holders of those interests to those presently occupying it. As a result, an action may in some cases be brought in the courts to prevent it taking place.

The first category is *permissive waste*, which comprises defaults of maintenance and repair leading to the dilapidation of buildings situated on the land. Note that this has nothing to do with activity (or inactivity) on the land leading to the dilapidation of buildings on neighbouring land. Nor does it seem to include the neglect of trees and other plants on the land[23] – it relates solely to buildings. However, a failure to carry out works to a tree which leads to the deterioration of

---

[23] *Hutton v Warren* (1836) 1 M. & W. 466 at p. 472.

a building on the land – such as by permitting tree roots to damage foundations, or allowing leaves to fill gutters or roots to fill drains,[24] thus causing damage to buildings – would amount to permissive waste.

The second category is *voluntary waste*, which includes any positive diminution in the value of the land. The two most frequently encountered examples are the quarrying of minerals and the felling of timber[25] – and it is significant that both minerals and trees are actually part of the land itself. In addition, both mining and felling timber are acts that are effectively irreversible. "Timber" in this context is a term of art, and is considered further below. To constitute voluntary waste, any destruction of the property must be negligent, such as by allowing a defective branch to fall on a building, or deliberate, and must not be in the course of the tenant's reasonable use of it.[26]

A particular example of voluntary waste is *equitable waste*, which consists of extreme acts of deliberate or wanton destruction of the land to the prejudice of the holder of any future interest. It has been described as "that which a prudent man would not do in the management of his own property".[27] It includes, in particular, cutting timber planted for ornament or shelter, except where the cutting of some such timber is necessary for the preservation of the remainder.

The third category of waste, in relation to which the courts are unwilling to intervene,[28] is the category known as *ameliorating waste*, which is any waste which actually improves the land and enhances its value. That would clearly apply to the planting of trees that are likely to be of value for amenity or forestry purposes. It would also, presumably, apply to the removal of trees, or the carrying out of other works to them, where that is necessary to solve or avoid a problem such as damage to the foundations of neighbouring buildings. Such a problem, if ignored, will in all probability involve future owners of the property in more expensive works (to the tree, the buildings or both) – and possibly litigation as well.

2.3.3 Definition of "timber"

It has already been noted that waste includes the cutting of timber. The precise definition of what is or is not "timber" for this purpose has been the subject of many cases over many years.

The general rule is explained by Sir George Jessel M.R. in his useful and clear judgment in *Honywood v Honywood*[29]:

"The question of what timber is depends, first, on general law, that is, the law of England; and, secondly, on the special custom of a locality.

"By the general law of England, oak, ash and elm are timber, provided they are of the age of twenty years and upwards, provided also they are not so old as not to have a reasonable quantity of useable wood in them, sufficient, according to a text writer,[30] to make a good post.

---

[24] *Herne v Bembow* (1813) 4 Taunt 764.
[25] *Honywood v Honywood* (1874) L.R. 18 Eq. 306
[26] As to the reasonable use of business premises, see *Manchester Bonded Warehouses Co v Carr* (1880) 5 C.P.D. 507.
[27] *Turner v Wright* (1860) 2 De G.F. & J. 234 at p. 243.
[28] *Doherty v Allman* (1878) 3 App. Cas. 709 at 722f (conversion of dilapidated premises into dwelling houses).
[29] (1874) L.R. 18 Eq. 306.
[30] Gibbons on Dilapidations, p. 215; *Countess of Cumberland's Case* (1610) Moo. K.B. 812; *Herlakenden's Case*, 4 Rep. 63b.

"Timber, that is, the kind of tree which may be called timber, may be varied by local custom. There is what is called the custom of the country, that is, of a particular county or division of a county, and it varies in two ways. First of all, you may have trees called timber by the custom of the country – beech in some counties, hornbeam in others, and even white-thorn and black-thorn, and many other trees, are considered timber in peculiar localities – in addition to the ordinary timber trees. Then again, in certain localities, arising probably from the nature of the soil, trees of even twenty years old are not necessarily timber, but may go to twenty-four years, or even to a later period, I suppose, if necessary; and in other places the test of when a tree becomes timber is not its age but its girth. These, however, are special customs."[31]

This judgment is worth reading in full. However, the reference to girth should be treated with caution. Only two cases appear to give any support to this idea; and both are unreliable authorities. In *Smythe v Smythe*,[32] Lord Eldon specifically rejected the use of volume as a test for whether particular oak trees were properly classified as timber. And in *Whitty v Lord Dillon*,[33] it was agreed by the witnesses for the two parties that "timber", in the sense of what a tenant for life would be allowed to fell, could be defined as trees of six inches [15 cm] diameter or two feet [60 cm] in girth (allowing for irregularities of shape); but this was not part of the decision of the Court. By contrast, Lord Ellenborough C.J. noted in *Aubrey v Fisher*[34] that if a tree were only to be timber if it had sufficient solid contents, this would lead to great uncertainty and inconvenience.

Some of the older cases relating to the meaning of timber arose in the context of the powers of a tenant for life[35] or tenant for years. Some of the cases related to which species were liable to tithes, since from the enactment of the statute *Sylva Coedua*[36] until the passing of the Tithe Commutation Act 1836 a tithe was payable on all trees that were not legally timber but which grew from stools.[37] In either context, the courts would enquire as to local custom in order to determine whether a particular species of tree was or was not "timber" in law. Thus in the sixteenth century case of *Soby v Molins*[38] it was explained that:

"The trees are of a base nature and are not timber, nor can be of any service in building, for they cannot in their nature endure long, but they are only fit for fuel and other trifling uses; and therefore if the hornbeams themselves had been cut down, tithes should have been paid for them, and by the same reason shall be paid for the boughs and branches of them."

The same logic was employed in two other cases of the same period.[39] Those decisions suggest that the definition of "timber" relates to whether wood from particular trees can be used for building purposes. But that cannot be the sole determinant, as many types of timber (for example, larch[40]) are now used for such purposes, but have never been classified as "timber".[41]

---

[31] See also **2.4.5**.
[32] (1818) 2 Swanst. 251.
[33] (1860) 2 F. & F. 67.
[34] (1809) 10 East 446 at p. 456.
[35] See **2.4.4**.
[36] 45 Edw. III, c. 3
[37] See Adkin, *The Law of Forestry*, 1914, Chapter XIV.
[38] (1575) Plowd 468 at p. 470.
[39] *Foster and Peacock v Leonard* (1582) 1 Cro. Eliz. 1; and *Countess of Cumberland's Case* (1611) Moo. 812.
[40] *Re Harker's Will Trust* [1938] Ch. 323.
[41] See **2.3.4**.

Finally, it should be noted that the definition of "timber" in the context of "waste" is also of importance for other purposes. Thus in *Re Tower's Contract*,[42] a contract for the sale of land included an extra sum for the "timber", but the only trees on the land concerned were spruce trees, which were not timber. Eve J. held as follows:

"[The court] had to decide what was the meaning of the word 'timber' in this contract. Did it mean every sort of tree which was growing on the property, either in Crabtree Plantation or in the hedgerows, or in the orchards, or did it mean timber as strictly construed? It was said that timber was only strictly construed when the question was as between tenant for life and remainderman, and that in a contract of this nature it would be astonishing to affix to it its real and primary meaning. No authority had been cited for that proposition, and it was one to which he [the judge] did not assent."

When persons entered into a formal contract to sell property for a large sum, and included in the parcels a quantity of timber of such importance as to be valued at £500, his Lordship was of opinion that they used the word "timber" in its primary and proper meaning, that was to say, as referring to trees which were recognised as timber throughout the whole country, namely, oak, ash and elm. It might be, of course, that according to the custom of a particular locality, other trees, such as beech, were included as timber, but it was not suggested that there was any such extension of the meaning of the word here.

"Then it was said that there was a custom amongst auctioneers and surveyors of using the word 'timber' as a loose expression for describing timber trees or timber-like trees of all descriptions, and a person purchasing at an auction, or by private contract under auction particulars, ought to be acquainted with the fact that there was this secondary meaning attached to the word 'timber' in the minds of auctioneers, surveyors, and others. It was for the applicants here [the vendors] to establish to some reasonable degree of satisfaction the existence of such a custom. In his Lordship's opinion they had wholly failed to do so, and he thought that 'timber' in this contract bore its primary and strict meaning."

Adkin submitted in 1914[43] that "the legal definition of timber is entirely unsatisfactory, and could be amended with advantage". That seems to be as true now as it was then.

2.3.4 Particular species

All the cases make it clear that species other than oak, ash and elm may be "timber" by local custom. As might be expected, there are a number of old authorities on particular species, of which the following are only a representative sample; many of them contain references to other decisions. It should be pointed out that the reports of these cases are often in very obscure language, at least to modern readers.

The species most frequently discussed is beech. It has been found that this is timber in Buckinghamshire,[44] once it is 20 years old, and in particular parishes in

---

[42] (1924) W.N. 331.
[43] *The Law of Forestry*, p. 36.
[44] Co Litt 53a; and see *Aubrey v Fisher* (1809) 10 East 446 at pp. 455 and 456.

Hampshire,[45] Gloucestershire,[46] Surrey[47] and Bedfordshire.[48] The Court of Appeal in *Dashwood v Magniac*,[49] however, held that beech is not timber in Oxfordshire – although that is surprising, given that it is timber in the immediately adjacent parts of Buckinghamshire.

As for birch, this was held in one very early case not to be *gros bois*, a term that appears to be synonymous with "timber", in Sevenoaks in Kent,[50] on the grounds that it was only used for fuel, and not for building. Shortly afterwards, however, it was decided that it was timber in Yorkshire, because it appeared that it was used there for "sheep houses, cottages and other mean buildings"[51]; and it has also been held to be timber in Berkshire.[52]

Horse chestnuts and aspens (poplars) may be timber in some locations.[53] It has also been held that it is waste to cut whitethorn[54] or blackthorn[55] in certain cases; and willow has been found to be timber in Hampshire.[56] On the other hand, alder is generally liable to tithes, and thus is not timber[57]; the same is true of stub oak and ash – at least in Essex[58] – and hornbeams, sallows, hazels and maples.[59] Hazel is probably generally classified as underwood, rather than timber.[60]

It seems that no coniferous tree has ever been held to be either timber or underwood. Thus it was noted in one old case[61] that "of all plantations, fir is perhaps the least valuable, being chiefly, I believe, intended for protection rather than profit". And in *Harrison v Harrison*, an important case in the Court of Appeal on timber estates, it was noted that "it has repeatedly been decided by the courts that larch trees are not timber".[62] As for spruce, it appears to have been simply assumed, without the need for any explicit judicial comment, that it is not timber strictly so called.[63]

Fruit trees in general, and apple trees in particular, were considered in *Bullen v Denning*, which related to a lease of land which excepted to the lessor "all timber trees and other fruit trees, but not the annual fruit thereof". It was noted by Bayley J.[64] that a grant of "timber trees and other trees" will not transfer fruit trees (in the conventional sense of that term); and it was considered that the reference to "the annual fruit thereof" did not alter that, since "fruit" could refer to the produce of oak, elm and walnut trees. It would also in practice be highly inconvenient for the tenant in the management of his farm, which was situated in a county (Dorset) where cider is made and where apples constitute a great part of

[45] *Layfield v Cooper* (1694) 1 Eag. & Y. 591.
[46] *Abbot v Hicks* (1696) 1 Wood 319; *R v Minchinhampton* (1762) 3 Burr. 1309.
[47] *Walter v Tryon* (1751) 2 Gwill. 827.
[48] *Biye v Huxley* (1824) 1 Eag. & Y. 805.
[49] [1891] 3 Ch. 306 at p. 351.
[50] *Foster and Peacock v Leonard* (1582) 1 Cro. Eliz. 1.
[51] *Countess of Cumberland's Case* (1611) Moo. 812.
[52] 2 Roll's Ab 814.
[53] *R v Ferrybridge (Inhabitants)* (1823) 1 B. & C. 375 at pp. 378, 379.
[54] *Lashmer v Avery* (1605) Cro. Jac. 126; *Palmer's Case* (1612) Co Litt 53a.
[55] *Cook v Cook* (1639) Cro. Car. 531.
[56] *Guffly v Pindar* (1617) Hob. 219.
[57] *Goodall v Perkins* (1694) 2 Gwill. 543
[58] *Turnor v Smith* (1680) 2 Gwill. 526.
[59] *Soby v Molins* (1575) Plowd 468 at p. 470; *Abbot v Hicks* (1694–6) 1 Wood 319.
[60] *R v Ferrybridge (Inhabitants)* (1823) 1 B. & C. 375 at p. 384.
[61] *R v Ferrybridge (Inhabitants)* (1823) 1 B. & C. 375 at p. 384.
[62] (1884) 28 Ch.D. 221 at p. 227; and *Re Harker's Will Trusts* [1938] Ch. 323 at p. 328.
[63] *Re Tower's Contract* (1924) W.N. 331.
[64] [1826] 5 B. & C. 842 at p. 847.

the annual produce, if the apple trees were not included in the tenancy.

It was incidentally in *Bullen v Denning* that Littledale J. held that "the word 'trees', generally speaking, means wood applicable to buildings, and does not include orchard trees".[65] This has sometimes been used to support the proposition that the word "trees" never includes fruit trees; but it should be treated with caution in the context of modern statutes.

Finally, walnut trees were considered in *Duke of Chandos v Talbot*. The logic of that decision is not entirely clear, but is summarised in the side note to the report as follows:

". . . walnut trees, where of considerable value, to be estimated as timber. Where trees are of value, and the parties cannot agree in the valuation of them as timber, the Court will send it to be tried whether by the custom of the country any and which of these are timber trees." [66]

This is a somewhat surprising decision, since there appears to be no other authority suggesting that the value of the wood is of any particular relevance.

2.4 Trees on land held under a trust

2.4.1 *Trusts of land*

By virtue of the Trusts of Land and Appointment of Trustees Act 1996, a *trust of land* is any trust of property, however worded, which consists of or includes land.[67] It thus includes any trust for sale[68] created before the end of 1996, which will have automatically become a trust of land at the start of 1997. In addition, no new strict settlement[69] can be created after that date, other than by way of a resettlement of existing settled land. Any other arrangement coming into existence after the start of 1997 purporting to be either a trust or a strict settlement is deemed to be a trust of land, even if the instrument creating it explicitly provides otherwise.

In general, trustees of land held under the 1996 Act can together deal with any land that is subject to the trust as if they were the freeholders,[70] subject to any restrictions set out explicitly in the trust declaration. It follows that the old rules as to what trustees could do in relation to timber no longer apply.

However, it should not be forgotten that these theoretically almost unlimited powers are still significantly limited by the duty laid upon all trustees to act in the interests of the trust as a whole and those of the beneficiaries in particular.[71] In the present context, this could mean that it would be a breach of trust to fell trees where this would have the effect of reducing the value of an estate to beneficiaries entitled to future occupation and enjoyment of it. To ensure that this happens, trustees, before exercising any of their powers, are required to consult so far as

---

[65] At p. 851.
[66] (1731) 2 P. Wms. 601 at p. 606.
[67] 1996 Act, s. 1.
[68] See **2.4.2**.
[69] See **2.4.3**.
[70] See **2.2.1**.
[71] 1996 Act, s. 6(5).

practicable all adult beneficiaries entitled to an interest in possession.[72]

Finally, where timber, or even a single tree, is felled on land subject to a trust of land, the proceeds of sale presumably constitute capital money, to be applied by the trustees as with any other moneys arising from the sale of land subject to the trust.

2.4.2 Land held under a trust for sale

By statute, the trustees of a trust for sale were given "all the powers of a tenant for life and the trustees of a settlement under the Settled Land Act 1925".[73] Those powers, which are the subject of the following sections of this Chapter, could be and frequently were added to by the instrument creating the trust.

In practice, therefore, the trustees had substantial powers to cut and sell timber and other trees. Their powers thus included those given to the trustees of a settlement where the beneficiary was a child, which included the power "to fell timber or cut underwood from time to time in the usual course for sale, for repairs or otherwise"[74] As to the definition of "underwood", see *R v Inhabitants of Ferrybridge*.[75] Following a sale, the proceeds were to be applied as with settled land, save that capital money was to be applicable as if it were the proceeds of sale arising under the trust for sale.

2.4.3 Settled land

Strict settlements are not often found nowadays, and can no longer be created.[76] However, those created prior to the end of 1996 (under the Settled Land Acts of 1882 or 1925) remain in being, and the relevant law will therefore still be relevant for a number of years yet, not least in situations involving large estates which may contain many trees. In addition, many of the early cases relating to trees arose in the context of settled estates, and it is useful to understand the basis for them – not least because they are sometimes used to support propositions to which they are only questionably relevant.

The person who has the beneficial interest in a property under a strict settlement is known as the *tenant for life*. The general rule is that the person who is the current tenant for life, and thus the owner of the equitable interest in the land, will usually also hold the legal interest in the land upon trust for him or herself and the other (future) beneficiaries. It follows that, when exercising any statutory powers, the tenant for life does so as trustee, and must have regard to the interests of all parties entitled under the settlement.[77] Subject to that, the tenant has more or less unfettered powers to deal with the land that is subject to the settlement, subject to any terms to the contrary in the instrument creating the settlement. This is however subject to a number of restrictions in practice, some of which are particularly relevant to trees.

Note that there are special rules relating to the granting of a lease of settled land for the purposes of forestry. Forestry leases used to be subject to the same maximum length as other types of lease but since 1925 it has been possible to

---

[72] 1996 Act, s. 11(1).
[73] Law of Property Act 1925, s. 28(1), repealed by 1996 Act, s. 25.
[74] Settled Land Act 1925, s. 102(2)(a).
[75] (1823) 1 B. & C. 375.
[76] 1996 Act, s. 2(1); see **2.4.1**.
[77] Settled Land Act 1925, s. 107.

grant a 999-year lease for forestry (as for building).[78] A forestry lease is a lease to the Secretary of State for purposes authorised by the Forestry Act 1967[79] – which in practice refers to land that is then placed by the Minister at the disposal of the Forestry Commission.

In addition, whilst the tenant for life is generally under an obligation to obtain the best rent possible, it is possible in the case of forestry to reserve a nominal or reduced rent for the first ten years of the term, and to vary the rent thereafter by reference to the amount of timber growing on the land, or the amount actually felled in any year – and for this purpose "timber" includes all forest products, not just the product of those trees which are "timber" at common law or by custom.[80]

Finally, the tenant for life is entitled to enter into a forestry dedication covenant – either for a consideration or otherwise – and doing so amounts to a disposition of land for the purposes of the 1925 Act.[81]

2.4.4 Entitlement of life tenant to fell timber

It has already been noted that felling timber is classified as "waste".[82] It follows that the extent to which a life tenant under a settlement is entitled to cut timber on the settled land depends on whether he or she is "impeachable of waste".

In practice, most settlements make life tenants "unimpeachable of waste".[83] This means that the tenant for life is not liable for voluntary waste, and there is thus almost no restriction on the felling of any trees on the estate by the tenant, whether or not they are strictly "timber". Further, once trees have been felled, and the timber sold, the tenant may keep the entire proceeds.[84]

However, even where a life tenant is unimpeachable of waste, he or she may not commit equitable waste, and may be restrained at equity from doing so.[85] This principle may be overridden by an express provision to the contrary in the instrument creating the settlement.[86] This means, in particular, that the life tenant may not normally cut down trees planted for ornament or shelter, or grub up an entire wood.

Where the person entitled under a settlement is an infant, the trustees of the settlement have the same power to fell timber and underwood[87] as would the infant if of full age; and they may put the proceeds of any resulting sale towards the general management of the estate.[88] In particular, they may only commit waste (in particular, by felling timber) if the infant would be entitled to do so if of full age.

---

[78] Settled Land Act 1925, s. 41(3).
[79] Settled Land Act 1925, s. 117, amended by FA 1967, Sched. 6, para. 5; the reference to the Secretary of State (in place of the Ministry of Agriculture, Fisheries and Food) is the result of S.I. 2002 No. 794. See **11.2.3**.
[80] Settled Land Act 1925, s. 48.
[81] FA 1967, Sched. 2, para. 1; as to forestry dedication covenants, see **12.6**.
[82] See **2.3.2**.
[83] Megarry's Manual of the Law of Property, fifth edn, 1975, p. 48.
[84] *Lewis Bowles's Case* (1615) 11 Co. Rep. 79b.
[85] Law of Property Act 1925, s. 135; and see (1573) 2 Plowd 547 at 555, 75 E.R. 805 at 816f.
[86] 1925 Act, s. 135.
[87] See **2.4.2**.
[88] Settled Land Act 1925, s. 102.

2.4.5 Liability of tenant impeachable of waste

The rights of a tenant for life under a strict settlement are more restricted where the instrument creating the settlement explicitly makes the tenant "impeachable of waste". And where a settlement is silent on the point, a life tenant will automatically be liable for waste.[89] In either case, the tenant will then generally only be able to fell trees where this does not constitute "voluntary waste".

First, a tenant who is impeachable of waste may only cut and sell timber that is ripe and fit for cutting having first obtained either the consent of the trustees of the settlement or an order of the court.[90] As to what is "timber" for this purpose, this has already been considered;[91] see in particular the judgment of Sir George Jessel M.R. in *Honywood v Honywood*.[92] Once the timber has been sold, the tenant for life may only retain one quarter of the proceeds. The remaining three-quarters are to be set aside as capital money – that is, the trustees of the settlement hold the money (together with any other assets of the settlement) on trust for all persons having any interest in the land, paying only the interest to the current life tenant.[93]

Secondly, even a life tenant who is impeachable of waste may cut, at least in theory, all trees which are not timber (such as, in most areas, willows or larches[94]), as well as "dotards" – that is, dead trees not fit for use as timber or trees which do not still contain sufficient wood to make a good post.[95] In practice, this apparent freedom should be considered alongside with the requirement of a tenant for life to act as trustee of his or her powers for future beneficiaries.[96] In addition, it is voluntary waste (and therefore unlawful for a life tenant impeachable of waste) to fell:

- trees which would be timber but for their immaturity, unless the felling of some trees is necessary thinning to allow for the proper growth of those remaining[97];

- fruit trees in a garden or orchard[98]; or

- trees that it is imprudent to cut, such as willows which help to hold together a river bank.

Nor, obviously, is it permissible for such a tenant to fell trees where that would be equitable waste (see above).

Thirdly, special rules apply where trees are severed before they are ripe for cutting, as a result of abnormal circumstances such as extraordinary gales or wartime conditions. Thus, for example, where a plantation of larch trees (which are not timber strictly so-called) was destroyed in a storm, and the land had to be

---

[89]   *Woodhouse v Walker* (1880) 5 Q.B.D. 404 at 406f; *Re Ridge* (1885) 31 Ch.D. 504 at p. 507.
[90]   Settled land Act 1925, s. 66(1).
[91]   See **2.3.3**.
[92]   (1874) L.R. 18 Eq. 306.
[93]   s. 66(2).
[94]   *Re Harker's Will Trust* [1938] Ch. 323 at p. 328.
[95]   *Manwood's Case* (1573) Moo. 101; *Herlakenden's Case* (1588) 76 E.R. 1025 at p. 1029; 4 Co. Rep. 62a at p. 63b; *Honywood v Honywood* (1874) L.R. 18 Eq. 306 at p. 309.
[96]   Settled Land Act 1925, s. 107.
[97]   *Honywood v Honywood* (1874) L.R. 18 Eq. 306 at p. 310; *Re Harker's Will Trust* [1938] Ch. 323 at p. 329.
[98]   *Kaye v Banks* (1770) Dick. 431.

replanted, the Court of Appeal ordered that the proceeds of the sale of the trees should be paid to the trustees of the settlement, who must invest them, and pay part (only) of the income to the tenant for life.[99] In another case, the court directed that the tenant for life could retain part of the proceeds of sale, but that the remainder should be held on trust as capital money.[1]

Fourthly, special rules also apply where the land concerned is a timber estate – that is, an estate cultivated mainly for the produce of saleable timber which is cut periodically. The tenant, even if impeachable of waste, may cut and sell timber according to the rules of proper estate management, since the timber properly cut on such an estate is part of the annual fruits of the land rather than part of the inheritance.[2]

Fifthly, only if the terms of his or her grant so stipulate can a tenant for life – even if impeachable for waste – be made liable for permissive waste.[3]

Finally, where a life tenant carries out improvements to the estate, he or she may cut down and use timber and other trees on the estate for purposes directly connected with those improvements – other than trees planted or left standing for shelter or ornament.[4]

2.4.6 Estovers

Whether or not "impeachable of waste" (see above), a tenant for life is entitled to take reasonable *estovers* from the land. These consist of the following:

- *house-bote*, or *greater house-bote*, that is, timber or other wood for repairing the tenant's house or rebuilding it after accidental destruction;

- *fire-bote*, or *lesser house-bote*, that is, the tops and lops of pollards and other trees, shrubs, dead wood and underwood for burning in the house;

- *hay-bote*, for repairing gates and fences; and

- *plough-bote*, for making and repairing wagons and agricultural implements.

"Estover" derives from the Old French word for "necessary"; "bote" from the Old English word for "useful".

The tenant's right to house-bote relates only to timber used in connection with the house on the land that is subject to the settlement. It does not authorise the cutting of more timber than is necessary for the present needs of the tenant. So, for example, the life tenant may not cut timber to use in future, or to sell – even if the proceeds of such sale are used to pay for carrying out repairs, or to buy other timber more suitable for use in repairs.[5]

Note that the concept of estovers is also of significance in relation to leasehold land generally,[6] and in relation to profits and commons.[7]

---

[99] *Harrison v Harrison* (1884) 28 Ch.D. 221.
[1] *Re Terry* (1918) 87 L.J. Ch. 577.
[2] *Honywood v Honywood* (1874) L.R. 18 Eq. 306 at pp. 309, 310; *Dashwood v Magniac* [1891] 3 Ch. 306.
[3] *Re Cartwright* (1889) 41 Ch.D. 532 at 535f. And see **2.3.2**.
[4] Settled Land Act 1925, s. 89.
[5] Co Litt 41b, 53b.
[6] See **2.5.3**.
[7] See **2.7.1** and **2.7.2** respectively.

2.4.7 Ownership of timber and other crops

Until a tree falls or is felled, it remains part of the land. It follows that a tenant for life has no claim to it; so that, if land is sold with uncut timber on it, and the timber is subsequently sold, the life tenant cannot claim any share of the proceeds even if he or she could lawfully have felled the timber.[8]

Once timber has been severed from the land, the proceeds of sale belong to the life tenant if he or she was entitled to sever it by felling; and this is regardless of whether the severance was in fact by the tenant, by a stranger or by an act of God (such as a storm). However, if the life tenant was not entitled to sever the timber (presumably because impeachable of waste), the proceeds belong to the owner of the next vested estate or interest of inheritance.[9]

A tenant for life only holds an interest in the land for the duration of his or her own life. It follows that the tenant does not know when the tenancy will end, and might therefore (at least in theory) be discouraged from sowing crops lest he or she might not be around to reap the harvest. To encourage the tenant to cultivate the land, therefore, the law allows the tenant's personal representatives after his or her death to enter the land and remove the crops sown by the tenant and growing at the date of death – known as *emblements*.[10] This applies to annual crops artificially produced, such as corn, but not to fruit trees or timber, even if the tenant "by good husbandry and industry, either by overflowing, or trenching, or compassing of the meadows, or digging up of bushes and such like, makes the grass to grow in more abundance".[11]

However, as with the distinction between *fructus naturales* and *fructus industriales*,[12] the distinction between emblements and other crops is becoming increasingly artificial with modern agricultural methods.

2.4.8 Trusts relating to the sale of timber or wood

There is a general principle (known as the *rule against accumulations*) whereby no property may be settled or disposed of in such a way that the income arising accumulates in trust for more than a certain period[13] – as to the calculation of that period, the standard textbooks on property law should be consulted.

One exception to this rule is that it does not apply in relation to the produce of timber or wood[14]; even then, however, a direction will be void if it exceeds the perpetuity period.[15] This provision is said to have originated due to the need for naval timber in 1800,[16] and is unlikely to be of much significance now; it is thus included here purely for completeness.

The Law Commission has sensibly suggested that the rule against accumulations should be scrapped altogether.[17]

---

[8] *Re Llewellin* (1887) 37 Ch.D. 317.
[9] *Bewick v Whitfield* (1734) 3 P. Wms. 267; *Honywood v Honywood* (1874) L.R. 18 Eq. 306 at p. 311.
[10] Co Litt 55b; *Grantham v Hawley* (1615) Hob. 132.
[11] *Graves v Wedd* (1835) 5 B. & A. 105; 110 E.R. 731.
[12] See **2.1.3**.
[13] Law of Property Act 1925, s. 164; Perpetuities and Accumulations Act 1964, s. 13.
[14] 1925 Act, s. 164(2)(iii).
[15] *Ferrand v Wilson* (1845) 4 Hare 344.
[16] Megarry, p. 132.
[17] *The Rule Against Perpetuities and Excessive Accumulations* (Law Comm No. 251, March 1998).

2.5 Trees on land subject to lease or licence

2.5.1 General principles

In principle, the owner of a freehold interest in land (or the trustees of a trust of
land or a tenant for life of settled land) can grant a leasehold interest in all or any
part of that land. And since "land" includes any trees, shrubs or other plants
whose roots are in it, those will be included in the lease unless they are specifically
excluded. This is clear from the older cases:

"When a lease of land is granted by a lessor to a lessee, the woods and trees are parcel of the
lease and pass to the lessee as well as to the land, if they are not excepted by it; and, in proof
of this, all fruits and profits arising from the fruit trees shall be the lessee's, and the shadow,
and also the branches and loppings for fuel or enclosure of fences."[18]

And the leaseholder or tenant must take the responsibility as well as the
benefit. That approach has been confirmed more recently by the Court of Appeal,
when it dismissed an argument that, because trees were not mentioned in a
demise, they remained the property of the freeholder, and maintained that the
occupier of land is in general responsible for the trees – whether holding the land
under a long lease or a weekly tenancy.[19]

Where land is used for the growing of timber, the trees will frequently be the
subject of specific provisions in any lease, or may be excluded altogether.[20]
However, other land that is the subject of a lease, for residential or other
purposes, may happen to contain trees; and it then becomes important to
ascertain who is responsible for their maintenance and who has the right to carry
out works to them and, in due course, fell them.

The first thing to be determined in relation to any lease is precisely what land
and, therefore, what trees and hedges are the subject of the tenancy. It should be
possible to discover this from the actual terms of the lease – although it may well
have been drawn up with less precision than a conveyance of freehold property.
As with such a conveyance,[21] inspection of a lease may discover some wording
such as "all that house known as 23 Acacia Avenue, together with outbuildings
and appurtenances"; which is fine, so long as there is no dispute as to the
boundaries of the land thereby granted – either as to their location or as to the
responsibility for the maintenance of each of them. The lease may contain a plan
stated to be "for identification purposes only", but again this is likely to be of little
help. It should of course be remembered that a freeholder cannot let (and a
leaseholder cannot sub-let) more than he or she owns; so if a freeholder is
responsible for the south boundary of a garden but not the north one, so too will
the leaseholder. Otherwise, in the event of a dispute, the court must take into
account evidence of the surrounding circumstances in order to dispel the
vagueness[22] – although such evidence cannot override the terms of the written
lease itself.

---

[18] *Mervyn v Lyds* (1553) 1 Dyer 90a; see also *Liford's Case* (1615) 11 Coke's Rep. 48b; *Anon* (1550)
Moo. 23, p. 6.
[19] *Edge v Briggs* (1961) 178 E.G. 261, CA.
[20] See **2.5.4**.
[21] See **2.2.1**.
[22] *Willson v Greene, Moss (Third Party)* [1971] 1 W.L.R. 635; *Wigginton & Milner Ltd v Winster
Engineering Ltd* [1978] 3 All E.R. 436.

Particular problems may arise where only part of the landlord's own interest is being let. This will be the case with, for example, agricultural property where the lease only extends to certain fields forming part of a larger farm, or a farmhouse redundant after the amalgamation of two farms. In such cases, a careful check will need to be made to ascertain the location of (and responsibility for) the boundary with the retained land, including any new hedges planted to mark the division.

2.5.2 Rights and duties of landlord and tenant

The most important principle in practice is that the tenant of leasehold property is of course entitled to take and enjoy the fruit, shelter and shade of all the trees growing upon the land, the landlord being unable to touch them. And the tenant is also entitled to plant new trees. As against that, the tenant will generally be responsible for the trees[23]; and any trees planted on the land during the course of a tenancy will revert to the landlord when the land itself does.

More specifically, the rights and duties of the landlord and tenant of leasehold property will be subject to any express covenants in the lease, which may include stipulations as to the planting, care and felling of any trees on the land, where these are not excepted from the lease altogether. These will need to be considered carefully to ascertain their effect.

Note that the Court of Appeal has held in *George v Reeves*[24] that a covenant "not to cut down any trees without consent of the landlord, such consent not to be unreasonably withheld" prevents the carrying out of damage to trees which leads to their death. In that case, the landlady had declined to grant consent for the felling of an elm and six macrocarpas, and the local authority had then imposed a tree preservation order on the trees. As a result, the tenant:

". . . in a temper then unwisely took the matter into his own hands and ring-barked [the trees]. The elm fell down, and [the tenant] interfered in an unfair and disgraceful manner with attempts by tree experts to save the macrocarpas. . . . When there was a risk of the trees recovering after tree experts had attended to them, the tenant ring-barked them again".

The court unanimously agreed that "if one ring-barked a tree so that it died, that was equivalent to cutting down or felling the tree"; the lease was accordingly forfeited, and the defendant was lucky to have to pay only £1 damages in the circumstances.

Where the trees are excepted or reserved from the land that is let, there will usually be a covenant forbidding the tenant from harming them.[25]

In the absence of any express covenants to the contrary, the rights and duties of a tenant are governed by rules under the common law, as explained below.[26] It will be clear from the analysis of those rules, many of which are of great antiquity, that in practice, where there any trees or hedges of any consequence on a piece of land that is to be let, it will usually be appropriate for the lease to make specific provisions for trees and hedges and works to them, particularly in the case of property let under a long lease. And where there is no relevant provision in a lease, or simply no written lease at all, it is always prudent for a tenant at least to notify the landlord in writing of any proposed works.

[23] See **2.5.1**, and **Chapters 3** and **5**.
[24] (1969) 210 E.G. 211, CA.
[25] See **2.5.4**.
[26] See **2.5.3**.

As to the duties of tenants of agricultural land in relation to hedgerows, this is considered later.[27]

2.5.3 Liability at common law

In the absence of any express covenants to the contrary, however, the rights of a tenant at common law are similar to those of a tenant for life under a settlement who is impeachable of waste.[28] And, not surprisingly, there have been a number of decisions exploring the extent of those common law rights.

The court will not, in principle, interfere to stop a tenant committing ameliorating waste – that is, alterations that improve the state of the land – although it will uphold covenants prohibiting the carrying out of alterations or the construction of new buildings. Such covenants are not often found relating to trees and plants, although there would seem to be no reason in principle why one should not be inserted into a lease prohibiting the tenant from planting new trees or from making any substantial alteration to the layout of a garden; and the court would presumably enforce it by the award of damages or, in an appropriate case, the grant of an injunction.

Otherwise, there is a general duty on tenants (whether under a lease for a fixed term of years, or a yearly or other periodic tenancy) not to commit voluntary waste.[29] Nor must they allow others to do so, since they are deemed to be in a position to prevent it.[30] The meaning of "waste" has already been considered.[31]

An important Irish case, *Dunn v Bryan*[32] highlighted points relating to waste in trees as between landlord and tenant. In particular, a tenant may cut down and appropriate trees of any age which are not timber or fruit trees, except those which have been planted or left standing for ornament or shelter, or which hold up banks and the like, provided that they will reproduce themselves from their stools. Secondly, a tree must attain twenty years before it can be classified as timber. However, the cutting of a younger tree, even if of a species such that it would be timber if over twenty years,[33] is not necessarily waste unless it is done unseasonably or so as to prevent regrowth of the stools – especially if the tree has been cut before. Thirdly, the cutting of a hedge in such a manner that it will grow again is not waste. Nor will the court enquire into the manner in which trees or stools are cut, but only as to the result.

The tenant may also cut coppices and underwood at proper age and in a husbandlike manner, and take the proceeds of sale. Here too, the key principle is that underwood is a crop, albeit only harvested every ten years or so, and so belongs to the tenant; whereas the stools – which must be left – belong to the landlord.[34] On the same basis, a tenant is probably, at least in the case of a long lease, to make such thinnings of any plantations as may be necessary.[35]

A tenant at sufferance is liable for voluntary waste[36]; a tenant at will is

---

[27] See **24.5.4**.
[28] Adkin, *Law of Forestry*, pp. 113, 114; and see **2.4.5**.
[29] *Yellowly v Gower* (1855) 11 Exch. 274 at 293f, 156 E.R. 833 at 841f.
[30] *Attersoll v Stevens* (1808) 1 Taun. 183.
[31] See **2.3.2**.
[32] (1872) Ir. R. Eq. 143 at p. 153.
[33] See **2.3.4**.
[34] *Hoe v Taylor* (1594) Cro. Eliz. 413.
[35] Adkin, *Law of Forestry*, pp. 113, 114.
[36] *Burchell v Hornsby* (1808) 1 Camp. 360.

theoretically not liable, but is in practice, since the committing of any damage to the property terminates the tenancy and makes the former tenant liable in trespass.[37] For the meaning of these different types of tenancy, a standard text on landlord and tenant law should be consulted.

In principle, no lease ever entitles a tenant to commit equitable waste – such as, in particular, felling trees planted for shelter or ornament. It seems, however, that the cutting of saplings and young timber unfit to be felled, provided that the cutting is seasonable, does not amount to equitable waste as between landlord and tenant.[38]

A tenant for years has the same right to estovers – that is, timber required for routine purposes[39] – as does a tenant for life under a settlement.[40] In particular, where there is a liability imposed on the tenant to repair the house and the principal buildings, that will carry with it a right to cut down such timber trees as may be necessary for the purpose of carrying out those repairs. Where, on the other hand, the landlord is liable for repairs, but fails to carry them out, the tenant may cut down trees for the repairs, after first having given notice to the landlord of the need for the repairs.[41]

Finally, windfalls of sound timber belong to the landlord, but windfalls of decayed timber trees and trees that are not timber belong to the tenant.[42] The tenant probably also has the right to fell dead trees and to take the wood, if not ornamental timber.[43]

2.5.4 Timber owned or let separately from the remaining land

Because timber forms part of the land on which it grows, it may form the subject of a separate holding. It follows that – particularly in the case of land used for commercial forestry – timber may be, and in appropriate cases frequently is, reserved from land being let. The precise wording of the clause in the lease purporting to reserve the timber may be of crucial importance.

Such a reservation will carry with it the right to cut, remove and, of course, sell the timber.[44] The extent of any reservation is always strictly construed in favour of the tenant and against the landlord[45]; and it will only cover subject matter that was in existence at the time of the grant of the lease. The word "trees" in a reservation will not include fruit trees.[46] "Merchantable" timber means timber that would be saleable or marketable when the owner desires to deal with it.[47] The reservation of timber may also involve the reservation of a right of way across the land that is let, or at least a licence to enter it, in order for the landlord to reach the timber and remove it; indeed, if the landlord leaves the fallen timber, the tenant can take steps to have it removed.[48]

[37] *Countess of Shrewsbury's Case* (1600) 5 Co. Rep. 13.
[38] *Dunn v Bryan* (1872) 7 Ir. R. Eq. 143 at p. 154.
[39] See **2.4.6**.
[40] Co Litt 41b.
[41] 1 Brownl. & G. 240; (1561) Dyer 198b; Co Litt 54b; *Maleverer v Spinke* (1537) Dyer 36b.
[42] *Herlakenden's Case* (1589) 4 Rep. 63b.
[43] Adkin, *Law of Forestry*, p. 114.
[44] *Liford's Case* (1614) 11 Co. Rep. 46b; [1558–1774] All E.R. Rep. 73; *Stukely v Butler* (1615) Hob. 168.
[45] *Cardigan (Earl) v Armitage* (1823) 2 B. & C. 197; [1814–23] All E.R. Rep. 33; *Bullen v Denning* (1826) 5 B. & C. 842.
[46] *Bullen v Denning* (1826) 5 B. & C. 842 at p. 847.
[47] *Smith v Daly* [1949] 4 D.L.R. 45 at pp. 52–53, Ontario High Court.
[48] *Hewitt v Isham* (1851) 7 Exch. 77.

As to whether a reservation of trees will extend to the soil in which they are growing, this must be ascertained in the light of the probable intention of the parties at the time when the lease was made, and the entire context of the document.[49] It is in principle possible for the soil to be owned by one person, while the trees, although still attached to it, are owned by another[50]; the Ontario High Court, after reviewing the earlier authorities, expressed it thus: "by a grant of trees *simpliciter* no soil passes but sufficient nutriment to sustain the vegetative life of the trees".[51]

If, following a reservation of timber, the land on which it is growing changes hands by adverse possession, the timber will not necessarily also pass – in one American case, it has been held that:

". . . there must be such possession of the timber evidenced by acts of ownership and control as will amount to an open, notorious, distinct, and hostile adverse claim and possession as required by the statute".[52]

In particular, the leasehold owner of the ground in which trees are growing may not obtain adverse possession of the freehold interest in the trees as against the original lessor, even though no attempt has been made to cut and remove the trees for more than 10 years after the grant.[53]

It is usual to find that, where land is let subject to an exception relating to the timber, there is an express covenant whereby the tenant undertakes not to cut the trees, or more generally to preserve them from injury. Breach of that covenant will then entitle the landlord to re-enter – for trespass, not waste.[54] Thus in *Smith v Smale*[55] a landlord had reserved to herself trees and underwood on the farm which she had let to the defendant, and was able to regain possession of land when he had allowed his cattle to enter the wood and damage the trees – and had even tied back a gate to enable them to do so more easily.

Any timber felled before the start of the lease will not be part of the land, and therefore will not be subject to the lease; but the landlord should stipulate a right of entry onto the land if he or she wishes to recover it after the tenant has gone into occupation.

Quite apart from the doctrine of waste, the right of a tenant to exclusive occupation of the land does not mean that a landlord is unable to restrict the use to which the tenant can put the land. Where, for example, A grants to B a lease of land on which there is timber, it is perfectly possible for A also to grant C a licence to enter the land and remove the timber; and B cannot exclude C from the land. Such an arrangement would also necessarily mean that, even if C does not exercise his right, B has no right to fell and remove the timber.[56]

[49] *Leigh v Heald* (1830) 1 B. & Ad. 622.
[50] *Herlakenden's Case* (1589) 4 Rep. 63b; *Liford's Case* (1614) 11 Co. Rep. 46b; [1558–1774] All E.R. Rep. 73; followed in *Eastern Construction Co Ltd v National Trust Co Ltd* [1914] A.C. 197.
[51] *Smith v Daly* [1949] 4 D.L.R. 45 at p. 49, Ontario High Court.
[52] *Southwestern Lumber Co v Evans* 275 SW 1078 at p. 1082, following *Liford*.
[53] *John Austin & Sons Ltd v Smith* (1982) 132 D.L.R. (3d) 311, Ontario Court of Appeal.
[54] *Goodright v Vivian* (1807) 8 East 190.
[55] (1954) E.G., October 30.
[56] *Glenwood Lumber Co Ltd v Phillips* [1904] A.C. 405 at p. 408; *Re British American Oil Co Ltd and de Pass* (1960) 21 D.L.R. (2d) 110 at pp. 117ff.

2.5.5 Dangerous or harmful trees at the start of a tenancy

Where there are trees on, overhanging or immediately adjacent to land at the start of a tenancy, the incoming tenant must satisfy himself that they are not in any way dangerous. As it was expressed by the court in *Erskine v Adeane*[57]:

"With respect to what the Master of the Rolls seems to have rested his judgment upon, namely, that there was a warranty that no noxious trees should grow on the demised premises, I have never heard of such a warranty. The law of this country is that a tenant, when he takes a farm, must look and judge for himself what the state of the farm is. Just as in the case of a purchaser of a business the rule is *caveat emptor*, so in the case of taking the lease of property the rule is *caveat lessee*; he must take the property as he finds it. I never heard that a landlord warranted that the sheep should not eat his yew trees. Yew trees, it appears, are not at all times poisonous; and although it is not uncommon for them to grow in plantations, or about a farm, it is very rare for any accident to happen on account of them. In my opinion, the lessee must take his chance of such a damage, or ask for an express warranty if he thinks there is reason to fear that his cattle or sheep may be injured."

In that case, the appellant was the tenant of a farm; and his landlord had reserved to himself certain plantations[58] in which were yew trees. In one plantation, the branches of the yews overhung the surrounding fence, and in another the surrounding fence was insufficiently maintained. In both cases, the appellant's cattle browsed the yews and died. The court held that the claim was in the event time-barred but that, even if it had not been, it would not have been sustainable since the owner of the yews was the appellant's landlord.

That decision was followed by the Court of Appeal in *Cheater v Cater*[59] which concerned very similar facts – a horse owned by a tenant of a field died after eating the overhanging branches of a yew tree on neighbouring land owned by his landlord. Here too, the court found that, since the shrubbery containing the yew was retained by the landlord, and since the branches had apparently been overhanging the field at the start of the tenancy, the tenant was unable to obtain damages: "a clear distinction must be drawn between disputes between adjoining owners and disputes between landlord and tenant".[60]

That case was itself followed by the Court of Appeal in *Shirvell v Hackwood Estates Co Ltd*,[61] which concerned a tree on the defendant's land that shed a branch onto adjacent land that the plaintiff had leased from the defendant. On the facts of the case,[62] the court (albeit only by a majority) found that the defendant had not been negligent; but whether or not there had been negligence, it was agreed that no action could succeed due to the landlord-tenant relationship between the parties.

It is thus clear that if a dangerous or harmful tree is on land owned by B, and at the start of the tenancy overhangs land leased by A from B, then A may not recover damages from B. But if a tree is not harmful at the start of the tenancy, but becomes harmful later, then it may be that damages might be recoverable – that at any rate seems to be the way the court in *Cheater* was moving, although it specifically declined to decide the point. And if the land on which the tree is

[57] (1873) L.R. 8 Ch. 756, per Sir George Mellish L.J. at p. 761.
[58] See **3.4.4**.
[59] [1918] 1 K.B. 247, affirming [1917] 2 K.B. 518.
[60] Per Bankes L.J. at p. 254.
[61] [1938] 2 K.B. 577, 2 All E.R. 1.
[62] See **5.7.2**.

growing is owned by C, then whilst A may still not sue B (the landlord), an action by A against C will be determined according to the normal principles governing disputes between neighbours.[63]

2.5.6 Licences to remove timber

As an alternative to a lease, it is possible for the owner of land to grant a "licence coupled with the grant of an interest". This is particularly relevant in the context of timber. Thus the decision in the old case of *Thomas v Sorrell* is often cited as a foundation for the modern law of licences:

"A dispensation or licence properly passeth no interest, nor alters or transfers property in any thing, but only makes an action lawful, which without it had been unlawful."[64]

However, that statement is followed almost immediately by this:

"But a licence to hunt in a mans park, and carry away the deer kill'd to his own use; to cut down a tree in a mans ground, and to carry it away the next day after to his own use, are licences as to the acts of hunting and cutting down the tree; but as to the carrying away of the deer kill'd and tree cut down, they are grants."

Thus where, for example, A grants to B a lease of land on which there is timber, it is perfectly possible for A also to grant C a licence to enter the land and remove the timber; and B cannot exclude C from the land – not least since C has a legal interest in the trees, even if not in the land on which they are growing. Such an arrangement would also necessarily mean that, even if C does not exercise his right, B has no right to fell and remove the timber.[65] And C's licence is irrevocable, assignable and enforceable against A's successors in title.

This may appear to be a licence somehow having the force of a legal interest in property; or it may be that the grant of the licence to cut the trees of necessity implies the grant of a right of way across the grantor's land to reach the trees and then to remove them, so that it is actually enforceable as an easement rather than as a licence as such.

And it has already been noted that a contract to purchase standing timber – which is of course, at least in theory, "land" – is nevertheless valid even if it is only oral.[66] That may suggest that it is in effect only a type of licence, rather than an interest in land as such.

2.5.7 Other land held under a licence

A freeholder may grant to another person a right to enter and remain on land, without thereby creating a formal legal interest. This is known as a "licence" and the basis for such an arrangement has already been considered.[67]

One variety of licence, known as a "bare licence", is granted frequently in practice, such as where a householder invites a friend to a barbecue or allows a

---

[63] See **Chapters 3 and 4**.
[64] (1673) Vaughan 330 at p. 351; 124 E.R. 1098 at p. 1109.
[65] *Glenwood Lumber Co Ltd v Phillips* [1904] A.C. 405 at p. 408; *Re British American Oil Co Ltd and de Pass* (1960) 21 D.L.R. (2d) 110 at pp. 117ff.
[66] *Marshall v Green* (1875) 1 C.P.D. 35.
[67] See **2.5.6**.

neighbour's children to retrieve their ball. It is also granted by implication to persons such as postmen, election canvassers, and others having a genuine and legitimate reason to be present or wishing to conduct lawful business with the householder. A business similarly grants an implied licence to those who wish to enter its premises and acquire information or do business.

A second situation is where a contract entitles A to enter onto B's land and remain there. Such a contract can serve either a short-term function (where, for example, a person buys a ticket to enter a stately home and view the gardens), a medium term function (where an owner of land pays a builder to enter onto it and erect a building) or a long-term function (where a house owner takes in a paying guest). The latter situation is in some cases difficult to distinguish from a lease.[68]

Either a bare licence or a contractual licence only entitles the licence holder to be on the land for the relevant purpose that is the subject of the grant or the contract, and not for any other. It therefore does not confer any entitlement to damage or destroy trees or other plants on the land – unless of course that was the purpose of the licence, such as where a tree surgeon is employed to cut down a householder's tree.

2.6 Trees on mortgaged land

If money is borrowed on the security of land, by way of a mortgage, and the borrower fails to repay the loan on demand, the lender has the right to enter into possession of the land. Where this happens, the lender (mortgagee) becomes the owner of the land at law and in equity.

Once it has entered into possession, and provided that the mortgage was made by deed, a mortgagee may then cut and sell timber[69] and other trees ripe for cutting, other than those planted or left standing for shelter or ornament, or contract for this to be done within twelve months of the date of the contract.[70] Although generally not liable for waste, a mortgagee will be liable if it improperly cuts timber save that, if it becomes apparent that the property is no longer sufficient security for the money due, the court will not interfere if timber is cut, except in the case of wanton destruction (a phrase presumably equivalent to equitable waste).[71]

2.7 Profits, estovers and common rights

2.7.1 Profits and estovers

An alternative to a licence to enter a land to remove timber[72] is a *profit à prendre*. This is a right for one person to take for his or her own use from the land of another some of that land, or something growing on it. This may include, in particular the right to take the branches and boughs of growing trees,[73] acorns

---

[68] *Street v Mountford* [1985] A.C. 809; and see any general work on landlord and tenant law.
[69] See **2.3.3, 2.3.4**.
[70] Law of Property Act 1925, section 101(1)(iv).
[71] *Millett v Davy* (1863) 31 Beav. 470 at pp. 475, 476; see **2.3.2**.
[72] See **2.5.6**.
[73] *Willingdale v Maitland* (1866) L.R. 3 Eq. 103.

and beech mast (presumably to feed animals).[74]

In particular, a profit of "estovers" is the right to take wood from the land of another, as house-bote, hay-bote or plough-bote. The meaning of those terms has been considered already.[75] Thus, quite apart from the rights to estovers possessed by a tenant for life under a settlement, and by a tenant under a lease, it is possible too for the owner of land quite separately to grant to another person a right to estovers, or for such a right to arise automatically.

Any profit may exist as "appurtenant" or "in gross". A profit appurtenant is linked to the ownership of another property, so that, for example, the owner of X may have the right to take timber from property Y; but in that case the right will be limited to as much timber as is required in connection with the use of Y.[76] A profit in gross is a right for a particular person to take from the land, not by virtue of his or her ownership of any other land, and the amount that may be taken can be limited or unlimited.

Such a right may be the subject of an explicit grant – which must be in writing, since a profit is an interest in land.[77] Alternatively, it may be by prescription – essentially after it has been exercised for 30 years as of right, without secrecy, and not by force.[78] Once it has come into existence, it may be given by will, or sold, or otherwise dealt with as any other interest in land – and, again, any transfer must be evidenced in writing. A profit may exist either for a specified period of time, or in perpetuity; and may be limited to certain times of the year.

In addition, a profit may be exclusive, or it may be enjoyed in common with others (including the grantor). Where a profit such as a right to cut timber is both perpetual and exclusive, there is a danger that the exercise of it will render valueless the land on which the timber is growing. There is thus a general (but rebuttable) presumption that a grantee's exercise of his or her rights are restricted to a "reasonable" time following the date of the grant.[79]

2.7.2 Common land

Common land is land owned by one person over which two or more owners of other land (the dominant tenements) possess rights that they may exercise in common with each other and the landowner. Such rights will be in the nature of profits,[80] but are usually known as "rights of common". Any land that was subject to any rights of common on or before July 31, 1970 had to be registered under the Commons Registration Act 1965, or it ceased to be common land.[81] The general law of commons is complex and somewhat obscure; but it is of relevance in the present context in that one category of common right is the common of estovers.

A substantial number of commons of estovers were registered under the 1965 Act[82]; but usually the registration did not specify which category of estovers[83] was

---

[74] *Chilton v London Corpn* (1878) 7 Ch.D. 562.
[75] See **2.4.6**.
[76] *Harris v Earl of Chesterfield* [1911] A.C. 623.
[77] Law of Property Act 1925, s. 53.
[78] Prescription Act 1832, s. 1; *R v Oxfordshire County Council, ex p. Sunningwell PC* [1999] 3 W.L.R. 160, H.L.
[79] *Reid v Moreland Timber Co Pty Ltd* (1946) 73 C.L.R. 1, per Dixon J. at p. 13.
[80] See **2.7.1**.
[81] 1965 Act, s. 1(2)(a); Commons Registration (Time Limits) Order 1996 (S.I. 1996 No. 1470), amended by S.I. 1970 No. 383.
[82] Gadsden, *Law of Commons*, 1988, paragraph 3.66.
[83] See **2.4.6**.

being claimed. The common right may be attached to a particular building; in which case the courts will not sever the right – so, for example, the owner of a right to wood for burning in a particular house cannot transfer the right to enable the wood to be burned elsewhere.[84] Nor can the amount of wood that can be taken be increased when the building is enlarged.[85] It is however probably permissible to apportion a right of estovers for fencing, when the land to which the right attaches is itself divided.[86]

Again, the exercise of an appurtenant right of estovers is strictly limited to the amount of wood that can be used for the relevant purpose on the dominant tenement.[87]

It may be noted that at the time of writing there are proposals by the Government for the reform of the law relating to common land,[88] but past experience suggests that even if they are universally accepted to be desirable, it is unlikely that their implementation will be given high priority.

---

[84] *Sir Henry Nevil's Case* (1570) 1 Plowden 377 at p. 381, 75 E.R. 572 at p. 579; *Att-Gen v Reynolds* [1911] 2 K.B. 888 at pp. 904 and 919.

[85] *Luttrel's Case* (1601) 4 Co. Rep. 86a, 76 E.R. 1065; *Brown v Taylor* (1610) 4 Leon 241, 74 E.R. 847; *Bryers v Lake* (1655) Style 446, 82 E.R. 850.

[86] Gadsden, paragraph 3.67.

[87] *Earl of Pembroke's Case* (1636) Clayton 47.

[88] *Greater Protection and Better Management of Common Land in England and Wales*, DETR, February 2000.

Chapter 3

Trees on or near Boundaries

3.1 Introduction

It is no coincidence that many trees are on or near property boundaries. Land is in most cases acquired and used for an activity other than merely growing trees; and that activity – whether it be in a house, an office block, a church, or any other building, or in a garden, on a playing field, or any other open space – will generally be carried on in the middle of a site, or at any rate not at the edge of it; trees, therefore, will tend to be round the edge.

Secondly, of course, hedges and trees have always traditionally provided a way of marking property boundaries.

Unfortunately, boundaries have two sides; and the owners of neighbouring properties may have differing views as to the way in which boundary trees and hedges should be maintained, and indeed as to the desirability of retaining them at all. The trees that make such a pleasing backdrop to the perfectly maintained garden may be seriously undermining the foundations of the house next door. Trees and hedges are thus often the focus of disputes, and litigation, between warring neighbours. And neighbours may be at loggerheads for reasons entirely unconnected with the boundary tree or hedge, which then becomes a convenient excuse for a dispute rather than the true reason for it.

It should therefore come as no surprise that there have been many reported cases over the centuries considering the rights and duties of neighbouring property owners in relation to the trees on or near the boundary between them – at **1.5** is an account of one such dispute from the early seventeenth century.[1]

Most of this Chapter considers the role of the law in relation to trees on or near boundaries which cause difficulties by their very existence or, rather, by their location – because of, for example, branches which overhang neighbouring land, roots which undermine structures and so forth. The tree concerned, in other words, is not defective in any way; it is merely (seen from the point of view of a potential complainant) in the wrong place. Such a situation is generally dealt with by reference to the law of nuisance, although there are various other mechanisms that may be relevant, considered in outline at **3.3**.

The application of the law of nuisance to trees is discussed in detail at **3.4**, in relation to branches and trunks encroaching into the airspace over neighbouring land, and at **3.5** in relation to roots encroaching into the neighbouring land itself.

[1] *Masters v Pollie* (1620) 2 Roll. 141.

An understanding of the principles involved should hopefully avoid the need to trouble the courts; and the most readily available remedy is self-help ("abatement"), considered at **3.6**. However, litigation may sometimes be unavoidable; the principles involved are considered at **3.7** and **3.8**, in relation to claims for damages or an injunction. An alternative approach, that may sometimes yield results even though it has been little tried to date, is to rely on the doctrine of "statutory nuisance". This is explored at **3.9**.

Finally, the provisions of the Access to Neighbouring Land Act 1992, as they relate to trees, are explored at **3.10**.

Chapter 4 considers those problems in the specific context of boundary hedges.

Where a tree or hedge causes problems to those on neighbouring land because it is harmful or dangerous in some way, this is generally considered in relation to the law of negligence, which is the subject of **Chapter 5**.[2] Special problems also arise where a property shares a boundary with highway land. These are considered in **Chapter 6**.[3]

Before proceeding any further, however, the first matter to be considered in relation to any dispute between neighbouring landowners concerning trees and hedges is the apparently simple question of who actually owns them.

3.2 Ownership of trees on or close to boundaries

3.2.1 Trees on a boundary

It has already been pointed out that a tree (or indeed any other plant) is owned by the person who owns the soil surrounding the base of its stem.[4] But what is the position where that soil is owned by more than one person – where, in other words, the tree is actually on a property boundary?

This question was considered in passing by the Court of Appeal in the celebrated case of *Lemmon v Webb*[5]:

"In 20 Vin Abr, under the head 'Trees' and 'Disputes between Neighbours', I find:

'A tree grows in A's close, and roots in B's, yet the body of the main part of the tree being in the soil of A, all the residue belongs to him also.'[6]

There is added in a note:

'But if it grows in a hedge which divides the land of A and B, and the roots take nourishment of both their lands, it was adjudged that they are tenants in common of it.'[7]

This shews that the roots, though in another man's land, belong to the owner of the tree, and it is only where the tree is on the boundary line, so that the trunk is partly in the land of each of the adjoining owners, that they become joint owners of the tree: see *Holder v Coates*.[8]"

---

²   See, in particular, **5.3.1**.
³   See also **5.3.2**.
⁴   See **2.1.1**.
⁵   [1894] 3 Ch. 1, per Kay L.J. at p. 20.
⁶   2 Roll. 141; Hill 17 Jac B R; *Masters v Pollie*.
⁷   2 Roll. 255; Mich 20 Jac B R.
⁸   Mood. & M. 112; and see *Waterman v. Saper* (1697) 1 Ld. Ray 737.

The case proceeded to the House of Lords,[9] but the judgment of the Court of Appeal was not questioned at all on the issue of ownership (or indeed on any other issue).[10] It is therefore clear that a plant which is planted so that the base of the stem is actually intersected by the line between two properties, is jointly owned by the owners of both of them – who are thus, at least in theory, tenants in common of the tree under a trust of land (since 1997).[11] This was also the approach of the Lord Ordinary in the later Scottish case of *Heatherington v Gault*, upheld on appeal by the Court of Session:

". . . I think the sole question here is whether the trees proposed to be cut are on the march, in which case they are common property, or on the respondent's ground, in which case they are wholly his." [12]

More recently, the issue was considered by the Chancery Division of the High Court in *Richardson v Jay*,[13] which concerned a dispute between the owners of two neighbouring properties whose mutual boundary was formed by a fence that ran between two trees. The fence had been there "for years and years" and so, whether or not it had originally been erected in the correct position, it undoubtedly now marked the true boundary, which left half of each tree in the garden of each property. Cross J. (as he then was) held that "the result was that the two trees were owned by the parties in common". And see the judgment of Millett L.J. in *Stanton v Jones*.[14]

In the case of a party wall, other than a wall forming part of a larger structure such as a building, section 38 of the Law of Property Act 1925 provides that the wall is deemed to be severed into two equal parts, both with cross-rights of support and user. That provision does not explicitly apply to trees or other plants, and it is not clear whether the same principles could simply be assumed to be apply; but it would seem to be logical that they should.

Generally, with land held under a tenancy in common, both tenants have full use of the whole of the shared property, and neither can, for instance, sue the other in trespass. Thus where a field was owned by tenants in common, the House of Lords held that:

". . . it is idle to talk of trespass as a consequence of a man making hay upon his own field – for it is his own – or a moiety of it at least, and no definite portion of it is mapped out as his moiety".[15]

That would suggest that where a tree is a genuine "boundary tree", the owners of both properties have equal rights to carry out works to it. However, if one owner fells the whole tree, that would destroy the subject of the tenancy in common, which would amount to "ouster", and thus to trespass.[16] Thus in *Heatherington v Gault*, the Lord Ordinary held that:

9   [1895] A.C. 1.
10 See **3.6**.
11 See **2.4.1**.
12 (1905) 7 F. 706, per Lord Stormonth-Darling, Ordinary at p. 710.
13 (1960) E.G. July 9.
14 October 6, 1994, unreported, CA; see extract at **4.2.4**.
15 *Jacob v Seward* (1872) L.R. 5 H.L. 464, per Lord Hatherley L.C. at p. 473.
16 *Cubitt v Porter* (1828) 8 B. & C. 257 at p. 268, 108 E.R. 1039 at p. 1043.

"If the trees are on the line of march, they are undoubtedly common property, and cannot be removed without consent of both proprietors."[17]

And in *Richardson v Jay*, Cross J. commented as follows:

"A difficult question might arise as to what exactly the rights of owners of trees in common were. The plaintiff was entitled to cut the roots on his own side. Whether he could cut down half the trees longitudinally, he (the judge) did not know. At any rate he had no right to cut down the whole tree without the consent of the defendant."[18]

That suggests that the position is not – yet – entirely clear, so that there may be scope for further litigation (or, better, legislation) to clarify the rights and duties of all concerned.

Finally, where a building is located so that one of its walls is right on the boundary of two properties – where, for example, a house owned by A immediately adjoins a garden owned by B (as in *Pickering v Rudd*[19]) – a creeper planted in the soil owned by B, and growing up the wall of A's building, will belong to the owner of the soil (B), not to the owner of the building (A).

3.2.2 Trees close to a boundary

Where a tree is located close to a property boundary, but not actually on it, some of its roots may still extend into the soil of the neighbouring property, and its branches into the air over that soil. In such a case, the ownership of the whole of the tree, including those encroaching roots and branches, will remain unchanged; that is, the plant will still be owned by the owner of the land on which it was originally planted.

Nor is there any question of the owner of the tree acquiring an easement to permit the roots or branches encroach into or over neighbouring land. The position is summarised thus in *Gale on Easements*:

"As regards boundary trees, there is no authority in the English law that an easement can be acquired to compel a man to submit to the invasion of his land by the roots or branches of a tree planted on his neighbour's soil. The principal objections to the acquisition of such an easement by user consist in the perpetual change in the quantity or inconvenience imposed by it and, in the case of penetrating roots, the secrecy in the mode of enjoyment. It is now settled that the encroachment of boughs or roots of trees (whether planted or self-growing) over and within the land of an adjoining owner, is not a trespass or occupation which by lapse of time can become a right but is (or may be) a nuisance."[20]

As will be seen, the word "nuisance" does not mean a mere inconvenience, but has a very specialised meaning.[21]

Where there is no co-operation between neighbours, a plant (including a hedge plant or a tree) should generally not be planted actually on or very close to a boundary. That is, it should be planted so that the whole of the ball of soil containing the root system of the plant is sunk into the soil of the land owned by the person doing the planting. This is particularly so in the case of a tree. It is then clear that the plant belongs to the person in whose soil the roots are first buried;

[17] (1905) 7 F. 706, at p. 708.
[18] (1960) E.G. July 9.
[19] (1815) 1 Stark. 56, 4 Camp. 219.
[20] 16th edn, 1997, para. 11–54.
[21] See **3.3.2**.

and when, as will inevitably happen, the branches and roots on one side grow across the boundary, the ownership will not change. See, for example, the speech of Kay L.J. in *Lemmon v Webb*,[22] quoted above, and the opinion of the Lord Ordinary in the later Scottish case of *Heatherington v Gault*.[23]

Thus, if a tree is planted very close to the boundary, so that even initially at least some of its roots are within the neighbouring land, it is likely that a court would consider that it still belonged to the owner of the soil surrounding the base of the stem – if only because, once the planting is complete, it is impossible to know with certainty how far the roots extend in any direction without excavating the soil and, probably, damaging the tree. And, in theory at least, the person doing the planting would need to have excavated the hole to receive the roots of the plant partly on his or her own land, and partly on the neighbour's – and the latter would amount to trespass. An additional problem is that the owner of the neighbouring property is entitled to cut encroaching roots back to the boundary line,[24] and could in principle probably do so as soon as the tree had been planted, which would clearly be unsatisfactory.

In practice, of course, where there is co-operation between neighbours, a tree or other plant can be planted wherever it is convenient to all concerned. But to avoid problems of the kinds outlined above – particularly following a change in the ownership of the property on one or other side of the boundary – it may be best to agree and set out in writing the initial intentions of the two parties. This is probably unnecessarily elaborate in the case of a small shrub, but may well be advisable in the case of a tree of any size, or a hedge, either of which may in years to come attain a size currently undreamed of, with problems of corresponding magnitude arising as a result.

3.2.3 Fruit and leaves

It is now settled law that, where a branch of a tree projects over a boundary, any fruit on that overhanging branch belongs to the owner of the tree, not the owner of the airspace in which it is hanging. That still applies even where the fruit has been severed from the branch – "whether it has fallen from being ripe, or been blown off by the wind, or severed by the act of man"[25] – or where the branch has itself been severed from the remainder of the tree (for example, by way of abating a nuisance[26]). And if fruit falls onto adjoining land, its owner is entitled to enter that land and recover it.[27]

If anyone other than the owner finds on his or her land branches or fruit that has been accidentally separated from a neighbour's tree (for example, by the wind), there is no obligation to keep it safe. However, if the finder removes, destroys or sells it, or gives it away (or eats the fruit), that amounts to conversion, which can be the subject of a civil action in the courts; it will also usually be theft, which is a criminal offence.[28]

That leaves unresolved the question of who owns dead leaves, which can be a real source of annoyance each autumn. It would seem that they probably belong,

---

[22] [1894] 3 Ch. 1, at p. 20.
[23] (1905) 7 F. 706, per Lord Stormonth-Darling, Ordinary at p. 710.
[24] See **3.6.1**.
[25] *Mills v Brooker* [1919] 1 K.B. 555, *per* Lush J. at p. 558.
[26] See **3.6.5**.
[27] *Mitten v Faudrye* (1625) Poph. 161; *Patrick v Colerick* (1838) 3 M. & W. 483 at p. 485.
[28] See **9.6.1**.

in theory, to the owner of the tree; but it is most unlikely that a court would grant an injunction requiring the owner to come and collect them! See also the discussion below[29] on harm caused by leaves.

3.2.4 Disputes

It will be obvious that the question of who owns trees on or near a boundary will often be of great importance to the owners of the land on either side – if only so as to determine the question of who has the duty to maintain them, or the right to fell them.

Most of the disputes reaching the courts, in which the issue of ownership has been a crucial (or the only) element, have tended to be in the context of boundary hedges rather than trees as such. They are accordingly considered in the following Chapter. But the principles outlined there[30] are in general as relevant to disputes relating to the ownership of trees as they are to those as to the ownership of hedges. And of course trees on or close to a boundary are often growing in a hedge, or indeed may be the only survivor of an earlier hedge long since gone; so the two issues cannot be wholly separated.

Finally, it should not be forgotten that seeking a declaration as to the ownership of a tree will usually form part of more extensive litigation – either as to the ownership of a piece of ground on which the tree is growing, or as to the rights and duties of the possible owners with regard to maintenance and felling. As to the latter, this forms the subject of the remainder of the Chapter.

3.3 Liability for boundary trees

3.3.1 Introduction

It has already been noted that trees on or near boundaries often give rise to problems.[31] There are a number of legal mechanisms for dealing with these, of which the most significant is the common law remedy of nuisance. The basic principles underlying this are therefore considered first, followed by a brief glance at the principle in *Rylands v Fletcher* (which is anyway linked closely to nuisance).

Later in this Chapter, these principles are applied generally to problems involving incursion by branches[32] and roots.[33] Where there is potential liability in nuisance, the available remedies may be self-help (abatement)[34] or litigation; and the latter may be seeking either an award of damages[35] or an injunction.[36] Each of these is considered in turn.

The related topic of statutory nuisance is considered towards the end of the Chapter.[37]

---

[29] At **3.4.3**.
[30] At **4.2.5**.
[31] See **3.1**.
[32] See **3.4**. The anomalous case of incursion by a whole tree – trunk, branches, roots and all – into neighbouring land (as occurred in *Elliot v Islington LBC* [1991] 1 EGLR 167, CA) is considered with branches.
[33] See **3.5**.
[34] See **3.6**
[35] See **3.7**.
[36] See **3.8**.
[37] See **3.9**.

3.3.2 Nuisance at common law

Many things in life are a "nuisance", in the colloquial sense of that term. To lawyers, however, it has a much more specific meaning. The scope of the law of nuisance has recently been considered by the House of Lords in the landmark case of *Hunter v Canary Wharf Ltd*, in which it was held:

"Private nuisances are of three kinds. They are:

(1) nuisance by encroachment on a neighbour's land;
(2) nuisance by direct physical injury to a neighbour's land; and
(3) nuisance by interference with a neighbour's quiet enjoyment of his land."[38]

The encroachment of trees into neighbouring land is always cited as the principal, if not the only, example of the first of these categories.

Also in *Hunter*, the House approved the thesis of Professor Newark, who explained the historical origin of the tort as follows:

"*Disseisina, transgressio* [trespass] and *nocumentum* [nuisance] covered the three ways in which a man might be interfered with in his rights over land. Wholly to deprive a man of the opportunity of exercising his rights over land was to disseise him, for which he might have recourse to the assize of novel disseisin. But to trouble a man in the exercise of his rights over land without going so far as to dispossess him was a trespass or a nuisance, according to whether the act was done on or off the plaintiff's land."[39]

That tends to suggest that a nuisance is where A does something on his land which interferes with the enjoyment by B of her land; whereas a trespass is where A goes onto B's land to cause the interference. Plants are unique in that a plant on A's land, which is therefore A's property, can nevertheless spread so as to intermingle with B's land, or the airspace above it. An invading plant might therefore appear to be properly the subject of an action in either trespass or nuisance or, possibly, both. In fact, however, the courts, as will be demonstrated, have consistently maintained that the proper cause of action in relation to the encroachment of the boughs and roots of a tree over and within the land of an adjoining owner is not trespass but nuisance.[40]

The first of the three categories identified in *Hunter*, encroachment, is the subject of much of the remainder of this Chapter.[41] The third category (interference with quiet enjoyment of land) may arise in the context of trees, but is more likely to do so in the context of high hedges; it is accordingly considered in the following Chapter.[42]

Before going any further however, it may be appropriate to consider the current state of the law regarding general liability for natural phenomena.

---

[38] [1997] A.C. 655, H.L., reversing [1996] 1 All E.R. 482, CA; per Lord Lloyd of Berwick at p. 695B ([1997] 2 All E.R. 426, at p. 441c).

[39] (1949) 65 L.Q.R. 480 at pp. 481, 488–489; approved by Lord Goff at [1997] A.C. 6687G–688D (2 All E.R. 434g).

[40] See, for example, *Lemmon v Webb* [1894] 3 Ch. 7, CA, per Kay L.J. at p. 24 (upheld at [1894] A.C. 1, H.L.).

[41] See **3.3.4**, and for more detail **3.4** (branches) and **3.5** (roots).

[42] See **4.3.3**.

3.3.3 Liability for things naturally on land

The liability in nuisance for the existence of natural phenomena, as opposed to human activities, was considered authoritatively by Professor Goodhart in an influential article with the above title written in 1930.[43] That was cited with approval in a number of subsequent judgments, but most significantly by the Court of Appeal in *Leakey v National Trust*,[44] which considered the whole issue in some depth.

The court in *Leakey* thus explicitly overruled *Giles v Walker*,[45] a brief decision that had been followed by the courts with increasing reluctance in spite of criticism by Goodhart and others. *Giles* had held that there could be no duty as between adjoining occupiers to cut thistles, which are the natural growth of the soil. The Australian decision of *Sparke v Osborne*,[46] which relates to the spread of prickly pears (a noxious weed), and which followed *Giles*, is thus also no longer good law. Indeed, both were not followed in the more recent New Zealand case of *French v Auckland Corporation*,[47] in which it was held that there could be liability for harm caused by weeds and thus, by implication, harm caused by other natural causes. The decision in *Pontardawe RDC v Moore-Gwyn*,[48] which also followed *Giles*, was similarly overruled by the Court of Appeal in *Leakey*.

Instead, both *French* and *Leakey* followed the decision of the Privy Council in *Goldman v Hargrave*,[49] which accepted that there does exist "a general duty upon occupiers in relation to hazards occurring on their land, whether natural or man-made".[50] That acceptance also enabled the Court of Appeal in *Leakey* to harmonise the approach to be taken in relation to any case involving natural occurrences, whether mineral (such as the landslip in *Leakey* itself) or vegetable (such as trees). It thus adopted the approach of Rowlatt J. in *Noble v Harrison*,[51] relating to hazardous trees, and that of the Court of Appeal in *Davey v Harrow Corporation*,[52] which concerned encroaching tree roots. Thus in *Davey*, the court had held:

"In our opinion, it must be taken to be established law that, if trees encroach, whether by branches or roots, and cause damage, an action for nuisance will lie."[53]

That case also established that there was no logical distinction between planted and self-sown trees[54]; nor was it any defence to such an action to say that the harm was caused by natural growth or natural causes. That approach was echoed by the Privy Council shortly afterwards in *Morgan v Khyatt*:

"It has in their Lordships' opinion long been established as a general proposition that an owner of land may make any natural use of it; but also (and by way of qualification of the

---

[43] *Liability for things naturally on the land*, Prof. A.L. Goodhart, 4 C.L.J. 13.
[44] [1980] 1 Q.B. 485, CA.
[45] (1890) 24 Q.B.D. 656.
[46] (1908) 7 C.L.R. 51, High Court of Australia.
[47] [1974] 1 N.Z.L.R. 340, Supreme Court, Auckland.
[48] [1929] 1 Ch. 656.
[49] [1967] A.C. 645, P.C.; see **5.1.2**.
[50] *ibid.*, at pp. 661–662, considered in *Leakey* [1980] 1 Q.B. 485, CA, at p. 515.
[51] [1926] 2 K.B. 332 at pp. 338, 341; considered in *Leakey* at pp. 516E and 518C respectively; see **5.1.2**.
[52] [1958] 1 Q.B. 60; considered in *Leakey* at p. 522A-D.
[53] [1958] 1 Q.B. 60, CA, per Lord Goddard at p. 73.
[54] *ibid.*, at p. 71.

general rule) that if an owner of land grows or permits the growth on his land in the natural way of trees whose roots penetrate into adjoining property and thereby cause and continue to cause damage to buildings upon that property, he is liable for the tort of nuisance to the owner of that adjoining property."[55]

The court in *Leakey*, whilst generally following *Davey*, did however add the important proviso that:

". . . the duty arising from a nuisance which is not brought about by a human agency does not arise unless and until the defendant has, or ought to have had, knowledge of the existence of the defect and the danger thereby created".[56]

As to the scope of the duty owed by a landowner under the law of nuisance, in respect of things naturally on the land, this was explained (by Megaw L.J. in *Leakey*) as follows:

"The duty is a duty to do that which is reasonable in all the circumstances, and no more than what, if anything, is reasonable, to prevent or minimise the known risk of damage or injury to one's neighbour or to his property. The considerations with which the law is familiar are all to be taken into account in deciding whether there has been a breach of duty and, if so, what that breach is, and whether it is causative of the damage in respect of which the claim is made. Thus there will fall to be considered:

- The extent of the risk: what, so far as reasonably can be foreseen, are the chances that anything untoward will happen, or that any damage will be caused?
- What is to be foreseen as to the possible extent of the damage if the risk becomes a reality?
- Is it practicable to prevent, or to minimise, the happening of any damage?
- If it is practicable, how simple or how difficult are the measures which could be taken, how much and how lengthy work do they involve [sic], and what is the probable cost of such works?
- Was there sufficient time for preventive action to be taken, by persons acting reasonably in relation to the known risk, between the time when it became known to, or should have been realised by, the defendant and the time when damage occurred?

Factors such as these, so far as they apply in a particular case, fall to be weighed in deciding whether the defendant's duty of care requires, or required, him to do anything, and, if so, what?"[57]

There thus seems now to be no doubt whatsoever as to the existence of at least some liability on the part of landowners for any harm caused by trees and other plants (even weeds) growing on their land. Nor is there any defence that the owner of the affected land acquired it in full knowledge of the existence of the thing causing the harm.[58]

More recently, the Court of Appeal has re-visited the decision in *Leakey*, in the context of a well-publicised incident in which a landslip on land owned by a local authority caused catastrophic failure of a hotel on neighbouring land.[59] The

---

[55] [1964] 1 W.L.R. 475, per Lord Evershed at p. 477.
[56] [1980] 1 Q.B. 485, CA, per Megaw L.J. at p. 522.
[57] *ibid.* per Megaw L.J. at p. 524 E.
[58] *Sturges v Bridgman* (1879) 11 Ch.D. 852.
[59] *Holbeck Hall Hotel Ltd v Scarborough BC* [2000] Q.B. 836, CA.

Court held that the duty of a landowner was confined to an obligation to take care
to avoid danger to the neighbour's land which it ought to have foreseen without
further, extensive geological investigation. Clearly a landslip caused by a hidden
underground geological fault is similar in concept to the fall of a tree or a branch
caused by a hidden defect within the body of the tree. How much investigation
would be appropriate in any case, however, must presumably be a matter of fact
and degree, to be determined in the light of all relevant circumstances.

Finally, it may be noted that the decision of the Court of Appeal in *Wringe v
Cohen*[60] should be treated with caution in the present context, insofar as it decides
that there is no liability where a nuisance is created by a "secret and unobservable
operation of nature", a phrase earlier applied to trees.[61] That might appear to
mean that there is never, or only rarely, liability for harm caused by root action,
since roots are normally unseen. But that is manifestly not the true position, as
witnessed by the stream of cases noted later in this Chapter.

3.3.4 Encroachment by roots and branches

It has already been noted that the first of the three categories of nuisance
identified by the House of Lords in *Hunter v Canary Wharf Ltd* is "nuisance by
encroachment on a neighbour's land"[62]; and that encroachment by trees is always
taken as the most significant, if not the only, example of this category of nuisance.
But the principles are the same as with other types of nuisance.

The encroachment of a branch of a tree into a neighbour's airspace is thus a
"nuisance", not simply because it drops leaves onto neighbour's path and shades
his plants, but because its mere existence impedes the neighbour's enjoyment of
his land. It might prevent him from erecting a children's climbing frame, or
extending his lawn; the fact that he may not wish to do any of these things is
irrelevant – if only because he might later sell the land to someone who does wish
to use the land in a particular way that is impeded by the branch. Similarly the
encroachment of a root into the neighbour's soil is a nuisance not just because it
harms the foundations of his house, but because it limits the use of the land that is
affected by the roots.

In *King v Taylor*,[63] a case of harm caused by roots, Eveleigh J. held that the
view that "if there was no damage, there was no nuisance" was a misconception.
However, that was in the context of a dispute where a tree was threatening to
cause harm to the foundations of a bungalow on neighbouring land,[64] and he
went on to find that although no harm had yet been caused directly to the
bungalow (so that no damages were payable), harm had been caused in that the
soil had been affected so as to make it less suitable to support the bungalow (so
that an injunction was granted). It follows that, strictly speaking, his dictum
quoted above is therefore *obiter* – that is, it did not form an essential part of the
reasoning which led to the decision.

Similarly, in *Elliott v Islington LBC*,[65] the Court of Appeal came close to
accepting that a tree could be a nuisance "in the technical sense of the word"

[60] [1940] 1 K.B. 229, CA, per Atkinson J. at p. 233.
[61] By Wright J. in *Noble v Harrison* [1926] 2 K.B. 332 at p. 341.
[62] [1997] A.C. 655, H.L., reversing [1996] 1 All E.R. 482, CA; per Lord Lloyd of Berwick at p. 695B
      ([1997] 2 All E.R. 426, at p. 441c); see **3.3.2**.
[63] [1976] 1 EGLR 132 at p. 132H
[64] See **3.8.2**.
[65] [1991] 1 EGLR 167, CA; see **3.8.3**.

merely because it was invading the plaintiff's property – "it is his garden, and there is no reason why he should not have full enjoyment of it". However, here too there was a finding that harm had in fact been caused to the boundary wall itself – albeit in a way that could be avoided in future by making adjustments to the construction of the wall.

In practice, of course, cases tend to come to court only where harm – caused, or alleged to have been caused, by a tree – has actually occurred or is imminent. That is because the remedy in such cases, damages or an injunction, will only be obtainable in court. Where the problem is merely that branches are encroaching into air space over neighbouring land, the remedy (abatement) is, literally, in the hands of the owner of that land – with only rarely any need for judicial intervention (as in *Lemmon v Webb*[66]). However, even that "remedy" would not be available if there was not, in principle, a cause of action.

So the Court of Appeal in *Lemmon v Webb* held (in the context of encroachment by branches):

"The encroachment of the boughs and roots over and within the land of the adjoining owner is not a trespass or occupation of that land which by lapse of time could become a right. It is a nuisance.
"For any damage occasioned by this, an action on the case would lie.
"Also, the person whose land is so affected may abate the nuisance if the owner of the tree after notice neglects to do so."[67]

And the same is true of roots. The observations of the Court of Appeal in *Lemmon v Webb* regarding roots, quoted above, were of course strictly *obiter*, but they were effectively adopted by that court in *Davey v Harrow Corporation*, which was a case relating to encroachment by roots:

"[*Lemmon v Webb*] has been cited again and again and has never been the subject of adverse comment. In our opinion, once it is established that encroachment by roots is a nuisance, it must follow that, if damage is thereby caused, an action on the case will lie."[68]

It logically follows from this that there may be cases of encroachment by roots where harm is not caused, so that no action will lie, but that such encroachment is still a "nuisance" in law. And the principles in *Lemmon v Webb* have recently been upheld by the House of Lords, in *Delaware Mansions Ltd v Westminster CC*.[69]

The rule is thus that any encroachment by the root of a tree (or of a hedge plant) into the soil of neighbouring property, or by a branch into the airspace above it, is a "nuisance" in law, which may be abated by the owner of that property; and that an action for damages or an injunction will be possible where damage is caused. It follows that the general principles developed over many years in relation to the law of nuisance may be applied in such cases.

The Court of Appeal has indeed recently confirmed that encroachment is simply one form of nuisance; and also that there is no reason why, where a defendant has not created a nuisance but has merely adopted or continued it, different principles should apply. In either case, liability only arises if there has

---

[66] [1894] A.C. 1, H.L., upholding [1894] 3 Ch. 1, CA; see **3.6.1.**
[67] [1894] 3 Ch. 1, per Kay L.J. at p. 24.
[68] [1958] 1 Q.B. 60, CA, per Lord Goddard at p. 71.
[69] [2001] 3 W.L.R. 1007, H.L.; see paragraph 12 at p. 1013A.

been negligence, and the duty to abate the nuisance arises from the defendant's
knowledge of the hazard that would affect his neighbour.[70]

3.3.5 Infringement of light

Where something on A's land prevents light reaching B's land, that may
constitute a nuisance at law, which may enable B to seek redress in the courts.
However, there appears to be no reported case of such an action being brought,
let alone succeeding, in the context of trees. This is because the remedy is available
only in very limited circumstances.

This is considered further in the following Chapter,[71] since it is more likely to be
of use (if at all) in the context of high hedges than in connection with individual
trees. But the same principles would seem to apply in the latter case.

3.3.6 Strict liability: the rule in Rylands v Fletcher

The rule in *Rylands v Fletcher* was first stated as follows:

"We think that the true rule of law is that the person who, for his own purposes, brings on
his land and collects and keeps there anything that is likely to do mischief if it escapes, must
keep it in at his peril; and if he does not do so, is *prima facie* answerable for all the damage
which is the natural consequence of its escape.   . . . It seems but reasonable and just that
the neighbour who has brought something on his own property (which was not naturally
there), harmless to others so long as it is confined to his own property, but which he knows
will be mischievous if it gets on his neighbour's, should be obliged to make good the
damage which ensues if he does not succeed in confining it to his own property."[72]

That statement of law was adopted without demur by the House of Lords.[73] It has
been authoritatively re-considered by the House of Lords in *Cambridge Water Co
v Eastern Counties Leather plc*, where it was held that foreseeability was an
essential ingredient under the rule in *Rylands v Fletcher* as in nuisance.[74]

Subject to that modification, the distinctive feature of the rule in *Rylands v
Fletcher* is that liability, if it can be established, is strict; that is, it is not dependant
on any proof of fault. In that respect it echoes the approach of the French *Code
Civil*, which imposes a relatively strict liability on owners for anything in their
charge.[75]

Because of this, many litigants over the last century have based claims on the
rule in *Rylands* as well as in nuisance or negligence; but it has been held to be the
basis of liability in comparatively few cases. In particular, the Courts have placed
much emphasis on the need for the cause of the harm to be a non-natural use of
the land. However, *Rylands* itself concerned the escape of water from a reservoir
on the defendant's land; and water is after all a natural substance, rendered
harmful only by its quantity and location. It is thus not entirely surprising that a
number of cases relating to harm caused by trees have been framed in relation to
the rule.

---

[70] *Holbeck Hall Hotel Ltd v Scarborough BC* [2000] Q.B. 836, CA; see **3.5.3**.
[71] See **4.3.2**.
[72] (1866) L.R. 1 Ex 265, per Blackburn J. at pp. 279–280.
[73] (1868) L.R. 3 H.L. 330, per Lord Cairns L.C. at pp. 339–340.
[74] [1994] 2 A.C. 264, per Lord Goff at p. 301.
[75] *cf.* Art. 1384 of the *Code*.

In relation to encroaching branches and roots, *Rylands v Fletcher* was considered in *Wilson v Newberry* – one of the earliest cases relating to poisonous foliage, decided shortly after *Rylands* itself – but it was held that *Rylands* had no relevance.[76] In *Erskine v Adeane*,[77] *Rylands* was cited by counsel, but not discussed. The claim in *Crowhurst v Amersham Burial Board*,[78] on the other hand, succeeded on the basis of liability under *Rylands v Fletcher*; apparently because the trees in question were poisonous yews. And in *Ponting v Noakes*,[79] which also concerned yews, such liability was not discounted (although that claim failed on its facts[80]). The same approach was followed, with considerable reluctance, in *Smith v Giddy*.[81]

In only two of the many subsequent encroachment cases,[82] however, has liability under *Rylands v Fletcher* been considered; and in both instances liability was established solely on the basis of nuisance. And even on the facts in *Crowhurst* it would seem that a claim framed solely in nuisance would succeed today, since the danger of harm being caused to animals on neighbouring land by eating foliage on the overhanging branch of a yew tree is both foreseeable and avoidable.

As to the cases relating to hazardous trees, considered in **Chapter 5**, Wright J. in *Noble v Harrison* stated clearly "I see no reason whatever to apply the principle in *Rylands v Fletcher*" [83]; and in none of the subsequent decisions has the possibility even been canvassed.

The conclusion thus seems to be that the principle in *Rylands v Fletcher* has little continuing relevance to cases involving trees and hedges.

3.3.7 Negligence

It is obvious that one property owner owes to the owner and occupiers of nearby property a duty of care. In the present context, this largely becomes a duty to ensure that trees and other plants do not cause harm to those on other land. The distinction has been expressed thus (in the context of the escape of noxious weeds) in the New Zealand case of *French v Auckland City Corporation*:

"Insofar as any claim is based on nuisance, a claimant, in order to merit legal intervention, will have to demonstrate that the annoyance or damage which he suffers is substantial and, in any case, the law will be concerned to strike a tolerable balance between the conflicting claims of landowners to enjoy their properties and the interests of surrounding occupiers. Insofar as the claim is based on negligence, a claimant will have to demonstrate the breach on the part of an occupier of a duty to take reasonable care to avoid the spread of weeds or their seeds."[84]

---

[76] (1871) L.R. 7 Q.B. 31, at p. 33.
[77] (1873) L.R. 8 Ch. App. 756.
[78] (1878) 4 Ex D 5, per Kelly C.B. at p. 10.
[79] [1894] 2 Q.B. 281.
[80] See **3.4.4**.
[81] [1904] 2 K.B. 448, per Wills J. at p. 450.
[82] *Davey v Harrow Corporation* [1958] 1 Q.B. 60 at pp. 72–73; also *Hawkins v Coulsdon and Purley UDC* (1953) E.G., June 13, Digest p. 192.
[83] *Noble v Harrison* [1926] 2 K.B. 332, per Wright J. at p. 342; followed in *Cunliffe v Bankes* [1945] 1 All E.R. 459;
[84] [1974] 1 N.Z.L.R. 340, per McMullin J. at p. 351, lines 46–54.

However, where that harm consists of harm caused by encroaching branches and roots, that is usually the subject of a claim in nuisance rather than negligence. In those few cases where a claim has been made in negligence as well as nuisance,[85] including a number of the cases relating to street trees,[86] little if any comment is made by the court as to the claim in negligence, or as to the distinction between them. In *Low v Haddock*, HH Judge John Newey Q.C. summed up thus the position in relation to "natural processes":

"Nuisance, when knowledge and foresight of consequences are required for it, bears a strong resemblance to negligence; but because it is a continuing wrong, it is much more difficult to establish a limitation defence to it."[87]

In *Hurst v Hampshire County Council*, the Court of Appeal noted that a free-standing claim founded in negligence relating to a street tree "would present great difficulties in the light of *Stovin v Wise*".[88] And in the most recent of these cases, *Delaware Mansions v Westminster CC*, another street tree case, that court confirmed at the outset that "there is no doubt that the appropriate action when there is encroachment by roots is in nuisance",[89] a conclusion that was not doubted when the case went on to the House of Lords.[90]

It follows that where a claim is founded in nuisance in relation to encroachment by branches or roots, either in relation to a street tree or in any other case, the broad principle is that an additional claim in negligence adds little. The only slight qualification to that is that the Court of Appeal has, perhaps unfortunately, recently muddied the water by pointing out that, in the case of any encroachment amounting to a nuisance, liability arises only if it can be proved that there has been negligence.[91] However, in spite of the broad proposition on which the judgment was based, that was in the context a considering liability for a latent defect in land, which is more akin to a defective or inherently hazardous tree, rather than a perfectly healthy one that is "merely" encroaching onto neighbouring land.

Thus, where harm arises as a result of the condition of the tree – where, for example, the whole tree or a part of it falls so as to harm buildings on neighbouring land – a claim will generally be brought in negligence[92]; and, as will be seen, the same principles apply whether the potential victim is on the same property as the tree or is on neighbouring land.[93] It follows that there is nothing special about boundary trees in that context; and disputes will be governed by the normal rules as to liability in negligence.

---

[85] See, for example, *Coupar v Heinrich* (1949) E.G., March 19, Digest p. 176.
[86] Including *Russell v Barnet LBC* [1984] 2 EGLR 44; *Low v Haddock* [1985] 2 EGLR 247; *Hurst v Hampshire County Council* (1997) 44 E.G. 206 [1997] 2 EGLR 164, CA; *Delaware Mansions Ltd v Westminster CC* [1999] 46 E.G. 194, [1999] 3 E.G.L.R. 68, [2000] B.L.R. 1, CA, reversing (1998) 88 B.L.R. 99 (decision of CA upheld at [2001] 3 W.L.R. 1007, H.L.).
[87] [1985] 2 EGLR 247, at p. 251 J.
[88] [1997] 2 EGLR 164, CA, *per* Stuart-Smith L.J. at p. 69B; for a full consideration of *Stovin v Wise*, see **6.4.6**.
[89] [1999] 46 E.G. 194, CA, per Pill L.J. at p. 195.
[90] [2001] 3 W.L.R. 1007, H.L.
[91] *Holbeck Hall Hotel Ltd v Scarborough BC* [2000] Q.B. 836, CA; see **3.3.3**.
[92] See **5.1.2**.
[93] See **5.4.1**.

3.4 Encroaching branches and trunks

3.4.1 The nature of the problem

There are various problems that may result from the encroachment of trees into neighbouring property. Those caused by roots are the subject of the next section. This section concerns those caused by the parts of a tree above the ground – that is, trunks, branches, leaves and fruit. The most notable are:

- unwanted intrusion into airspace;

- overshadowing of crops (and gardens), harm to buildings and walls, and shedding of leaves, needles, cones, and bird and insect droppings;

- poisoning of animals from eating foliage of certain species; and

- branches (or even whole trees) falling.

The first of these may include any or all of the others. There may thus be a general feeling that an overhanging tree is a "nuisance", in the popular sense of that term, without particularising any further. The right to abate a nuisance, in the strict legal sense, arises from that concern, in that the removal of encroaching branches will automatically sort out most of the other problems too. Although, they may still arise to a lesser extent due to the remaining part of the tree on the neighbouring land (which of course cannot generally be touched). Abatement is accordingly the first possible remedy to be considered.[94]

The next two of the above situations concern the occurrence of actual harm, rather than mere encroachment. Here the result is likely to be an award of damages (where harm has already occurred) and an injunction, to prevent future harm.[95] The third, in particular, applies only where horses, cattle, sheep and other animals have access to parts of trees which are harmful, such as the leaves of yew trees (or clippings from such trees). This is clearly a limited problem but one which, where it does occur, notably in farming areas, is potentially very serious.[96]

The first three of the categories listed above are the result of the natural characteristics of a healthy tree. However, additional problems may arise where a tree on or near a boundary is defective, as a result of disease, decay, storm damage or just simply old age, and may fall or shed branches onto neighbouring land, causing property damage, injury or even death.[97] Any litigation that arises in such cases is more properly framed in negligence rather than nuisance, and is accordingly dealt with in **Chapter 5**.[98]

3.4.2 Encroachment

The most common situation – which occurs routinely, up and down the country, and especially in urban areas – is where the branches of a tree extend into the

---

[94] See **3.6**.
[95] See **3.7** and **3.8**.
[96] See **3.4.4**.
[97] See for example *Bruce v Caulfield* (1918) 34 T.L.R., CA; *Shirvell v Hackwood Estates* [1938] 2 K.B. 577, CA; *Knight v Hext* [1980] 1 EGLR 111, CA.
[98] See, in particular, **5.1.2** and **5.3.1**.

airspace over a neighbour's land. This is the classic case of a tree constituting a "nuisance" at common law, and has already been dealt with.[99]

The remedy to this is usually for the owner of the land into which the tree is encroaching to take direct action, by cutting back some or all of the offending branches, possibly up to the boundary. This is known as "abatement", and will be dealt with later in the Chapter.[1]

Occasionally, it is not just a branch but a whole tree that causes a problem by encroaching into neighbouring property, with the boundary wall or fence usually being the first victim, as occurred in *Elliott v Islington LBC*.[2] In this situation, in the absence of co-operation from the owner of the tree, it may be that the only remedy will be an injunction to bring about its removal.[3]

3.4.3 *Harm caused (other than by encroachment)*

In some cases, of course, the parts of a tree above ground – notably branches – will not only encroach into the airspace above neighbouring land, so as to give rise to a right to abatement, but will also cause actual harm. Examples are –

- overshadowing of crops (and gardens);
- harm to buildings and walls; and
- shedding of leaves, needles, cones, and bird and insect droppings.

The first was the subject of a claim for damages and an injunction in *Smith v Giddy*, which concerned a group of elm and ash trees on G's property whose branches overhang S's land, and interfered with the growth of his fruit trees. It was noted that there was no precedent for any action in such a case, except where the trees were poisonous,[4] but it was held that:

"If trees, although projecting over the boundary, are not in fact doing any damage, it may be that the plaintiff's only right is to cut back the overhanging portions; but where they are actually doing damage, I think that there must be a right of action. In such a case, I do not think that the owner of the offending trees can compel the plaintiff to seek his remedy in cutting them. He has no right to put the plaintiff to the trouble and expense which that remedy might involve."[5]

The case was sent back to the County Court for a new trial, and it is not known what the eventual outcome was; but there seems to be no reason to suppose that there was not at least an award of damages.

Smith v Giddy was decided on the basis that it was analogous to *Crowhurst v Amersham Burial Board*,[6] which in turn had been decided on the basis of the rule in *Rylands v Fletcher*. But Wills J. in *Smith*[7] also rested his judgment on the decision of the Court of Appeal in *Lemmon v Webb*,[8] which rested solely on

---

[99] See **3.3.4**.
[1] See **3.6**.
[2] [1991] 1997 1 EGLR 197, CA; see **3.8.3**.
[3] See **3.8**.
[4] See **3.4.4**.
[5] [1904] 2 K.B. 448, *per* Kennedy J. at p. 451.
[6] (1878) IV Ex D 5; see **3.4.4**.
[7] See [1904] 2 K.B. 448, at p. 451.
[8] [1897] 3 Ch. 7, CA; upheld at [1895] A.C. 1, H.L.

nuisance. Such an action would now be best brought in nuisance, and would in an appropriate case lead to damages and an injunction.

Finally, trees are inevitably a source of irritation to neighbouring landowners in the autumn, when they shed leaves. And harm may be caused (particularly to parked vehicles) by falling blossom in the spring, and by aphids and other insects related to the trees. The courts are in general unlikely to be quick to grant a remedy – sweeping leaves, and parking away from cherry trees, may be tiresome, but they are part of normal life; and the law takes no note of trifles.[9] However, it seems that damages (and possibly an injunction) may be granted where leaves block gutters and cause mould inside a building.[10] And it may be that a tree that leads to problems with aphids and other insects may be a statutory nuisance.[10a]

3.4.4 Poisonous foliage or fruit

Particular problems may arise where trees whose foliage is poisonous are allowed to grow so that their branches overhang neighbouring property, so as to be eaten by animals, or where clippings from such trees are allowed to lie where they can be eaten. Obviously, the normal rules[11] will apply here too; but there may be a stronger claim to an award of damages, probably without proof of any fault on the part of the tree owner, under the rule in *Rylands v Fletcher*.[12] This emerges from a series of cases at the end of the nineteenth century – all of which relate to yew trees.

In *Wilson v Newberry*,[13] clippings from a tree on the defendant's land were allowed to fall onto the plaintiff's land, resulting in the death of the plaintiff's horses. The plaintiff's claim failed because there was no evidence as to who had actually cut the clippings, nor any indication that the defendant even knew that they had been cut at all. Nor was the plaintiff more fortunate in *Erskine v Adeane*,[14] which related to the death of E's sheep from cuttings thrown over their common boundary by A's gardener – but here, too, it seems, only because of a technicality, in that A (the defendant) had died before the action came to trial.

In the latter case, in particular, it seems that such a claim might have succeeded in other circumstances. It follows that, in general, it is important that poisonous clippings are not placed where animals on neighbouring land may reach them and suffer or die as a result.

Erskine also related to the death of E's cattle as a result of eating branches of the yew overhanging the boundary, and straying onto A's land (through a gap in the fence) and eating yew branches and clippings there. The claim as to the overhanging branches was dismissed on the basis that E had been A's tenant and knew, or could have discovered, the existence of the yews when first entering on the land.[15] The claim as to the straying failed too, because A had no duty to fence his land; whereas a similar claim succeeded in *Lawrence v Jenkins*,[16] even though

---

[9]   *De minimis non curat lex* (pre-Woolf).
[10] *Fusco v Georgiou*, February 9, 1994, unreported, Ilford County Court (noted in *Gardens and the Law*, Blackburn, 1998 (p. 31)).
[10a] *R. v. Test Valley BC, ex p. Anne* [2001] EWHC Admin 1019; see **3.9.3**.
[11] See **3.4.2** and **3.4.3**.
[12] Law Rep. 1 Exch. 265; but see **3.3.6**.
[13] [1871] VII Q.B. 31.
[14] (1873) L.R. 8 Ch. App. 756.
[15] See **2.5.5**.
[16] Law Rep. 8 Q.B. 274.

J's fence was broken down without his knowledge by a third party, because J was under a duty to maintain it.

Where trees with poisonous foliage are planted on or close to boundaries, therefore, it may be important to ascertain whether there is any liability on one or other party to maintain a stock-proof fence between them. Such a liability may be by a grant or contract, or by prescription, or by statute. As to the latter, Mellish L.J. in *Erskine* noted that an obligation to repair fences is constantly found in inclosure Acts[17]; and recent litigation[18] suggests that it is just possible that such an obligation may still be binding two centuries later.

Erskine was also followed, both at first instance and by the Court of Appeal, in *Cheater v Cater*,[19] another landlord and tenant case.[20] Although that case explicitly left open for further consideration the question of whether a landlord who retains adjacent land is liable for the growth of poisonous branches across the boundary subsequent to the start of the tenancy.[21]

All of the earlier cases were explicitly distinguished in *Crowhurst v Amersham Burial Board*,[22] which is perhaps the most significant of these decisions. It concerned a yew planted by the Board 1.2 metres (4 ft) from a wall forming the boundary of a cemetery; after some years, its branches grew so as to overhang a neighbouring field. A horse grazing there ate the foliage, and died. It was established that it is generally known that cattle frequently browse on the leaves and branches of yew trees when within reach, and that they are not infrequently poisoned thereby[23]; the court also noted that:

". . . if the trees were innocuous, it might well be held, from grounds of general inconvenience, that the occupier of land projected over would have no right of action, but should be left to protect himself by clipping. Such projections are innumerable throughout the country, and no such action has ever been maintained; but the occupier sought, from similar grounds of general convenience, to be allowed to turn out his cattle, acting upon the assumption that none but innocuous trees are permitted to project over his land."[24]

Accordingly, the Board was found liable for allowing the yew to overhang the boundary, but on the principle in *Rylands v Fletcher* rather than in nuisance as such.

Crowhurst was itself distinguished in the last case in this series, *Ponting v Noakes*.[25] Here, P's horse died as a result of eating yew leaves; but there was some uncertainty as to whether these came from a tree on N's land, or one on the land of H (at third party), or a bush on P's own land. The jury accepted the evidence of the veterinary surgeon that the death was most likely to have been caused by N's tree, and that was not overturned on appeal. But P's land and N's land were separated by a ditch (on the actual boundary) and a fence (on N's side of the ditch); N's tree overhung his part of the ditch, but did not overhang the actual boundary. It followed that P's horse must have been trespassing when it ate the yew leaves, and that as a result there was no liability.

---

[17] (1873) L.R. 8 Ch. App. 756, at p. 763.
[18] See **23.3**.
[19] [1918] 1 K.B. 247, CA, affirming [1917] 2 K.B. 518.
[20] See **2.5.5**.
[21] See [1918] 1 K.B. 247, CA, per Bankes L.J. at p. 255.
[22] (1878) IV Ex D 5.
[23] At p. 12.
[24] At p. 10.
[25] [1894] 2 Q.B. 281.

The conclusion seems to be that trees such as yews should not be planted close to boundaries where they are liable to be browsed by livestock on adjacent property; and that any branches that do grow across such boundaries should be regularly checked and trimmed back. It is not sensible to wait for a passing animal to feel hungry.

Where such harm has occurred, damages should be sought by the landowner who has suffered loss and, where it is likely in the reasonably near future, an injunction. However, although the action in *Crowhurst* was brought under the principle in *Rylands v Fletcher*,[26] there seems to be little if any distinction between the results and those which would have occurred had the action been in nuisance. Arguably, therefore, these cases are in fact merely a particular example of the general category of instances where the above-ground parts of trees cause harm to neighbouring property.[27]

3.5 Encroaching roots

3.5.1 The nature of the problem

The fact that tree roots may cause problems, particularly to paths, walls and foundations, is now widely known – in particular, by engineers, insurers, property owners and householders. And it has long been known to judges: in the words of one county court judge just after the war, "the roots of the poplar spread very fast, and their depredations were in the nature of a land octopus, thrusting on regardless of any obstruction".[28]

However, the emphasis in the first sentence in the previous paragraph should be on the word *may*: problems are not inevitable and, when they do occur, there are in many cases several possible ways of resolving them. It is perhaps helpful, therefore, before considering in detail the lessons to be learnt from the numerous cases that have reached the courts relating to root damage, to consider in outline what is actually happening to give rise to such problems in the first place.[29]

In the spring, when a tree starts to produce leaves, photosynthesis starts too and, more importantly, so does transpiration – that is, the process by which moisture is lost by evaporation through the leaves. That loss is replenished through the take up, via the roots of the tree, of water from the soil. Peak rates of water uptake from the soil can be the equivalent of more than 5 mm of rainfall per day. Rainfall is usually much less than this, so that the soil becomes progressively drier, typically reaching its driest state in September. From then on, rainfall will usually exceed the loss of moisture through transpiration, so that the soil will start to rehydrate, typically returning to full moisture capacity at the end of the year.

As a result, there is an annual cycle of drying during the summer, and rehydrating during the winter. However, if clay dries, it will shrink; and as it rehydrates, it will swell. Clay soil will therefore be subject to considerable movement through the year, and that will cause movement in any structure resting on the soil – such as a path, a garden wall or the foundations of a building.

---

[26] See **3.3.6**.
[27] See **3.4.3**.
[28] *Attfield v Wilson* (1949) E.G., June 18, Calne County Court.
[29] The material here is based on work by Dr Giles Biddle, with permission; for more details, see his encyclopaedic work *Tree Root Damage to Buildings*, published in 1998 by Willowmead Publishing, Wantage.

The same phenomenon can occur as a result of any vegetation, be it trees, shrubs or even grass. The key feature of trees is that the depth and lateral spread of their root system means that they can penetrate beneath the foundations of buildings.

In theory, therefore, a building will subside during the summer as the soil beneath its foundations dries out, and it will rise during the winter as the soil completely rehydrates. This is broadly what does in fact happen, except that the constant movement of foundations causes a gradual long-term settlement (sometimes referred to as "dynamic settlement"). Many buildings – particularly those of more traditional construction – will tolerate considerable movement, so that there may be no harm done (or none that cannot be tolerated); but excessive movement of foundations can lead to serious harm to the building above. And where the soil has very low permeability, roots will have to go ever further and deeper to find the necessary moisture to support the tree, and this will lead to a "persistent deficit", causing greater subsidence of foundations and thus potentially more serious harm to buildings.

To remedy the cause of such problems, it may be appropriate (or necessary) to underpin the building, that is, to increase the depth of the foundations to below the zone where movement occurs, so that the problem will not recur. However, that is inevitably both very disruptive and very expensive; and insurers will usually demand that the offending tree is removed as well, so that this method, whilst it may stop the recurrence of the harm, does not save the tree. In addition, where the building affected is part of a terrace, or one of a pair of semi-detached houses, there may be further problems if part of a block is underpinned and the remainder is left to continue moving.

Alternatively, it may be that heavy pruning of the tree will reduce the leaf area, and thus the amount of transpiration, so as to reduce the uptake of moisture and thus the annual movement of the soil. That too is not without drawbacks, as most trees respond to pruning by vigorous production of new shoots and leaves, in order to restore the original leaf area as soon as possible. And if pruning is insufficient, it may be necessary to fell the tree altogether, although even that will not reduce the result of dynamic settlement, and the building may never entirely recover its original form.

In addition, once the tree has gone, there will of course be no transpiration to balance the intake of rainfall, so the clay may swell and cause further problems as a new equilibrium is achieved (this is the phenomenon known as "heave").

One further feature of subsidence is that it is very difficult to predict with any accuracy. As it was put in one text book:

"Whoever expects from soil mechanics a set of simple hard and fast rules for settlement computation will be deeply disappointed. The nature of the problem strictly precludes the possibility of establishing such rules."[30]

And whether damage will occur is even more unpredictable. So, for example, it is known that in 50 per cent of cases involving harm caused by oak trees, the distance between the tree and the building is less than 9.5m, in 90 per cent it is less than 18m; and the maximum distance recorded is 30m (the corresponding figures for the much-maligned poplar are slightly greater). However, that does not mean

---

[30]   Terzaghi, *Settlement of Structures* (1936) – cited in *Bunclark v Hertfordshire County Council* [1977] 2 EGLR 114, at p. 120A.

that it is necessary to fell every oak closer than 9.5m to a building – since, even at that distance, probably less than one per cent of oak trees on clay soils will cause harm.[31]

3.5.2 Points to be considered

Many cases involving tree root damage have come before the courts since the first English decision (*Butler v Standard Telephone and Cables Co Ltd*[32]) in 1939. The underlying principles, however, were considered more thoroughly by the Court of Appeal in *Davey v Harrow Corporation*[33]; and that decision was then approved by the same court in *Leakey v National Trust*,[34] subject to the proviso that a defendant must have had knowledge of the hazard.

Following *Leakey*, the court once again re-visited the matter of root damage in *Solloway v Hampshire County Council*.[35] At first instance, the judge had formulated the position as follows:

"I therefore find that the law which I have to apply to the facts of the present case to be that the duty in respect of the nuisance created by the roots arises if the encroachment of those roots is known, or ought to be known, to the owner, occupier, or other person responsible for the tree and its maintenance, if the encroachment is such as to give rise to a reasonably foreseeable risk that such encroachment will cause damage."[36]

That was adopted as an accurate statement of the law by Dunn L.J., who gave the leading judgment when the case went on to the Court of Appeal – albeit after some hesitation (since there had been no mention of foreseeability in *Davey*). He also repeated the observations of Megaw L.J. in *Leakey* as to the scope of the owner's duty in nuisance,[37] and summarised it thus:

"In considering whether there is a breach of duty, the extent of the risk and the foreseeable consequences of it have to be balanced against the practicable measures to be taken to minimise the damage and its consequences."[38]

The approach adopted by the Court of Appeal in *Solloway* has been elaborated in subsequent judgments, but not basically questioned (save in *Butcher v Perkins*[39]). More recently, the need for the type (if not the extent) of harm to be foreseeable was confirmed by the Court of Appeal in *Holbeck Hall Hotel Ltd v Scarborough BC*.[40]

Finally, in what must currently be the definitive statement of the law in this area, the House of Lords in *Delaware Mansions Ltd v Westminster CC*[41] agreed with the approach that had been adopted in *Solloway*, which it saw as "a salutary

---

[31] See also Cutler and Richardson, *Trees, Roots and Buildings* (2nd ed., Longman, 1989) (the Kew root survey).
[32] [1940] 1 All E.R. 121.
[33] [1958] 1 Q.B. 60, CA.
[34] [1980] 1 Q.B. 485, CA; see **3.3.3**.
[35] (1981) 79 L.G.R. 449, [1981] 1 EGLR 129, CA; for the facts, see **3.5.4** and **3.5.6**.
[36] (1980), February 20, unreported, per Stocker J.; cited with approval at 79 L.G.R. 449, CA, p. 452.
[37] Quoted at **3.3.3**.
[38] (1981) 79 L.G.R. 449, CA, per Dunn L.J. at 457.
[39] (1994) 10 Const L.J. 67; see **3.5.4**.
[40] [2000] Q.B. 836, CA.
[41] [2001] 3 W.L.R. 1007, H.L., upholding [1999] 46 E.G. 194, [2000] B.L.R. 1, CA, reversing (1998) 88 B.L.R. 99.

warning against imposing unreasonable and unacceptable burdens on local authorities or other tree owners".[42] The *Delaware* decision went further, however, in that it made it clear that it is not just harm to buildings that must be considered:

"I think that there was a continuing nuisance . . . until at least the completion of the underpinning and the piling in July 1992. It matters not that further cracking of the superstructure may not have occurred after March 1990. The encroachment of the roots was causing damage to the land by dehydrating the soil and inhibiting rehydration. Damage consisting of impairment of the load-bearing qualities of residential land is, in my view, itself a nuisance . . . . Cracking in the building was consequential."[43]

That same decision also established that the response to the harm caused or threatened by the tree must be reasonable.[44]

It follows that the questions to be considered in any root damage case are now as follows:

- Did the roots of A's tree actually cause harm to B's structure?

- Was that harm reasonably foreseeable?

- Were there any practicable measures that could have been taken to minimise or avoid the harm and its consequences?

- Was it reasonable to take the steps that were actually taken?

Each of these is now considered in turn, indicating how it has been dealt with by the courts in practice.

It should be noted that some of these decisions (including *Solloway* itself) relate to harm caused by street trees to buildings on adjacent land; others relate to disputes between private landowners. The principles are the same, however, in either case – except insofar as there is an issue as to whom is responsible for highway trees, which is dealt with in **Chapter 6**.

3.5.3 Causation

The key issue under this heading is whether the harm to the structure on A's land was caused by one or more trees on B's land; or whether it was caused either by one or more trees on A's land, or by something else. That is, there is no need to show that trees of a particular species may cause harm if at a given distance to a building; it is the actual cause of this particular harm that is of concern.

So, for example, in the first reported case of root damage (*Middleton v Humphries*), which related to the collapse of a garden wall near Dublin separating the properties owned by the parties, allegedly as a result of nearby oaks, elms and other forest trees, the judge noted:

"The only question I have to decide is one of fact. I have heard all the evidence, and am not bound by the testimony of any expert, good, bad, or indifferent. I am allowed to use my own experience as to what I have seen, and what I understand about trees and such

---

[42] [2001] 3 W.L.R. 1007, H.L., per Lord Cooke of Thorndon at p. 1019, paragraph 34.
[43] [2001] 3 W.L.R. 1007, H.L., per Lord Cooke of Thorndon at p. 1019, paragraph 33.
[44] See **3.5.6** for more details on this.

matters. I have spent a good portion of my life in the country. The one question I have to decide is – what brought down the wall?"[45]

He concluded that it was "the growing action of the roots of the trees that brought down this wall", and awarded a declaration, an injunction and damages. In the light of the significant increase over the subsequent years in the understanding of the mechanism of root growth, such reliance on judicial experience over technical expertise might now be somewhat frowned upon.

The court often has to consider whether there are any alternative reasons for the harm. Thus, in *Coupar v Heinrich*,[46] which concerned harm alleged to have been caused by tree roots to a house which had also been damaged by a war-time bomb, the court found that the bomb had caused harm, but that that had been properly repaired. However, the house had then continued to suffer harm as a result of the tree, so that damages were payable. The fall of a bomb nearby was also blamed for harm in *Niklaus v Moont*,[47] as was "general subsidence of the house, of which there had been no real evidence at all"; the judge was not convinced by either of them. And in *Lumb v United Utilities Water Ltd*,[48] the Lands Tribunal accepted that damage to a house had occurred due to blasting carried out in connection with the construction of a sewer, rather than because of the drying out of soil due to a nearby tree.

And sometimes there will be two incompatible theories as to the cause of harm, each of which is plausible. The burden of proof then is on the plaintiff to substantiate his or her case; and the requirement (on both sides) is merely to demonstrate the likelihood of each theory on the balance of probabilities, not beyond reasonable doubt. This makes sense, as it will in some cases be impossible to determine with absolute certainty what caused harm; but it will still be necessary to say which of the possible causes is most likely.

So, for example, where the foundations of a ground floor extension were severely harmed (in *Holloway TCHA v Islington LBC*[49]), the owner argued that the cause was a large horse-chestnut tree next door abstracting water from the clay sub-soil, causing desiccation leading to subsidence. The owner of the tree, on the other hand, argued that the harm was due to ground water seepage as well as drainage problems causing the sub-soil to be unduly moist and soft, thus reducing its bearing capacity. Each side produced expert evidence to support its theory. The court held that, on the balance of probabilities, the plaintiff's theory (blaming the tree) was inherently more convincing. A poplar tree was also found to be the principal, if not the only, cause of the problem in the earlier case of *Brown v Bateman*.[50]

Poor foundations were also cited as a possible cause of subsidence in *Bunclark v Hertfordshire County Council*.[51] However, at the conclusion of a lengthy and careful judgment, the deputy judge concluded:

---

[45] (1912) XLVII ILT 160, per Ross J. at p. 160.
[46] (1949) E.G., March 19, 1949; E.G. Digest, p. 176
[47] (1950) E.G., July 29, 1950.
[48] *Jack Lumb v United Utilities Water Ltd (formerly North-West Water Ltd)* Lands Tribunal, June 7, 2001, unreported.
[49] *Holloway Tenant Co-operative Housing Association v Islington LBC* (1997) 57 ConLR 160, Q.B.D. Official Referees' Business
[50] (1955) 115 E.G. 261.
[51] [1977] 2 EGLR 114.

"I have examined the evidence in great detail from both sides in order to answer the first question: was the damage caused by the roots of the defendants' trees? I have come to the conclusion that on the balance of probability the answer must be yes. I do not utterly dismiss the defendants' suggestion that the insufficiency of the foundations, exaggerated in the later years by some leakage from drains, was a factor, but I think it was a contributory one . . . It is no defence for the plaintiffs, who have caused damage on the defendants' land, to say, 'Oh well, the structure that was damaged was not robust, or was of its nature not likely to survive long' (see *Hoare & Co v McAlpine*[52]). . . . I doubt whether the contributory effect of faulty construction should be taken into account and weighed against the root effect, unless, of course, the former was of so overwhelming a nature as to reduce the tree root effect to insignificance. If that were the case, it might be possible for the court to say that the bad foundations were the only true cause of the damage, or if the roots had begun causing damage only a few months or so before the inevitable collapse of the building, that might be reflected in the measure of damages."[53]

Occasionally, however, the court may decide that the harm has been caused by more than one factor. Thus in *Murray v Hutchinson*, Gorman J. noted that:

"Poplar trees have often been blamed for so denuding the soil of moisture that they cause it to crumble, but one has to be careful not to jump to the conclusion that because they have a bad name they are always responsible for this damage."[54]

He went on to conclude that, on the evidence, the harm had been caused by several factors: faulty construction, settlement common to the area, dry summers, the effect of war damage and the effect of tree roots. He accordingly decided that the defendant tree owner was responsible for 25 per cent of the harm, and awarded damages accordingly.

In *Mayer v Deptford and Lewisham Councils*,[55] on the other hand, the judge concluded that there were other factors responsible for subsidence – and that the roots of a nearby plane tree ("a weak one, with weak roots") had accelerated the settlement, but had not started it. In this case, however, he did not split the award of damages, but simply gave judgment to the defendants.

Most recently, in *Paterson v Humberside County Council*, it was found that the encroachment of roots from street trees were an effective and substantial cause of the harm to the plaintiff's house, albeit not the sole cause:

"Other causes are the poor foundations of the property and the drought. The superior quality of construction of 42 Park Avenue may well explain why that property has suffered less damage. But it is sufficient to establish causation that the trees were an effective cause of the damage: *Banque Bruxelles Lambert SA v Eagle Star Insurance Co Ltd*. The foundations were not so poor that the damage was bound to happen in any event. That is evidenced by the facts not only that the property had stood for over a hundred years, but also that the structure was in a stable condition at the time of the plaintiffs' purchase and for several years after. That being so, the fact that the property had shallow foundations and was therefore more susceptible to damage from soil shrinkage caused by invasion of

[52] [1923] 1 Ch. 167.
[53] [1977] 2 EGLR 114 at p. 121C.
[54] (1955) 116 E.G. 467; E.G. Digest, p. 202; quoted also in subsequent decisions such as *Wallace v Clayton* (1962) 181 E.G. 569 (Bloomsbury County Court).
[55] (1959) 173 E.G. 961.

tree roots is no more relevant to liability than the fact that a plaintiff has a thin skull: *Smith v Leech Brain & Co Ltd.*[56] The roots take their victim as they find it."[57]

That is clear, but must now be treated with caution. For one thing, the *Banque Bruxelles* decision referred to (that of the Court of Appeal[58]) has since been overturned on appeal. And secondly, the application of the "thin skull" principle is doubtful. The plaintiff in a personal injury case cannot increase the thickness of his skull so as to be more resistant to unexpected personal injuries; whereas the purchaser of a house with poor foundations may reasonably expect that his house will be less resistant to root damage than the superior house next door (as was indeed the case in *Paterson*), and would presumably pay less for it.

More frequently, however, although two or more theories are canvassed as to the cause of the harm, the court has little difficulty in deciding which is to be preferred. In *Butler v Standard Telephones and Cables*,[59] for example, it was admitted that the plaintiffs' houses were being severely harmed as a result of subsidence, which in turn was the result of the drying of the clay beneath them; and it was admitted that the roots of a nearby row of fine poplar trees were beneath the foundations. The plaintiffs claimed that the drying of the clay was due to the poplars; the defendants that it was due to the drought, and to the fact that the clay in that area was particularly wet. The judge had no doubt that the plaintiffs were correct.

3.5.4 Foreseeability of harm

It must be remembered that it was not until the decision of the Court of Appeal in 1981 in *Solloway v Hampshire County Council*[60] that the courts reached the view that harm caused by tree roots must be foreseeable if it is to result in an award of damages. It follows that cases decided prior to *Solloway* might be decided differently now – in many of them, foreseeability was not considered as an issue at all; and there is therefore no way of knowing what the outcome would have been.

Secondly, the extent of general knowledge as to the part played by tree roots in harm to buildings is increasing; what was unforeseeable in 1981, let alone 1951, may well be entirely foreseeable now – especially to public bodies (including highway authorities). But this is an area that remains uncertain. Thus, one deputy judge could say in 1977[61] (as it happens, prior to *Solloway*) that "damage by tree roots is *always* foreseeable" (emphasis added), whereas another could conclude four years later[62] (after *Solloway*) that "it would be quite wrong to attribute either the plaintiff or the defendant with foresight of the possibility of any real risk existing because of the underlying clay bed". Both cases related to litigation between neighbouring householders with no specialist technical expertise.

Where the tree concerned is growing in the highway, on the other hand, the owner is in practice presumed to be the highway authority[63]; and it is very difficult

---

[56] [1962] 2 Q.B. 405.
[57] (1995) 12 Const L.J. 64, per Roger Toulson QC, sitting as deputy judge, at p. 68.
[58] [1995] Q.B. 375, CA
[59] [1940] 1 K.B. 399, 1 All E.R. 121.
[60] (1981) 79 L.G.R. 449, E.G., May 30, [1981] 1 EGLR 129, CA; see **3.5.2**.
[61] *Tajika v Sturgess* (1977) December 19, unreported, per Sir Douglas Frank QC, sitting as deputy judge.
[62] *Greenwood v Portwood* (1984) January 4, unreported; [1985] C.L.Y. 2500, per HH Judge Fallon, sitting as deputy judge.
[63] See **6.2.5**.

for such authorities now to escape liability on the grounds of not knowing about the mechanics of tree root damage. This was the clear conclusion drawn by the court from the technical evidence in *Russell v Barnet LBC*.[64] That case was decided in 1984, after the drought of 1975–76 had significantly increased awareness of the problem. Such awareness must now be universal amongst authorities whose area contains any clay soil.

Thus, what is foreseeable means, presumably, what would be capable of being predicted by a tree owner, properly advised, once the matter had been drawn to his or her attention. The latter qualification is necessary because it would be perverse to require an owner of trees to consider in advance whether any of them might cause harm in the future. As already noted, the incidence of harm is notoriously difficult to predict, and to make predictions with any degree of probability would require a full knowledge of the foundations of all nearby buildings.

It follows that, as soon as a property owner notices cracks which might be due to trees growing on neighbouring land, the matter should be drawn to the attention of the owner of that land, preferably in writing, so that it will not be possible thereafter for the tree owner to claim that subsequent harm was unforeseeable. In a number of cases the problem was first noticed in the form of cracks to paths – which were not in themselves particularly serious, but which could (and should) have put everyone on notice of likely harm to buildings and, in particular, houses.[65]

In *Solloway* itself,[66] the house that had been harmed by the roots of a chestnut tree in the adjacent street was in an area where the topsoil was generally plateau gravel, which is unlikely to be affected by the intrusion of tree roots. There were, however, amongst the gravel a few pockets of clay, too small to appear on the relevant geological plan, and completely randomly distributed. This particular house was founded upon plateau gravel at the rear and clay at the front – which would have meant that it was at greater risk of subsidence, since the foundations would not be resting on a homogenous sub-soil.

The first argument raised by the defendant (the highway authority) was that the harm occurred during the drought of 1975–76, and that a drought of that duration had only occurred once in the last 200 years. However, the various experts agreed that, given the existence of the clay under some of the house, the tree roots would certainly have caused subsidence eventually, so that the drought merely accelerated the process. The Court of Appeal thus agreed with the judge at first instance that the key question was, therefore, whether the existence of the pocket of clay under the house was foreseeable.

The evidence of all the various experts was that they were surprised at the presence of the clay, and they would have thought, prior to seeing the evidence, that subsidence would be most unlikely. The judge at first instance appeared to have misunderstood one of them, and concluded that intrusions of clay were likely in the area. But when the case proceeded to the Court of Appeal, Dunn L.J. (who delivered the leading judgment) reviewed the evidence carefully, and concluded that:

---

[64] [1984] 2 EGLR 44, at pp. 51H–52G (the evidence was given by the arboriculturist, Dr Biddle).
[65] See, for example, *Tajika v Sturgess*.
[66] *Solloway v Hampshire County Council* (1981) 79 L.G.R. 449, [1981] 1 EGLR 129, CA.

"The possibility of an intrusion of clay under No 72, which is the real question, was unlikely. I would hold that it was no more than a vague possibility, not a real risk, in the words of Lord Reid in *Wagon Mound (No 2)*,[67] but assuming that there was a real risk or chance, I would say that it was an outside chance, and that outside chance has to be balanced against the practical steps which could reasonably have been taken by the defendants to minimise the damage."[68]

(The second point mentioned there is considered below.[69]) Sir David Cairns summarised the position this way:

". . . it appears to me not surprising that the defendants clearly never directed their minds to the question of whether any particular house in that road was liable to be damaged by such roots. If they had considered the matter, I am of the opinion that they could have reasonably taken the view that any risk of such damage was so remote that it could be disregarded. To say that a risk of damage is reasonably foreseeable means that it is foreseeable not merely as a theoretical possibility but as something the chance of which occurring is such that a reasonable man would consider it necessary to take account of it. The risk of being struck by lightning when one goes for a walk is not a reasonably foreseeable risk. I should be prepared to hold that the risk in this case was not a reasonably foreseeable risk."[70]

Stephenson L.J. cited the words of Lord Dunedin in *Fardon v Harcourt-Rivington*: was the risk more than a mere possibility that would never occur to the mind of a reasonable man.[71]

From this it is clear that, for an action in nuisance to succeed, the possibility of root damage must be a "real risk", and not just a "vague possibility"; it must be such that a reasonable man would consider it necessary to take account of it. In practice, it seems that it is now difficult for a defendant to avoid liability on the basis that it is unforeseeable that tree roots might cause harm to buildings built on clay. But it might in rare cases be possible to avoid liability if it can be shown that the presence of clay at this location was itself unforeseeable (as in *Solloway*).

Damage can also occur if the extent to which a tree is pruned is reduced, leading to an increase in transpiration, and thus an increase in the uptake of water from the ground and consequential drying up of the ground. This was found to be the cause of the increased root growth which caused foundation damage in the recent case of *Delaware Mansions v Westminster City Council*.[72] That case related to a plane tree, growing in the street, that had been heavily pruned from at least the mid-1950s, until the mid-1970s when severe tree-pruning went out of fashion. The tree was allowed to become bushier, and as a result its roots grew more extensively. On that basis, it was foreseeable that there would be an increased chance that foundations of neighbouring buildings would be harmed.

And note that foreseeability can only apply once there is reasonable general knowledge of the possibility of the type of harm that has occurred.

---

[67] *Overseas Tankship (UK) Ltd v Miller Steamship Co Pty (Wagon Mound) (No. 2)* [1967] 1 A.C. 617, H.L. at p. 642G.
[68] (1981) 79 L.G.R. 449, CA, at p. 458.
[69] See **3.5.5**.
[70] (1981) 79 L.G.R. 449, CA, at p. 460.
[71] (1932) 146 L.T. 391 at p. 392, quoted (1981) 79 L.G.R. 449, CA, at p. 461.
[72] (1998) 88 B.L.R. 99, overturned at [1999] 46 E.G. 194, 3 EGLR 68, [2000] B.L.R. 1, CA; decision of CA upheld at [2001] 3 W.L.R. 1007, H.L.

Finally, reference should be made to *Butcher v Perkins*, a slightly maverick decision of a county court in which the decisions of the Court of Appeal in *Davey*, *Leakey* and *Solloway* were considered with the following result:

"I think that there are two things that can be said about *Leakey*. So far from putting a gloss on the *Davey* case, the dictum [as to the proviso to be added[73]] actually conflicts with it; and if *Leakey* is said to be the modern law, then I do have two conflicting authorities. I prefer [the plaintiff's] argument, that the *Leakey* case did not decide the question of whether the foreseeability test applied in cases of nuisance arising from trees, so that the Court in *Solloway* was misled, and Tudor Evans J. in *Russell* also. I can see the force in that argument, but I also think that it would be odd if the test of foreseeability were to be applied to some nuisances and not to others. If I am forced to chose between the two lines of authority I would prefer *Davey*. . ."[74]

The judge explicitly recognised that he was on thin ice ("there is a strong possibility that I may not be upheld"), and so went on to consider whether, if foreseeability did have to be shown, the harm was in fact foreseeable anyway (it was). It is indeed likely that the decision would not have survived on appeal; but someone else may wish to run the argument on another day.

3.5.5 *Possibility of avoiding or minimising harm*

Stephenson L.J. in *Solloway* held that there were two questions to be considered in an action for nuisance caused by tree roots. The first was as to foreseeability.[75] But the second was whether there were any reasonable precautions that the defendants could have taken to prevent or minimise the risk of harm being caused by the tree roots in question to the plaintiff's house. Both he and Dunn L.J. concluded that, even if they were wrong as to foreseeability, there was in effect nothing that could reasonably have been done to minimise the risk:

". . . to have prevented or minimised the plaintiff's damage would have required correspondence with many of the property owners in the county, wholesale inspection of and boring under properties, and the felling of many trees, which would have put the defendants to very great expense and produced many complaints from property owners upset by warnings of dangers which might not exist and from a wide public deprived, perhaps needlessly, of the amenity provided by trees like those lining Shirley Avenue.
  "Such precautions would not, in my opinion, be reasonable; and no less would have been required, without exceptional good luck, to discover and deal with the pocket of clay which unhappily underlay a crucial part of the plaintiff's house before the abnormally long, dry season of 1975/1976 made it too late to stop the subsidence and damage."[76]

On the other hand, both in *Nagioff v Barnet LBC*[77] and *Russell v Barnet LBC*,[78] two cases decided shortly after *Solloway* where this issue came up again, the court considered that it would have been perfectly possible for the offending trees (in both cases, oaks) to be pollarded or pruned so as to avoid the subsidence occurring to adjoining houses. The same conclusion was reached in *Bridges v*

---

[73] See **3.3.3**.
[74] (1994) 10 Const L.J. 67, per Judge Nicholas Brandt at p. 70.
[75] See **3.5.4**.
[76] (1981) 79 L.G.R. 449, CA, per Stephenson L.J. at p. 461.
[77] October 22, 1984, unreported, Westminster County Court.
[78] [1984] 2 EGLR 44, 271 E.G. 699 and 779.

Harrow LBC[79] (decided before *Solloway*). Evidence was given in *Nagioff* as to the Council's other commitments, but the court was unconvinced.

The issue is clearly bound up with foreseeability. The difficulty (and expense) of taking precautions sufficient to discover the problem usually arises where the pockets of clay are so small, or so unpredictably located, that to take precautions sufficient to discover one problem would mean in practice taking steps in relation to many, possibly many hundreds, of other potential problems. Thus if the size and location of the clay in *Solloway* had been otherwise, then not only would the harm have been more foreseeable, but the taking of sufficient precautions would have perhaps been more manageable.

And this issue is also linked to the reasonableness of any steps that actually were taken in response to the problem – as highlighted in the *Delaware Mansions* case, considered below.[80]

One further problem that may arise is where the tree has been planted in such a way that its retention is itself necessary for structural reasons – as happens with, for example, some older railway embankments. In such cases, there may be no option but to underpin any buildings that are affected by roots, since the removal of the tree will not be realistically possible without a great deal of other work.

3.5.6 Reasonableness of steps taken in response to harm

Finally, the steps taken by a property owner in response to harm, or the threat of harm, caused by a neighbouring tree must be reasonable. In other words, it is not reasonable to underpin a large building because of a small tree a long way away (on the grounds that there might in the future be some settlement) and then to claim from the tree owner the cost of the underpinning.

In reality, the first thing to do when a property owner discovers a problem which appears to be due to a tree on neighbouring land is to notify the owner of the tree, to enable him or her to take appropriate action to avoid the problem becoming any worse, and thus to limit the damages payable. In the absence of any satisfactory response to such notification, the property owner can take reasonable action to cure past damage and to prevent re-occurrence, and claim the cost from the owner of the tree.

Thus in the *Delaware Mansions* case, the tree owners (the local highway authority) were made aware of the potential problem in 1990, but declined to remove the tree. Instead, in 1991 they inserted a root barrier between the tree and the mansion block allegedly being affected by its roots. The owner of the building did not agree that that was a sufficient response, and underpinned the building in 1992. There was a dispute between the experts called by the two sides as to whether that underpinning, costing £570,735, was necessary; but the judge at first instance found that the claimants (the new owner of the block) had acted reasonably in executing the works.[81]

The dispute centred on whether the owner was entitled to claim, a point on which both the Court of Appeal and the House of Lords found in its favour.[82] But

---

[79] [1981] 2 EGLR 143 at p. 147D, 260 E.G. 284.
[80] (1998) 88 B.L.R. 99, overturned at [1999] 46 E.G. 194, 3 E.G.L.R. 68, [2000] B.L.R. 1, CA; decision of CA upheld at [2001] 3 W.L.R. 1007, H.L. See **3.5.6**.
[81] (1998) 88 B.L.R. 99, at p. 118, noted at [2001] 3 W.L.R. 1007, H.L. at paragraph 10, p. 1012D.
[82] See **3.7.2**.

the House of Lords also went on to consider whether the claimant had been reasonable in taking the action that it had:

"Having regard to the proximity of the tree to Delaware Mansions, a real risk of damage to the land and the foundations was foreseeable on the part of Westminster, as in effect the judge found. It is arguable that the cost of repairs to the cracking could have been discovered as soon as it became manifest. That point need not be decided, although I am disposed to think that a reasonable landowner would notify the controlling local authority or neighbour as soon as tree root damage was suspected. It is agreed that, if the plane tree had been removed, the need to underpin would have been avoided and the total cost of repair would have been only £14,000. On the other hand, the judge has found that, once the Council had declined to remove the tree, the underpinning and piling costs were reasonably incurred, despite the Council's trench.

". . . If reasonableness between neighbours is the key to the solution of problems in this field, it cannot be right to visit the authority or owner responsible for a tree with a large bill for underpinning, without giving them notice of the damage and the opportunity of avoiding further damage by removal of the tree. Should they elect to preserve the tree for environmental reasons, they may fairly be expected to bear the cost of underpinning or other reasonably necessary remedial works; and the party on whom the cost has fallen may recover it, even though there may be elements of hitherto unsatisfied pre-proprietorship damage, or protection for the future. But, as a general proposition, I think that the defendant is entitled to notice and a reasonable opportunity of abatement before liability for remedial expenditure can arise. In this case, Westminster had ample notice and time before the underpinning and piling, and is in my opinion liable."[83]

3.5.7 Conclusion

None of the above means that every tree near a property boundary should be felled, or drastically pruned. Still less does it mean that such action should be taken in relation to every street tree. After all, even where the soil type is known, the possibility of harm being caused by any particular tree to any particular building is still very unpredictable. And to fell every tree that just might be responsible for harm would lead to a severe loss of amenity.

What it does mean is that owners of trees near to buildings should be aware that there might be a problem at some stage. When building owners discover cracks or other evidence of possible subsidence damage, they should promptly notify the owners of any nearby trees. Appropriate investigative work should then be carried out. This will generally be the responsibility of building owners (or their insurers).[83a] If, and only if, a tree is (or probably is) responsible, then either:

- the tree should be either pruned or felled as appropriate; or

- the building should be underpinned, or otherwise strengthened, to allow for movement.

Either will have to be at the expense of the tree owner. Which would be appropriate in any particular case will depend, obviously, on the comparative cost, and also on the desirability of retaining the tree. Where the problem is caused by an over-mature forest tree now growing in a back garden, extremely

---

[83] [2001] 3 W.L.R. 1007, H.L. per Lord Cooke of Thorndon at paragraphs 33, 34, p. 1019B to F.

[83a] See para. 1 of Association of British Insurers, "Domestic Subsidence Tree Root Claims Agreement", reproduced in Biddle, *Tree Root Damage to Buildings*, p. 347.

close to a house with shallow foundations, it would probably be better to fell the tree, and possibly replace it with a more appropriate one at a more suitable location. Where, on the other hand, it is a fine specimen with many years life ahead of it, some way from a building, it may be better to monitor carefully any further movement, and to underpin as and when necessary.

However, in several of the reported cases it emerged that action would have been possible, relatively cheaply, at an early stage (usually pruning or felling the tree). But once there had set in an intransigent attitude on the part of the tree owner, frequently a public body, the passage of time meant that the only realistic option for the owner of the affected building was underpinning, which by then was relatively expensive:

"The case that [British Railways] knew, or ought to have known, of the dangers posed by tree roots in an area such as Colchester is, in my opinion fully made out, even in respect of the period before the complaints started to be made. After complaints were made on the plaintiff's behalf, their neglect to deal with the situation was, in my view, inexcusable and incomprehensible and, I believe, effectively converted a trivial problem of superficial cracks into something more serious."[84]

And, of course, that was true to a spectacular degree in the *Delaware* litigation.[85]

The court has usually recompensed the building owner by way of an award of damages equal to the cost of the work that actually was carried out; but the tree owner would have been much better off if he or she had been willing to carry out the lesser action earlier – which would also have avoided the costs of litigation!

The one thing that is certain, as always, is that litigation should be only considered when all else fails.

3.6 Abatement

3.6.1 The right to abate a nuisance

There is a long line of cases establishing that branches of trees overhanging another's land constitute a nuisance at law, and may be cut back by the owner or occupier of that land. This is known as "abatement". It is "an exception to the general law of England that a man has no right to take the law into his own hands"[86]; and is thus a remedy which the law does not favour, because "this many times occasions tumults and disorders".[87] The latter sentiment would certainly seem to be borne out in relation to disputes as to boundary trees.

Thus, in the leading case of *Lemmon v Webb* (decided towards the end of the nineteenth century), it was held in the Court of Appeal:

"The right of an owner to cut away the boughs of trees which overhang it, although those trees are not his, is too clear to be disputed. This has been declared to be the law for centuries . . . and there is no trace of the age of the tree or its branches being a material circumstance for consideration."[88]

---

[84] *Hart v British Railways Board* (1989) July 28, unreported, Official Referees' Business.
[85] See **3.5.6**.
[86] *Jones v Jones* (1862) 1 H. & C. 1, per Wilde B. at pp. 5–6.
[87] Per Sir Matthew Hale, in *De Portibus Maris*, Pt 2, Chap VII; and see *Lagan Navigation Co v Lambeg Bleaching, Dyeing and Finishing Co Ltd* [1927] A.C. 226 at p. 244.
[88] [1894] Ch. 7, CA, per Lindley L.J. at p. 12; upheld at [1895] A.C. 1, H.L.

Nor has there been any dispute since.

The earliest authority generally quoted is *Earl of Lonsdale v Nelson*, which was a case relating to trespass, rather than nuisance, but in the course of his judgment Best J. noted as follows:

"Nuisances by an act of commission are committed in defiance of those whom such nuisances injure, and the injured party may abate them, without notice to the person who committed them; but there is no decided case which sanctions the abatement, by an individual, of nuisances from omission, except that of cutting the branches of trees which overhang a public road, or the private property of the person who cuts them. The permitting these branches to extend so far beyond the soil of the owner of the trees is a most unequivocal act of negligence, which distinguishes this case from most of the other cases that have occurred."[89]

Those remarks are clearly *obiter*[90]; and should also be treated with caution in the light of the courts' tendency in subsequent cases to reject the use of "negligence" as a cause of action in encroachment cases.[91]

The matter was then considered more thoroughly by the Court of Appeal and the House of Lords in *Lemmon v Webb* itself. The case concerned a number of large trees, oaks and elms, growing in a hedge separating the properties owned by L and W. The hedge was on L's land, so that the trees in it were owned by L; but their branches had overhung W's farm for many years. W then removed some of those branches back to the boundary line, without giving notice to L, in reliance upon what he supposed to be his common law right.[92] The litigation in that case turned on the narrow point of whether L had a right to be notified of the impending works (a point considered below); but there was so suggestion by anyone that W had a right to carry out the works.

Perhaps the most striking comment in the various judgments given in the case, seen from a century on, was the prescient observation by Lord Herschell L.C.:

"It might be very reasonable that there should be some law regulating the rights of neighbours in respect of trees, which, if planted near the boundary, necessarily tend to overhang the soil of a neighbour. It may be, and probably is, generally a very unneighbourly act to cut down the branches of overhanging trees unless they are doing some substantial harm. The case is a very common one; such trees constantly do overhang, and it certainly might call for the intervention of the legislature if it became at all a common practice for neighbours to exercise what may be their legal rights in thus cutting off what would frequently be a considerable portion of the trees which grow on the other side of the boundary."[93]

And, whilst the entitlement to abatement is generally well known only in relation to branches, it applies equally to roots. A typical statement of the position is thus that of Harman J. in *McCombe v Read*[94]:

---

[89] (1823) 2 B. & C. 302, at pp. 311–312.
[90] That is, not part of the essential reasoning which led to the decision.
[91] See **3.3.7**.
[92] It may not be without significance that the solicitors acting for the defendant (Walter Webb) were Walter Webb & Co; so he presumably was justified in feeling reasonably confident of his position.
[93] *ibid.*, at p. 4.
[94] [1955] 1 W.L.R. 635 at p. 637.

"It is very old law that if my neighbour's tree encroach on my ground, either by overhanging boughs or by undermining roots, I may cut the boughs or the roots so far as they are on my side of the boundary."

As to who may carry out the abatement, this is considered below, in the context of litigation.[94a]

3.6.2 No duty to give notice to tree owner

The question that may sometimes arise is whether the person carrying out the works to abate the nuisance – by removing the encroaching branches or roots – has to give notice of the impending works to the owner of the tree.

As has been noted already, this was the main point at issue in the leading case of *Lemmon v Webb*[95] in which L did not dispute that his neighbour had a right to cut the overhanging branches, but simply claimed that he should have been notified first. L won at first instance,[96] and W appealed. L placed considerable reliance on the comparison between a building and a tree: a building that overhangs a neighbouring property constitutes a nuisance and may be removed, but not without notice, and if it survives undisturbed for long enough, its owner may acquire a prescriptive right for it to remain indefinitely. But the Court of Appeal was not impressed:

"According to our law, the owner of a tree which gradually grows over his neighbour's land is not regarded as insensibly and by slow degrees acquiring a title to the space into which its branches gradually grow . . . Considering that no title is acquired to the space occupied by new wood, and that new wood not only lengthens but thickens old wood, and that new wood gradually formed over old wood cannot practically be removed as it grows, and considering the flexibility of branches and their constant motion, it is plain that the analogy sought to be established between an artificial building or a projection hanging over a man's land and a branch of a tree is not sufficiently close to serve any useful purpose."[97]

Lopes L.J. observed that "as there is always some risk of committing a trespass in removing overhanging boughs, it is a wise precaution to give notice".[98] Kay L.J. said that "it is reasonable and more likely to promote good feelings between neighbours that notice should be given before cutting, in order . . . that the owner may have an opportunity of removing the encroachment himself"[99] – sensible and well-intentioned advice that may not always be very realistic in the context of a heated neighbour dispute. Nevertheless, after considering all of the earlier cases, and noting that there was no distinct statement in any of them as to whether notice had to be given, Kay L.J. reluctantly concluded that their true meaning was that notice did not have to be given, providing that the abatement could be carried out without any trespass onto the land of the tree owner[1]. The other members of the court agreed.

The case proceeded to the House of Lords – slightly surprisingly, in view of the almost complete absence of judicial support for any requirement for notice to be

[94a] See **3.7.2**
[95] [1894] Ch. 7, CA; upheld at [1895] A.C. 1, H.L.
[96] [1894] Ch. 1.
[97] [1894] Ch. 7, CA, per Lindley L.J. at p. 12.
[98] *ibid.*, at p. 18.
[99] *ibid.*, at p. 19.
[1] *ibid.*, at p. 24.

given – and the decision of the Court of Appeal was upheld without anything of great significance being added. Lord Macnaghten did however question whether perhaps notice should have to be given "in the case of trees so young that the owner might remove them intact if he chose to lift them, or in the case of shrubs capable of being transplanted".[2] That aside might yet prove to be of significance, particularly now that it is possible (if cost is no object) to move surprisingly large shrubs and trees intact.

Where a tree falls over a boundary, perhaps due to a defect at its base, the owner of the land onto which it falls may remove whatever can be reached from his land. Here, too, an effort should be made to contact the owner of the tree, but a failure to do so will not negate the entitlement to abate.[2a]

3.6.3 Duty of care to the owner of the tree

It should not be forgotten that, whilst the owner of land that is the subject of encroachment has a right to abate the nuisance, he or she also has a duty of care to the owner of the land from which the nuisance emanates.[3] Thus, A may have a right to drive on the street outside B's house (because it is a public highway), but that is still subject to her duty not to knock him over when he comes out of his front door. A person abating a nuisance must thus still exercise reasonable care, and failure to do so may lead to liability in negligence. Such a person is also, presumably, responsible for his own safety, and may not blame the owner of the tree if, for example, it sheds a branch as a result of the works carried out.

In particular, the removal of the branches or, more especially, roots of a tree up to the boundary between two properties may lead to the tree being unstable, and thus more likely to fall in the future. In addition, if the work is carried out incompetently, it may lead to decay at the points where the branches were removed, thus shortening the life of the tree. It is for these reasons unwise to carry out abatement – other than at a trivial level – without first taking professional advice from an arboriculturist.

It has also recently been pointed out that "where there are two ways of abating a nuisance, the less mischievous is to be followed".[3a] This echoes the *obiter* remark of Lord MacNaughten in *Lemmon v. Webb*, suggesting that in cases where some alternative remedy could be effected without mischief to the tree owner, that remedy ought to be preferred.[3b]

It is in any event prudent wherever possible to negotiate with the neighbour, rather than simply doing the work unannounced. And where relations between neighbours have reached the point that civilised negotiation is no longer a realistic option, experience suggests that an arboriculturist (as an unbiased but knowledgeable outsider) may be able to act as a mediator and bring about a solution that achieves at least most of what the two neighbours want whilst not excessively butchering the tree. Such an approach is certainly more likely to lead to a generally satisfactory outcome than an exchange of letters between solicitors.

---

[2] [1895] A.C. 1, H.L., at p. 7.
[2a] *Dayani v. Bromley LBC* [2001] B.L.R. 503.
[3] See **Chapter 5**; in particular **5.2.1** and **5.3.1**. And see *Dayani v. Bromley LBC* [2001] B.L.R. 503.
[3a] *Logan Navigation v. Lamberg Bleaching, Dyeing and Finishing Co Ltd* [1927] ACC.226, *per* Lord Atkinson at p. 245.
[3b] *Lemmon v. Webb* [1895] A.C. 1, H.L. at p. 7.

3.6.4 Need for consent under other legislation

The carrying out of works to prevent or abate a nuisance does not require a felling licence.[4]

If the encroaching tree is subject to a tree preservation order, the consent of the planning authority is not required[5]; and if, exceptionally, the works necessary to abate the nuisance lead to the loss of the tree, no replacement has to be planted.

If the tree is in a conservation area, the work does not need to be notified to the planning authority, but – oddly – if the works lead to the loss of the tree, a replacement must be planted unless the authority dispenses with the requirement.[6] The precise extent of these provisions is considered in more detail later in this book.[7]

3.6.5 Procedure following abatement

It should not be forgotten that the owner of the tree – that is, the owner of the ground surrounding the base of its trunk[8] – owns overhanging branches, both before and after they have been severed from the remainder, just as much as any other part. It follows that, whilst a person is entitled to remove the branch, that is solely in order to abate the nuisance; and there is no entitlement to dispose of either the branch itself or any fruit. As to the latter, this was the subject of *Mills v Brooker*, in which it was held as follows:

"The owner of a fruit tree, the branches of which grow over his land, is the owner of the fruit of the overhanging branches while it is still growing on the tree. It is equally his property after it has been detached from the tree, whether it has fallen from being ripe, or been blown off by the wind, or been severed by the act of man. The adjoining owner is entitled to sever the overhanging fruit in the exercise of a right of abatement of the nuisance, but the exercise of that right cannot divest the owner's right of property in the fruit so severed."[9]

Once a branch has been severed, therefore, it should be offered back to its owner, and only disposed of with the owner's consent.

To do otherwise is, technically at least, theft.

3.7 Litigation: a claim for damages

3.7.1 When the cause of action arises

Generally, litigation must be started within a fixed period after the need for it has arisen. Thus, where a building is defectively constructed in such a way that the defect is not apparent for some years, the cause of action in negligence accrues when the actual harm appears.[10] However, where there is a continuing nuisance, as in most cases of harm caused by trees, time does not start to run against the

---

[4] FA 1967, s. 9(4)(a).
[5] TCPA 1990, s. 198(6)(b).
[6] TCPA 1990, s. 198(6)(b), 212; TCP(T) Regulations 1999, reg. 10(1)(a).
[7] See **14.2.5** (felling licences), **17.5** (tree preservation orders), and **21.2.2** (conservation areas).
[8] See **3.2.1** as to trees that are actually on a boundary.
[9] [1919] 1 K.B. 555, per Lush J. at p. 558.
[10] *Sparham-Souter v Town and Country Devts (Essex) Ltd* [1976] 1 Q.B. 858, CA at p. 867.

plaintiff. That at least seems to be the conclusion to be drawn from the decision of the Court of Appeal in *Delaware Mansions v Westminster City Council* (although the reasoning is not altogether clear):

". . . where there is a continuing nuisance, the owner is entitled to a declaration, to abate the nuisance, to damages for physical injury and to an injunction. He is, in my judgment, and on the same principle, entitled to the reasonable cost of eliminating the nuisance if it is reasonable to eliminate it. . . . A nuisance is present during Flecksun's ownership; acceptance of the need for remedial work establishes that. The actual and relevant damage is the cost of the necessary and reasonable remedial work. Underpinning has been held to be a reasonable way of eliminating the nuisance, and the owner can recover the cost of doing it. There is no need to prove further physical damage resulting from the nuisance".[11]

And in *Low v Haddock*, another root damage case, HH Judge John Newey Q.C. summed up thus the position in relation to "natural processes":

"Nuisance, when knowledge and foresight of consequences are required for it, bears a strong resemblance to negligence; but because it is a continuing wrong, it is much more difficult to establish a limitation defence to it."[12]

However, given that foreseeability is a key element in the establishment of a claim for nuisance, no claim can be sustained where all the harm occurred prior to the date when it would have been foreseeable. So in *Low v Haddock* it was considered that the type of harm which had occurred would not have been generally known about until the mid-1960s, and the particular instance of harm was not notified to the defendant Council until the mid-1970s. Thus the court held that a new situation arose from then.

3.7.2 Who may take action in nuisance

"The general rule is that he alone has a lawful claim [in private nuisance] who has suffered an invasion of some proprietary or other lawful interest in land".[13] This was recently reaffirmed by the House of Lords in *Hunter v Canary Wharf Ltd*,[14] which also approved the statement by Newark that:

". . . In true cases of nuisance, the interest of the plaintiff which is invaded is not the interest of bodily security but the ability to exercise rights over land in the amplest manner. It is for this reason that the plaintiff in an action for nuisance must show some title to realty."[15]

That would seem to mean that action can be taken by a person who is the owner and occupier of the land affected by the nuisance, or by a tenant or a person who effectively has exclusive possession of the land, but not by the occupier's family, guests, lodgers or employees. It may also be taken by the owner of a reversionary interest in leasehold land (that is, the person to whom the rent is paid and who will regain a right of occupation at the end of the lease). This is as long as the nuisance will affect the value of the reversionary interest – as would clearly be the case with harm caused by tree roots.

---

[11] [1999] 3 EGLR 68, 46 E.G. 194, per Pill L.J. at p. 69M, upheld [2001] 3 W.L.R. 1007, 4 All E.R. 737, H.L.
[12] [1985] 2 EGLR 247 at p. 251 J.
[13] *Read v J. Lyons & Co* [1947] A.C. 156, H.L., per Lord Simonds at p. 183.
[14] [1997] A.C. 655, H.L.
[15] (1949) 65 L.Q.R. 480 at pp. 481, 488–489; approved by Lord Goff at [1997] 2 All E.R. 434g.

Where it is proposed to abate the nuisance,[16] therefore, those other than the person with the right to exclusive possession (such as, for example, an occupier's wife) may only take action as the agent of that person.

Where the remedy sought is an injunction, of course, that will benefit all those entitled to occupy the land, as well as the owner and occupier.

Where the remedy sought is damages, only one set of damages may be claimed. It follows that where a leasehold occupier and the owner of a reversionary interest both wish to claim, any damages recovered will have to be apportioned between them in proportion to the amount by which each interest is diminished in value.[17]

Problems may also occur where there is a change in the ownership of the land affected by a problem tree – and here too only one set of damages may be claimed in respect of any particular harm. This was first considered in *Masters v Brent LBC*,[18] which related to harm caused by a lime tree, planted in the street by the local authority, to a house which was subsequently transferred to M by his father. After considering a number of earlier authorities, the judge considered that the son, the present owner, was entitled to recover damages, even though the harm had occurred only in the time of the previous owner (his father).

That decision was doubted, and not followed, at first instance in *Delaware Mansions v City of Westminster*, where harm was caused by the roots of street trees to a block of flats before it was sold to a new owner, who carried out the remedial works at its own expense. The position was explained as follows:

"If A owns a house which is damaged by tree roots, such that it will cost £100,000 to repair, and wishes to sell it to B, it seems to me that A can do one of two things. He can have the repairs carried out, sell the house to B fully repaired and sue the tree owner for the cost of repairs (plus any residual loss of value which he can prove); or he can sell the house as it is, at a lower price, and sue for the whole of the diminution in value. Either way round, that cause of action belongs to A and not B.

"If the house has already been repaired by A before B buys it, B has suffered no loss. If B buys it in its defective state, again he has suffered no loss, because he has or ought to have paid a lower price for it, and any expenditure which B incurs will rank as improvement and not compensatable loss. That position does not seem to me to be altered if A and B are unaware of the damage at the time of the sale; but fortunately that problem does not arise on the facts of the present case."[19]

The logic of that seems impeccable, as far as it goes. However, the Court of Appeal reversed the decision, and explained it this way:

"A nuisance is present during the second appellant's ownership; acceptance of the need for remedial work establishes that. The actual and relevant damage is the cost of the necessary and reasonable remedial work. Underpinning has been held to be a reasonable way of eliminating the nuisance, and the owner can recover the cost of doing it. There is no need to prove further physical damage resulting from the nuisance.

"If the council had agreed to remove the trees when asked, the damages would have been very small. In the circumstances, which are probably unusual, the fact that the nuisance existed before the second owner became the owner is irrelevant. Had it been the case that the purchase price was reduced to reflect the existence of a continuing nuisance, the loss would have been that of the vendor. It would have been a matter of evidence as to how the

---

[16] See **3.6**.
[17] *Hunter* at p. 709.
[18] [1978] Q.B. 841, 1 EGLR 128.
[19] (1998) 88 B.L.R. 99, per Mr Recorder Derek Wood Q.C., sitting as deputy judge, at pp. 119–120.

loss was to be apportioned between the vendor and the purchaser who did the remedial work.

"I have been glad to avoid a conclusion under which the right to recover a large sum would have depended on the accident of who was owner when slight physical damage resulting from the nuisance occurred, rather than depending on upon where the loss of eliminating the nuisance actually fell."[20]

That approach was supported when the case went on to the House of Lords.[21]

In other words, using the language of the decision at first instance, if the harm occurs during the time A owns the house, A may then transfer the house at full value to B on the basis that B will have to carry out the necessary remedial works at his own expense but can claim the cost of them by way of compensation from the owner of the tree. Alternatively, A may reduce the transfer price by a sum equal to the cost of the works which will have to be carried out and paid for by B; in which case the compensation will be payable to A. Either way, neither A nor B loses out. And if the price was reduced, but by less than the actual cost of the works carried out by B at his expense, the compensation will have to be split between A and B. But in any of these three scenarios, there is no reason of principle to prevent the action being brought by B rather than A. And the first scenario (in which the house is transferred at full value) is what would in practice occur if neither A nor B was aware of the problem at the time of the transfer.

The result seems to be that, where a property that has been affected by a tree subsequently changes hands, either the previous owner or the new owner may bring an action for damages against the owner of the tree. And any compensation awarded will then be split between them as appropriate, in the light of the price paid for the transfer and who actually paid for the remedial works.

3.7.3 Who may be sued in nuisance

The general rule is that it is the occupier of land who is responsible for a nuisance created by something arising on the land. That is obvious where land is occupied by the freehold owner, as there is no one else who could be responsible. But it is also generally true where the land is occupied by a tenant – whether under a long lease or a weekly tenancy. A tenant is thus normally responsible for any harm caused by trees to neighbouring property, even though no mention of any trees is made in the lease.[22]

On the other hand, it seems that an owner may, exceptionally, be liable even where he or she is not the occupier, if the owner has assumed responsibility for and control of the land – as, for example, where a property company buys land to let out on leases to others.[23]

Where there are two possible causes for harm to a building, which are the responsibility of different people or bodies, there may be two defendants bringing cross-proceedings against each other, for indemnification in the event of one being found liable.[24]

Once again, problems may arise where there is a change in the ownership of the land on which the problem tree is growing. The rule then is generally that the

---

[20] (1999) E.G. November 20, 1999, per Pill L.J. at p. 196.
[21] [2001] 3 W.L.R. 1007, H.L.
[22] *Edge v Briggs* (1961) 178 E.G. 261, CA, per Willmer L.J.
[23] *Davis v Artizans Estates* (1953), E.G., May 16, 1953; E.G. Digest, p. 190.
[24] See, for example, *Mayer v Deptford and Lewisham Borough Councils* (1959) 173 E.G. 961.

incoming owner takes over liability for any harm caused by trees, including that caused prior to the change of ownership:

"It might be that the occupier did not create the nuisance, but, as soon as he knew, or ought to have known, of the nuisance, he became liable in respect of it."[25]

Where a person purchases land, or an interest in land, even if he does not become the occupier, he may therefore take over liability for harm done to neighbouring property by tree roots before he acquired the land.[26] A nuisance of this kind is a continuing one, and the new landowner may be liable for allowing to continue the state of affairs causing the problem – although there may be an issue as to whether he could reasonably be supposed to have knowledge of it at the time of sale. It is in any event likely that the harm will continue after the sale, and it would be somewhat artificial to apportion the harm according to whether it occurred before or after that date.

In one recent case, however, it was apparently accepted that an incoming owner was not liable for harm that had been caused by trees on the land to neighbouring property prior to the change of ownership, and indeed for a month or two after the change.[27]

It follows that where there is a transfer of land on which trees are growing, especially if they are near to a boundary, it is prudent for a prospective purchaser to check whether there are any possible nuisance claims in prospect, and to reduce the purchase price accordingly (or to seek a suitable indemnity from the vendor, if necessary backed up by insurance).

One other result of the occupier of land generally being responsible for a nuisance arising from the state of it, rather than the owner, concerns the position in relation to insurance. Where the same person is both the owner and occupier of land, and has taken out two policies, one of which indemnifies him against claims against him as owner and one in relation to claims against him as occupier, it will normally be the latter policy that will be relevant in relation to claims arising as a result of harm caused by trees on the land.[28]

Where the problem is caused by a tree growing on highway land, the highway authority is presumed to be liable, as the owner of the tree, even though the sub-soil is notionally owned by the owner of the adjoining property. This has been the subject of considerable litigation; see **Chapter 6** for further details.[28a]

3.7.4 Remedies: an award of damages

Where harm has been caused to property as a result of trees, the owner of the property will normally be able to win damages from the owner of the trees in an action for nuisance. This is demonstrated by the numerous root damage claims over the years.

So, for example, in *Bunclark v Hertfordshire CC*,[29] the deputy judge considered carefully the issue of damages in respect of the subsidence caused to a block of flats by a row of trees growing on the property next door, owned by the County Council. He summarised the principles as follows:

[25] *Edge v Briggs* (1961) 178 E.G. 261, CA, per Danckwerts L.J.
[26] *Davis v Artizans Estates* (1953), E.G., May 16, 1953; E.G. Digest, p. 190.
[27] *Hough v Cheshire County Council* October 17, 1994, unreported.
[28] *Rigby v Sun Alliance* [1979] 2 EGLR 30; see also **8.4.2**.
[28a] See in particular **6.5**.
[29] [1977] 2 EGLR 114.

"A fair measure of damages in an action for nuisance is the cost of replacement or repair of the damaged parts of the plaintiff's property, plus general damages for annoyance, inconvenience or discomfort of the occupier. (See *McGregor on Damages*, 13th edition, paragraphs 1059 to 1063.[30]) It is well established that the plaintiff's impecuniosity can have no bearing on the measure of damages, for it is extraneous to the defendant."[31]

He accordingly awarded by way of special damages a sum equal to the (undisputed) cost of underpinning the block – even though that had risen from £7,300, at the time the first estimate was obtained, to £58,625, partly due to the continuing harm to the building and partly to the increase in building costs – split between the plaintiffs, who were the owners of the flats. He also awarded each of them a figure of £500, by way of general damages, and a further sum varying according to the physical harm suffered by each flat.

Similarly, the Court of Appeal in *Delaware Mansions v City of Westminster* – which related to harm caused by tree roots to a block of flats prior to its transfer to the present owner (Flecksun Ltd) – did not question the summary of the position as to damages by the deputy judge at first instance:

"The ordinary measure of damages would be the diminution in the value of Flecksun's interest. The cost of repair would be taken as *prima facie* evidence of the amount by which that value had been reduced, if it were reasonable for Flecksun to have the repairs done. Again, Mr Cooper [counsel for the Council] conceded that that would be reasonable in the present case." [32]

When that case went on to the House of Lords, Lord Cooke concluded that the key to the measure of damages that may be recovered is "applying the test of reasonableness between neighbours (real or figurative) and reasonable foreseeability". This has already been considered.[33]

So a claim for damages must be justified. As Gorman J. put it in *Davis v Artizans Estates*,[34] before deciding that the plaintiff's claim was "obviously" exaggerated:

"It is not right that, because a man has a claim which is right in law, he should put forward a claim for damages which he cannot justify. He has a duty to put forward a claim which he can justify, and the law demands that he should mitigate his damages."

The first step in assessing damages will be to consider what remedial work is actually required – in the case of root damage, either underpinning or some other method of stabilising the foundations (there being no point in carrying out other remedial works if the structure is continuing to move). There will then be the cost of repairs (including temporary repairs) to remedy the harm caused, which will need to be considered carefully so as to provide compensation for expense that is genuinely due to the tree but not for improvements to make the building better than it was when the harm started. The plaintiff will also be entitled to damages for annoyance, discomfort and inconvenience – which will inevitably be a somewhat arbitrary sum.[34a] Finally there may be an item for contingencies –

[30]   Now 16th ed., 1997, paragraphs 1484 to 1485.
[31]   [1977] 2 EGLR 114, per Judge Brian Gibbens QC, sitting as deputy judge, at p. 121L.
[32]   [1999] E.G. November 20, CA (reversing (1998) 88 B.L.R. 99), at p. 195.
[33]   See **3.5.6**.
[34]   (1953), E.G., May 16, 1953; E.G. Digest, p. 190.
[34a] *Bone v Seale* [1975] 1 W.L.R. 797, CA, at p. 804F.

particularly in view of the possibility that the defendant's approach to the necessary works might prove to be too optimistic. For a detailed example of how this works in practice, see *Pettifer v Cheshunt UDC*.[35]

Sometimes "remedial" work will be carried out by the plaintiff in a way, or to an extent, that seems excessive to the defendant. So, for example, in *Tajika v Sturgess*,[36] where the court found in favour of the plaintiff on the question of causation, there then arose the question of whether the underpinning that had actually been carried out was necessary. However, the plaintiff had given the defendant ample notice of the proposed work, allowing full access to experts to assess whether it was necessary, and no complaint had been made at the time. The deputy judge accordingly allowed the expense – even though perhaps suspecting that the work might not have been entirely necessary. In doing so, he relied on the speech of Lord Macmillan in *Banco de Portugal v Waterlow*:

"It is often easy after an emergency has passed to criticise the steps which have been taken to meet it, but such criticism does not come well from those who have themselves created the emergency. The law is satisfied if the party placed in a difficult situation, by reason of the breach of duty owed to him, has acted reasonably in the adoption of remedial measures, and he will not be disentitled to recover the cost of such measures merely because the party in breach can suggest that other measures less burdensome to him might have been taken."[37]

And see *Low v Haddock*, where again the court had sympathy for the view that it might not have in fact been necessary to carry out full underpinning, but considered that it was not unreasonable to have done so at the time of the harm.[38]

A defendant will generally be under a duty to mitigate his or her loss, but this duty probably does not extend to severing encroaching roots (or branches).[39]

As for the payment of damages where land changes ownership, this has been considered above.[40]

Finally, it may be possible in many cases for the parties to reach a settlement, avoiding the need to go through with litigation right to the bitter end. This may be particularly appropriate where the defendant tree owner has limited means.[41]

3.7.5 Defence to a claim

The most common response to an action in nuisance is to allege the absence of one or more of the essential ingredients to establish a claim. These have largely been discussed already.

One further matter that is sometimes raised by defendants is the issue of contributory negligence. That is, for example, the owner of the building that was harmed by tree roots was the author of his own misfortune, as he should have carried out a structural survey when he bought it. This was accepted in principle in *Low v Haddock*, where two householders had bought houses near to an oak tree growing in the street:

---

[35] (1970) 216 E.G. 1508.
[36] December 19, 1977, unreported.
[37] [1932] A.C. 452, H.L. at p. 506.
[38] [1985] 2 EGLR 247, at p. 252J,K
[39] *Attfield v Wilson* (1949) E.G., June 18, 1949, Calne County Court.
[40] See **3.7.2** and **3.7.3**.
[41] See, for example, *Watson and Roberts v Smith and Wakeham*, (1956) 168 E.G. 39.

". . . it does seem to me that a purchaser who commits his life's savings and undertakes to repay a large loan, in order to buy a house which he has not had surveyed, is taking a terrible chance. Time had passed between the building of the houses and the date of purchase and, therefore, despite Haddocks' [the builders'] reputation, I think that [the defendants] were both contributorily negligent."[42]

As it happened, the carrying out of a survey would have made no difference on the facts of that case, as the harm had not occurred by then; so the award of damages was not reduced. But it may occasionally be relevant.

3.8 Litigation: a claim for an injunction

3.8.1 The purpose of an injunction

In many cases, harm will already have been caused (at least in the claimant's view) by the tree – and for that, damages will be the appropriate remedy. However, prevention is obviously better than cure; and in most cases the claimant will seek an injunction to prevent future harm – in addition to damages where harm has already occurred. Further, boundary disputes often involve neighbours between whom there is little if any civilised communication. Once matters have got as far as litigation, therefore, an injunction may be the only way to bring a dispute to a conclusion.

In practice, an injunction may be awarded by the court in response to a claim in nuisance, either as an alternative or in addition to a claim for damages. Frequently, after all, a litigant will be seeking damages, as a form of monetary compensation for past harm, and also an injunction, to prevent future harm. So, for example, in the first reported decision relating to harm caused by tree roots, *Middleton v Humphries*,[43] elms, oaks and other trees, and ivy, had been planted by the defendant or predecessor near the wall separating her land from that of the plaintiff. The wall (owned by the plaintiff) had collapsed and an injunction was awarded, to prevent recurrence of the problem, as well as a declaration and damages.

It follows that the discussion above as to who may sue and who may be sued[44] would apply equally in the context of an injunction.

3.8.2 Principles on which the court will grant an injunction

In the first English case on root damage, *Butler v Standard Telephones and Cables Ltd*,[45] the decision in the (earlier) Irish case of *Middleton v Humphries*,[46] was mentioned with approval. In *Butler*, an injunction was originally claimed, but that was abandoned at trial. It was not until 1955, in *McCombe v Read* that the position as to the availability of an injunction in such cases was clarified:

"If an action on the case will lie, then the remedy of injunction must be available if the nuisance be a continuing one, as is clearly the case here. It could not be right to throw upon the plaintiff the burden of watching for further subterranean encroachment. In my

---

[42] [1985] 2 EGLR 247, at p. 253 A.
[43] (1913) ILT 160, Ch.D. (Ireland).
[44] See **3.7.2** and **3.7.3**.
[45] [1940] 1 K.B. 399.
[46] (1913) ILT 160, Ch.D. (Ireland).

judgment, however, the plaintiff is not entitled to an unqualified injunction, for he has no remedy unless a nuisance be caused. The injunction will therefore be to restrain the defendants from allowing the roots from any tree on their property so to encroach on the plaintiff's land as to cause a nuisance."[47]

That approach has been followed in subsequent cases, such as *Tajika v Sturgess*, in which the deputy judge said that he felt reluctant to order the destruction of what was undoubtedly a very attractive mulberry tree, but would instead make an order following the one in *McCombe v Read*.[48]

This leaves open the question as to whether "mere" encroachment across the boundary, without causing any harm, is a nuisance, and thus to be prevented by such an injunction.[49] The terms of any order may thus need to be considered carefully in order to minimise the possibility of further dispute.

In *Paterson v Humberside County Council*, a standard case of root damage by street trees, it was agreed that a remedial scheme of regular pruning could be devised to make the house safe even if the trees were to stay, but the highway authority was not willing to undertake to carry out any pruning. The court was thus faced with the options of refusing an injunction or ordering the trees to be felled; it felt that it had little choice but to grant the order.[50] This should be contrasted with *Elliot v Islington LBC*,[51] considered in more detail below,[52] in which an injunction was granted requiring the tree to be felled in spite of strong resistance by the tree owner, the local authority, which had sought to retain the tree on the grounds of its contribution to amenity. The court was unsympathetic.

However, an injunction will not always be granted. Thus in one case property owners sought an injunction to restrain an alleged threat of harm to their property by the roots of poplar trees on neighbouring land. Following expert evidence indicating that harm was not likely to occur for at least three years, the neighbour gave an undertaking to cut down the tree at the end of that period. The trial judge concluded that the apprehended harm was not imminent, and dismissed the application for an injunction, with costs. The Court of Appeal confirmed that the test for granting an injunction was the imminence of the apprehended danger. Accordingly, although there was risk of future harm if nothing were done, the plaintiffs had failed to take sufficient steps to find out what the position was at the time of issuing the writ, which was accordingly premature. They therefore dismissed the appeal, and upheld the order as to costs.[53]

In a more recent case, *King v Taylor*,[54] Eveleigh J., in the context of a dispute where lime and elm trees had caused harm to a path and a garage on neighbouring land, and was threatening to cause harm to the foundations of a bungalow on that land, noted:

"Although no damage had been done to the bungalow, the plaintiffs sought an injunction to restrain further encroachment from the roots. The defence argued that if there was no damage, there was no nuisance, but that was a misconception. The word nuisance had many different shades of meaning. It could accurately be said that there could be no claim

---

[47] [1955] 1 W.L.R. 635, per Harman J. at p. 637.
[48] December 19, 1977 unreported; see also, for example, *Wallace v Clayton* (1962) 181 E.G. 569 (Bloomsbury County Court).
[49] See **3.3.4**.
[50] (1995) 12 Const L.J. 64, at p. 72.
[51] [1991] 1 EGLR 167, CA.
[52] See **3.8.3**.
[53] *Lemos v Kennedy Leigh Devt*, CA (1960) 105 S.J. 178.
[54] [1976] 1 EGLR 132 at p. 132H.

for damages unless it was established that damage had been caused, but he (his Lordship) thought it was sufficient to establish damage that the tree roots were shown to be abstracting water from the soil and making it less suitable than it was before they encroached. . . . It was clear, in his (Eveleigh J.'s) view, that even the defence witnesses accepted that the soil under the foundations of the bungalow had been affected. The presence of the roots did present a serious threat to the structure, and the roots presented all the ingredients necessary for damage to foundations. Therefore, as the roots presented a threat, the plaintiffs were entitled to their injunction."

These decisions make it clear that a court will grant an injunction, either in addition to damages or as the sole remedy, but only where harm is imminent.

And frequently an injunction will not be needed where the defendant is ready to give an undertaking in the event of being found at fault.[55]

3.8.3 *An example:* Elliott v Islington

The celebrated case of *Elliott v Islington LBC*[56] concerned a street tree (an ancient horse chestnut) growing very close to a front garden wall. As the judge put it:

". . . the tree and the plaintiff's wall have manifestly been on a collision course for a number of years. That collision has now taken place, and the wall has been deflected into the plaintiff's property, both at its base and, to a greater extent, further up the wall. Furthermore, the branches of the tree apparently extend over the wall into the plaintiff's property.

"Prolonged negotiations have taken place between E and the his advisers and the local authority and their advisers because the authority passionately desire to keep this tree and appear to be prepared to go to almost any lengths to do so, including visiting this court. There is no suggestion that this tree is not a nuisance in the technical sense of the word, or that it is not invading the plaintiff's property. There is an issue as to how serious the matter is, but that there is a cause of action in nuisance is not disputed."[57]

The plaintiff, the property owner into whose garden the tree was growing, sought a mandatory injunction compelling the Council to remove the tree, and was indeed successful at first instance. Upon the authority's appeal:

"The local authority say that the proper way to deal with this matter is to leave the tree where it is, and to give E assistance in the matter of his wall. They have offered to do two things in the alternative. They are quite prepared to rebuild the wall in such a way as to provide for an alcove for the greater happiness and further growth of the tree. The alcove would necessarily be built entirely on the plaintiff's land. Alternatively, they say, if the plaintiff does not like that, they are prepared to put a pre-cast concrete bar slightly above ground level and rebuild the wall on top of that with pillars at each end. In effect this would create what I suppose would be the arboreal equivalent of a cat-flap for the tree."[58]

The plaintiff was not impressed, and persisted in seeking an injunction.

The Court of Appeal applied the classic tests as to the desirability of granting an injunction, set out in *Shelfer v City of London Electric Lighting Co*[59] and adopted in numerous subsequent cases, and held as follows:

[55] As in, for example, *Bunclark v Hertfordshire CC* [1977] 2 EGLR 114 at p. 122N.
[56] [1991] 1 EGLR 167, CA.
[57] [1991] 1 EGLR 167, CA, per Lord Donaldson M.R. at p. 167K.
[58] *ibid.,* at p. 168A.
[59] [1895] 1 Ch.D. 287.

". . . it is not the function of the courts to license breaches of the rights of citizens. Compulsory purchase under statute is a well-known concept and is subject to well-known protections, but it is not for the courts to add to that burden on the citizen a system whereby, as in this case, they will grant, for a fee payable to the plaintiff, a compulsory lease of land to accommodate the roots of this tree in addition to putting up with the nuisance it creates.

"That there are exceptional circumstances in which it would be right to refuse an injunction and to grant damages is not gainsaid but, if one looks at these tests, I am far from satisfied that the injury to the plaintiff's legal rights is small. I think it is very considerable. In inches, no doubt, his wall has only been moved a relatively small distance, but nobody who has sat in these courts and has any experience whatsoever of these boundary disputes would be under the slightest misapprehension as to the strong feelings of emotion and, indeed, irrationality which flow from any incursion over the boundary of somebody's property."[60]

Whether the court should be seen to support a person's concern if it is in fact irrational may be open for debate on another occasion. However, the principle is clear; an award of damages on its own will not always – or even often – suffice. The court accordingly upheld a mandatory injunction, requiring the tree to be felled within 28 days.[61]

This decision has been highlighted because it is likely to be of relevance in other boundary disputes. As it happens, the defendant in this case was a local authority acting on behalf of what it perceived to be the public interest in preserving the tree for its amenity value. But the principle in this case would apply equally, and arguably even more strongly, where a dispute is between two private landowners.

3.9 Statutory nuisance

3.9.1 General principles

In addition to the common law tort of nuisance, which has been the subject of the bulk of this Chapter so far, there is the related but separate topic of "statutory nuisance", which is now dealt with in sections 79 to 82 of the Environmental Protection Act 1990.[62]

The law of statutory nuisance is essentially a mechanism whereby, once a state of affairs exists which comes within certain defined categories, action may be taken by a local authority to bring it to an end. This is usually by the service of an abatement notice, so that there is not the requirement on the person affected by the nuisance to take action in the courts. Indeed, an authority is under a duty to serve an abatement notice where it is satisfied on the balance of probability that a statutory nuisance exists[63]; and it must inspect its area from time to time to detect any statutory nuisances which ought to be the subject of a notice.[64]

Failure to comply with a notice is a criminal offence; and, since notices are of indefinite duration, recurrence of the nuisance may lead to a subsequent

---

[60] [1991] 1 EGLR 167, CA, at p. 168J-K.

[61] For what it is worth, it may be noted that the tree is currently (some 12 years later) still flourishing.

[62] This replaced the Public Health Act 1936, which was in similar but by no means identical terms. For further wisdom in relation to statutory nuisance generally, see McCracken, Jones, Pereira, Payne, *Statutory Nuisance* (Butterworths, 2002).

[63] 1990 Act, s. 80; *R v Carrick DC, ex p. Shelley* [1996] Env L.R. 273.

[64] 1990 Act, s. 79.

prosecution without the need for another notice to be served. Further, if the authority does not serve a notice, anyone aggrieved by the existence of the statutory nuisance may apply to the magistrates' court for an abatement order, in the same terms.[65]

3.9.2 Application to trees

A statutory nuisance is defined by section 79(1) of the Environmental Protection Act 1990 to include, amongst other things,

"(a) any premises in such a state as to be prejudicial to health or a nuisance, [or] . . .
(e) any accumulation or deposit which is prejudicial to health or a nuisance."

"Premises" is defined to include "land"[66] – and thus trees and hedges. Further, it has been held (in *National Coal Board v Neath Borough Council*[67]) that:

". . . a nuisance coming within the meaning of the Public Health Act 1936 [the predecessor to the 1990 Act] must be either a private or public nuisance as understood by common law".

From this it might appear that any encroachment by the roots or branches of a tree into a neighbour's land – whether or not causing any physical harm – would constitute a statutory nuisance under section 79(1)(a), since it is undoubtedly a common law nuisance.[68] And if it is correct that the obstruction of a right of light by a tree or hedge might also constitute a nuisance at common law,[69] it would logically follow that it might also be a statutory nuisance.

However, there appears to have been no judicial decision settling the matter one way or the other – it seems that no one has yet been brave (or foolish) enough to bring an action alleging that an encroaching branch or tree constitutes a statutory nuisance. For it is by no means certain that an attempt to take such action against encroaching trees would be successful. Thus in the *Neath* case (above), the court found "attractive" the proposition that:

". . . not only must a statutory nuisance be either of a private or public kind at common law, but the act of nuisance itself must be such as comes within the spirit of the 1936 Act . . . whatever is complained about must in some way be directed to the question of the health of the person who claims to be or who has been affected by the nuisance".[70]

However, it explicitly declined to resolve the point. And it must be questionable whether it was right, since the Act refers to a health hazard *or* a nuisance – implying that the two terms are distinct.

More recently, in the context of nuisance consisting of dust or other effluvia, the Court of Appeal in *Wivenhoe Port v Colchester Borough Council*[71] upheld a judgment of the Chelmsford Crown Court in which it was said that:

"To be within the spirit of the Act a nuisance to be statutory nuisance had to be one interfering materially with the personal comfort of the residents, in the sense that it

---

[65] 1990 Act, s. 82.
[66] s. 79(7).
[67] [1976] 2 All E.R. 478, per Watkins J. at p. 482c.
[68] See **3.3.4**.
[69] See **3.3.5**.
[70] [1976] 2 All E.R. 478, per Watkins J. at p. 482e.
[71] [1985] J.P.L. 396.

materially affected their well-being although it might not be prejudicial to their health. Thus, dust falling on motor cars might cause inconvenience to their owners; it might even diminish the value of their motor car; but this would not be a statutory nuisance. In the same way, dust falling on gardens or trees, or on stock held in a shop, would not be a statutory nuisance. But dust in eyes or hair, even if not shown to be prejudicial to health, would be so as an interference with personal comfort."[72]

That decision did, however, recognise the great uncertainty of this area of law.

And it might be difficult to persuade someone living in a house falling apart as a result of root-induced subsidence, or cowering under an excessively high hedge, that their personal comfort was not being interfered with.

However, if it be correct that a tree that is a nuisance at common law is also a statutory nuisance, the consequences would be very unfortunate, given the extensive duties and powers of local authorities to take action, and the number of cases potentially involved. A court is therefore unlikely to be enthusiastic in reaching such a conclusion – but that does not, of course, mean that that it is wrong.

3.9.3 Deposits from insects and spores in trees

The only case examining the question of whether a tree could be a statutory nuisance (albeit only indirectly) was a recent decision of the High Court, *R v Test Valley BC, ex parte Anne.*[73] This case concerned the related issue of whether a tree could be a statutory nuisance where it possesses features which injure the health of those living on neighbouring land.

The case concerned a very large lime tree which harboured aphids which excreted honeydew which fell onto the thatch of the cottage next door, and was a source of moulds and spores which also harmed the thatch, accelerating its decay and having a seriously adverse effect on the health of those living in that cottage. The owners of the tree had notified the local authority of their intention to top and reshape it, since it was in a conservation area. The authority in response made a tree preservation order to protect it, which was confirmed in spite of objections from the owners of the neighbouring cottage on health grounds. The neighbours then sought consent to fell the tree, which was refused by the authority and by the Secretary of State on appeal.

The affected neighbours then made a formal complaint to the authority that the tree was a statutory nuisance under section 79(1)(e) of the 1990 Act ("any accumulation or deposit which is prejudicial to health or a nuisance"[74]), and asked it to serve an abatement notice. They also obtained a number of reports detailing the effects of the presence of the lime tree on their health. The authority's environmental health officer noted those reports, and carried out further research, but declined to serve a notice.

The court accepted that natural materials are capable of being a statutory nuisance.[75] However, it considered that the authority had carried out adequate investigation and that the relevant officer of the authority had been well qualified to reach conclusions of her own on the basis of that investigation. The key question was not whether the health of the actual occupiers of the thatched

---

[72] [1985] J.P.L. 175, per Butler J.
[73] [2001] EWHC Admin 1019.
[74] See **3.9.2**.
[75] [2001] EWHC Admin 1019, at paragraph 43.

cottage had been prejudiced by the accumulation of honeydew or the incidents of mould spores, but whether the health of the average person would be prejudiced for those reasons. On that basis it was not possible to stigmatise as *Wednesbury* unreasonable or irrational[76] the conclusions of the officer, and thus those of the authority, that the tree was not prejudicial to the neighbours' health and that any damage to the roof was insufficient to constitute a statutory nuisance.

The reasoning of the judgment is succinct, and it is not possible readily to discern the principles on which its conclusions were reached, so as to predict what might be the outcome of future challenges. However, it seems that it is probable that a local authority would in principle be entitled to serve an abatement notice in such circumstances, but that it is unlikely to do so in practice.

3.10 Access to neighbouring land

Finally, the provisions of the Access to Neighbouring Land Act 1992 may occasionally be relevant in enabling the carrying out of work to trees and other plants on neighbouring land, where a person (A; usually the neighbour) seeks but cannot obtain the consent of the owner of that land (B).

The first step is that A should make an application to a county court.[77] The court, before making an order, must be satisfied that:

- It is reasonably necessary for the preservation of A's land to carry out "the treatment, cutting back, felling, removal or replacement of any hedge, tree, shrub or other growing thing which is [comprised in, or situate on, B's land] and which is, or is in danger of becoming, harmed, diseased, dangerous, insecurely rooted or dead";

- The work cannot be carried out, or would be substantially more difficult to carry out, without access to B's land; and

- B would not be unreasonably suffer a disproportionate degree of hardship or inconvenience.[78]

The work may include preliminary survey and investigation.

If the court is so satisfied, it may make an "access order", which will specify what may be done, where, on what date (or during what period), and on what terms. And, in the case of work carried out on non-residential land, those terms may include the payment of compensation by A to B.[79] Damages may be payable for any non-compliance with the order.

The order will bind B's successors in title.

The Act is the result of a recommendation by the Law Commission,[80] and it essentially provides a sensible mechanism to secure the carrying out of works which are necessary, but which were in the past difficult to achieve – such as pruning trees on boundaries. It is to be hoped that it will seldom be necessary to invoke its provisions; the knowledge that a court will grant an order in the last resort should persuade neighbours not to be difficult at an earlier stage.

---

[76] [2001] EWHC Admin 1019, at paragraphs 61 to 64; *Associated Provincial Picture Houses v Wednesbury Corporation* [1948] 1 K.B. 223; [1947] 2 All E.R. 680.
[77] 1992 Act, s. 7.
[78] s. 1(4)(c),(2),(3).
[79] ss. 2, 3.
[80] *Rights of Access to Neighbouring Land*, Law Commission No. 151.

Chapter 4

Boundary Hedges

4.1 Introduction

4.1.1 Disputes over boundary hedges

Hedges are generally found on, or at least along, property boundaries, not least between residential properties in built-up areas. It is hardly surprising, therefore, that they are the focus of much litigation.

Such litigation may arise from a dispute that has (or at least originally had) nothing to do with the hedge itself – neighbours, after all, not uncommonly fall out over any of a wide variety of issues – and the hedge may thus be merely a convenient focus for the final confrontation after a long war of attrition. At **1.5** is the sorry tale of three such disputes in the last ten years which ended up in the courts, to the benefit of no one but the lawyers involved.

But not all disputes arise from warring neighbours. Sometimes there may be a genuine disagreement as to the correct way in which to maintain a hedge, or as to the size to which it should be allowed to grow. And some property owners, particularly those who are older, allow hedges to get out of hand, not out of malice but merely because they cannot cope with the work involved; and this can lead to resentment on the part of neighbours, which may give rise to a dispute in spite of previously amicable relations.

This Chapter accordingly considers first the position in law as to who owns boundary hedges (see **4.2**), and then examines various existing and proposed remedies for dealing with, or avoiding, potential disputes (**4.3** and **4.4**). As will be seen, none of these are entirely satisfactory. The Government has therefore supported the idea of new legislation, in particular the High Hedges Bill in 2001. The provisions of the Bill are thus considered in outline at **4.5**, as they give an indication of the likely form of any future Act to deal with this problem.

4.1.2 Hedges: other provisions

It may be noted hedgerows are also considered at Part V of this book. **Chapter 23** outlines the process by which hedges were created under the inclosure Acts and awards, and considers the rather more topical issue of whether such provisions are still enforceable today. **Chapter 24** describes the special regime to control the loss of important hedgerows, under the Environment Act 1995 and the Hedgerows Regulations 1997.

4.2 Ownership of boundary hedges

4.2.1 Introduction

As always with any matter relating to trees and hedges on boundaries, the first matter to be resolved is ownership. It has already been noted, in the context of boundary trees, that:

- a tree actually straddling a boundary is owned by the two owners in common,[1] whereas

- a tree growing on one side of a boundary is owned by the owner of the land surrounding the base of its trunk, even if its branches or roots subsequently grow across the boundary.[2]

There would seem to be no reason in theory why this should not apply equally to woody plants grown so as to form a hedge. In practice however, the strict application of that approach would lead to the conclusion that, where the centre-line of a thick hedge is approximately along a boundary between properties owned by A and B, some plants in it would be owned by A, some by B, and some in common by both A and B – with the plants in each of the three categories freely intermingling. That would be highly unsatisfactory, so the courts have tended to assume that the whole of a hedge is in the same ownership – either the undivided ownership of one or other landowner or the joint ownership of both.

The first point in resolving any ownership dispute is to consider whether the hedge in question is along the line of a boundary that is subject to an inclosure award. Where it is, the position is straightforward (see **4.2.2**).

A second line of approach is to apply the "hedge and ditch" rule. This has been the subject of a number of judicial decisions and is therefore widely noted in textbooks; but it is of relatively little application in practice other than in relation to agricultural land; it is dealt with at **4.2.3**. Two relatively recent decisions of the Court of Appeal on the issue of boundary hedges, both of which have unfortunately not been reported, deal with the more normal situation of hedges without ditches; see **4.2.4**.

More general issues arising in litigation in relation to ownership are covered at **4.2.5**.

4.2.2 Inclosure Act hedges

First, then, it needs to be appreciated that a significant number of hedges in rural areas, and some which are now in urban and suburban areas, were planted under the provisions of inclosure Acts and awards, principally in the eighteenth and nineteenth centuries. This is particularly so in certain parts of the country.[3]

The process of inclosure is considered in slightly more detail later in this book.[4] The relevance in the present context, however, is that where an award required a hedge (or indeed a fence) to be planted, and maintained thereafter, there can be no doubt but that the present-day hedge – along with any trees growing in it – will be

---

[1]   See **3.2.1**.
[2]   See **3.2.2**.
[3]   See **23.2.1**.
[4]   See **23.2.2**.

owned by the owner of the parcel of land whose predecessor in title was required to plant it in the first place, unless the relevant award explicitly provides otherwise.

The most complete list available of such Acts and awards appears to be that assembled by W E Tate, in his comprehensive work *A Doomsday of English Inclosure Acts and Awards*.[5] The awards themselves may be available in the Public Record Office and individual county record offices.

4.2.3 *The hedge and ditch presumption*

Where a boundary between two properties is marked by a hedge or by a hedge and ditch, some care will be needed to determine where the precise boundary is, and who owns the hedge. This may also be important to determine the ownership of trees growing in the hedge.

The first situation that may be found is where a boundary already exists, but only on paper, and it is then desired to mark that boundary on the ground. In the context of agricultural land, this may be done by digging a ditch and planting a hedge along the top of the bank formed by the soil excavated to make the ditch. In such a case, the presumption is that:

"No man, making a ditch, can cut into his neighbour's soil, but usually he cuts it to the very extremity of his own land: he is of course bound to throw the soil which he digs out upon his own land; and often, if he likes it, he plants a hedge on top of it."[6]

It follows that both the whole of the ditch and the mound and the hedge alongside it are in the ownership of the owner of the land on the side of the hedge away from the ditch.

This is known as "the hedge and ditch presumption". But it should be noted that it assumes that the land on the two sides of the physical feature was in separate ownership before the feature was constructed, and also that the construction was carried out by one party entirely on his or her own land with no co-operation from the other party. Both assumptions, but particularly the latter, seem doubtful. The presumption is nevertheless applied in any case where a boundary is of considerable antiquity, unless it can be showed that there is a reason to presume otherwise; its utility has thus been upheld as recently as 1999 by the House of Lords in *Alan Wibberley Building Ltd v Insley*.[7] This is so even if, as in that case, the Ordnance Survey plan indicated simply the line of the centre of the hedge as the boundary.

Secondly, by contrast, it may be that a physical feature, such as hedge, a row of trees, a ditch or some combination of these, already exists on land in a single ownership, and it is desired to divide that land into two portions. In that situation, it is highly likely that the new boundary will simply follow the line of the pre-existing feature. It follows that the hedge and ditch presumption will not apply, and the ownership boundary will be "along" the general line of the physical feature. As to precisely where it lies, the relevant conveyancing documents will need to be considered carefully to see whether the new boundary was intended to be down the centre line of the feature, or along one edge or the other.

---

[5] Reading University Press, 1967. A similar work, *Guide to Parliamentary Enclosures in Wales* by John Chapman, was published by the University of Wales Press in 1992, in relation to inclosures in Wales.

[6] *Vowles v Miller* (1810) 3 Taunt. 137 at p. 138.

[7] [1999] 1 W.L.R. 894, 2 All E.R. 897, *The Times*, April 30, 1999.

So, for example, in *Fisher v Winch*,[8] a large estate was divided in the 1920s, with the first parcel to be carved out of the estate specified in the relevant conveyance by reference to the Ordnance Survey plan. That plan indicated the centre line of a hedge, alongside which ran a ditch; both hedge and ditch had existed before the conveyance. Evidence was given as to the universal practice of the Ordnance Survey that, where there is a hedge or fence running along the edge of a parcel of land, the boundary marked on the plan is the centre of the hedge or fence. The Assizes had simply applied the hedge and ditch presumption; but the Court of Appeal made it plain that since the conveyance referred to the plan, and since that plan related to the pre-existing hedge, that should take precedence, so that the presumption would not operate. The boundary was therefore down the centre line of the hedge.

That decision was followed by the Court of Appeal in *Davey v Harrow Corporation*,[9] where judicial notice was taken of the Ordnance Survey practice referred to in *Fisher v Winch*. In *Davey*, the house owned by D had been built on part of a field, which was separated from land to the south owned by the Council (the predecessor of the defendant) by an old hedge and, to the south of it, a ditch. A post and wire fence had been erected along the north face of the hedge (on D's side) when D's house had first been built, and the whole of the hedge had from then on been treated by the Council as its own. As in *Fisher*, all the subsequent conveyances all referred to the Ordnance Survey plans. The Court of Appeal agreed that the hedge was on the Council's land, at least from the date of the erection of the fence. It followed that the trees in the hedge were also owned by the Council.

The Court of Appeal took the same approach in *Falkingham v Farley*,[10] where a carefully prepared plan drawn for an earlier conveyance of the land in question was sufficient to rebut the hedge and ditch presumption.

4.2.4 More recent decisions

There have been a number of more recent decisions of the Court of Appeal dealing with the ownership of boundary features other than by reference to the hedge and ditch presumption. The most notable of these, not least because of the publicity it attracted, was *Stanton v Jones*.[11] Unfortunately, the decision has not been reported (other than as a news item in the general press); and it should in any event be treated with some caution, because the facts were not entirely straightforward.

It concerned the boundary between two residential gardens in Bournville Village, which was marked by a wire fence. Shortly afterwards, a line of beech saplings was planted on S's side, approximately 30 cm from the fence. Five years later, S planted on his side a row of ten Leyland cypress plants[11a], about 90 cm apart and also 30 cm from the fence, interspersed between the beeches. A scheme of management was in existence covering the entire estate, which provided that hedges "on and along" the boundary were to be deemed a party wall and kept properly trimmed and in good condition.

---

[8] [1939] 1 K.B. 666, 2 All E.R. 144, CA.
[9] [1958] 1 Q.B. 60, CA.
[10] *The Times*, March 11, 1991.
[11] October 6, 1994, unreported, CA.
[11a] See **4.4.1**, n.47.

The Recorder hearing the case in the Birmingham County Court first defined what he understood to be a hedge:

"A number of woody plants, whether capable of growing into trees or not, which are so planted as to be intended to be in line and . . . , when mature, to be so integrated together as to form both a screen and a barrier."

He then found that the row of cypress plants was a hedge, being intended to replace the previous beech hedge, and that, whilst not precisely "on" the boundary, it was "along" the boundary. It was accordingly a party hedge within the meaning of the scheme and subject to the maintenance requirement.

In the Court of Appeal, Millett L.J. held as follows:

"If it is decided to plant a hedge to form a boundary between two properties, it may be planted on the boundary line so that that line runs through the mid-point of the hedge. As the hedge grows in thickness, it will be a party hedge which divides two properties and belongs to both adjoining owners, divided on the line of the notional boundary line running through the middle of the hedge.

"Alternatively, the hedge may be planted within the line of the boundary and on the land of the person who planted it, with the intention that, when mature, its furthermost face will run along the boundary line and constitute the line marking the boundary. In such a case it would belong wholly to the party on whose land it was planted, though his neighbour would be entitled to trim it on his side, back to the line of the boundary. It would not, in the ordinary case, be a 'party hedge' unless by agreement or otherwise it was deemed to be a 'party hedge'."

The questions as to whether the cypress plants were a hedge or a tree screen, and as to whether they were intended to be a party hedge, were to be determined (objectively) on the basis of the intention of the person who planted them.

On the particular facts in the case, the court found that both the original beeches and the cypresses which were intended to replace them, being planted 30 cm from the boundary, were intended to form a boundary hedge rather than a tree screen, and were intended to be a hedge on S's land, the furthermost face of which was to be on the line of the actual boundary. It would thus not normally be a party hedge (although it was in fact deemed to be one in that case because of the terms of the scheme).

In *Burns v Morton*,[12] the Court of Appeal resolved a boundary dispute by considering the conveyancing history back to the time when the two properties had been in common ownership. It held that the true boundary had been established at that stage, as being a party fence actually on the boundary. Subsequently M had built a wall, on his land, just to one side of the fence; and B's predecessors had then planted a Leyland cypress hedge on their side of the wall, which M had then sought to cut back. The court found that the boundary between the two properties had moved from the line of the original fence to the line of the wall once the latter had been constructed, so that the hedge was indeed wholly on what was now B's land.

In *Clarke v Oates*,[13] the court similarly resolved a dispute by looking at the history of the land. It held that the true boundary had been established at the time when the ownership of the two properties had first been severed, as being at that

---

[12]   [2000] 1 W.L.R. 347, CA.
[13]   June 11, 1999, unreported, CA.

stage a fence just to one side of the hedge. The fact that a conveyance of the property on that side of the boundary had purported to include the land between the fence and the centre of the hedge was not conclusive – it was not possible to convey more than was owned; and anyway that conveyance could not bind the neighbour, who was not party to it.

And in the most recent of these cases, *Nelson v Nicholson*,[14] the Court of Appeal established that where a hedge is planted wholly on a neighbour's land so as to constitute a trespass, the owner of that land may normally simply remove it without further ado. However, where for some reason that is impossible (for example, because of a restrictive covenant), an injunction is likely to be appropriate, requiring the hedge to be removed rather than just restricted to a particular height – and an award of damages will not be an adequate substitute.

4.2.5 Disputes

It will be obvious that the question of who owns a hedge along, on or near a boundary will often be of great importance to the owners of the land on either side – if only so as to determine the question of who has the duty to maintain the hedge (and any trees in it), or the right to fell them.

Thus in *Alan Wibberley Building Ltd v Insley*,[15] both parties were keen to claim ownership of the hedge in question – the appellant because he had already grubbed it up, and wanted to avoid paying damages, the respondent company because it wanted to claim damages. In *Davey v Harrow Corporation*,[16] on the other hand, both parties were keen to avoid having ownership of the hedge, and thus of the trees in it, since it was accepted that the latter had caused subsidence damage to D's house, and each party wanted to transfer the liability to the other.

It is not always a straightforward issue to determine, however. So, for example, in *Hamilton v Weston*,[17] two small claims courts separately considered the question of who owned a particular boundary hedge; one went one way and one the other.

As will be clear from the cases noted above, the only rule is to consider very carefully the whole of the relevant conveyancing history, if possible back to the time when the two properties were in common ownership, and to make from that whatever deductions are justified. The principles decided by those cases will hopefully assist in determining the question of ownership, but there is no substitute for a patient examination of the particular facts in each new situation.

Actual litigation should always be the last resort. In *Davey*, the Court of Appeal noted that the damages eventually awarded would probably be less than the cost of the litigation. In *Hamilton* the cost of the litigation was likely to ruin the unsuccessful party, and render life a misery even for the successful party. And in practice, by no means all of the costs of litigation can be recovered even by the successful party. It is therefore always better to resolve disputes by agreement if at all possible – long before they reach the point where civilised resolution is no longer an option.

If court intervention is to be sought, it should be in the form of an action for a declaration – either in the County Court or (exceptionally) in the Chancery

---

[14] December 1, 2000, unreported, CA.
[15] [1999] 1 W.L.R. 894, 2 All E.R. 897, *The Times*, April 30, 1999; see **4.2.3**.
[16] [1958] 1 Q.B. 60, CA.
[17] [1997] E.G.C.S. 10, CA; see **1.5**.

Division of the High Court. It is important to consider all possible outcomes, so as to avoid the problem encountered in *Stanton v Jones* (above), where the litigants did eventually obtain a declaration in the Court of Appeal that the group of ten Leyland cypress plants constituted a party hedge, but Millett L.J. noted that "such a declaration will leave it open to the parties to dispute, if they must, the question whether what the Respondent did was within the rights granted by the conveyancing documents or not". If necessary, therefore, the scope of the declaration sought should cover all the issues on which there could be any dispute, so as to minimise the risk of having to come back to court.

4.3 Boundary hedges as a common law or statutory nuisance

4.3.1 Encroachment

Where a hedge is entirely on one side of a boundary, so that it is considered to be owned wholly by the owner of the land on that side, any encroachment across the boundary constitutes a "nuisance".[18] In practice, this may be avoided by the owner of the neighbouring land taking advantage of the self-help remedy of abatement – that is, he or she may cut the encroaching roots or branches back to the boundary. This has already been considered, in the context of trees.[19]

Alternatively, it would be possible to claim for damages if the roots or branches had caused actual harm, for example to foundations or to drains[20] or for an injunction to prevent future harm.[21] However, it is unlikely that a hedge, as opposed to a tree growing within it, would cause sufficient harm to justify recourse to the courts rather than simply resorting to abatement.

These remedies may be of some use where D's hedge is getting out of control, as it enables C, the owner of the neighbouring land, to cut it back to the actual boundary. But it cannot prevent such a hedge growing thicker and higher on the far side of that boundary, since any attempt by C to interfere would involve trespass onto D's land, which would doubtless be met with some form of resistance.

4.3.2 Interference with right to light

In addition to a hedge itself constituting a nuisance by virtue of encroaching into or over neighbouring land, it is – theoretically at least – possible that it might amount to a nuisance by impeding a right to light reaching a building on that land.

A right to light is an easement – that is, it is a right over one piece of land for the benefit of another.[22] For example, C may have a right to light in relation to a particular window of a building on his land, and D, the owner of adjoining land, may not obstruct that light. If D does obstruct it excessively, she is then liable to be sued by C in nuisance.

---

[18] See **3.3.4**.
[19] See **3.6**.
[20] See **3.7**.
[21] See **3.8**.
[22] For more details, see appropriate specialised works such as *Gale on Easements*, 16th ed., 1997, Chap. 7.

That general principle is, however, subject to several caveats. First, a right to light must actually be created; its existence cannot just be assumed. Thus it must either be created by a specific grant – which is very unusual – or arise as a result of prescription. The latter occurs where the right has been enjoyed uninterruptedly for 20 years[23]; although this whole area of law has been criticised as being marked by "much unnecessary complication and confusion".[24] Secondly, a right can only be enjoyed in relation to a specified opening (such as a window); it must therefore be associated with a building,[25] even if only a greenhouse[26]; and there can thus be no right to light in connection with open land, such as a garden.

Thirdly, even where there is a right of light, there is only a limited right of action if it is obstructed. The courts will look not at the size of the obstruction, but at the amount of light remaining after its introduction[27]; and will judge that remaining amount according to the ordinary use of the building – so that, for example, a greenhouse or a photographic studio may require more than other buildings.[28] The owner of the building is thus "entitled to such access of light as will leave his premises adequately lit for all purposes for which they may reasonably be expected to be used".[29]

There does not seem to have been any reported decision of an action brought to seek the removal of either a tree or hedge unreasonably obstructing a right of light.[30] In principle, however, there would seem to be no reason why such an action should not be brought, provided that it can be shown that the window in question did indeed receive light for at least 20 years prior to the obstruction. That will inevitably not be particularly straightforward since, particularly in the case of a tree, the obstruction will only have come into existence gradually. But it might be feasible in the case of a rapidly growing high hedge where the situation at different dates is likely to have been be more clear-cut, and where there may be sufficient evidence on which to base a claim.

4.3.3 Interference with right of enjoyment

The House of Lords in *Hunter v Canary Wharf Ltd*[31] identified three categories of nuisance. The third of these is "nuisance by interference with a neighbour's quiet enjoyment of his land".[32] It was also in *Hunter* that the House of Lords approved the statement by Professor Newark that:

". . . In true cases of nuisance, the interest of the plaintiff which is invaded is not the interest of bodily security but the ability to exercise rights over land in the amplest manner.

---

[23] Prescription Act 1832, s. 3.
[24] *Tehidy Minerals Ltd v Norman* [1971] 2 Q.B. 528, per Buckley L.J. at p. 543 F; the Law Reform Committee recommended the abolition of the concept of prescriptive acquisition of easements in its 14th Report (Cmnd 3100, 1966), paragraph 32.
[25] *Harris v De Pinna* (1886) 33 Ch.D. 238 at pp. 250 f, 262; *Levet v Gas Light & Coke Co* [1919] 1 Ch. 24 at p. 27.
[26] *Allen v Greenwood* [1980] Ch. 119, CA, per Goff L.J. at p. 129C.
[27] *Higgins v Betts* [1905] 2 Ch. 210, per Farwell J. at p. 215.
[28] *Allen v Greenwood*, at pp. 131–136.
[29] *Carr-Saunders v Dick McNeil Associates* [1986] 1 W.L.R. 922, per Millett J. at pp. 928H; 2 All E.R. 888 at p. 894.
[30] But see *Viewpoint: a Right to a View*, by John A Good, published by University of West of England, ISBN 18043-1968.
[31] See **3.3.2**.
[32] [1997] A.C. 655, H.L., reversing [1996] 1 All E.R. 482, CA; per Lord Lloyd of Berwick at p. 695B ([1997] 2 All E.R. 426 at p. 441c).

A sulphurous chimney in a residential area is not a nuisance because it makes householders cough and splutter but because it prevents them taking their ease in their gardens."[33]

One way in which householders are prevented from taking their ease in their gardens is by the existence of very high hedges on the edge of neighbouring gardens. This may occur even though there is no encroachment by roots or branches, justifying abatement or an action for nuisance on that count,[34] no actionable interference with a right to light,[35] and no physical danger, justifying an action in negligence.[36]

It might therefore be possible, at least in theory, to argue that the mere existence of a tree or (more likely) a high hedge on D's land, even where it does not encroach across a boundary, might amount to a nuisance at common law if it prevents his neighbour C enjoying her property to the full. That could in turn lead to a claim for damages, by way of compensation for harm already caused, and an injunction to prevent its repetition. After all, if an action can succeed in respect of noise on neighbouring land, there seems to be no reason in principle why one should not succeed in respect of an overbearingly high hedge.

As to the basis on which a court might intervene, the right approach would seem to be that outlined by Knight Bruce V-C in *Walter v Selfe*:

". . . ought this inconvenience to be considered in fact as more than fanciful, more than one of mere delicacy or fastidiousness, as an inconvenience materially interfering with the ordinary comfort physically of human existence, not merely according to elegant or dainty modes of living, but according to plain and sober and simple notions among the English people".[37]

Nor should a hypersensitive claimant be allowed to impose excessive restraints on a defendant:

". . . a nervous, or anxious, or prepossessed listener hears sounds which would otherwise have passed unnoticed, and magnifies and exaggerates into some new significance, originating within himself, sounds which at other times would have been passively heard and not regarded".[38]

4.3.4 Common law nuisance: litigation

It might, therefore, be possible to mount an action in nuisance if a boundary hedge is interfering either with a neighbour's right to light or more generally with his or her right to enjoy property "in the amplest manner".[39]

Having said that, it must readily be admitted that no such action is known to have been instituted, let alone succeeded; and the courts may well prove in practice to be reluctant to encourage what might turn out to be a fruitful source of potentially acrimonious litigation.

---

[33] (1949) 65 L.Q.R. 480 at pp. 481, 488–489; approved by Lord Goff at [1997] 2 All E.R. 434g.
[34] See **3.3.4** and **4.3.1**.
[35] See **4.3.2**.
[36] See **5.1.2**.
[37] (1851) 4 De G. & Sm. 315, at p. 322; 20 L.J. Ch. 433.
[38] *Gaunt v Finney* (1872) 8 Ch. App. 8, at p. 13; 42 L.J. Ch. 122.
[39] *Hunter v Canary Wharf Ltd* [1997] 2 All E.R. 426, H.L., per Lord Goff at 434g.

If such an action were to be mounted, the relevant principles would be as already explained in the context of trees.[40]

4.3.5 Statutory nuisance

If it is true that a hedge that is interfering either with a neighbour's right to light (or more generally with his or her right to enjoy property) is a nuisance at common law, it follows that it may also be a statutory nuisance.

This, too, has already been considered in the context of trees.[41] Thus, a local authority has a duty (not just a power) to serve an abatement notice where it is satisfied that a statutory nuisance exists[42]; and it must inspect its area and from time to time to detect any statutory nuisances which ought to be the subject of a notice.[43] Failure to comply with a notice is a criminal offence; and, since notices are of indefinite duration, recurrence of the nuisance may lead to a subsequent prosecution without the need for another notice to be served. Further, if the authority does not serve a notice, anyone aggrieved by the existence of the statutory nuisance may apply to the magistrates' court for an abatement order, in the same terms.[44]

It is therefore unlikely that, under the law as it stands at the moment, a court would be very sympathetic to a claim that a hedge on neighbouring land is a statutory nuisance, with all that follows from that. Thus there is no reported instance of such a claim succeeding, even though the possibility of one has been mooted on a number of occasions.[45] And it is to be hoped that Parliament does not prescribe by legislation that a high hedge would in all circumstances, or in certain prescribed situations, constitute a statutory nuisance; as that would impose on local authorities a major burden which would probably not be justifiable. Several of the private member's bills to deal with the issue of high hedges[46] attempted to use such a mechanism, but the Government has, wisely, so far chosen not to pursue that approach.

Of course, if such a claim were to be made in relation to a boundary hedge, it could be argued by its owner that a statutory nuisance can only exist where there is a danger to health. A court might nevertheless find that the existence of a high hedge next to a small garden could led to depression or other psychological disorders; but it would be necessary for the person alleging the existence of a nuisance to obtain convincing medical evidence that such illness had in fact occurred or was likely if such a claim was to succeed.

---

[40] See **3.7** and **3.8**.
[41] See **3.9**.
[42] Environmental Protection Act 1990, s. 80.
[43] 1990 Act, s. 79.
[44] 1990 Act, s. 82.
[45] See, for example, *High Hedges: Possible Solutions*, DETR, 1999 (and note 50 below), particularly paragraph 3.14.
[46] The Control of Residential Hedgerows Bill, introduced by Jim Cunningham in 1998–1999 and 1999–2000 and the Statutory Nuisances (Hedgerows in Residential Areas) Bill, introduced by Baroness Gardner of Parkes in the same sessions.

4.4 High hedges: the need for new legislation

4.4.1 The problem

The problem of disputes over boundary hedges has become worse in recent years. This is partly because the increasing density of urban areas means that new houses and gardens are smaller, and the extent of overshadowing correspondingly greater. But it has been exacerbated in recent years by the more ready availability at nurseries and garden centres of fast-growing dense hedging plants. The most notable of these is the Leyland cypress,[47] but other species[48] may cause the same problems to a lesser extent.

As will be clear from the analysis earlier in this Chapter,[49] an action in the civil courts for nuisance is at best a very uncertain remedy to this problem, as is reliance on the provisions of the Environmental Protection Act 1990 relating to statutory nuisance.

This has given rise to a great deal of public concern, particularly in the late 1990s, leading to the issue by the Government in 1999 of a consultation paper entitled *High Hedges: Possible Solutions*.[50] This recognised that high hedges, either Leyland cypress or of any other species, might be entirely appropriate in certain situations – in particular where a rapidly-growing dense hedge is required to mark boundaries between gardens in a new development, or to hide an unsightly view – but that in other circumstances they could cause a major problem. The Government therefore, rightly, did not rush forward with new legislation, but first sought to explore the use of existing procedures.[51]

4.4.2 Non-legislative approaches

Given that the basic difficulty arises primarily because of people, and only secondarily because of hedges, the first option considered in the 1999 consultation paper was reliance on neighbourly co-operation. That is, of course, the best approach where all concerned agree to its use, but equally obviously it will only work in certain cases. The next step is to seek the intervention of local mediation services; but, again, that is effective only where there is at least some good will on both sides.

Advice from nurseries and garden centres on the characteristics of hedging plants would be welcome, but may be counter-productive in some cases (merely enabling those intent on causing trouble to do so with maximum effectiveness).[52]

It would, in theory, be possible under existing law to place legal restrictions on future planting by imposing a restrictive covenant, but yet again that would

---

[47]   *X Cupressocyparis leylandii* (often referred to simply as *Leylandii*), a hybrid of the Nootka cypress (*Chamaecyparis nootkatensis*) of Alaska and Western Canada and the Monterey cypress (*Cupressus macrocarpa*) of California; the original cross occurred naturally on the Leighton estate in mid-Wales, many years before the species was commercially grown.

[48]   For example, Lawson cypress (*Chamaecyparis lawsoniana*), western red cedar (*Thuja plicata*), yew (*Taxus*), holly (*Ilex*) and privet (*Ligustrum*).

[49]   See **4.3**.

[50]   Department of the Environment, Transport and the Regions (DETR), November 1999; separate consultation exercises were undertaken in Scotland and Northern Ireland.

[51]   *High Hedges: Possible Solutions*, DETR, 1999 (see previous note), Chapter 3, and paragraphs 5.2 to 5.15.

[52]   See in particular the well-meaning *The Right Hedge for You: A Guide to Choosing a Garden Hedge*, DETR, June 1999.

require co-operation between the two parties which is most unlikely to exist, and would assist not at all in relation to existing hedges. Possibly of marginally greater use may be the imposition by planning authorities of suitable landscaping conditions on planning permissions for new development[53]; but this too will at best prevent future problems, and will not solve existing ones.

4.4.3 New legislation

The first legislative option canvassed by the Government in its 1999 Consultation Paper was to amend the law relating to easements of light so that they could exist in relation to open land as well as defined openings in buildings.[54] However, it recognised that this approach was by no means without its own problems.[55]

The Paper therefore went on to consider in some detail the possibility of introducing a new mechanism to enable complaints to be made to a third party, presumably a local authority.[56] It highlighted the need to define what constituted a hedge, and noted the definition emerging from the County Court judgment in *Stanton v Jones*.[57] It also suggested that any new system should be restricted to conifers, and to hedges on boundaries of residential properties – although neither restriction seems either necessary or desirable, if hedges of other types or in other locations are causing problems.

The next problem would be to define the circumstances in which complaints could be made. To prescribe these in too much detail (for example, by reference to the height of hedges or the distance from buildings or other features) could lead to great complexity whilst still leaving certain situations beyond control. On the other hand, to rely solely on general formulae such as "loss of amenity" would lead to uncertainty – although that could be the subject of guidance from central Government to authorities responsible for administering the system. Once a complaint had been made, there would then have to be a procedure for the issuing of a notice by the local authority, requiring remedial work to be carried out.

Then there would need to be some form of appeal mechanism, either to the courts or an independent tribunal (neither of which was recommended), or to the planning inspectorate. The Consultation Paper also suggested a form of appeal within the authority, but that would almost certainly not comply with article 6 of the European Convention on Human Rights. And there would also have to be a method of enforcing the system – probably by the authority carrying out the necessary works at the expense of the hedge owner if they had not already been carried out within a reasonable time after the notice had been served.

Following the issue of the Consultation Paper, 97 per cent of those responding thought that the Government should take action; and 94 per cent felt that new laws were needed. The clear preference was for a system of complaints dealt with by local authorities, as outlined above. Accordingly, the Government has committed itself to introduce legislation.[58] That commitment bore fruit in the form of the High Hedges Bill, introduced at the start of the following year.

---

[53] See **15.9.1**.
[54] See **4.3.2**.
[55] *High Hedges: Possible Solutions*, DETR, 1999 (see note 50 above); see particularly paragraphs 5.16 to 5.19.
[56] *High Hedges: Possible Solutions*, DETR, 1999; see particularly paragraphs 5.20–5.83.
[57] See **4.2.4**.
[58] See *Hansard*, **4.2.4**, H.C., October 15, 2001, col. 884W.

4.5 The High Hedges Bill

4.5.1 Introduction

The High Hedges Bill was a private member's Bill, introduced into the House of Commons by Mr John M Taylor M.P. on January 17, 2001, but with Government support. It was to apply to England and Wales only – similar legislation may be brought forward in Scotland in due course, but there is apparently no high hedge problem in Northern Ireland and thus no plans to legislate there.[59]

The Bill was briefly debated, but it failed to get enacted prior to the general election in July 2001. It is likely to re-emerge, however, when a suitable opportunity arises – possibly in association with the legislation that will be required to implement the Government's proposals to reform the planning system,[60] or perhaps together with the improvement of the tree preservation order system.[61] The brief discussion which follows here is accordingly based on the Bill as introduced; but, obviously, if primary and secondary legislation is actually enacted, it will be necessary for anyone potentially affected to check its terms in detail.

4.5.2 Situations in which the Bill would have applied

Clause 1 of the Bill stated that it would apply in the first instance where a complaint was made by an owner or occupier of domestic property who alleged that his reasonable enjoyment of that property was being affected by an unreasonable obstruction of light caused by a high hedge situated on land owned or occupied by someone else.

The definition of "unreasonable obstruction of light" was the subject of guidance issued by the Building Research Establishment in December 2001, entitled *Hedge Height and Light Loss*:

"The aim of this document is to provide an objective method for assessing whether high hedges block too much daylight and sunlight to adjoining properties, and to provide guidance on hedge heights to alleviate these problems. The document introduces the concept of 'action hedge height' above which a hedge is likely to block too much light. It then gives a procedure to calculate this height both for windows to main rooms in a dwelling, and for a garden. The minimum action hedge height is 2 metres. The procedure is intended to be simple enough for householders to use. It involves multiplying the distance from a window to the hedge, or the depth of a garden, by a factor; for gardens this factor depends on hedge orientation. Corrections can be made for site slope or where the hedge is set back from a garden boundary."[62]

The guidance, which is also available on the internet,[63] will presumably be still used as and when legislation is finally enacted. It may be noted that 2 metres is

---

[59] See *High Hedges Bill: Briefing Pack*, issued by the DETR, March 7, 2001.
[60] See Delivering a Fundamental Change: The Planning Green Paper (December 12, 2001), and other associated consultation papers.
[61] See **16.2.7**.
[62] *Hedge Height and Light Loss*, December 7, 2001, Summary.
[63] www.regeneration.dtlr.gov.uk/info/env/treeshedges/height/01.htm.

the height of walls and fences that may generally be erected without specific planning permission.[64]

The Secretary of State was given power to amend clause 1 by regulations, so as to extend the scope of the new procedures beyond just domestic property, and to include situations where the enjoyment of the property was being affected by more than just obstructions of light.[65] That would enable the procedures in the Bill to be used to deal with other categories of properties, such as nursing homes, and situations such as where a hedge was causing psychological distress.

By virtue of clause 2 of the Bill, a "high hedge" was defined as meaning two or more adjacent evergreen trees or shrubs which together formed all or part of a barrier, and whose height exceeded 2 metres. This definition too could be amended by regulations made by the Secretary of State, if it seemed appropriate in the light of experience – for example, to include broadleaved hedges.

4.5.3 Complaints procedure

The broad principles of the complaints procedure were set out at clauses 4 to 9 of the Bill, with (as might be expected) powers for the Secretary of State to prescribe details in regulations.

Before making a formal complaint under the new system, the person affected by the high hedge was required to take all reasonable alternative steps to resolve the matters complained of.[66] This would doubtless include informal negotiations with the owner of the hedge and, if appropriate, mediation. The Department indicated at the time of the Bill that it would probably issue guidance requiring complainants at least to make two written requests to the owner of the hedge asking him or her to cut it back by a specified deadline.[67] And, of course, once the legislation had come into operation, a complainant would be negotiating from a position of strength rather than, as hitherto, weakness. The BRE guidance already referred to would clearly be relevant in determining what sort of action it would be reasonable to suggest.

If all such approaches had failed, the complainant could then make a complaint in writing to the appropriate local authority (the district council in areas with two tiers of authorities[68]). A fee would be required along with the initial complaint, but an authority could refund it in an appropriate case – for example, where the complainant was of limited means.[69]

On receipt of a complaint, the authority was to satisfy itself that sufficient efforts had been made to resolve the matter informally, and that the complaint was not frivolous or vexatious. The authority was then to consider (where relevant):

- the extent to which the hedge in question afforded privacy to its owner

- the extent to which it contributed to the amenity of the neighbourhood, and

---

[64] Under TCP (General Permitted Development) Order 1995 (S.I. No. 1995/418), article 3 and Schedule 2, Part 2, Class A.
[65] High Hedges Bill, cl. 16.
[66] High Hedges Bill, cl. 4(2).
[67] *High Hedges Bill: Briefing Pack*, March 7, 2001, FAQ 2.
[68] High Hedges Bill, cl. 15.
[69] High Hedges Bill, cl. 4(1), (8); *High Hedges Bill: Briefing Pack*, March 7, 2001, FAQ 12.

- any relevant legal obligations relating to it.[70]

As to the second question, this is probably equivalent to the exercise carried out by authorities when considering whether to grant consent for works to a tree protected by a tree preservation order.[71]

In the light of these considerations, the authority was then to decide whether there was indeed a justified cause for complaint, and what (if anything) should be done about it. Having made that decision, it must be communicated to the complainant and, more importantly, to the owner of the tree, in the form of a remedial notice, together with the reasons for it. If, however, the authority decided that nothing needed to be done, either because informal negotiations had not yet been exhausted, or because the hedge was not in fact a problem, that decision too should be notified as appropriate.[72]

A remedial notice must specify what action must be taken in relation to the hedge, and by when – but the action was not to involve the removal of the offending hedge, or a reduction in its height to less than 2 metres.[73] The notice could also require continuing action to be taken indefinitely into the future, so as to prevent the problem recurring. It would obviously be a local land charge, and binding on the owner or occupier of the land for the time being. A remedial notice could be varied or withdrawn by the authority on the joint application of the owner of the hedge and the complainant, or where circumstances had changed.[74]

There was to be a right of appeal against decisions of the local authority to issue a remedial notice, or to vary or withdraw one, or not to pursue a complaint[75] – although, oddly, no explicit provision for the parties to opt to be heard at an inquiry. Regulations were to prescribe the detailed procedure for appeals[76] – no doubt very much in line with planning appeals. The Government envisaged that such appeals would be determined by the Planning Inspectorate.[77]

4.5.4 Enforcement

As to the enforcement of all this, the Bill essentially adapted the provisions relating to the enforcement of planning control.

It thus provided that, where a remedial notice had been served, and had come into force (possibly following an unsuccessful appeal), it would be an offence for the person responsible to fail to comply with its requirements.[78] Such an offence would be punishable on summary conviction with a fine of up to level 3.[79] In addition, the court would be able to order the owner of the hedge to carry out the specified works – with a further fine in the event of continuing non-compliance.

Alternatively, or in addition to mounting a prosecution, an authority would be entitled, after giving notice, to enter the relevant land and carry out the required works itself, and reclaim the cost from the person responsible.[80]

---

[70] High Hedges Bill, cl. 4(4).
[71] See **18.3.3**.
[72] High Hedges Bill, cl. 4.
[73] High Hedges Bill, cl. 5.
[74] High Hedges Bill, cl. 6.
[75] High Hedges Bill, cl. 7, 9.
[76] High Hedges Bill, cl. 8.
[77] High Hedges Bill, Explanatory Notes, paragraphs 36, 37.
[78] High Hedges Bill, cl. 10.
[79] See **Appendix C**.
[80] High Hedges Bill, cl. 11.

Chapter 5

Hazardous Trees

5.1 Introduction

5.1.1 General principles

It has already been shown that there are a number of different situations in which harm may be caused by a tree.[1] These may be broadly divided into three categories:

- harm due to the mere existence of a tree because of its position[2];
- harm due to the natural characteristics of a healthy tree[3]; and
- harm due to a tree or part that is in some way defective.[4]

The first category above is where a tree is in the wrong place – notably that its branches are hanging over, or its roots are extending into, a neighbour's land or a public highway. Litigation in these cases is likely to be in the form of a claim for nuisance or under the principle in *Rylands v Fletcher*[5]; this is the subject of **Chapter 3**. This Chapter deals with the principles underlying claims relating to the second and third categories.

The second category above is where a tree is in good health, but behaves in a way that is hazardous or inconvenient. One example of this is where a healthy tree is blown over in an exceptionally heavy storm; as will be seen, the distinction between this and a tree that is blown over because it was defective is not always straightforward in practice. Here, litigation may well arise if only in the hope that it will be possible to show that the tree was in fact defective – *Caminer v Northern & London Investment Trust*[6] is an example of a claim for damages which went, unsuccessfully, all the way to the House of Lords, where it was ultimately held that the fall of the tree was not the fault of the owner.

Other examples are trees which shed leaves or fruit, causing a path to become

---

[1] See **1.3**.
[2] See **1.3.3**.
[3] See **1.3.4**.
[4] See **1.3.5**.
[5] (1868) L.R. 3 H.L. 330
[6] [1951] A.C. 88, H.L., upholding [1949] 2 K.B. 64, CA.

slippery, or which have poisonous berries, or which enable people (particularly children) to gain access to hazards such as electric wires. In cases such as these, the harm is not usually significant enough to justify litigation, but it does occasionally arise.

However, even if actual resort to the courts is rare, owners and occupiers of land and their advisers should be aware of their rights and duties in law.

As to the third category, one example is where a tree falls or sheds a branch because it is diseased, defective or dead, and causes injury to people or animals or harm to vehicles or other property. The defect in the tree may or may not have been visible on careful inspection prior to the failure. Such an incident is likely to give rise to litigation, which may in the form of a claim either in negligence or, where the injury is to a person on the same land as the tree, under the Occupiers' Liability Acts. It may also, or alternatively, be framed as a claim in nuisance; but this is likely to add little.[7]

With incidents in this third category, the allegation is usually not that the owner of the tree has omitted to take sufficient care of the tree, but that he or she has simply allowed it to remain in spite of its location and condition which mean that it is inherently hazardous. Again, therefore, litigation may be framed either in nuisance or under the principle in *Rylands v Fletcher*,[8] or in negligence or under the Occupiers' Liability Acts, or both.

The basic principle underlying both the law of negligence and the Occupier' Liability Acts is that the owner of land, including trees, owes a duty to take reasonable care to protect those reasonably likely to be affected.[9] And the Court of Appeal, considering the extent of a landowner's liability for defects in the state of his property which cause harm to neighbouring property, considered that the defect must be such that a reasonable man would foresee that it would lead to harm of the type (if not the extent) that did in fact occur.[10]

But what, in each case, is "reasonable"? Section **5.2** considers the nature of the duty of care, and by whom it is owed; and the following section (**5.3**), to whom it is owed. The extent of that duty is then examined (at **5.4**), along with particular factors that may be relevant in relation to the tree in question and any potential victim (**5.5** and **5.6**). The following sections (**5.7** and **5.8**) consider possible remedial measures that should be taken to avoid or minimise liability; and **5.9** looks at possible litigation.

The last section of the Chapter (**5.10**) highlights various other statutory provisions relating to "dangerous" trees.

The rules in this Chapter also apply to trees on or adjacent to highways, and many of the decided cases relate to them; but there are special features of highways which are considered in **Chapter 6**.

Finally, it is important to be clear as to the meaning of the various terms used, notably "harm", "damage", "danger", "risk", "hazard" and "safe". This has been considered at the start of this book,[11] but should be referred to particularly in relation to this Chapter.

---

[7]   See **5.1.2**.
[8]   See **Chapter 3**.
[9]   See **5.2.1**.
[10] *Holbeck Hall Hotel Ltd v Scarborough BC* [2000] Q.B. 836, CA.
[11] See **1.3.2**.

5.1.2 The relationship between negligence and nuisance

The law of nuisance relates to the carrying out of an activity, or the existence of a state of affairs, on one piece of land that materially interferes with the enjoyment of another piece of land. In the context of trees, this principally refers to encroaching branches and roots.[12] It may be noted, however, that some of the cases discussed in this Chapter, involving hazardous trees, related to actions that were brought in both negligence and nuisance.

Indeed, one of the earliest of the cases, *Bruce v Caulfield*, was brought in negligence, nuisance and trespass. The Court of Appeal held as follows:

"The action has been brought on three grounds, but that of nuisance – namely, that the trees were overhanging the plaintiff's premises – had really nothing to do with the case. As to the alleged trespass, the fact that the tree fell was no evidence that the defendant caused it to fall, and if the case came to anything at all it was one of negligence."[13]

In *Noble v Harrison*,[14] which predated the decision of the House of Lords in *Donoghue v Stephenson*,[15] Rowlatt J. held at the outset that, since the county court judge had found that the failure of the branch was due to a latent defect not discoverable by any reasonably careful inspection, a claim for negligence was "out of the question". He accordingly went on to consider whether there was any liability as for nuisance or under the principle in *Rylands v Fletcher*.[16] He decided that the latter had no relevance either[17]; and went on to consider liability for nuisance, and concluded as follows:

"A person is liable for a nuisance caused by the state of his property:

(1) if he caused it;
(2) if by the neglect of some duty he allowed it to arise; and
(3) if, when it has arisen without his own act or default, he omits to remedy it within reasonable time after he did or ought to have become aware of it."[18]

As will be seen, that is a classic statement of the test to determine liability for negligence, as much as nuisance, and has been cited in almost all of the subsequent cases, as if it directly related to liability in negligence.

Thus in *Cunliffe v Bankes*, the court adopted the same approach. It concluded that there was no negligence,[19] and that disposed of the claim in nuisance: "what has to determined is the same, whether the claim be in negligence or nuisance".[20] In *Shirvell v Hackwood Estates*, the claim was in negligence and nuisance, but the defendant at trial abandoned the claim in nuisance.[21]

In the important case of *Caminer v Northern & London Investment Trust*, Lord Goddard C.J. at first instance followed *Noble v Harrison*, holding that "it seems to

---

[12] See **Chapter 3**.
[13] (1918) 34 T.L.R. 20, per Pickford L.J.
[14] [1926] 2 K.B. 332
[15] [1932] A.C. 562.
[16] (1868) L.R. 3 H.L. 330.
[17] See **3.3.7**.
[18] [1926] 2 K.B. 332, at p. 338.
[19] See **5.3.2**.
[20] [1945] 1 All E.R. 459 at pp. 464H and 465D.
[21] [1938] 2 All E.R. 1 at p. 5H.

me to be immaterial whether the cause of the action is laid in negligence or in nuisance".[22] That approach (although not his conclusion) was upheld in the Court of Appeal.[23] The case had initially been brought both in nuisance and negligence, but here, too, no case of nuisance was maintained on the further appeal to the House of Lords[24]; although Lord Porter did agree that there was no distinction between the tests to be adopted.[25]

In *Brown v Harrison*,[26] it is not clear whether the action was in nuisance, negligence, or both; but in both *Lambourn v London Brick Co*[27] and *Lane v Tredegar Estate Trustees*,[28] it appears that only negligence was relied on. In *Quinn v Scott*, the action against the landowner was brought in negligence and/or nuisance, but the judge treated it solely as a "charge of negligence".[29] All four cases related to trees falling across highways. And in *Knight v Hext*,[30] which concerned a tree falling onto neighbouring property, the action was solely in negligence.

Finally, of the actions against highway authorities, that in *Mackie v Dumbartonshire County Council*[31] was brought only in negligence; but the much more recent claim in *Chapman v Barking and Dagenham LBC*, on not dissimilar facts, was (surprisingly) brought in nuisance, negligence and breach of statutory duty. The Court in the latter case noted that negligence added nothing to the plaintiff's submission, and confirmed that, for the purposes of identifying the duty, there is no difference as between nuisance and negligence[32]; as to the statutory duty, this is considered in relation to highway trees.[33]

More generally, the interface between nuisance and negligence was considered by the Privy Council in *Goldman v Hargrave*, which concerned a bush fire in Western Australia. The fire was initially caused by lightning, but the landowner chose to adopt a method of extinguishing it which was "unreasonable, or negligent in the circumstances".[34] Lord Wilberforce summarised the matter as follows:

". . . the case is not one where a person has brought a source of danger onto his land, nor one where an occupier has so used his property as to cause a danger to his neighbour. It is one where an occupier, faced with a hazard accidentally arising on his land, fails to act with reasonable prudence so as to remove the hazard."[35]

This is of course precisely the situation that arises where an occupier of land discovers that there is on it a tree that is for some reason dangerous.

"The issue is therefore whether in such a case an occupier is guilty of legal negligence, which involves the issue of whether he is under a duty of care and, if so, what is the scope of

[22] [1949] 2 K.B. 64 at p. 66.
[23] Per Tucker L.J. at p. 70.
[24] [1951] A.C. 88 at p. 105.
[25] At p. 99.
[26] (1947) E.G., June 28, 1947, CA.
[27] (1950) E.G., July 28, 1950.
[28] (1954) E.G., November 27, 1954.
[29] [1964] 1 W.L.R. 1004 at p. 1008H.
[30] [1980] 1 EGLR 111.
[31] (1927) 91 J.P. 158.
[32] [1997] 2 EGLR 141 (upheld in CA (1998) unreported) at p. 145F–G.
[33] See **6.4.7**.
[34] [1967] A.C. 645, P.C., at pp. 656D.
[35] At p. 656F.

that duty. Their Lordships propose to deal with these issues as stated, without attempting to answer the disputable question whether if responsibility is established it should be brought under the heading of nuisance or placed in a separate category. As this Board has recently explained [36], the tort of nuisance, uncertain in its boundary, may comprise a wide variety of situations, in some of which negligence plays no part, in others of which it is decisive. The present case is one where liability, if it exists, rests upon negligence and nothing else; whether it falls within or overlaps the boundaries of nuisance is a question of classification which need not here be resolved."[37]

The conclusion would seem to be that the substantive cause of action in all these cases is in fact now best categorised as negligence, and that the addition of a claim in nuisance adds little if anything.

5.2 The duty of care: who is responsible?

5.2.1 General liability

The common law imposes on everyone a duty, known to lawyers as "the duty of care", not to injure his or her neighbour. In what is still the leading case on this area of civil liability, *Donoghue v Stevenson*, Lord Atkin elaborated the scope of that duty as follows:

"The rule that you are to love your neighbour becomes, in law, you must not injure your neighbour; and the lawyer's question, Who is my neighbour? receives a restricted reply. You must take reasonable care to avoid acts or omissions which you can reasonably foresee would be likely to injure your neighbour. Who, then, in law is my neighbour? The answer seems to be – persons who are so closely and directly affected by my act that I ought reasonably to have them in contemplation as being so affected when I am directing my mind to the acts or omissions which are called in question."[38]

If on that basis A has a duty of care to B, then a breach of that duty may give rise to a civil action for negligence by B against A if it causes foreseeable harm to B.

It will be rare that a tree is the subject of a positive "act" causing injury to someone, although, for example, the carrying out of works incompetently so as to lead to decay which subsequently causes a branch to fall might be categorised as actionable negligence – the situation where the negligent carrying out of works leads immediately to harm (for example, to bystanders or to those up the tree) is dealt with in a later Chapter.[39]

More likely in practice to be the subject of an action in negligence is the omission to take sufficient care of a tree, where it leads to foreseeable harm. The owner of a tree may thus be liable in negligence if:

- the tree falls or sheds a branch[40];

- injury or harm is caused as a result;

---

[36] *Overseas Tankship (UK) Ltd v Miller Steamship Co Pty Ltd (The Wagon Mound No. 2)* [1967] A.C. 617, P.C.

[37] [1967] A.C. 645, P.C., at pp. 656G–657B; followed by Megaw L.J. in *Leakey v National Trust* [1980] 1 Q.B. 485 at p. 514G.

[38] [1932] A.C. 562, H.L., at p. 580.

[39] See **9.5**.

[40] See **1.3.5**.

- the injury or harm was foreseeable;

- the person who was injured, or whose property was harmed, is someone to whom the tree owner had a duty of care; and

- the injury or harm was caused by a breach of that duty.

The same may apply in some circumstances to a failure to remove a tree that is poisonous or otherwise dangerous,[41] where that failure actually leads to harm.

It follows that, to avoid liability, the owner should take steps to ensure that he or she is aware of whether a tree is likely to cause such problems and, if it is, should take appropriate avoiding action as necessary.

The approach of Lord Atkin in *Donoghue v Stevenson* (where the harm arose from a positive act by a wrongdoer) was thus followed in subsequent years in a line of important cases relating to natural hazards (where the harm arose from a hazard not being abated): by the Lords in *Sedleigh-Denfield v O'Callaghan*[42] (a nuisance case), by the Privy Council in *Goldman v Hargrave*,[43] which confirmed:

". . . the existence of a general duty of care upon occupiers in relation to hazards occurring on their land, whether natural or man-made",[44]

and by the Court of Appeal in *Leakey v National Trust*, which defined the scope of the duty as:

". . . a duty to do that which is reasonable in all the circumstances, and no more than what, if anything, is reasonable, to prevent or minimise the known risk of damage or injury to one's neighbour or to his property".[45]

It will have been noted that, having formulated the "rule" that "you must not injure your neighbour" – which on the face of it is an absolute rule – Lord Atkin immediately recast it in somewhat more realistic terms. You are thus only under a duty to protect those who are "reasonably" likely to be affected by any omission on your part, and only if you can "reasonably" foresee that they are likely to be injured as a result; and even then you are only required to take "reasonable" care to avoid such omissions. And Megaw L.J. in *Leakey* (above) only envisaged a duty to do that which is "reasonable in all the circumstances".

5.2.2 Those by whom a duty of care is owed: the occupier of land

The first question is: upon whom is laid the duty of care in relation to trees? The remainder of this Chapter, and much of the relevant case law, refers blandly to "the tree owner". As has been seen earlier in this book, however, there may be more than one owner of land – freeholder, tenant, sub-tenant and so on; and the land may be occupied by one or more others.[46]

---

[41] See **1.3.4**.
[42] [1940] A.C. 880, H.L.
[43] See **5.1.2**.
[44] *Goldman v Hargrave* [1967] A.C. 645, P.C., at p. 662G; followed by Megaw L.J. in *Leakey v National Trust* [1980] 1 Q.B. 485 at p. 524D.
[45] [1980] 1 Q.B. 485, CA at p. 524E.
[46] See **Chapter 2**.

In the context of the liability of the owners and occupiers of land for the safety of others on the land, the Occupiers' Liability Acts of 1957 and 1984 place the duty of care on "the occupier" of land; a phrase that is not defined. However, the House of Lords in *Wheat v Lacon*[47] held:

"In the [1957 Act], the word 'occupier' is used in the same sense as it was used in the common law cases on occupiers' liability for dangerous premises. It was simply a convenient word to denote a person who had a sufficient degree of control over premises to put him under a duty of care towards those who came lawfully on to the premises. . . . This duty is simply a particular instance of the general duty of care which each man owes to his 'neighbour'. . . . When Lord Atkin eventually formulated the general duty in acceptable terms, he too used occupier's liability as an illustration: see *Donoghue v Stevenson*."

In other words, whilst the 1957 Act may have altered the identity of those to whom a duty of care was owed, it did not alter the common law position as to who owed that duty. It follows that if someone has sufficient control over land (and in particular over any trees on that land) to be responsible for the safety of visitors under the 1957 Act, he or she will equally have sufficient control to ensure the safety of those on neighbouring land and highways under the general common law duty of care.

And the 1984 Act specifically adopts the definition of occupier used for the 1957 Act.[48]

5.2.3 Liability under the Occupiers' Liability Acts

As to the identity of the occupier by whom a duty is owed under the 1957 and 1984 Acts, and thus at common law generally, this was authoritatively considered in *Wheat v Lacon*:

"Wherever a person has a sufficient degree of control over premises that he ought to realise that any failure on his part to use care may result in injury to a person coming lawfully there, then he is an 'occupier' and the person coming lawfully there is his visitor: and the 'occupier' is under a duty to his 'visitor' to use reasonable care. In order to be an occupier it is not necessary for a person to have entire control over the premises. He need not have exclusive occupation. Suffice it that he has some degree of control. He may share the control with others. Two or more may be 'occupiers'. And whenever that happens, each is under a duty to use care towards persons coming lawfully onto the premises, dependent on his degree of control. If each fails in his duty, each is liable in consequence of his failure, but each may have a claim to contribution from the other."[49]

In that case, for example, which related to the safety of the interior of a public house, the disagreement was as to the responsibility of the brewer landlord as against that of the resident tenant manager and his wife who took in paying guests in the summer. Lord Denning considered that each was an occupier, but each only owed a duty of care in respect of the extent of his or her occupation.

Thus in the simplest situation, where a house with a small garden is owned by a private individual and lived in by him and his family, he is the occupier for the purposes of the Act; and where he lets the house to another who has exclusive

---

[47] [1966] A.C. 552, per Lord Denning at pp. 577G to 578C.
[48] Occupiers' Liability Act 1984, s. 1(2)(a).
[49] [1966] A.C. 552 at p. 578D to F.

possession, that tenant is the occupier. Suppose, however, that the Duke of Barchester owns a house that is so large that he passes it to the National Trust, but rents and continues to live with his family in a flat in the east wing and enjoy the rose garden immediately outside it. In that situation, the Duke remains the occupier of the east wing and the rose garden, but the Trust becomes the occupier of the remainder – and if the Trust maintains the flat and the garden on behalf of the Duke, they may be in the joint occupation of him and the Trust. If the Duke goes to the Bahamas for the winter and lets his part of the house and the rose garden to his brother, his brother may be an occupier of them for that period.

The key to seeing who is responsible under the Act is thus to look not just at the legal interest, if any, of the possible contenders,[50] but at the degree of control able to be exercised. Note, too, that the concept of "occupation" for the purposes of the 1957 Act is somewhat wider than the concept of "possession" which is necessary to found an action for nuisance.[51]

It will be noted that there may be more than one occupier for the purposes of the Act. *Wheat v Lacon*[52] also established that, in such instances, it is necessary to consider how much control each occupier had in relation to the part of the premises that proved to be defective, in order to ascertain the extent of the duty laid upon him or her. It is thus not possible for each of the occupiers to pass the liability to the others, and for the claimant thus to be deprived of any remedy at all – someone must be liable.

Thus, in the example postulated above, if a decaying tree in the rose garden finally blows over and kills the postman delivering letters, or a cyclist on an adjacent road, the liability may fall on the Trust, the Duke or the brother – depending on who at the relevant time actually had sufficient control that they ought to have realised that the tree needed to be dealt with. If the Duke's brother was only in residence for a fortnight, he would probably not be considered the relevant occupier; if his visit extended to several years, he almost certainly would. If the Duke was senile, and never ventured into the garden, so that the Trust in practice had full responsibility, he might be considered the occupier, but would not be considered in breach of his duty for failing to deal with the tree. If, on the other hand, the Duke was a keen gardener and ran the rose garden entirely as a private garden, the Trust might be the joint occupier but, again, would be exonerated if it was unaware of the problem.

It is also possible for one "occupier" to sue another – so if in the above example the Duke in practice relied on the Trust to maintain the garden, and the falling tree injured him rather than the postman, he could sue the Trust. So, for example, in one case decided in the Exeter County Court[53] (prior to the 1957 Act, and thus under the general common law rules), the occupier of a caravan on a caravan site sued the owner of the site following the fall of a branch onto her caravan.

Finally, it may be noted that "premises" includes any fixed or moveable structure,[54] and the "occupier" of such a structure would be the person occupying or having control of it. It follows that, where a tree is allowed to grow in such a way that it provides easy access for a child to climb it and thus come into contact

---

[50] Explored in more detail in **Chapter 2**.
[51] See **3.7.2**.
[52] [1966] A.C. 552.
[53] *White v Carruthers* (1954) 172 E.G. 229.
[54] 1957 Act, s. 1(3)(a).

with a dangerous electricity cable,[55] it may be possible for an action to be brought against not only the occupier of the land under the 1957 or 1984 Act (depending on the status of the child) but also the electricity company, as "occupier" of the cable.

5.2.4 Trees growing on highway land

The ownership of and responsibility for trees growing on highway land (either carriageways or, more commonly, footways and verges) is not altogether straightforward, but broadly the highway authority is almost always responsible in practice. For further details, see **Chapter 6**.

5.3 Those to whom a duty is owed

5.3.1 Those on neighbouring land

If a tree is not inspected, or if necessary remedial works are not carried out, the persons who are "so closely and directly affected by that omission that they ought reasonably to be contemplated by the owner of the tree" (to adapt the words of Lord Atkin, quoted above) are those who may be injured, or whose property may be harmed, by any resulting failure. Such injury or harm may be direct or indirect.

Atkin used the biblical concept of a "neighbour" to depict the person to whom a duty of care is owed; and whoever may be a neighbour in law, it must almost inevitably include someone who is a neighbour in fact – that is, the owner or occupier of land adjoining that on which a tree is growing, and the users of a highway, railway or other facility abutting such land.

Other than in relation to highways, however, there have in fact been very few instances of trees falling onto people and buildings on adjoining land in circumstances leading to litigation in the higher courts. This is hardly surprising. It will be relatively rare that a tree is so close to a property boundary as to fall onto neighbouring land in such a way as to cause sufficient harm to justify litigation.

Usually a defective tree will be noticed either by its owner or by the neighbour, and appropriate action taken in sufficient time to prevent problems. If the defect is not noticed, however, provided that it is such that it could have been detected without undue effort, any liability clearly rests on the owner; and the extent of any harm will be readily quantifiable. The matter can therefore be promptly resolved without recourse to the courts. Indeed it is likely that the only outstanding issue will be the quantum (amount) of any damages recoverable, which will be relatively simply ascertained, usually by agreement or, if necessary, in the county court.

Thus, in both *Bruce v Caulfield*,[56] where a neighbour's stable was seriously damaged by the top of a poplar that blew off in a gale, and in *Knight v Hext*,[57] where a neighbour's barn was damaged by a falling beech tree, the potential for harm had been spotted, but action had not been taken in time. In both cases,

---

[55] As in *Buckland v Guildford Gas Light & Coke Co* [1948] 2 All E.R. 1086 (another case prior to the 1957 Act).
[56] (1918) 34 T.L.R. 204, CA.
[57] [1980] 1 EGLR 111, CA.

however, there was held to be no liability – in the first case, the gale had been exceptional; and in the second, there had been no time for action to be taken.[58]

In *Shirvell v Hackwood Estates*,[59] it was a neighbour's workman who was unfortunately hit by a dead branch falling from a beech tree into the field where he was working. Here too there was no liability.[60]

This does not mean that trees on boundaries do not cause problems. They do; and care should be taken by those responsible for them, as with any other trees, to ensure that they are not dangerous. And of course their roots may well cause problems by extending under or into the foundations of buildings on neighbouring land – but that has already been considered at length in **Chapter 3**.

Finally, where trees on or close to boundaries have foliage that causes injury or harm to livestock (for example, cattle being poisoned as a result of eating the foliage from a yew tree), there may be liability under the rule in *Rylands v Fletcher*.[61]

5.3.2 Those on the highway

The most common examples of harm caused by trees relate to injuries to users of the highway and damage to their vehicles. This too is unsurprising, for several reasons. First, the users of a highway – particularly those in vehicles – perfectly properly are likely to pay no attention whatsoever to the condition of nearby trees, either those on highway or those on neighbouring land, particularly after dark. When a branch or a whole tree falls onto or in front of them, therefore, it does indeed come (literally) out of a clear sky.[62] Secondly, because there are vehicles involved, sometimes moving at considerable speed, the resulting harm or injury is likely to be greater, which makes litigation justifiable. And thirdly, for the same reason, any resulting litigation is likely to be driven by insurance companies.

The simplest, and rarest, situation is where a falling branch actually hits a person outright – as in *Brown v Harrison*,[63] where the unlucky victim was walking along the road when he was hit by a horse chestnut that was blown down by a heavy gust of wind; his skull was injured.

Somewhat more common are cases where a branch or a whole tree hits a vehicle, causing damage and (usually) injury. The first reported cases appear to be *Noble v Harrison*[64] and *Mackie v Dumbartonshire County Council*,[65] which both related to accidents in or around 1925. In the former, a diseased branch of a beech tree fell and damaged a motor coach in Sussex. The passengers in that incident, none of whom were injured, were fortunate. In *Mackie*, in the same year, a whole elm fell across a road in Scotland, striking a charabanc, killing some passengers and injuring others. A similar incident, concerned a milk van, whose driver was killed by an elm tree falling in a storm.[66]

---

[58] See **5.7.3**.
[59] [1938] 2 All E.R. 1, CA.
[60] See **5.7.2**.
[61] See **3.4.4**.
[62] Except, perhaps, for the fact that trees tend to fall when the weather is windy and wet, and often at night, so the sky will usually be neither clear nor blue.
[63] (1947) E.G., June 28, 1947, CA.
[64] [1926] 2 K.B. 333.
[65] (1927) 91 J.P. 158, H.L.
[66] *Kent v Marquis of Bristol* (1940), unreported; noted in the *Quarterly Journal of Forestry*, January, 1947.

The most notorious of these cases (because it reached the House of Lords) was *Caminer v Northern and London Investment Trust*,[67] in which an elm fell across the road, hitting the car in which Mr and Mrs Caminer were driving, and injuring them. More recently, in *Chapman v Barking and Dagenham* LBC,[68] the branch of a horse chestnut planted on the verge between the footpath and the carriageway fell on a van, which veered across the road into a parked car, and knocked over a lamp post; the driver of the van was rendered a paraplegic.

A further category of cases are those where a tree falls so as to obstruct a highway, and a motorist subsequently drives into the fallen tree – usually in the dark or the rain or, not infrequently, both. A particularly unfortunate case was *Cunliffe v Bankes*,[69] where an elm tree fell across a wall adjoining a road, resting on it, some while before the plaintiff arrived at the spot on his motor bike. He did not see the tree in his lights, hit it, and continued some 6 or 7 metres before stopping; his bike continued the same distance further. He died a week later, leaving a wife who had her fourth child three days after the accident. That incident occurred at around 5 a.m., as did a similar collision involving a motor cyclist and a fallen elm in *Lambourn v London Brick Co.*[70]

In *Lane v Tredegar Estate Trustees*,[71] a van collided after dark, during a gale and in heavy rain, with an elm tree that had just fallen across the road. In the earlier case of *Hudson v Bray*,[72] it took four days to remove an elm tree that had also blown across a road, and a car collided with the branches which had not been cleared (or lit). In each case the vehicle was damaged and the occupants injured.

In all of the cases above, the base of the tree was relatively close to the point of impact. In *Quinn v Scott*,[73] on the other hand, a beech tree was growing some 16 metres from the highway, across which a large part of it fell. The plaintiff was driving a mini-bus, saw the tree fall, and stopped just short of the fallen branches; but a car coming the other way was not so fortunate, and crashed into the branches and the mini-bus, injuring the driver.

In many of the reported cases, the owner of the tree was not in fact held to be liable, on the particular facts at issue (considered below[74]); but it was in every case found, or assumed, that the owner had been under a duty of care to the victim of the accident – whether the person was directly struck by the tree, or the driver coming upon it later, or the driver whose car was struck by another as a result of the fall, or the landowner whose building was damaged.

On highway trees generally, see **Chapter 6**.

5.3.3 Visitors to the land on which the tree is growing

The next obvious category of people who may thus be affected are those who are actually on the land on which the tree is growing. Here too, as with harm to those on neighbouring land,[75] there have been almost no reported cases – for the same

---

[67] [1949] 2 K.B., 65, CA; upheld at [1951] A.C. 88, H.L.
[68] [1997] 2 EGLR 141, upheld in CA (unreported).
[69] [1945] 1 All E.R. 459.
[70] (1950) 156 E.G. 146.
[71] (1954) E.G., November 27, 1954.
[72] [1917] 1 K.B. 520.
[73] [1964] 1 W.L.R. 1004.
[74] See **5.7**.
[75] See **5.3.1**.

reasons, and also because the potential victims of a defective tree are likely to be known to or related to the occupier of the land who is responsible for it.

The liability of the occupier of land to those on his or her land is governed by the Occupiers' Liability Acts of 1957 and 1984. These replace the common law which used to apply, and have been the subject of litigation mainly in the context of liability for defective buildings and structures; but they clearly apply equally to liability for the condition of the land itself – including, of course, any trees growing on it.

The key provision of the 1957 Act is that the "common duty of care" (a phrase considered below[76]) is owed by the occupier of land to all his or her "visitors". The latter is defined as those who would before the coming into the force of the Act have been treated as either invitees or licensees.[77]

In practice, an invitee is a person who, without any contract, enters on the land on business of interest both to himself or herself and to the occupier of the land – for example, a customer visiting a garden centre to view the wares on sale, a tradesman visiting a house by invitation to estimate for work, a child visiting for tea, or an elderly aunt on a visit for the foreseeable future.

A licensee is any person entering with the occupier's express or implied permission but without any community of interest. In relation to private land, this would include, for example, an election canvasser, a policeman seeking information, or a child recovering a ball. It would seem that other family members, living permanently on the land, are probably "licensees" in the eyes of the law.[78] In relation to "public" land (that is in fact owned by local authorities and similar bodies), such as parks, those members of the public making use of them do so as licensees.[79] Prior to the Act, invitees were owed a higher duty of care than "mere" licensees, but they are now treated identically.

It will be noted that the 1957 Act extends the same protection as is owed to visitors to those who have a contractual relationship with the occupier.[80] In practice, therefore, the most significant distinction now is between licensees (including in particular those with implied permission to enter onto the land), who are owed the common duty of care under the 1957 Act, and trespassers, who are owed only the lesser duty under the 1984 Act.

The simplest, and commonest, example of an implied permission is where someone enters land with the intention of communicating with the occupier. This will not apply where the entrant knows (or ought to know) that he or she has been forbidden to enter; but where the occupier revokes the implied permission by refusing to speak or deal with the entrant, the entrant has a reasonable time to leave the land before becoming a trespasser.[81]

It is also important to note that an entrant may often be (explicitly or implicitly) permitted to be on some of the occupier's land, but not necessarily on all of it. As one judge put it graphically, "when you invite a person into your house to use the staircase, you do not invite him to slide down the banisters"[82]; so the election canvasser is (thankfully) not entitled to inspect your garden. Where a person who is a lawful visitor to part of premises strays onto a part to which he or

---

[76] See **5.4.1**.
[77] 1957 Act, section 1(2).
[78] See, for example, Gray, *Elements of Land Law*, second edn, pp. 906–909.
[79] *Glasgow Corporation v Taylor* [1922] 1 A.C. 44, at pp. 51, 60, 63.
[80] See **5.3.5**.
[81] *Robson v Hallett* [1967] 2 Q.B. 393.
[82] *The Carlgarth* [1927] p. 93, per Scrutton L.J. at p. 110.

she is not invited, he or she ceases to be a "visitor", protected by the 1957 Act, and becomes instead a trespasser, protected only by the 1984 Act.[83]

Generally, it will be necessary to examine the facts of each case to establish whether or not there indeed exists an implied permission; and the onus of proof lies on those who claim that there does[84] – although the courts have seemed in the past to be very willing to support such a claim. For example, in one case, members of the public habitually took a short-cut across a farmer's field; he attempted to dissuade them, but did not actually take legal action as they were potential customers for his milk. The court accepted that they had implied permission to be on the land, and could therefore recover damages when they were attacked by a savage horse that the farmer introduced into the field.[85] The same would presumably have applied if he had failed to inspect and deal with a defective tree.

So children playing in a public park were held to be entitled to protection (from poisonous plants) in *Glasgow Corporation v Taylor*[86]; and those climbing trees (from contact with electric wires) in *Buckland v Guildford Gas Light & Coke Co.*[87] Both these cases preceded the 1957 Act. And in the only known case since the Act relating to a tree, *Thomas v Miller*,[88] a holiday-maker parked his car in a lane which he admitted he knew was private property. The landowner did not try to stop holiday-makers parking there, considering it almost impossible, but he would on his occasional visits remind those he found that the property was private and that they parked at their own risk. An elm tree fell onto the parked car, ruining it. The court found that those who parked in the lane were visitors (presumably as licensees), and not trespassers, and thus entitled to the full protection of the 1957 Act.

This attitude may be gradually changing, however, particularly since the Occupiers' Liability Act 1984 has improved the lot of a trespasser. Indeed, all earlier authorities (and particularly those prior to 1957) must be read with caution.[89a] As to the nature of the duty under the 1984 Act, see below.[89]

5.3.4 Those on the land under a contract

The second category of people (other than the "occupier" himself or herself) who may be on land are those who are present as a result of a contract with the occupier. The Act now provides that any such contract, in either category, is deemed to include a provision that the occupier owes to the entrant the same "common duty of care"[90] as is owed to visitors.[91] The most common examples of such a contract are a licence, a lease, a contract of employment or a contract for sale.

The most common category of person with a contractual relationship with the occupier is the licensee – that is, a person whose presence on the land in question

---

[83] *Hillen v ICI (Alkali) Ltd* [1936] A.C. 65 at pp. 69–70. See **5.3.5** and **5.6.4**.
[84] *Edwards v Railway Executive* [1952] A.C. 737; also *Buckland v Guildford Gas Light & Coke Co*, above, at p. 1090C.
[85] *Lowery v Walker* [1911] A.C. 10.
[86] [1922] A.C. 44, H.L.
[87] [1948] 2 All E.R. 1086.
[88] Decision of the Exeter County Court, (1970), unreported (except as news item in *Western Morning News*, February 3, 1970), noted in *The Arboriculturalist's Companion*, NDG James.
[89a] The 1957 Act came into force on January 1, 1985 (s. 8(3)); the 1984 Act on May 13, 1984 (s. 4(2)).
[89] See **5.6.4**.
[90] See **5.4.1**.
[91] 1957 Act, s. 5(1).

arises as a result of a contract that is not a lease, but is specifically aimed at allowing and regulating such entry.

The holder of a leasehold interest in land – the tenant – is likely to be the occupier of the land for the purposes of the Act if he or she has exclusive possession, as will generally be the case. Otherwise, it is possible, although unlikely, that the lease will itself provide for matters relating to the safety of the land (as where a landlord undertakes to repair the lift in a block of flats), but this is unlikely to be relevant to trees. More common will be the situation where the landlord and tenant are both at least to some extent "occupiers".[92]

A contractual relationship may also arise where the occupier of land engages the services of someone – either as an employee or as an independent contractor – for a purpose that necessarily involves that person being on the land.

Examples of such contracts include those enabling a single visit by a guest at a country house hotel or a series of visits by a member of the golf club attached to the hotel (each of which would be a licence). And the owner of the hotel may employ on a permanent basis a chambermaid to clean the bedrooms, and may occasionally call on the services of a local plumber to un-block the drains. Some such arrangements may be the subject of written agreements, others are more likely to arise from a telephone call, but nothing turns on that. It is also probable that none of the agreements will say anything with regard to the safety of the premises, including the grounds; but each will be deemed to include the common duty of care. If, therefore, a mulberry tree outside the main door of the hotel deposits large quantities of fruit on the ground, which are not cleared up and cause the guest, the golfer, the chambermaid and the plumber to slip and fall, each will be able to rely on the Act to sue the hotel.

It is possible to restrict or exclude liability by a term in a contract or by a notice, but only in limited circumstances.[93] In particular, where a contract contains a term that purports to reduce the occupier's duty below the common duty of care, that will usually be void.[94]

5.3.5 Others on the land

It has been shown that the Occupiers' Liability Act 1957 applies directly to protect any "visitor", and indirectly anyone with a contract with the occupier. There will, however, be various other categories of people on the occupier's land, and these are protected by the Occupiers' Liability Act 1984, which prescribes the (lesser) duty that is owed by an occupier of land to "persons other than his visitors".[95] The nature of that duty, and the overlap between the two Acts, is considered below.[96]

The principal category of people covered by the 1984 Act is usually considered to be trespassers, who, prior to the 1984 Act, were sometimes in a difficult position if harmed or injured by the state of land.[97] The same principles apply, however, to:

---

[92] As in *Wheat v Lacon*, above.
[93] See **5.4.4**.
[94] Unfair Contract Terms Act 1977, s. 2.
[95] 1984 Act, s. 1(1).
[96] See **5.6.4**.
[97] See, for example, *Robert Addie & Sons (Collieries) v Dumbreck* [1929] A.C. 358, overruled by *British Railways Board v Herrington* [1972] A.C. 877.

- those using a private right of way across the land[98];

- members of the public exercising rights under section 2 of the Countryside and Rights of Way Act 2000 ("the right to roam"); or

- those exercising rights conferred by an access agreement made under Part V of the National Parks and Access to the Countryside Act 1949.[99]

These three groups may well be relevant in the context of possible liabilities for dangerous trees. Unsurprisingly, therefore, at least in the context of the right to roam under the 2000 Act, liability under the 1984 Act is explicitly excluded in respect of "a risk resulting from the existence of any natural feature of the landscape"[1] – which would obviously include any trees.

As for those using public rights of way, they are protected neither under the 1957 Act[2] nor under the 1984 Act[3]; they will instead be protected under the Highways Act 1980[4] and under the general common law duty of care.

5.4 The nature and extent of the duty of care

5.4.1 The nature of the duty of care

As already indicated,[5] the general common law duty of care is:

". . . to take reasonable care to avoid acts or omissions which you can reasonably foresee would be likely to injure your neighbour".[6]

The somewhat similar duty under the Occupiers' Liability Act 1957 ("the common duty of care") is:

". . . to take such care as in all the circumstances is reasonable to see that the visitor is reasonably safe in using the premises for the purposes for which he is invited or permitted by the occupier to be there".[7]

That the two duties are in practice very similar in the context of trees is hardly surprising. Liability to someone on land adjacent to that on which a tree is growing will only arise if he or she is harmed, and then only if that harm is the fault of the tree owner – usually the result of an omission to take proper care. That is, the duty of the owner is to ensure that such harm does not occur or, in other words, that the neighbour is safe. Normally a defect in the condition of premises (which is the mischief at which the 1957 Act is aimed) will only affect those on that premises; a tree (which is, as has already been shown,[8] part of the

---

[98] *Holden v White* [1982] 2 Q.B. 679.
[99] 1957 Act, s. 1(4), as substituted by Countryside and Rights of Way Act 2000, s. 13(1); 1949 Act, s. 66(2).
[1] 1984 Act, s. 1(6A), inserted by 2000 Act, s. 13(2).
[2] *Greenhalgh v British Railways Board* [1969] 2 Q.B. 286.
[3] 1984 Act, s. 1(7).
[4] See **Chapter 6**.
[5] See **5.2.1**.
[6] *Donoghue v Stevenson* [1932] A.C. 562, H.L., at p. 580.
[7] 1957 Act, s. 2(2)
[8] See **Chapter 2**.

land on which it is growing) is a rare example of a situation where the defective condition of one property will affect those on neighbouring properties.

Another way to look at it is to consider the case of a tree situated so near a boundary that half of its branches overhang the land (owned by X) on which it is planted, while the other half overhang neighbouring land (owned by Y). It would be surprising – and unjust – if X owed a lesser duty to those on that neighbouring land than to those on his own land. Again, Y will owe a duty under the 1957 Act to those on his land to make sure that they are reasonably safe – which will include protecting them from any dangers likely to be caused by X's overhanging tree. The result of these interlocking duties is that Mrs Z, the potential victim, is equally safe (in relation to the tree) whether she is on X's land or Y's land – X will be under a duty to protect Z from danger as far is it lies in his power, wherever she is, and Y will be under a similar duty as far as it lies in his power.

And to ensure that a visitor is "reasonably safe" is presumably in effect the same as to protect a neighbour from "omissions which you can reasonably foresee would be likely to injure [him or her]".

On the face of it, if a branch or a whole tree falls, it is clearly foreseeable that it may hit someone or something; and the bigger the tree, the larger the area, and thus the greater the number of potential victims. And even if it does not actually hit someone or something directly, it is equally foreseeable that someone or something may subsequently collide with it. Further, if the unlucky victim is in a vehicle, it is foreseeable that the shock of the impact will cause him or her to lose control, so that the vehicle may then cause further damage.[9]

But will the branch or the whole tree fall? And, if it does, will it hit or be hit by someone or something?

And with risks such as poisonous berries, it is obvious that, if they are eaten, illness or death may follow – but will they in fact be eaten?

5.4.2 The extent of the duty of care

The duty under the 1957 Act, which has been shown to be in this respect the same as the common law duty, is only to ensure that visitors (and thus neighbours, too) are "*reasonably* safe". This does not mean "as safe as they possibly could be"[10] – it is in any event impossible to ensure that anyone or anything is completely safe. This is important, as it may often be possible, after the event, to point to something that would have made the visitor slightly safer; but that does not of itself prove that the visitor was not in fact *reasonably* safe.

To ensure that degree of safety, the duty under the common law is simply to take "reasonable" care. This is expanded by the 1957 Act to require "such care as is reasonable in all the circumstances"[11]; but nothing turns on the distinction, as it is clear from the cases that the courts do indeed (as would be hoped) examine all the circumstances to see what level of care was reasonable. There is thus no absolute rule as to the extent or scope of the duty of care. As to what those circumstances might be, the Act further mentions three specific matters (the degree of care likely to be exercised by visitors,[12] the existence of any warning of

---

[9] *Chapman v Barking and Dagenham LBC* [1997] 2 EGLR 141, upheld in CA (unreported).
[10] *Phillis v Daley* (1988) 15 N.S.W.L.R. 65; *Unger v City of Ottawa* (1989) D.L.R. (4th) 98.
[11] 1957 Act, s. 2(2)
[12] 1957 Act, s. 2(3).

the danger,[13] and whether works already carried out have been executed competently[14]); but these are explicitly stated to be by way of example, so that the factors explicitly mentioned are not to constitute an exclusive list.

And the whole issue needs to be considered with a degree of common sense. For example, in one recent county court case, children aged around seven were playing in a school playground where a tree was growing so that its branches were just within reach. One child pulled down a branch, which sprang back injuring another boy in the eye. To the allegation that the trees were a dangerous allurement, the judge sensibly responded that there was:

". . . absolutely nothing whatsoever to put any reasonable person on notice of any danger, in the absence of some previous [incident] or special knowledge that children might pull them down".[15]

And in another such case, where a child climbed a tree and fell to the ground, the judge noted that the tree was not defective, and pointed out "that there were trees the length and breadth of the country which may be an allurement to children". Climbing trees is what children do. The question here is:

". . . is this a particularly dangerous tree, so as the local authority [the landowner] ought to have a high burden placed upon them? . . . This is, in my opinion, . . . an accident rather than an situation where any liability attaches to the authority."[16]

It is thus self-evident that not all trees are equally likely to cause harm. For harm to occur, there must be two elements present:

- *a tree or a part of a tree that constitutes a hazard*, in that it may cause harm; and

- *a potential target* – a person, an animal or an inanimate object – located so as to be at risk of harm.

As to the first, there must exist a tree that behaves in a particular way – having roots and branches that grow; having poisonous fruit, or thorns; dropping branches, twigs, or berries; or falling.[17] Whether this will lead to a problem may depend on the age, size, species and (in particular) the condition of the tree; and on whether any works have been carried out to it in the past. This is considered in more detail below.[18]

And as to the second, there must be someone or something to be harmed or damaged by that behaviour. It will therefore be important to consider the number and frequency of potential impacts, and the nature of any likely victims; this will depend principally on the location of the tree. Particular problems arise in this context in relation to the possibility of incidents involving children. Special considerations also apply in the case of those with special expertise; and where the

---

[13] 1957 Act, s. 2(4)(a).

[14] 1957 Act, s. 2(4)(b).

[15] *Bassett v Surrey CC*, Reading County Court, January 2000, unreported. Compare *Glasgow Corporation v Taylor* [1922] A.C. 44 (see **5.6.2**). And see also *Gough v Upshire Primary School*, February 2, 2001.

[16] *Beddow v Cleveland CC*, Middlesborough County Court, August 16, 1999, unreported.

[17] See **1.3.4**, **1.3.5**.

[18] See **5.5**.

only potential victims are trespassers. These too are all considered in more detail.[19]

But it must never be forgotten that there will be no harm without the presence of *both* a hazardous tree and a potential target. A tree in a botanical garden that has highly poisonous berries, but which is in a securely fenced area inaccessible to anyone except trained staff, is no danger; nor is a tree that overhangs a footpath regularly used by small children, if it is in perfect condition. Taking the two elements together enables one to assess the likely risk of harm occurring.

5.4.3 *Damage to property*

Although the discussion in this chapter is largely framed by reference to "injury" and "victims", in practice trees are very much more likely to cause harm to property, in particular vehicles (not least parked ones), than directly to people – essentially because people get out of the way of falling trees, whereas inanimate objects do not.

The Occupiers' Liability Act 1957 thus explicitly applies to damage to property on land (whether owned by visitors or by others) as much as it does to death or injury.[20] As for the general duty of care under the common law, Megaw L.J. noted in *Leakey v National Trust*[21]:

"If, as a result of the working of the forces of nature, there is, poised above my land, or above my house, . . . a rotten tree, which is liable to fall at any moment of the day or night, perhaps destroying my house, and perhaps killing or injuring me or members of my family, am I without remedy? (Of course, the standard of care required may be much higher where there is risk to life and limb as contrasted with mere risk to property, but can it be said that the duty exists in the one case and not in the other?)"

This might tend to suggest that there is a lesser duty to avoid damage to property; and this might indeed be the case in relation to certain types of property such as, for example, unimportant garden sheds or agricultural barns. And damage caused by trees to occupied buildings, such as houses – although sometimes spectacular – is in fact fairly unlikely to cause death or injury (simply because the structure absorbs the impact of the falling tree).

Damage by trees to vehicles, on the other hand, is likely to occur in locations, such as car parks, where people are also directly at risk, albeit for much shorter periods of time; and there may be large numbers of people involved. The standard of care in such cases would therefore probably be determined in relation to the possibility of trees harming people directly; if that incidentally gave protection to their vehicles, that would be an added bonus.

And note that, in many circumstances, liability for damage to property may not be excluded unreasonably; whereas liability for death and injury may not be excluded at all, unreasonably or otherwise.[22]

[19]   See **5.6**.
[20]   1957 Act, s. 1(3)(b).
[21]   [1980] 1 Q.B. 485, at p. 523F.
[22]   See **5.4.4**.

5.4.4 Exclusion of liability

The Occupiers' Liability Act 1957 explicitly allows an occupier of land to extend, restrict, modify or exclude his or her duty under the Act to visitors, by agreement or otherwise, but only in so far as he or she is free to do so and does in fact do so.[23] And there is no reason in principle why the general duty of care (to those other than visitors, such as those on neighbouring land or adjacent highways) should not be excluded from liability. In practice, however, there are relatively few situations in which this occurs; and the freedom of a landowner, other than a private person, to exclude liability in this way has been substantially curtailed by the Unfair Contract Terms Act 1977 (which was itself amended by the Occupiers' Liability Act 1984).

In particular, where people are allowed onto land as part of the business of the occupier of that land, or as part of another business, the occupier may not exclude liability for death or personal injury, and may not unreasonably exclude or restrict liability for other damage (for example, to parked cars).[24] "Business" for this purpose includes the activities of "any government department or local or public authority".[25] Where access to land is granted for recreational or educational purposes, that will only come within these provisions if the allowing of such access itself falls within the business activities of the occupier.[26]

So, for example, A (the owner of a private house) may allow B onto his land on the strict understanding that A is not liable for any harm that may occur due to dangerous trees, since occupying a house is not a business; it is then up to B to decide whether to take up the offer – and, if harm does in fact occur, it would then be up to A to establish the existence of the agreement. But C (the proprietor of a hotel) may not exclude liability for harm caused by the state of trees in the hotel gardens, since the hotel is a business. Nor may a local authority seek to exclude liability for dangerous trees in a public park – for example, by erecting a notice to that effect at the entrance.

A farmer may allow children onto his land for educational purposes (for example, to view particular plants and animals on the farm) on the basis that he takes no responsibility for any harm arising from the state of the land, including any dangerous trees, because his business is farming, not education. An education authority, on the other hand, would not be able to exclude liability for trees on its playing fields. And the National Trust would not be able to allow access to its land on similar terms, as enabling children to study flora and fauna in the countryside is (probably) part of its business. If a landowner makes a charge for entry onto his land, therefore, he will probably only be able to escape liability on this basis if he can show (by reference to accounts and so on) that the charge was solely to cover expenses, so that there was no element of profit which might be interpreted as a "business".

Where it is permissible to exclude liability on the basis of the above principles, it may be done either by a clause in a contract, or by a notice, or an oral agreement, or any other way that seems appropriate. However, merely because a person agrees to a term in a contract, or is aware of a notice, does not mean that he or she

---

[23] 1957 Act, s. 2(1).
[24] Unfair Contract Terms Act 1977, s. 2(1),(2).
[25] 1977 Act, s. 14.
[26] 1977 Act, s. 1(3), as amended by Occupiers' Liability Act 1984, s. 2.

has voluntarily accepted the risk.[27] It would, after all, be absurd if a landowner, either a business, a public authority or a private person, could, for example, simply erect a notice on the boundary of his property stating that members of the public walking or driving on the adjacent highway did so entirely at their own risk.

Notices are also considered further below, in the context of possible remedial action.[28]

5.5 The nature and location of the tree

5.5.1 The nature of the tree

The nature of the tree itself is clearly relevant to any consideration of whether reasonable care has been taken to ensure that it does not lead to the land on which it is growing being unreasonably dangerous. Some trees, that is, are clearly more dangerous than others. The problem is that defects in trees are not always readily discoverable: they are the result of "a secret and unobservable operation of nature".[29]

The first consideration will be whether all or some of the tree is likely to fall. This will depend on its age and species, but more importantly on its condition. A tree that is apparently free from serious defects may suddenly shed a branch, or blow over altogether in a severe storm,[30] but that is a risk that cannot reasonably be predicted, and any harm thereby caused will, by definition, be unforeseeable, and thus will not render its owner liable in negligence. What is required is to consider the risks that are apparent, or which could become apparent with reasonable care; and these will largely relate to discernible defects such as fungal infection and malformation. Thus trees may develop defects for a wide variety of reasons. This may be as a result of pruning (considered in more detail below). But it may be due to natural causes, such as branches breaking in storms and leading to decay; or unbalanced crowns; weak forks; or through disease or pests.

There have, for example, been a number of cases in which the courts have decided that the failure of the tree in question was caused by a defect of some kind, which would have been discoverable on a proper inspection: a hole in the elm tree in *Kent v Marquis of Bristol*,[31] the decay in the branch of the chestnut which fell onto the road in *Lane v Tredegar Estate Trustees*,[32] the decay causing die-back and thinness of foliage which caused a large section of a beech tree to fall across a road in *Quinn v Scott*,[33] and the decay which caused an elm to shed a branch onto a parked car in *Thomas v Miller*.[34]

Trees that are dying or dead, as opposed to merely diseased or otherwise defective, may also be dangerous – as with the old and partly dead horse-chestnut

---

[27] 1977 Act, s. 2(3).
[28] See **5.8.2**.
[29] *Noble v Harrison* [1926] 2 K.B. 332 per Wright J. at p. 341; *cf. Wringe v Cohen* [1940] 1 K.B. 229, CA, per Atkinson J. at p. 233.
[30] *Bruce v Caulfield* (1918) 34 T.L.R. 204, CA.
[31] (1940), unreported, noted in the *Quarterly Journal of Forestry*, January 1947; see **5.3.2**.
[32] (1954) E.G., 27 November, 1954.
[33] [1964] 1 W.L.R. 1004.
[34] (1970), unreported, noted in the *Western Morning News*, February 3, 1970.

tree in *Brown v Harrison*,[35] and the beech tree in *Shirvell v Hackwood Estates*[36] that was dead from 5 metres above the ground to its top.

And of course each tree must be considered individually. It is no use saying that old trees, or trees of a particular species, are statistically more likely to be defective; that may well be true as a generality, and may suggest that inspections should be carried out more frequently, but what matters is the particular tree in question. Conversely a young tree of a species that is generally problem-free may be seriously defective, perhaps because of an earlier pruning wound,[37] or a blow by a vehicle.

It may incidentally be noted that judges, particularly in the past, were prone to make unsupported statements about trees, which may or may not have been justified. So, for example, the comment of Lord Goddard C.J.[38] that "elms are notoriously treacherous trees" appears not to have been based on any evidence; and the statement by MacKinnon L.J.[39] that "the fear of branches falling from a beech is nothing like as great as that of their falling from an elm" was based on his knowledge "as one who lives in the country".

Once a fall has occurred, that may suggest that the tree had been defective, and thus dangerous, before it fell; but that does not of itself prove that reasonable care had not been taken to see that visitors were safe, since the defect may have been invisible. A tree may thus be apparently safe from all outward evidence, but actually defective inside, so that even a slight breath of wind will cause it to fall – it is therefore dangerous before it falls, even though no one could tell that until after the fall has occurred.

Thus in *Noble v Harrison*, which concerned a beech tree, it was found that the branch that fell had at some time developed a crack at the place about 4.5 m from the trunk where it broke off, but that the defect would not have been observable by any reasonably careful inspection.[40] In *Cunliffe v Bankes*,[41] the cause of the elm tree falling was honey fungus at the base of the trunk, which would probably not have been detected by inspection; in *White v Carruthers*,[42] it was elm heart rot – also undetectable.

In *Caminer v Northern & London Investment Trust*,[43] the situation was slightly more complex, in that it was subsequently discovered that the roots of the tree that had fallen were badly affected by elm butt rot, but it was held both at first instance and in the House of Lords that there was nothing in the appearance of the tree to indicate that it was in any way diseased; nor would an expert have discovered it. That case therefore turned on what was described as a "broader and more general" issue:

"In the case of an apparently healthy elm tree, which was of obviously mature age although by no means old, ought its owners either to have had it lopped and topped or should they at any rate have called in an expert to advise them as to its treatment, and was this course the more imperative in the case of a tree standing near a public and well-used road? The answer

---

[35] (1947) E.G., June 28, 1947, CA.
[36] [1938] 2 All E.R. 1, CA, see **5.7.2**.
[37] See **5.5.2**.
[38] In *Caminer v Northern and London Investment Trust* [1949] 2 K.B. 66 (at first instance).
[39] In *Shirvell v Hackwood Estates* [1938] 2 All E.R. 1, CA, at p. 9.
[40] [1926] 2 K.B. 332 at p. 339.
[41] [1945] 1 All E.R. 459.
[42] (1958) 172 E.G. 229.
[43] [1951] A.C. 88, H.L.

in this particular case is somewhat complicated by the controversy as to whether the crown was a very large one or not."[44]

That is, the problem was not the disease which in fact existed, but which was unknown and unknowable, but simply the size and age of the apparently healthy tree. Lord Normand summarised the matter as follows:

"The Court of Appeal applied . . . the proper test – the conduct to be expected of a prudent and reasonable landowner – and held on the evidence that the [owner] had satisfied this test because there was nothing dangerous in the appearance of the tree, no sign of disease, advanced age, disproportion of crown to stem, or rising roots."[45]

That provides a useful checklist, although it may not be complete. Particular species may be prone to particular problems which will suggest that other features should be looked for. The expert retained by the Council in *Chapman v Barking and Dagenham LBC*,[46] for example, suggested that a more thorough inspection of an elm would be justified in the event of features such as fruiting bodies, decay, weak forks, or crossed or broken branches.

The same position occurred in *Knight v Hext*,[47] in that after the beech tree had fallen, it was discovered that it had been subject to butt rot; but, as in *Caminer*, that could not have been discovered by external inspection, and the question was again whether the top heavy crown would or should have led an expert to recommend that the tree be either topped or felled.

The matters mentioned above largely relate to abnormal growth, or disease, decay or death of the tree. The remaining factors under this heading are simply evidence of a tree behaving in a way that is entirely normal, but which could in certain circumstances be dangerous to people – such as having poisonous fruit, or thorns at eye level, or dropping branches, twigs, cones, leaves and berries.

All of these features – abnormal (such as disease) or normal (such as dropping berries) – do not necessarily in themselves make a tree, and thus the land on which it stands, "dangerous"; but all are potential sources of danger if the tree is in certain locations.[48] They are therefore all matters that should be considered carefully by occupiers. For further information, see texts such as *Principles of Tree Hazard Assessment and Management* by David Lonsdale.[49]

5.5.2 Danger due to works carried out in the past

One particular source of problems is the effect of work having being carried out at some stage in the past. Where a tree is pruned so that a wound is caused which leads to decay, this may some while later lead to a branch falling onto the ground. Or a building may be constructed in such a way as to harm the root system of a tree so that it is much less stable; it may then fall in a subsequent storm.

---

[44] Per Lord Porter at p. 94.
[45] At p. 99.
[46] [1997] 2 EGLR 141 at p. 145E
[47] [1980] 1 EGLR 111, CA.
[48] See **5.5.3**.
[49] 2nd ed., 2001, Stationery Office; part of the Research for Amenity Trees series published by DTLR (formerly DETR).

The same result may follow from alterations being made to the ground surrounding the base of the tree, as in *Mackie v Dumbartonshire County Council*,[50] where about a year before the accident[51] the Council had widened the road, in the process removing a great deal of the soil which had supported an elm tree growing on a very steep bank at the side of the road. The House of Lords held that the Council was liable "either for the negligence which did not disclose the obvious danger or for the negligence which did not in fact deal with the obvious danger after it had been disclosed".[52]

This type of scenario will not necessarily lead to the tree owner being liable for any consequent damage or harm, provided that he or she was reasonable in entrusting the earlier work to the contractor concerned, and took all reasonable steps to check that the contractor was competent and that the work had been done properly[53] – although the contractor may be liable in negligence.[54] It is thus not appropriate to rely on a tree pruning exercise that was done at some stage in the past by a general contractor with no special expertise.

And it may be that it is not known who did the earlier work, as in *Lambourn v London Brick Co*,[55] where the judge noted that the roots of the tree had been severed, and that this had undoubtedly contributed to its fall; but he also held that this was not an obvious feature of the tree, and there was no evidence as to who had done the work or when.

Or it may be that a trespasser or a vandal harmed the tree in such a way as to leave it unsafe. Once the owner is – or should be – aware of the potential hazard, it should be dealt with. That was the situation in *Sedleigh-Denfield v O'Callaghan*,[56] albeit that that was a claim based on liability in nuisance rather than negligence.

However, there is an important difference between works to trees and those to buildings. Where a building has been constructed or altered, any defect arising from faulty workmanship will not (usually) become any worse with the passage of time; and it may thus be entirely reasonable to justify the fact that a building has collapsed by pointing to faulty workmanship of many years earlier which could not have become apparent on intermediate inspection. Trees, by contrast, grow and decay; the effect of faulty work will therefore change, and possibly increase, with time. Indeed, work carried out perfectly competently may have the effect that some while later the tree develops a structural weakness or other defect.

The law recognises this by, in effect, requiring occupiers to continue to inspect their trees from time to time (how often depends on the circumstances) – and to pay particular attention where past works may have subsequently caused defects. Thus in *Chapman v Barking and Dagenham LBC*,[57] the Court of Appeal confirmed that where works are carried out to a tree such that it is no longer in its natural state there is a special duty to inspect the result. Even if, as claimed by the Council, the earlier pruning works had been carried out in accordance with the relevant British Standard that was applicable at the time, that did not absolve the Council from its duty to continue to inspect the tree. And in the earlier case of

---

[50] (1927) 91 JP 158; see also *Sheen v Arden* (1945), unreported, noted in the *Journal of the Land Agents' Society*, January, 1946.
[51] See **5.3.2**.
[52] Per Viscount Dunedin at p. 159.
[53] Occupiers' Liability Act 1957, s. 2(4)(b).
[54] See **9.5.1**.
[55] (1950) E.G., July 28, 1950.
[56] [1940] A.C. 880.
[57] [1997] 2 EGLR 141, upheld by CA (1998) unreported.

Caminer v Northern & London Investment Trust, it was noted that evidence had been given to the effect that lopping a tree may be appropriate, but that it would make it more dangerous in the end, so that it should be inspected "every five or seven years" after the works.[58]

5.5.3 The location of the tree

It has already been noted that none of the features considered above necessarily in themselves make a tree "dangerous". The location is also crucial. A tree that has a decaying branch, or poisonous berries, is not dangerous if it is in the middle of a dense forest to which the public have no access; but an identical tree may be potentially lethal if it is immediately adjacent to the main entrance to a large primary school. The location is not of itself a source of danger – there must be an inherent hazard in the tree – but it is the location that might turn a diseased branch from a low risk of harm into a high risk.

Further, there are features of trees (notably roots, and fallen leaves and berries) which are of themselves not dangerous at all, but which can lead to harm or danger in certain situations. Roots can disrupt the surface of a path, creating a trip hazard; fallen leaves and berries can make playgrounds slippery; either can be a danger to those affected. But there must be a path, or a playground, in a location such that it will be affected.

Amongst the factors that will need to be considered, the number of people likely to frequent the vicinity of the tree will be crucial. The level of care that is required in connection with a tree on a remote mountainside is clearly much less than with one in a public park. There may also be seasonal discrepancies; a part of a park that is normally almost deserted may be used twice each summer for concerts attended by thousands. And as well as people, there may be property involved – notably vehicles (either moving or stationary).

So, for example, trees on or adjacent to land that is used for any public or semi-public purpose (such as roads, schools, parks, railways and cemeteries) need to be the subject of particular care. It is thus no surprise that many of the reported cases relating to the duty laid upon tree owners relate to trees causing harm to users of the highway.[59] This is partly because there are many trees adjacent to highways and because claims involving vehicles are funded by insurers. But it also reflects the fact that there are more people on highways likely to be affected by the failure of a tree; they usually are not aware of its existence, let alone its condition, until after it has failed, and any accident involving a moving vehicle is likely to be serious.

This view was expressed by Lynskey J. in *Lane v Tredegar Estate Trustees*[60]:

"If a bough of a tree was overhanging a highway, there might be an extra degree of care required as compared with the case of a tree in a park to which there was no public access and where, if a bough fell, it might not cause any particular damage."

But not all roads are equally well used. Lord Radcliffe pondered this question in *Caminer*:

---

[58] [1951] A.C. 88 at p. 108.
[59] See, in particular, **5.3.2**.
[60] (1954) E.G., November 27, 1954.

"It would be conceded, I believe, that there is somehow a difference between the legal responsibilities of the owner of a mature forest tree, in a built-up area, immediately adjacent to a busy street, and the responsibilities of the owner of a stand of timber bordering a country lane. But is the difference only this, that the latter is entitled to take more chances at the expense of his neighbours than the former? I am not certain of the logic, for a tree or its branch only falls once; and it must be poor consolation to an injured passer-by in the country lane to be assured that the chances were all against his being at the place of the accident at the moment when it occurred. The accepted test that liability only begins when there is apparent in the tree a sign of danger has the advantage that it seems to ignore, or to a large extent to ignore, the distinction between a spot that is much, and the spot that is little frequented."[61]

There is also the problem that an accident on a very minor road in the remote countryside, particularly if at night, is likely to remain undiscovered for longer than one on a busy road, and it will take longer for the victims to obtain medical assistance.[62] Any injuries in such a case are likely to be aggravated.

And not all cases involve roads. The other things that are likely to be hit by trees are parked vehicles and buildings – since they cannot see the danger or get out of the way. A residential caravan was thus hit by an elm tree in *White v Carruthers*,[63] and a parked car by a branch of another elm in *Thomas v Miller*[64] – the two cases, by coincidence, were decided twelve years apart in the same county court by the same judge.

Buildings near trees are also high-risk targets in some circumstances. Thus a neighbour's stable was damaged in *Bruce v Caulfield*[65] – as had been predicted by the plaintiff's wife. And in *Knight v Hext*,[66] the plaintiff pointed out to his neighbour that his barn was directly beneath her beech tree, which was leaning in that direction – and which indeed fell in that direction a few days later.[67] The lesson is that it is prudent to ensure that trees are carefully inspected where there is a building, particularly one that is occupied, that would be within range if it were to fall.

5.6 The nature of the potential victims

5.6.1 General principles

The nature of those frequenting the area will require consideration. It has already been noted that the Occupiers' Liability Act 1957 specifically states that amongst the circumstances that must be borne in mind are the degree of care, and of want of care, which would ordinarily be looked for in those who are likely to be visitors to the land on which the tree is growing.[68] And there would seem to be no reason why the same approach should not be adopted in relation to trees affecting those on neighbouring land. So, for example, are they likely to be elderly, adults, older

---

[61] [1951] A.C. 88 at p. 111.
[62] See, for example, *Cunliffe v Bankes* [1945] 1 All E.R. 459.
[63] (1958) 172 E.G. 229.
[64] (1970), unreported, noted in the *Western Morning News*, February 3, 1970.
[65] (1918) 34 T.L.R. 204, CA.
[66] [1980] 1 EGLR 111, CA.
[67] See **5.7.3**.
[68] 1957 Act, s. 1(3).

children or toddlers? Are they fully sighted or blind, fully mobile or disabled? Will they have special knowledge?

Children present special problems, which are considered in the following section. But many of the same problems arise in the context of the elderly, the blind and other disabled people. Those who have less mobility, partial sight or impaired intelligence are thus more likely to trip or slip and fall on uneven or slippery ground. They may also be less able to heed warning notices or take avoiding action. Clearly this will be more of a problem in some locations than others – a tree that drops squishy fruit is likely to cause problems if it is next to a stone path in the grounds of an old people's home, for example, as will a tree with thorns at head height in a garden frequently used by the visually impaired.

Essentially, the rule laid down with respect to children in *Phipps v Rochester Corporation*[69] (see below) would seem to apply equally to other groups needing special attention – the occupiers of land to which the public habitually have access need to take special care to ensure that those in such groups are reasonably safe; others can assume that they will have guardians insofar as they need them. So, for example, a tree owner cannot accurately tell what special problems may arise as a result of a visitor having impaired intelligence, but it can be assumed that such visitors will either be able to look after themselves or will have companions who will assist them as necessary.

These obligations will be reinforced by the Disability Discrimination Act 1995, the relevant provisions of which (relating to the obligations of service providers not to discriminate against disabled people by the nature of their premises[70]) will come into force in 2004.

Finally, it should be noted that there is no liability on an occupier to provide for the safety of a visitor in relation to a risk that has been willingly accepted as his or hers by the visitor.[71] In deciding whether the risk was so accepted, the normal rules relevant to negligence are to be applied (that is, the principle known to lawyers as *volens non fit injuria*[72]). If, therefore, a person knows that a branch is weak, but chooses to crawl along it to rescue a cat or spy on a neighbour, he cannot complain if it collapses beneath him; if another is warned that berries are poisonous, she cannot claim for illness resulting to her from eating them – provided, that is, that she is old enough to understand the warning.

Thus, in one recent case, a person protesting against the construction of a road was chained to a branch of a tree, or at least he thought he was, but fell to the ground when the contractors started to fell it. He was not able to claim damages in respect of his injuries under the 1957 Act.[73]

5.6.2 Children

It will be obvious from a moment's thought that children present special problems, particularly in the context of trees. There have been only two reported cases (*Glasgow Corporation v Taylor*[74] and *Buckland v Guildford Gas Light & Coke Co*[75]) where a tree has caused injuries, as opposed to property damage, on the

---

[69] [1955] 1 Q.B. 450.
[70] See particularly sections 19–21 of the 1995 Act.
[71] 1957 Act, s. 1(5).
[72] See Winfield & Jolowicz, *op. cit.*, Chapter 25.
[73] *Ellis v Dept of Transport* (2000) unreported.
[74] [1922] A.C. 44, H.L.
[75] [1948] 2 All E.R. 1086.

land on which it is growing; and it is perhaps significant that both of them involved children. And the two unreported cases noted earlier also involved young boys.[76]

The 1957 Act itself requires occupiers to be prepared for children to be less careful than adults.[77] Children are thus less aware of potential hazards – they will not necessarily assume that a branch hanging limply from a tree is likely to fall, or that it is dangerous to climb trees, or certain parts of them, or (as in *Glasgow*) to eat certain berries; they do not appreciate the problems that may arise where an electricity cable is very close to a tree (as in *Buckland*).

Children are also, no doubt in many ways to their great advantage, blissfully ignorant of the finer points of land law, and accordingly sometimes go where they should not. Nor will they necessarily be able (or willing) to read notices prohibiting or restricting entry to certain areas of land – the reference above[78] to sliding down banisters highlights the problem. And, once on the land, they are more likely to attempt feats that those who are older (such as judges?) would not:

"A tree visible from a nearby footpath which may be easily climbed may, to the gaze of a bright and healthy schoolgirl, present an alluring attraction which would not suggest itself to those who are either no longer nimble or for whom heights have no fascination."[79]

The risks and the resulting problems will be greater with younger children: the girl who was electrocuted by high voltage wires too close to a tree in *Buckland* was aged 13; the boy who died from eating the poisonous berries in *Glasgow v Taylor* was aged seven. It might be that older children would not have succeeded – particularly in the case of the electricity cable, the perils of which should have been obvious to an adult – although even adults may not know what is and is not poisonous. And the very young present the problem in an acute form:

"The child must take the place as he finds it, and take care of himself. But how can he take care of himself? If his injury is not to go without legal remedy altogether, by reason of his failure to use a diligence which he could not possibly have possessed, the owner of the close might be practically bound to see that the wandering child is as safe as in a nursery."[80]

The problem was addressed in *Phipps v Rochester Corporation*,[81] which concerned a building site that had been left unfenced by the Corporation, even though it had been aware that people crossed the land. A five-year-old boy had ventured onto the land together with his seven-year-old sister, in order to go blackberrying, and fell into a large trench that had been dug to contain sewer pipes. The court considered that, unlike the berries in *Glasgow v Taylor*,[82] the trench was neither an allurement to a child nor a danger concealed from an adult or older child – but that it was dangerous to a little child. It held that a landowner who indiscriminately allows the public onto his land must assume that the public may include little children:

---

[76] *Bassett v Surrey CC* , Reading County Court, January 2000 – which involved a 7-year-old boy – and *Beddow v Cleveland CC*, Middlesborough County Court, 16 August 1999 – a 9-year-old boy – both noted at **5.4.2**.

[77] 1957 Act, s. 2(3)(a).

[78] See **5.3.3**.

[79] *ibid.*, at p. 1092H.

[80] *Latham v R Johnson & Nephew Ltd* [1913] 1 K.B. 398, per Hamilton L.J. at p. 414.

[81] [1955] 1 Q.B. 450.

[82] Above.

"But as a general rule he will have discharged his duty towards them if the dangers which they may encounter are only those which are obvious to a guardian or of which he has given a warning comprehensible by a guardian. . . . the responsibility for the safety of little children must rest primarily upon parents; it is their duty to see that [little] children are not allowed to wander about by themselves, or at least to satisfy themselves that the places to which they do allow their children to go unaccompanied are safe for them to go to. It would not be socially desirable if parents were, as a matter of course, able to shift the burden of looking after their children from their own shoulders to those of persons who happen to have accessible bits of land. Different considerations may well apply to public parks or to recognised playing grounds where parents allow their children to go unaccompanied in the reasonable belief that they were safe."[83]

An occupier will thus have discharged his or her duty if the place is reasonably safe for a child accompanied by the sort of guardian whom the occupier is in all the circumstances entitled to expect. The question would then be whether the source of a child's injury is one which could and should have been foreseen, taking into account the guardian's responsibility for the child's safety – and in an appropriate case, the liability may have to be shared between the occupier of the land and the child's guardian.

This is why it is in general not possible for children to sue if they climb trees and fall out of them. Lord Atkinson thus noted in *Glasgow* that:

". . . there is no resemblance between this case and those cases where mischievous boys sustain injury by interfering with or misusing natural objects, such as trees in public parks up which they may be tempted to climb, or water, ornamental or other, into which they may accidentally fall or be tempted deliberately to enter. The appearance of such objects as these is well known and unmistakable. There is nothing deceptive or misleading about them. They cannot be mistaken for things other than, or different from, what they really are."[84]

And in a more recent case in the Court of Appeal, relating to a seven year old who was injured while playing on a grassy slope,[85] Dunn L.J. observed as follows:

"[It cannot be] suggested that an occupier should fence off every climbable tree in case a child climbed too high up it and fell out of it, and as far as I know a climbable tree has never been held to be dangerous to children.
    ". . . [T]here are many parts of the country with open spaces adjacent to houses where children play unattended, and this is to be encouraged."

The rule thus seems to be that where a tree is in a place of such a character that it is likely that small children will climb it, or attempt to do so, unsupervised, it must be made safe. Given that no tree can be made even moderately safe for a small child climbing it, the only sensible way to deal with a tree in a public park or recreation ground is thus to prune it in such a way that it is effectively impossible to climb (usually by simply removing the lowest branches). Elsewhere, however, it is reasonable to assume that young children will be accompanied by those who will be able to point out the dangers of climbing trees; older children – that is those old enough not to be accompanied – should be aware of such dangers themselves.

---

[83] *Phipps*, above, per Devlin J. at p. 472.
[84] [1922] A.C. 44 at p. 52.
[85] *Simkiss v Rhondda BC* [1982] 81 L.G.R. 460, at p. 470.

Otherwise, occupiers only have to deal with features or defects of trees which lead to dangers which will not be obvious to guardians of children or to older children unaccompanied by guardians; and they may do so by giving warnings that will be obvious to those guardians or older children.

5.6.3 Those with special expertise

Another special group of people likely to be affected by a defective tree are those with particular expertise. The 1957 Act thus provides that "an occupier may expect that a person, in the exercise of his calling, will appreciate and guard against any special risks ordinarily incident to it, so far as the occupier leaves him free to do so".[86]

This means firstly that there will be people who, in the normal course of events, come into contact with sources of danger; but that is not a problem if it is an inevitable part of their job. So, for example, a tree surgeon can be expected to know which branches will support his or her weight; a curator of a botanical garden will know which trees and shrubs have poisonous berries; an electricity worker pruning a tree so that it does not come into contact with a cable will know that a live cable is dangerous.

Secondly, if an occupier of land becomes aware of a dangerous tree, he or she must take steps to avoid visitors to the land being put unacceptably at risk; but if those steps involve hiring experts to undertake remedial work, they do not need protection from the very danger which they are removing.

In each of these situations, the specialist workers may themselves provide such protection, of course; and if they are employees, their employer will need to ensure that they have a safe system of work.[87] That has been the subject of much detailed regulation in recent years, but is considered in outline later in this book.[88] The key point for present purposes is that the safety of specialist workers is their own responsibility, or that of their employer, but not that of the occupier of the land where they are working.

5.6.4 Trespassers and others on the land

It has been pointed out[89] that a lesser duty is owed to people on the land who are neither "visitors" nor in a contractual relationship with the occupier. In particular, prior to 1984, trespassers were protected not under the Occupiers' Liability Act 1957, but simply as a result of "the common duty of humanity" laid upon the occupier to protect them from dangers of which the occupier was or should have been aware.[90] However, the Occupiers' Liability Act 1984 now requires the occupier of premises to protect a person on his premises other than a visitor if:

"(a) he is aware of the danger or has reasonable grounds to believe that it exists;
(b) he knows or has reasonable grounds to believe that the other is in the vicinity of the danger concerned or that he may come into the vicinity of the danger (in either case, whether the other has lawful authority for being in that vicinity or not); and

---

[86] 1957 Act, s. 2(3)(b).
[87] Health and Safety at Work etc Act 1974; *Wilsons and Clyde Coal Co v English* [1938] A.C. 57; see also the relevant secondary legislation.
[88] See **9.5**.
[89] See **5.3.5**.
[90] *British Railways Board v Herrington* [1972] 1 All E.R. 749, H.L.

(c) the risk is one against which, in all the circumstances of the case, he may reasonably be expected to offer the other some protection".[91]

In other words, the occupier is required to offer those other than visitors protection against risks that are known or suspected, but not against those which could only be discovered as a result of unreasonable effort. Once a hazard has been discovered, the occupier's duty is, once again, to take "such care as is reasonable in all the circumstances of the case" to ensure that the potential victim does not suffer injury.[92] The distinction between the two Acts lies thus not in the extent of the duty, but in the circumstances in which it is owed.

The significance of this distinction will not be great in most instances – if a tree is in a location, such as overhanging the path to the front door, where its fall is liable to cause harm to lawful visitors, it must be maintained accordingly (see above); the fact that this may incidentally protect trespassers and others walking up the path is an added bonus. But there may be more remote parts of larger plots of land which would only rarely if ever be frequented by lawful visitors, but which may be occasionally used by trespassers, even if only as a short cut to reach other land. If there is a defective tree in such a location, and it causes harm, any trespasser injured as a result would not be able to claim damages from the occupier of the land unless it could be shown that the occupier knew of the danger.

It follows that trees in locations that are not frequented by "visitors" (within the meaning of the 1957 Act) will require a lower standard of maintenance, except in the case of those which are in fact known (by the occupier) to be dangerous.

5.6.5 Those visiting national parks and the open countryside

The Occupiers' Liability Act 1984[93] applies also in the case of land in national parks which is subject to access agreements enabling the public to wander at will – so that the owner of the land is only required to provide protection against hazards of which he or she is aware.

The 1984 Act does not apply, however, in relation to members of the public exercising a right to roam under the Countryside and Rights of Way Act 2000. Instead, occupiers of "access land" under that Act are explicitly relieved of any duty in respect of any risk arising from the existence of "any natural feature of the landscape"[94] – which is explicitly defined to include "any plant, shrub or tree, of whatever origin".[95]

5.7 Inspection and risk assessment

5.7.1 Introduction

Given that neither the common law nor statute requires an occupier to make his or her land *completely* safe, and given that it is not practical to inspect every tree on the land every day, what then is the occupier to do?

[91] 1984 Act, s. 1(3).
[92] s. 1(4).
[93] See **5.6.4**.
[94] 1984 Act, s. 1(6A), inserted by Countryside and Rights of Way Act 2000, s. 13(2).
[95] 1984 Act, s. 1(6B), inserted by 2000 Act, following an amendment introduced in the Lords.

It should be remembered that the duty is (only) "to take reasonable care" or, as it is elaborated in the Occupiers' Liability Acts 1957 and 1984, "such care as in all the circumstances of the case is reasonable . . .".[96] This reflects the classic definition of negligence just over a century earlier in *Blyth v Birmingham Waterworks*[97]:

"[Negligence is] the omission to do something which a reasonable man, guided upon those considerations which ordinarily regulate the conduct of human affairs, would do, or doing something which a prudent and reasonable man would not do."

As to what is reasonable, this will obviously vary with circumstances:
  Even if an occupier has no special expertise in matters relating to trees, he or she will still be expected to act as a "reasonable and prudent landowner".[98] That will mean that, in the case of potential dangers such as poisonous berries, thorns, fallen leaves, moss caused by shade, and so on, an occupier should be generally aware of the state of his or her property, and immediately adjacent land, and particularly of those parts most frequented by visitors (such as roads, paths, driveways and patios), and promptly remove any hazard. That is, either the problem branches should be cut back, or the fallen leaves removed, or whatever else is appropriate.
  More substantial measures may be required in some cases, including completely felling the tree where there is no alternative, but this will rarely be necessary.
  The first step is, in the light of the above considerations, to assess the risk of injury or harm being caused by the tree in question or by any part of it.[99] Where it is justified, an inspection must then be carried out by someone with sufficient knowledge and experience – which may be the owner himself or herself, or an appropriate expert.[1] Once the problem has been properly assessed, it will then be possible to decide whether further action is required.[2]

5.7.2 Assessment of risk

In the light of all the above considerations – the nature of the tree, its location and those likely to be affected by it – it should be possible for the owner to begin to make some assessment of the potential risk presented. It has thus already been noted that not all trees are equally dangerous; some, for example, are more liable to shed branches than others. Perhaps more importantly, hazards arising from trees are more likely to cause harm and danger in locations more frequented by people than elsewhere.
  This problem was considered briefly by the House of Lords in *Caminer v Northern & London Investment Trust*, particularly in the thoughtful speech of Lord Radcliffe, quoted above.[3] He was clearly troubled by the whole issue of risk, however, because he revisited the matter later in the same year in his speech in

---

[96] 1957 Act, s. 2(2); 1984 Act, s. 1(4) is virtually identical.
[97] (1856) 11 Ex. 781, per Alderson B. at p. 784.
[98] *Caminer v Northern & London Investment Trust* [1951] A.C. 88, per Lord Normand at p. 99 (following the Court of Appeal).
[99] See **5.7.2**.
[1] See **5.7.3**, **5.7.4**.
[2] See **5.8**.
[3] [1951] A.C. 88 at p. 111; see **5.5.3**.

Bolton v Stone[4] – albeit in the context of cricket balls landing on the highway rather than trees (or parts of them) landing on surrounding land. His speech in that case is worth quoting at length:

"If the test whether there has been a breach of duty were to depend merely on the answer to the question whether this accident was a reasonably foreseeable risk, I think that there would have been a breach of duty, for that such an accident might take place some time or other might very reasonably have been present to the minds of the appellants. It was quite foreseeable, and there would have been nothing unreasonable in allowing the imagination to dwell on the possibility of its occurring. But there was only a remote, perhaps I ought to say only very remote, chance of the accident taking place at any particular time, for, if it was to happen, not only had a ball to clear the fence round the ground but it had also to coincide in its arrival with the presence of some person on what does not look like a crowded thoroughfare and actually to strike that person in some way that would cause sensible injury.

"Those being the facts, a breach of duty has taken place if they show the appellants guilty of a failure to take reasonable care to prevent the accident. One may phrase it as 'reasonable care' or 'ordinary care' or 'proper care' – all these phrases are to be found in decisions of authority – but the fact remains that, unless there has been something which a reasonable man would blame as falling beneath the standard of conduct that he would set for himself and require of his neighbour, there has been no breach of legal duty. And here, I think, the respondent's case breaks down. It seems to me that a reasonable man, taking account of the chances against an accident happening, would not have felt himself called upon either to abandon the use of the ground for cricket or to increase the height of his surrounding fences. He would have done what the appellants did: in other words, he would have done nothing. Whether, if the unlikely event of an accident did occur and his play turned to another's hurt, he would have thought it equally proper to offer no more consolation to his victim than the reflection that a social being is not immune from social risks, I do not say, for I do not think that is a consideration which is relevant to legal liability."[5]

Some years later, the House of Lords revisited its earlier decision. Lord Reid (who had been a member of the Judicial Committee in both *Caminer* and *Bolton*) said this:

"The House of Lords [in *Bolton v Stone*] held that the risk was so small that in the circumstances a reasonable man would have been justified in disregarding it and taking no steps to eliminate it.

"But it does not follow that, no matter what the circumstances may be, it is justifiable to neglect a risk of such a small magnitude. A reasonable man would only neglect such a risk if he had some valid reason for doing so, e.g. that it would involve considerable expense to eliminate the risk. He would weigh the risk against the difficulty of eliminating it."[6]

The question is thus not "was the harm foreseeable?" but "was the conduct unreasonable?".

That is clearly relevant to questions of how much care should be taken to avoid harm being caused by trees; and suggests that action need not be taken where the risk is very small. And just as the cricket accident required both the abnormal shot (to provide the missile) and the person passing by at the relevant moment (to provide the target), so the chance of a person being hit by a tree (or by part of it)

---

[4]   [1951] A.C. 850.
[5]   Per Lord Radcliffe at p. 868.
[6]   *The Wagon Mound (No. 2)* [1967] 1 A.C. 617, per Lord Reid at p. 642E.

may be extremely remote if the tree is unlikely to fall or shed a branch and the number of people passing by is very small – so remote indeed as to not require any precautions to be taken. But that will be a matter for consideration on the facts of each case.

This issue had earlier been considered by the Court of Appeal in *Shirvell v Hackwood Estates*, in which Lord Camrose took possession on February 10 of an estate on which were some 56,000 trees (excluding young plantations), and among them were thousands of dead and dying trees. Mackinnon L.J. considered what landowners exercising reasonable care would do in those circumstances:

"I think that they would resort to expert advice as to how to deal with these neglected woods, and that, perhaps without waiting for that, they would put on men to cut down the most obviously dead and dangerous trees. The latter would obviously be properly done where such trees were near thoroughfares or footpaths."[7]

As ill luck would have it, the tree that actually caused the death of the workman (on May 30) fell onto an arable field, where there was no footpath, and it was one of the last places where anyone might expect to be working; the deceased and his colleague were probably "the only beings who had been within range of the tree for a year". The court accordingly held that the Estate was not negligent in failing to get round to dealing with that tree before it fell.

Of course this level of analysis is not appropriate in every instance; in some cases it is patently obvious that people are at risk from a tree. This may occur because of the normal state of affairs – such as a bush that has thorns at head height – or as the result of an abnormal event – where, for example, large quantities of leaves have fallen over a weekend onto a much-used path, or a storm has left a branch only loosely attached to the remainder of a tree, overhanging a car park. In each case, the risk is clear; and in the last two, at least, so is the remedy.

Equally, in other cases, it may be wholly unnecessary to take any action, because the risk is so small – as where claims were brought by a gas fitter who had injured his knee on a needle hidden in a carpet,[8] and by a child who fell over a banister at a school[9]; in each case the court considered that the risk had been insignificant, and dismissed the claim. So too with trees that have very recently been inspected, or that are in very remote locations; in either case, there could be a theoretical risk of harm occurring, but the risk is insignificant and does not justify action of any kind.

But in other cases, it will be necessary to consider a range of possible remedies.

5.7.3 The need for an inspection

The first duty of the owner of trees is clearly to inspect them at appropriate intervals. Indeed, it is probably prudent to inspect trees on first acquiring a new property, and to ascertain at that stage how frequently and how thoroughly they should be inspected thereafter.

But there are limits on what must be done immediately. In *Knight v Hext*,[10] the defendant had bought a property, and had moved in on December 12. Her

[7] [1938] 2 All E.R. 1, CA, at p. 9H
[8] *Fryer v Pearson, The Times*, April 4, 2000, CA.
[9] *Gough v Upshire Primary School*, February 2, 2000, Q.B.D., unreported.
[10] [1980] 1 EGLR 111, CA.

husband went into hospital on December 14. She was warned by a neighbour of
the dangerous state of one of her trees, overhanging his barn, on Saturday
December 16. There were then five working days before Christmas; but she had
not arranged for the tree to be inspected by the time it fell, on December 27. The
Court of Appeal, reversing the decision of the judge at first instance, held that all
that was required of her was that, within a reasonable time, she should go and
make an inspection; and, in all the circumstances, a failure to do so before
Christmas was not unreasonable. See also the analysis by the Court of Appeal in
the earlier case of *Shirvell v Hackwood Estates*.[11]

A failure to inspect at all will usually be a powerful indication of negligence. In
Brown v Harrison, for instance, the owner had failed to notice a partly dead horse
chestnut tree in a spinney. The Court of Appeal approved the formulation of the
test by the judge at first instance:

"Having regard in each particular case to the circumstances of the particular case, if there is
a danger which is apparent not only to the expert but to the ordinary layman, which the
ordinary layman can see with his own eyes, if he chooses to use them, and he fails to do so,
with the result that injury is inflicted . . ., the owner is responsible because, in the
management of his property he has not acted as a normal, reasonable man should act." [12]

And in *Chapman v Barking & Dagenham LBC*, there was a clear failure to
inspect:

"I am satisfied that, despite all encouragement and advice both from external sources and
to some extent from their own officers, the defendant council did not at any relevant time
appreciate the distinction between making lists of trees and routine maintenance, as
opposed to systematic expert inspection as often as would reasonably be required. I find
that no such inspections were ever made, that it was a clear duty on the defendants to make
them, and that they have failed in that duty."[13]

In that case, the court also found that an inspection, if it had been made, would
have discovered the defect that caused a branch to fall; the failure to inspect was
accordingly fatal.

On the other hand, it may be that a tree is suffering from a defect that will not
be revealed by inspection. In *Caminer v Northern & London Investment Trust*, the
House of Lords considered that the question was whether the owners of the tree in
question performed the duty of inspection that a prudent and reasonable owner of
such a tree – bearing in mind both its size and age and its proximity to a highway
– would have performed. "Plainly they did not." But, continued Lord Normand,
"it is no less plain that, if they had, it would have made no difference. The tree was
just such a tree as [the expert witness] says the owner might consider safe."[14] In
other words, the failure to inspect was negligent, but that negligence had not
caused the harm.

The limitations of inspection are highlighted by the fact that, in several of the
cases, the tree in question had been inspected, but that inspection had failed to
disclose the problem that led to the failure of the tree or part of it shortly

[11] [1938] 2 All E.R. 1, CA; see **5.7.2**.
[12] (1947) E.G., June 28, 1947, CA.
[13] [1997] 2 EGLR 141, per Judge Viscount Colville of Culross QC, at p. 145G; upheld in the Court of
Appeal (1998) unreported.
[14] [1951] A.C. 88 at p. 103.

afterwards.[15] Thus in *Noble v Harrison*, which concerned a beech tree, it was found that the branch that fell had at some time developed a crack at the place about 4.5 m from the trunk where it broke off, that the tree had actually been the subject of inspection "not long previously", but that the defect would not have been observable by any reasonably careful inspection.[16] And in *Cunliffe v Bankes* the defective tree was on a large estate of some 2,000 hectares, where the agent inspected all the trees every summer, and marked with signs of disease or decay. In this case, too, the court decided that there was nothing like certainty that any examination in the previous summer would have disclosed that this tree was affected by honey fungus:

"The onus is upon the plaintiff . . . of showing that there was something wrong with the tree of such a kind that the occupier or his agent either knew it or ought to have known it."[17]

Nevertheless, an inspection should be carried out if in any doubt, particularly if the tree in question is close to a highway or other high-risk target. The passing comment of Finnemore J. in *Lambourn v London Brick Co*,[18] that "it was neither the duty nor the practice of an ordinary prudent landowner to make a meticulous examination of individual trees" may be correct as to the normal practice of typical landowners; but it is very doubtful as a statement of the duty in law of the hypothetical "prudent and reasonable landowner". The comment may have arisen from that which immediately followed, to the effect that "there was nothing at all to indicate that the trees were dangerous. They appeared to be sound, of good quality and of comparatively young growth".

The need to carry out a proper inspection is highlighted by the fact that there have been a number of cases in which the courts have decided that the defect that led to the failure of the tree in question would have been discoverable on a proper inspection. In *Brown v Harrison*,[19] the Court of Appeal upheld a decision that a landowner was responsible for the fall of a tree since it was partly dead; the judge at first instance had decided that the evidence showed that the tree was so old that it had become a danger and that that danger should have been apparent to its owners. Proper inspection would also have revealed a hole in the elm tree in *Kent v Marquis of Bristol*,[20] the decay in the branch of the chestnut which fell onto the road in *Lane v Tredegar Estate Trustees*,[21] the decay causing die-back and thinness of foliage that caused a large section of a beech tree to fall across a road in *Quinn v Scott*,[22] and the decay that caused an elm to shed a branch onto a parked car in *Thomas v Miller*.[23]

Useful advice on the inspection of highway trees is given in the Department of the Environment Circulars 52/75 and 90/73.[24]

---

[15] See **5.5.1**.
[16] [1926] 2 K.B. 332 at p. 339.
[17] [1945] 1 All E.R. 459 at p. 464H.
[18] (1950) E.G., July 28, 1950.
[19] (1947) E.G., June 28, 1947, CA.
[20] (1940), unreported, noted in the *Quarterly Journal of Forestry*, January 1947; see **5.3.2**.
[21] (1954) E.G., November 27, 1954.
[22] [1964] 1 W.L.R. 1004.
[23] (1970), unreported, noted in the *Western Morning News*, February 3, 1970.
[24] And see **Chapter 6**.

5.7.4 The nature of an inspection

Of course, it is no good having a tree inspected if the inspection is inadequate or incompetent. But what is "adequate" in this context? Where a Council was aware that land in its ownership was unstable, through no fault of its own, it was held to be liable only to take care to avoid harm that it ought to have seen without further geological investigation.[25] The same would seem to apply to liability for defective trees. A landowner is thus liable for harm caused by a defect in his land that is patent and not merely latent. It is no answer for him to say that he had not observed the defect if a responsible servant had seen it, or should have seen it.

The first consideration, therefore, is to make sure that any investigation is indeed carried out properly. So, for example, it is not enough to rely solely on the advice of a forester who has been in practice for 53 years, who makes no detailed examination of a tree, but who passes under it two or three times a week on his bicycle – as was the case in *Lane v Tredegar Estate Trustees*,[26] where the forester unfortunately failed to spot the decay that caused a branch of the roadside horse-chestnut tree to fall. As the judge put it:

"I think that the condition of those two branches, with their degree of decay, ought to have put the defendants on inquiry. I do not suggest for one moment that they would be called upon to make a branch to branch examination of that tree; but I do think that when one has a tree with heavy branches like that overhanging a highway, if one finds evidence which ought to make one suspicious, then one ought to make a branch to branch examination of those branches which overhang a highway."

In that case, the decay in the branch that actually fell would probably only have been visible from above, on inspection by climbing a ladder. But the same decay also affected a neighbouring branch, in such a way as to be visible from the ground; and that should have put the owner on notice to get a proper examination.

The first key question facing the owner of trees is whether, and if so how often, to call in an expert. After all, in practice most owners of trees, rightly or wrongly, decide themselves whether works should be done, and merely engage the services of an "expert" to carry them out. This was considered by the House of Lords in *Caminer*. Lord Reid phrased the question thus:

"Would a reasonable and careful owner, without expert knowledge but accustomed to dealing with his trees and having a countryman's general knowledge about them, think it necessary to call in an expert to advise him or would he think it sufficient to act at least in the first instance on his own knowledge and judgment?"[27]

Fifty years later, it is not perhaps immediately obvious what would have been the extent of "a countryman's general knowledge of trees" at the time of the Second World War.

But an owner who is not confident as to his or her own expertise should, if in any doubt, find someone at least a bit more knowledgeable (and, just as important, experienced), for advice – partly as to whether to obtain an opinion from a genuine expert. Lord Reid again:

---

[25] *Holbeck Hall Hotel Ltd v Scarborough BC* [2000] E.G.C.S. 29, CA.
[26] (1954) E.G., November 27, 1954.
[27] *Caminer* [1951] A.C. 88, H.L., at p. 108.

"I think the question is whether a person with general knowledge and experience of trees would or should have advised the respondents that this elm tree, notwithstanding its normal healthy appearance, ought to be lopped or at least that there was such doubt that expert advice should be sought if it was desired to keep the tree untouched."

Note the reference to the need for expert advice, particularly if the intention of the owner is to do nothing – after all, if something is to be done, the person doing the work will at least probably give some advice.

The Court of Appeal had summarised the proper approach as being that of "a reasonable landowner" or "a reasonably careful man".[27a] By the time the case reaches the House of Lords, Lord Normand misquoted this as "a reasonable and prudent landowner". However, he continued:

"The test of the conduct to be expected from a reasonable and prudent landlord sounds more simple than it really is. For it postulates some degree of knowledge on the part of landlords which must necessarily fall short of the knowledge possessed by scientific arboriculturists but which must surely be greater than the ordinary urban observer of trees or even of the countryman not practically concerned with their care."[28]

Clearly not all countrymen, even then, had a general knowledge of trees.

Lord Radcliffe, in the same case, propounded a slightly different test:

"The accepted test that liability only begins when there is apparent in the tree a sign of danger . . . does end by making the standard of the expert the test of liability. Anyone can own a tree: there is no qualifying examination; but to how many people in this country can be credited as much general knowledge as will warn them that a tree's top is unusually large or that it is in fact diseased, dangerously or otherwise?"[29]

On reflection, this seems to be the most logical, although the most onerous, test – litigation of this kind will almost always occur following an "accident" of some kind; and the tree owner must be confident that he or she will then be able to justify fully the works that were done (or not done). The only way to be certain is to employ the services of an expert: if the expert turns out to be incompetent, anyone affected can sue him or her for negligence, but at least the owner is covered.

And even an expert must be looking for the right things. In *Quinn v Scott*,[30] the beech tree in question was owned by the National Trust, who employed a land agent, a forester and seven woodmen. The tree was the subject of a limited inspection; but unfortunately no one looked up and noticed the thinness and die-back of the foliage, which would have caused a reasonable landowner to have the tree cut down at once.

In a relatively recent case, *Chapman v Barking and Dagenham LBC*,[31] there was a dispute between the two expert witnesses as to the level of the inspection required. The expert appearing for the Council (the owner of the tree) had stated that there were no abnormal features justifying such inspection; the tree was not any more of a risk than thousands of other trees. But the judge accepted the view

[27a] [1949] K.B. 64, CA, *per* Tucker L.J. at p. 70 and Singleton L.J. at p. 76.
[28] [1951] A.C. 88, H.L., at pp. 99–100. The references to "landlords" should presumably have been to "landowners".
[29] At p. 111.
[30] [1964] 1 W.L.R. 1004.
[31] [1997] 2 EGLR 141, upheld in CA (1998) unreported.

that the tree would have exhibited features that would have warranted a climbing inspection; and considered that it was unnecessary, as well as impossible, for him to decide whether, and if so how many, other trees in the road would also have deserved such attention. This would seem to place a high duty on those with trees in high-risk locations.

As to what should be covered in any specialist inspection, appropriate technical literature should be consulted. See, in particular, the three manuals published by the Department of the Environment and the Forestry Commission in the series *Research for Amenity Trees*:

- *Diagnosis of Ill-Health in Trees*, by R G Strouts and T G Winter[32];

- *The Body Language of Trees: a Handbook of Failure Analysis*, by C Mattheck and H Breloer[33]; and

- *Principles of Tree Hazard Assessment and Management*, by D Lonsdale.[34]

In all cases, however, it should be borne in mind that professional opinion is by no means unanimous as to the causes of particular types of failure, nor as to the results of particular types of remedial works. Technical evidence should be written and read accordingly, and terms such as "undoubtedly" and "inevitably" viewed with caution.

A tree owner may thus obtain a report by an appropriately qualified and experienced expert stating that inspection indicates that no works need to be carried out to a tree. If the tree in fact falls shortly afterwards, another expert may appear on behalf of the victim stating that he now considers, not least with the benefit of hindsight, that it must have been clear at the time of the owner's inspection that the tree should have been felled. That does not mean that the owner was negligent, since all that a prudent and reasonable landowner can be expected to do is to obtain an expert opinion – not a range of opinions.[35] It may, of course, suggest that the original expert can now be shown to have been negligent, but that is a different issue.[36]

Further, professional knowledge is constantly improving, so that when reading older decisions of the courts, it should be borne in mind that the professional evidence on which the analysis of the court was based may now be discredited in detail – it is the underlying principles that must be discovered, not (necessarily) the practical outworking of those principles.

5.8 Possible remedial measures

5.8.1 Removing the target

Having considered the risk posed by a tree and, if appropriate, had the tree inspected, the next step for the owner is to consider what (if any) remedial action is required.

[32] HMSO, London, second edn, 2000 TSO.
[33] HMSO, London, first edn, 1995.
[34] The Stationery Office, London, second edn, 2001.
[35] *Caminer* [1951] A.C. 88, per Lord Oaksey at p. 104; and see *Quinn v Scott* [1964] 1004 per Glyn-Jones J. at p. 1009C.
[36] See **8.2.1**.

If a tree constitutes a hazard, that will usually be in the context of a particular "target". That is, it will be above or next to a road, building, picnic area or whatever. The tree may have grown in that location for many decades, and may have many more ahead; to replace it with a new sapling, either in the same location or elsewhere, will be normally be no kind of substitute.

The first possible remedy, therefore, since it will be impossible to move the tree, may be to move the target.

This will obviously not often be possible, but should be considered in the case of, for example, a greenhouse, a path, or a seating area that might be hit by a tree if it were to fall. Or, in the case of a veteran tree standing in open parkland, it may be possible to allow the grass underneath it to be left alone, thus making the immediate vicinity of the tree less suitable for picnics.

And in some cases it may be possible to prevent (or limit) access to the target zone, through the use of suitable fencing – either a simple rope barrier or a secure fence, depending on the circumstances. This may need to be supplemented with an appropriate notice (see below).

5.8.2 Warning of danger

Another simple (and cheap) way in which to lessen danger is to give warning of it. It is accordingly provided in the Occupiers' Liability Act 1957 that the occupier may be able to rely on the fact that he or she had warned visitors of potential dangers to escape liability, but only where "in all the circumstances [the warning] was enough to enable the visitor to be reasonably safe".[37]

This is not unreasonable; the existence of a warning notice ("Beware: poisonous berries"; or "Warning: these are old trees, and may occasionally shed branches"), or an oral warning on a specific occasion, may be sufficient to enable a visitor to take appropriate avoiding action. Apart from anything else, it may enable the occupier to justify a defence on the basis that the visitor, after receiving the warning, had voluntarily assumed the risk, so that the occupier was no longer liable.[38]

But the fact that a warning has been given is not necessarily sufficient for the occupier to discharge his or her duty of care; someone who keeps a tiger in his garden needs to do more than put up a notice pointing out the danger. Thus no warning was given of the poisonous berries in *Glasgow v Taylor*[39]; but it is arguable that a warning notice would have made no difference. There is similarly no point in erecting a sign to point out that a tree overhanging a path is dangerous, if no alternative route is provided.

On the other hand, a warning may not always be necessary, if the danger is self-evident; a Council in Derbyshire was thus not required to put up a sign warning people not to fall off a cliff[40]; and, perhaps more relevantly, another Council was held not liable for failing to warn people about the danger of slipping on algae at the Cobb at Lyme Regis in Dorset.[41] It is thus presumably not necessary to warn people that holly has sharp leaves, or to highlight the danger of slipping on autumn leaves or fallen fruit; but whether the dangers of climbing on or walking

---

[37] 1957 Act, s. 1(4)(a).
[38] 1957 Act, s. 2(5); see above.
[39] [1922] A.C. 44, H.L.
[40] *Cotton v Derbyshire Dales DC, The Times*, June 20, 1994
[41] *Staples v West Dorset DC, The Times* (1995) 93 L.G.R. 536.

underneath a veteran tree are sufficiently self-evident as to need no warning must be a matter of judgment in each case.

Nor was the National Trust held to be liable for failing to warn visitors not to swim in the lake at Hardwicke Park; erecting a notice to warn of the dangers of swimming would only had told the deceased what he already knew.[42] From that it would follow that there is no need to erect a sign warning simply of the general danger of climbing trees, or walking under them; a sign would only be needed if there was some special danger that was not self-evident.

The position therefore seems to be: if in doubt, an occupier should erect a sign warning of a source danger that is not self-evident; but should then ensure that a visitor, thus warned, is in fact able to avoid the danger.

And of course all of the above is subject to the limitations imposed by the Unfair Contract Terms Act 1977.[43]

5.8.3 Carrying out works to the tree

The next possible step for an owner anxious to avoid future liability for the failure of a tree, obviously, is to carry out some works to the tree.

It is not possible for a landowner to escape liability merely by showing that some works were carried out in the distant past. Indeed, as highlighted in *Chapman v Barking and Dagenham LBC*,[44] the fact that works to a tree were carried out in the past may make its owner more, not less, liable.[45] What is important is to show that the right works were carried out, in the right way, at the right time.

Where a professional inspection has been carried out, the owner would need to have good reasons not to implement any recommendations that result. Where a great deal of work is recommended, judgment will obviously be needed as to how quickly it is done, and in what order – see the extract from the judgment of the Court of Appeal in *Shirvell v Hackwood Estates*,[46] cited above.[47] It would, presumably, usually be reasonable to obtain a second opinion – provided that it was done promptly. And just as the defendant in *Knight v Hext*[48] was found not to have acted unreasonably in postponing the inspection of trees on newly acquired property due to exceptional circumstances,[49] so it would not necessarily be unreasonable to postpone action following the receipt of a report recommending it – but, again, there would need to be sufficient justification for so acting.

Where an inspection is not carried out, an owner would still not be liable if he or she could show that everything was in fact done that would have been recommended by a professional. So, for example, an expert might recommend that a tree belonging to A's friend is treated in a particular way, so that A then does the same work to his tree, which he considers to be similar. Or B may prune her tree in a particular way simply because that is what she always does, or what she vaguely remembers being told to do years ago by her mother. In either

---

[42] *Darby v National Trust, The Times*, February 23, 2001, CA (following *Steeples*).
[43] See **5.4.4**.
[44] [1997] 2 EGLR 141, upheld by CA (1998) unreported.
[45] See **5.5.2**.
[46] [1938] 2 All E.R. 1, CA, per Mackinnon L.J. at p. 9H.
[47] See **5.7.2**.
[48] [1980] 1 EGLR 111, CA.
[49] See **5.7.3**.

situation it might be possible to maintain that the owner was not taking sufficient care; but the owner would be able to escape liability for a subsequent collapse of the tree if an expert brought in subsequently were to agree that the work that was actually done was what he would have recommended anyway – because the breach of duty did not actually cause the harm.

Even if no work (or not enough) is carried out, there will presumably be no liability if it can be shown that the defect that led to the subsequent failure would not have been discoverable on inspection.[50] Again, on one analysis, there would have been a breach of the duty of care (in that no work was done), but that breach would not have been the cause of the harm.

But it is obviously safer to rely on a professional inspection, and then to carry out the works recommended.

Finally, it is not of course necessary to carry out more works than recommended – if a branch is defective, that does not of itself justify felling the whole tree.

5.8.4 The cost and difficulty of works

Two factors that will determine whether and, if so, what works are done to trees may be the cost and difficulty of them.

There is one line of authority that suggests that the means of the owner of the trees is a relevant consideration. Thus the Privy Council in *Goldman v Hargrave*, after noting that "the present case is one where liability, if it exists, rests upon negligence and nothing else,"[51] went on to consider the scope of the duty laid upon a landowner faced with a naturally occurring hazard:

". . . the standard ought to be to require of the occupier what it is reasonable to expect of him in his individual circumstances. Thus, less must be expected of the infirm than the able-bodied: the owner of a small property where a hazard arises which threatens a neighbour with substantial interests should not have to do so much as one with larger interests of his own at stake and greater resources to protect them: if the small owner does what he can and promptly calls upon his neighbour to provide additional resources, he may be held to have done his duty: he should not be liable unless it is clearly proved that he could, and reasonably in his individual circumstances should, have done more."[52]

This approach was followed by the Court of Appeal in *Leakey v National Trust*[53]:

"Just as where physical effort is required to avert an immediate danger, the defendant's age and physical condition may be relevant in deciding what is reasonable, so also logic and good sense require that, where the expenditure of money is required, the defendant's capacity to find the money is relevant. But this can only be in the way of a broad, and not a detailed, assessment; and, in arriving at a judgment on reasonableness, a similar broad assessment may be relevant as to the neighbour's capacity to protect himself from damage, whether by way of some form of barrier on his own land or by way of providing funds for expenditure on agreed works on the land of the defendant."

---

[50] See **5.5.1**.
[51] [1967] A.C. 645, P.C., at p. 657A; see **5.1.2**.
[52] *Goldman v Hargrave* [1967] A.C. 645, per Lord Wilberforce at p. 663E.
[53] [1980] 1 Q.B. 485 at p. 526F.

However, these dicta need to be followed with caution. Both *Goldman v Hargrave* and *Leakey* related to situations where an abnormal natural hazard had arisen unexpectedly (in one, a fire started by lightning, in the other, an unexpected landslip). Trees, by contrast, do not suddenly appear from nowhere. The owner of the land on which a tree is growing knows, or should know, that it may at some stage become hazardous, and should take appropriate professional advice at appropriate intervals. Remedial work, if carried out promptly, is not particularly expensive when compared to all the other costs arising from the ownership of property; and the cost can, if necessary, be borrowed against the value of the land.

It would also be slightly surprising if the safety of the postman delivering letters, the neighbour sunning herself in her garden, or the child walking along the adjacent highway, was dependant on whether the owner of a tree that was in fact visibly dangerous and required remedial work was a public authority, a wealthy private individual, a charity dependant on public support, or a widow with almost no income. If the widow invited her neighbour to inspect the trees on their mutual boundary, and to carry out any works he considered necessary, and he agreed to do so, that might be sufficient to discharge her duty of care – at least to him. But there seems to be no logical reason why he should be forced to do so; and even less reason why passers-by or visitors should accept a lesser degree of safety because of the poverty of the owner.

On the other hand, the personal circumstances of the owner were clearly considered relevant in *Shirvell v Hackwood Estates*[54] and *Knight v Hext*.[55] And the constraints upon a highway authority were considered to be relevant in deciding whether it should exercise its discretionary powers under the Highways Act 1980 with the aim of improving road safety – see the decision of the House of Lords in *Stovin v Wise*,[56] discussed in the next Chapter in more detail.[57]

On balance, therefore, it would seem that the personal circumstances (including the financial resources) of the owner are only relevant where works are required abnormally or urgently, or where there is a real element of discretion in whether they should be carried out.

5.8.5 *The amenity value of the trees*

One other factor that may appear to be relevant in some cases is that a hazardous tree may be of some amenity value. Its owner, and others who enjoy looking at it, may therefore be understandably reluctant to carry out drastic works to it.

This problem was considered by the Court in *Quinn v Scott*, which concerned a tree on the National Trust estate at Clumber Park, growing close to a busy road[58]:

"The good landowner – using the word 'good' in its moral sense – does not ruthlessly cut down every tree growing on his land as soon as it would pay him to do so. He has some regard for the beauty of the tree and of the countryside. The National Trust are, and must be, careful to have in mind what is called the amenity value of growing trees. . . . I am, however, as I see it, bound to take the view that in the present case the safety of the public must take precedence over the preservation of the amenities; and cannot hold that the

---

[54] [1938] 2 All E.R. 1, CA, per Mackinnon L.J. at p. 9H; see **5.7.2**.
[55] [1980] 1 EGLR 111, CA; **5.7.3**.
[56] [1996] A.C. 323, H.L.
[57] See **6.4.6**.
[58] See **5.3.2**.

Trust's duty to care for the countryside diminishes in any degree the duty not to subject users of this highway to unnecessary danger."[59]

Whilst it is therefore entirely proper to seek to minimise the extent of any works to those which are actually necessary, it should not be assumed that amenity will take precedence over safety.

This is so even where a tree may be subject to a tree preservation order,[60] or where it is in a national park or area of outstanding natural beauty.

However, nor should it be assumed that a tree which is partly or even wholly dead should necessarily be removed – it may in fact be perfectly safe for a number of years to come, possibly after the carrying out of relatively minor works from time to time, and may in the meanwhile provide a useful habitat for other flora and fauna.

5.8.6 Removal of the debris

Finally, it should not be forgotten that, once a tree or a branch has fallen, the danger is not over. The reported cases where motorists and pedestrians were hit by falling trees and branches are outnumbered by those where motorists, particularly motor cyclists, drove into ones that had already fallen.[61]

This is considered further in the following Chapter in the context of the removal of debris from a highway.[61a]

5.9 Litigation

5.9.1 Introduction

Finally, if all else fails, it may be necessary to resort to the courts – or at least to threaten doing so.

It has already been pointed out[62] that the liability for hazardous trees arises primarily under the law of negligence – even though, in some of the reported cases, actions have been brought also in nuisance, or under the rule in *Rylands v Fletcher*. It follows that, where harm has been caused by a tree in such a case, an action could be brought by the victim against the person apparently responsible. In addition, where such harm seems to be imminent, it would be possible for an action to be brought by anyone likely to be a potential victim.

This section of the Chapter brings together some of the threads from what has gone before, in order to provide at least some small measure of assistance to those contemplating such action. The tactics of litigation are generally outside the scope of this book; but it should be clearly borne in mind that litigation in the courts is itself an inherently hazardous activity, and should not be undertaken by the faint-hearted. Serious thought should therefore always be given to achieving a settlement (amicable or otherwise) out of court.

---

[59] [1964] 1 W.L.R. 1004 at p. 1010C,E.
[60] See **Pt. IV**.
[61] *Hudson v Bray* [1917] 1 K.B. 520; *Cunliffe v Bankes* [1945] 1 All E.R. 459; *Lambourn v London Brick Co* (1950) 156 E.G. 146; *Lane v Tredegar Estate Trustees* (1954) E.G., November 27; *Quinn v Scott* [1964] 1 W.L.R. 1004.
[61a] See **6.4.8**.
[62] See **5.1.2**.

Nor is this the place for a detailed discussion on civil procedure, on which numerous books, more or less detailed, have been published in recent years – following the coming into force of the new Civil Procedure Rules on April 1, 1999.

5.9.2 Liability

In summary, then, for an action in negligence to succeed, the plaintiff must be able to show that:

(1) the defendant owed him/her a duty of care;

(2) the defendant was in breach of that duty;

(3) the breach led to the plaintiff being harmed; and

(4) the harm was foreseeable.

Where harm is caused as a result of the failure of a tree (such as someone being injured by a falling branch), or as a result of its natural characteristics (such as poisonous berries), therefore, the first step is to identify the potential defendant, and who owed the victim a duty of care in respect of the tree concerned. Where the tree is (or was) growing on highway land, the most appropriate defendant will usually be the highway authority[63]; in other cases it will usually be the "occupier" of the land on which the tree was growing.[64]

It will usually be straightforward to establish that the defendant owed at least some duty of care to the plaintiff (the victim) – either at common law or under the Occupiers' Liability Acts 1957 and 1984.[65] The more difficult question will be to establish the extent and scope of that duty,[66] and whether the action, if any, taken by the defendant was sufficient to discharge it.[67] So, for example, where it can be shown that a landowner asked his gardener to inspect from ground level all the trees on his land once a year, was that sufficient to escape liability when one of them subsequently shed a branch onto a passing bus?

It may be even less straightforward to establish that a failure to take adequate care actually caused the harm. It has already been noted[68] that even a complete failure to inspect a particular tree, or to carry out any remedial work, will not assist a potential plaintiff if the defect that actually caused harm would not have been visible on any inspection. And the situation may be further complicated where there are potentially more than one "causes" of the eventual harm – where, for example, a drunk motorist, driving too fast, collides with a fallen branch across the road which he failed to see partly because the highway authority had omitted to repair a nearby street lamp.

In addition, the harm must be foreseeable, and must not be too remote – the two being often linked, so that the test of whether particular harm was too remote from the incident that theoretically caused it is often, in practice, whether it was foreseeable that the incident would lead to the harm. It is thus foreseeable that, if a tree is diseased so that a branch is only weakly attached to the trunk, the branch

---

[63] See **6.2**.
[64] See **5.2**.
[65] See **5.3**.
[66] See **5.4**.
[67] See **5.7, 5.8**.
[68] See **5.7.3**.

will fall in a high wind. It is further foreseeable that, if the branch overhangs a highway, its fall may cause a vehicle to collide with it, or with another vehicle, and that that in turn may cause a multiple pile-up. It is, however, probably not foreseeable that someone of a nervous disposition will suffer a heart attack due to nervous shock at hearing about the incident on the television.[69]

And although in theory the first three elements in the list above can be considered in isolation, they are of course heavily inter-linked. In practice, therefore, once an "accident" has occurred, and the potential defendant identified, there will not be an academic debate about what, in the abstract, the owner of the tree should have done, but rather a focussed consideration as to whether he had actually done enough to avoid responsibility for this particular incident.

5.9.3 Defences

It has already been pointed out that a particular incident may have more than one "cause". It follows that an owner of a tree on the receiving end of an action for negligence would do well to consider first of all whether there is some other cause. If that can be established, it may shift the blame altogether onto whoever is responsible for the other cause or, perhaps more likely, enable the blame, and thus any eventual award of damages, to be shared – in whatever proportions seem appropriate.

One possible additional cause that should not be overlooked is the negligence of the victim himself. Did he know about the dangerous state of the tree – was it obvious, or had he been warned? If he drove into a fallen branch, was he going too fast? Again, this will enable the damages to be reduced, by virtue of the Law Reform (Contributory Negligence) Act 1945.

Alternatively, it may be possible to show that the victim had voluntarily assumed the risk – where a neighbour crawls along a branch of your tree to rescue his cat, and explicitly says that he thinks it is strong enough to bear his weight, he cannot reasonably sue you if he is wrong. This is a general principle known for centuries, until 1999, as *volenti non fit inuria*, and thereafter as "voluntary assumption of risk".[70] It is also recognised, in the context of occupiers' liability, by the 1957 Act.

Finally, it may be possible for the defendant to show that he had excluded liability; although this may be difficult, and almost impossible in the case of commercial defendants.[71]

5.9.4 Damages

Where a plaintiff is able to establish liability in respect of harm that has already been caused, he or she will be able to claim damages.[72] That is, persons who have been injured, or who have suffered, should be able to recover a sum of money to put them in the same position as they would have been if they had not sustained the wrong in the first place.[73]

---

[69] As occurred in *Alcock v Chief Constable of South Yorkshire Police* [1992] 1 A.C. 310, H.L.
[70] See *McCluskey v Lord Advocate*, *The Times*, August 18, 1993.
[71] See **5.4.4**.
[72] *Leakey v National Trust* [1980] 1 Q.B. 485, at p. 523.
[73] *Livingstone v Raywards Coal Co* (1880) 5 App. Cas. 25, per Lord Blackburn at p. 39; cited in numerous subsequent cases.

Where a defective tree causes death or personal injury, the resulting damages will be assessed as in any other case of personal injury, according to complex rules long established; appropriate specialist texts should be consulted. Where chattels (such as vehicles) or buildings are damaged or destroyed, the usual measure of damages will be the value of the necessary repairs, replacement or re-building.

5.9.5 Injunctions

Where harm has not yet occurred, but is threatened, it may be possible in theory to obtain an injunction – that is, an order by the court requiring the owner of the tree to take whatever action is necessary to ensure that the threatened harm does not occur.

In practice, neighbours are likely to be able to remove many problems by the self-help remedy of abatement[74]; but where, for example, a landowner is worried that a tree on his neighbour's land near to, but not overhanging, the boundary, may be about to fall onto his greenhouse, he may be able to persuade a court to act.

Similarly, since highway authorities have special powers to deal with trees likely to endanger users of the highway[75]; an injunction will only rarely if ever be required.

It is therefore perhaps not surprising that there appears to be no reported instance of such an injunction being granted. In addition, in a situation where an injunction might be successfully sought, it will often be more appropriate to invite the relevant local authority to take action under the Local Government (Miscellaneous Provisions) Act 1976.[76]

5.10 "Dangerous" trees: other consequences in law

5.10.1 Introduction

As well as the principles of the common law discussed above, there are a number of other statutory provisions relating explicitly to "dangerous trees".

First, a local authority may take action to deal with dangerous trees under the Local Government (Miscellaneous Provisions) Act 1976. This is considered in more detail below.[77]

Secondly, a highway authority has powers under section 154 of the Highways Act 1980 to deal with hedges, trees and shrubs that endanger the passage of vehicles and pedestrians on the highway.[78]

Thirdly, where a tree is dangerous, works to remove the source of the danger may be carried out without the need for consents that might otherwise be required. That is, such works do not require a felling licence[79]: if the tree is subject to a tree preservation order, consent does not have to be obtained[80]; and if it is in

---

[74] See **3.6**.
[75] See **6.4**.
[76] See **5.10.2**.
[77] See **5.10.2**.
[78] See **6.4.3**, **6.4.7**.
[79] FA 1967, s. 9(4)(a); see **14.2.4**.
[80] TCPA 1990, s. 198(6)(a); see **17.3.2**.

a conservation area, the planning authority does not have to be notified beforehand.[81] In each case, there are specific procedural requirements to be considered – including in some cases a need to plant a replacement tree; the relevant Chapters should be consulted for further details.

In each of the above cases, "dangerous" is not defined; but the principles explored in this Chapter will hopefully assist in determining whether or not a tree is dangerous so as to come within the relevant statutory provision.

So, for example, if a tree on land adjoining a highway is sufficiently hazardous or dangerous so that works should be carried out without further ado under the common law principles of negligence, then a highway authority would presumably be justified in taking action under the 1980 Act. But that would not be the case if a healthy tree merely overhangs a highway, but at such a height that no vehicles would be endangered. And if a tree was sufficiently hazardous that an occupier of land would be liable to be pay damages to a visitor onto his land, or to the owner of neighbouring land, if it were to fall, then to carry out the necessary preventative works would not require consent under any tree preservation order that may apply. But the owner of a protected tree cannot fell it without consent simply because he fears that it *might* fall over.

It must therefore be doubtful whether the mere size of a tree, for example, is sufficient to justify the exemption – in spite of suggestions to the contrary by Tudor Price J. in *Smith v Oliver*:

"A tree has become dangerous at the moment when it constitutes a present danger to persons or property. That may be not only as a result of disease or damage; it may be by reason of its size and location. For example, a tree planted at a roadside may by its very size be judged to have become dangerous in the sense that in a high wind it, or part of it, may fall across the road to the danger of traffic. A common case is that of a forest tree planted in a suburban garden which begins to dominate and tower above the house roof so that in high wind it might fall and hole the roof or its roots begin to undermine the foundation. In each case it is a question of fact for the justices to see whether or not the person who has felled or lopped without the necessary permission is able to bring himself within the exemption of the Act."[82]

This seems, with respect, to be fallacious. In a strong enough gale almost any tree may fall across a road, provided it is near enough, but that does not mean that every tree within falling distance of a road is dangerous – if that were so, the word "dangerous" would almost have ceased to have any meaning. Somehow, a distinction must be made between the elm tree in *Caminer v Northern & London Investment Trust*[83] and the horse chestnut in *Chapman v Barking and Dagenham LBC*.[84] Of the former it was said:

"As a matter of fact, none of the experts called in the case, who had seen the tree before it fell, thought it appeared dangerous; and it is not at all clear, in my view, that even the expert witnesses who had not seen the tree in growth would have considered it dangerous."[85]

As to the latter:

[81]   TCPA 1990, s. 198(6)(a), 212; TCP(T) Regulations 1999, reg. 10(1)(a); see **21.2.2**.
[82]   [1989] 2 PLR 1 at p. 4H.
[83]   See **5.5.1**.
[84]   See **5.7.3**.
[85]   [1951] A.C. 88, H.L., per Lord Oakley at p. 104.

"The fact is that when the tree grew fairly large the defendants or their predecessors must have pruned it, so far as concerns the higher branches, to prevent danger. Thereby they altered the natural state of the tree and created a potential danger; there was plenty of information available whereby they could have known that the pruning wounds could lead to decay, yet they allowed the danger so caused to persist . . ."[86]

In other words, one tree was not considered to be dangerous, and the other one was (or should have been, if it had been inspected). In fact, of course, they both fell; but if it be true that the elm in *Caminer* was "dangerous", so that it should have been felled in spite of the views of all the experts, then every roadside tree in the country would need to be felled just in case it had a hidden defect, which cannot be right.

And see *Wandsworth Board of Works v United Telephone Company*,[87] which concerned the issue of whether a highway authority had the right to require the removal of a telephone cable suspended across a street in its area. It was held that the Board had no right to an injunction simply by virtue of trespass by the cable into its airspace, but that it would be able to remove the wire if it was "dangerous".[88] Brett M.R. continued:

"But whether this wire was a danger, and in that sense a nuisance to the street, was a question of fact. Upon that question of fact, I think there was evidence on both sides. . . . there was very strong evidence indeed . . . that it was not of any practical danger; there was very strong evidence, which really was not contradicted in the least, that this wire, put up as it was with ordinary care and being of ordinary material, would not begin to deteriorate so as to become dangerous for several years after it had been put up, and that even after several years it would take many more years before it became really dangerous. Upon that evidence, having considered it, the learned judge who saw the witnesses, and who had the means of estimating what credit ought to be given to their care and their truthfulness, came to this conclusion, that there was no appreciable danger in the wire at present, and for some considerable time to come. If there is no appreciable danger, that, in fact as well as in law, means that there is no danger at all."[89]

The test was thus whether there was "appreciable" danger, or whether the wire was "not of any practical danger". But again the emphasis is on "strong" evidence, as opposed to mere uninformed opinion – and the same would seem to be true of trees.

The conclusion, therefore, seems to be that, for a tree to be "dangerous", it would be necessary for there to be some evidence as to the existence of a properly informed opinion to that effect.

5.10.2 Action by local authority to deal with dangerous trees

A local authority (defined for this purpose as a district council, London borough council or the common council of the City of London[90]) has certain powers under the Local Government (Miscellaneous Provisions) Act 1976 to "deal with dangerous trees", to use the words of the marginal note to section 23.

---

[86] [1997] 2 EGLR 141, per Judge Viscount Colville of Culross QC, sitting as judge (upheld in CA, 1998, unreported).
[87] (1884) 13 Q.B.D. 904.
[88] See **6.2.1**.
[89] At p. 910.
[90] Local Government (Miscellaneous Provisions) Act 1976, s. 23(1).

First, an owner or occupier of land on which a tree is standing may give a notice to the council, requesting it to make the tree safe. Where the council is satisfied that the condition of the tree is indeed such that there is "imminent danger" of it causing harm to persons or property, it may under section 23(1) take such steps as it thinks are appropriate for making the tree safe, whether by felling it or otherwise, and may recover the cost of its action from the person giving the notice, together with interest.[91]

Note that the council may only take action under section 23(1) if it considers that the danger posed by the tree is "imminent". And even then, it does not have to take action; although, in such a situation, it would presumably want to ensure that at least something was done – either by the council or by the owner. If the owner was unable or unwilling to do the work (for example, in the case of the proverbial little old lady), it might well be easier for the council to do the work itself and reclaim the cost from the owner, rather than try and persuade the owner to do it himself or herself, with the risk that the feared "imminent" harm might in the meanwhile actually come to pass. There is no requirement for the council to notify the owner in advance of the likely cost of the works, although that would no doubt be good practice if time permitted.

Secondly, an owner or occupier of land may give a notice to the council, asking it to make safe a tree on land in other ownership. Where the council considers that the tree is indeed "likely to cause damage" (note: not necessarily imminently) to persons or property on the land of the person giving the notice, it may then take action – the nature of the action depending on whether or not it knows the name and address of any owner or occupier of the land on which the tree is standing. It may also take such action where it considers that damage is likely to be caused to persons or property on its own land by a tree on other land.[92]

If the council does not know of any owner or occupier of the land on which the tree is standing, it should make reasonable enquiries to find such a person.[93] If it is still unable to track down an owner or occupier, or if it considers that the danger posed by the tree is so imminent that there is no time to do so, it may itself without further ado carry out the appropriate action to make the tree safe, under section 23(2). Once the works have been done, it may then seek to recover the cost from anyone it subsequently discovers was an owner or occupier of the land on which the tree was standing at the time when the works were carried out.[94]

Where, on the other hand, the council is able to discover, or knows already, the owner or occupier of the land containing the dangerous tree, it may serve on that person a notice under section 23(3). Such a notice will specify:

- the steps which the council requires to be taken to make the tree safe; and

- the period within which they must be taken (which must be at least 21 days from the date on which the notice is served).[95]

Unsurprisingly, anyone who can show that he or she has been authorised by the council to do so has a right to enter any land to decide whether works should be carried out by the council to a tree under section 23(2), and in due course

[91]   1976 Act, ss. 23(1), 24(6).
[92]   1976 Act, s. 23(4).
[93]   1976 Act, s. 23(2)(c)(i).
[94]   1976 Act, ss. 23(2), 24(6).
[95]   1976 Act, s. 23(3).

actually to carry them out; or to decide whether a notice should be served under section 23(3).[96] A formal warrant is not required. Such a person may take colleagues onto the land, and any equipment as may be necessary; and it is an offence to obstruct those exercising such a right of entry. Where the land is unoccupied, any persons gaining entry under these provisions must leave the land as secured against trespassers as it was when they arrived. Any abuse of these powers of entry will entitle the owner of the land to claim compensation from the council concerned, to be settled if necessary by the Lands Tribunal.[97]

5.10.3 Action by tree owner on receipt of notice under section 23(3)

Where a notice has been served under section 23(3) of the 1976 Act, requiring work to be carried out to a tree to make it safe,[98] the person upon whom it is served may appeal against it to the county court, under section 24, within 21 days of the date of service of the notice. The grounds on which such an appeal may be made are as follows:

(a) that the person on whom the notice was served is neither an owner nor an occupier of the land on which the tree is situated;

(b) that the tree is not likely to cause damage to persons or property on the land of the person who originally alerted the council as to the problem;

(c) that there are less expensive ways of making the tree safe than those specified in the notice;

(d) that it would have been fairer to serve the notice on someone else who is also an owner or occupier of the land on which the tree is situated.[99]

Any owner or occupier of the land where the tree is, other than the person on whom the notice was actually served, may also appeal against the notice on ground (b) or (c).[1]

The procedure is then the same as for an appeal under section 21 of the 1976 Act against a notice under section 20.[2]

On determination of an appeal, the court may simply uphold the notice and dismiss the appeal, or allow the appeal and quash the notice.[3]

The respondent to the appeal will normally be the authority, save that where the appeal is on ground (d), the other person who it is alleged should have been served with the notice should also be made a respondent.[4] Where an appeal is on ground (d), the court may modify the notice so that it requires someone other than the original recipient to do the necessary works to make the tree safe (in which case the notice is deemed to have been served on that other person), or it

---

[96] 1976 Act, s. 24(1),(2).
[97] 1976 Act, s. 24(2)–(5).
[98] See **5.10.2**.
[99] 1976 Act, s. 23(5).
[1] 1976 Act, s. 23(5).
[2] By which a local authority may require the owner of a place of public entertainment to provide proper sanitary appliances.
[3] 1976 Act, s. 21(3)(a),(d), as applied by s. 23(6)
[4] 1976 Act, s. 21(2), as applied by s. 23(6); CPR Pt. 52; see Practice Direction, para. 24.1 (formerly County Court Rules Ord 49, r. 11).

may order that the appellant can recover the cost of those works from some other person.[5]

Except where a notice is simply quashed on appeal, the court may extend the time for compliance with it.[6]

If the person on whom the notice was served fails to carry out the required works within the specified period, the council may enter the land and carry them out itself, and recover the cost from that person together with interest.[7] Again, there is a right of entry to enable it to decide whether to carry out such works in default, and in due course actually to carry them out.[8]

In any event, it is probably sensible for the council to enter negotiations with the owner of the tree to decide on the best way forward.

5.10.4 Use of the 1976 Act powers in practice

The Minister responsible for the passage of the Bill said at Committee stage in the House of Commons:

"These are intended as powers of last resort. An owner or occupier should normally be able to find a private contractor to fell his dangerous tree for him, and neighbours should normally be able to reach agreement on the felling of a dangerous tree."

The Minister must have had a very rosy view of the general state of relations between neighbours.[9] He also added that these powers of last resort were intended to be used "where the public interest is affected, if ordinary agreement fails".

The relevant Government guidance on the use of powers under the 1976 Act, issued at the time, was as follows:

"Sections 23 and 24 enable district councils to take action in connection with a dangerous tree when asked to do so by the owner or occupier of the land on which the tree stands or by the owner or occupier of land threatened by the tree. The powers are intended though as a last resort. In general the responsibility for the removal or treatment of dangerous trees on private land should remain with the owner or occupier. They should normally be able to find a contractor to fell or treat their dangerous trees; when authorities are approached by a neighbour they should be particularly careful to ensure that he has made a genuine effort to reach agreement with the owner of the tree before they consider taking action."[10]

That may have been the intention of the Government, but there is nothing in the Act to indicate that these powers are only to be used as a last resort. And it may be in practice that it is in some cases a great deal easier (and more effective) for a local authority, once alerted to the existence of a dangerous tree, to serve a notice promptly, and then enter the land, do whatever is necessary to make it safe and charge those responsible.

---

[5] 1976 Act, s. 21(3)(b),(c), (4), as applied by s. 23(6).
[6] 1976 Act, s. 21(6), as applied by s. 23(6).
[7] 1976 Act, ss. 23(7), 24(6).
[8] 1976 Act, s. 24.
[9] See **1.5** for a different view.
[10] Department of the Environment Circular 9/77, *Local Government (Miscellaneous Provisions) Act 1976*, Appendix A, Pt. I.

In practice, however, it seems that these powers have rarely, if ever, been used.[11]

As for what is the meaning of "danger", and hence that of "safe", that has already been covered.[12]

5.10.5 Dangerous trees on highway land

Finally, dangerous trees on or affecting highway land are the subject of separate statutory provisions (sections 96 and 154 of the Highways Act 1980), dealt with in the following Chapter.[13]

[11] The author would welcome any information suggesting otherwise.
[12] See **5.10.1**.
[13] See **6.4**.

Chapter 6

Trees and Highways

6.1 Introduction

6.1.1 Trees on highway land

It will be obvious from a casual glance at any town or village, or from a drive
through any area of countryside, that trees are very often to be found on, or
immediately adjacent to, highways. It is not surprising, therefore, that they are
greatly valued by some as an amenity, enjoyed both by those living in the area and
by the public at large.

It is also unsurprising, given the propensity of tree roots to cause damage to
foundations of nearby buildings,[1] that trees growing on highway land are often
the subject of protracted litigation, particularly in urban areas where buildings are
close to the boundary of highway land. This is, no doubt, also connected with the
perception of those affected that highway trees are owned by – or at least the
responsibility of – public authorities, who have unlimited funds to compensate
home owners for underpinning their foundations.

Further, trees that are growing either on or close to highways are no more or
less prone than other trees to fall or shed branches, but the consequences of their
doing so can be particularly unfortunate.[2] Highways are frequented by people, on
foot or in vehicles, who quite properly take little or no notice of the trees to either
side of them, so that a falling tree will usually come as a complete surprise, with
little if any warning. And if the tree or branch falls at night, vehicles may well
collide with it. The results may be devastating. Here too, the eagerness to sue in
relation to highway trees may be linked to the apparent availability of funds to
meet claims.

So who is responsible for trees growing on highway land? After a review of all
of the principal reported decisions on the topic, one of which describes this as "an
unsatisfactory and difficult branch of the law",[3] the conclusion reached by the
leading authority on highway law in 1997 was that "it cannot be said that the law
on the ownership of trees in the highway is clear" – although he did add that "it
now appears that the question of liability based upon control is established".[4]

---

[1]   See **3.5.1**.
[2]   See **5.3.2**.
[3]   *Russell v Barnet LBC* [1984] 2 EGLR 44, per Tudor Evans J. at p. 49A.
[4]   Sauvain, *Highway Law*, second edn, Sweet and Maxwell, 1997, paragraph 3–49.

Thankfully, in the same month in which that was written, the Court of Appeal significantly both clarified and simplified the law.[5] The reason for the previous confusion, which arises from the very concept of a highway, and the process by which it came to be resolved, is considered at **6.2**.

The specific powers to plant trees and shrubs in highways are considered at **6.3**. The responsibility for highway trees, whether planted or self-sown, and whether before or after the adoption of the highway, is then considered at **6.4** (in relation to obstruction and danger to those using the highway) and **6.5** (in relation to encroachment onto to neighbouring property).

One specific problem arising in relation to highway trees concerns the activities of statutory undertakers. This is the subject of **Chapter 7**.

6.1.2 Trees on land adjacent to highways

It has already been noted[6] that trees are often planted or allowed to grow on, or close to, property boundaries. The same applies to land adjacent to highways; trees are often found along the front boundary. This provides a more pleasant outlook for those walking or driving along urban streets and country roads, and shade for parked cars. But problems can and often do arise where trees and shrubs encroach onto highway land; and less often, but more dramatically, where trees or branches growing on private land fall onto the highway.

The final section of this Chapter (**6.6**) therefore considers the special responsibilities of those owning trees on land adjacent to a highway.

6.1.3 Highway authorities

This Chapter makes frequent references to the "highway authority". This term is defined in some detail in Part I of the Highways Act 1980. Broadly speaking, however, the "highway authority" in relation to motorways, trunk roads and certain other major roads is the Secretary of State – that is, in theory, the Secretary of State for Transport in England, or the National Assembly for Wales[7] and, in practice, the Highways Agency. In relation to other roads, the highway authority is the county council (where there is one) or the unitary authority.[8] It may also be noted that a highway authority may, and frequently does, delegate its functions to another local authority.[9]

6.2 Ownership of and responsibility for highway trees

6.2.1 The nature and ownership of a highway: the general rule

A highway is in law not a strip of land, but essentially a right of way for the public at large to pass and re-pass along a defined route.

---

[5]   In *Hurst v Hampshire County Council* [1997] 2 EGLR 164, CA.
[6]   See **3.1**.
[7]   HA 1980, s. 1(1), S.I. 1999 No. 672 (Wales), art. 2, Sched. 1.
[8]   HA 1980, s. 1(2)–(5), for areas of unitary authorities, see **16.4.2**.
[9]   HA 1980, ss. 4 to 9. For the implications of this, see *L E Jones (Insurance Brokers) Ltd v Portsmouth City Council*, QBD Technology and Construction Court, March 11, 2002, unreported – see **6.5.3**.

It follows that, in theory at least, the ownership of that land does not normally change at the date on which the highway comes into being:

"That the king has nothing but the passage for himself and his people; but the freehold and all the profits belong to the owner of the soil."[10]

The rights of the owner of the soil are from then on subject to those of the public, so that they are of little use or value in practice – until, that is, the land ceases to be a highway, at which point full rights of ownership revert to the actual owner of the soil over which the highway previously passed. In practice, ownership is usually assumed to be split between the frontagers on either side, each of whom (at least in theory) owns the soil across which the highway runs, up to the middle line.[11] This is unless there is some reason to suppose that the ownership prior to the existence of the highway was wholly in the hands of one or other of them, or a third party.[12]

That at any rate is still the position at common law – the public have a right over land rather than an interest in the land as such.[13]

This was not particularly convenient in practice, so Parliament enacted section 149 of the Public Health Act 1875, in relation to urban areas, and section 29 of the Local Government Act 1929, in relation to rural areas, in an attempt to clarify the situation. These were replaced by section 226 of the Highways Act 1959, which contained the same formula as is found in the provision currently in force, section 263(1) of the Highways Act 1980:

". . . every highway maintainable at the public expense, together with the materials and scrapings thereof, vests in the authority who are for the time being the highway authority for the highway".

There is no definition of the word "scrapings". Nor is there any statutory definition of the extent (and in particular the depth) of the highway authority's interest in the land.

It is in any event not entirely clear how a highway – which is, after all, neither a piece of land nor an interest in one – can be said to "vest" in any normal sense of that word. However, it seems to have been accepted that the interpretation of the word "highway" in modern legislation should be on the same basis as that of the word "street" in the 1875 Act (and "road" in the 1929 Act).

The meaning of the provision in the 1875 Act,[14] which referred to the vesting of the "street" in the local board (the predecessor to the highway authority), was thus considered in several decisions of the courts in the nineteenth century. In the important case of *Coverdale v Charlton*, Bramwell L.J. commented:

"The meaning I should like to put upon it is, that the street vests in the local board qua street; not that any soil or any right to the soil or surface vests, but that it vests qua street. I find some difficulty in giving it a meaning, and I do not know how far it adds to the words, 'shall be under the control of'. The meaning I put upon the word 'vest' is, the space and the

---

[10] 1 Rolle's Abridgement 392, letter B.5, cited in *Goodtitle d Chester v Alker* (1757) 1 Burr. 133, per Lord Mansfield at p. 143 and Foster J. at p. 146 (Eng. Rep. 231 at pp. 236, 238).

[11] *Usque ad medium filum viae*; and see *St Edmundsbury and Ipswich Diocesan Board of Finance v Clark (No 2)* [1973] 1 W.L.R. 1572, at p. 1583.

[12] As in *Low v Haddock* [1985] 2 EGLR 247 (see p. 250C).

[13] And see *Russell v Barnet LBC* [1984] EGLR 44 at pp. 45M–46B.

[14] 1875 Act, s. 149.

street itself, so far as it is ordinarily used in the way that streets are used, shall vest in the local board."[15]

Brett L.J. by contrast, noting that the 1875 Act (unlike its present-day successor), stated that a street "shall vest in and be under the control of" the urban authority,[16] rightly sought to find some meaning for "vest in" that was distinct to "be under the control of". But he was scarcely more successful.[17] A little later on in the same judgment, he held as follows:

" 'Street' means more than the surface, it means the whole surface and so much of the depth as can be used, not unfairly, for the ordinary purposes of a street. It comprises a depth which enables the urban authority to do that which is done in every street, namely, to raise the street and lay down sewers.   . . . 'Street', therefore, in my opinion, includes the surface and so much of the depth as may be not unfairly used, as streets are used."[18]

The exact depth of the soil beneath the surface of the highway that is vested in the authority must depend on all the circumstances, including the nature of the sub-soil, the method of construction of the road, as well as the existence of any sewers and other services beneath it.[19] Lord Denning M.R. subsequently suggested that the corresponding provision in the Local Government Act 1929[20] referred to "the top spit, or perhaps, I should say the top two spits, of the road."[21]

The principles explored in *Coverdale* were subsequently applied in *Wandsworth Board of Works v United Telephone Co*[22] to the airspace above a highway in order to determine whether the Board of Works had any property in a telephone cable suspended across a street from a building on one side to one on the other. Brett M.R. held:

". . . the same rule applies to that which is above the surface, and therefore that [the word 'street'] includes only so much of the area which is above the surface as is the area of the ordinary user of the street as a street.
". . . I am of opinion that [the 1875 Act] by the use of the word 'street' does not pass any property *above or over* the street, it only passes property *in* the street. It therefore passes only that which is the ordinary space occupied by men or things, which use the street as a street. Under those circumstances, it appears to me that no property passed in that part of the air through which, or in which, this telephone wire was placed."[23]

In other words, an injunction would have been properly granted if the telephone wire had been dangerous to those using the "street" as thus interpreted, but not simply and solely on the ground that there was a trespass into the airspace above the roadway and footway, since that airspace was not vested in the Board.

---

[15] (1878) 4 Q.B.D. 104, at p. 116; and see note 41 below.
[16] 1875 Act, s. 149; compare HA 1980, s. 263(1) (above).
[17] (1878) 4 Q.B.D. 104, at p. 120.
[18] (1878) 4 Q.B.D. 104, at p. 121
[19] See *Schweder v Worthing Gas Light and Coke Company (No. 2)* [1913] 1 Ch. 119, per Eve J. at
      p. 124.
[20] 1929 Act, s. 29.
[21] *Tithe Redemption Commissioners v Runcorn UDC* [1954] 1 Ch. 383.
[22] (1884) 13 Q.B.D. 904, at p. 911.
[23] At pp. 916–917.

As to the width of a highway, this will be the full width of the land dedicated as a highway, or allocated in an inclosure award. This is so even if the usable carriageway[24] is only a part of that land, where the remainder has been allowed to become overgrown, as in *Turner v Ringwood Highway Board*.[25] The position was expressed in *Coverdale* as being that the street "includes the space between the houses which is used as the footway and roadway".[26] And the Court of Appeal has confirmed that drivers of vehicles are entitled to use the full width of the carriageway, so that, if a branch is allowed to overhang, even if only by a few centimetres, the highway authority may be liable in the event of a collision.[27]

Once a piece of land is no longer used as a highway, the normal rule is that ownership of it will revert to the owners of the adjacent land[28] – together, presumably, with ownership of any trees growing on it, whenever planted.

6.2.2 Trees in the highway: introduction

It will be recalled that the normal rule[29] is that a tree is owned by whoever owns the soil surrounding its base. In view of the uncertainty as to the ownership of the subsoil beneath most highways, it is not surprising that the courts have had some difficulty in resolving the question of who owns a tree growing on highway land.

The current position has, however, been authoritatively expressed by the Court of Appeal in *Hurst v Hampshire County Council*,[30] in which Stuart-Smith L.J. held as follows:

"There are no authorities binding on this court which preclude us from holding that pre-adoption trees vest in the highway authority for all purposes, though I appreciate that Brawell L.J.'s opinion[31] was to the contrary. The penal and compensatory provisions of section 149,[32] as he recognised, suggest that the property of all trees rests in the highway authority. I think that the time has come when the courts should adopt a consistent approach to all highway trees other than those already subject to the statutory scheme in section 96 of the 1980 Act. And I take this view, notwithstanding that it involves holding that my previous decision in *Bridge*'s case[33] was wrongly decided." [34]

It will be clear from the tone of that conclusion that the matter was far from straightforward; and, in order to assist both in understanding the decision in *Hurst* and in enabling the earlier decisions to be put in context, it may be helpful to consider in some depth how the position has evolved to where it is now.

It should be noted that to determine the ownership of a highway tree is not just of academic interest, because it will determine responsibility for its maintenance, and liability for the results of any failure to maintain it. In particular, harm caused by (for example) the whole or part of the tree falling onto the highway, branches overhanging the carriageway and roots damaging adjacent buildings.

---

[24]   Referred to as the *via trita* in older cases.
[25]   (1870) L.R. 9 Eq. 418, at p. 422; see **6.2.3**.
[26]   (1878) 4 Q.B.D. 104, per Brett L.J. at p. 121; and see Cotton L.J. at p. 123.
[27]   *Hale v Hants and Dorset Motor Services* (1947) 46 L.G.R. 55, CA; [1947] 2 All E.R. 628.
[28]   *Rolls v St George the Martyr Southwark Vestry* (1880) 14 Ch.D. 785, CA.
[29]   See **2.1.1**.
[30]   [1997] 2 EGLR 164, CA.
[31]   In *Coverdale v Charlton* (1878) 4 Q.B.D. 104, at p. 117.
[32]   Of the Public Health Act 1875.
[33]   *Bridges v Harrow LBC* [1981] 2 EGLR 143.
[34]   [1997] 2 EGLR 164, CA at p. 168M.

6.2.3 The older authorities

The earliest authorities were clear that not only did the freehold and all the profits belong to the owner of the soil, but "so do all the trees upon it, and mines under it (which may be extremely valuable)".[35] Further, the owner of the soil may cut down the trees.[36]

However, that position began to change with the passing of numerous inclosure Acts in the eighteenth and nineteenth centuries.[37] Thus in *Turner v Ringwood Highway Board*, inclosure commissioners had in 1811 allotted land as a highway, on part of which some thirty or forty years later trees had grown up. It was held[38] that the Board, on behalf of the public, had a right to deal with the trees so as to prevent them being or becoming an obstruction to the highway, just as it had to deal with telegraph posts.[39] In particular, the owner of the land adjacent to the highway had failed to make out any title to the trees – although the court specifically declined to determine the question of who would own the timber once the trees had been cut.

The position was subsequently clarified with the enactment of the Public Health Act 1875 and the Local Government Act 1929, the relevant sections[40] of which provided that a street that is a highway maintainable at public expense shall vest in and be under the control of the urban authority.[41] Those Acts also provided that any person who without the consent of the authority wilfully displaces, takes up or injures the trees of such a street shall be liable to a penalty, and in case of injury to the trees to pay to the authority such compensation as the court may award.

Bramwell L.J. in *Coverdale v Charlton* considered whether this meant that the local board had property in the tree and in the soil; he doubted that it did, but expressly declined to make a firm decision.[42] Brett L.J., on the other hand, clearly held that: "If the enactment gives the local board that property in so much of the land, it gives them the absolute property in everything growing on the land."[43]

The decision in *Coverdale* was reviewed 50 years later in *Stillwell v New Windsor Corporation*.[44] The latter concerned the common situation of a tree that must have been planted in land over which the public had for very many years had a right of passage, and which thus constituted an ancient highway, but before the date on which that highway was dedicated as such. The owner of the adjacent land argued that this meant that the land on which the trees actually stood had

---

[35] *Goodtitle d Chester v Alker* (1757) 1 Burr. 133, per Lord Mansfield at p. 143 (Eng. Rep. 231 at p. 236). The observations of Mansfield were probably *obiter*; see *Low v Haddock* [1985] 2 EGLR 247 at p. 250E.

[36] *Goodtitle* at p. 136 (Eng. Rep. p. 232).

[37] On the inclosure process generally, see **Chapter 23**.

[38] *Turner v Ringwood Highway Board* (1870) L.R. 9 Eq. 418 at pp. 422, 423.

[39] As in *R v United Kingdom Electric Telegraph Company* (1862) 31 L.J. (M.C.) 166.

[40] 1875 Act, s. 149; 1929 Act, s. 29.

[41] See **6.2.1**.

[42] (1878) 4 Q.B.D. 104, at p. 117. Of this judgment, it was later said by Brett M.R. (in *Wandsworth Board of Works v United Telephone Co* (1884) 13 Q.B.D. 904 at p. 911): "Much has been said, and much must always be said, of the judgment of Lord Bramwell upon this point. No more valuable judgment could be given upon any point than one given by Lord Bramwell." And much later it was noted (by Stuart-Smith L.J. in *Hurst v Hampshire County Council* [1997] 2 EGLR 164, CA at p. 167E): "I shall have to refer to it, but it does appear that it lacks somewhat the clarity that was the characteristic of that great judge."

[43] (1878) 4 Q.B.D. 104, at p. 121.

[44] [1932] 2 Ch. 155.

not been dedicated, since it could not be used for passing and re-passing. The court disagreed.

Clauson J. noted that, where a tree is injured, compensation is payable to the local authority, and that the authority had the right to grant consent for the moving of a tree; both suggesting that property in the tree would be in the authority. He accordingly held – notwithstanding the somewhat hesitant conclusion of Bramwell L.J. in *Coverdale* – that the trees formed part of the "street" that had been dedicated, and which was thus vested in the highway authority by the 1875 Act:

"In my view, for all the purposes of exercising the rights of the highway authority, these trees are to be treated as the highway authority's trees, and if they think it convenient to remove them it is proper that they should remove them. I am not called to decide to whom the timber would belong when the trees were removed."[45]

6.2.4 More recent decisions

Unfortunately, neither *Coverdale* nor *Stillwell* were cited to the court in *British Road Services v Slater*.[46] In the latter case, an oak tree had grown alongside an ancient highway after it had been dedicated as such. Lord Parker C.J. considered the factual evidence, which suggested that the tree had grown up either in the hedge bordering the highway, or (more likely) in the verge between that hedge and the carriageway. He concluded that it was not necessary to decide that question, since, even if the tree was within the dedicated portion of the verge, the owners of the adjacent land (who thus also owned the subsoil across which the highway ran) could still be liable for harm caused by it:

"The fact that the highway authority, and the Minister, can, or may have the duty to, remove obstructions, does not necessarily exonerate the adjoining owner, in whom the property in the tree still remains. It seems to me that he may be liable in certain circumstances for nuisance."[47]

That decision has not been overruled, but should be viewed with considerable caution in the light of subsequent decisions. Thus it was cited by Stuart-Smith J. (as he then was) in *Bridges v Harrow Corporation*[48] as being "an accurate statement of the law", in that it established that property in highway trees (at least those planted prior to its adoption) remained in the owner of the sub-soil. But the decision in *Bridges* was itself explicitly overturned by Stuart-Smith L.J. (as he had by then become) in the Court of Appeal in *Hurst v Hampshire CC*[49] (see below).

A few months before the decision in *Bridges*, a more realistic approach had been taken in *Solloway v Hampshire County Council*,[50] the first of a number of significant decisions relating to the responsibility for highway trees causing harm to buildings on adjacent land. Stocker J. considered that, whoever in law owned trees growing in the highway, planted either before or after its adoption, highway

---

[45] [1932] 2 Ch. 155, per Clauson J. at p. 165.
[46] [1964] 1 W.L.R. 498, 1 All E.R. 816, E.G. May 30, 1964.
[47] [1964] 1 W.L.R. 498, per Lord Parker C.J. at p. 502.
[48] [1981] 2 EGLR 143, at p. 146C,D.
[49] [1997] 2 EGLR 164, CA.
[50] (1981) February 20, unreported; overturned on other grounds (1981) 79 L.G.R. 449, [1981] 1 EGLR 129, CA.

authorities had sufficient control over them to make them liable for any nuisance they caused.[51]

The decision at first instance in *Solloway* was not reported, and was not cited in *Bridges*. It was followed in at least one county court decision later that same year, in which the judge sensibly observed:

"To hold that the rights and duties of the highway authority and of the community in general depended on ownership, arising from whether or not the tree was planted before the dedication of the road, or by whom it was planted, would be to determine rights and duties on unrealistic distinctions and on facts not easily determinable."[52]

Perhaps more significantly, it was heavily relied upon by Tudor Evans J. in *Russell v Barnet LBC*, another case concerning a pre-adoption tree. He first considered all the older decisions, and concluded:

". . . in many urban conditions, ownership of the subsoil to the middle line is, in practical terms, of little value, at least in relation to highway authorities. Although theoretically the owner's rights are unaffected, in reality it is very difficult to conceive of circumstances in which rights in relation to a tree growing in the highway and arising from presumption of law can be exercised. It is really nothing more than ownership without rights."[53]

He nevertheless concluded that, although the presumption of ownership by the frontagers was now "a meaningless relic", it could not be disregarded. He also considered section 149 of the Public Health Act 1875 (see above), and concluded that the section was not dealing with pre-adoption trees. However, he went on to consider section 82 of the Highways Act 1959, which was itself amended by section 5 of the Highways (Miscellaneous Provisions) Act 1961. Section 82, as amended, provided as follows:

"(1) Subject to the provisions of this section, a highway authority may in a highway maintainable at public expense by them, plant trees and shrubs and lay out grass verges and may erect and maintain guards or fences and otherwise do anything expedient for the maintenance and protection of trees, shrubs, grass verges planted or laid out [whether or not by them, in such a highway]. A highway authority may alter or remove any grass verges laid out [, whether or not by them, in such a highway,] and any guard, fence or other thing [provided, whether or not by them, for the maintenance or protection of any tree, shrub or verge in such a highway]
. . .

(5) No tree, shrub, grass verge, guard or fence shall be planted, laid out or erected under this section or, if planted, laid out or erected thereunder, allowed to remain, in such a situation as to hinder the reasonable use of the highway by any person entitled to the use thereof, or so as to be a nuisance or injurious to the owner or occupier of premises adjacent to the highway."[54]

The judge in *Russell* noted that the 1961 amendment to subsection (1) (indicated above by square brackets) had the effect of enabling the highway authority to maintain and protect all highway trees, whenever planted. He held that this extended to the duty under subsection (5) to preventing them from being a

[51] See **6.5.3** for an extract from his judgment.
[52] *Nagioff v Barnet LBC* October 22, 1981, unreported (Westminster County Court).
[53] [1984] 2 EGLR 44 at p. 47D.
[54] subss. (1),(2) and (5) of section 96 of the HA 1980 are in identical terms.

hindrance or causing a nuisance.[54a] The latter conclusion was subsequently held by the Court of Appeal to be wrong[55]; but he went on to hold that even subsection (1) on its own was sufficient to ensure that, in effect, the authority alone had the power to maintain the trees. He therefore agreed with Stocker J. in *Solloway* that the authority had sufficient interest in and control over a highway tree to make it liable for any nuisance caused.[56]

The next case in this sequence (*Low v Haddock*[57]) concerned a self-seeded tree that had been growing on land owned by housebuilders, which had been dedicated as a highway following the completion of new houses along either side. The court considered first the question of whether the tree was included in the dedication:

". . . there can be only one inference from what Haddocks [the builders] did, namely, that they intended that everything between the fences should form Blewbury Drive; they intended to dedicate the trees along with everything else. Any other conclusion would I think be wholly unrealistic. The public would not be able to pass where the actual bole of a tree was, but they would be able to benefit from the tree visually and obtain from it shelter from sun or rain. If the tree died, its site would not be excluded from the highway, but would continue as part of it."

That seems eminently sensible. It was then noted that section 82 of the 1959 Act (see above) was not relevant, since it did not apply to self-seeded trees; but the court followed *Solloway* and *Russell*, and held that, since the tree must have been dedicated along with the surrounding land, the authority had full legal powers and obligations in respect of it.

The trend in this sequence of cases has thus been to emphasise more and more the powers and duties of highway authorities, so that – whoever might in theory "own" the tree (either the authority of the owner of the adjacent land) – in practice all the responsibility lay on the shoulders of the authority.

6.2.5 *The present position:* Hurst v Hampshire CC

The final step was taken by the Court of Appeal in *Hurst v Hampshire CC*.[58] The decision in this case is the most recent, and the most authoritative, analysis of the law in this area, in relation to the three principal categories of highway trees:

- those planted and growing in the highway before its dedication/adoption by the inhabitants at large or the highway authority ("pre-adoption trees");

- those planted and growing in the highway after dedication/adoption, but not planted under statutory powers ("post-adoption trees");

- those planted under express statutory powers granted to the highway authority ("planted trees").

[54a] [1984] 2 EGLR 44.
[55] *Hurst v Hampshire County Council* [1997] 2 EGLR 164, per Stuart-Smith L.J. at p. 166H.
[56] [1984] 2 EGLR 44, at p. 49L.
[57] [1985] 2 EGLR 247.
[58] [1997] 2 EGLR 164, CA.

After considering all the most significant previous decisions,[59] Stuart-Smith L.J. concluded that there could be no doubt that the property in post-adoption trees vests in the highway authority for all purposes:

"If they were planted, albeit not under statutory powers as the tree in the present case possibly was, they are planted for highway purposes in that part of the soil which plainly vested. If they are self-seeded, again they are seeded in that part of the highway which vests in the local authority. If, as they mature, their roots encroach into the subsoil which remains the property of the adjoining owner, I do not see how that makes the tree the property of the owner of the sub-soil. And I can see no logical distinction between trees and smaller shrubs, plants or grass."[60]

It must follow that the property in trees planted under the statutory scheme also vests in the authority.

But the court then went on to consider the question of pre-adoption trees. It noted that:

". . . both counsel have urged upon us the view that there is no logical distinction between pre- and post-adoption trees so far as the liability of the highway authority is concerned.

". . . from a practical point of view, there is much to commend [this submission]. It may be very difficult to determine in any given case and without the expensive advice of dendrologists whether the tree is pre- or post-adoption. Much time and expense may be taken in litigating this issue. Second, in practice a highway authority cannot make any distinction in management between the two, and in this case did not attempt to do so.

"If there is any logical basis in the distinction, it depends on the fiction that, in the case of a pre-adoption tree, there is a reservation from the public's right to pass over the full extent of the highway [of] that part of the surface on which the tree is growing, and that the owner of the land at dedication intended to reserve the tree from dedication. That seems to me an unreal fiction, in the absence of an express reservation. . . . I think that the time has come when the courts should adopt a consistent approach to all highway trees other than those subject to the statutory scheme now contained in section 96 of the 1980 Act."[61]

In other words, for all practical purposes, the property in all highway trees, regardless of when or by whom they were planted, or whether they were in fact self-seeded, vests in the highway authority.[62]

The conclusion in *Hurst* was strictly *obiter* insofar as it related to pre-adoption trees and self-seeded trees, since the tree in question in that case was a post-adoption tree; but it must be highly likely that any court will follow it – not least because, as has been shown above,[63] the decision followed naturally from those which preceded it. It is perhaps not without significance that the one more recent decision of the courts relating to street trees (*Delaware Mansions v Westminster CC*[64]) did not raise the issue of ownership of, or responsibility for, the trees. As in the earlier cases, it was simply assumed to lie with the highway authority.

---

[59]   In particular, *Coverdale v Charlton* (1878) 4 Q.B.D. 104, *Stillwell v New Windsor Corporation* [1932] 2 Ch. 155, *Solloway v Hampshire County Council* February 20, 1981, unreported, *Bridges v Harrow LBC* [1981] 2 EGLR 143, and *Russell v Barnet LBC* [1984] 2 EGLR 44.

[60]   [1997] 2 EGLR 164, CA, at p. 168J.

[61]   [1997] 2 EGLR 164, CA, at p. 168K to 169A.

[62]   As to the identity of which, see **6.1.3**.

[63]   See **6.2.3** and **6.2.4**.

[64]   [2001] 3 W.L.R. 1007, H.L., upholding [2000] B.L.R. 1, [1999] 3 EGLR 68, CA, overturning (1998) 88 B.L.R. 99.

6.2.6 Ownership of highway trees: special cases

The discussion so far has related to the normal situation of a public highway running across land where the ownership of the sub-soil remains in the hands of the owners of adjacent land.

No such problems arise where a highway authority purchases a strip of land before constructing a road on it – as is the case with, for example, virtually all motorways and major new trunk roads, and most, if not all, road-widening schemes. In that situation, the authority simply owns the land (and therefore of course any trees growing on it) outright, and the fact that there is a highway across it is – at least from the point of view of ownership – irrelevant.

And land may sometimes be bought by an authority other than the highway authority, as for example in *Bridges v Harrow LBC*,[65] in which a strip of land was conveyed to Hendon Rural District Council for use in a road widening scheme, and simultaneously dedicated as a highway. The rights and duties of that Council as highway authority then devolved by a series of local government reorganisations onto the Greater London Council; and its other rights and liabilities onto Harrow London Borough Council. As it happens, the court in *Bridges* considered that the liability for a tree growing on the land rested on the owner of the sub-soil (by then Harrow) rather than on the highway authority (the GLC), and resolved the case accordingly – a decision that was later overturned by the Court of Appeal in *Hurst*.[66] It would now be held to be the highway authority that would be liable, not the landowner.

Nor is there a difficulty in the case of a private street – that is, one that is not maintained at public expense. In such a situation, the trees in the street belong to the owner of the soil, along with liability for them; and the highway authority has no liability.

6.2.7 Damage to highway trees

A number of the cases relating to the ownership of highway trees raised the issue of responsibility for damage to them.[67] This arose from the wording of section 149 of the Public Health Act 1875, which provided not only that the street (and thus the trees growing in the street[68]) was vested in the urban authority, but also that:

"Any person who . . . injures . . . the trees in any such street, shall be liable to a penalty . . .; he shall also be liable in the case of any injury to trees to pay the local authority such amount of compensation as the court may award."[69]

This provision was replaced by section 117 of the Highways Act 1959, the relevant parts of which were in turn subsumed into section 1 of the Criminal Damage Act 1971.[70] The provisions of the latter will be considered in more detail in relation to

---

[65] [1981] 2 EGLR 143.
[66] *Hurst v Hampshire County Council* [1997] 2 EGLR 164, CA, at p. 169A.
[67] See, for example, *Coverdale v Charlton* [1878] 4 Ch.D. 104, at p. 117; *Stillwell v New Windsor Corporation* [1932] 2 Ch. 155, at p. 165; *Hurst v Hampshire County Council* [1997] 2 EGLR 164, CA, at p. 167A.
[68] See **6.2.2**.
[69] Public Health Act 1875, s. 149.
[70] Criminal Damage Act 1971, s. 11(8), Sched.

the problem of criminal damage to trees,[71] along with section 132 of the Highways Act 1980, which deals with the problem of graffiti and fly-posters on highways, including on trees on the highway.

6.2.8 Maintenance of highway trees

The level of maintenance of highway trees will need to be decided – as in the case of any other trees – in the light of the principles explained in the remainder of this Chapter. The discussion on responsibility for hazardous trees, in the previous Chapter, will also obviously be relevant.

Useful guidance on inspection is given in Department of the Environment Circulars 52/75 and 90/73 – the latter dealing with rural roads.

6.3 Planting of trees on highway land

6.3.1 Planting by highway authorities

Public authorities have for many years had powers to plant trees in highways: urban authorities originally under section 43 of the Public Health Acts Amendment Act 1890[72]; and the Minister, county councils and highway authorities under section 1 of the Road Improvement Act 1925. Those powers were consolidated as section 82 of the Highways Act 1959 (reproduced above[73]), which in turn became section 96 of the Highways Act 1980.

Under this provision, which relates only to highways maintainable at public expense, the relevant authority may plant trees and shrubs (including plants of any description[74]), and may lay out, alter and remove grass verges. It may also erect and maintain guards and fences for the protection of trees, shrubs and grass verges, whether or not originally planted or laid out by that authority, and may alter or remove such guards or fences.

It may, in addition, plant trees and so forth on land acquired for highway purposes, even if not actually classified as a highway.[75] This allows for trees and shrubs to be planted on wide verges and accommodation land generally, and may be particularly relevant in the case of major new highways involving large grass areas possibly some distance from the road itself.

The authority must, however, make sure that all trees and shrubs planted under these powers do not hinder the use of the highway by the public or cause a nuisance to neighbouring land[76]; and if any damage is caused to any property (which presumably, in this context, includes vehicles) by the exercise of the authority's powers, its owner may seek compensation from the authority.[77] Any compensation payable, however, will be reduced to the extent that the damage is caused by the negligence of the owner of the property.[78] In practice, it is unlikely that the planting of a tree will cause problems under these heads; but the carrying

---

[71] See **9.6.5**.
[72] As to the position before 1890, see *R v Lewes Corporation, The Times*, March 9, 1886.
[73] See **6.2.4**.
[74] HA 1980, s. 96(10).
[75] HA 1980, ss. 96(3), 239(2)–(4).
[76] HA 1980, s. 96(6), see **6.5**.
[77] HA 1980, s. 96(7).
[78] HA 1980, s. 96(8).

out of works to a highway tree and, more significantly, the failure to do so, may well lead to claims.[79]

Where a street runs along the boundary between the areas of two highway authorities, they may by agreement exercise their powers under section 96 jointly, and apportion the costs between them accordingly.[80]

A specific power is also provided for highway authorities to plant "trees, shrubs and other vegetation", either for ornament or in the interests of safety, on the central reservation of dual carriageways and on traffic islands generally,[81] and on pedestrian refuges.[82]

6.3.2 *Planting by others*

A local authority other than the highway authority, with the consent of the latter, may plant trees on highway land[83] – although not on central reservations, traffic islands and pedestrian refuges.

In addition, the owner or occupier of any premises adjacent to a highway may plant (or retain) trees, shrubs, grass and other plants on highway land, and may subsequently maintain them, provided that he or she has first obtained a licence from the highway authority, under section 142 of the Highways Act 1980.

Such a licence, which must specify the part of the highway where the planting is to take place,[84] may be granted either to the owner of the adjacent land and his or her successors in title – in which case it will be subject to a condition that the highway authority must be informed within a month of any change of ownership – or to a specific person who is currently occupying the adjacent land.[85] The former will presumably be more appropriate in the case of trees, which are likely to outlast the ownership of any one owner of the land.

A licence will be subject to conditions necessary to ensure the safety and convenience of those using the highway, to prevent nuisance or annoyance being caused to the owners and occupiers of other adjacent land, and to protect the apparatus of statutory undertakers and telecommunications code operators.[86] This enables the highway authority to require any trees to be properly maintained – or, presumably, for the authority itself to carry out such maintenance as the agent of the licensee – but, either way, at no cost to the authority. If any condition is not complied with, the authority may withdraw the licence after giving seven days written notice.[87]

No charge may be made for the grant of a licence, other than by way of recovering the cost of drawing it up and subsequently administering it.[88]

Other than in the case of a breach of a condition, a licence may be withdrawn at any time, on three months' written notice, where the highway authority considers it necessary for it to carry out its functions.[89] This would enable an authority to require a tree to be removed where, for example, it was impeding visibility at a

---

[79] See **6.4**.
[80] HA 1980, s. 96(9).
[81] HA 1980, s. 64(2).
[82] HA 1980, s. 68(2).
[83] HA 1980, ss. 96(4) (district or borough council) and 96(5) (parish council).
[84] HA 1980, s. 142(1).
[85] HA 1980, s. 142(2), (4).
[86] HA 1980, s. 142(5); see **Chapter 7**.
[87] HA 1980, ss. 142(6)(a), 320 to 323.
[88] HA 1980, s. 142(3).
[89] HA 1980, ss. 142(6)(b), 320 to 323.

junction. Where a licence is withdrawn, for any reason, the authority may itself remove all or any of the trees concerned, and reinstate the highway, or may authorise the last licensee to do so – but, again, either way, the work will be at the expense of the last licensee.[90]

More generally, the licensee is to indemnify the highway authority against any claim arising in respect of injury, damage or loss arising out of either the planting or presence in the highway of the trees, shrubs, plants or grass to which the licence relates, or the carrying out of any works following the withdrawal of the licence – except, obviously, where the claim is attributable to the negligence of the authority.[91]

Where the sub-soil of the highway is owned by the highway authority,[92] it may authorise anyone to plant trees on highway land, and may, if it sees fit, make a charge for doing so.[93]

Finally, there are other, more general powers to plant trees, which could be used in relation to highway land, considered later in this Book.[93a] However, the exercise of those powers would still be subject to the restrictions under section 141 of the 1980 Act, considered below.

6.3.3 Unauthorised planting

The general rule in section 141 of the Highways Act 1980, is that a tree or shrub must not be planted within a made-up carriageway, or within 4.57 m (15 ft) of the centre of a carriageway.[94] However, that is subject to:

- the power of a highway authority or local authority to plant trees, etc., on a highway, under section 96 of the 1980 Act[95];

- the power of a highway authority to plant trees on traffic islands, etc., under sections 64 and 68 of the Act[96]; and

- the power of the owner of land adjacent to a highway to plant trees, etc., under the terms of a licence under section 142 of the Act.[97]

Where a tree is planted in the carriageway in any other circumstances, the highway authority may simply remove it, as an obstruction to the highway. Where the tree is on private land, but within 4.57 m of the centre of a carriageway, the authority may serve a written notice, under section 141 of the 1980 Act, on the owner or occupier of the land, requiring him or her to remove the tree or shrub within 21 days.[98] In certain, limited cases, where the liability to repair a highway rests with someone other than the highway authority, that person may serve such a notice on the owner of the land.

Failure to comply with a notice under section 141 is a criminal offence, punishable on summary conviction (in the magistrates' court) by a fine of up to

---

[90] HA 1980, ss. 142(7), 305, 306.
[91] HA 1980, s. 142(8).
[92] See **6.2.6**.
[93] HA 1980, s. 142(10).
[93a] See **Chapter 10**.
[94] HA 1980, s. 141(1); Interpretation Act 1978, s. 8.
[95] See **6.3.1**, **6.3.2**.
[96] See **6.3.1**.
[97] See **6.3.2**.
[98] HA 1980, ss. 141(2), 320 to 323.

level 1 on the standard scale.[99] On conviction, the court may allow a reasonable time for compliance; but continuing non-compliance with the notice after the expiry of that time is a further offence, albeit punishable on summary conviction at the rate of only 50p per day![1]

It is also an offence, under section 138 of the 1980 Act, to plant a hedge in a highway without lawful authority or excuse. This offence, which only applies in relation to highways used by vehicles, attracts a fine of up to Level 3. However, plenty a hedge may be the subject of a license under section 142.[2]

6.4 Trees obstructing highways

6.4.1 Introduction

It is fairly obvious that, as trees, shrubs and hedges grow, they may become an obstruction or a danger to users of the highway. The most common problem is where trees and other vegetation (particularly hedges) cause an obstruction – that is, they prevent the free and safe passage of pedestrians, bicycles and vehicles along the highway. That in turn may constitute a hazard, since highways are designed and maintained on the assumption that they are kept clear, so that danger may be caused by the excessive growth of vegetation leading to (for example) a constriction in the usable width of a carriageway, or the blocking of a footway requiring pedestrians to use the carriageway or to cross it at an unsafe location, or the hindrance of an important sign, or the distortion of light after dark.

It is therefore not surprising that there are a number of different powers and duties given to highway authorities and other local authorities to prevent or deal with such problems. These powers generally relate to any trees interfering with the use of a highway, whether they are growing on the highway itself or on adjacent land – or, of course, straddling the boundary between the two.

The starting point is the general duty of highway authorities under sections 96 and 130 of the Highways Act 1980 to prevent the stopping up or obstruction of highways.[3] However, there are in addition a number of other powers available to authorities, scattered in an apparently random pattern throughout the 1980 Act (which itself is a somewhat unsatisfactory piece of consolidating legislation[4]). They are as follows:

- power to require removal of danger or obstruction caused by a tree (section 154[5]);

- power to require removal of obstruction to visibility at corners and bends (section 79[6]); and

---

[99] HA 1980, ss. 141(3), 310.
[1] HA 1980, ss. 141(3), 311.
[2] See **6.3.2**.
[3] See **6.4.2**.
[4] In the long run, of course, it would be helpful for the Law Commission to reform these (and other) provisions of highways legislation, to bring them into line with modern requirements.
[5] See **6.4.3**.
[6] See **6.4.4**.

- power to require removal of cause of damage by exclusion of sun and wind (section 136[7]).

It should be noted that the terms of each procedure are slightly different, so that it is important to check on the precise wording of the relevant statutory provision to ensure that it does cover the particular situation concerned. Thus, for example, in *Walker v Horner*,[8] a landowner summoned under section 72 of the Highways Act 1835 (now section 137 of the 1980 Act), for wilfully obstructing a highway by allowing vegetation to grow so as to obstruct a bridleway, was able to escape conviction by showing that his action (or inaction) was not "wilful", as he considered that the path in question was not a highway. That particular problem should not occur now, as it would be possible for a highway authority to take action under section 130 of the 1980 Act (see above) whether or not the path was a "highway"; but it does emphasise the significance of the precise wording of each provision.

As to the consequences of failure by highway authorities to exercise these discretionary powers, they are now significantly diminished, following the decision of the House of Lords in *Stovin v Wise*.[9]

The relatively rare, but potentially very serious, problem of trees falling or shedding branches so as to cause personal injury or damage to property, can be the subject of action under section 96 of the 1980 Act or, more usually, by reference to the common law duty of care.[10] And once a tree or branch has fallen onto the highway, so as to constitute an obstruction, the authority must remove it under section 150.[11]

Finally, it may be noted that highway authorities have a duty (not merely a power) to maintain the highway, under section 41 of the 1980 Act, and may be required to carry out necessary works under section 56. However, it seems that neither the failure to prevent the encroachment of trees and shrubs onto a highway[12] nor the failure to inspect and remove a defective tree[13] is likely to constitute disrepair so as to bring these provisions into play. Nor is either likely to constitute a statutory nuisance, the existence of which would also require the authority to take action.[14]

6.4.2 Trees causing an obstruction: sections 96 and 130

Obstruction principally arises from the expansion of trees and bushes, including hedges, as they grow, particularly by sending out branches or foliage at lower levels. This can cause problems in the case of trees and bushes on footways, on grass verges, in hedges along the boundary of highway land, or on adjacent land, in that:

---

[7] See **6.4.5**.
[8] (1875) 1 Q.B.D. 4, Divisional Court.
[9] [1996] A.C. 323, H.L.; see **6.4.6**.
[10] See **6.4.7**.
[11] See **6.4.8**.
[12] *Westley v Hertfordshire County Council* (1998) 76 P. & C.R. 518, Div Court (an obstruction by a fence built in a highway does not constitute disrepair).
[13] *Chapman v Barking and Dagenham LBC* [1997] 2 EGLR 141 (upheld in CA (1998) unreported) at p. 146C.
[14] *Westley*, at p. 525.

- they physically obstruct the passage of pedestrians and vehicles along the highway; and

- they impede visibility at corners and junctions, or obscure signs.

Since the whole point of a highway is that it should be freely passable, it is not surprising that highway authorities have a duty to remove any obstructions to the use of a highway, and this includes trees in the "wrong" place.

This arises firstly as a result of section 96 of the Highways Act 1980, which empowers public authorities to plant trees in a highway that are maintainable at public expense,[15] but also requires such trees to be maintained properly:

"No tree, shrub, grass verge, guard or fence shall be . . ., if planted, laid out or erected under this section, allowed to remain, in such a situation as to hinder the reasonable use of the highway by any person entitled to use it."[16]

It has been held that this requires that trees planted under section 96 are not to be "dangerous" to members of the public using the highway[17] (which is considered below[18]). But it also, on its face, requires that they should not even "hinder" the reasonable use of the highway, which is a somewhat more exacting standard. It is, however, no more than a particular case of the general duty laid upon authorities by section 130 of the Act, which provides that:

". . . it is the duty of a council who are a highway authority to prevent, as far as possible, the stopping up or obstruction of –

(a) the highways for which they are the highway authority, and
(b) any highways for which they are not the highway authority, if, in their opinion, the stopping up or obstruction of that highway would be prejudicial to the interests of their area".[19]

The existence of section 130 means that there is no need for a highway authority to consider when a tree was planted, or by whom, or who is the owner of the sub-soil; if the tree is causing an obstruction, it must be dealt with. However, it should be noted that this requires the removal of the obstruction, not the felling of the tree. It may well be sufficient to remove or cut back a branch or two, or to prune over-enthusiastic foliage. And note too that the duty extends to highways for which the council concerned is not the highway authority.

In order to carry out that duty, a council may take legal proceedings – such as seeking an injunction – or may generally take such steps as it deems expedient.[20] As to the exercise of powers under this section, Lord Russell C.J. commented as follows (in *Reynolds v Presteign UDC*):

". . . it is desirable that the question whether a private individual has encroached should not be decided by the public body acting in a high-handed way, or taking the law into their own hands. Where the question is one of doubt and difficulty, I think a judicial decision should be obtained by the public authority. . . . The burden lies upon them of justifying

[15] See **6.3.1**.
[16] HA 1980, s. 96(6).
[17] See *Morrison v Sheffield Corporation* [1917] 2 K.B. 866, CA, per Viscount Reading C.J. at p. 871.
[18] See **6.4.7**.
[19] HA 1980, s. 130(3); formerly HA 1959, s. 116(3), replacing Local Government Act 1894, s. 26(1).
[20] HA 1980, s. 130(5).

their action; and, if they fail to justify by reason of their being unable to shew that there was an obstruction or encroachment, they become liable to damages for trespass."[21]

It is clearly sensible for an authority to act with caution, but it must be doubted whether Lord Russell's dictum in *Reynolds* is still good law, particularly in the light of the decision in *Stillwell v New Windsor Corporation*,[22] in which the court endorsed the right – indeed the duty – of a highway authority to keep the highway in proper condition by removing trees which were dangerous on account of their instability. In that case, the trees in question stood on the line separating the footway and the carriageway; but the same principle would clearly apply to trees growing anywhere in the footway or the carriageway (the latter are rare but not unknown, even now), or indeed encroaching from on private land so as to obstruct the highway.

The court in *Stillwell* held that the trees, being planted after the land had become a highway but before it was dedicated as such, constituted an obstruction to the highway, since the public had the right to use the whole width of it, and not just the made-up carriageway. The highway authority, if satisfied that the obstruction was a serious one, had the right, and possibly the duty, to remove them. Further, it was established that the owner of adjacent land had no right to prevent such action being taken.[23]

It should not be forgotten that where an authority carries out works to a non-highway tree, in the exercise of its duty under section 130, the arisings still belong to the owner of the tree. They should therefore, strictly speaking, be offered back to him or her – although this may not be practical in circumstances where the immediate priority is to clear the highway.

6.4.3 Obstruction and danger caused by trees on adjacent land: section 154

In addition to the general duty under section 130 of the Highways Act 1980,[24] there are specific powers in the Act that enable a highway authority to take action to prevent problems being caused by trees and shrubs growing on land adjacent to the highway to those using the highway.

Firstly, a notice may be served under section 154(1) of the 1980 Act[25] by any competent authority:

". . . where a hedge, tree or shrub [which includes vegetation of any description] –

[i]   overhangs a highway or any other road or footpath to which the public has access so as to endanger or obstruct the passage of vehicles or pedestrians, or
[ii] obstructs or interferes with the view of drivers of vehicles or the light from public lamp, or
[iii] overhangs a highway so as to endanger or obstruct the passage of horseriders".

[*numbering added for clarity*].

In any of the cases specified in section 154, the notice is to require the hedge, tree or shrub to be lopped or cut so as to remove the source of the danger, obstruction or interference.

---

[21] [1896] 1 Q.B. 604, at p. 608.
[22] [1932] 2 Ch. 155.
[23] See **6.2.3**.
[24] See **6.4.2**.
[25] Formerly HA 1959, s. 134(1).

The third of these categories was inserted by the Countryside and Rights of Way Act 2000, with effect from January 30, 2001.[26]

Secondly, a notice may be served under section 154(2)[27]:

". . . where it appears to a competent authority for any highway or for any other road or footpath to which the public has access –

   (a) that any hedge, tree or shrub is dead, diseased, damaged or insecurely rooted, and
   (b) that by reason of its condition it, or part of it, is likely to cause danger by falling on the highway, road or footpath".

The notice in this case is to require the hedge, tree or shrub to be cut or felled so as to remove the likelihood of danger.

The competent authority for the purpose of serving a notice under either section 154(1) or 154(2) is generally either the highway authority or the district or borough council.[28]

In either case, the notice is to be in writing, and must be served on the owner of the hedge or tree, or the occupier of the land on which it is growing, who will have to comply with it within 14 days.[29] If the notice is served on the owner, rather than the occupier, and the occupier obstructs the owner in carrying out the required works, there is a power for the owner to seek an order from the magistrates' court requiring the occupier to desist[30]; but it would usually in practice be more sensible for the authority to serve the notice on the occupier in the first place.[31]

The notice should make it clear what precisely is to be done[32]; and should only encompass enough works to remove the danger or obstruction to the highway – it may not require the carrying out of other works which might seem to the authority to be desirable. It is thus probably sensible for an authority, before serving a notice, to discuss the matter with the occupier of the land concerned and, if appropriate, the owner, so that the tree can, if possible, be treated as a whole rather than simply being cut back on one side only.

As for the meaning of the terms "lop", "cut" and "fell", Lord Esher M.R. in *Unwin v Hanson* held that the correct approach to interpretation was as follows:

"Now when we have to consider the construction of words such as this ['pruned' and 'lopped'] occurring in Acts of Parliament, we must treat the question thus: If the Act is directed to dealing with matters affecting everybody generally, the words used have the meaning attached to them in the common and ordinary use of language. . . .

"Now dealing with the cutting of trees in the country, is there not a language which all people in the country conversant with trees know and understand? It is not a question of mere forestry, but of what persons generally living in the country know and understand by the use of a particular term with respect to the cutting of trees there. Therefore, dealing with the cutting of trees in the country, this Act of Parliament uses language which everybody conversant with the cutting of trees in the country knows and understands. . . .

"Two words, 'lopping' and 'topping', which mean different things, are used in the country with respect to the cutting of trees. The Act . . . uses only one of those words,

---

[26] 2000 Act, s. 103.
[27] Formerly Highways (Miscellaneous Provisions) Act 1961, s. 10.
[28] HA 1980, s. 154(1).
[29] HA 1980, ss. 154(1),(2), 320 to 323.
[30] HA 1980, s. 304.
[31] See also *Woodard v Billericay Highway Board* (1879) 11 Ch.D. 214.
[32] See also *Woodard v Billericay Highway Board* (1879) 11 Ch.D. 214, at p. 218.

namely, 'lop'. That word is well known in the country to mean cutting off the branches of a tree; 'topping' is the cutting off its top. I think that the proper way to construe the Act, under these circumstances, is to say that was only intended to give power to cut off the branches."[33]

Fry and Lopes L.JJ. delivered concurring judgments.[34]

The notice must state that the recipient may appeal against it to a magistrates' court,[35] and from there to the Crown Court.[36] Perhaps more importantly, if the notice is not complied with, the authority may carry out the required works, and recover its expenses from the person in default,[37] – subject, again, to the (theoretical) duty to offer back the arisings to the owner of the tree.

The distinction between section 130 and section 154 is that section 30 requires an authority to take some action to remove any obstruction or danger. If that involves actually carrying out works to a tree encroaching onto the highway from neighbouring land, the authority would seem to have no power to recover the cost of those works from the owner of the tree. If, on the other hand, the authority considers the matter is less urgent, it can serve a notice on the tree owner under section 154. Unless the recipient of the notice successfully appeals against it, the result is that the cost of the required works to the tree is borne by its owner, rather than by the authority. Which procedure to use will clearly be a matter of judgment for the authority.

The existence of a power for an authority to take action under this section would only rarely if ever carry with it a duty to do so.[38] This is considered below.[39]

6.4.4 Trees and shrubs obstructing visibility at corners: section 79

As well as the more general powers under section 130 and 154 of the Highways Act 1980,[40] there is a specific procedure enabling a highway authority to prevent the view of drivers and pedestrians being obstructed by trees or shrubs growing on land at or near any corner or bend. This basically enables an authority to interfere with the private property rights of those owning land close to highways, by taking action in respect of trees and shrubs that are neither growing on the authority's land nor overhanging it.

An authority may thus serve a notice under section 79 of the 1980 Act[41]:

"(a)   on the owner or occupier of the land, directing him to alter any . . . tree, shrub or other vegetation on the land so as to cause it to conform with any requirements specified in the notice; or

---

[33] [1891] 2 Q.B. 115, CA, at p. 119.
[34] All three judges stressed that the statutory provision in question (now HA 1980, section 136) related to country matters. The site in question is now on the border of Ealing and Hounslow, in West London!
[35] HA 1980, ss. 154(3), 315, 316.
[36] HA 1980, s. 317.
[37] HA 1980, ss. 154(4), 305, 306.
[38] Stovin v Wise [1996] A.C. 923, H.L.
[39] See **6.4.6**.
[40] See **6.4.2** and **6.4.3** respectively.
[41] Formerly HA 1959, s. 81, replacing Roads Improvement Act 1925, s. 4.

(b) on every owner, lessee and occupier of the land, restraining them either absolutely or subject to such conditions as may be specified in the notice, from causing any or permitting any . . . tree, shrub or other vegetation to be . . . planted on the land".[42]

A notice under subsection (1)(a) thus requires the owner or occupier of the land to carry out works on a one-off basis, presumably to remove a problem that presently exists – either by removing the offending tree or shrub altogether, or by carrying out specified works to reduce its height or bulk. It would seem that a notice under this provision may not require further works to be carried out on a regular basis; but it would obviously be sensible for an authority serving a notice requiring the carrying out of works to a tree or shrub (as opposed to a building) to inform the recipient that a further notice would follow if the tree or shrub is allowed to grow significantly larger than the specified size. Because a notice under section 79(1)(a) is aimed at securing immediate action, it should be served on whoever is likely to carry out the works most expeditiously; but if it is for that reason served on the owner, a copy must be served on the occupier (and vice versa).[43]

A notice under subsection (1)(b) prevents anyone with any interest in the land from planting any trees or shrubs on the land – although such a restriction may be subject to conditions, so that it would presumably be possible to prevent the planting of any tree, or any shrub likely to have more than a specified height at maturity; or to prevent the planting of any tree or shrub without the prior written approval of the authority. But note that a notice may not restrict the growth of a tree or shrub, merely the planting of one. The existence of a notice under section 79(1)(b), being intended to be of permanent effect, is registrable as a local land charge.[44]

The works required by a notice under section 79 may be carried out even if they would otherwise be prohibited by the terms of a conveyance, lease or licence relating to the land concerned[45]; and the reasonable cost of them may, in any event, be recovered from the authority.[46] Further, if the carrying out of the works leads to a loss in the value of the land, the owner may seek compensation from the authority.[47]

A notice under section 79 must be in writing,[48] and comes into force immediately; it binds every subsequent owner, lessee and occupier of the land concerned.[49] A recipient may, however, serve a counter-notice on the authority, in which case the dispute shall be settled either by arbitration or in the county court, where the notice may, if appropriate, be modified.[50] Non-compliance with a notice is an offence, punishable on summary conviction by a fine of up to level 1 on the standard scale; and continuing non-compliance following conviction by a further fine of up to £2 per day.[51] Curiously, there is no provision for the authority to carry out the required works in default.

---

[42] HA 1980, s. 79(1).
[43] HA 1980, s. 79(4).
[44] Local Land Charges Act 1975; Local Land Charges Rules 1977.
[45] HA 1980, s. 79(9).
[46] HA 1980, s. 79(12), (13).
[47] HA 1980, ss. 79(11), 308, 309.
[48] HA 1980, ss. 320 to 323.
[49] HA 1980, s. 79(6).
[50] HA 1980, s. 79(7), (8).
[51] HA 1980, ss. 79(10), 310 to 314.

The consequences of a failure by a highway authority to exercise its powers under section 79 was recently considered by the House of Lords in *Stovin v Wise*[52] – albeit in the context of an obstruction to visibility at a junction caused not by a tree, but by a bank of earth topped by a fence. This is considered in a separate section,[53] as it is relevant more generally to a number of the topics discussed in this Chapter.

Finally, it may be noted that this power applies only to highways maintainable at public expense[54]; in the case of other highways, or private streets, it may still be possible to take advantage of the powers under section 154 of the 1980 Act.[55]

6.4.5 *Damage to highway by exclusion of sun and wind: section 136*

The provisions of section 136 of the Highways Act 1980[56] apply where a highway consisting of a carriageway is being damaged in consequence of the exclusion from it of sun and wind by a hedge or tree – other than a tree planted for ornament, or for shelter to a building, courtyard or hop ground.[57]

A complaint may be made to the magistrates' court either by the highway authority or, in the case of a highway not maintainable at public expense, by the person liable to maintain it.[58] The court may then by order require the owner or occupier of the land to cut, prune or plash (lay) the hedge or prune or lop the tree, so as to remove the cause of the damage – save that it may not require or authorise the cutting or pruning of a hedge except during the months of October to March.[59] "Lopping" means the removal of a branch by a vertical cut, as opposed to "topping".[60]

Non-compliance with an order under section 136 is an offence punishable on summary conviction by a fine of up to level 1 on the standard scale, and the authority or person initiating the complaint may then carry out the required works and recover the cost from the owner or occupier of the land.[61]

This provision dates from the days when carriageways (that is, roads for vehicles[62]) were unmetalled – the roads in rural Herefordshire, for example, were in many cases only surfaced with tarmac in the 1920s. In those days, roads quickly became rutted and unpassable in poor weather; and the first step in remedying this was to maximise the amount of sun and wind reaching the surface, so as to dry it out. That now applies only very rarely, if ever; and this provision is accordingly of little continuing utility.

---

[52] [1996] A.C. 323, H.L.
[53] See **6.4.6**.
[54] HA 1980, s. 79(1).
[55] See **6.4.3**.
[56] Formerly HA 1959, s. 120, replacing HA 1835, ss. 65 and 66, and Highways Acts Amendment Act 1885, ss. 1 and 2.
[57] HA 1980, s. 136(1).
[58] HA 1980, s. 136(2).
[59] HA 1980, s. 136(1), (4) (the latter subsection was amended by Wildlife and Countryside Act 1981, s. 72(13) by the insertion of the word "except"!).
[60] *Unwin v Hanson* [1891] 2 Q.B. 115, CA; see **6.4.3**.
[61] HA 1980, ss. 136(3), 310 to 314.
[62] HA 1980, s. 329.

6.4.6 *Failure to exercise discretionary powers:* Stovin v Wise

The consequences of a failure by a highway authority to exercise its powers under the Highways Act was recently considered by the House of Lords in the important case of *Stovin v Wise*.[63]

The dispute concerned an obstruction to visibility at a junction caused not by a tree but by a bank of earth topped by a fence. The highway authority (Norfolk County Council), joined as third party in the action, had been aware of the bank, and had considered taking action under section 79 of the Act,[64] but had not done so before two cars collided, due in part to the obstructed view. The question before the House was whether the existence of the power to take action under section 79 carried with it a liability in negligence for failure to act. The judge at first instance and the Court of Appeal[65] held that there was liability; the House of Lords (but only by a 3 to 2 majority) held that there was not.

Lord Nicholls of Birkenhead, dissenting, considered that a common law duty of care upon a highway authority would be to the same effect as its public law duty to act as a reasonable authority. Some statutory powers are of their nature more susceptible than others to a concurrent common law duty; and he noted that a power to remove dangers from public places must be near this end of the spectrum.[66] He also noted that:

"A highway authority is liable in damages for failing to take reasonable care to keep the highway safe. But no sound distinction can be drawn between dangers on the highway itself, where the authority has a statutory duty to act, and other dangers, where there is a statutory power but not a statutory duty. The distinction would not correspond to the realities of road safety. On the Council's argument, a highway authority would be liable if it carelessly failed to remove a dead tree fallen onto the road, but not liable if it carelessly failed to act after learning of a diseased overhanging tree liable to fall at any moment. Such a legalistic distinction does not commend itself. It would be at variance with ordinary persons' expectations and perceptions."[67]

He accordingly would have dismissed the appeal, although – significantly – even he explicitly reserved his view on what the position would be if an authority did not know, but ought to have known, of the existence of a danger.[68]

The appeal was allowed, however. Lord Hoffman, who delivered the leading speech, noted that there was no duty on a private owner of land across which ran a public right of way to maintain it in a safe condition,[69] and went on to consider whether a public authority should be under a more extensive duty. He concluded as follows:

". . . the minimum preconditions for basing a duty of care upon the existence of a statutory power, if it can be done at all, are,

- first, that it would in the circumstances have been irrational not to have exercised the power, so that there was in effect a public law duty to act, and

---

[63] [1996] A.C. 323, H.L.
[64] See **6.4.4**.
[65] [1994] 1 W.L.R. 1124, 3 All E.R. 467, CA.
[66] [1996] A.C. 323, H.L., at p. 338.
[67] [1996] A.C. 323, H.L., at p. 340.
[68] [1996] A.C. 323, H.L., at p. 341.
[69] *McGeown v Northern Ireland Housing Executive* [1995] 1 A.C. 233, per Lord Keith at p. 243; cited [1996] A.C. 323, H.L., at p. 345.

- secondly, that there are exceptional grounds for holding that the policy of the statute requires compensation to be paid to persons who suffer loss because the power was not exercised".[70]

As to the exercise of the power under section 79 of the 1980 Act, Lord Hoffman considered that it had not been unreasonable or irrational for the Council to have taken no action – even though there had been three accidents at that location. There were after all 3,500 personal injury accidents in Norfolk every year, and the Council had to make a decision as to where remedial work was most urgently required; that must be a matter for its discretion.[71]

But even if the failure to carry out the work had in this case been irrational, there was no liability to compensate those affected. It was quite clear that the junction had not been improved, even though it could have been, and the victim of this particular accident was thus treated in the same way as every other road user. To hold otherwise would be to distort the spending priorities of local authorities, by forcing them to spend more on highway improvements rather than education or social services. He concluded:

"Given the fact that the British road network largely antedates the highway authorities themselves, the court is not in a position to say what an appropriate standard of improvement would be. This must be a matter for the discretion of the authority. On the other hand, denial of liability does not leave the road user unprotected. Drivers of vehicles must take the highway network as they find it. Everyone knows that there are hazardous bends, intersections and junctions. It is primarily the duty of drivers of vehicles to take due care. And if, as in the case of Mrs Wise, they do not, there is compulsory insurance to provide compensation to the victims. There is no reason of policy or justice which requires the highway authority to be an additional defendant."[72]

This decision accordingly establishes that, at least in the case of powers to remove obstructions, or to require others to do so, there is no liability at common law for failure to act.

It therefore follows that, if a highway authority is not willing to take action under any of the discretionary powers considered above, there is little that can be done by someone adversely affected. Even sections 96 and 130 of the Act, both of which relate to duties rather than powers, are qualified – section 96 requires the authority only to take "reasonable" care,[73] and section 130 to take action only "as far as possible".[74]

And the position is even less clear with respect to hidden dangers, which are the subject of the following sections.

6.4.7 Danger to users of the highway

It has already been noted[75] that section 96 of the Highways Act 1980, which empowers public authorities to plant trees in a highway maintainable at public expense, also requires such trees to be maintained properly. This means that trees planted under section 96 (or its predecessors) must not be allowed to become an

---

[70] [1996] A.C. 323, H.L., at p. 353.
[71] [1996] A.C. 323, H.L., at p. 357.
[72] [1996] A.C. 323, H.L., at p. 358.
[73] *Morrison v Sheffield Corporation* [1917] 2 K.B. 866, CA, at p. 872; see **6.4.7**.
[74] HA 1980, s. 130(3); see **6.4.2**.
[75] See **6.4.2**.

obstruction. But it also means that they must not be allowed to become a danger to those using the highway.

This emerges from the decision of the Court of Appeal in *Morrison v Sheffield Corporation*.[76] Trees were planted by the Corporation under the powers in the predecessor legislation to section 96 of the 1980 Act,[77] and protected by iron guards with spiked tops facing outwards; and a black-out was ordered under the Defence of the Realm Regulations (it was 1916). Just over two weeks later, a pedestrian crossing the road in the pitch dark collided with one of the tree-guards, which was slightly out of perpendicular, and suffered injury. The Court of Appeal held that there was a continuing duty on the Corporation to take reasonable measures to ensure that the guards were not dangerous. Scrutton L.J. noted:

"It is said that our decision will involve a hardship upon local authorities, and will impose on them an obligation to guard or to paint every post and kerb, but in truth it only imposes an obligation to take reasonable care that what they have put in the roadway shall not become a nuisance and a danger under altered conditions."[78]

As it happens, the luckless Mr Morrison collided in the dark with a leaning tree guard. But the same duty applies to trees and shrubs; and there is no reason why the same principle should not apply. That is, the authority is under a duty to take "reasonable" care to protect users of the highway – which is of course the same standard that applies to the duty of care owed to visitors to land, under the Occupier's Liability Act 1957, and to potential victims in general.[79] Which is, no doubt, why street trees are generally pruned so as to have no branches protruding at lower levels into which hapless pedestrians might wander on dark nights (especially when the highway authority has also failed to maintain a nearby street lamp).

The Court of Appeal did, in fact, consider some years later the provision[80] in relation to trees overhanging the carriageway, in *Hale v Hants and Dorset Motor Services*.[81] A tree that had been planted by the local council, as highway authority, was allowed to grow so as to overhang the carriageway very slightly (by some 18 cm or so), so that a bus, driven very close to the kerb, hit it, resulting in injuries to some of the passengers. Lord Greene M.R. considered that it was immaterial whether the action was based on breach of statutory duty or "merely" on nuisance or negligence at common law. Either way, the authority was liable, since drivers were entitled to use the full carriageway without having to spot obstructions – particularly, as in this case, after dark.

The decision in *Hale* appears not to have been cited in *British Road Services v Slater*,[82] which also concerned a tree, growing in a highway verge, such that a branch just overhung the carriageway. Neither the Minister, as the highway authority, nor the county council, as the previous highway authority, had ever considered the tree to be a hazard, otherwise it would have been removed; nor did the local police. But it became one solely by the fortuitous circumstance that two tall lorries had to pass one another, in the dark, at precisely that spot, so that the

---

[76] [1917] 2 K.B. 866, CA.
[77] Public Health Acts Amendment Act 1890, s. 43.
[78] [1917] 2 K.B. 866, CA, at p. 872.
[79] See **5.4.1**.
[80] By then section 1 of the Roads Improvement Act 1925.
[81] (1947) 46 L.G.R. 55, [1947] 2 All E.R. 628, CA.
[82] [1964] 1 W.L.R. 498, 1 All E.R. 816, E.G. May 30.

branch caused one to shed its load, leading to the other veering off the road and being damaged.[83] Lord Parker C.J. considered that, on that basis, the owner of the adjacent land – whom he had, surprisingly, held as being capable of being responsible for the tree[84] – was not liable for the harm caused.

Of the two decisions *Hale* and *Slater*, which cannot easily be reconciled, the former would seem to be preferable. The fact that a vehicle, apparently being driven perfectly lawfully, did in fact hit the branch in each case shows that each tree was growing in such a way as to impede the reasonable use of the highway. But, presumably, the branch in *Hale* had also not come into contact with any vehicle before the bus collided with it – indeed it is likely that a branch will be cut back immediately after any serious accident of this kind, so that any branch will only ever hit one vehicle before it is removed (in all this analysis, the occasional brushing against a vehicle by the light foliage of a tree is ignored). It seems more satisfactory to require highway authorities in principle to cut back trees to allow all vehicles, even tall ones, to pass at all times – even if they do so by driving right up to the edge of the carriageway. That conclusion was also reached in the Irish case of *Lynch v Dawson*,[85] even though that case concerned a tree growing on private land.[86]

The duty under what is now section 96(6) of the 1980 Act strictly applies only in relation to trees planted under section 96 and its predecessors. However, the requirement (following *Morrison*) to take "reasonable" care is, unsurprisingly, the same as the common law duty of care owed to "neighbours" generally, following subsequent decisions such as *Donoghue v Stevenson*.[87] And the observations of the court in *Hale* confirm that the statutory duty adds little to the duty at common law. There is therefore no need for a highway authority to consider when or by whom the tree in question was planted; and the usual rules as to liability in negligence will apply to determine its liability.[88]

Thus, in the earlier Scottish case of *Mackie v Dumbartonshire County Council*, which related to a tree falling as a result of works carried out a year previously by the road authority, the action was based in negligence, without reference to any duty under statute. And in *British Road Services v Slater*,[89] the action was founded on nuisance and negligence – with, surprisingly, no claim against the highway authority.

In *Chapman v Barking and Dagenham LBC*,[90] a claim was made against the highway authority in relation to a street tree that was found to have been diseased at the time it shed a branch and caused harm. It succeeded in negligence, and probably in nuisance too, on the basis that the authority had failed to carry out a sufficient (or indeed any) inspection of the tree[91]; but the court specifically declined to resolve the question as to whether the Council was also liable under section 41 of the 1980 Act, by failure to maintain the highway.

---

[83] [1964] 1 W.L.R. 498, at p. 504.
[84] See **6.2.4**.
[85] [1946] I.R. 504.
[86] See **6.6.2**.
[87] [1932] A.C. 562, H.L.; see **5.4.1**.
[88] See **Chapter 5**; in particular **5.5**.
[89] [1964] 1 W.L.R. 498, 1 All E.R. 816, E.G. May 30.
[90] [1997] 2 EGLR 141, upheld in CA (1998) unreported.
[91] See **5.7.4**.

6.4.8 Removal of fallen branches and trees

Once a branch, or a whole tree, has fallen onto the highway, the highway authority is under a duty to remove it.[92] It may also take reasonable steps to warn users of the highway of the obstruction (such as by lights, signs and fences).[93] It has already been noted that the reported cases where motorists and pedestrians were hit by falling trees and branches are outnumbered by those where motorists, particularly motor-cyclists, drove into ones that had already fallen.[94]

If the authority fails to take action, anyone may make a complaint to a magistrates' court, which may then order the authority to act within such time (not less than 24 hours) as the court thinks reasonable in all the circumstances.[95] In deciding what (if any) order to make, the court should have regard in particular to the character of the highway concerned, the nature of the obstruction and the resources for the time being available to the authority.[96] As might be expected, therefore, the court is unlikely to be too excited about a small branch across a remote country lane after a gale has caused widespread havoc.

Where the obstruction is the fault of the owner of the tree, the authority may recover from him or her the cost of removing it – but not where the owner has taken reasonable care to ensure that the tree did not cause an obstruction.[97] This does not mean that the owner is under a duty to get on and remove the tree before the authority's contractors arrive, merely that if the falling of the tree was the fault of the owner,[97a] the owner will also have to bear the cost of removing it – as well as any damages that may be payable in any action by anyone harmed by its fall. Where a tree is sound and healthy, therefore, but falls or sheds a branch due to abnormally high winds, the owner is under no liability to reimburse the authority.[98]

Where someone other than the highway authority is liable to maintain the highway in question, that person is under a similar duty to remove obstructions.[99]

Of course, these duties also apply where debris falls onto the highway as a result of works carried out by the highway authority itself (in the exercise of its general duty under section 130 of the Act) or by the owner of a tree on neighbouring land.

6.4.9 Conclusion

It seems that the consensus of judicial authority (with the notable exception of *British Road Services v Slater*[1]) is that it is the highway authority, not the owner of adjacent land, that is responsible for trees growing on the highway.

Further, that authority has a duty, both at common law in negligence and under the 1980 Act,[2] to ensure that such trees do not become either an obstruction or a danger (in so far as the two can be distinguished) to those making reasonable

---

[92] HA 1980, s. 150(1); formerly HA 1959, s. 129.
[93] HA 1980, s. 150(4)(a); formerly Highways (Miscellaneous Provisions) Act 1961, section 9(1).
[94] See **5.8.6**.
[95] HA 1980, s. 150(2).
[96] HA 1980, s. 150(3).
[97] HA 1980, s. 150(4)(c).
[97a] As to which, see **6.4.7**.
[98] *Williams v Devon County Council* (1966) 200 E.G. 943, 65 L.G.R. 119.
[99] HA 1980, s. 150(6).
[1]   [1964] 1 W.L.R. 498.
[2]   HA 1980, ss. 96 and 130.

use of the highway. However, that duty is to take reasonable care, which means that the authority does not have to inspect every tree in its area every day, to check for possible defects and cut back every twig that might extend into the path of oncoming buses in a high wind.

In addition to that duty, there are also powers, which should be exercised reasonably,[3] in relation to trees and shrubs that either encroach onto the highway from neighbouring land[4] or impede visibility at junctions and bends.[5]

As with so many matters relating to trees, the choice as to how and when to exercise these duties and powers will in practice be a matter of assessing priorities, not losing sight of competing claims on resources.

It will take account of local circumstances. So, for example, trees are normally pruned to allow for the passage of vehicles, but the height clearance will vary as between a major road or bus route (to allow the passage of a double-decker bus) and a housing estate road (to allow a dustcart). And the choice will take account, too, of changing times – thus in one Irish case the court noted that the County Council had not required the owners of adjacent land to lop overhanging branches during the period of emergency caused by the war; on the other hand, it later noted that the size of lorries in common use had increased:

"Although the principles of the Common Law remain the same, the application of these principles must move with the times."[6]

That approach remains as valid now as it was half a century ago.

Finally, it may be noted that in some cases a highway authority such as a county council delegates the exercise of its various functions to another body, such as a district or borough council.[7] Where the agreement governing such an arrangement so provides, this delegation may extend to the planting of new trees and/or management of existing trees on and adjacent to the highways in the area concerned. In such a case, it is probable that all the responsibilities of the highway authority are either passed to or at least shared with that other council. Certainly, the council actually carrying out the maintenance of highway trees may be held responsible for the results of their encroachment onto neighbouring land,[8] and there seems no reason not to follow the same approach in relation to other functions transferred in this way.

6.5 Encroachment of highway trees onto adjacent land

6.5.1 Introduction

Trees are frequently planted, or allowed to grow, on highway land – and, in particular, on footways or on the grass verges adjacent to them. Buildings, especially in urban areas, are often placed at the front of sites, close to or immediately adjoining the back edge of the footway or verge. It is therefore not at

---

[3]   *Stovin v Wise* [1996] A.C. 323, H.L., at p. 357.
[4]   HA 1980, s. 154.
[5]   HA 1980, s. 79.
[6]   *Lynch v Dawson* [1946] I.R. 504.
[7]   Using powers under Local Government Act 1972, s. 101.
[8]   *LE Jones (Insurance Brokers) Ltd v Portsmouth City Council*, Q.B.D. Technology and Construction Court, March 11, 2002, unreported; see also **6.5.3**.

all surprising that highway trees often cause problems for the owners and occupiers of adjacent property.

It has already been noted that section 96 of the Highways Act 1980, which empowers public authorities to plant trees in a highway maintainable at public expense, also requires that trees planted under that section shall not be planted or allowed to remain "so as to be a nuisance or injurious to the owner or occupier of premises adjacent to the highway".[9]

Where the branches or trunk of a highway tree intrude into the airspace above a neighbouring property, or its roots grow into the soil of such a property, that constitutes a nuisance at common law. The general provisions outlined in **Chapter 3** will thus apply as in any other case of encroachment. This section simply summarises the position.

6.5.2 Encroaching branches and trunks

Where the branches of highway trees overhang adjacent property, they will of course cause all the usual problems such as blocking out light, dropping leaves which may in turn block gutters, and so on.[10] Such problems do not happen overnight, however, but gradually, as the trees grow; and by definition they are perfectly obvious to all. In practice, therefore, the remedy lies in the hands of the property owner, who is perfectly entitled to abate the nuisance[11] by simply cutting back the offending branches to the boundary.

However, in the case of highway trees, even more than trees overhanging from other types of property, it is always advisable to consult the owner, the highway authority, before taking any action other than the most trivial pruning.[12] The right to abatement does not do away with the duty of care to all who may be affected – which in this case may include all those using the highway. And the highway authority may therefore be willing – it may even prefer – to do the work itself, possibly as part of its routine programme of street tree maintenance.[13]

And sometimes the encroachment may take the form of a tree growing in such a way as to damage the wall or fence on the boundary between the highway and the neighbouring property. This was considered by the Court of Appeal in *Elliott v Islington LBC*,[14] in which an injunction was granted requiring the offending tree to be removed. In that case, the tree was itself on highway land, encroaching onto a neighbouring garden; but the principles would seem to apply equally to a tree on neighbouring land encroaching onto the highway.

6.5.3 Encroaching roots

Encroachment by roots is likely to be more problematic, partly because they are – normally – invisible, and partly because they may cause very substantial (and expensive) damage.

The liability in nuisance in respect of damage caused, or likely to be caused, by the roots of street trees is in principle as in the case of any other trees. This has been analysed fully at **3.5**; and of course many of the cases noted there concerned

---

[9] HA 1980, s. 96(6), replacing HA 1959, s. 82(5); **6.3.1**.
[10] See **3.4.1**.
[11] See **3.6**.
[12] See **3.6.3**.
[13] Even if not necessarily to pay for it!
[14] [1991] 1 EGLR 167, CA; see **3.8.3** for a full discussion.

street trees. The position can perhaps best be summed up in the dictum of Stocker J., who decided *Solloway v Hampshire County Council* at first instance:

"The duty in respect of the nuisance created by the roots arises if the encroachment of the roots is known, or ought to be known, to the owner, occupier or other person responsible for the tree and its maintenance, if the encroachment is such as to give rise to a reasonably foreseeable risk that such encroachment will cause damage."[15]

The questions of causation and foreseeability have already been considered.[16]

There is, however, still the question of who is "the owner, occupier or other person responsible for the tree and its maintenance" in the case of a tree growing on highway land. In the early cases,[17] it was simply assumed that the highway authority was responsible for any harm caused by the roots of street trees, subject to issues such as causation and quantification of damages.

But the issue was raised explicitly at first instance in *Solloway*, which led Stocker J. to conclude:

"In my view, the issue with regard to the position of the defendants [the highway authority] is whether or not they have sufficient interest in and control over the trees to make them responsible for the nuisance created by it. In my judgment, they have. Even if it be correct (and for my part, in modern conditions I rather doubt the proposition) that a highway authority does not own the trees planted in the pavement or the verges where they alone have power to maintain the trees and, if damage is caused, to cut them down, then this is sufficient control over the tree to render them liable for nuisance if such occurs.. . . .

"I can see no valid reason to suppose that such a duty does not exist, either under the statute [or] independently of it, where the trees are taken over by the highway authority which previously existed in the highway. It seems to me that the legislation cannot be intended to make the highway authority liable for nuisance to adjoining owners arising from trees planted by them, but not for a similar nuisance arising from trees for which they become liable under the 1961 Act."[18]

That conclusion was not questioned when the case proceeded to the Court of Appeal,[19] even though the decision of Stocker J. was overturned on other grounds; and his approach has been followed in several subsequent cases relating to harm caused by the roots of highway trees,[20] including (at least by implication) that of the Court of Appeal in *Hurst v Humberside County Council*.[21]

The question of ownership of highway trees has already been considered at length[22]; and it is significant that most of the more recent cases raising the issue of ownership arose in the context of root damage. It is not necessary to repeat that analysis here, save to re-emphasise that the decision in *Hurst* – that the property in all highway trees, regardless of when or by whom they were planted, or whether indeed they were self-seeded, rests in the highway authority – means that in any

---

[15] *Solloway v Hampshire County Council* (1980), unreported, per Stocker J., approved by Court of Appeal (1981) 79 L.G.R. 449, at p. 452, [1981] 1 EGLR 129, at p. 130B.

[16] See **3.5.3** and **3.5.4**.

[17] *Mayer v Deptford & Lewisham Councils* (1959) 173 E.G. 961, *Pettifer v Cheshunt UDC* (1970) 216 E.G. 1508, and *Masters v Brent LBC* [1978] 1 EGLR 128.

[18] Transcript, p. 29; quoted in *Russell v Barnet LBC* [1984] 2 EGLR 44, at p. 49.

[19] (1981) 79 L.G.R. 449, CA.

[20] *Nagioff v Barnet LBC* (1981), unreported (county court); *Russell v Barnet LBC* [1984] 2 EGLR 44; and *Low v Haddock* [1985] 2 EGLR 247.

[21] [1997] 2 EGLR 164, CA; see **6.2.5**.

[22] See **6.2.3** to **6.2.5**.

action for root damage alleged to be caused by a tree growing in the highway, the defendant should be the highway authority.[23]

The only qualification to that is that where, as sometimes occurs, the highway authority delegates to another council its functions under the Highways Act, and where the agreement explicitly transfers responsibility for (amongst other things) the routine maintenance of highway trees, that other council may be sued in respect of harm caused by such trees encroaching onto neighbouring land.[24]

6.5.4 Liability under the Highways Act 1980

In some of the cases, it has been suggested that highway authorities might be liable for harm due to the roots of street trees not just in nuisance but also by virtue of section 96 of the Highways Act 1980. This provision, which empowers authorities to plant and maintain trees in highways, has been considered above.[25] It will be noted that it requires authorities not just to ensure that trees planted under section 96 do not hinder the use of the highway, but also to prevent any such tree from being a nuisance or injurious to the owner or occupier of premises adjacent to the highway.[26]

It was pointed out in *Paterson v Humberside County Council*[27] that any duty that might exist under section 96 in relation to nuisance to adjacent land would only apply to trees planted under the provisions of the section, referred to in *Hurst v Hampshire County Council*[28] as "planted trees"; and it has generally been supposed that the duty under the common law was co-terminous with that under the statute. On the other hand, the court in *Hurst* specifically left open the question of whether, in an action for breach of statutory duty relating to harm caused by planted trees, it would be necessary to demonstrate that the harm had been foreseeable.[29]

It follows that, where the tree causing harm was, or might have been, planted later than 1890 in an urban area, or 1925 elsewhere, it may be worth a claimant basing any claim on breach of statutory duty as well as nuisance, as that will maximise the chances of success in the event that the highway authority is able to show that the harm was not reasonably foreseeable (as in *Solloway v Hampshire County Council*[30]).

6.6 Trees on land adjacent to highway

6.6.1 Ownership and responsibility

Trees on land adjacent to a highway are, obviously, owned by the owner of that land. The only feature of note relates to the parts of such trees that overhang the highway.

---

[23] See **6.1.3**.
[24] *LE Jones (Insurance Brokers) Ltd v Portsmouth City Council*, Q.B.D. Technology and Construction Court, March 11, 2002, unreported.
[25] See **6.3.1** and **6.4.2** and **6.4.7**.
[26] HA 1980, s. 96(6).
[27] (1995) 12 Const L.J. 64, at p. 71.
[28] [1997] 2 EGLR 164, CA, at p. 166F.
[29] [1997] 2 EGLR 164, CA, at p. 168H.
[30] (1980), unreported, per Stocker J., approved by Court of Appeal (1981) 79 L.G.R. 449, [1981] 1 EGLR 129.

The usual rule is that a tree that is growing on A's land is owned by A, even if its branches or roots grow over or under neighbouring land owned by B – subject to B's right to abate the resulting nuisance by cutting back the encroaching branches or roots to the boundary. That common law right of abatement on the part of B arises not least, of course, because B has absolute ownership of the airspace above his land.

However, it would seem to follow from the decision in *Wandsworth Board of Works v United Telephone Company*[31] that the "ownership" of the airspace above a highway is not absolute, and is limited to that extent of airspace which is "the ordinary space occupied by men or things, which use the street as a street". It follows that a highway authority has no absolute right to take abatement action in respect of encroaching branches or roots, but only to do so to the extent that they are causing a danger to those using the highway. In practice, where such a branch or tree is either a hindrance or a danger, specific statutory powers are granted to the authority.[32]

In the subsequent case of *Reynolds v Presteign UDC*,[33] it was pointed out that a highway authority had a statutory duty to prevent the obstruction of public rights of way,[34] and the view was expressed that it would be in general desirable that an authority should exercise that duty with caution.[35] However, it was held that it did still have a residual common law right of abatement – as had then been recently established by the House of Lords in the context of private land, in *Lemmon v Webb*.[36] The Council had therefore acted correctly in cutting back some hedges and removing others where they had become an obstruction to the highway; although it would have been in some difficulty if the owner of the hedges had been able to prove that they were not an obstruction.

6.6.2 Encroachment by trees and hedges onto the highway

Trees, bushes and hedges growing on land adjacent to a highway will frequently start to encroach onto the highway – in practice, either by roots growing into the subsoil beneath the finished surface of the highway or by branches and foliage extending into the airspace above that surface. That will frequently cause no problems for a while, as pedestrians will walk round the obstacle created, and vehicles will either avoid it or brush past – sustaining, in either case, at most a few minor scratches.

However, if no remedial action is taken, sooner or later a more serious problem will occur, when the tree or hedge causes a more substantial obstruction and, in turn, a real danger. At that point the highway authority has power to act. In theory, it might be possible for an authority to enter into litigation against the tree owner in nuisance; in practice, however, it is much more likely to use one or more of its statutory powers to achieve the required result. The various powers available to it in this regard have been considered at length[37]; see in particular the earlier discussion of the duty laid upon the highway authority to remove

---

[31] (1884) 13 Q.B.D. 904; see **6.2.1**.
[32] See **6.4**.
[33] [1896] 1 Q.B. 604.
[34] Under s. 26(1) of the Local Government Act 1894.
[35] See **6.4.2**.
[36] [1895] A.C. 1; see **3.6.1**.
[37] See **6.4**.

obstructions to the highway, under what is now section 130 of the Highways Act 1980.[38]

Alternatively, a motorist or pedestrian may take action to bring about the removal of an obstacle. Such action can be taken against the highway authority, alleging a failure to carry out its statutory duty, or against the owner of the tree, in nuisance. It is of course possible that in the first case a court may find that the authority had not acted unreasonably in failing to exercise its duty, which is only to prevent obstructions "as far as possible", or its powers.[39] If the owner is sued, it may be possible to establish liability (as in the Irish case of *Lynch v Dawson*[40]), but the risk is that the victory will prove fruitless if the owner proves to have no funds.

Such litigation is only ever likely to be started following the occurrence of actual damage, such as a lorry hitting an overhanging branch,[41] or a collision between two cars as a result of reduced visibility caused by a tree or hedge. It is therefore greatly preferable for the highway authority to act – possibly at the instigation of the tree owner – before such damage occurs.

In addition, it should be noted that the powers of certain statutory undertakers[42] apply to "any" tree, and not just one growing on highway land. It follows that a telecommunications operator may require a tree to be lopped where it is obstructing wires, poles and other apparatus, or to enable such items to be erected.[43] Similar but more extensive powers are available to public electricity suppliers, in that they may require branches to be lopped or roots to be cut back where they are obstructing plant.[44]

In practice, of course, rather than wait for action to be taken by highway authorities or statutory undertakers, let alone for damage to occur, it is almost always best for the owners of land bordering highways to keep any trees and hedges under control themselves, so that they do not become a problem. As to the precautions to be taken in carrying out such works, this is considered later.[45]

6.6.3 Trees falling onto the highway

Much less common, but much more dramatic, than a mere obstruction is where a tree or a branch growing on neighbouring land falls onto the highway, and either hits something or someone or is not removed before someone drives into it.

From the point of view of the tree owner, the liability relating to trees falling onto a highway is no different to that relating to trees falling onto any other land (including that on which the tree is growing) where the use of that land is such that there is a high risk of harm. A tree owner should thus take equal care in relation to trees close to boundaries with schools, parks, railways or roads.

However, the great majority of the decided cases that have considered the liability arising in such situations, which have already been considered at length in **Chapter 5**,[46] have in fact concerned trees adjacent to highways. It is perhaps

---

[38] See **6.4.2**; and in particular *Stillwell v New Windsor Corporation* [1932] 2 Ch. 155.
[39] As in *Stovin v Wise* [1996] A.C. 923, H.L.
[40] [1946] I.R. 504.
[41] As in *Lynch v Dawson* [1946] I.R. 504.
[42] Considered in more detail in **Chapter 7**.
[43] Telecommunications Act 1984, s. 10 and Sched. 2, paragraph 19.
[44] Electricity Act 1989, s. 10 and Sched. 4, paragraph 9.
[45] See **Chapter 9**.
[46] See **5.3.2** in particular.

relevant, therefore, to note that, of the cases cited in that Chapter, only two[47] related to trees actually growing on highway land[48]; the remaining ten all related to trees or branches falling from on adjacent land. In some cases they actually hit a person or a vehicle,[49] and in others they caused a vehicle to collide with the fallen branches before they had been cleared out of the way.[50] The tree owner was found to be liable in six cases.

Because such "accidents" are very traumatic for all concerned, whether or not legal liability is actually established (and very expensive if it is), it is particularly important for owners of trees close to highways to have them regularly inspected; and the more heavily used the highway, the more frequent (and thorough) should be the inspection.

It is also for that reason that a highway authority has special powers, under section 154 of the Highways Act 1980, in relation to any tree that seems to the authority to be dead, diseased, damaged or insecurely rooted, such that all or part of it is likely to fall onto a highway, road or footpath. It may in those circumstances serve a notice requiring the tree or shrub to be felled so as to remove the likelihood of danger; and if the required works are not done, the authority may enter the land and carry them out itself – at the owner's expense.[51]

Once again, therefore, rather than waiting for the service of such a notice, owners should take action themselves to remove danger. If a tree does fall or shed a branch, and it is found that the cause was a defect that would have been apparent upon a reasonable inspection, it will not assist the owner to point to the failure of the authority to serve a notice.

[47] *Mackie v Dumbartonshire* (1927) 91 J.P. 158, H.L. and *Chapman v Barking and Dagenham LBC* [1997] 2 EGLR 141.
[48] See also **6.4.7**.
[49] *Noble v Harrison* [1926] 2 K.B. 332; *Kent v Marquis of Bristol* (1940), unreported; *Brown v Harrison* (1947) 177 L.T. 281, CA; *Caminer v Northern & London Investment Trust* [1951] A.C. 88, H.L., upholding [1049] 2 K.B. 64, CA; *Quinn v Scott* [1964] 1 W.L.R. 1004, 2 All E.R. 588.
[50] *Hudson v Bray* [1917] 1 K.B. 520; *Cunliffe v Bankes* [1945] 1 All E.R. 459; *Sheen v Arden* (1946), unreported; *Lambourn v London Brick Co* (1950) 156 E.G. 146; *Lane v Tredegar Estate Trustees* (1954) E.G., November 27, 1954.
[51] See **6.4.3**.

Chapter 7

Trees and Statutory Undertakers

7.1 Introduction

One significant source of potential conflict is between trees and cables, pipes and sewers. Overhead wires (transmitting either electric power or telecommunications) and their supports may become tangled with branches of trees, leading to both being damaged. And roots similarly cause problems to underground cables. This has long been recognised, and the statutory codes governing electricity and telecommunications providers each contain a system to prevent excessive harm being caused, and to protect trees of special value. These provisions are described at **7.2**.

Possibly more of a problem in theory, because they are invisible, subterranean sewers and other pipes (for drainage, water supply, other liquids or gas) may damage or be damaged by the roots of trees and shrubs. However, this seems to be less explicitly dealt with by the law – perhaps because the operators of the relevant utilities are usually concerned solely with getting the system repaired as soon as possible, without time for the service of notices and counter-notices.

In many cases these potential conflicts will relate to highway trees, which have been considered in more detail in **Chapter 6**; but cables and pipes cross private land too, and the same principles will apply (save that they will do so in relation to private landowners rather than highway authorities).

And, finally, there are specific mechanisms provided by the relevant legislation (set out at **7.3**) to prevent trees getting in the way of trains and aeroplanes.

These various provisions will not often be come across in practice, since they are all designed to prevent problems occurring, or to enable them to be rectified before they become too serious; and those in the relevant industries will in practice, rightly, get on and sort out such difficulties without recourse to lawyers. But it is perhaps as well, if only for sake of completeness, to describe them all briefly.

A further source of difficulties is trees or branches blocking watercourses and drainage channels. This, too, is the subject of special statutory provisions, but since such problems are likely to occur principally in the context of works being carried out to trees, they are described later.[1]

---

[1] See **9.4.3**.

7.2 Trees, cables and pipes

7.2.1 Branches and roots affecting electricity equipment

It is obvious that trees are likely to interfere with overhead electricity cables, both existing and proposed – see *Buckland v Guildford Gas Light & Coke Co*[1a] for a particularly gruesome case of a child climbing a tree and coming into contact with an electricity cable. Unsurprisingly, therefore, there has for many years been a provision whereby those responsible were empowered to remove trees or branches causing, or likely to cause, such problems – either to the equipment itself or to those coming into contact with it.

The relevant provisions used to be contained in section 34 of the Electricity (Supply) Act 1926; they were carried forward, largely unaltered, into the code, found as Schedule 4 to the Electricity Act 1989, which is applied to any public electricity supplier or holder of a licence to transmit electricity.[2] The procedure relating to problems caused by trees is at paragraph 9 of Schedule 4. It applies:

". . . where any tree is or will be in such close proximity to an electric line or electrical plant which is kept installed or is being or is to be installed by a licence holder as –

(a) to obstruct or interfere with the installation, maintenance or working of the lines or plant; or
(b) to constitute an unacceptable source of danger (whether to children or to other persons) . . .".[3]

From this it will be noted that the potential obstruction, interference or danger may be caused by a tree, not just by its branches. Interference by tree roots with subterranean cables is thus covered. It also relates to any trees, wherever they are growing, and not simply to those with branches overhanging highways. And "tree" is defined to include "shrub",[4] so that in effect all vegetation of any consequence is covered.

Where a tree is causing or is likely to cause such obstruction, interference or danger, the licence holder may serve a notice on the occupier of the land on which the tree is growing, requiring him or her to fell or lop it or cut back its roots so as to remove the problem.[5] The notice must also offer up-front to pay any expenses incurred in complying with it – there is, in other words, no need to apply for compensation after the works have been carried out. A copy of the notice must also be served on the owner, where he or she is not also the occupier.[6] It may also be noted that the notice can require the tree to be felled, as well as simply lopped, or a shrub to be uprooted. It can also require the roots of a tree or shrub to be cut back; although this may cause instability, and such a requirement should only be imposed after careful research into the likely effects of the proposed works on the above-ground portion of the tree.

On receipt of such a notice, the occupier of the land then has a 21-day period within which either:

[1a] [1948] 1 K.B. 321; and see **5.6.12**.
[2] Electricity Act 1989, s. 10(1).
[3] 1989 Act, Sched. 4, para. 9(1).
[4] 1989 Act, Sched. 4, para. 9(8).
[5] 1989 Act, Sched. 4, para. 9(2).
[6] 1989 Act, Sched. 4, para. 9(3).

- to carry out the required works, or
- to give the operator a counter-notice objecting to the requirement.

If by the end of that period neither has happened, the operator may itself cause the necessary works to be carried out without further ado.[7] If the recipient of a notice has objected to the required works and served a counter-notice on the operator, the matter is to be referred to the Secretary of State (not to the court).[8] The Secretary of State on such a reference may confirm or reject the notice, after holding an inquiry if either the operator or the owner requires one, and determine how the relevant expenses are to be paid – and may in particular empower the operator to carry out the works.[9]

The operator, once authorised to do the works, must carry them out in accordance with good arboricultural practice, and in such a way as to cause minimum damage to any tree, fence or hedge (or any growing crops). It must remove felled trees or shrubs, lopped branches and root cuttings as required by the owner, and must make good any consequential damage.[10] No compensation is payable, other than the reimbursement of any expenses incurred.

7.2.2 Branches affecting telecommunications equipment

A somewhat similar statutory provision relates to the interference by trees with telecommunications equipment, save that for some reason its scope is considerably narrower, and the details are somewhat more loosely drafted.

Where a company is authorised to run a telecommunications system, it will be given a licence under the Telecommunications Act 1984.[11] Almost all such licences will apply the telecommunications code,[12] subject to such exceptions and conditions as may be required to ensure:

"(a) that the physical environment is protected, and in particular that natural beauty and amenity of the countryside is conserved,
(b) that there is no greater damage to streets or interference with traffic than is reasonably necessary; and
(c) that funds are available for meeting any liabilities which may arise from the exercise of rights conferred by or in accordance with the code".[13]

All of those clearly have relevance in the context of trees.

The code, which is set out at Schedule 2 to the 1984 Act, essentially provides a code of practice for enabling the operator of a telecommunications system to deal effectively with a variety of commonly occurring practical problems. One such problem is ensuring that trees do not impede the efficient operation of the system; the provisions designed to achieve that are at paragraph 19 of Schedule 2 to the Act.

The provisions of the code are, however, surprisingly limited in scope. They

[7] 1989 Act, Sched. 4, para. 9(4).
[8] 1989 Act, Sched. 4, para. 9(5).
[9] 1989 Act, Sched. 4, para. 9(6).
[10] 1989 Act, Sched. 4, para. 9(7). See *Planning Overhead Power Line Routes*, Carruthers, 1987, for an indication of how these powers can be used in practice.
[11] Telecommunications Act 1984, s. 7.
[12] 1984 Act, s. 10(1).
[13] 1984, s. 10(4)

apply only where a tree overhangs a street, and obstructs or interferes with the working of any existing telecommunication apparatus, or is considered likely to obstruct or interfere with any such apparatus that the operator is about to install.[14] "Telecommunication apparatus" is defined so as to include any apparatus constructed or adapted for transmitting messages[15]; any line (that is, any wire, cable, tube, pipe or other similar thing) designed or adapted for use in connection with a telecommunications system, and any structure, pole or other thing supporting or carrying such apparatus.[16] "Street" means the whole or any part of any highway, road, lane, footway, alley, passage, square, court or other land laid out as a way.[17]

Where the code does apply, the operator may serve a notice on the occupier of the land on which the tree is growing, requiring the tree to be lopped so as to prevent the obstruction or interference.[18] "Lopping" a tree presumably has the same meaning as it does in section 136 of the Highways Act 1980[19]; that is, it means making a lateral cut so as to remove or shorten a branch, as opposed to "topping" a tree by removing the upper part of its growth, including part of its central stem or trunk.[20] A notice may not require a tree to be felled.

On receipt of such a notice, the occupier of the land then has a 28-day period (not 21 days as with the electricity code) within which either:

- to carry out the required works, or

- to give the operator a counter-notice objecting to the requirement.

If by the end of that period neither has happened, the operator may itself cause the tree to be lopped without further ado.[21] Where the recipient of a notice objects to the requirement to lop the tree (the most obvious basis for such an objection being that the required work is not necessary), and serves a counter-notice on the operator, the original notice takes effect only once it has been confirmed by an order of the court.[22] If such an order is indeed made, but is not complied with, the operator may again carry out the works. Either way, the operator must carry out the work in a husband-like manner, and in such a way as to cause the minimum damage to the tree.[23]

If works are carried out as required by the original notice, either by the occupier of the land or by the telecommunications operator, and if anyone suffers loss as a result (such as a diminution in the value of land), or incurs expenses in complying with it, the operator must pay that person "such compensation . . . as it thinks fit",[24] which seems a curiously imprecise piece of drafting.

The result of these provisions is that, where the branch of a tree is interfering with an existing or proposed telephone pole or wire on or over a street – but not, it

---

[14] 1984 Act, Sched. 2, para. 19(1).
[15] 1984 Act, s. 4(3).
[16] 1984 Act, Sched. 2, para. 1(1).
[17] 1984 Act, Sched. 2, para. 1(1), as amended by New Road and Street Works Act 1991, Sched. 8; 1991 Act, s. 48(1).
[18] 1984 Act, Sched. 2, para. 19(1).
[19] See **6.4.3**.
[20] *Unwin v Hanson* [1891] 2 Q.B. 115.
[21] 1984 Act, Sched. 2, para. 19(3).
[22] 1984 Act, Sched. 2, para. 19(2).
[23] 1984 Act, Sched. 2, para. 19(4).
[24] 1984 Act, Sched. 2, para. 19(5).

should be noted, where a root is interfering with a subterranean cable – the operator can take action to remove the problem, subject to the payment of at least some compensation.

In other cases, such as where a pole or wire is on or over a private garden or other land, presumably the operator is reduced to negotiating with the owner. It might well be that in those circumstances an operator would endeavour to be guided by the code on a non-statutory basis; and the landowner would then be well advised to do the same.

7.2.3 Pipes and sewers

By contrast with the well-established codes relating to above-ground cables, there appears to be no explicit powers for those charged with installing and maintaining underground pipelines (notably for the carriage of gas, water and sewage) to require works to be carried out to tree roots considered to be causing a danger to the pipework.

It may be possible for the owner of a pipe (whether for water supply or drainage) to mount an action in nuisance against the owner of any tree that is allowed to get so large that its roots cause damage to the pipe.

The Gas Act 1986 lays a duty on gas suppliers to maintain pipes,[25] although that does not explicitly authorise the removal of any roots casing damage. It also provides that it is an offence, attracting on summary conviction a fine of up to level 3 on the standard scale, to injure by culpable negligence any gas fitting or service pipe.[26] The latter could in theory provide the basis for a criminal prosecution where the owner of a tree allows its roots to grow so as to damage a pipe; but it is much more likely that the gas supplier will simply get on with the necessary works without further ado. In either case, it is of course important for anyone carrying out such works to ensure that any roots discovered are not cut back to such an extent as to lead to serious instability in the tree, as that could itself lead to an action against the supplier.

7.2.4 Underground cables and pipes: codes of practice

In many cases, where a statutory undertaker carries out works to underground cables and pipes, they will be within highway land, and not infrequently underneath footways. Unfortunately, footways are of course where street trees are almost always found, and it is therefore no surprise that roots are often found alongside cables and pipes.

In order to avoid some of the more frequently occurring problems relating to the carrying out of works to the apparatus of statutory undertakers in streets, the Secretary of State has power under the New Roads and Street Works Act 1991 to issue various codes of practice. Where such a code has been complied with, that will be sufficient to prove that the statutory undertaker has complied with its duties under the relevant section of the Act.[27] Several of these codes contain provisions that are relevant to trees.

The relevant codes issued to date include the following:

---

[25] Gas Act 1986, Sched. 2B, para. 25.
[26] 1986 Act, Sched. 2B, para. 10, inserted by Gas Act 1995, Sched. 2.
[27] See, for example, 1991 Act, s. 71(4).

- *Co-ordination of Street Works and Works for Road Purposes*[28];
- *Specification for the Re-instatement of Openings in Highways*[29];
- *Safety at Street Works and Road Works*[30]; and
- *Code of Practice for Inspections.*[31]

Also relevant will be some of the publications of the National Joint Utilities Group (NJUG), in particular Number 10, *Guidelines for the Planning, Installation and Maintenance of Utility Services in Proximity to Trees*,[32] and the code of practice on the need for consultation and publicity to be undertaken on a non-statutory basis by planning authorities in relation to development by statutory undertakers, at Appendix B to Department of the Environment Circular 9/95. The main points of these two documents are summarised at Annex 4 to the *DETR Guide*.[33]

7.2.5 General environmental duties

Many statutory undertakers and similar bodies – in particular, those relating to water, drainage, harbours, electricity, telecommunications and coal – are subject to general duties, under a wide range of statutes, to have regard to environmental matters, which would obviously include trees.

These duties are most likely to be of relevance in the context of trees and woodlands of particular value. They are accordingly briefly noted in **Chapter 15**.[34]

7.3 Railways and airfields

7.3.1 Trees likely to endanger railways

Where a tree is growing near a railway, and is in danger of falling onto it so as to obstruct rail traffic, the company which works such railway may make a complaint to the local magistrates under the Regulation of Railways Act 1868[35]; and the magistrates may order the tree to be removed or otherwise dealt with. The order may also require the company to pay compensation. In the context of national railways, the company that could take action under the Act would now seem to be Railtrack, rather than the train operating companies.

This provision, which is still in force, applies to any railway – whether owned by Railtrack, London Underground, or another body. It is unlikely to be used much in practice, but it may provide a useful back-up for railway operators seeking to have trees removed by agreement, in their negotiations with intransigent owners of neighbouring land.

[28] HMSO, ISBN 0-11-551162-8, £7.50, authorised under the New Roads and Street Works Act 1991, s. 59.
[29] HMSO, ISBN 0-11-551143-1, £5.95, authorised under 1991 Act, s. 71.
[30] HMSO, ISBN 0-11-551144-X, £3.95, authorised under 1991 Act, s. 65.
[31] HMSO, ISBN 0-11-551148-2, £3.15, authorised under 1991 Act, s. 71.
[32] April 1995, available from NJUG at 30 Millbank, London SW1P 4RD.
[33] *Tree Preservation Orders: a Guide to the Law and Good Practice*, DETR, 2000 (see **16.2.6**).
[34] See **15.11**.
[35] 1868 Act, s. 24.

Unfortunately, however, neither that Act nor any other deals with the perennial problem of leaves falling onto the line.

7.3.2 Trees likely to endanger aviation

Where land is used as a civilian airfield, the Secretary of State may make an order under section 46 of the Civil Aviation Act 1982 to ensure safety. The effect of such an order is that the Secretary of State may then issue a direction that (amongst other things) restricts the height of any trees upon any land within the area, or requires any tree upon any such land to be cut down or reduced in height.[36] The order may also empower a named person to carry out any necessary works to achieve its intention.[37]

Such an order is to be made under the special parliamentary procedure[38]; and may not be made until the Secretary of State has consulted any local authorities in the area affected[39] (which, in the present context, entitles them to make representations in respect of particular trees of value). Once an order has been made, the Act does not require the carrying out of any further consultation in connection with the making of directions under the order; but there is no reason why such a requirement should not be inserted into the order itself.

Anyone injuriously affected by a direction made under an order under the Act is entitled to claim compensation.[40]

[36] Civil Aviation Act 1982, s. 46(2).
[37] 1982 Act, s. 46(3).
[38] 1982 Act, s. 46(4).
[39] 1982 Act, s. 46(5).
[40] 1982 Act, Sched. 9.

Chapter 8

Other Forms of Liability for Trees

8.1 Introduction

It has been noted already[1] that trees can cause a great deal of harm. It follows that, when they do, those who are affected may seek redress against those whom they consider to be responsible.

The two situations which have in practice given rise to the greatest amount of litigation are trees on or near boundaries, and trees that are defective. These have already been considered at greater length, in **Chapters 3 and 5** respectively, with the particular problems arising in the context of highways being considered at **Chapter 6**. In all these cases, the person adversely affected by the tree is not the owner or occupier of the land on which the tree is growing, and will therefore attempt to recover the cost of any damage from the owner or occupier in an action for nuisance or negligence.

But there are other situations in which it may appear that there is a cause of action, even where the tree by which a person is (or may in the future be) adversely affected is on his or her own land. So, for example, is there any way for the owner or prospective owner of land to verify that trees growing on it are not currently likely to cause harm – either actually to the property itself (including any buildings on it) or to neighbouring property, or to those visiting or passing by – and that such harm is unlikely to occur in the foreseeable future? And, in particular, to what extent can such a person rely on professional advice given by surveyors or others as to the likely effect of trees on nearby buildings or the need for any remedial works to them? This is the subject of **8.2**.

Section **8.3** then considers the particular problem of the extent to which those responsible for building works are liable to ensure that the resulting building is designed so that it is not subsequently harmed by any trees nearby. The converse problem of ensuring that the trees of value are not lost or damaged by building works is considered in **Chapter 15**.[1a]

Finally, if all else fails, there is always the possibility of looking to insurers to compensate for loss – either by paying the cost of rectifying harm directly caused by a tree or giving an indemnity in respect of damages payable to someone else to compensate them for such harm. This is considered at **8.4**.

---

[1] See **1.3**.
[1a] See **15.9.4**.

This and the previous three Chapters are principally concerned with liabilities relating to trees that are growing, and to which no works are proposed (other than, possibly, to avoid or minimise those very liabilities). Duties arising in connection with the carrying out of works to trees are considered in the following Chapter.

8.2 Advice on possible problems due to trees

8.2.1 Introduction

An owner of land will from time to time need advice in connection with trees. He or she should thus strive to avoid some of the liabilities discussed in previous Chapters in this book, by ensuring that all the trees on the land are in good condition, and not likely either to damage neighbouring property or to fall or shed branches. Advice may also be required even where there is no such liability, for example, to determine the cause of cracks newly appearing in an existing building on the land, or the advisability of constructing a new one. In each case, advice must be sought, and paid for; but how much can it be relied on?

One particular example of the need for advice is where someone is proposing to acquire land. It is well known that the basic rule as to liability is "let the buyer beware".[2] This applies to the existence and consequences of any trees on or near the land as it does to anything else. It is thus up to the purchaser of property to make such investigations as he or she thinks fit, to adjust the price offered if necessary and, once the property has changed hands, to live with the consequences.

That in turn means that a prospective purchaser needs to rely heavily on those advising him or her. In most cases, the purchaser will not have the experience to carry out a sufficient survey. Hiring experts also has the advantage that, if they are subsequently found to have got it wrong, they can be sued, since they should be covered by professional indemnity insurance – indeed this is required of surveyors by the RICS[3] (and other professions have similar requirements of their members in their codes of conduct).

And it is important for the professionals concerned, just as much as for their clients, to know the extent to which they are liable for the advice they give.

In practice, in the present context, it is usually surveyors and arboricultural experts who will most often be required to identify the presence of trees likely to cause harm and to advise on possible remedial works. This section thus attempts to highlight the principal issues which arise – largely in the context of surveyors advising those considering the purchase of property, since that is the situation in which litigation seems to arise most frequently in practice. But these principles in general apply equally to other situations where professional advice is sought and given; and the liability of surveyors is merely a particular example of the wider issue of the extent to which professionals and experts are liable for the advice they give. This is covered in greater depth, in the context of many different factual situations where such conflicts can arise, generally in texts on tort and more specifically in texts on professional negligence.

---

[2]　*Caveat emptor*; see, for example, *Perry v Sharon Development* [1937] 4 All E.R. 390, CA, per Romer L.J. at p. 394, cited in *Jennings* at pp. 773–774.

[3]　Royal Charter and Byelaws, RICS, 1973, amended to 2002 reg. 27.6. Byelaw 19, reg. 27.6.

8.2.2 The duty of care

The issue of whether professionals are liable for their statements has been frequently considered by the courts, the present law being formulated initially by the House of Lords in *Hedley Byrne v Heller & Partners*[4] and summarised most recently in *Caparo Industries v Dickman*[5]. In the latter case, it was suggested that for a relationship between a client and professional adviser to be such as to give rise to a duty of care, the breach of which would lead to a successful claim in damages, the following characteristics would be typically found:

> "(1) The advice is given for a purpose, whether particularly specified or generally described, which is made known, either actually or inferentially, to the adviser at the time when the advice is given;
> (2) the adviser knows, either actually or inferentially, that his advice will be communicated to the advisee, either specifically or as a member of an ascertained class, in order that it should be used by the advisee for that purpose;
> (3) it is known, either actually or inferentially, that the advice so communicated is likely to be acted upon by the advisee for that purpose without further inquiry; and
> (4) it is so acted upon by the advisee to his detriment."[6]

This would clearly apply in the case of an arboricultural or other expert asked for specific advice relating to the possible effect of trees on nearby persons and property. It would also apply to a surveyor, engineer or other professional hired by a prospective purchaser of a property specifically to carry out a survey, where the professional knows that the client will use the survey to inform his or her decision as to whether to go ahead with the purchase and, if so, at what price.[7]

It usually applies too in the case of a surveyor carrying out a survey for a building society or other prospective lender, where it is known (or suspected) that the purchaser will also rely on the survey.[8] And this is so even where the surveyor's report contains a disclaimer including words such as the following:

"No responsibility is implied or accepted by the Society or its valuer for either the value or condition of the property by reason of the Inspection or Report. The Society does not undertake to give advice as to the value or condition of the property, and accepts no liability for any such advice that may be given. The inspection carried out by the Society's valuer was not a structural survey, and there may be defects which such a survey would reveal."

Such a disclaimer (which is saying, in effect, that the surveyor's report is more or less worthless) was considered in *Beaton v Nationwide Building Society*.[9] The court noted that, under the terms of the Unfair Contract Terms Act 1977, it is for someone relying on such a disclaimer to show that it is "fair and reasonable to

---

[4]   [1964] A.C. 465, H.L.
[5]   [1990] 2 A.C. 605, H.L.
[6]   [1990] 2 A.C. 605, H.L., per Lord Oliver at p. 638.
[7]   *Daisley v B S Hall & Co* (1972) E.G., Mar 3, 1973; *Cross v David Martin & Mortimer* [1989] 1 EGLR 154, 10 E.G. 110, *The Times*, November 24, 1988; *Cormack v Washbourne* [1996] E.G.C.S. 196, CA; *Smart v Royal Insurance* [1998] E.G.C.S. 129.
[8]   *Smith v Eric S Bush* [1990] 1 A.C. 831, H.L., [1989] 2 All E.R. 514, 1 EGLR 169; followed in *Beaton v Nationwide Building Society* [1991] 2 EGLR 145, *The Times*, October 8, 1990.
[9]   [1991] 2 EGLR 145, *The Times*, October 8, 1990.

allow reliance on it, having regard to all the circumstances obtaining when the liability arose or (but for the notice) would have arisen".[10]

The court in *Beaton* followed the approach of Lord Griffith in *Smith v Eric S Bush*,[11] noting that it was to be anticipated that the prospective purchasers would not commission an independent survey – since only 10 to 15 per cent of all purchasers of "modest" dwelling-houses trouble to do so. Further, the terms of the report in question, which contained details of structural matters and recommendations as to work to be carried out, went much further than simply approving the application for a mortgage. It was accordingly perfectly reasonable for the purchaser to rely on the contents of the report, which had been positively reassuring on the critical question of structural movement.

This suggests that such a disclaimer is unreasonable in the context of a modest dwelling-house, and may not be relied on by the surveyor or valuer. But that would not necessarily be so in the case of a house at the upper end of the market, or a commercial property, where it is reasonable to expect a prospective purchaser to commission an independent survey.

Purchasers of property should thus exercise caution. If they are concerned about the effect of trees, they could make a specific request of the lender that any report deals explicitly with the question of structural movement and subsidence. That, however, leads to the possibility that the lender may simply play safe and require all nearby trees to be felled (regardless of possible problems resulting from ground heave). Alternatively, it is possible to commission an independent survey, just in case – but again the surveyor may also play safe in relation to his or her indemnity insurers, and recommend felling.

And the same applies more generally to anyone seeking professional advice – the more the advice is relied on, the greater is the possibility that the professional will offer advice that is "safe" (that is, unlikely to generate a claim against the professional's indemnity insurers) but not necessarily helpful. To offer advice that is both safe and helpful is of course possible, but requires greater care and takes more time, and thus costs more.

8.2.3 *The standard of care required*

Having established that a surveyor, arboricultural consultant or other profes-sional owes a duty of care to prospective purchasers and other clients, what then is the scope of that duty? This has been the subject of some litigation in the last 30 years in the context of the purchase of houses that were later found to have been the subject of subsidence caused by the presence of trees nearby on clay soil.[12]

The first consideration is that the duty imposed on the surveyor or other professional is not to get it right every time, but to exercise the care of a "reasonably skilled" member of that profession. Thus, for example, in *Daisley v BS Hall & Co*, the court found that:

". . . a reasonably skilled surveyor, alive to the fact that this house was built on shrinkable clay soil, would have suspected that crack 3.5.11 [that had been visible at the time of the inspection] might have been caused by subsoil shrinkage. . . . Any reasonable surveyor must then take the view that the shrinkage of the subsoil might be caused by the adjacent

---

[10] 1977 Act, s. 11(3).
[11] [1990] 1 A.C. 831, H.L., [1989] 2 All E.R. 514, 1 EGLR 169
[12] See **3.5.1**.

poplar trees which, applying the Building Research Station rule of thumb, were well in range. He would then take into account the age of the house, the size and number of the trees within range, and the likelihood of damage from swelling of the clay if the trees were cut down, and advise his client on the extent of the risk accordingly." [13]

Unfortunately, the surveyor in that case had only 18 months experience and, although he knew of the "poplar-tree-plus-shrinkable-clay hazard", he did not recognise the trees in question as poplars (they were in fact *Populus canadensis* Moench, a close relation of the black poplar) and thought the subsoil in the area was chalk, not shrinkable clay.

In *Cross v David Martin & Mortimer*,[14] the court held that a house purchaser could properly expect to be informed of any feature of the property which involved uncertainty as to its condition, even if the surveyor's opinion as to its significance was reassuring. In that case, the surveyor should have considered with particular care the possibility of subsidence due to the fact that the house in question was built on clay, the existence of poplar trees standing in the vicinity, and the fact that the house was built on a slope which required an unusually large amount of fill underneath the floor slab.

On the other hand, in the absence of any relevant warning signs, a reasonable surveyor is entitled to assume that building foundations are adequate. For example, where a surveyor noted that a house had been extended, he was entitled to consider that the cracks which he had noticed had arisen as a result of the building of the extension rather than because of the nearby oak trees. He was thus not negligent.[15]

Where a survey of a bungalow was carried out by an employee of a building society, in circumstances where it was going to be disclosed to the prospective purchaser, the court held (in *Beaton v Nationwide BS*) that the duty of the surveyor in carrying out his inspection and reporting on it was:

". . . to value the property after taking into consideration major defects which were, or ought to have been, obvious to him in the course of a visual inspection of so much of the exterior and interior of the bungalow as were accessible to him without undue difficulty. His inspection was not, nor do I approach it as if it should have been, a structural survey. His inspection was limited, but it was a limited inspection made by a skilled professional man. The standard of care required of [the surveyor] was that of the ordinary skilled man exercising the same skill as himself. The degree of skill required to be exercised can be described as the abilities of a reasonably skilled, competent building society surveyor." [16]

In that case, the surveyor admitted that he had been aware of the clay sub-soil, the shallow foundations and the presence of oak trees nearby. He was also aware from his training, his experience and from comment in various professional journals (even in 1981) that certain trees on clay subsoil close to buildings constitute a potential danger. The court expressed the view that:

"The rule of thumb of which, I am satisfied, any competent building society valuer should have been aware in 1981 is to the effect that there is a risk of subsidence causing structural

---

[13] (1972) E.G., March 3, 1973, per Bristow J.
[14] [1989] 1 EGLR 154, 10 E.G. 110, *The Times*, November 24, 1988.
[15] *Smart v Royal Insurance* [1998] E.G.C.S. 129.
[16] [1991] 2 EGLR 145, per Neil Butterfield QC, sitting as deputy judge, at p. 149C.

movement where an oak tree is growing at a distance less than its own height from the building under consideration." [17]

This conclusion should be treated with caution. Past judgments are statements of law, not of arboricultural practice. And it is important to remember that the principle is that the valuer in that case was liable not because of the distance between the house and the oak tree, but because he failed to take into account the rule of thumb of which any competent building society valuer should have been aware at the time. If expert advice current at the time of a survey is that the critical distance is 1.5 times the height of the tree, or half of the height, then that is what should be taken into account; and of course the relevant principles will differ as between trees of different species, and as between trees of the same species in different circumstances (such as on sloping or level ground).

On the other hand, current thinking is that such rules of thumb are themselves of limited value in many cases, as a matter of principle; and arguably the risks are too unpredictable to justify a blanket preventative policy. In most situations, therefore, it may be better to accept that damage will be caused by a small proportion of trees, and to deal with these by prompt and appropriate remedial action.[18] A good report should therefore assess what action is needed in the particular case, rather than simply apply a general arithmetic rule.

Nor are the obligations of a surveyor carrying out a less extensive RICS House Buyers Report any different to those that would have been incurred by one carrying out a full structural survey.[19]

Finally, one particular factor that should be taken into account is the geological survey map of the area. It may not always reveal the presence of clay or other soil likely to cause problems in the context of trees,[20] but it must be inspected – and failure to do so is likely to be categorised as negligence.[21]

8.2.4 Damages for breach of duty of care

As for the damages allowable following a finding that a survey has been carried out negligently, this was considered in *Daisley v BS Hall & Co*[22] in which a house was surveyed prior to its purchase. The surveyor failed to notice the presence of trees nearby which would then have seemed likely to require the house to be underpinned.

It was held, following the decision of the Court of Appeal in *Philips v Ward*,[23] that the proper measure of damages was the difference between what was actually paid for the house and what would have been its market value if the presence of the trees and their potential for harm had been known.[24] In *Daisley*, as it turned out, the trees were removed and the damage that had at one time been feared did not materialise, so that underpinning was not in the event necessary. But that was irrelevant – just as it would have been if the underpinning had, as feared, been

[17] [1991] 2 EGLR 145, at p. 150F.
[18] See *Tree Root Damage to Buildings*, Biddle, Vol. 1, p. 354.
[19] *Smart v Royal Insurance* [1998] E.G.C.S. 129.
[20] See, for example, *Solloway v Hampshire County Council* (1981) 79 L.G.R. 449, [1981] 1 EGLR 129, CA, considered at **3.5.4**.
[21] *Cormack v Washbourne* [1996] E.G.C.S. 196, CA.
[22] (1972) E.G., March 3, 1973.
[23] [1956] 1 W.L.R. 471, CA.
[24] See also *Perry v Sidney Philllips & Son* [1982] 1 W.L.R. 1297 and, in the context of trees, *Cormack v Washbourne* [1996] E.G.C.S. 196, CA.

necessary and had in fact cost considerably more than the loss in market value. As the judge in *Daisley* put it, what is sauce for the goose is sauce for the gander. A similar conclusion was reached, albeit *obiter*, in *Smart v Royal Insurance*.[25] And a plaintiff may also be able to recover damages for the inconvenience of living elsewhere while repair works are carried out.[26]

Since the cost of repair works may in some cases significantly exceed the loss in market value, even though interest will be payable on the latter, it may be wise for a property owner to consider rapid action so as not to be too much out of pocket.

8.3 Harm caused by trees to new buildings

8.3.1 Introduction

Where a building is being designed and built on a site close to trees, it is sensible for all concerned to take appropriate precautions to ensure that the trees do not cause harm to the building once it is completed – prevention being, after all, better than cure. The purchaser of a building that is under construction is, however, in a different position to that of a completed building already occupied by another, or even a completed but unoccupied building. This is because there is no possibility of such a person, or any professional acting on his or her behalf, knowing what the position will be when the building is finished, and the maxim "let the buyer beware"[27] therefore cannot apply.[28]

It follows that someone buying a half-completed building necessarily has to rely on the adequacy of the design and the competence of the builders executing it. Where the building is near trees, he or she might thus feel entitled to assume that, when completed, it will have been constructed in such a way as to avoid any damage being caused by any tree – either by the tree being removed or pruned, or by suitable foundations being provided, or in some other way – and to seek compensation if that proves not to be the case. In fact, however, this is only true to a limited extent.

It used to be thought that there was a fairly general liability in respect of building work – on the part of both the builders and professionals involved and the local authority building inspectors who checked it for compliance with the Building Regulations. This followed the decision of the Court of Appeal in *Dutton v Bognor Regis UDC*[29] and that of the House of Lords in *Anns v Merton*.[30] However, those were both overturned[31] by the Lords in *Murphy v Brentwood DC*,[32] which made it clear that local authorities were not liable for negligently performing their duties in relation to inspecting building works; and that decision was itself applied by the Lords on the same day to builders.[33]

---

[25] [1998] E.G.C.S. 129, following *Watts v Morrow* [1991] 2 EGLR 152.
[26] *Perry v Sidney Philllips & Son* [1982] 1 W.L.R. 1297.
[27] *Caveat emptor*; see **8.2.1**.
[28] *Jennings v Tavener* [1955] 2 All E.R. 769, E.G. May 21, 1955.
[29] [1972] 1 Q.B. 373, CA.
[30] [1978] A.C. 728, H.L.
[31] At least in respect of the United Kingdom; Canada and New Zealand have declined to follow suit.
[32] [1991] 1 A.C. 398, H.L.
[33] *Department of the Environment v Thomas Bates & Son* [1991] 1 A.C. 499, H.L.

It follows that those cases decided between *Dutton* and *Murphy* must now be treated with caution. Thus, in *Acrecrest v WS Hattrell & Partners*,[34] the architects concerned accepted liability for damage caused by trees to a block of flats that had been defectively constructed, and the local authority was found liable on the basis of the decision in *Anns*. The former decision would still be reached today – albeit under the Defective Premises Act 1972, rather than on the basis of negligence at common law; but the latter would not.

Thus in situations to which the Defective Premises Act 1972 applies there is still a considerable degree of protection; but there is little if any protection otherwise – notably in the case of commercial buildings.

8.3.2 Defective Premises Act 1972

In relation to dwellings, the position is now largely covered by the Defective Premises Act 1972, which provides that:

"A person taking on work for or in connection with the provision of a dwelling (whether the dwelling is provided by the erection or by the conversion or enlargement of a building) owes a duty –

    (a) if the dwelling is provided to the order of any person, to that person, and
    (b) without prejudice to paragraph (a) above, to every person who acquires an interest (whether legal or equitable) in the dwelling,

to see that the work which he takes on is done in a workmanlike or, as the case may be, professional manner, with proper materials and so that, as regards that work, the dwelling will be fit for habitation when completed."[35]

The duty under the Act thus applies both to the builder who actually builds the dwelling (and any sub-contractors), and to the professionals who design it and supervise its construction. It does not apply to houses that are protected by an approved scheme,[36] and thus did not until recently apply to those erected under the terms of the scheme operated by the National House Building Council (NHBC). Nor, obviously, does it apply to buildings other than dwellings.

Any cause of action under the 1972 Act is deemed to have accrued at the date when the dwelling is completed (or, where appropriate, the date on which were completed any follow-up works – such as rectifying defects).[37] There is then a 6-year period in which to bring an action.[38] Alternatively, it is possible to bring an action in negligence within three years of the date on which the plaintiff could reasonably have known about the damage[39] – subject to a long-stop of 15 years from the date of the last negligent act.[40]

The application of the 1972 Act in relation to trees is illustrated by the earlier decision of *Jennings v Tavener*.[41] The court confirmed – albeit with some hesitation (it was after all only 1955) – that a builder should know that poplar trees some 10 metres from a bungalow were likely to cause damage (as much

---

[34] [1979] 2 EGLR 95; for the facts, see **8.3.2**.
[35] Defective Premises Act 1972, s. 1(1).
[36] 1972 Act, s. 2.
[37] 1972 Act, s. 1(5).
[38] Limitation Act 1980.
[39] 1980 Act, s. 14A, inserted by Latent Damage Act 1986.
[40] 1980 Act, s. 14B, inserted by 1986 Act.
[41] [1955] 2 All E.R. 769, E.G. May 21.

literature had, even then, been published) and that, if the builder had employed an architect, the architect would certainly have known of the danger. That must surely now be absolutely beyond doubt. Jones J. thus held that the bungalow in that case was not fit for human habitation, by virtue of the cracks caused by the subsidence that was itself caused by the trees. It followed that there was a breach of the implied warranty, which was not confined to the building of those parts of the bungalow above the ground, but extended to the provision of proper foundations in a place where they would not settle or collapse:

"The defendant assumed the responsibility of supervision of the siting and building of the bungalow without the assistance of an architect, and failed to provide the plaintiff's husband with a bungalow fit for habitation, as he omitted to consider or guard against the well-recognised danger that the proposed site of a house may be unfit for that purpose because moisture has been extracted from it by the roots of such quick-growing trees as poplars growing in the immediate neighbourhood of the site. I find that the defendant could have prevented the occurrence of these cracks by cutting the roots of the trees at a distance from the bungalow, or by asking the [owner of the neighbouring land, on which the trees grew,] to do so, or by putting in a concrete bed under the foundations."

The builder was accordingly liable to the purchaser.

A subsequent case, *Acrecrest v WS Hattrell & Ptnrs*,[42] related to a block of flats which has been built on a site on which there were a large number of trees (all the subject of tree preservation orders), so located as to cause severe damage to the foundations of the flats. The developers claimed against the architects responsible, on the basis of negligent design and supervision, and against the local authority for negligence in the exercise of its powers of inspection and approval of the foundations under the Building Regulations.

As to the claim against the architects, it was accepted that some of the damage was caused by the drying out of the soil due to some of the nearby trees; but some was the result of ground heave caused partly by the removal of some fruit trees before the start of construction and partly by the death of a number of elms due to Dutch elm disease. The block had originally been designed with foundations 0.91 m (3 ft) deep, subsequently increased to 1.07 m (3 ft 6 in) in the light of possible problems with the trees; but the Council's building inspector had required this to be increased to 1.52 m (5 ft) where he found tree roots. The architects subsequently accepted that they had been negligent in not specifying foundations 1.52 m deep throughout, in view of the number of trees on the site and the presence of London clay, and accordingly consented to judgment – unsurprisingly, in view of the principles enunciated in *Jennings*, not to mention those of the 1972 Act (although neither was cited in *Acrecrest*) – half way through the action, and damages awarded along with 75 per cent of the plaintiffs' costs.

The Latent Damage Act 1986 also gives some protection for subsequent purchasers of dwellings, by providing that a new cause of action (against the original builders) is deemed to accrue to a subsequent owner on the date on which he or she acquires an interest in the property, but subject to the same overall limitation periods.

---

[42] [1979] 2 EGLR 95.

8.4 Insurance

8.4.1 Introduction

In many cases where damage to property is caused by trees, the tree is on the same land as the property damaged. It follows that there is no possibility of transferring liability onto any other landowner; the only hope of the tree owner avoiding having to pay out of his or her own pocket is therefore to rely on some form of insurance. As to whether it will be possible to recover in such circumstances, that will of course depend on the wording of the policy.

Thus, for example, most domestic policies will cover damage caused by falling trees or parts of trees. They will normally also cover damage caused to buildings or contents either by subsidence or ground heave; but that may be subject to restrictions in the case of ancillary structures such as garden walls, patios, terraces, fences, gates and drives. Frequently, when a property changes hands, the new owner is required to remove a tree or trees thought likely to cause subsidence; the fact that the removal may cause ground heave is usually ignored. Similarly, damage to vehicles caused by falling trees or branches will usually be recoverable under an appropriate comprehensive vehicle insurance policy. And commercial property will usually be subject to some form of insurance cover, the terms of which will vary as appropriate.

Where such damage does occur, and a claim is made, its recovery will be subject to the normal procedures and law governing any insurance claim – which is beyond the scope of this book.

Where damage to property is caused by a tree on neighbouring land, the owner of the damaged property may be able to succeed in a claim for nuisance against the owner of the tree – as considered at length in **Chapter 5**. In some cases, such a claim may be brought by one individual owner against another – often as part of a protracted and sometimes bitter dispute – but in many cases any litigation will be brought between their respective insurers.[43] This is because an insurance policy will usually indemnify the insured against any damages they may be found liable to pay. In practice, therefore, a claim will be brought by the owner of the damaged property (or by his insurer on his behalf) against the owner of the tree, who will then seek to involve as a third party to the action his own insurance company, in reliance upon such an indemnity.[44]

8.4.2 Availability of insurance

The applicability of insurance cover to damage caused by tree roots was considered by the court in *Mills v Smith (Sinclair Third Party)*.[45] The dispute concerned damage caused to M's house by the desiccation of the underlying soil, caused in turn by the excessive take-up of moisture by an oak tree on neighbouring land owned by S. The court found that S was liable, but he brought third party proceedings against the underwriters to his insurance policy, claiming that they were liable to indemnify him for an damages awarded against him in favour of M.

---

[43] See, for example, *Greenwood v Portwood*, 1984, unreported, [1985] CLY 2500.
[44] Under Civil Procedure Rules, Pt 20.
[45] [1963] 3 W.L.R. 367, 2 All E.R. 1078, [1964] 1 Q.B. 30, (1963) E.G. May 14.

The policy concerned was in the usual form of a Lloyd's householder's policy, which contained the following provision:

"*Liability to Public.* All sums for which the assured . . . as occupier . . . may be held legally liable . . . in respect of claims made by any person . . . for . . . damage to property . . . caused . . . by accident or by defective sanitary arrangements in or about the premises. . . . The [insurer's] liability shall not exceed £25,000 any one accident or any series of accidents."

The insurers contested liability, on the basis that the drying out of the soil as a result of the presence of the tree roots was not an "accident"; it was rather a result of the entirely natural growth of the tree and its consequent natural desire for water. The judge considered that the phrase "damage caused by accident" in this context was to be interpreted in the same way as "injury caused by accident" in the Workmen's Compensation Acts; and considered that "if, so far as the property is concerned, unexpected misfortune happens and damage is caused, the insured is to be indemnified".[46] He concluded:

"I would ask and seek to answer two questions.
  "One: has there been at any moment of time (or at particular moments of time) some unexpected event (or events) which have (or has) led to damage? My answer to that question is, yes. It is true that foundations settle, that is, tend to drop a little at one or more points, and that that settling may be gradual. In this case, however, there has come a point in time when the movement has overstepped the safety limit, if I may use that expression, and a crack in the concrete or in the brickwork at or near the south-east corner of the house has started. This may have happened several times, that is, there may have been more than one crack. In humans, the overstepping of the safety limit of movement may cause a fracture, a rupture, or a haemorrhage. In a building, it may cause a fracture of the concrete or of the brickwork. There is no 'accident' until the overstepping takes place.
  "The second question is: what was the cause of the overstepping of the safety limit? My answer is that the cause was the nuisance of the roots of the tree penetrating into the plaintiff's soil and draining away the moisture necessary to keep the movement of the house from overstepping that safety limit."

He accordingly gave judgment in favour of the defendant, for a declaration that the underwriter was bound to pay him against the damages which he had to pay to the plaintiff.

Some forty years later, insurance policies still refer to "accidents", and thus claims of this kind are in general still covered.

A further problem may arise where there are in existence two policies in relation to a single piece of land owned and occupied by a single person – one policy indemnifying him in relation to claims against him as owner, and one relating to claims against him as occupier. Because claims in nuisance and negligence will tend to be properly made against the occupier of land, rather than the owner, it will be the latter policy that will be relevant.[47]

---

[46] 2 Q.B. 429, per Paull J., at p. 38; following *Trim Joint District School Board v Kelly* [1914] A.C. 667, H.L., per Lord Haldane at p. 676.
[47] *Rigby v Sun Alliance* [1979] 2 EGLR 30.

Chapter 9

Carrying Out Works to a Tree

9.1 General principles

9.1.1 Introduction

It is inevitable that from time to time works are carried out to trees. This may be for any of a wide variety of reasons.[1] And the works may be perceived as being either "necessary" or "desirable" or both. In the first category would be works to benefit a tree itself, through the removal of weak forks, or of damaged or diseased branches. Alternatively, the need for the works may arise as a result of some of the matters considered in the earlier chapters of this book – such as to prevent branches interfering with existing buildings, passing vehicles, overhead cables and so forth, or roots interfering with foundations.

Sometimes proposed works may be (at least primarily) cosmetic – for example, to help the tree form a satisfactory well-balanced crown, or to make a given length of the main stem or trunk free from branches; although the latter is also an example of works that may be undertaken for safety reasons (to prevent climbing). It will often be considered desirable to raise or to thin the canopy of a tree, so as to help it to form a well-shaped crown or to reduce the leaf area and thus to decrease the uptake of moisture by the roots.[2]

And there will eventually come a time when it is necessary (or at least, other things being equal, highly desirable) to fell the tree – either for one or more of the above reasons, or simply because it has reached the end of its life.

In other cases works may not be necessary in any absolute sense, but merely desirable. An example would be the removal of a tree or branch whose existence is in some way or other impeding the implementation of a project (whether a multi-million pound development or a new flowerbed). Or the owner of a tree may wish to remove it simply because he or she does not like it – perhaps because it blocks out the light or because the owner wishes to replace it with one of a different species.

In all these situations, there are a number of considerations to be borne in mind – whether the proposed works affect a single branch or a forest of a thousand trees, and whether the trees involved are of great value (as an amenity or otherwise) or of none.

---

[1] See, for example, *The Arboriculturist's Companion*, NDG James, Blackwell, second edn, 1998.
[2] See **3.5.1**.

9.1.2 *The right to carry out works to trees*

The first question to be considered is who has the right to carry out any works to a tree. The remainder of this Chapter refers, for simplicity, to works being carried out by, or on behalf of, "the owner"; but to determine the identity of the relevant owner is occasionally less than straightforward.

The general question of who owns a tree has already been considered at some length.[3] The basic rule is that a tree is part of the land (soil) surrounding the base of its trunk. It follows that whoever "owns" that land – that is, has sufficient rights over it – owns the tree, and may in principle carry out any works to it. There may be more than one owner of any particular parcel of land; and if any one of them wishes to carry out works to a tree on it, it may be necessary to consult some or all of the others (for example, where land is subject to the terms of a trust or settlement[4] or held under a lease or licence[5]).

Uncertainty may arise where a tree is growing on more than one parcel of land, or near the boundary between them. This situation, which is commonly found in practice and has on occasion been the subject of prolonged and acrimonious disputes, has also been considered earlier in this book.[6] Here the basic rule is that a tree planted or allowed to grow so as to straddle a boundary will be owned in common by the owners of the two properties concerned. But, surprisingly, the law is not altogether clear as to the rights – if any – of either owner to carry out works to the tree without the consent or knowledge of the other.[7]

By contrast, a tree near to a property boundary belongs to the owner of the soil in which it was initially planted (or allowed to grow, if self-seeded), even if its roots or branches subsequently stray across that boundary. But the owner of the land into or over which they have strayed is in principle entitled to cut them back to the boundary without notice to the owner of the tree.[8]

Where land is subject to restrictive covenants, their precise wording should be checked to ensure that they do not restrict the carrying out of works to trees – or, possibly, the carrying out of such works without having first obtained the permission of some named person.

And the law has now been – relatively recently – settled in relation to trees growing on highway land: they are owned by the highway authority.[9]

However, it is vitally important to appreciate that the above rules determine merely who has the right, in principle, to carry out works to a tree. That right is in practice subject to a plethora of other restrictions and duties, which form the subject of the remainder of this Chapter – and, indeed, the remainder of this book.

9.1.3 *Restrictions on the right to carry out works to trees*

First, both the person causing the works to be carried out and the person actually carrying them out must consider: whether they require to be authorised; from whom such authorisation may be obtained; what are the remedies if it is not forthcoming; and what are the consequences of carrying out the works without it.

---

[3] See **Chapter 2**.
[4] See **2.4**.
[5] See **2.5**.
[6] See **Chapter 3**.
[7] *Richardson v Jay* (1960) E.G. July 9, 1960; and see **3.2.1**.
[8] *Lemmon v Webb* [1895] A.C. 1, H.L.; and see **3.2.2**, **3.6**.
[9] *Hurst v Hampshire County Council* [1997] 2 EGLR 164, CA; and see **Chapter 6**.

The principle types of authorisation are considered briefly at **9.2**, and in greater depth in **Parts III** and **IV** of this book. They are:

- the need for an environmental impact assessment in relation to major forestry proposals[10];

- a felling licence for the felling of trees in any quantity[11];

- consent from the local planning authority for works to trees protected by a tree preservation order[12] or in a conservation area[13]; and

- a faculty for works to trees in a churchyard.[14]

Secondly, it is a feature of works to trees that they sometimes have side-effects – intended or otherwise – which may cause considerable problems in practice. In some cases, these can be resolved by obtaining a licence or consent of some kind. But in others, these problems may effectively mean that certain types of works simply cannot be carried out in a particular way or at a particular time, or at all. And indeed failure to comply with such restrictions is in most cases a criminal offence. It is therefore important to be aware of the relevant legislation, both in determining whether any such authorisation is required at the outset (in addition to the consents noted at **9.2**) and in deciding the way in which the works should be done. The legislative codes relating to the protection of wildlife (birds, animals and plants) and habitats generally are therefore considered at **9.3**; and a miscellany of other relevant legislation at **9.4**.

Thirdly, even once any necessary permits and consents have been sought and obtained, the works themselves must be carried out so as not to cause any unnecessary problems. This is partly because those carrying out any building or similar works owe a duty of care to anyone who might be affected, and partly due to the various requirements of health and safety legislation. Both of these are largely outside the scope of this book, but they are considered in outline at **9.5**.

Finally, some works to trees may most appropriately be categorised as criminal damage or even theft. The application of the criminal code to such situations is the subject of **9.5**.

9.2 Principal consents needed

9.2.1 Introduction

There have been for half a century two separate legislative codes controlling the carrying out of works to trees:

- the need to obtain a felling licence, under the Forestry Act 1951 and later the Forestry Act 1967, and

- the need to obtain consent under a tree preservation order, under the various planning Acts since 1947.

---

[10] See **Chapter 13**.
[11] See **Chapter 14**.
[12] See **Chapters 16 to 20**.
[13] See **Chapter 21**.
[14] See **Chapter 22**.

The former applies, in principle, in relation to any tree (albeit subject to numerous exemptions); the latter only to trees of particular amenity value.

The relationship between forestry and amenity controls is not always straightforward, but the theory is that the former was, at least originally, designed to ensure the continuing existence of an adequate stock of home-grown timber, whereas the latter is part of the general control over land use in the interests of amenity. Since, however, both systems are now operated almost entirely in the interests of amenity,[15] it must be open to serious question whether it is still really necessary to retain two such overlapping codes. But for the moment at least they should both be borne in mind by anyone contemplating any works to any tree.

Forestry legislation generally is the subject of detailed consideration in **Part III** of this book, and the relevant provisions of planning legislation in **Part IV**. They are briefly summarised here, however, so that this Chapter may provide a more or less complete outline of all the law relating to works to trees and hedges.

9.2.2 Felling licences

To fell growing trees in any quantity generally requires a felling licence under the Forestry Act 1967.[16] A felling licence is thus not needed for lopping, topping or pruning operations,[17] or to fell trees which are dead. Nor is it needed for small felling operations – involving up to 5 cubic metres of timber in any quarter – or for the felling of small trees.[18]

This requirement is also subject to various other exemptions. It does not apply in inner London.[18a] It does not apply to the felling of trees in an orchard, garden, churchyard or public open space.[19] Nor does it apply to felling which is necessary to prevent a danger or to prevent or abate a nuisance, to comply with an Act of Parliament, or to carry out development for which planning permission has been granted.[20] Further exemptions are contained in regulations[21]; the most significant of these are that a licence is not required where the felling is on land subject to a forestry dedication agreement or for the felling of elms subject to Dutch elm disease.[22]

Where a felling licence is needed, it should be sought from the Forestry Commission by the owner of the land, or by the tenant if his or her lease permits felling without the landlord's consent.[23] Special provisions apply where the trees are subject to a working plan approved by the Commission,[24] and where they are subject to a tree preservation order.[25] Where a licence is issued, it may be subject

---

[15] See **14.1** (felling licences) and **15.6.2** (tree preservation orders).
[16] FA 1967, s. 9; see **14.2**.
[17] FA 1967, s. 9(2)(c).
[18] FA 1967, s. 9(2)(a), (3).
[18a] FA 1967, s. 36; see **14.2.1**.
[19] FA 1967, s. 9(2)(b).
[20] FA 1967, s. 9(4).
[21] Made under FA 1967, section 9(5)(a); see Forestry (Exceptions from Restriction of Felling) Regulations 1979 (S.I. 1979/ No. 792), amended by S.I. 1981 No. 1476, S.I. 1985 No. 1572, S.I. 1986 No. 1356, S.I. 1988 No. 970, S.I. 1996 No. 252, S.I. 1998 No. 603.
[22] 1979 Regulations, reg. 4.
[23] FA 1967, s. 10; see **14.3**.
[24] FA 1967, s. 14.
[25] FA 1967, s. 15; see **14.4**.

to conditions,[26] and in particular to a condition requiring the land to be restocked with new trees.[27] An unsuccessful applicant may be entitled to compensation, or to appeal against a decision to refuse a licence, or to impose conditions, to the relevant Minister.[28]

To carry out felling operations without having obtained a licence, where one is needed, is a criminal offence.[29] The Commission may serve a notice requiring compliance with a restocking condition – against which there is a right of appeal to the minister – and may if necessary enter the land and carry out the necessary works itself, and recover its costs from the person in default.[30] Failure to comply with such a notice is a criminal offence, as is failure to comply with a notice requiring land to be restocked following unauthorised felling.[31-32]

These provisions are all explored in greater depth in **Chapter 14**.

9.2.3 Environmental impact assessment of forestry projects

A new requirement, introduced for the first time in 1998,[33] is that consent must be obtained from the Forestry Commission for any forestry project (including deforestation) which is likely to have a significant effect on the environment by virtue of factors such as its nature, size or location. The relevant legislation is now in the Environmental Impact Assessment (Forestry) Regulations 1999.[34] Thresholds have been introduced to define those projects that will not normally require consent under these provisions, with lower thresholds in sensitive areas.[35] It may be noted that the need for consent under these provisions is wholly independent of any requirement for a felling licence.

The key feature of these provisions, which are considered in more detail in **Chapter 13**, is that an application for consent under the 1999 Regulations must be accompanied by an environmental impact assessment. If in doubt, an applicant may seek the opinion of the Commission as to what should be included.[36] Consent may be granted subject to conditions, or refused, and there is a right of appeal to the Minister against any refusal or against the imposition of non-standard conditions.[37]

9.2.4 Consent under a tree preservation order

In addition to the above provisions, which in principle apply equally to any tree, certain trees are subject to special protection regimes, described in **Part IV** of this book, and these too generally impose criminal liability. Of these, the most important in practice is the need for consent under a tree preservation order.

---

[26] FA 1967, s. 12.
[27] FA 1967, s. 12.
[28] FA 1967, ss. 11, 16; see **14.5**.
[29] FA 1967, s. 17; see **14.7**.
[30] FA 1967, s. 24; see **14.6**.
[31-32] FA 1967, ss. 17C, 24 to 26.
[33] Environmental Assessment (Forestry) Regulations 1998 (S.I. 1998 No. 1731), superseded and revoked by EIA (Forestry) Regulations 1999 (S.I. 1999 No. 2228) ("EIA Regulations").
[34] For Scotland, see now EIA (Forestry) (Scotland) Regulations 1999 (S.I. 1999 No. 43).
[35] EIA Regulations 1999, Sched. 2; see **13.3**.
[36] EIA Regulations 1999, regs. 9 to 12; see **13.4**.
[37] EIA Regulations 1999, regs. 15 to 18; see **13.4.6**.

In summary, the Town and Country Planning Act 1990 provides that it is an offence to cut down, top, lop, uproot, wilfully damage or wilfully destroy any tree that is the subject of a tree preservation order, without having obtained the consent of the relevant local authority.[38] The order in question should be checked to ascertain its precise terms – it will have been drafted in line with the Model Order provided in the relevant set of regulations in force at the time, each of which was amended before being superseded.[39]

As with felling licences, there are a number of exemptions from the need for consent, both in the Act and in the order itself. The 1990 Act thus provides that no consent is necessary for works to trees which are dying or dead or have become dangerous, or for works necessary to comply with an Act of Parliament, or to prevent or abate a nuisance,[40] or works in accordance with a forestry dedication covenant or a plan approved by the Forestry Commission.[41] And no consent under a tree preservation order will be needed for works that are the subject of a felling licence.[42]

The order will exempt from the need for consent certain works by various public bodies – largely in circumstances where works to trees are necessary to ensure the safe and efficient operation of their undertakings.[43] Consent will also not be needed where works to protected trees are required to enable the carrying out of development for which planning permission has been granted.[44] And consent will not be required for some works to fruit trees.[45]

An application for consent should be made to the appropriate local planning authority, and will be processed much in the same way as a planning application; and where consent is refused or granted subject to conditions, including as to replanting, an appeal may be made to the Secretary of State.[46] Further, if any loss is suffered in consequence of a decision relating to an application for consent, compensation may be payable.[47]

Finally, if a tree subject to a tree preservation order is removed without consent, or if a tree other than one in a woodland is removed because it is dead, dying or dangerous, the owner of the land must plant a replacement unless the planning authority agrees to dispense with the requirement.[48] If the owner fails to comply with such a requirement, or with a condition on a consent requiring a replacement to be planted, the authority may serve a notice requiring compliance, against which there is a right of appeal to the Secretary of State. And if that notice is itself not complied with, the authority may enter the land, carry out the replanting and recover its costs.[49]

These provisions are considered fully in **Chapters 16 to 20**. They are also the subject of an explanatory leaflet produced by the Department of the Environment, Transport and the Regions (DETR), entitled *Protected Trees: a Guide to*

---

[38] TCPA 1990, s. 210.
[39] See **16.3**.
[40] TCPA 1990, s. 198(6); see **17.3 to 17.5**.
[41] TCPA 1990, s. 200(3); 1969 Model Order, Sched. 2, para. (1), (2); see **17.6.1**.
[42] TCPA 1990, s. 198(7)(b); FA 1967, s. 15(6); see **17.6.2**.
[43] See **17.7**; also **Chapter 7**.
[44] See **17.8**
[45] See **17.9**
[46] See **18.2 to 18.6**.
[47] TCPA 1990, ss. 203, 204.
[48] TCPA 1990, s. 206; see **20.2**.
[49] TCPA 1990, ss. 207 to 209; see **20.3 to 20.5**.

Tree Preservation Procedures, and a more comprehensive publication *Tree Preservation Orders: a Guide to the Law and Good Practice*.[50]

9.2.5 Notification of works to trees in conservation areas

Even where a tree is not subject to a tree preservation order, it is still an offence to carry out works to it if it is in a conservation area, unless the local planning authority has first been given six weeks' notice in writing.[51]

This requirement is, unsurprisingly, subject to numerous exceptions, all contained in regulations – currently Part III of the Town and Country Planning (Trees) Regulations 1999.[52] All of the exemptions to the need for consent under a tree preservation order apply here too.[53] In addition, notice does not have to be given for works by, or on behalf of, a planning authority; nor for works to small trees.[54]

The replanting duties relating to trees subject to a tree preservation order[55] apply generally to trees in a conservation area, subject to some minor variations.[56]

These provisions are considered fully in **Chapter 21**.

9.2.6 Faculties for works to trees in churchyards

Finally, whether or not there is any need to obtain consent from or to notify the local authority under the Town and Country Planning Act 1990, a faculty will be needed for any works of any consequence to any existing trees in a Church of England churchyard. This may not apply to minor works such as routine pruning, provided that the detailed specification of the works is in accordance with the relevant guidance applying in the diocese concerned.[57]

This is considered in more detail in **Chapter 22**.

9.3 Harm to protected wildlife and habitats

9.3.1 Introduction

This Chapter concerns the carrying out of works to trees, not nature conservation generally; and only one species of tree has yet been protected as such in the United Kingdom.[57a] Nevertheless, the provisions of the law relating to species protection should not be ignored, since trees (including dead and dying ones) will often provide valuable habitat for a variety of animals and birds, and will usually if not always be found close to other plants. It follows that the carrying out of works to trees – particularly, but not only, felling – may have the unintended result of killing protected birds or animals, or at the very least disturbing their habitats or destroying protected plants.

---

[50] Both available from the Office of the Deputy Prime Minister (ODPM), Rural Development Division, Zone 3/C5, Eland House, Bressenden Place, London SW1E 5DU, or at www.wildlife-countryside.detr.gov.uk.
[51] TCPA 1990, s. 211.
[52] S.I. 1999 No. 1892, reg. 10.
[53] TCP (Trees) Regulations 1999, reg. 10(a)–(c); see **21.2.2, 21.2.3**.
[54] TCP (Trees) Regulations 1999, reg. 10(d)–(f); see **21.2.4, 21.2.5**.
[55] See **9.2.4, 20.2**.
[56] TCPA 1990, s. 213; see **21.5**.
[57] CCEJM 1991, ss. 6(3) and 11(8).
[57a] Plymouth pear (*Pyrus Cordata*); see **9.3.4**.

The principal legislation is contained in Part I of the Wildlife and Countryside Act 1981, which replaced, amongst other Acts, the Protection of Birds Acts 1954 to 1967[58] and the Conservation of Wild Creatures and Wild Plants Act 1975. The enforcement provisions of the 1981 Act were strengthened with effect from February 1, 2001 by the Countryside and Rights of Way Act 2000[59] (and accordingly references here to the 1981 Act are to that Act as amended by the 2000 Act).

The provisions of the 1981 Act should be read in conjunction with those of the Conservation (Natural Habitats, etc.) Regulations 1994,[60] which transpose into United Kingdom domestic legislation the provisions of EC Directives on Habitats and Wild Birds.[61] The 1994 Regulations provide somewhat stronger protection for those few species that are considered to be of international, rather than simply national importance.

In each case, the legislation provides that it is an offence to do certain things without a licence, but that there are certain defences to a prosecution for such an offence. The most significant of these in practice is that a person can avoid a conviction if he or she is able to prove that the act that would otherwise have been unlawful was the incidental result of a lawful operation and could not reasonably have been avoided. This is therefore considered in more detail below.[62]

It seems that relatively few prosecutions have been mounted in practice; but this may change as the climate of public opinion changes – as evidenced by the tightening up introduced in the 2000 Act. It is therefore increasingly necessary for those dealing with trees to be aware of the relevant provisions and, in particular, which species are currently given special protection.

As already noted, these considerations should be borne in mind in deciding both whether and how to carry out particular works. At one level, the decision will be simply whether a licence or other consent is required; but obtaining such authorisation may be difficult or impossible – certainly if, for example, the works to the trees are required solely to facilitate the carrying out of development. It may therefore be necessary simply to avoid the problem – for example, by programming a construction project so as to leave untouched during the breeding season a branch on which there is a protected birds' nest, or felling a tree in such a way as to leave undisturbed a clump of protected wildflowers growing to one side.

It is also important to remember that the provisions considered here apply equally in the case of works to a tree which is dead or dying – indeed, such trees frequently provide particularly valuable habitats for other forms of wildlife. It thus cannot be assumed that, after a tree has been uprooted in a gale, or where a tree is still standing but dying due to its advanced age, it can be simply removed with impunity. This is particularly important in the case of veteran trees.[63]

And in addition to the protection given to birds, animals and plants as such, protection is also afforded to habitats generally. Almost all of the significant habitats have been designated as sites of special scientific interest (SSSIs); and the legislation relating to these has recently been significantly strengthened.[64] The

---

[58] Protection of Birds Act 1954, Protection of Birds Act 1954 (Amendment) Act 1964, Protection of Birds Act 1967.
[59] 2000 Act, ss. 81(1), 103(2), Sched. 12.
[60] S.I. 1994 No. 2716, amended (slightly) by S.I. 2000 No. 192.
[61] Respectively Council Directives 92/43 and 79/409; see **9.39**.
[62] See **9.3.5**.
[63] See **15.4**.
[64] 1981 Act, ss. 28 to 28R, inserted by 2000 Act, s. 75; see **9.3.8**.

most important have also been designated as special areas of conservation (SACs) or special protection areas (SPAs) under the 1994 Regulations, implementing the European Habitats Directive.[65]

9.3.2 Protected birds

The most extensive protection is afforded by the law to birds – both rare and otherwise. This is important in the context of trees, as of course many birds live in trees.

First, then, a person is guilty of an offence under section 1(1) of the Wildlife and Countryside Act 1981 if he or she intentionally:

- kills, injures or takes *any* wild bird;

- takes, damages or destroys its nest while under construction or in use; or

- takes or destroys any of its eggs.

For these purposes, "wild birds" excludes game birds and poultry.[66]

Secondly, it is an offence under section 1(5) to disturb intentionally or recklessly[67]:

- any bird listed in Schedule 1 to the Act[68] while it is building a nest or is in, on or near a nest containing eggs or young; or

- the dependent young of such a bird.

The species listed in Schedule 1 obviously include rare ones, but some of those included are reasonably common, at least in certain parts of the country.

For a conviction to succeed, it is necessary for the prosecution to be able to prove the required state of mind – either intention or recklessness, as appropriate. This is not likely to be easy where the harm to the birds, nests or eggs occurs solely as an incidental result of works carried out – otherwise perfectly lawfully – to trees. Indeed, there are a number of defences to a charge of committing an offence under section 1; and one of those, under section 4(2)(c), provides that a person is not guilty of an offence if the harm was the incidental result of a lawful operation and could not reasonably have been avoided.[69] That defence is important in the present context, and is considered in more detail below.[70]

A further defence is available to an "authorised person" if he or she can prove that the action that caused the harm was necessary to preserve public health or safety or prevent the spread of disease or serious damage to (amongst other things) growing timber.[71] In order for such a defence to succeed, however, it will also be necessary for the accused to prove:

---

[65] See **9.3.9**.
[66] WCA 1981, s. 27(1). As to game birds, see also s. 2 of the Act.
[67] The reference to recklessness was inserted by Countryside and Rights of Way Act 2000, Sched. 12, para. 1.
[68] The offence under s. 1(5) only applies to the handful of birds in Part II of Sched. 1 during the close season: see s. 1(7).
[69] WCA 1981, s. 10(3)(c).
[70] See **9.3.5** below.
[71] WCA 1981, s. 4(3).

- that there was no other satisfactory method of preventing that damage;

- that he or she had obtained a licence,[72] or at least sought one if the need for the action could have been predicted; and

- that he or she had notified DEFRA as soon as possible after taking the action.[73]

An "authorised person" includes the owner or occupier of the relevant land, and any person authorised by the owner or occupier, and any person authorised in writing by (amongst others) the local authority, English Nature or the Environment Agency.[74] This defence is further limited in that it does not apply in relation to the rarer birds, listed in Schedule 1.[75]

9.3.3 Wild animals

The approach taken by the 1981 Act to the protection of animals[76] is similar to that adopted in relation to wild birds[77] – save that there is no offence applying to *all* animals; those discussed (briefly) here apply only to the wild animals listed in Schedule 5 to the Act.

Most of the species listed in Schedule 5 are unlikely to be relevant in the context of trees, but a few may well be – including a variety of types of beetles, butterflies and moths, the red squirrel and, above all, horseshoe and typical bats[78] (of any species). Note that some species are listed in the Schedule only in relation to certain offences: stag beetles, for example, are only the subject of the offences under section 9(5) relating to the sale of animals, which are not relevant in the present context. Note too that the Secretary of State has power to vary the Schedule by order[79] – and has indeed exercised that power on several occasions, both to include and to exclude species.[80] At the time of writing, research is under way which may, in due course, lead to further changes, so the current position needs to be checked carefully.

A person is guilty of an offence under section 9(1) if he or she intentionally kills, injures or takes any wild animal listed in Schedule 5; although merely to do any of those things recklessly is not an offence. Possibly more significant is section 9(4), which provides as follows:

"Subject to the provisions of this Part, if any person intentionally or recklessly –

(a) damages or destroys, or obstructs access to, any structure or place which any animal included in Schedule 5 uses for shelter or protection; or

---

[72] See **9.3.6** below.
[73] WCA 1981, s. 4(4)–(6), inserted by S.I. 1995 No. 2825, reg. 2.
[74] WCA 1981, s. 27(1) (amended by Environment Protection Act 1990, Sched. 9, and Water Act 1989, Scheds. 25, 27).
[75] WCA 1981, s. 4(3).
[76] That is, all animals other than birds or human beings.
[77] See **9.3.2** above.
[78] *Rhinolophidae* and *Vespertilionidae*.
[79] WCA 1981, s. 22.
[80] See S.I. 1988 No. 288, S.I. 1989 No. 906, S.I. 1991 No. 367, S.I. 1992 No. 2350 and S.I. 1998 No. 878.

(b) disturbs any such animal while it is occupying a structure or place which it uses for that purpose,

he shall be guilty of an offence."[81]

As with the offences relating to wild birds, it is necessary for the prosecution to be able to prove the required state of mind – either intention or recklessness, as appropriate.

Defences are available (under section 10) to a charge under section 9 relating to a wild animal, similar to those available in relation to birds.[82] In particular, a person will usually be able to escape conviction if he or she can show that the act made unlawful by section 9 was the incidental result of a lawful operation and could not reasonably have been avoided.[83]

The only exception to this relates to bats. Thus, where proposed operations would have the incidental effect of killing, injuring or disturbing bats, or damaging, destroying or obstructing access to bat roosts, the defence under section 10(3)(c) is available if the person responsible first notifies the relevant nature conservancy council[84] and allows it a reasonable time to give advice as to whether and, if so, how the operation should be carried out.[85] Oddly, there seems to be no duty to take any particular notice of the advice, once offered; but it would be difficult to rely on the defence that harm to the bats could not reasonably have been avoided if the advice from English Nature suggested otherwise. Further guidance in relation to bats may be obtained from the Bat Conservation Trust.[86]

A further defence is available, but only to an authorised person, if he or she can prove that the action that caused the harm was necessary to prevent serious damage to (amongst other things) growing timber, and that he or she had obtained or at least sought a licence.[87] Although in this case it is not necessary to notify DEFRA or to prove that there was no satisfactory alternative solution.

In the case of animals of the rarer species, protected under the EC Habitats Directive, it is a further offence, under the Conservation (Natural Habitats, etc.) Regulations 1994, to deliberately disturb them, take or destroy their eggs, or damage or destroy their breeding sites or resting places.[88] The species whose natural range includes any area in Great Britain are helpfully listed in Schedule 2 to the 1994 Regulations. For present purposes, the most relevant ones are, once again, horseshoe bats and typical bats, of all species. There are exceptions and defences to liability under the Regulations, more or less identical to those applying under the 1981 Act.[89]

---

[81] The reference to recklessness was inserted by Countryside and Rights of Way Act 2000, Sched. 12, para. 5.
[82] See **9.3.2** above.
[83] WCA 1981, s. 10(3)(c); see **9.3.5** below.
[84] English Nature, Countryside Council for Wales (Cyngor Cefn Gwlad Cymru), or Scottish Natural Heritage: WCA 1981, s. 27(3A), inserted by Environmental Protection Act 1990, Sched. 9, and amended by Natural Heritage (Scotland) Act 1991, Sched. 2, and 2000 Act, Sched. 8.
[85] WCA 1981, s. 10(5).
[86] For contact details, see Appendix D. See in particular the free leaflet *Bats and Trees*, produced by the Trust in 1997.
[87] WCA 1981, s. 10(4).
[88] 1994 Regulations, reg. 38.
[89] 1994 Regulations, reg. 39.

9.3.4 Wild plants

Limited protection for wild plants[90-91] is afforded by the Wildlife and Countryside Act 1981. A "wild plant" is defined for these purposes as:

". . . any plant which is or (before it was picked, uprooted or destroyed) was growing wild and is of a kind which ordinarily grows in Great Britain in a wild state."[92]

In relation to rare plants, an offence (under section 13(1)(a)) occurs where any person intentionally picks, uproots or destroys any wild plant included in Schedule 8 to the Act. It will be noted that "any person" includes the owner of the land on which the plant is growing. As with the other Schedules, the Secretary of State has power to amend the list in Schedule 8; and a significant number of species were added in 1988, 1992 and 1998.[93]

Only one tree is included in Schedule 8: the Plymouth pear (*Pyrus cordata*). It was indeed one of the relatively few plants selected when the Act was first passed. Rather more significantly, however, a number of lichens, mosses and puff-balls are included. And the Act also protects many types of wildflowers and other plants that may be found growing close to trees and hedges.

The second offence (under section 13(1)(b)) occurs where anyone other than an authorised person intentionally uproots any wild plant not included in the Schedule. This might at first sight seem to provide a measure of protection for trees and hedgerows, since a tree or a hedging plant may well be a "wild plant" for the purposes of the Act. However, it will be recalled that an "authorised person" includes an owner or occupier of the land,[94] and anyone authorised by either of them; and most trees are lost through the action of one or more of those, rather than at the hand of a stranger.

As with birds and animals, there is a statutory defence to a charge under section 13(1) – that the act thus made unlawful was the incidental result of a lawful operation and could not reasonably have been avoided.[95]

As with animals, further protection is given to plants of the rarer species, protected under the EC Habitats Directive, listed in Schedule 4 to the Conservation (Natural Habitats, etc.) Regulations 1994.[96] In practice, however, this does no more than to duplicate the protection afforded under the 1981 Act.

9.3.5 Harm arising as incidental result of lawful operation

It has already been noted that one of the defences available to a charge of committing an offence under Part I of the Wildlife and Countryside Act 1981 is for the person responsible for the act to prove that it was the incidental result of a lawful operation and could not reasonably have been avoided.[97] The same applies to a charge under the Conservation (Natural Habitats, etc.) Regulations 1994.[98]

The reason for this defence is presumably that, if the operation which led

[90-91] Which for this purpose includes fungi.
[92] WCA 1981, s. 27(1).
[93] By S.I. 1988 No. 288, S.I. 1992 No. 2350 and S.I. 1998 No. 878.
[94] WCA 1981, s. 27(1); see **9.3.2**.
[95] WCA 1981, s. 13(3); see **9.3.5**.
[96] 1994 Regulations, amended (slightly) by S.I. 2000 No. 192; reg. 43.
[97] WCA 1981, ss. 4(2)(c) (birds), 10(3)(c) (animals), 13(3) (plants).
[98] 1994 Regulations, regs. 40(3)(c) (animals), 43(4) (plants).

unavoidably to the harm being caused was indeed lawful, it is likely to have been the subject of some form of official authorisation – licence, permission, consent or whatever – and that the agency granting that authorisation would have, or at least should have, considered the harm to protected species that would follow its implementation. So, for instance, where a person carrying out works to a tree has obtained a felling licence and consent under any tree preservation order which may apply, he or she may proceed to carry out those works even if they lead to harm being caused to protected wildlife, provided that the harm could not reasonably be avoided.

And the same would apply where, for example, a developer wishes to build a housing estate on a site on which are currently growing trees that provide the habitat for a particular species of rare butterfly. The planning authority, in deciding whether or not to grant planning permission, will have to weigh up (alongside any other considerations) the importance of preserving the butterflies. As it ponders its decision, it should take into account that a grant of permission will make the development lawful, and that if the implementation of the permission leads to the loss of the trees and thus inevitably to the loss of the butterflies, there is nothing further that can be done to protect them.

If someone who has been charged with harming wild birds, animals or plants of a protected species wishes to rely on this defence, as with all statutory defences of this kind, it is for him or her to show in any trial – on the balance of probabilities – that it does apply (rather than for the prosecution to show that it does not).[99] In particular, the accused has to prove that:

- the operation that led to the harm being caused to the birds, nest, eggs or whatever was lawful;

- the harm caused was the incidental result of that operation; and

- the harm could not reasonably have been avoided.

As to the first element, it will normally be necessary to point to a licence, permission or consent of some kind for the relevant operation. Alternatively, it would be sufficient to show that as a matter of law no such authorisation was required – for example, because works to a tree protected by a tree preservation order were covered by one of the statutory exemptions in that order[1] or because any building operations which led to the loss of a tree were permitted development under the General Development Order.

As to the second element of the defence, that will be for the defence to prove on the basis of appropriate factual evidence.

The most important issue in practice is likely to be the third element of the defence, which requires the accused person to prove that the harm could not be avoided. It is of course in principle difficult to prove a negative; and thus it may be that it is up to the prosecution to suggest ways in which they say that the harm could have been avoided – for example, by felling being delayed until after the nesting season, or by the area around a group of protected plants being fenced off to prevent harm. It would then be open to the owner of the land or the contractor

---

[99] See **19.4.2**.
[1] See **17.7 to 17.9**.

responsible for the works to show why such protective measures would have been unreasonable.

The special rules that apply in the case of proposed operations affecting bats have already been considered.[2]

9.3.6 Licences under the 1981 Act

The offences under section 1 of the 1981 Act relating to harm caused to wild birds[3] do not apply to an act done under a licence obtained from the appropriate authority under section 16(1) of the Act. However, such a licence may only be granted where the proposed act is for one of the purposes listed in that subsection. Most of those relate to the well-being of birds or to other ornithological concerns,[4] and so are not relevant where the harm is caused as the incidental result of works to trees.

A licence may also be granted, however, where the act causing the harm to the protected birds is for the purposes of preserving public health, or public or air safety, preventing the spread of disease, or preventing serious damage to livestock, foodstuffs for livestock, crops, vegetables, fruit, growing timber, fisheries or inland waters.[5] That would include the felling of a tree that is considered hazardous – either to those on the land where it is growing or to those on neighbouring land, particularly where it overhangs a highway.[6]

Similarly, a licence may be granted, under section 16(3), to authorise works affecting wild animals or wild plants that would otherwise be an offence under section 9 or section 13. Again, the act authorised must be either for various purposes (principally zoological or botanical) not relevant in the present context,[7] or for the purposes of preserving public health or public safety, preventing the spread of disease or preventing serious damage to livestock, foodstuffs for livestock, crops, vegetables, fruit, growing timber or any other form of property or to fisheries.[8]

Where a licence is sought (under either section 16(1) or section 16(3)) for an act undertaken for any of the various purposes spelt out above – heath, safety or the prevention of serious damage – the appropriate authority is the Secretary of State for the Environment, Food and Rural Affairs in relation to England, and the National Assembly for Wales concurrently with the Secretary of State for Wales.[9]

9.3.7 Breaches of 1981 Act

Any of the offences under the Wildlife and Countryside Act 1981 may be the subject of a prosecution mounted by a local authority[10] or by the police. The nature conservancy councils[11] may assist,[12] but they may not bring a prosecution in their own right. In practice, most investigations under the Act (or the

---

[2]   See **9.3.3**.
[3]   See **9.3.2**.
[4]   WCA 1981, s. 16(1)(a)–(h), amended by S.I. 1995 No. 2825, reg. 3.
[5]   WCA 1981, s. 16(1)(i)–(k), amended by S.I. 1995 No. 2825, reg. 3.
[6]   See **Chapters 5 and 6**; particularly **5.8.3**.
[7]   WCA 1981, s. 16(3)(a)–(e).
[8]   WCA 1981, s. 16(3)(f)–(h).
[9]   WCA 1981, ss. 16(9), 27(1); S.I. 1999 No. 672, art. 2, Sched. 2; S.I. 2000 No. 794, art. 2.
[10] WCA 1981, s. 25(2).
[11] See **9.3.3** and note 84 above.
[12] WCA 1981, s. 24(4).

Conservation (Natural Habitats, etc.) Regulations 1994) are carried out and prosecutions mounted by the police; and a number of police forces now have wildlife liaison officers, with special knowledge and experience, to deal with them.

In the case of all these offences, the 1981 Act only refers to the actual interference with the wild bird, animal or plant itself as being an offence; that is, there is no offence of causing or permitting the act in question. It follows that where works are carried out to a tree by a tree surgeon or other contractor, under the instructions of the owner of the land, on the face of it only the contractor is liable to prosecution. However, by virtue of the Magistrates Courts Act 1980,[13] those who aid, abet, counsel or procure the commission of a summary offence may be prosecuted as if they had actually committed the offence themselves. A landowner (or developer, etc.) who instructs a contractor to fell a tree knowing that, for example, it contains a birds nest, may therefore be prosecuted under section 1 of the 1981 Act just as if he or she had felled the tree him/herself. If, on the other hand, the contractor knows about the nest but the owner does not, the owner could probably escape conviction on the basis that he or she lacked the necessary intention.[14]

All the offences under the 1981 Act are summary only – that is, they may only be the subject of prosecution in the magistrates court. However, the time limit for mounting a prosecution is (unusually[15]) six months from the date on which evidence sufficient to warrant the proceedings came to the knowledge of the prosecutor – subject to a limit of two years from the date of the actual commission of the offence.[16]

The penalties for the various offences are as follows. Offences under Part I of the 1981 Act relating to wild birds (under section 1), wild animals (section 9) and wild plants (section 13) are punishable on conviction with a prison sentence of up to six months or a fine of up to level 5 on the standard scale.[17] And where a charge under the Act relates to harm caused to more than one bird, animal or plant, the maximum sentence on conviction is determined as if each bird, etc. was the subject of a separate charge.[18] This is the result of amendments made to the 1981 Act by the Countryside and Rights of Way Act 2000. No similar amendments have (yet) been made to the 1994 Regulations. For the moment, therefore, offences under the Regulations relating to wild animals and wild plants attract a fine of up to level 5 or level 4 respectively.[19]

9.3.8 Trees in sites of special scientific interest (SSSIs)

In addition to the protection afforded to various forms of wildlife, described above,[20] the law also recognises a number of different types of habitat which require more general protection. Many of these will contain trees and hedges, and

---

[13]   MCA 1980, s. 44.
[14]   *Callow v Tillstone* (1900) LT 411.
[15]   The time limit for mounting a summary prosecution is normally six months from the commission of the offence.
[16]   WCA 1981, s. 20(2).
[17]   WCA 1981, s. 21(1), substituted by Countryside and Rights of Way Act 2000, Sched. 12, para. 10.
[18]   WCA 1981, s. 21(5).
[19]   Conservation (Natural Habitats, etc.) Regulations 1994, regs. 39(6), 43(7).
[20]   See **9.3.2 to 9.3.4**.

works to those may as a result require special authorisation – and some types of works may in practice be impossible.

The most significant designation for present purposes is where land is notified as a site of special scientific interest (SSSI); it may be noted that over 2 million hectares of land in Great Britain[21] has been designated as an SSSI – which represents around 8 per cent of the total land area. The relevant legislation is contained in sections 28 to 28R of the Wildlife and Countryside Act 1981, which were inserted into that Act by section 75 of and Schedule 9 to the Countryside and Rights of Way Act 2000 with effect from February 1, 2001.[22] References below to the 1981 Act are to it in its amended form.

An SSSI is an area of land which is of special interest by reason of any of its flora, fauna, or geological or physiographical features, and has been notified as such by the relevant nature conservancy council[23] to the local planning authority, the owner and occupier of the land concerned, and the Secretary of State.[24] That notification is also to specify the flora, fauna, or geological or physiographical features that cause the land to be of special interest, and any operations appearing to the conservancy council to be likely to damage that flora or fauna or those features[25] – and those operations may well include works to trees (including dead ones) or hedges in the area.

Thereafter, the owner or occupier of land in the SSSI may not carry out any of those potentially damaging operations without first obtaining written consent from the conservancy council, unless (as is not very likely) they are in accordance with a management agreement, scheme or notice.[26] Such consent may – indeed, is likely to be – subject to conditions; so that, for example, consent might be given to undertake limited pruning to a veteran tree in an SSSI, but only provided that the works do not disturb particular habitats for rare invertebrates. There are provisions for appealing in the event that consent is refused.[27]

A public body (including a department of central Government or a local authority) similarly has to notify the relevant conservancy council before carrying out any potentially damaging operations. But, if the council declines to give its assent, it can proceed anyway as long as the operations are carried out in such a way as to give rise to as little damage as is reasonably practicable in all the circumstances.[28]

It is an offence to carry out potentially damaging operations without having first obtained written consent from the conservancy council (or its assent in the case of operations by a public body). Such an offence carries a sentence of a fine of up to £20,000 on summary conviction or an unlimited fine on conviction on

---

[21] 1,053,796 ha in England by 2000.

[22] The new provisions replaced WCA 1981, ss. 28 and 29 as originally enacted, which were described in the House of Lords as being "toothless" (see *Southern Water v Nature Conservancy Council* [1992] 3 All E.R. 481, H.L., per Lord Mustill at p. 484).

[23] English Nature, Countryside Council for Wales (Cyngor Cefn Gwlad Cymru), or Scottish Natural Heritage; see **9.3.3** and note 84 above.

[24] WCA 1981, s. 28(1). Note that a notification made before the amended legislation came into force is deemed to have been made under the new rules: see 2000 Act, Sched. 11, para. 2.

[25] WCA 1981, s. 28(4).

[26] WCA 1981, s. 28E.

[27] WCA 1981, s. 28F.

[28] WCA 1981, s. 28H. Such bodies also have a general duty, in carrying out their functions, to further the conservation and enhancement of the special flora, fauna and other features of the SSSI (s. 28G).

indictment.[29] It is, however, a defence to prove that an operation was carried out in an emergency, and was notified to the council as soon as possible.[30]

9.3.9 Other designations

Some SSSIs are designated under international conventions or directives, such as Ramsar sites under the Ramsar Convention,[31] special protection areas (SPAs) under the Birds Directive,[32] and special areas of conservation (SACs) under the Habitats Directive.[33] These receive special protection under the Conservation (Natural Habitats, etc.) Regulations 1994 as "European sites".[34]

All the land designated under any of these provisions is also notified as an SSSI; and in the present context, that it is the controls which flow from the latter that are the most significant. However, it is likely that those controls will be exercised with more vigour in the case of European sites, and it may be noted that a number of the habitat types that are defined to be of Community interest relate to forests.[35] Those found in the United Kingdom include the following (with the estimated total area in hectares):

"Atlantic acidophilous beech forests with *Ilex* and sometimes also *Taxus* in the shrublayer (6,000-8,500); *Asperulo-Fagetum* beech forests (11,000-13,500); sub-Atlantic and medio-European oak or oak-hornbeam forests of the *Carpinion betuli* (1,000); *Tilio-Acerion* ravine forests (8,000-15,000); old acidophilous oak woods with *Quercus robur* on sandy plains (4,000-5,000); old sessile oak woods with *Ilex* and *Blechnum* (96,000-111,000); Caledonian forest (25,440); bog woodland (less than 1,200); residual alluvial forests with *Alnus glutinosa* and *Fraxinus excelsior* (4,500-8,000); *Taxus baccata* woods (less than 1,500)."[36]

Other areas of land which are being managed as a nature reserve and are of national importance may be declared as national nature reserves, under section 35 of the Wildlife and Countryside Act 1981.[37] These will almost all contain trees or hedges; but, again, they are all notified as SSSIs.

9.4 Other controls

9.4.1 Trees in hedgerows

This Chapter generally concerns works to trees, rather than works to hedgerows as such. However, where trees to be removed are in a hedgerow, and are sufficient

---

[29] WCA 1981, s. 28P(1)–(3).

[30] WCA 1981, s. 28P(4)(b).

[31] The Ramsar Convention on Wetlands of International Importance, ratified in 1976 and amended in 1982 by the Birds Directive (see below).

[32] EC Council Directive on the Conservation of Wild Birds; Directive 79/409.

[33] EC Council Directive on the Conservation of Natural Habitats and of Wild Flora and Fauna; Directive 92/43.

[34] 1994 Regulations, reg. 10.

[35] See Annex I to the Habitats Directive (reproduced as Annex G to PPG 9).

[36] JNCC Report 312: *Handbook on the UK status of EC Habitats Directive interest features: provisional data on the UK distribution and extent of Annex I habitats and the UK distribution and population size of Annex II species.* The figures for the areas (in brackets) are estimates based on expert opinion.

[37] See also National Parks and Access to the Countryside Act 1949, ss. 15 to 22.

in number to constitute "a stretch of hedgerow forming part of a hedgerow", they would be properly classified as a hedgerow subject to the Hedgerows Regulations 1997,[38] and their felling would thus need to be notified to the appropriate local planning authority.

The removal of a hedgerow without notice having been given to the relevant planning authority, or where a hedgerow retention notice has been issued, is an offence under the 1997 Regulations.[39] See **Chapter 24** for further details.

9.4.2 Trees in or near archaeological sites

Particular care may be needed where works are proposed to a tree that is close to a scheduled ancient monument; or indeed where a tree is to be planted in such a location.

The Ancient Monuments and Archaeological Areas Act 1979 provides that references in that Act to a monument include references to the site of the monument in question[40]; and that the site of a monument includes not only the land in or on which it is situated but also any land comprising or adjoining it which appears[41] to be essential for the monument's support and preservation.[42] The "land" thus referred to will of course include any trees (and hedges) growing in it. Further, references to a monument include references to part of the monument, as so defined.[43]

By virtue of section 2 of the Act, scheduled monument consent is needed for works in any of the following categories:

"(a) any works resulting in the demolition or destruction of or any damage to a scheduled monument;
 (b) any works for the purpose of removing or repairing a scheduled monument or any part of it or of making any alterations thereto; and
 (c) any flooding or tipping operations on land in, on or under which there is a scheduled monument".

This means, in particular, that consent will be needed for almost any works which interfere with the ground (such as soil moving, and grubbing up tree roots and hedges). It would also be required, at least in theory, for works of any consequence to the above-ground portions of a tree. Although in practice it would probably be appropriate to seek consent where such works were likely to affect either the ground itself or any man-made structures – thus, for example, consent should be sought for up-rooting but not (normally) for felling or pruning. Consent may also be needed to plant a tree or hedge.

This is unlike the position with listed building consent, which is only required for the carrying out of works that actually affect the listed building itself, not the ground in its curtilage.[44] In addition, by virtue of section 2(2)(a), consent is required for works that actually result in the demolition or destruction of or

---

[38] S.I. 1997 No. 1160; see reg. 3(2).
[39] reg. 7.
[40] 1979 Act, s. 61(10)(a).
[41] To the Secretary of State or English Heritage or to a local planning authority, in the exercise in relation to that monument of any of their functions
[42] 1979 Act, s. 61(9).
[43] 1979 Act, s. 61(10)(a).
[44] *Cotswold DC v Secretary of State* [1985] J.P.L. 407.

damage to all or part of a monument (including the ground surrounding it), even if the person responsible has no intention to bring about such a result.

Just as planning permission is granted automatically for certain categories of relatively minor development, there are a number of operations affecting scheduled monuments which are normally of little consequence, and for which as a result scheduled monument consent is granted automatically, by means of an order made by the Secretary of State under powers in section 3(1) of the 1979 Act. The categories of works that are currently granted consent in this way are listed in the Schedule to the Ancient Monuments (Class Consents) Order 1994.[45] The 1994 Order should be consulted for the detailed wording of the various classes and the exceptions to each class.

Class 1 comprises agricultural, horticultural and forestry works. This is on the basis that such works are carried out regularly, so that they will not cause any new damage. Unsurprisingly, therefore, the consent applies only where the works are carried out at the same spot as others of the same kind that have been carried out at some time in the previous six years. Further, there are a number of specific categories of works that are excluded from the general consent under this Class – largely those which cause greater disturbance to the ground, including, in particular:

". . . sub-soiling, draining works, the planting or uprooting of trees, hedges or shrubs, the stripping of top soil, tipping operations, or the cutting and removal of turf".[46]

Class 5 is works urgently necessary for safety or health. They are only granted consent in this way, however, if they are limited to the minimum measures immediately necessary and if they are notified in writing (together with a justification for them) to the Secretary of State as soon as is reasonably practicable. In deciding whether proposed works to a tree are indeed necessary for safety, the considerations already identified in the context of hazardous trees[47] would seem to be relevant.

Where consent is required, but is not granted automatically by the Class Consents Order, an application should be made to the Secretary of State on form AM112, which is available (together with supporting guidance) from the Department of Culture, Media and Sport in London[48] or from Cadw: Welsh Historic Monuments in Cardiff.[49]

If works are carried out for which scheduled monument consent was required but without it having first been obtained, that is a criminal offence punishable with a fine of up to the statutory maximum on summary conviction or an unlimited fine on conviction on indictment.[50]

The above is inevitably only a brief summary; for a fuller account, a specialist text should be consulted.[51]

---

[45] S.I. 1994 No. 1381.
[46] 1994 Order, Schedule, Class 1, restriction (c).
[47] See **5.10**.
[48] 2–4 Cockspur Street, London SW1Y 5DH (www.culture.gov.uk).
[49] Cathays Park, Cardiff, CF10 3NQ (www.cadw.wales.gov.uk).
[50] Ancient Monuments and Archaeological Areas Act 1979, s. 2(10).
[51] See, for example, *Listed Buildings, Conservation Areas and Monuments*, Mynors (Sweet & Maxwell, third edn, 1999); see especially Chapters 4 and 12.

9.4.3 *Works affecting watercourses and land drains*

By virtue of section 90 of the Water Resources Act 1991, a person is guilty of an
offence if he or she:

- causes or permits a substantial amount of vegetation to be cut or uprooted
  in any inland freshwaters, or to be cut or uprooted so near to any such
  waters that it falls into them; and

- fails to take all reasonable steps to remove the vegetation from those
  waters.[52]

It is, in theory, possible to obtain from the Environment Agency a licence to
authorise such a course of action, but it is difficult to imagine why one would ever
be granted. Otherwise, the offender is liable on summary conviction to a fine of up
to level 4 on the standard scale.[53]

Similarly, it is an offence to cause a blockage of any ordinary watercourse – see
section 25 of Land Drainage Act 1991.

9.4.4 *Trees in environmentally sensitive areas*

The Secretary of State for Environment, Food and Rural Affairs (and the
National Assembly for Wales) may designate "environmentally sensitive areas"
under section 18 of the Agriculture Act 1986.[54] The purpose of such a designation
is (amongst other things) to conserve and enhance the natural beauty of an area,
and to conserve its flora, fauna or geological or physiographical features, through
the maintenance and adoption of particular agricultural methods.

Designation is usually followed by the drawing up of management agreements,[55] which provide for the making of payments by the Secretary of State in
exchange for an undertaking by a landowner to manage his or her land in a
particular way. The preparation of such an agreement is subject to the same
procedures as that of forestry dedication covenants.

The relevance of this for the present purposes is that an agreement under the
1986 Act may well prohibit or limit the felling of trees – for example, to maintain
shelter belts or wildlife habitats, or to retain woodlands which form important
landscape features.

9.4.5 *Planning permission*

The conventional view is that planning permission is not required for the carrying
out of works to trees, since such works do not constitute "development".

The definition of "development" includes the carrying out of building,
engineering, mining or other operations in, on, over or under land[56]; and it
could be argued that the carrying out of major works to a tree – including felling –
constitutes "other operations".[57] A tree is part of the land, but so are minerals

---

[52]   Water Resources Act 1991, s. 90(2).
[53]   Water Resources Act 1991, s. 90(3).
[54]   See S.I. 1999 No. 672, art. 2, Sched. 1, and S.I. 2002 No. 794.
[55]   Under 1986 Act, s. 18(3); see **12.6.1**.
[56]   TCPA 1990, s. 55(1).
[57]   Or possibly "engineering operations".

before they are extracted; there is therefore no conceptual difference between the extraction of minerals and the carrying out of works to trees. And, whereas there is, for example, a specific provision exempting advertising from the need for planning permission even if it happens to be development,[58] there is no corresponding provision relating to trees. However, in practice no such argument is known to have ever been advanced before the courts; and the conventional view, even if not strictly logical, is universally assumed to be correct.

Of greater concern in practice is that some trees were originally planted to comply with a condition imposed on a grant of planning permission either by the local planning authority or (usually on appeal) by the Secretary of State. The carrying out of works to such a tree may well require the permission of the local planning authority. And trees may also be protected during the carrying out of development. This is considered further in due course.[59]

9.5 Carrying out works to trees: the duty of care

9.5.1 General duty of care

Once a felling licence has been obtained from the Forestry Commission (if the works are on a sufficient scale) and consent under any tree preservation order from the local authority, and once the works have been planned so as to avoid or minimise harm to conservation areas, wildlife, protected habitats, hedgerows, archaeological monuments and watercourses, it is then possible to start work. But care is still required; works to trees – whether the removal of a single branch or the felling of several hectares of conifers – are potentially hazardous, and those responsible must avoid causing harm.

As already explained, everyone has a duty at common law to take reasonable care to avoid acts or omissions which they can reasonably foresee would be likely to injure their neighbour – that is, anyone so closely and directly affected that he or she should be taken into account.[60] If on that basis A has a duty of care to B, then a breach of that duty may give rise to a civil action for negligence by B against A if it causes foreseeable harm to B.

The outworking of that principle in practice has been considered at length in numerous specialist texts,[61] which should be consulted as appropriate; but one obvious example of it would be the carrying out of works to a tree, where it is obvious (or at the very least reasonably foreseeable) that a false move may have potentially disastrous consequences – both to those on the ground (bystanders, including users of any highway affected, and owners of property) and to anyone in the tree. It is thus inevitable that those harmed (or whose property is harmed) directly or indirectly as a result of the carrying out of such works may seek to recover damages in a civil law action in negligence.[62]

Advice as to the conduct of such litigation, and the calculation of damages in the event that negligence is established, should be sought elsewhere.

---

[58] TCPA 1990, s. 222.
[59] See **15.9**.
[60] *Donoghue v Stevenson* [1932] A.C. 562, H.L., per Lord Atkin at p. 580; see **5.2.1**.
[61] See, for example, Winfield and Jolowicz, *Tort*, fifteenth edn, 1998, Chapter 5; Clerk and Lindsell, *Torts*, eighteenth edn, 2000, Chapter 7.
[62] See **9.5.2 to 9.5.4**.

In addition to those common law principles, there is a whole raft of health and safety legislation, principally in the form of regulations made under the Health and Safety at Work, etc. Act 1974.[63] A breach of these regulations, or indeed of the Act itself, would in principle lead to a criminal prosecution of the employer – which might help to prevent a recurrence of the problem, but would be of little assistance to an injured employee. But since the enactment of the 1974 Act, such regulations may impose civil as well as criminal liability[64]; and this has indeed happened, more especially since a series of EC Directives.

It follows that both strands of the law must be considered to obtain a true picture as to the incidence of liability. The outline below is inevitably only a very brief summary; for further details, including the text of all the various statutory instruments and directives, a good source of reference is the *Encyclopedia of Health and Safety at Work, Law and Practice.*[65]

Finally, reference should be made to BS 3998, the stated purpose of which is to give general recommendations for tree work, for owners of established trees, for agents of the owners, and for those responsible for planning, specifying and undertaking work on maturing trees.[66] Compliance with a British Standard does not of itself confer immunity from legal obligations, but it does minimise the risk of problems arising. Compliance with the standard may also be a requirement of the contract governing the carrying out of works to trees.

9.5.2 *Liability of contractors to bystanders*

It is, in general, difficult for a contractor to escape liability for injuries sustained as a result of works to trees negligently carried out. It is, after all, not difficult to attack a tree with a chain saw; the skill lies in knowing what will happen next. Any damage that results should thus be reasonably foreseeable by any competent contractor. It should also be avoidable with reasonable care, either by selecting the most appropriate way in which for the work to be done, or by erecting and maintaining suitable protective barriers. Indeed, such foresight and care is precisely what is being paid for.

One of the earlier reported cases involving works to trees, *Mourton v Poulter,*[67] concerned the felling of a large elm tree on a piece of unfenced waste land adjoining the highway. The owner of the land, a developer, engaged the defendant (a nurseryman) to fell the tree. Unsurprisingly, in an age with few other forms of amusement, a large number of children gathered round to watch, and several times had to be driven back. By the end of the day, the tree was held up by one root only, and the defendant, knowing that when that root was cut the tree would fall within two minutes, and without giving any further warning to the children, cut that last root, whereupon the tree fell, injuring a 10-year-old boy.

Even at that time, two years before the decision in *Donoghue v Stevenson,*[68] there was no doubt as to the negligence of the nurseryman; the only uncertainty was as to liability for negligence in relation to harm caused to those who, as in this case, were trespassers. And it is noteworthy that the Divisional Court in *Mourton,*

---

[63] See **9.5.5 to 9.5.7.**
[64] 1974 Act, s. 47(2).
[65] Sweet and Maxwell.
[66] BS 3998: 1989 (British Standards Institution); amended December 21, 1990.
[67] [1930] 2 K.B. 183.
[68] [1932] A.C. 562, H.L.; see **9.5.1.**

faced with two very recent and mutually contradictory decisions of the House of Lords, chose to follow the one that imposed liability,[69] rather than the one that did not.[70] That debate was of course in any event rendered academic by the enactment of the Occupiers' Liability Act 1984[71]; but for present purposes the key fact is that a person felling a tree is liable in negligence to anyone injured, including bystanders – whether trespassers or not – and, of course, particularly to children. The fact that it may be difficult to prevent them being in the way is irrelevant.

A further example is provided by the tragic case of *Salsbury v Woodland*,[72] in which a tree felling contractor removed a hawthorn tree in a suburban front garden, but did it in such an incompetent manner that the tree fell onto a pair of telephone wires, which in turn fell into the road, causing an obstruction. S, a friend of the occupier of the house next door, who had been watching the whole operation out of curiosity, ran into the road to remove the wires and thus obviate the hazard; but before he could do so, a car approached at high speed, and S realised that it was bound to collide with the wires. He accordingly threw himself onto the grass verge so as to be out of the way, but this caused a tumour in his spine to bleed; and the result of this on the adjacent spinal chord was to give S all the symptoms of paraplegia.

As in *Mourton*, here there was no dispute as to the negligence on the part of the contractor; he had offered no defence to the claim and did not seek to escape liability. The only question in issue was whether that liability (and thus responsibility for the payment of damages) should be shared between him, the householder who had employed him, and the motorist; this is considered further below.[73] *Salsbury* is thus in no way determinative as to the liability in law of tree contractors; but it does illustrate the potential extent of that liability – and there can be little doubt that if, for example, there had indeed been (as feared by S) a major collision as a result of the wires falling onto the road, so that one or more motorists or their passengers had been injured, they would have been joining S to sue the contractor.

A more recent example of the kind of problem that can arise, especially in the context of works to trees on or near the highway, was *Koyn v Department of Transport*.[73a] Contractors were working in the highway at night, to remove a diseased and dangerous poplar, and a motorist collided with the workmen, due to the incompetent way in which the works had been laid out.

But there are limits. One new hazard is that bystanders are occasionally found in the trees themselves, rather than merely on the ground. Thus, in *Ellis v Department of Transport*[74] the claimant (E) was in a tree, securely (as he thought) attached by ropes, protesting against the construction of the Bath By-Pass and the consequent destruction of trees. The lower branches of the tree were being removed both by the main contractor building the road and a tree surgeon, using a chain saw from a hydraulic hoist. The protestors, including E, were standing on branches which were to be cut. E then fell when the branch he was on gave way

---

[69] *Excelsior Wire Rope Co v Callan* [1930] A.C. 404, H.L.
[70] *Addie (Robert) & Sons (Collieries) Ltd v Dumbreck* [1929] A.C. 358, H.L.
[71] See **5.3.5** and **5.6.4**.
[72] [1970] 1 Q.B. 324, CA.
[73] See **9.5.3**.
[73a] January 30, 2001, unreported, QBD.
[74] July 21, 2000, unreported (Queen's Bench Division).

– his rope turned out not to have been adequately secured after all – and sustained very serious injuries.

The court held that the contractors were not liable under the 1984 Act (E was a trespasser). Further, although both they and the tree surgeons had owed E a duty of care not to enhance the danger that E had created for himself by climbing the tree, they had not breached that duty, so there was no negligence. The contractor, and probably the tree surgeon, should have produced a risk assessment, but their failure to do so had not contributed to E's fall. E had voluntarily exposed himself to the whole risk as a matter of deliberate policy, and could not now hold the contractors liable for it; their conduct was not disproportionate. This may be contrasted with the position of the injured child in *Mourton*. And this decision emphasises (albeit *obiter*) the need for a contractor, before undertaking works, to prepare a risk assessment – in relation to not just those carrying out the works but also any others potentially involved such as bystanders and passers-by.

Finally, it may be noted that to fell a tree, or indeed to carry out any works to it, in such a manner as to endanger life (or reckless as to whether the life of another would be thereby endangered) would be an offence under the Criminal Damage Act 1971,[75] carrying a maximum sentence on conviction in the Crown Court of imprisonment for life.[76]

In general, litigation arises out of people being injured as a result of works to trees negligently carried out, but the same principles would apply to property being damaged – the most likely problems in practice being falling branches hitting vehicles, or structures such as walls, greenhouses and sheds.

9.5.3 Liability of property owners to bystanders

The discussion above has considered the liability of a contractor for harm caused by works to trees negligently carried out. But it may be that an owner too is liable in some situations – either as well as, or instead of, the contractor.

This was the main point considered by the Court of Appeal in *Salsbury v Woodland*, the facts of which have already been outlined. It was accepted that it was perfectly reasonable for the householder to have hired the contractor in question, who was apparently competent to carry out the works. However, given that the contractor in the event achieved what Sachs L.J. described as a "near miracle of incompetence",[77] the question was then whether the householder was vicariously liable. Widgery L.J. noted that it is trite law that one who employs an independent contractor is in general not vicariously liable for any negligence of that contractor; but that there are cases where the employer owed a direct duty to the person injured, a duty which he or she cannot delegate to a contractor on his or her behalf.[78]

The court considered that cases in the latter category fell into two groups. The first was where hazards arose on highway land as a result of works carried out under statutory powers (by highway authorities, statutory undertakers or others) – which might indeed include works to highway trees,[79] but would not necessarily, or even often, include works to trees which were merely near to highways. The second was where the works being done are so inherently dangerous, or "extra

---

[75] CDA 1971, s. 1(2); see **9.6.2**.
[76] CDA 1971, s. 4(1).
[77] [1970] 1 Q.B. 324, CA, at p. 347.
[78] [1970] 1 Q.B. 324, CA, at pp. 336–337.
[79] See **Chapter 6**.

hazardous", in relation either to those on a highway or to neighbours generally, that the public interest demands absolute responsibility.

In the present case, the contractor had been told that no stump was to be left, which involved bringing up the roots as well. Having lopped the tree to some extent but not so significantly as to affect its total height, he then dug a trench round the root bole of the tree, severed some of the roots, and proceeded by means of a tractor to push and pull the tree with a view to loosening it and causing it to fall. This method of removing the stump gave him no real control over the direction in which the tree fell, so it was not entirely surprising that one long branch fell so as to foul the telephone wires, with the unfortunate results already described.

The judge at first instance held that "there can be no doubt that there was an inherent risk of injury to others when the tree was felled unless proper care was taken to get rid of the risk." Widgery L.J. commented upon those words as follows:

"[T]he evidence makes it perfectly clear that the tree could have been felled by a competent contractor, using proper care, without any risk of injury to anyone. The undisputed evidence of an expert was that the proper way to fell it, in its confined situation, was to lop the branches respectively until there was left a stump of only eight to ten feet in height. All that could be done without any danger to anyone, if, at any rate, all appropriate precautions were taken, and the resultant stump eight to ten feet high could then have been winched out of the ground, again without risk to anyone. So when the judge referred to it as being an operation in which 'there was an inherent risk', he was, in my view, putting the matter too high. If he meant that there was a risk which even due care could not avoid, he was, in my judgment, quite wrong upon the undisputed evidence that was before him."[80]

The Court thus considered that there was nothing inherently dangerous in the works to be done in this case.

Sachs L.J., however, went on to note, albeit *obiter*, that:

"[T]he whole position as regards 'inherent danger' might be very different if the case was concerned with the removal of a 60-foot tree. The appropriate operation in the instant case was, incidentally, as different from what is usually termed 'tree-felling' as a hawthorn differs from the single-trunk, tall trees to which, of course, the word 'felling' is normally an appropriate word to apply."[81]

That suggests that an owner may in principle retain liability where he or she proposes the carrying out of felling or other works to a tree which is unusually high or in an unusually confined or exposed location, or where the nature of the works themselves is such that they are "inherently dangerous" – by which is presumably meant that there is an element of danger however carefully the works are carried out. Examples might be the felling of an exceptionally tall tree, or the lopping of a branch overhanging a major road, or the removal of a major part of a tree that is known to be diseased.

It may of course be perfectly appropriate for an owner of a tree in such circumstances to seek a written indemnity from the contractor, whereby the contractor voluntarily assumes any risk of liability that would otherwise be borne by the owner.

---

[80] [1970] 1 Q.B. 324, CA, at p. 337.
[81] [1970] 1 Q.B. 324, CA, at p. 348.

An owner should in any event select carefully the person who is to do works to any particular tree. It may be entirely reasonable to rely on a teenage son or daughter to remove a small branch of an apple tree overhanging a flower bed; but the felling of a large tree standing next to a major railway line after partial storm damage should only be carried out by a very experienced tree surgeon.

Finally, problems may arise where a fence is damaged by fall of tree. Quite apart from liability for the repair of the fence itself, there may be further liability for any damage caused by livestock who are now able to stray through the resulting gap. Normally, such responsibility will rest with the person actually carrying out the work, but where (exceptionally) the owner of a fence has repaired it for so long that a quasi-easement had arisen by prescription, that owner would then be liable.[82]

9.5.4 Liability to those carrying out the works

Quite apart from the general duty of care on the part of anyone responsible for works to trees not to harm bystanders and others,[83] there is a specific duty on those organising such works to ensure the safety of those actually carrying them out.

The classic formulation of the duty of an employer to his or her workers was set out by the House of Lords 60 years ago – "the provision of a competent staff of men, adequate material and a proper system and effective supervision."[84] More recently it has been expressed as follows:

". . . a duty not to subject the employee to any risk which the employer can reasonably foresee, or, to put it slightly lower, not to subject the employee to any risk which the employer can reasonably foresee and which he can guard against by any measure the convenience and expense of which are not entirely disproportionate to the risk involved".[85]

In the context of tree surgery, one key aspect of the employer's duty is to take reasonable care to provide his or her workers with the necessary plant and equipment[86] and, no less important, to maintain it in proper condition.[87] This extends to the installation of necessary safety devices on dangerous machinery[88] (such as, presumably, chainsaws) and the provision of protective equipment when required.[89] The employer is indeed also liable for defective equipment even where the defect was caused by the manufacturer of the equipment.[90]

The place of work will be the actual tree to which the works are to be carried out, and the ground surrounding it – both of which (and in particular their layout and their inherent safety) are obviously outside the control of the employer. Equally obviously, however, working up a tree with a heavy chainsaw, and getting from one place to another in a tree by means of rope harnesses, are inherently

---

[82] *Lawrence v Jenkins* (1873) Law Rep. 8 Q.B. 274; see also **3.4.4**. See also *Jones v Price* [1965] 2 Q.B. 618, CA.
[83] See **9.5.3**.
[84] *Wilsons and Clyde Coal Co v English* [1938] A.C. 57, per Lord Wright at p. 78.
[85] *Harris v British Asphalt Contractors* [1953] 1 Q.B. 617, per Slade J. at p. 626.
[86] *Ross v Associated Portland Cement Manufacturers* [1964] 1 W.L.R. 768.
[87] *Baxter v St Helena Hospital Management Committee, The Times*, February 14, 1972.
[88] *Jones v Richards* [1955] 1 W.L.R. 444.
[89] *Qualcast Ltd v Haynes* [1959] A.C. 743, H.L.
[90] Employer's Liability (Defective Equipment) Act 1969; as to the manufacturer's liability, see also Consumer Protection Act 1987.

hazardous activities unless sensible precautions are taken. It follows that the other crucial area in which the employer is liable in relation to tree surgery is in the provision of a safe system of working. That is, an employer should exercise reasonable care to devise a system of working that as far as possible minimises the danger of a worker's own foreseeable carelessness, and to see that the system is in fact implemented and complied with by those for whose safety it is instituted.

Finally, it should be remembered in this context that section 47(2) of the Health and Safety at Work, etc. Act 1974 provides that a breach of a requirement of some (but not all) of the various regulations made under that Act is actionable at common law, so far as the breach leads to damage, unless the relevant regulations provide otherwise.[91] It follows that a detailed consideration of their terms will almost always be necessary to obtain a full picture of the potential liability of an employer in any particular situation.

9.5.5 Liability under Health and Safety at Work, etc. Act 1974

The general purposes of the Health and Safety at Work, etc. Act 1974, so far as is relevant to the carrying out of works to trees, are:

- securing the health, safety and welfare of persons at work; and

- protecting persons other than persons at work against risks to health or safety arising out of, or in connection with, the activities of persons at work.[92]

It may be noted that in this context, and in relation to all the regulations made under the 1974 Act, persons at work includes the self-employed.[93] Also, although the term "health and safety at work" is sometimes thought to refer solely to the health and safety of those actually doing the work, the Act and the Regulations do in fact apply equally to ensuring the safety of anyone (such as a bystander) who might be affected.

Section 2 of the Act sets out in general terms the duties of employers to ensure the health, safety and welfare of their employees. Section 3 deals with the duties of employers and the self-employed to avoid exposing to risks persons other than their employees (such as by-standers); and section 7 makes similar provision as to the duties of employees. Section 6 sets out the duties of the manufacturers of equipment used at work. These sections are in similar, but by no means identical, terms to the corresponding common law duties, but do not of themselves provide a basis for a civil action for negligence.[94]

Failure to comply with one of the above provisions of the Act is a criminal offence.[95] Such an offence is triable either way; the maximum penalty for a breach of sections 1 to 6 is £20,000 on summary conviction, or an unlimited fine on conviction in indictment; for a breach of section 7, the penalty is generally lower.[96] In practice, prosecutions are usually bought by the Health and Safety

---

[91]   1974 Act, s. 47(2).
[92]   1974 Act, s. 1(1)(a),(b).
[93]   1974 Act, s. 52.
[94]   1974 Act, s. 47(1).
[95]   1974 Act, s. 33(1)(a).
[96]   1974 Act, s. 33(1A),(3).

Executive (HSE), or occasionally by local authorities.[97] Unsurprisingly, given the inherently hazardous nature of the work involved, the HSE keeps a close eye on the arboriculture and forestry industries.

9.5.6 Regulations and codes of practice under the Act

Of greater importance in practice, perhaps, than the general duties set out in the opening sections of the Health and Safety Act 1974 are the regulations made under section 15 of the Act, and the codes of practice made by the Health and Safety Commission under section 16.[98] The notes below are only a very brief commentary; in every case the Regulations themselves should be consulted to ascertain their precise wording – for example, as to whether they would apply to work carried out in the garden of a private dwellinghouse. This is particularly so in view of the fact that almost none of the Regulations explicitly refer to tree surgery or forestry, the circumstances of which are inevitably somewhat different to those of many other occupations.

The overall approach to an operation should be in accordance with the Management of Health and Safety at Work Regulations 1999[99]; there is an approved Code of Practice providing useful general guidance. In essence, these Regulations provide that every employer must prepare an assessment of risks to the health and safety both of his or her employees and of others, and every self-employed person must assess any risks to him/herself and to others; and they must then set about eliminating or at least minimising those risks.[1] Care must also be taken to protect employees under the age of eighteen.[2]

As for the manner in which operations are carried out, the Manual Handling Regulations 1992,[3] and more especially the HSE guidance,[4] provide a useful checklist of principles affecting the manual handling of loads – which would obviously include tree branches (or sections of them) or whole trunks.

More specific requirements are in the Lifting Operations and Lifting Equipment Regulations 1998[5] (sometimes referred to as LOLER) – every operation involving the lifting or lowering of a load must be properly planned by a competent person, appropriately supervised, and carried out in a safe manner.[6] That would obviously be relevant to the way in which felling and other operations are planned, to avoid problems being caused by the raising and lowering of equipment (including, in particular, chainsaws and other tools) and workers up into and down from a tree, and the lowering to the ground of sections of a tree as they are removed. The Regulations also require that lifting equipment (including,

[97] 1974 Act, s. 18; see ss. 19 to 28 and 34 to 46 for further details of enforcement procedure.
[98] As to the status of such codes, see **9.5.7**.
[99] S.I. 1999 No. 3242, implementing EC Directive 89/391/EEC (OJ L183 June 29, 1989, p. 1); replacing S.I. 1992 No. 2051.
[1] S.I. 1999 No. 3242, regs. 3, 4.
[2] S.I. 1999 No. 3242, reg. 19, replacing Health and Safety at Work (Young Persons) Regulations S.I. 1997 No. 135. Note that the Health and Safety (Training for Employment) Regulations 1990 (S.I. 1990 No. 1380) extend to trainees and students on sandwich courses the general protection given to employees.
[3] S.I. 1992 No. 2793, implementing EC Directive 90/269/EEC (OJ L1156/9).
[4] *Manual Handling: Guidance on Regulations* (L23), HMSO.
[5] S.I. 1998 No. 2307, partially implementing EC Directive 89/655/EEC (OJ L393, December 30, 1989, p. 13), as amended by 95/63/EC (OJ L335, December 30, 1995, p. 28).
[6] S.I. 1998 No. 2307, reg. 8.

presumably, ropes, harnesses, slings, karabiners and other anchorages, friction brakes and pulleys) be thoroughly examined for any defects at regular intervals.[7]

As for the equipment itself, including in particular chainsaws, chippers, stump grinders, but including more generally the whole range of equipment used, that will be governed by the Provision and Use of Work Equipment Regulations 1998[8] (PUWER). The Regulations require that all equipment must be suitable for the task in hand, well maintained, and used by operators who are sufficiently trained. This may well determine (or at least influence) the decision by contractors as to whether, for example, tree work is carried out using traditional techniques involving climbing or from a mobile elevated work platform (MEWP).

No approved Code of Practice appears to have been issued by the HSE in relation to either set of 1998 Regulations, but it has in each case issued "Open Learning Guidance", available from HSE Books. And of course there are various booklets and other guides available from the relevant trade-based training bodies, all of which may provide useful practical guidance applicable in particular situations.

Personal protective equipment (PPE) is governed by the Personal Protective Equipment at Work Regulations 1992[9] and Personal Protective Equipment (EC Directive) Regulations 1992.[10] The former, in particular, require that chainsaw operators are provided with and wear the appropriate PPE, to minimise the risk of injury.[11] The risk of damage from noise is dealt with by the Noise at Work Regulations 1989,[12] which require the provision of personal ear protectors to those exposed to high levels of noise. The Health and Safety (First-Aid) Regulations 1981[13] require that adequate and appropriate first-aid equipment, facilities and personnel are provided by employers and the self-employed.

The Workplace (Health Safety and Welfare) Regulations 1992[14] require, amongst other things, that suitable and effective measures be taken, so far as reasonably practicable, to prevent any person falling a distance likely to cause personal injury, or being struck by a falling object so as to cause such injury.[15] The obvious precaution to be taken to avoid the latter problem is to provide suitable temporary fencing – although it must be a matter of judgment as to whether that is suitable or practicable where the risk only applies for a short period.

The 1992 Regulations (which also impose general requirements, for example, as to the provision of washing facilities) only apply to a limited extent to forestry operations.[16] "Forestry" for these purposes would seem to bear the same meaning as in the Social Security (Industrial Injuries) (Prescribed Diseases) Regulations 1995, which relates to the availability of compensation in respect of vibration white finger suffered as a result of "the use of a hand-held chain saw in forestry".[17]

---

[7] S.I. 1998 No. 2307, reg. 9.
[8] S.I. 1998 No. 2306, implementing EC Directives noted above; replacing S.I. 1992 No. 2932.
[9] S.I. 1992 No. 2966; the HSE has produced Guidance on these Regulations: see L25, pub HMSO.
[10] S.I. 1992 No. 3139, implementing EC Directive 89/686/EEC OJ L399/18), amended by 93/95: [1993] OJ L276/11. The amended Directive is set out at the Schedule to the Regulations.
[11] HSE Guidance (see note 9 above), Table 1.
[12] S.I. 1989 No. 1790, implementing EC Directive 86/188/EEC (OJ L137, May 24, 1986, p. 28).
[13] S.I. 1981 No. 917; a HSC Code of Practice, revised in 1987, is available from the HSE.
[14] S.I. 1992 No. 3004, implementing EC Directive 89/654/EEC (OJ L393, December 30, 1989, p. 1); the HSE has produced Code of Practice and Guidance on these Regulations: see L24, pub HMSO.
[15] S.I. 1992 No. 3004, reg. 13.
[16] S.I. 1992 No. 3004, reg. 3(4).
[17] S.I. 1985 No. 967, Sched. 1, Pt I, para. A11.

The Court of Appeal has recently held that in that context "forestry" means "the management of growing timber" – regardless of whether that growing timber is in a forest, parkland or elsewhere, or for what purpose it is being grown.[18]

Other regulations which may be relevant to the carrying out of works to trees include the Control of Substances Hazardous to Health Regulations 1999[19] (COSHH), the Reporting of Injuries, Diseases and Dangerous Occurrences Regulations 1995[20] (RIDDOR), and the Working Time Regulations 1998.[21] The Construction (Design and Management) Regulations 1994[22] could also potentially apply where tree felling is carried out as part of the process of site clearance prior to construction work.[23]

9.5.7 Breaches of Health and Safety legislation

Failure to comply with regulations made under the Health and Safety at Work, etc. Act 1974[24] is an offence under section 33. Such an offence is triable either way; the maximum penalty varies according to the precise nature of the breach, but may in an appropriate case be a high fine or imprisonment. Again, prosecutions are usually bought by the Health and Safety Executive or local authorities.[25] Where there exists a relevant Code of Practice issued by the Health and Safety Commission, that will be admissible as evidence in any such prosecution; and if a breach of the Code can be shown, that will generally be evidence of a breach of the regulations to which the Code relates.[26]

In almost every case, the Regulations noted above do not exclude civil liability – that is, in general, a breach of any of their requirements will found a civil action in negligence as well as a criminal prosecution. The principal exceptions are the Management of Health and Safety at Work Regulations 1999 and the Construction (Design and Management) Regulations 1994, which both explicitly exclude civil liability.[27]

9.6 Theft and criminal damage

9.6.1 Theft of trees and other plants
Theft is defined (by the Theft Act 1968[28]) as the dishonest appropriation of property belonging to another with the intention of permanently depriving the other of it, and "property" includes all real property.[29] It has been shown that a

---

[18] *Davis v Secretary of State for Social Security* [2001] EWCA Civ 105, para. 26.
[19] S.I. 1999 No. 437, replacing S.I. 1994 No. 3246, S.I. 1996 No. 3138, S.I. 1997 No. 11, and implementing a range of EC Directives relating to particular products.
[20] S.I. 1995 No. 3163, replacing S.I. 1985 No. 2023.
[21] S.I. 1998 No. 1833, implementing EC Council Directive 93/104/EC (OJ L307, December 13, 1993, p. 18).
[22] S.I. 1994 No. 3140.
[23] S.I. 1994 No. 3140, reg. 2(1): definition of "construction work".
[24] See **9.5.6**.
[25] 1974 Act, s. 18; see ss. 19 to 28 and 34 to 46 for further details of enforcement procedure.
[26] 1974 Act, s. 17.
[27] S.I. 1999 No. 3242, reg. 22; S.I. 1994 No. 3140, reg. 21.
[28] 1968 Act, s. 1(1).
[29] 1968 Act, s. 4(1).

plant generally forms part of the land out of which it grows, and is in the same ownership as that land[30]; it is thus "real property".

The general rule is that it is not possible to steal "land".[31] However, it is theft when someone who does not own a piece of land appropriates something forming part of the land, either by severing it or causing it to be severed, or by removing it after it has been severed.[32] On the face of it, therefore, to remove a plant from the soil in which it is growing, or to remove part of it (such as fruit or flowers, or the branch of a tree) from the remainder, would be theft – unless, obviously, the act is done with the consent of the owner of the soil.

However, this principle is qualified by section 4(3) of the Theft Act 1968, which provides as follows:

"A person who picks mushrooms growing wild on any land, or who picks flowers, fruit or foliage from a plant growing wild on any land, does not (although not in possession of the land) steal what he picks, unless he does it for reward or for sale or other commercial purpose. For the purposes of this subsection, 'mushroom' includes any fungus, and 'plant' includes any shrub or tree."

The result of the provisions explained above is as follows.

First, to pull up out of the ground without consent a whole plant (even a sapling), including its roots, is the appropriation of property; further, it is not the removal of anything from a plant, but the removal of the entire plant, and is thus not exempted by section 4(3). It follows that it constitutes theft, and can be the subject of a criminal prosecution. This is clear in the case where a stranger, after uprooting a plant, removes it altogether from the land (either with the intention of planting it elsewhere, or to destroy it). But it applies equally where someone other than the owner uproots a plant and leaves it there to die, since that is to usurp the rights of its owner, which is part of the concept of "appropriation" of property.[33]

Fungi are normally considered to be botanically distinct from green plants. But the pulling up of a whole mushroom is in any event specifically exempted from the definition of theft by section 4(3), unless it is for commercial purposes.

Secondly, to pick "flowers, fruit or foliage" from a plant growing wild is not theft. Again, this exemption does not apply if the removal is for commercial purposes. That last phrase clearly includes depredation on a fairly large scale – such as removing substantial quantities of holly in order to sell it in a florist's shop at Christmas – but would presumably not include the removal of dead foliage from a tree by a schoolchild in order to earn extra pocket money. The meaning of the phrase "a plant growing wild" is considered below, in the context of the Criminal Damage Act 1971.[34]

Thirdly, it is theft to remove without consent flowers, fruit or foliage by an act which could not be described as "picking" – such as cutting grass with a scythe, or sawing off the top of a Christmas tree. This is so whether or not the act is for commercial purposes.

Fourthly, it is theft to appropriate – that is, in practice, to remove, consume or destroy – all or part of a plant after it has been severed from the ground. So, for example, where apples have fallen from the overhanging branch of a neighbour's

---

[30] See **2.1**.
[31] 1968 Act, s. 4(2).
[32] 1968 Act, s. 4(2)(b), see **3.2.3**.
[33] 1968 Act, s. 3(1); and see *R v Morris* [1983] 3 All E.R. 288.
[34] See **9.6.2**.

tree or have been removed by someone else, it is an offence to eat them, give them away or sell them. This effectively replaces the old offence of "fraudulent conversion" under the Larceny Acts of 1861 and 1916; although the removal of all or part of a plant, even where it does not constitute theft, may still amount to the tort of trespass and conversion.[35]

Note that many acts that in theory constitute theft may be more appropriately classified as criminal damage.[36]

9.6.2 Criminal damage

The Criminal Damage Act 1971[37] makes it an offence to destroy or damage any property belonging to another without lawful excuse, either deliberately or recklessly. The Act defines "property" to include all property of a tangible nature, but it specifically does not include:

". . . mushrooms growing wild on any land, or flowers, fruit or foliage of a plant growing wild on any land. For the purposes of this subsection, 'mushroom' includes any fungus, and 'plant' includes any shrub or tree".[38]

This clearly echoes the provisions of the Theft Act 1968, considered above.[39]

It follows that it is in principle an offence to destroy or damage a plant, including a tree or shrub, belonging to someone else; but not if the damage is only to the flowers, fruit or foliage of a plant growing wild. The dictionary[40] definition of "foliage" is "plant leaves, collectively". It follows that it is an offence to snap off a branch of a tree growing wild, to remove the bark from its trunk, or to carve messages on either branch or trunk.

What is more uncertain is the meaning of the phrase "a plant growing wild". It obviously includes a plant (such as a tree) that is self-seeded, and thereafter left to grow without any human intervention. It equally obviously does not include any plant planted deliberately and thereafter intensively cultivated. The use of the word "growing" tends to suggest that the phrase would include a plant that was once planted deliberately but has for many years been left entirely untended, but conversely not one that was self-seeded but is now consciously maintained. That would mean that the unauthorised removal of foliage from, say, a tree that was once in open countryside but is now in a domestic garden would be theft.

It may be noted that the Wildlife and Countryside Act 1981, which contains a prohibition on picking, uprooting, destroying or selling certain "wild" plants,[41] provides that a plant shall be assumed to be wild unless the contrary is shown.[42] However, that Act is designed to protect wild plants, whereas the Criminal Damage Act and the Theft Act are designed to protect those that are not wild, so it may be that a contrary presumption would be more appropriate. On the other hand, the 1981 Act refers only to a "wild plant", rather than a "plant growing

---

[35] *Mills v Brooker* [1919] 1 K.B. 555 at p. 558; see **3.6.5**.
[36] See **9.6.2**.
[37] Criminal Damage Act 1971, s. 1(1).
[38] 1971 Act, s. 10(1).
[39] See **9.6.1**.
[40] New Oxford Dictionary of English, 1998
[41] WCA 1981, s. 13; see **9.3.4** above.
[42] WCA 1981, s. 13(4).

wild", so caution should be used in assuming that a particular plant is necessarily classified identically under the two statutes.

It is only an offence to damage or destroy the plant with the intention of doing so, or being reckless as to whether it would in fact be destroyed or damaged.[43] The House of Lords has held that "reckless" in the 1971 Act "is an ordinary English word", not "a term of legal art".[44] More generally, as to the necessary degree of intention that must be proved in order to secure a conviction under the Act, general texts on criminal law should be consulted.

9.6.3 The "ownership" of trees and shrubs

It will have been noted that the offence of criminal damage only applies to damage, etc. carried out to property "belonging to another". This does not necessarily refer to the actual ownership as understood for other purposes, since the 1971 Act provides that:

"Property shall be treated for the purposes of this Act as belonging to any person

    (a) having the custody or control of it;
    (b) having in it any proprietary right or interest . . ."[45]

The ownership of a tree has already been considered at some length,[46] from which it will be apparent that the identification of the true owner in law will not always be straightforward. However, given the much more wide-ranging definition in the 1971 Act, it will usually be easy to determine whether a tree that has been damaged or destroyed is the property of someone other than the person doing the damage or destruction.

And it is clearly possible for a particular item (including a tree or shrub) to belong for the purposes of the Act to more than one person – for example, a tenant and a landlord. It follows that it would be possible for a tenant to be prosecuted for damaging or destroying a tree belonging to the landlord without his or her consent.

The property in a tree or shrub growing on a highway would be in the highway authority, since the authority clearly has the custody or control of it, whether or not it has a proprietary right or interest.[47]

9.6.4 Justification for works

Works that might seem to be criminal damage are only an offence under the 1971 Act if they are carried out "without lawful excuse". This would obviously exclude from criminal liability the carrying out of works to a tree by a contractor with the consent of its owner. In addition, however, the Act specifically provides that someone shall be deemed to have a lawful excuse to carry out what would otherwise be criminal damage if he or she honestly believed, at the time of the

---

[43] 1971 Act, s. 1(1)(a).
[44] *R v Caldwell* [1982] A.C. at p. 353H, per Lord Diplock.
[45] Criminal Damage Act 1971, s. 10(2).
[46] See **Chapter 2**.
[47] Confirmed by the Court of Appeal in *Hurst v Hampshire County Council* [1997] 2 EGLR 164 at p. 168M.

carrying out of the works, that the owner of the property (or the person entitled to authorise works to it) had consented to the works, or would have consented if they had known of the works and the reasons for them.[48]

If, therefore, a contractor is instructed to cut down tree A, but in fact fells tree B because he misunderstood his instructions, he may be liable to its owner in a civil action for negligence or breach of contract, but he cannot be prosecuted for criminal damage.

It is also permissible to carry out works that might otherwise be categorised as criminal damage where they are immediately required for the purpose of protecting property, and were reasonable in all the circumstances.[49] A prosecution would thus not be possible where a branch of a tree is removed in the genuine (even if mistaken) belief that it was about to fall onto a greenhouse.

Finally, it is possible that the carrying out of unlawful works to a tree or other plant would not be an offence if they were regarded as an improvement[50]; but this defence should clearly be used only as a last resort!

9.6.5 Damage to highway trees

The Public Health Act 1875 provided not only that the street (and thus the trees growing in the street[51]) was vested in the urban authority, but also that

"Any person who . . . injures . . . the trees in any such street, shall be liable to a penalty . . .; he shall also be liable in the case of any injury to trees to pay the local authority such amount of compensation as the court may award."[52]

This was replaced by section 117 of the Highways Act 1959, which removed the explicit entitlement of the highway authority to receive compensation for damage to highway trees, but instead provided that "wilful" damage to a tree, hedge or shrub planted in a highway was an offence, in relation to which a prosecution might be mounted as for any other criminal offence.

That was itself replaced by section 1 of the Criminal Damage Act 1971,[53] which made it an offence intentionally or recklessly to damage any property – which includes trees and shrubs other than the flowers, fruit or foliage of those growing wild.[54] In the case of a conviction for damage to a highway tree, an order for compensation in favour of the highway authority could be made by the court under the provisions of the Criminal Courts Act 1973.[55]

A further specific procedure is provided by section 132 of the Highways Act 1980 to deal with the problem of graffiti and fly-posters on highways, including on trees on the highway. Under this section, it is an offence to paint, inscribe or affix any picture, letter, sign or other mark upon any tree on or in a highway, without either the consent of the highway authority or some other proper authorisation or reasonable excuse. Summary conviction (in a magistrates' court) may lead to a

---

[48] Criminal Damage Act 1971, s. 5(2)(a).
[49] 1971 Act, s. 5(2)(b).
[50] R v Fancy [1980] Crim. L.R. 171.
[51] See **6.2.2**.
[52] Public Health Act 1875, s. 149.
[53] 1971 Act, s. 11(8), Sched.
[54] 1971 Act, ss. 1, 10(1).
[55] 1973 Act, s. 35; see Hurst v Hampshire County Council [1997] 2 EGLR 164, CA, at p. 167A.

fine of up to level 4 on the standard scale.[56] In addition, whether or not a prosecution has been mounted or is intended under section 132, the authority may simply remove the offending item without further ado.[57]

9.6.6 Sentencing

The offence of theft is triable either way – that is, in the Crown Court or by magistrates – with a maximum penalty on conviction in the Crown Court of imprisonment for ten years.

To destroy or damage a tree by means of fire is known as arson,[58] and carries a maximum possible sentence (on conviction in the Crown Court) of life imprisonment.[59] However, unlike other offences attracting such a maximum, arson is triable either way, and may therefore be dealt with by magistrates, with the usual maximum penalties. Other forms of criminal damage, and indeed any offences under the 1971 Act not involving actual or possible danger to life, attract a maximum sentence of ten years. These include the offences of threatening to damage property[60] and possessing an article with the intention of using it to destroy or damage property.[61]

In the present context, prosecution for any of the above offences is much more likely to take place in the magistrates' court, leading to a relatively mild fine, the size of which will depend on the circumstances. For further details, either as to the principles of the criminal law or as to prosecution procedure, appropriate general texts should be consulted.

9.6.7 Trees and other plants on access land

Under the Countryside and Rights of Way Act 2000, access may be obtained to common land, land more than 600 metres above sea level, and other land shown as open land on the relevant map maintained under the Act. However, a person may only avail himself or herself of that right of access on condition that he or she observes the restrictions set out in Schedule 2 to the Act, which include a prohibition on (amongst other things) intentionally removing, damaging or destroying any plant, shrub, tree or root or any part of one.[62]

---

[56] HA 1980, ss. 132(1), 310.
[57] HA 1980, s. 132(2).
[58] 1971 Act, s. 1(3).
[59] 1971 Act, s. 4(1).
[60] Under Criminal Damage Act 1971, s. 2.
[61] Under Criminal Damage Act 1971, s. 3.
[62] 2000 Act, Sched. 2, para. 1(l); see also **11.3.6**.

Chapter 10

Planting Trees and Hedges

10.1 Introduction

10.1.1 Avoidance of future problems

Much the most important requirement for anyone contemplating planting a tree is to consider carefully its likely life-span and eventual size, and whether, as a result, any of the problems identified in the earlier chapters of this book are likely to arise. Arguably, this applies with even more force when considering planting a hedge – this is touched on again at the end of this Chapter.

The most significant problems almost always occur in relation to trees close to property boundaries, roads, buildings or wires. Essentially, a tree growing across a boundary remains the property of the person in whose land it was first planted; but the owner of the land into or over which the roots and branches subsequently penetrate may, without notice, cut them back to the boundary.[1] Tree roots growing under buildings may cause subsidence, leading to possible liability in nuisance.[2] And trees (or parts of them) may fall onto highways or elsewhere – either in a high wind or due to structural failure – with unfortunate or disastrous consequences, and liability in negligence.[3] Any of these situations may lead to litigation that may be, at best, acrimonious and time-wasting and, at worst, extremely costly.

Prevention is almost always better than cure – and always better than litigation. Neighbour disputes, in particular, can sometimes be extraordinarily difficult to solve, without one or other party moving, whereas it may often be relatively easy to avoid a dispute arising in the first place, by the use of only a modicum of common sense. It follows that care in the choice of the species and location of trees may pay ample dividends in the long term, not least in ensuring that future purchasers of the property (and their mortgagees) are not put off by potential disputes over trees.

---

[1] See **3.2** and **3.6**.
[2] See **3.5**.
[3] See **Chapter 5**.

10.1.2 Restrictions on planting of trees

Apart from the desirability of avoiding future problems, there are very few legal constraints relating to the planting of new trees, as opposed to the carrying out of works to existing ones. However, a few of those described in **Chapter 9** may also occasionally apply in relation to planting.

In particular, the terms of any leases, licences and restrictive covenants may restrict the planting of trees, or may in effect prohibit such planting without the consent of some named person.[4] And byelaws made by river authorities, drainage boards, and such bodies as the Conservators of the River Thames and the Lee Valley Catchment Board may contain restrictions on planting trees – even though in some cases these will be administered by successor bodies such as the Environment Agency.

A faculty will usually be needed for new planting (of any number of trees) in a churchyard; and the chancellor of each diocese is required to issue guidance on the subject.[5]

The relevant nature conservancy council will need to be notified before the carrying out of tree planting on land in an SSSI where planting has been specified as a potentially damaging operation.[6] And care may be needed when planting in proximity to a scheduled ancient monument; it is possible that scheduled monument consent may be needed (from the Department of Culture, Media and Sport).[7]

Special considerations apply to the planting of trees on or near highway land. In particular, sections 138 and 141 of the Highways Act 1980 make it an offence to plant hedges and trees on highway land, without a licence under section 142.[7a] And the existence of various powers in that Act by which the highway authority may prune or remove altogether trees and shrubs interfering with the free use of the highway[7b] means that trees should not be planted (or allowed to grow) in inappropriate locations in the first place. These issues have been explored in greater detail in **Chapter 6**.

10.1.3 Planning permission for tree planting

Planning permission will rarely if ever be required for planting a tree as such – or indeed for planting any number.

If the number of trees planted on a piece of land is enough for the operation to amount to a material change of use, that could in theory constitute development, but not if the new use amounts to "forestry". The latter exception arises because section 55(2) of the Town and Country Planning Act 1990 provides that:

"The following . . . uses of land shall not be taken for the purposes of this Act to involve development of land –

. . .

---

[4]   See **Chapter 2** and **9.1.2**.
[5]   See **Chapter 22**, in particular **22.3.5**.
[6]   See **9.3.8**.
[7]   See **9.4**.
[7a] See **6.3**.
[7b] See **6.4**.

(e) the use of any land for the purposes of agriculture or forestry (including afforestation) and the use for any of those purposes of any building occupied together with land so used; . . ."

The term "forestry" is not defined in the 1990 Act, other than by the reference to afforestation.[8] Whether, for example, it would include simply planting a small number of trees on a previously vacant patch of land is uncertain. The Court of Appeal has recently decided that "forestry" means "the management of growing timber"[9] – regardless of whether that timber is growing in a forest, parkland or elsewhere. However, that was in a different context, relating to compensation for injuries caused by the use of a chainsaw,[10] and it is by no means certain that a similar approach would be taken should the point arise under planning legislation, which is concerned with the proper use of land.

Having said which, no litigation is known to have arisen on the point.

10.2 Powers to plant trees

10.2.1 General powers of local planning authorities

A local planning authority has specific powers to plant trees on land in its area "for the purpose of preserving or enhancing the natural beauty thereof", under section 89(1) of the National Parks and Access to the Countryside Act 1949. It is not clear whether the word "thereof" refers to the land on which the trees are to be planted or to the authority's area generally; but probably little turns on that.

More significantly, it may be noted that the powers relate to any land, and not just land owned by the authority. However, the power does not operate so as to override any relevant prohibition or restriction having effect under any enactment or rule of law.[11] This would mean that, for example, before the authority exercised the power in relation to land that it did not own, it would require the consent of the owner. Similarly, a tree should not be planted in a location such that – bearing in mind its eventual size and other characteristics – it is likely to give rise to a hazard, either immediately or at some time in the future.[12]

There is of course little point in planting trees if they will not be looked after, at least in their early years. The Act therefore provides that, where trees are planted by an authority under this power on land which it does not own, their subsequent care and maintenance may be undertaken (and paid for) either by the authority or by the owner of the land, as may be agreed between them.[13]

---

[8] TCPA 1990, s. 55(2)(e); also TCP (General Permitted Development) Order 1995, Sched. 2, Pt 7, para. A; see also **11.4.1**.
[9] *Davis v Secretary of State for Social Security* [2001] EWCA Civ 105, para. 26.
[10] Under Social Security (Industrial Injuries) (Prescribed Diseases) Regulations 1985 (S.I. 1985 No. 967), Sched. 1, Pt I, para. A11; see **9.5.6**.
[11] 1949 Act, s. 89(4).
[12] See **Chapter 5** on hazardous trees generally, and **Chapter 6** on hazards relating to highways.
[13] 1949 Act, s. 89(6).

The definition of a "local planning authority" for the purposes of these provisions is, in principle, the same as in the Town and Country Planning Act 1990[14]: the general rule is thus that in England it is the district or borough council in metropolitan counties,[15] and the district or county council elsewhere[16]; and in Wales it is the county or county borough council.[17] In areas in England where there are still both a district council and a county council, either or both may exercise the powers of a local planning authority under section 89 of the 1949 Act.[18] In a national park in England, those powers may be exercised either by the national park authority or the district council; but in a national park in Wales, only by the national park authority.[19] In the Norfolk and Suffolk Broads, the powers may also be exercised by the Broads Authority.[20]

The reference to planting trees includes planting bushes (and thus, presumably, hedges), planting or sowing flowers, sowing grass and laying turf.[21]

10.2.2 Other powers

A local authority which has acquired an open space or burial ground under the provisions of the Open Spaces Act 1906 may plant, ornament and otherwise improve it[22] – which presumably includes planting trees and shrubs. Similar powers, in respect of any land used as a public walk or pleasure ground, are available to district councils[23] and county councils.[24]

More frequently used in practice are the powers relating to the planting – by highway authorities and others – of trees on highway land. These have been considered already.[25]

10.3 Acquisition of land for tree planting

The National Parks and Access to the Countryside Act 1949 gives local authorities powers to compulsorily acquire land for the purpose of planting trees on it[26] – which might be useful in the case of odd left-over patches of land on which a few trees could be planted.

Useful general guidance on the exercise of compulsory purchase powers is given in Department of the Environment Circular 14/94. Appendix M to that Circular makes specific reference to the 1949 Act provisions, but adds nothing.

[14] 1949 Act, s. 114(1); Planning (Consequential Provisions) Act 1990; Town and Country Planning Act 1990, Pt I.
[15] Greater London, Greater Manchester, Merseyside, South Yorkshire, Tyne and Wear, West Midlands, West Yorkshire: Town and Country Planning Act 1990, s. 1(2); the Common Council in the City of London (1990 Act, s. 336(1)).
[16] TCPA 1990, s. 1(1).
[17] TCPA 1990, s. 1(1B), inserted by Local Government (Wales) Act 1994.
[18] Local Government Act 1972, s. 184(4).
[19] TCPA 1990, ss. 1(5)(a), 4A(2); Environment Act 1995, s. 68(6)(a).
[20] 1949 Act, s. 111A, inserted by Norfolk and Suffolk Broads Act 1988.
[21] 1949 Act, s. 114(3).
[22] Open Spaces Act 1906, s. 10.
[23] Public Health Act 1875, s. 164.
[24] Open Spaces Act 1906, s. 14.
[25] See **6.3**.
[26] 1949 Act, s. 89(5).

10.4 Powers to require trees to be planted by others

10.4.1 Planting in connection with development

There appears to be no general power for any public authority to require landowners to plant trees on their land. A power was, however, introduced in the Civic Amenities Act 1967[27] whereby planning authorities were not just empowered but actually required to ensure, whenever appropriate, that where planning permission was granted for any development, adequate permission was made for the preservation and planting of trees.

This power (now in section 197 of the Town and Country Planning Act 1990) is regularly used to require developers to provide new trees in connection with developments, through the imposition of appropriate conditions on permissions. **Appendix A** contains a number of suggested conditions, based on the wording of those in the Circular providing general advice on the use of conditions.[28] Sample condition [A4] in that Appendix requires the specification of new trees to be planted, in connection with a grant of outline planning permission. Condition [A6] does the same in relation to a detailed permission. Condition [A8] then requires that the trees thus specified are actually planted, and conditions [A9] and [A10] that they are subsequently protected.

It will be noted that the protection thus afforded for the new trees lasts only for the specified period (two years in the example). The guidance sensibly suggests that the long-term protection of such trees is secured by the use of tree preservation orders rather than by relying on a condition. The 1990 Act accordingly provides that a tree preservation order may be made, in relation to a tree required to be planted by a condition under section 197(a), so as to apply from the moment that it is planted.[29]

There are also special provisions to ensure the protection of existing trees during the carrying out of building works.[29a]

10.4.2 Enforcing a requirement to plant trees

The planting of one or more trees may thus be required as a condition of a planning permission – either to replace other trees (which may or may not have been protected by a tree preservation order) lost in consequence of implementing the permission, or simply as part of the general requirements as to the landscaping of the new development. Such a condition, if not complied with, is enforced by the normal methods used in connection with any planning condition.

The most effective mechanism open to a local planning authority is to serve a breach of condition notice, under section 187A of the 1990 Act,[30] which requires the condition to be complied with in the time specified in the notice. Such a notice may be served either on the person carrying out the development or on the person

---

[27] Civic Amenities Act 1967, s. 12.
[28] Department of the Environment Circular 11/95 (Welsh Office 35/95), *The Use of Conditions in Planning Permissions*, Annex, Appendix A (models of acceptable conditions), particularly conditions 73, 74.
[29] TCPA 1990 Act, s. 198(5).
[29a] See **15.9.4**.
[30] Inserted by Planning and Compensation Act 1991, s. 2.

having control of the land[31]: in the case of a tree planting condition, the latter is likely to be more appropriate. There is no right of appeal against such a notice.

A failure to comply with a breach of condition notice is a criminal offence, attracting a fine of up to level 3.[32] There are two statutory defences to a charge of such an offence:

- that the defendant took all reasonable steps to secure compliance with the notice; or

- that the defendant is no longer in control of the land.[33]

The existence of this procedure should be sufficient in most cases to ensure that such conditions are complied with.

Alternatively, it is possible for an authority to issue an enforcement notice, under section 172. This carries with it a right of appeal to the Secretary of State.[34] However, unless such an appeal is made, and succeeds, the authority may enter the land and carry out the necessary planting in default.[35]

For further details of planning enforcement procedure, which is a complex area of law and procedure, a standard planning law textbook should be consulted.

10.4.3 Replacement for existing trees

Where consent is needed for the felling of a tree, there are powers for the relevant authority, in granting consent, to ensure that a new tree is planted in its place.

Thus, where a felling licence is issued by the Forestry Commission it will usually be subject to a condition requiring the land to be restocked.[36] The applicant may be entitled to compensation in the event of financial loss arising from complying with such a condition, and may be able to appeal against it.[37] However, where necessary, the Commission may serve a notice requiring compliance – against which, again, there is a right of appeal to the minister – and may if necessary enter the land and carry out the necessary planting works itself, and recover its costs from the person in default.

Failure to comply with such a notice is a criminal offence.[38] And where trees are felled without a licence being obtained at all, the Commission may still require the land to be restocked.[39] These requirements are described in **Chapter 14**.

Similarly, if consent is granted for the felling of a tree subject to a tree preservation order, it may be granted subject to a condition requiring a replacement to be planted.[40] An appeal may be made to the Secretary of State against a condition[41]; and if any loss is suffered in consequence, compensation may be payable.[42] If such a tree is removed without consent, or if a tree other than

---

[31] TCPA 1990, s. 187A(2).
[32] TCPA 1990, s. 187A(9),(12); for levels of fines, see **Appendix C**.
[33] TCPA 1990, s. 187A(11).
[34] TCPA 1990, s. 174.
[35] TCPA 1990, s. 178.
[36] FA 1967, s. 12(1); see **14.3.4**.
[37] FA 1967, ss. 11, 16; see **14.5**.
[38] FA 1967, ss. 24 to 26; see **14.6**.
[39] FA 1967, ss. 17A to 17C; see **14.7.6 to 14.7.8**.
[40] The power to impose conditions is in the relevant tree preservation order; see **18.3.7**.
[41] See **18.5**.
[42] 1990 Act, ss. 203, 204; 1969 sample order, arts. 5, 9; 1999 sample order, arts. 9 to 12.

one in a woodland is removed because it is dead, dying or dangerous, the owner of the land must plant a replacement unless the planning authority agrees to dispense with the requirement.[43]

If the owner fails to comply with such a requirement, or with a condition on a consent requiring a replacement to be planted, the authority may serve a notice requiring compliance, against which there is a right of appeal; and if that notice is itself not complied with, the authority may enter the land, carry out the replanting and recover its costs.[44]

These requirements are dealt with in detail in **Chapters 18** and **20**.

10.5 Planting woodlands and forests

The above considerations are essentially those which apply to the planting of a single tree, or a small group. Where the number to be planted is such as to amount to woodland or forest, further issues arise.

In particular, the planting and management of woodlands and forests have two distinctive features that are of consequence when considering the way in which they are treated by the law. First, they involve major expenditure with no immediate reward, which leads to the need for financial assistance; and, secondly, afforestation in particular is likely to have considerable environmental impact, which may need to be controlled. The special legal regime which has evolved as a result of these considerations is the subject of **Chapters 12** and **13**.

Perhaps not the least important consideration in achieving a greater extent of tree cover is not the existence of control over planting, but the consistent expression of Government policy in favour of it, over many decades. The position is currently as follows:

"Woodland occupies about 7.5 per cent of the land area of England, and is increasing. The Government would like to see woodland cover double over the next half century. Well planned and managed woodland will improve the appearance of the countryside, create new jobs, enrich wildlife habitats, open up new opportunities for recreation, and help improve air quality and carbon dioxide absorption."[45]

Planning authorities are also encouraged to give sympathetic consideration to afforestation initiatives in urban fringe areas, taking into account nature conservation interests.[46]

It is likely that this approach will also be reflected in policies in development plans produced by local planning authorities.

And, of course, the latest initiative is the promotion of Community Forests in various parts of the country, and the National Forest in the Midlands.[47]

---

[43] 1990 Act, s. 206.
[44] 1990 Act, ss. 207 to 209.
[45] PPG 7, *The Countryside: Environmental Quality and Economic and Social Development*, 1997, para. 1.8.
[46] PPG 17, *Sport and Recreation*, 1991, para. 33.
[47] See PPG 7, Annex D.

10.6 Planting a hedge

All of the issues outlined in this Chapter apply equally to the planting of hedges.

In particular, it is essential to think ahead, and to consider carefully the rate of growth, maintenance requirements and eventual size of a proposed hedge. It is also sensible to check whether there are any planning conditions or restrictive covenants that may restrict or prevent planting.

The problems (sometimes severe) that can be caused by existing hedges have already been explored.[48] It is up to those contemplating planting a new one to ensure, preferably in conjunction with their neighbours, that future problems are not unnecessarily created. The DETR has issued sensible guidance,[49] which should be studied carefully.

Note that planning permission is never required for the planting of a new hedge. Some have suggested that it should be, but it is to be hoped that such a move will be resisted, as being both undesirable in principle and impractical to enforce. Conditions on planning permissions (for example, for new houses) may sometimes be found restricting or preventing future policy; any variation of such a condition would need to be agreed with the planning authority.

---

[48] See **Chapter 4.**
[49] *The Right Hedge for You,* DETR, 1999.

Part III

Forestry

". . . In the nineteenth century, the nation had got into the habit of obtaining its cellulose by plundering other countries' wildwood. When this activity was interrupted by German submarines, the Government's reaction was to encourage the growing of conifers at home, a policy put into effect by the Forestry Commission founded in 1919."

– Oliver Rackham, in *Trees and Woodlands in the British Landscape* (1990).

". . . A new generation of foresters has grown up, as I put it, with other things to do with their lives than grow millions of identical trees. And the economic basis for the Forestry Commission's former activities has collapsed . . . it's hardly worth cutting the trees down."

– Rackham, interviewed in *Tree News* (2001).

"Trees have to be cut down and replanted."

– Rt Hon Nicholas Ridley, M.P. (Secretary of State for the Environment) (1989).

Chapter 11

Commercial Forestry

11.1 Introduction

11.1.1 Forests in history

No one knows the true origin of the word "forest". Today it almost always means "a large area covered chiefly with trees and undergrowth".[1] Historically, however, it had a rather different meaning: "an area, typically owned by the sovereign and partly wooded, kept for hunting and having its own laws". That earlier concept was widespread in Europe long before it reached England. Thus, throughout the Middle Ages a forest was a place of deer, not necessarily a place of trees.[2]

A "forest" was indeed a legal concept, a tract of land within which *forest law* operated and people could be prosecuted before special forest courts. Nearly always the legal forest was much wider than the physical forest, that is, the area of wood-pasture or other roughland on which the deer actually lived. Thus forests might be wooded, but few were entirely woodland; many were heathland, with or without scattered woods, or open moorland. Indeed, forests (as thus defined) may have had a similar amount, proportionately, of woodland to other parts of the country.

The forest system started shortly after the Norman Conquest. Some 25 forests (including the New Forest, the Forest of Dean and Wychwood) are recorded in Domesday; others (including Epping and Sherwood Forests) were first heard of in the eleventh century. By 1200 there were some 143 forests, of which 90 belonged to the King; this was indeed one of the causes of the discontent that led to Magna Carta, after which forests began to decline.

The forest laws were harsh in theory, but little enforced in practice; and the interest of successive monarchs in forests, either as places for hunting or as collections of trees, was small. By the sixteenth century the administration of forest laws was in a state of decay.[3] After 1600 forests became notorious as the haunts of armed poachers and highwaymen, leading to the passing of the ferocious Black Act of 1723.

Few of the medieval forests (in the sense of collections of trees) still survive,

[1] *New Oxford Dictionary of English*, Clarendon Press, Oxford: first edn, 1998.
[2] See Rackham, *Trees and Woodland in the British Landscape*, Weidenfeld & Nicholson, revised edn, 1990, from whose work most of the historical material in this chapter is derived.
[3] Manwood's Forest Laws (1598 edn), preface.

although there are exceptions – there are, for example, numerous veteran trees in Sherwood Forest, the New Forest, and Windsor Great Park (the remainder of Windsor Forest). Other older forests (including, notably, the Forest of Dean) survive on paper, but the planting regime is that of the nineteenth century. And the natural forest ("wildwood") that once covered most of Britain has long since gone.[4]

The proportion of the land area of the United Kingdom devoted to woodland, on the other hand, although still low by European standards, is steadily rising. At the beginning of the twentieth century, woodland cover was 5 per cent; one hundred years later, that figure had risen to 10 per cent (2.5 million hectares).[5] Of that resource, around two-thirds is privately owned – by individuals, family trusts, charitable trusts and companies – with very few ownerships extending to more than 1,000 hectares. The remaining one-third, mainly new planting established since 1900, is publicly owned – principally by the Forestry Commission,[6] but also by other public agencies including local authorities.

11.1.2 Special forest laws

The numerous forest laws that used to exist in relation to royal and private forests had become largely obsolete by the time they were repealed by the Wild Creatures and Forest Laws Act 1971, which abolished all "franchises of forest, free chase, park or free warren" and abrogated the forest law, except in so far as it related to the appointment and functions of verderers.[7]

The only two exceptions are the New Forest and the Forest of Dean – although only the New Forest survives in anything like its medieval form.[8] There the verderers still regularly hold a Court of Swainmote, at which the rights of commoners and other interested parties (by whom they are appointed) are upheld.[9] And they may make byelaws relating to animals in the Forest.[10] They must be consulted in relation to byelaws made by the Forestry Commissioners,[11] and the verderers' court may punish any breach of them (in which respect it is to be treated as though it was a magistrates' court).[12]

The Forestry Commission upholds the rights of the Crown in relation to the New Forest; it also is required to register all rights of common over any of the forest.[13] It may secure the drainage of the forest, and the clearance of seedlings and forestry debris.[14] Subject to the consent of the verderers, the Commission may enclose forestland to encourage the growth of timber, and may enclose the

---

[4] As to ancient semi-natural woodland, see **15.2**.
[5] The figures for England and Wales are 8 per cent and 14 per cent respectively.
[6] Or the Department of Agriculture for Northern Ireland (DANI).
[7] Wild Creatures and Forest Laws Act, s. 1(4), Schedule; see also Crown Estate Act 1961, s. 9(4), Sched. 3.
[8] Dean and New Forests Act 1808; New Forest and Forest of Dean Act 1819; New Forest Acts 1877 to 1947; New Forest Act 1964; and New Forest Act 1970.
[9] New Forest Act 1949, s. 8.
[10] New Forest Act 1877, s. 25; such byelaws have to be confirmed by the Ministry of Agriculture, Fisheries and Food: New Forest Act 1949, s. 9(5). The current byelaws are set out in the Schedule to the New Forest (Confirmation of the Byelaws of the Verderers of the New Forest) Order 1999 (S.I. 1999 No. 2134), which replace those confirmed in S.I. 1978 No. 1277 and the amendments to them confirmed in S.I. 1981 No. 550 and S.I. 1990 No. 1202.
[11] See **11.3.7**.
[12] FA 1967, s. 47.
[13] New Forest Act 1949, s. 4.
[14] New Forest Act 1949, s. 11.

ancient and ornamental woods in the forest for the purpose of regeneration, and may carry out in those enclosures any appropriate forestry operations.[15] And, not least important, the Forestry Commission (subject to the approval of the Treasury) may make grants to the verderers in relation to any expenditure incurred by them in the carrying out of any of their functions under the New Forest Acts 1877 to 1970.[16]

As for the Forest of Dean, it retains a vestige of its old legislation[17]; but much has been amended or repealed. As in the New Forest, the verderers must be consulted in relation to Forestry Commission byelaws,[18] and may punish any breach of them.[19]

Since the other special laws, including the byelaws, applying to the two forests are largely unrelated to trees as such, they are not the subject of any further comment here.[20]

11.1.3 *The Forestry Acts*

The first of the "modern" forestry Acts was the Forestry Act 1919, which set up the Forestry Commission.[21] The Commissioners were charged with the general duty of promoting the interests of forestry, the development of afforestation, and the production and supply of timber, in the United Kingdom. The Commission's principal powers were thus to acquire and dispose of land suitable for afforestation, to acquire and dispose of standing timber, to give grants and loans, and to give general assistance to forestry.[22] It was also given a specific power to deal with damage to trees by rabbits, hares and vermin.[23] The 1919 Act also established the Forestry Fund.[24]

As to the royal forests, control over them (including forest courts) had since 1832 vested in the Commissioners of Woods, Forests, Land Revenues, Works and Buildings.[25] It had passed in 1851 to the Commissioners of Woods, Forests and Land Revenues[26] (later the Commissioners of Crown Lands).[27] Under the Forestry (Transfer of Woods) Act 1923, land vested in the Commissioners could be transferred to the new Forestry Commission[28] – and extensive transfers were in fact made under that power.

The Forestry Act 1927 then increased the number of Commissioners from eight to ten,[29] and gave them powers to make byelaws.[30] The Forestry Act 1945 reconstituted the Commission, and transferred all land that had been previously

---

[15] New Forest Act 1949, ss. 12, 13.
[16] Agriculture and Forestry (Financial Provisions) Act 1991, s. 4, amended by S.I. 1999 No. 1747, para. 7.
[17] Dean and New Forests Act 1808; New Forest and Forest of Dean Act 1819; Dean Forest (Mines) Acts 1838, 1871 and 1904; Forest of Dean Act 1861; and Dean Forest Act 1906.
[18] See **11.3.7**.
[19] FA 1967, s. 47.
[20] See Halsbury's Laws, fourth edition, Vol. 19(1), *Forestry*, paras 4 to 6.
[21] FA 1919, ss. 1, 2.
[22] FA 1919, s. 3.
[23] FA 1919, s. 4.
[24] FA 1919, s. 8; see **11.3.3** below.
[25] Crown Lands Act 1832, s. 1.
[26] Crown Lands Act 1851, s. 2.
[27] The predecessors of the modern Crown Estate Commissioners.
[28] 1923 Act, s. 1.
[29] FA 1927, s. 1.
[30] FA 1927, s. 2.

owned by it to the relevant minister.[31] Forestry dedication covenants were introduced by the Forestry Act 1947,[32] and controls over felling by the Forestry Act 1951.[33] The latter Act also widened the duty of the Commission, to include a general duty to promote the establishment and maintenance in Great Britain of adequate reserves of growing trees[34]; it also required the setting up of a Home Grown Timber Advisory Committee, and regional advisory committees.[35]

All of the above Acts[36] were repealed and replaced by the Forestry Act 1967, which was a consolidation measure – that is, it did not introduce any new substantive law. The 1967 Act has itself been amended, but not significantly. In particular, new duties were laid on ministers (in 1981[37]) and on the Forestry Commission (in 1985[38]); and the Forestry Act 1986 introduced a power to require land to be restocked with trees following felling.[39]

Other minor amendments have been made in addition to those necessary as a result of devolution (particularly in Scotland[40]). The Trees Act 1970 tightened up the law relating to the grant of felling licences on land subject to a forestry dedication covenant or agreement.[41] The Forestry Act 1979 restated the powers of the Forestry Commission to give grants,[42] and introduced metric measurements into the requirements relating to felling licences.[43] The Forestry Act 1981 amended the law relating to the disposal of land[44] and the Forestry Fund,[45] and increased the number of Commissioners.[46] Finally, the Forestry Act 1991 increased the size of regional advisory committees.[47]

11.1.4 Environmental assessment

Wholly independently of the Forestry Acts, there has been introduced a requirement for major forestry projects to be the subject of environmental impact assessment, in response to an EC Directive on environmental assessment.[48] Since planning permission is not required for forestry activity,[49] the normal procedures requiring environmental assessment of major development

---

[31] FA 1945, s. 4(5); see **11.2.1**.
[32] See **12.6.1**.
[33] FA 1951, ss. 2 to 17; see **Chapter 14**.
[34] FA 1951, s. 1.
[35] FA 1951, s. 15.
[36] As well as the Forestry (Sale of Land) (Scotland) Act 1963; for list of repeals, see FA 1967, Sched. 7.
[37] FA 1967, s. 41, inserted by FA 1981, s. 4, and amended by S.I. 1999 No. 1756, art. 2, Sched., para. 3 (see **11.2.2**).
[38] FA 1967, s. 1(3A), inserted by Wildlife and Countryside (Amendment) Act 1985, s. 4.
[39] FA 1967, ss. 17A to 17C, inserted by FA 1986, s. 1; see **14.7.6 to 14.7.8**.
[40] See Scotland Act 1998 (Cross-Border Public Authorities) (Adaptation of Functions, etc.) Order 1999 (S.I. 1998 No. 1747), art. 3, Sched. 12, Pt II, para. 4.
[41] FA 1967, s. 12(2), amended by Trees Act 1970, s. 2.
[42] FA 1979, s. 1, Sched. 2; see **12.7.2**.
[43] FA 1967, s. 9, amended by FA 1979, s. 2, Sched. 1; see **14.2.2**.
[44] FA 1967, ss. 39(2) and 40(4), amended by FA 1981, ss. 1 and 2; see **11.2.3**.
[45] FA 1967, s. 41, amended by FA 1981, s. 3; see **11.3.3**.
[46] FA 1967, s. 2(1), amended by FA 1981, s. 5; see **11.3.2**.
[47] FA 1967, s. 38(3), amended by FA 1991, s. 1. Why is this sort of detail in primary legislation?
[48] Directive 85/337/EEC, amended by Directive 97/11; see **13.1**.
[49] See **13.2**.

proposals[50] do not apply. Accordingly, a special regime has been introduced for forestry – initially requiring an assessment to be made where a grant was sought,[51] but subsequently widening this so as to require assessment of any major forestry project.[52]

11.1.5 The current position

The law relating to forestry is thus now almost entirely contained within one statute, the 1967 Act. It has hardly changed at all during the last fifty years,[53] and has given rise to almost no litigation.

This reflects the fact that the law plays, in the words of one commentator, a remarkably small role in determining the way in which forestry operates.[54] There have indeed been major shifts in practice over the last half-century; but these have been achieved with very little assistance from either the legislature or the courts. In particular, there has been a move away from timber production as being the sole purpose of forestry, in favour of a more broadly based approach which encompasses the making of improvements to the landscape, protecting wildlife, facilitating recreation and sport, enhancing the economy of rural areas, and providing a land use in place of agriculture. And of course the large, insensitively located single-species plantations of conifers, so common in the past, are gradually being replaced by more diverse woodlands containing native broadleaf trees.

These changes have been reflected in the general policies and approach of the Forestry Commission, not least in the way in which it operates its grant schemes.[55] But they have not resulted in any major change to the law – even the new requirements as to environmental assessment apply in practice to a relatively small proportion of forestry projects.

The remainder of this Chapter sets out the law regulating the administration of forestry by central Government (**11.2**), by the Forestry Commission (**11.3**), and the short-lived rural development boards (**11.4**). It also describes briefly other relevant statutory codes including those relating to plant health, and the import and export of plants, seeds and cones (**11.5 and 11.6**). The following Chapters then consider how the law responds to particular aspects of forestry. **Chapter 12** looks at the law relating to financial matters; in particular, the special treatment of woodlands in respect to national and local taxation, and the schemes of grants available from the Forestry Commission. And **Chapter 13** looks at the impact of forestry on the environment, and the way in which forestry is treated by the planning system, and the environmental assessment code that has arisen more recently. Finally, **Chapter 14** describes in detail the legislation relating to felling licences.

---

[50] See currently TCP (Environmental Impact Assessment) (England and Wales) Regulations 1999 (S.I. 1999 No. 293), replacing S.I. 1988 No. 1199 (amended by S.I. 1990 No. 367, S.I. 1992 No. 1494, S.I. 1994 No. 677).

[51] EIA (Forestry) Regulations 1988 (S.I. 1988 No. 1207).

[52] EIA (Forestry) Regulations 1999 (S.I. 1999 No. 2228), reg. 3; see **13.3**.

[53] The only change of any significance since the introduction of felling control in the FA 1951 has been the introduction of restocking notices in 1986 and, perhaps, the change of central Government Departmental responsibility in 2001.

[54] See the chapter on forestry by Professor Colin T Reid, in *Scottish Countryside Law* (ed Rowan-Robinson, McKenzie), Edinburgh, 1999. The author is indebted to Professor Reid for assistance in relation to forestry generally.

[55] See **12.7**.

11.2 Central Government involvement in forestry

11.2.1 Responsible departments

As noted above, the Forestry Act 1945 transferred all land which had been previously owned by the Forestry Commission to the relevant minister – that was, the Minister for Agriculture and Fisheries in relation to England and Wales, and the Secretary of State in relation to Scotland[56] – who was then to place the land at the disposal of the Commission.[57] In other words, "Forestry Commission land" is not actually owned by the Commission; it is merely managed by it.

In 1965, land vested in the Minister was transferred to the Minister of Land and Natural Resources (if in England) and the Secretary of State (if in Wales)[58]; and on the dissolution of the former, land in England passed to the Minister for Agriculture, Fisheries and Food.[59] As a result of the devolution of power in Wales, functions of the Secretary of State were generally transferred to the National Assembly for Wales – including almost all those in the Forestry Act 1967.[60] In Scotland, the responsibilities of the Secretary of State were transferred to the Scottish Ministers.[61]

Following the 2001 general election, the Ministry of Agriculture, Fisheries and Food (MAFF) was abolished. Its responsibilities, together with many of those of the Department of the Environment, Transport and the Regions, were merged into a single new Department.[62] The current position therefore is that the interests of central Government in forestry matters fall generally under the aegis of:

- the Department for Environment, Food, and Rural Affairs (DEFRA) in respect of England;

- the National Assembly of Wales Agriculture Department (NAWAD); and

- the Rural Affairs Department of the Scottish Executive (SERAD).

The 1967 Act still refers to "the Minister", but now defines that term so as to achieve the above result.[63] This book follows the same convention. References in this Part of the book to "the Minister" and "the Department" should be construed accordingly.

In terms of policy, the lead Department in relation to forestry has in the past been the Scottish Office, which was to a large extent responsible for strategy throughout the United Kingdom – it was thus a "cross-border authority" in terms of the Scotland Act 1998.[64] It remains to be seen what will be the position in the long-term following the devolution of power from London to Wales and

---

56 FA 1945, s. 10; S.I. 1955 No. 554.
57 FA 1945, s. 4(5).
58 S.I. 1965 No. 319, arts. 4, 8, 9.
59 S.I. 1967 No. 156, art. 2.
60 National Assembly for Wales (Transfer of Functions) Order 1999 (S.I. 1999 No. 672), art. 2, Sched. 1. The exceptions are those relating to the Treasury, in FA 1967, ss. 33(5), 38(4), 41(4A), 45, and Sched. 1, paras 2(2), 6(1),(2), 10(1), 12.
61 See Scotland Act 1998 (Cross-Border Public Authorities) (Adaptation of Functions, etc.) Order 1999 (S.I. 1999 No. 1747), art. 3, Sched. 12, Pt II, para. 4.
62 Ministry of Agriculture, Fisheries and Food (Dissolution) Order 2002 (S.I. 2002 No. 794)
63 FA 1967, s. 49, amended by S.I. 1999 No. 1747, art. 3, Sched. 12, Pt II, para. 4(38) and S.I. 2002 No. 794, Sched. 1, para. 13.
64 S.I. 1999 No. 1319.

Scotland; although it is noticeable that documents are now routinely produced separately for each of the three parts of Great Britain.

Finally, it should be realised that the above outline, while it reflects the legal position in relation to the 1967 Act, is somewhat theoretical. In practice, for all purposes the Forestry Commission is the Government department responsible for forestry policy throughout Great Britain.

11.2.2 Forestry policy

The duty of ministers in performing any functions under the 1967 Act is "[to] have regard to the national interest in maintaining and expanding the forestry resources of England and Wales and . . . Scotland".[65] This has resulted over the last ten years or so in a stream of policy documents. All broadly declare two main aims:

- the sustainable management of the existing woods and forests, and

- a steady expansion of tree cover, to increase the many diverse benefits that forests provide.

These two concerns were highlighted in *Forestry Policy for Great Britain*, published in September 1991 by the Forestry Commission, setting out the Government's strategy.

The United Nations Conference on Environment and Development (the "Earth Summit") at Rio de Janeiro in 1992, the Ministerial Conference on the Protection of European Forests at Helsinki in 1993,[66] and a report by the House of Commons Select Committee on the Environment in 1992-93,[67] led to the production of *Sustainable Forestry: the UK Programme*[68] (January 1994), again emphasising the aims set out in the 1991 strategy. That in turn was followed by a general review of forestry policy, the conclusions of which were published in August 1994 as *Our Forests: the Way Ahead*.[69]

A further review led to *The UK Forestry Standard: the Government's Approach to Sustainable Forestry*, published by the Commission in 1998, which is now the key document.

The year 1998 also saw the launch by the Forestry Commission and the Government of a forest strategy for England, *A New Focus for England's Woodlands*. Following devolution, Scotland's first *Forestry Strategy* was launched by the Scottish Forestry Minister in November 1999, and a *Wales Woodland Strategy* by the National Assembly in the spring of 2001. These documents between them represent the most up-to-date statement of Government policy on all aspects of forestry.

---

[65] FA 1967, s. 41, inserted by FA 1981, s. 4, and amended by S.I. 1999 No. 1756, art. 2, Sched., para. 3.

[66] The Statement of Principles for a Global Consensus on the Management, Conservation and Sustainable Development of All Types of Forests, from the Rio summit, and the General Guidelines for the Sustainable Management of Forests in Europe, from the Helsinki conference, are reproduced as Annexes to *Sustainable Forestry: the UK Programme*, HMSO, 1994.

[67] The Government's response was presented to Parliament in June 1993: Cm 2259.

[68] Cm 2429.

[69] Cm 2644.

11.2.3 Acquisition and disposal of land for forestry

Forests and woodlands in public ownership may appear to be owned by the Forestry Commission. In strict legal terms, however, they are owned by the Crown, and merely at the disposal of the Commission.[70]

Where land is to be acquired for afforestation or for other purposes connected with forestry, therefore, the acquisition is carried out by the relevant minister rather than by the Commission. The 1967 Act accordingly provides that the Minister may acquire (by purchase, lease or exchange) land which in his or her opinion is suitable for such purposes, together with any other land that necessarily goes with it.[71] And the Minister may also acquire land which ought to be used for the planting of trees in the interests of amenity as well as, or instead of, for timber production,[72] and land that seems to be suitable for tourist, recreational and tourist facilities.[73]

In the case of settled land, the Minister may acquire a lease of up to 999 years lease for any of the above purposes.[74]

Where land is acquired by agreement, the normal conveyancing rules will apply, save that some of the features of a compulsory acquisition (contained in the Compulsory Purchase Act 1965[75]) will also apply where appropriate.[76] Where land is acquired by compulsory purchase, the process will be more or less as with any compulsory acquisition, although, unusually, it is not governed by the Acquisition of Land Act 1981 but by Schedule 5 to the 1967 Act, which is in broadly similar terms[77]: the making of the order, and objections to it, in Part I of that Schedule, challenges to the High Court as to the validity of the order in Part II, and the procedure for the actual acquisition by Part III of that Schedule and by Part I of the 1965 Act.[78]

Land may not, however, be compulsorily acquired under the 1967 Act if it is in any of the following categories:

- part of the site of an ancient monument or other object of archaeological interest (not necessarily a scheduled monument);

- part of a park garden, or pleasure ground attached to a dwellinghouse;

- land owned by a local authority;

- operational land of statutory undertakers; or

- land owned by one of the National Trusts.[79]

Nor may land be the subject of compulsory purchase if it is subject to a forestry dedication covenant,[80] and is being used and managed in accordance with a plan

[70] FA 1967, s. 3(1).
[71] FA 1967, s. 39(1).
[72] Countryside Act 1968, s. 24(2).
[73] Countryside Act 1968, s. 23(3); and see **11.3.6**.
[74] Settled Land Act 1925, ss. 41(3), 117, amended by FA 1967, Sched. 6, para. 5; see **2.4.3**.
[75] Compulsory Purchase Act 1965, ss. 1 to 3, 9, 11 to 30; and the corresponding provisions of the Lands Clauses (Scotland) Act 1845.
[76] FA 1967, s. 39(5), Sched. 3.
[77] FA 1967, s. 40(5).
[78] FA 1967, Sched. 5, para. 11.
[79] FA 1967, s. 40(2),(4); subs. (4) was substituted by FA 1981, s. 2.
[80] See **12.6**.

approved by the Forestry Commission. Where there is an issue as to whether an owner is in breach of the provisions and conditions of such a plan, that is to be determined by an arbitrator appointed by the President of the RICS.[81]

Where land is acquired in respect of which a grant has been paid by the Commission after March 26, 1945 (that is, two years before the coming into effect of the Forestry Act 1947), the amount of that grant, with interest at the rate of 3 per cent compound, but less any payments made more than 30 years before the service of the notice to treat, shall be repayable by way of a deduction from the compensation payable for the purchase.[82]

The Minister may then place any land thus acquired at the disposal of the Commission, for it to manage. Land that is not passed to the Commission may be managed by the Minister as seems appropriate, or disposed of for any purpose – this might apply where, for example, a larger estate is purchased as a single holding but only those parts suitable for afforestation are to be managed by the Commission.[83] The one exception to this is that within the Forest of Dean land may only be disposed of, either by sale or by exchange with other, more suitable land, if it is not needed or not suitable for forestry.[84]

11.2.4 Finance

The financing of central Government involvement in forestry is largely the responsibility of the Forestry Commission. It is accordingly dealt with here at **11.3.3**.

11.3 The Forestry Commission

11.3.1 General duties and functions

In practice, as already noted, it is the Forestry Commission rather than any Government department that takes the lead in forestry matters.

By virtue of section 1 of the Forestry Act 1967, as originally enacted, the Commissioners are under a duty:

- to promote the interests of forestry, the development of afforestation, and the production and supply of timber and other forest products[85]; and

- to promote the establishment and maintenance of adequate reserves of growing trees.[86]

In addition, in common with every other Government department and public body, the Commissioners are under a duty when exercising any of their functions to have regard to the desirability of conserving the natural beauty and amenity of

---

[81] FA 1967, s. 40(3); in Scotland by an arbiter appointed by the Chairman of the Scottish Committee of the RICS.
[82] FA 1967, s. 40(6).
[83] FA 1967, s. 39(2),(3).
[84] FA 1967, s. 39(2A), inserted by FA 1981, s. 1.
[85] FA 1967, s. 1(2); formerly FA 1919, s. 3(1).
[86] FA 1967, s. 1(3); formerly FA 1945, s. 1(1).

the countryside.[87] "Amenity" means "pleasant circumstances or features, advantages".[88] To this has been added more recently – in line with current thinking – an explicit requirement that the Commissioners are under a further duty, so far as is consistent with the proper discharge of their functions, to endeavour to achieve a reasonable balance between:

(a) the development of afforestation, the management of forests, and the production and supply of timber; and

(b) the conservation and enhancement of natural beauty and the conservation of flora, fauna and geological or physiographical features of special interest.[89]

The Commissioners are also, unsurprisingly, required to comply with directions given to it by the Minister.[90] They are in fact answerable to Parliament, but operate in partnership with the Department of the Environment, Food and Rural Affairs (DEFRA) in respect of England, the National Assembly of Wales Agriculture Department (NAWAD), and the Rural Affairs Department of the Scottish Executive (SERAD).[91]

More specifically, the Commission is given powers to manage land for the purposes of carrying out its functions relating to forestry, to manage (or to assist owners to manage) private woodlands, and to buy and sell timber and other forest products[92]; to enter forestry dedication covenants with the owners of private woodlands[93]; to ensure that sufficient haulage facilities exist for the haulage of timber[94]; to take steps to deal with vermin[95]; to amass relevant statistics and to promote the instruction and training in forestry[96]; and to give grants.[97]

In practice, the principal functions of the Commission are now as follows:

- to manage publicly owned forests and woodlands[98];

- to administer various grant schemes[99];

- to administer the new system of environmental assessment of forestry projects[1]; and

- to administer the felling licence system.[2]

---

87 Countryside Act 1968, s. 11.
88 Re Ellis and Ruislip-Northwood UDC [1920] 1 K.B. 343, per Scrutton L.J. at p. 370, upheld in FFF Estates Ltd v Hackney LBC [1981] Q.B. 503, CA; see **15.6.2**.
89 FA 1967, s. 1(3A), inserted by Wildlife and Countryside (Amendment) Act 1985, s. 4.
90 FA 1967, s. 1(4), amended by S.I. 1999 No. 1747; formerly FA 1945, s. 2.
91 See **11.2.2**.
92 FA 1967, s. 3, amended by S.I. 1999 No. 1747, Sched. 12, para. 4(5); see **11.3.4**.
93 FA 1967, s. 5, amended by S.I. 1999 No. 1747, Sched. 12, para. 4(6); see **11.12.6**.
94 FA 1967, s. 6, amended by S.I. 1999 No. 1747, Sched. 12, para. 4(7); see **11.3.5**.
95 FA 1967, s. 7, amended by S.I. 1999 No. 1747, Sched. 12, para. 4(8); see **11.3.5**.
96 FA 1967, s. 8, amended by S.I. 1999 No. 1747, Sched. 12, para. 4(8).
97 FA 1979, s. 1; see **12.7**.
98 See **11.3.4**.
99 See **12.7**.
1 See **Chapter 13**.
2 See **Chapter 14**.

Its policy as regards the carrying out of these duties and functions is contained in the various statements already referred to.[3]

Finally, it should be noted that the Secretary of State for Wales may by order provide for the carrying out of any of the activities of the Forestry Commission separately in so far as they relate to Wales, although he has not in fact yet done so; and those activities may be carried out in Wales in a manner that is different from the manner in which they are carried out in England or Scotland.[4]

11.3.2 Structure of the Forestry Commission

There is a maximum of 11 Forestry Commissioners, appointed by the Crown. Of these, at least three have special knowledge and experience of forestry, one knows the timber trade, and one has relevant scientific and technical knowledge.[5] The detailed rules as to the Commissioners are contained in Schedule 1 to the 1967 Act.[6]

The Commissioners are to appoint committees for England, Scotland and Wales, each to consist of a mixture of Commissioners, officers of the Commission and persons from outside the Commission.[7] These Committees may carry out any of the functions of the Commission that may be delegated to them by the Commissioners; but they have met rarely, if ever, in recent years. The Act also provides that there is also to be a Home Grown Timber Advisory Board, of up to 25 members, of whom between six and eight shall be appointed after consultation with those representing woodland owners, and between six and eight after consultation with those representing timber merchants.[8] The Board is to be consulted by the Commissioners when they come to make any regulations under the Act (notably as to the need for felling licences and the procedures for obtaining them).[9] This role is in practice filled by the Forestry Commission Advisory Panel.

The Commission may, and in practice does, operate on the basis of a series of "conservancies"[10] – there are eight conservancies in England (some with one or two area offices), and six in Scotland. Wales operates as a single conservancy. There is a regional advisory committee for each conservancy, which is to have between seven and 12 members, of who at least four shall be appointed after consultation with those with relevant special interests (woodland owners, timber merchants and forestry experts).[11] The function of the regional advisory committee is to advise in relation to applications for felling licences and proposals to give felling directions.[12]

In addition to these formal decision-making bodies, the Commissioners may appoint and dismiss staff, subject to the approval of the Treasury[13]; and such staff

---

[3] See **11.2.2**.
[4] Government of Wales Act 1998, Sched. 7, para. 1.
[5] FA 1967, s. 2(1),(2), Sched. 1, paras 9 to 13A amended by FA 1981, s. 5.
[6] FA 1967, Sched. 1, paras 1 to 5, 9 to 13A.
[7] FA 1967, s. 2(3), Sched. 1, para. 7.
[8] FA 1967, ss. 37(1)(a), 38(1),(2),(4),(5).
[9] FA 1967, ss. 32(1), 37(2); see **Chapter 14**.
[10] FA 1967, s. 35.
[11] FA 1967, ss. 37(1)(b), 38(1),(3)–(5).
[12] FA 1967, s. 37(3); see **14.3.4**, **14.5.4** and **14.8.1**.
[13] FA 1967, Sched. 1, para. 6.

are generally to have the same benefits as civil servants in respect of the principal civil service pension scheme.[14]

In the mid-1990s, the "Forestry Commission" was split into two sections: Forest Enterprise, which was responsible for managing its own woodlands; and the Forest Authority, which dealt with the Commission's statutory functions (notably the giving or withholding of grants and licensing). In practice, that led to confusion rather than clarity; and the regulatory section accordingly quietly dropped the "Forest Authority" tag in the late 1990s, although references to the Authority may sometimes be found in older material.

11.3.3 Finance and annual report

A key provision of the original Forestry Act of 1919, continued under the 1967 Act, was the setting up of the Forestry Fund.[15] Money was paid into the Fund annually by Parliament, as were any sums received by the Forest Commission (whether in respect of sales of timber or otherwise). From the Fund were paid the salaries of the Commissioners and the Commission staff, their expenses, as well as the expenses incurred by the Minister in connection with administering the felling licence system, any grants made by the Commission, and the cost to the Minister of acquiring and managing land.[16] It was, in other words, a rare example of a hypothecated fund.

However, on the coming into force of the Scotland Act 1988 on July 1, 1999, the Fund was wound up and the funds within it transferred to the Forestry Commission.[17] Thereafter, the expenses noted above, together with the cost of superannuation benefits for Commission staff, are to be met from money provided by Parliament (or from the Scottish Consolidated Fund) or from money received by the Commission – save that the Minister may direct that receipts in the latter category are to be paid into the Consolidated Fund or the Scottish Fund.[18]

The new arrangements, which are in reality very similar to the old, are the result of the tortuous amendments made to the Forestry Act 1967 by the Scotland Act 1998 (Cross-Border Public Authorities) (Adaptation of Functions) Order 1999[19] and, a few months later, by the Scotland Act 1988 (Cross-Border Public Authorities) (Forestry Commissioners) Order 2000.[20]

The Forestry Commission is to submit an annual report and accounts to the Minister, who is to lay them before Parliament, in respect of its activities in England and Wales[21]; and another to the Scottish Ministers, who are to lay them before the Scottish Parliament, in respect of Scotland.[22] In fact, the Commission produces a range of annual reports, which are available on its web-site.[22a]

---

[14] FA 1967, Sched. 1, paras 9 to 13A, as amended by the Superannuation Act 1972.

[15] FA 1919, s. 8; replaced by FA 1967, s. 41(1), as originally enacted.

[16] FA 1967, ss. 41, 42, , as originally enacted; for grants, see **12.7**.

[17] FA 1967, s. 41(1), as substituted by Scotland Act 1998 (Cross-Border Public Authorities) (Adaptation of Functions) Order 1999 (S.I. 1999 No. 1747), Sched. 12, para. 4(33).

[18] FA 1967, s. 41(2)–(4), (6)–(11), as substituted by S.I. 1999 No. 1747, Sched. 12, para. 4(33), and S.I. 2000 No. 746, Sched., para. 5.

[19] S.I. 1999 No. 1747.

[20] S.I. 2000 No. 746.

[21] Exchequer and Audit Departments Act 1921, s. 5; FA 1967, s. 45(3), as substituted by S.I. 1999 No. 1747, para. 4(36), and amended by S.I. 2000 No. 746, Sched. para. 5(6).

[22] FA 1967, s. 45(1),(2), as substituted by S.I. 1999 No. 1747, para. 4(36).

[22a] www.forestry.gov.uk.

As for Wales, with effect from May 14, 2001, the activities of the Forestry Commission are funded by the National Assembly (following consultation with the Commission itself).[23] Any money received by the Commission in respect of its functions in Wales has to be spent on those functions,[24] and the Commission has to keep separate accounts in respect of its income and expenditure relating to Wales.[25]

11.3.4 Management of Forestry Commission land

Once land has been placed at its disposal by the relevant minister, the Forestry Commission may manage, plant and use it for the purpose of exercising any of its functions under the 1967 Act; and that power includes a power to build on or otherwise develop the land.[26] Any timber produced on such land belongs to the Commission, and may be sold or otherwise disposed of.[27] The result is that, for almost all purposes, the land itself may be considered as belonging to the Commission, even though technically it still belongs to the Crown. The Commission in its role as owner and manager of woodland generally uses the name "Forest Enterprise".

One result of the classification of Forestry Commission land as Crown land is that the provisions of Part II of the Forestry Act 1967 (relating to felling licences) do not apply to it.[28] However, felling proposals by Forest Enterprise, known as forest design plans, are still publicised on the public register.[29]

Obviously the principal function for which such land will be used is the planting and management of trees, that being, after all, what the Forestry Commission is in business to achieve.[30] However, so as to avoid the hillsides of Britain being uniformly clothed with serried ranks of conifers, it was many years ago made explicit that the functions of the Commission includes the planting, caring for and management of trees in the interests of amenity as well as or instead of in the interests of timber production.[31] The duties of the Commission in relation to the countryside generally and features of special interest have already been noted.[32]

Equally obviously, large tracts of woodland, generally in rural areas, constitute a major resource both as a habitat for various forms of wildlife and for recreation. As to the former, the relevant law (in the main contained in the Wildlife and Countryside Act 1981[33]) is generally beyond the scope of this book, although it has been considered in outline in **Chapter 9**. As to the latter, this is the subject of section 23 of the Countryside Act 1968, which empowers the Forestry Commission to provide, manage, maintain and improve tourist, recreational and sporting facilities on its land. Such facilities may include items such as visitor accommodation, camping and caravan sites, facilities for meals and refreshments,

[23] Government of Wales Act 1998, s. 105, brought into force (together with most of Sched. 7) by S.I. 2001 No. 1756.
[24] Government of Wales Act 1998, Sched. 7, para. 4.
[25] Government of Wales Act 1998, Sched. 7, para. 5.
[26] FA 1967, s. 3(1), amended by S.I. 1999 No. 1747, para. 4(5).
[27] FA 1967, s. 3(1)(b), (3)(a).
[28] FA 1967, s. 33.
[29] See **14.2.1**, **14.3.2**.
[30] FA 1967, s. 1; see **11.3.1**.
[31] Countryside Act 1968, s. 24(1).
[32] See **11.3.1**.
[33] As amended, principally by CROWA 2000.

picnic places, viewpoints, car parks, information and study facilities, shops and
toilets.

11.3.5 Private woodlands

In relation to private woodlands, the most important powers of the Forestry
Commission in practice are those that enabled it to enter into forestry dedication
covenants with owners[34] and now to give grants (currently under the Woodland
Grant Scheme).[35]

More generally, the Commission may produce statistical information relating
to forestry; it may promote education in forestry; it may undertake enquiries,
experiments and research, and publish the results, with the aims of promoting
forestry and teaching it, and securing an adequate supply of timber. In reliance
upon these powers, the Forestry Commission has over the years produced a large
number of helpful books and pamphlets on a wide variety of topics related to trees
and forestry; and it makes available both general and specific advice through the
medium of the Arboricultural Advice and Information Service.[36]

In addition, the 1967 Act contains a number of other general and miscellaneous
powers. These are briefly described here, if only for completeness – but many of
them are somewhat theoretical, or at least rarely if ever formally relied on in
practice.[37]

First, as well as its general advisory role, the Forestry Commission may give
any advice in relation to the planting or management of any specific woods or
forests, whoever they are owned by (including private owners, the Crown Estate,
Government departments and local authorities); it may indeed undertake itself the
management and supervision of such woods and forests, on terms agreed with the
owner.[38] It may also purchase standing timber growing on private land; or may
sell on behalf of the owner of such land any timber or other forest products, again
on agreed terms.[39] The Commission may also set up and carry on woodland
industries generally, and assist others to do so.[40]

Secondly, where the Commission forms the view that there exist insufficient
facilities for the haulage of timber from a wood or forest to the nearest road,
railway or waterway, it may make an order requiring the owner of any relevant
land to make the necessary facilities available.[41] On receipt of such an order in
draft, the landowner is entitled to make representations to the Commission; and
once an order has actually been made, the owner may appeal to the minister, who
may revoke or vary the order if that seems appropriate. If an order is made, rent is
payable to the owner of the land over which the haulage facilities are provided,
together with compensation for any damage caused; and any disputes as to the
amount payable under either heading is to be determined by arbitration. It is
believed that no order has in fact ever been made under these provisions; certainly
the minister has never exercised his or her power to prescribe the procedures for
appeals.[42]

[34] See **12.6**.
[35] See **12.7**.
[36–37] Alice Holt Lodge, Wrecclesham, Farnham, Surrey, GU10 4LH.
[38] FA 1967, s. 3(2).
[39] FA 1967, s. 3(3)(a), (4).
[40] FA 1967, s. 3(3)(b).
[41] FA 1967, s. 6.
[42] Halsbury's Statutes, fourth edn, vol. 18, Forestry, p. 604.

Thirdly, in addition to its powers under the Plant Health Act 1967[43] to deal with pests and diseases, the Forestry Commission has powers under section 7 of the Forestry Act 1967 to deal with rabbits, hares and vermin – the latter being defined to include squirrels.[44]

Where the Commission considers that trees are being damaged by the attention of such vermin, or are likely to be damaged, and that the occupier of the land is not doing enough to deal with the problem, it must first give the occupier and the owner of the land a reasonable opportunity to take action. However, if that does not achieve the desired result, it may then authorise a competent person to enter the land and kill and take the offending animals, and recover the cost from the occupier of the land – if necessary, as a civil debt. The person carrying out the killing must produce his or her authority if challenged, but anyone obstructing him or her may be fined up to level 2 on the standard scale.[45] This procedure is apparently seldom, if ever, used in practice.

Finally, the Commission's officers, or others on its behalf, may enter any land to see whether it is suitable for afforestation, and to inspect timber growing on the land, or for any other purpose under the 1967 Act.[46]

11.3.6 Public access to woodlands

After the war, until the coming into force of the Countryside and Rights of Way Act 2000, an owner of land in the open country could enter into an access agreement with a local authority, allowing the public to have access to the land for the purpose of open-air recreation; or the authority could unilaterally make an order having that effect.[47] "Open country" was initially defined to include only mountains, moors and cliffs; but the definition was extended in 1968 to include woodlands (other than Epping Forest and Burnham Beeches).[48]

In fact, of course, very few access agreements or orders were ever made. Under the 2000 Act, therefore, members of the general public were given a new right to roam over any "access land" in England and Wales – that is, broadly speaking, common land, land more than 600 metres above sea level, and other land shown as open land on the relevant map maintained under the Act.[49] Such land might well include woods and forests.[50]

Where that land consists wholly or predominantly of woodland, whether or not under the control of the Forestry Commission, the Commission may become the relevant authority for the purposes of the Act, by giving notice to the authority which would otherwise have that role.[51]

---

[43] See **11.5**.
[44] FA 1967, s. 7(5).
[45] FA 1967, s. 7.
[46] FA 1967, s. 48(1).
[47] National Parks and Access to the Countryside Act 1949, Part V (ss. 59 to 83).
[48] Countryside Act 1968, s. 16(1); for the exclusion of the two forests under the control of the Corporation of London, see National Parks and Access to the Countryside Act 1949, s. 112.
[49] 2000 Act, ss. 1, 2.
[50] Not excluding Epping Forest and Burnham Beeches – perhaps surprisingly, the exemption in s. 112 of the 1949 Act does not apply.
[51] 2000 Act, s. 21(6), (7); the relevant authority would otherwise be the national park authority or, elsewhere, the Countryside Agency or the Countryside Council for Wales.

The owner of access land may seek to exclude the public for up to 28 days a year, by giving notice to the relevant authority.[52] The authority may also exclude access for longer periods where it is satisfied that exclusion is necessary for the management of the land (whatever that means).[53] And the authority may itself exclude the public where that is necessary to avoid a risk of fire or other danger, or to protect flora, fauna, ancient monuments and other features of special interest.[54] If the authority wishes to act under any of these powers so as to exclude access for a longer period, it must first consult the local access forum where one exists.[55]

It has already been noted that a person may only avail himself or herself of the right to roam, and must not intentionally remove, damage or destroy any plant, shrub, tree or root or any part of one.[56]

11.3.7 Byelaws

The Forestry Commission is empowered by section 46 of the Forestry Act 1967 to make byelaws with respect to any land which is under its management or control and to which members of the public have, or may have, a right of access. Such byelaws are likely to apply principally to land that is in Crown ownership and placed at the disposal of the Commission; but they also regulate the use of land in private ownership which the Commission has agreed to manage.[57]

Byelaws under section 46 are to regulate the use of the land by the public for exercise and recreation, and in particular to provide for the preservation of the trees and timber on the land, to protect the property of the Commission; and to avoid injury or disfigurement of the land.[58] They may also regulate the reasonable use by the public of any tourist, recreational and sporting facilities provided on Forestry Commission land under the provisions of the Countryside Act 1968.[59]

Such byelaws are to be in the form of a statutory instrument, laid before Parliament in draft.[60] Those affecting the New Forest or the Forest of Dean must also be the subject of consultation with the relevant Verderers.[61]

Those currently in force are the Forestry Commission Byelaws 1982.[62] These make unlawful a wide variety of activities, including the following: entering restricted areas; leaving gates open; lighting fires; damaging Forestry Commission property; displaying notices; digging up trees, shrubs or plants, whether living or dead; disturbing archaeological remains; operating metal detectors; setting up caravans or tents; grazing animals; riding horses; having dogs or other animals

---

[52]   2000 Act, s. 22; there are limits to the extent to which access may be prevented under this provision
        on public holidays and at weekends.
[53]   2000 Act, s. 24.
[54]   2000 Act, ss. 25, 26.
[55]   2000 Act, s. 27(1).
[56]   2000 Act, Sched. 2, para. 1(l); see **9.6.7**.
[57]   See **11.3.5**.
[58]   FA 1967, s. 46(1), (2).
[59]   Countryside Act 1968, s. 23(4); see **11.3.6**.
[60]   FA 1967, s. 46(4); those affecting land in Scotland will be laid before the Scottish Parliament; see
        Scotland Act 1998 (Cross-Border Public Authorities) (Adaptation of Functions, etc.) Order 1999
        (S.I. 1999 No. 1747), art. 3, Sched. 12, Pt II, para. 4(36).
[61]   FA 1967, s. 47(1).
[62]   S.I. 1982 No. 648. They replace the general Forestry Commission Byelaws of 1971 (S.I. 1971 No.
        997) and 1975 (S.I. 1975 No. 919), as well as the Bedgebury Pinetum Byelaws 1969 (S.I. 1979 No.
        312), the New Forest Byelaws 1970 (S.I. 1970 No. 1068), the Westonbirt Arboretum Byelaws 1972
        (S.I. 1972 No. 303) and the Forest of Dean Byelaws 1975 (S.I. 1975 No. 918).

out of control; selling articles; setting up beehives; disturbing wildlife or habitats; using firearms or bows and arrows; damming watercourses; operating aircraft, balloons, or model aircraft, boats or cars; causing a disturbance by playing sports, playing music, or otherwise; leaving broken glass or rubbish; polluting land or water; delivering speeches or holding meetings or festivals; evading charges levied for the use of roads and car parks.[63]

In addition, there are specific rules restricting the use of vehicles on Forestry Commission land.[64] It is thus generally unlawful to bring a vehicle onto such land, other than a child's pushchair, a wheelchair or an electrically powered invalid carriage. But this does not apply to vehicles using lay-bys at the side of the highway, or those using or gaining access to official car parks.

Whilst the majority of the provisions of the byelaws now relate to all land under the control or management of the Commission, there are still some which relate solely to particular areas. Thus in relation to Westonbirt Arboretum and Bedgebury Pinetum there are further restrictions on the recreational activities that may be lawfully carried out and a prohibition on introducing plants.[65] And there is a general speed limit throughout the New Forest,[66] and restrictions on grazing there and in the Forest of Dean.[67]

Any act forbidden by the byelaws may be carried out lawfully if authorised in writing by the Commission.[68] Subject to that, any breach of the byelaws is an offence, punishable on summary conviction by a fine of up to level 2 on the standard scale, with a further fine of 50p per day in the case of continuing offences.[69] The Commission's officers, or others on its behalf, may enter any land to enforce any byelaws made under the 1967 Act, and to remove or exclude (after due warning) anyone in breach of the byelaws and any vagrant. Anyone obstructing the exercise of such a right of entry is guilty of an offence, punishable by a fine of up to level 3 on the standard scale.[70]

11.4 Rural development boards

Under Part III of the Agriculture Act 1967, the Government was empowered to set up rural development boards in areas of hills and uplands, to deal with the special problems and needs of such areas and to draw up an overall programme for guidance in making decisions as to the use of land for agriculture and forestry – having regard, amongst other things, to the special economic considerations and the long-term nature of forestry.[71] Each rural development board was to co-ordinate its proposals and programmes with those of the Forestry Commission,

---

[63] S.I. 1982 No. 648, byelaw 5; see the byelaw for the detailed wording. Note that many of these activities were only previously prohibited in relation to specific areas.

[64] S.I. 1982 No. 648, byelaws 6, 7.

[65] S.I. 1982 No. 648, byelaws 8, 9.

[66] S.I. 1982 No. 648, byelaw 10.

[67] S.I. 1982 No. 648, byelaws 11, 12; see also the byelaws of the Verderers of the New Forest, set out in the Schedule to S.I. 1999 No. 2134, relating to animals in the Forest.

[68] S.I. 1982 No. 648, byelaw 3(3).

[69] FA 1967, s. 46(5). The maximum fine was originally £10 in respect of breaches in the New Forest, and £5 elsewhere (why?); these were both increased to £20 by the Criminal Justice Act 1967, and to level 2 (currently, since 1991, £500) by the Criminal Justice Act 1982. The fine for a continuing offence was substituted in s. 46(5)(c) by the Decimal Currency Act 1969.

[70] FA 1967, s. 48(2),(3).

[71] Agriculture Act 1967, s. 45(1)–(3).

and the board and the Commission were "to consult together at all stages and, where necessary, to act in concert".[72]

The reason for such close co-operation was that, although the principal function of the boards (in line with thinking at the time) was to be to stimulate voluntary amalgamation and modernisation of small holdings, so as to increase the number of "commercial" farms,[73] this would inevitably involve woodlands. The Government envisaged that:

". . . although they will no doubt work very largely by advice and persuasion, nevertheless to enable them to carry out their tasks effectively it is thought right to give them powers to control . . . tree planting that could prejudice their programme".[74]

The Act accordingly provided that no person was to plant trees in the area of a rural development board except under the authority of a licence granted by the board. As might be expected, that requirement was subject to numerous exceptions – notably planting by the Forestry Commission itself, or in accordance with a scheme approved by it; planting on land which had been woodland within the previous ten years; and planting on small areas of land, orchards and public open spaces. The Act further provided for the making of applications for such licences, and for their determination; and unauthorised planting was to be a criminal offence, attracting a fine of up to level 3.[75]

The mechanism to establish (and to dissolve) a board is in Schedule 5 to the Act; and in the event, only one board was ever set up, in the Northern Pennines.[76] But farming and landowning opinion was mistrustful of the idea, however democratic and benevolent it might have been in intention, as it appeared to be the harbinger of land nationalisation. A second proposed board, in mid-Wales, was thus the subject of campaigns by the Farmers Unions, mistrustful of it as a foreign implant from Whitehall, and the Northern Pennines Board was arbitrarily dissolved on the return to power of the Conservatives in 1970.[77]

There are thus currently no rural development boards in existence, and there have not been for many years. But the legislation requiring consent for tree planting is still on the statute book, and could (at least in theory) be reactivated by a future government.

11.5 Plant health

11.5.1 Introduction

Nearly 90 per cent of the timber used in Britain is imported from overseas, and a vast range of other goods are imported along with timber packing material (known as "dunnage"). This presents a serious risk to the health of the trees

---

[72] Agriculture Act 1967, s. 46(3).
[73] Agriculture Act 1967, ss. 48 to 51. On the background, see T Beresford, *We Plough the Fields: British Farming Today*, Penguin, 1975, pp. 66–67.
[74] Hansard, H.L., vol. 280, cols 445–446 (Lord Hilton); see also the speech of the Duke of Bucleuch and Queensberry at cols 491–493.
[75] Agriculture Act 1967, s. 52.
[76] Northern Pennines Rural Development Board Order 1969 (S.I. 1969 No. 1095).
[77] Northern Pennines Rural Development Board Order 1971 (S.I. 1971 No. 224). See Beresford, *op cit.*

growing in Britain, because imported wood may carry tree pests and diseases not currently found here, which could easily establish populations in growing forests. The Plant Health Service of the Forestry Commission accordingly endeavours to minimise this problem by controlling the import and export of forestry material (trees, timber and timber products), and the movement of such material within the EC and within Britain.

The legal basis for such control is the Plant Health Act 1967, which came into force on the same date as the Forestry and Agriculture Acts 1967, and was a consolidating statute which has effect "for the control . . . of pests and diseases injurious to . . . trees or bushes". References to pests in the Act (and thus in the Regulations[78]) are to insects, bacteria, fungi and other vegetable or animal organisms, viruses and all other agents causative of any transmissible disease of trees or bushes, and to such pests in any stage of existence.[79]

The Act authorises the relevant competent authority to make such orders as it considers expedient, or as are called for by any EC obligation:

- for prevent the introduction of pests into Great Britain; or

- for preventing the spread of pests within Great Britain.[80]

It further provides that the Forestry Commission is the competent authority as regards the protection of forest trees and timber (including all timber products) from attack by pests.[81]

Orders under the 1967 Act are to be made by statutory instrument.[82] The orders currently in force that have been made under these provisions are the Plant Health (Forestry) (Great Britain) Order 1993[83] and the Treatment of Spruce Bark Order 1993.[84] They are in fulfilment of the requirements of European Directive 2000/29/EC, on protective measures against the introduction into the Community of organisms harmful to plants or plant products and against their spread within the Community.[85]

11.5.2 Restrictions on the import, export and movement of forestry material

The first step in controlling pests and diseases is to try to stop them being imported into the country, or spreading within it. The import and export into and from Great Britain of various types of "forestry material" (that is, trees, wood, isolated bark, used forestry machinery, soil or growing medium), and the spread of such material within Great Britain, is regulated by the Plant Health (Forestry) (Great Britain) Order 1993[86] (referred to here as "the 1993 Order"), as amended.

[78] Interpretation Act 1978, s. 11.
[79] Plant Health Act 1967, s. 1(1). The Act replaces (principally) the Destructive Insects Act 1877, and the Destructive Insects and Pests Acts of 1907 and 1927.
[80] Plant Health Act 1967, ss. 2, 3, amended by European Communities Act 1972, Sched. 4. It is of course unthinkable that the making of an order called for by an EC obligation would not be expedient.
[81] Plant Health Act 1967, s. 1(2)(a).
[82] Plant Health Act 1967, s. 6.
[83] S.I. 1993 No. 1283, as amended by S.I. 1994 No. 3094, S.I. 1995 No. 1989, S.I. 1996 No. 751, S.I. 1998 No. 2206, S.I. 1998 No. 3109, S.I. 2001 No. 2995 and S.I. 2002 No. 295, and S.I. 2002 No. 927.
[84] S.I. 1993 No. 1282, as amended by S.I. 2002 No. 296.
[85] OJ No. L169, July 10, 2000 (replacing Directive 77/93/EC); amended by Directive 2001/33/EC (OJ No. L127, May 9, 2001, p. 42; see also notes to S.I. 2002 No. 295 and S.I. 2002 No. 927.
[86] See note 83 above.

As might be imagined, the provisions of the Order are detailed and technical; they are also subject to change every year or two, as new pests are discovered. The notes below, therefore, attempt only to provide a very broad outline of the structure of the control; for the details, it is necessary to consult the Orders themselves – or, probably better, to consult the Plant Health Service of the Forestry Commission at its headquarters in Edinburgh.

First, there is an absolute prohibition on the import into Great Britain of:

● any of the tree pests specified in Schedule 1;

● any of the trees specified in Part A of Schedule 2 if they are harbouring specified pests;

● an item of forestry material in any of the categories specified in Schedule 3 (mainly trees or isolated bark) if it has come from certain countries; and

● any other tree pest likely to be injurious.[87]

There is also a prohibition on keeping, storing, selling, planting, moving or otherwise disposing of within Great Britain an item which is in any of the first three categories, without the authority of the Forestry Commission or an inspector.[88]

Secondly, an item in the categories specified in Part A of Schedule 4, which includes various types of wood, packing material and dunnage, as well as trees, may not be imported from outside the EC unless the conditions laid down in that Schedule have been complied with – notably it must almost always be accompanied by a phytosanitary certificate.[89] And, again, such items may not be kept, stored, sold, planted, moved or otherwise disposed of within Great Britain without the authority of the Forestry Commission or an inspector authorised by the Commission.[90]

Thirdly, there is a prohibition on the following, unless authority has been obtained from the Forestry Commission or from an inspector:

● the import into the *dendroctonus micans* protected zone[91] of conifers infected with *dendroctonus micans* (the great spruce bark beetle);

● the import into the protected zone from elsewhere within the EC (including elsewhere within Great Britain) of an item in any of the categories specified in Part C of Schedule 4,[92] unless the conditions in that Schedule have been complied with – notably that the item must almost always be accompanied by a plant passport;

● the import into Great Britain of conifers infected with other types of spruce bark beetle[93]; and

---

[87]   1993 Order, art. 3(1).
[88]   1993 Order, art. 5.
[89]   1993 Order, art. 3(2); see also arts. 9 to 13 as to phytosanitary certificates generally (art. 11 as substituted by S.I. 1994 No. 3094).
[90]   1993 Order, art. 5.
[91]   Specified in Sched. 6, as substituted by S.I. 2002 No. 295 – broadly, Scotland, and the north, east and south of England.
[92]   As substituted by S.I. 1994 No. 3094, Sched. 1.
[93]   Sched. 2, Pt B, item 2.

- the import into Great Britain from an EC member state of the items specified in Part B of Schedule 4,[94] unless the specified conditions have been complied with – notably the material must almost always be accompanied by a plant passport.[95]

Unsurprisingly, there is a restriction on the keeping, storing, selling, planting, moving or otherwise disposing of an item in either of the first two categories within the protected zone or one within either of the second two within Great Britain, without the authority of the Forestry Commission or an inspector. And, again, an appropriate plant passport will always be required.[96]

There is also a separate restriction (under the Treatment of Spruce Bark Order 1993[97]) on the movement of any bark from a tree of the genus *picea* (spruce) within the area of Great Britain outside the protected zone, unless the bark has been treated against infestation by *dendroctonus micans*.

An item within one of the categories specified within Part A of Schedule 5 may not be exported to other EC member states, nor an item within Part B of Schedule 5[98] to specified areas within the EC, unless they are accompanied by a certificate as to its origin or as to the treatment it has received, and a plant passport.[99]

11.5.3 Plant health: supplementary provisions

In order for any system of control to operate satisfactorily, the role of traders importing, producing or distributing forestry material is crucial. The Forestry Commission therefore maintains a register of such traders; and in order to remain on the register, traders must maintain certain standards, and in particular must fully co-operate with the Commission.[1] Registered traders may then apply to the Commission to issue plant passports to allow particular items of forestry material to be moved from their premises.[2]

It is also important for any new outbreak of pests or disease to be reported promptly. Accordingly, where the occupier of any premises becomes aware of or suspects the presence of any of the tree pests listed in Schedule 1, Part A of Schedule 2, or Parts A or B of Schedule 4, or any other pest likely to be injurious to trees in Great Britain, he or she is to notify the Commission immediately (presumably by telephone if appropriate), and as soon as practicable confirm the notice in writing.[3]

The Commission's officers, or others on its behalf, have wide powers to take appropriate action to stop the entry into Great Britain, or the spread within it, of any tree pest or any forestry material being transported unlawfully. They may, in particular, enter any land or premises (including a dwellinghouse if a warrant has

---

[94] As substituted by S.I. 1994 No. 3094, Sched. 1.
[95] 1993 Order, arts. 4, 8, as substituted by S.I. 1994 No. 3094.
[96] 1993 Order, art. 6, 8.
[97] S.I. 1993 No. 1282, amended by S.I. 2002 No. 296. It is not clear why this is not in the main 1993 Order.
[98] As substituted by S.I. 1995 No. 1989, and amended by S.I. 2002 No. 295 and S.I. 2002 No. 927.
[99] 1993 Order, arts. 7, 8.
[1] 1993 Order, arts. 14 to 16.
[2] 1993 Order, arts. 17, 18. Applications are to be accompanied by a fee: see S.I. 1996 No. 2291, amended by S.I. 1997 No. 655 and S.I. 1999 No. 783.
[3] 1993 Order, arts. 19, 20.

been obtained), in connection with any of the Commission's functions under the Plant Health Act 1967 and the 1993 Orders.[4]

Finally, any contravention of the Plant Health Order 1993 or the Treatment of Spruce Bark Order 1993 is an offence, attracting a maximum penalty on summary conviction of up to Level 5 on the standard scale.[5]

11.5.4 Pesticides

Sometimes, of course, a cure can be worse than the disease. And the unrestricted use of pesticides has, rightly, provoked much concern. The European Commission has accordingly operated for some years a rolling programme of authorisation, which now applies throughout the European Economic Area, to ensure that no new product is placed on the market without having been authorised by the EAA country concerned. Authorisation will only be given where the relevant agency is satisfied that the product in question will be effective without causing harm to human or animal health and without adversely affecting plants, ground water or the environment in general.

The principal legislation is Directive 91/414/EC,[6] as updated by a constantly increasing number of EC directives, the current list of which is to be found in the most recent British amending regulations.[7] Included at Annex I to the Directive, as amended, is a list of the currently approved substances.

The use of pesticides in Great Britain is controlled by the Plant Protection Regulations 1995,[8] made under powers in the European Communities Act 1972.[9] These are amended at frequent intervals, with amendment regulations often incorporating and revoking previous regulations.[10] Pesticides may not be placed on the market nor used without a licence having been issued by the Secretary of State.[11]

Further details may be obtained from the Pesticides Safety Directorate of DEFRA.[12]

11.6 Seeds, cones and cuttings

11.6.1 Registration of seed stands and poplar beds

The quality of seeds, plants and cuttings marketed for forestry purposes is controlled by the Forestry Commission, under the Forest Reproductive Material Regulations 1997.[13] The Regulations were made under powers contained in the

---

[4]   FA 1967, s. 48(1); 1993 Order, arts. 21 to 28, 30; S.I. 1993 No. 3093, arts. 5, 6.
[5]   1993 Order, art. 31; S.I. 1993 No. 3093, art. 8. For standard scale, see **Appendix C**.
[6]   OJ No. L230, August 19, 1981.
[7]   See currently S.I. 2001 No. 1112 and S.I. 2001 No. 161, art. 2.
[8]   S.I. 1995 No. 887, replacing the Control of Pesticides Regulations 1986 (S.I. 1986 No. 1510).
[9]   European Communities Act 1972, s. 2(2).
[10] The amendments in force as at June 1, 2001 were S.I. 1997 No. 7, S.I. 1997 No. 2499, S.I. 2001 No. 1112 (England and Wales), and SS.I. 2001 No. 161 (Scotland).
[11] S.I. 1995 No. 887, reg. 3.
[12] Room 308, Mallard House, King's Pool, 3 Peasholme Green, York, YO1 2PX. Or visit www.defra.gov.uk.
[13] S.I. 1997 No. 891, amended (but only very slightly) by S.I. 1977 No. 1264 and S.I. 1992 No. 3078.

Plant Varieties and Seeds Act 1964,[14] and implemented two EC directives on forest reproductive material.[15]

Under Part II of the Regulations, the Commission maintains a national register of approved "basic material" – that is:

- stands of trees and seed orchards of silver firs, beeches, European larches, Japanese larches, Norway spruces, sitka spruces, Austrian and Corsican pines, Weymouth pines, Douglas firs, red oaks, pedunculate oaks and sessile oaks; and

- clones and mixtures of clones of poplars.[16]

In order to be registered, material must be such as to make it suitable for reproductive purposes, with no characteristics making it undesirable for forestry purposes. It must also be either:

- selected reproductive material, conforming to the requirements set out at Schedule 2 to the Regulations, or to similar requirements imposed in Northern Ireland or by other EC member states; or

- tested reproductive material, conforming to the requirements set out at Schedule 3 to the Regulations, or to similar requirements imposed in Northern Ireland or by other EC member states.[17]

Where the Commission decides to register material submitted for registration, or to remove from the register material already included, there is a right of appeal to the Plant Varieties and Seeds Tribunal.[18]

The significance of the register is that no seeds or cones are to be collected, and no parts of plants shall be taken, for the purpose of marketing, unless they have been derived from basic material that has been included in the register.[19] Once the Commission is satisfied that seeds, cones or plants are from material that has been registered, it will issue a certificate of provenance, which enables a dealer to provide its customers with details of the origins of the collections. Sample certificates are at Schedules 4 and 9 to the Regulations.

11.6.2 Marketing, import and export of material

No forest reproductive material produced by sexual means from the genera and species listed above (other than poplar) is to be marketed unless it is selected reproductive material or tested reproductive material, as defined above. And no reproductive material produced by vegetative means from poplars is to be

---

[14]   1964 Act, s. 16, as amended by the European Communities Act 1972, Sched. 4.

[15]   Council directive 66/404/EEC (OJ No. C 125 July 11, 1966, p. 2326), as amended by 69/64/EEC (OJ No. L 48 February 26, 1969, p. 12) and 75/445/EEC (OJ No. L 196, June 26, 1975); and Council directive 71/161/EEC (OJ No. L 87 April 17, 1971, p. 14), amended by 74/13/EEC (OJ No. L 15 January 18, 1974, p. 35).

[16]   1977 Regulations, reg. 4. For the botanical names and synonyms, see Sched. 1 to the 1977 Regulations.

[17]   1977 Regulations, reg. 5; definitions in reg. 2.

[18]   1977 Regulations, reg. 6. The Tribunal is established under s. 10 of and Sched. 4 to the 1964 Act, and is under the supervision of the Council on Tribunals; its procedure is governed by Plant Varieties and Seeds Tribunal Rules 1974 (S.I. 1994 No. 1136).

[19]   1977 Regulations, reg. 8.

marketed unless it is tested reproductive material.[20] "Forest reproductive material" means seeds, cones and parts of plants intended for the production of plants, and young plants raised from seed or from parts of plants, natural seedlings and sets. Seeds and parts of plants are to be marketed under the description "EEC standard", and must comply with the conditions laid down in Schedules 5 to 7 – Schedule 7 contains rules as to the testing of seeds.[21]

In practice, however, if there is likely to be a shortage of registered material, the Commission will seek an exemption from the EC, to permit the marketing of other material.

Reproductive material is not to be imported from another EC Member State unless it is accompanied by an official certificate of provenance.[22] Material from elsewhere may not be imported without such a certificate, and an import licence issued by the Commission, and those documents must be produced to customs at the time of import.[23]

The above provisions regarding marketing and import do not apply to small quantities of seed not intended for forestry purposes (such as those destined for garden centres); or to those intended for export to other countries outside the EC.[24] Indeed, none of the Regulations apply to material taken, raised or marketed for purposes other than timber, or to seeds or cones marketed to other countries outside the EC.[25] Subject to that, any breach of the 1977 Regulations is a criminal offence under the Plant Varieties and Seeds Act 1964.

11.6.3 Future change

A new European directive, replacing and revising the two current directives, was published in January 2001.[26] National regulations to implement this will have to be in place by January 1, 2003. A consultation paper on the new Regulations is available on the Commission's web-site.[27]

---

[20] 1977 Regulations, reg. 11.
[21] See also 1977 Regulations, reg. 13.
[22] 1997 Regulations, reg. 14, amended by S.I. 1999 No. 3078.
[23] 1997 Regulations, reg. 15.
[24] 1997 Regulations, reg. 3(2).
[25] 1997 Regulations, reg. 3(1).
[26] Directive 1999/105/EC.
[27] www.forestry.gov.uk/cs/repro.html.

Chapter 12

Financial Considerations

12.1 Introduction

One inherent problem of forestry is that the creation and management of woodlands and forests requires the expenditure of considerable sums of capital on land acquisition, preparation and planting, and of further sums regularly thereafter on maintenance, before a single penny is reaped by way of return in the form of receipts from the sale of timber following felling. The only possible exception is, in some cases, limited income from tourism or the lease of sporting rights, or limited sales of timber following thinning. This also applies, of course, to very many other commercial activities; but the difference is that, in the case of forestry, the pay-back comes not months or years but decades or even centuries later.

The result is that, in the absence of any other incentives, landowners would only be likely to consider afforestation if they were planning their estate management on the basis of a very long time scale, or if the scale of their landholding were such that the expenditure necessary on planting in one part could be funded by the income from felling in another. And the State is unlikely to be willing to fund the creation of woodlands unless it has some guarantee that its investment will be safeguarded.

Considerations such as this were partly what led after the First World War to the establishment of state-owned forestry, long in advance of most other forms of publicly owned enterprises, under the Forestry Act 1919.[1] They have also over the years led to a generally favourable taxation regime for woodlands, so as to maximise the incentive to plant trees. And they have given rise to a system of grant aid coupled with agreed plans of operations as the preferred mechanism for the financial support by the State of private forestry.

The taxation regime was significantly altered in 1988, leading to the position whereby woodlands are at present generally outside the income and corporation tax system. However, there are still a number of distinctive features of the way in which woodlands are dealt with for taxation purposes, particularly in relation to inheritance tax. There are also special rules relating to farm woodlands. The details of the legal provisions relating to the taxation of woodlands (let alone

---

[1] See **11.1**.

those relating to tax generally) are beyond the scope of this book;[2-6] but a brief account of their principal features is at **12.2** (taxes on income and capital gains), **12.3** (VAT) and **12.4** (inheritance tax).

Woodlands have also generally been exempt from local taxation – currently business rates. The relevant provisions are described at **12.5**.

As for grant aid, various schemes have been introduced over the years. One of the most significant of these, introduced after the Second World War, was a mechanism (under the Forestry Act 1947) whereby owners could enter into forestry dedication covenants. The relevant statutory provisions, now in section 5 of and Schedule 2 to the 1967 Act, are still in force; and even though the Commission no longer operates the dedication scheme – that is, it is not available for new applicants, and has in effect been replaced by the grant schemes considered below – practitioners may come across it. For one thing, existing covenants remain in force until terminated and are still, at least in theory, capable of being enforced; and they will, in any event, have been registered. And other legislation makes reference to the dedication system. The relevant legislation is therefore considered briefly in this Chapter (at **12.6**).

The final sections (**12.7** and **12.8**) outline the various ways in which financial assistance is currently given to the creation and management of woodlands – including the grant schemes that were in the past associated with dedication covenants and agreements (and which may still be operated in connection with those covenants which remain). More recently, incentives have been offered under various other grant schemes; the principal ones currently in operation being the Woodland Grant Scheme and the Farm Woodland Premium Scheme.

12.2 Taxation of income and capital gains

12.2.1 General principles

There are a number of taxes that need to be considered in relation to both the ownership of woodlands and the exploitation of woodlands for profit. This section deals with income tax, corporation tax and capital gains tax; value-added tax (VAT) and inheritance tax (IHT) are considered in the following sections. It should be emphasised that the details of the various rules are constantly shifting. In any event, in relation to any specific taxation problem, it is usually wise to seek specific advice from accountants with appropriate specialised experience; but the following notes may help by way of background.

First, however, it is necessary to define what constitutes "woodlands" for tax purposes. The term is not statutorily defined, but the view expressed in the recent case of *Jaggers (t/a Shide Trees) v Ellis*[7] is generally accepted as authoritative. In that case, which concerned the general income tax exemption that now applies to the commercial occupation of woodlands, it was held that "woodlands" connotes a sizeable area of land covered to a significant extent by growing trees of some maturity, height and size, probably for use as timber. There is no mathematical or scientific formula for determining the minimum area of land or density of trees;

[2-6] For more details, see, for example, Simon's Direct Tax Service, and in particular Divisions A5 (Schedule B taxation) and I7.4 (IHT on non-agricultural woodlands).
[7] [1997] STC 1417, *The Times*, December 10, 1997.

and whether the trees on a particular area of land could be described as woodland was a matter of impression.

Secondly, it may be noted that income tax is levied on income accruing to an individual taxpayer, whereas corporation tax is payable in respect of the income accruing to a corporation – whether a multi-million pound company or a small plumber's business. The rules are more or less identical as between the two taxes – other than minor distinctions that arose for a while, as a result of the introduction of self-assessment, with respect to the period over which the income was to be calculated (either the fiscal year or the financial year). It may therefore be assumed that the comments here, relating to income tax, apply, in general, equally to corporation tax.

12.2.2 Taxation on income from non-agricultural woodlands

Non-commercial amenity woodlands have always been outside the scope of income tax.

Until relatively recently, however, income from commercial woodlands – that is, woodlands managed on a commercial basis with a view to the realisation of profits – was subject to income tax. In order to understand when a charge might arise, it is necessary to consider in outline the scheme of the tax charging provisions. These are organised under several heads of charge, known as "Schedules".[8] Each of these contains rules regulating how specific types of income are measured and charged to tax; some are sub-divided into more specific heads of charge ("Cases").

Until April 6, 1988, income arising from the occupation of such woodlands was generally chargeable to tax on a completely different basis from any other income – that is, under Schedule B.[9] This provided that tax was payable on one third of the annual value (rateable value) of the land. All income and profits from the occupation of woodlands as such were thus ignored, as were grants and insurance recoveries. Conversely, no expenditure was allowable against the assessment under Schedule B, and no capital allowances were available.

Alternatively, a taxpayer could elect, in relation to any accounting period ending before April 6, 1993, to be assessed not under Schedule B but under Schedule D – and specifically under the first sub-head (Case 1), that applies to the taxation of income from trades. An election generally had to be made prior to April 6, 1988,[10] but could also be made not later than April 6, 1993 in certain limited cases, in relation to any period starting before that date.[11]

The practical benefit of making the election was often to obtain tax relief, by setting off any loss made in the woodlands business against other income, or carrying it forward to be set off against future profits; such relief would not arise under the Schedule B rules. In the calculation of such a loss, it was permissible to claim capital allowances in respect of plant and machinery or other expenditure incurred in the forestry operation.[12] An election for assessment under Schedule D was thus clearly advantageous in the early years of a forestry operation, when expenses were high and there was little if any income.

---

[8]   Set out at Income and Corporation Tax Act 1988, ss. 15 to 18.
[9]   Income and Corporation Tax Act 1988, s. 16(1); repealed by Finance Act 1988, Sched. 14, Pt V.
[10] Finance Act 1988, Sched. 6, para. 3.
[11] Finance Act 1988, Sched. 6, para. 4.
[12] Finance Act 1971, s. 47(1)(b), Capital Allowances Act 1990, s. 122.

The charge to tax under Schedule B was abolished with effect from April 5, 1988,[13] and elections for assessment under Schedule D ceased to be valid after April 5, 1993. Since then, therefore, income from the commercial occupation of non-agricultural woodlands has been effectively exempt from any charge to income or corporation tax, either under Schedule D, Case I[14] or under Schedule A.[15] On the other hand, of course, there is no relief for the cost of establishing or maintaining woodlands; and capital allowances, which used to be available to be set against income in respect of forestry buildings and works, were discontinued for chargeable periods ending after June 19, 1989.

12.2.3 Taxation of other income relating to woodlands

In addition to the basic rule that income from commercial woodlands is outside the tax system, there are a few other special provisions which apply in particular cases.

First, extraneous income, such as from the grant of a lease, a right of way, a wayleave or of sporting rights, was outside the general woodlands exemption, and has always been assessable as general income arising from the exploitation of land, under Schedule A. This was accordingly unaffected by the abolition of Schedule B, and remains taxable.

Secondly, where the occupier of woodlands engages in a separate but related business, income from the latter may be taxable. Thus, for example, where timber is processed up to the planking stage in a sawmill occupied along with the woodlands from which it came, that is included in the occupation of the woodlands as such, and any income arising is accordingly exempt from tax.[16] But that principle does not extend to the conversion of planks into wooden boxes.[17]

Thirdly, the profits (or losses) of land dealers are generally chargeable (or allowable) to tax as trading income, under Case 1 of Schedule D. However, there is a special statutory regime applicable where dealers' transactions involve woodlands.[18] The purpose of this is to isolate and exclude the cost of timber originally purchased by the vendor along with the land it was growing on, but not felled at the time of sale. Accordingly, where woodlands are acquired in the course of such a business, so much of the cost as is attributable to growing trees or saleable underwood is not deductible as a trading expense to be set against other income; and where such woodlands are subsequently sold, that same amount is disregarded again in computing the taxable income.[19] This does not extend to new planting – that is, trees that did not exist at the time the land was purchased – and applies only in relation to woodlands purchased under a contract entered into on or after May 1, 1963. "Saleable underwood" includes any wood that is so treated as to produce periodical profits from the same stools and roots.[20]

Fourthly, income from agriculture is taxable, as trading income, under Schedule D, Case I. This may include items relating to trees and woodlands.

[13] Finance Act 1988, Sched. 6, para. 2.
[14] Income and Corporation Tax Act 1988, s. 53(4), as substituted by Finance Act 1988, Sched. 6, para. 4(3).
[15] Income and Corporation Tax Act 1988, s. 15(1).
[16] *Christie v Davies* (1945) 26 T.C. 398.
[17] *Collins v Fraser* (1969) 46 T.C. 143.
[18] Income and Corporation Tax Act 1988, s. 99.
[19] Income and Corporation Tax Act 1988, s. 99(1).
[20] *Lord Fitzhardinge v Pritchett* (1867) L.R. 2 Q.B. 135, 36 L.J.M.C. 49.

Thus, the planting of shelter belts of trees and the removal of hedges are included within the scope of agricultural works, in respect of which capital allowances will be available to be offset against profits from the occupation of land in agricultural use when computing liability to taxation.[21] Expenditure on establishing a new orchard (such as planting and staking of trees), on the other hand, is a capital item, and thus not deductible; whereas subsequent expenditure (for example, cultivating trees) is deductible as a revenue item.[22]

Further, since November 29, 1994, income from "short rotation coppice" has been assessable under Schedule D, Case I as a farming receipt rather than being exempt as income from commercial woodland.[23] "Short rotation coppice" is defined as a perennial crop of trees planted at high density, the stems of which are harvested above ground level at intervals of less than ten years.[24] The views of the Inland Revenue on this are contained in its Tax Bulletin issued in October 1995. And income from trees which are grown so as to form, in effect, a nursery (such as a plantation of Christmas trees), rather than a woodland, will be taxable – again, under Schedule D.[25]

Finally, where standing timber is acquired by a company (for example, by the owner of a sawmill) as part of trading stock, the money paid will be chargeable as a trade expense, and accordingly deductible from taxable income.[26] Similarly, if such timber is subsequently sold before being felled, any increase in value will be taxable along with other trading income under Schedule D, Case I.[27] Where, however, the acquisition of timber is more in the nature of an acquisition of an interest in land, the money paid for it may be treated as a capital expense and thus not allowable against income.[28] The latter principle has also been applied where a fruit-grower purchased an orchard with a fruit crop ripe for picking; the whole of the price paid was for an interest in land, and thus not deductible.[29] The right for a timber merchant to enter land and select, fell and remove timber (without any time limit) has also been held to be a capital expense.[30]

12.2.4 Capital gains tax

The basis of capital gains tax (CGT), as its name implies, is a charge to tax of any profit made on the disposal of a capital asset. There are, as might be expected, a host of exemptions and reliefs that apply in calculating the gain (or loss) that is chargeable (or allowable) to tax; one of these applies to woodlands, and more specifically to the sale of trees standing, felled or cut. The underlying land remains a chargeable asset.

---

[21] Revenue Capital Allowances Manual CA 4535. The general code is in Part V of the Capital Allowances Act 1990, introduced by the Finance Act 1986.
[22] *IRC v Pilcher* [1949] 2 All E.R. 1097, 31 T.C. 314, CA.
[23] Finance Act 1995, s. 154(1).
[24] Finance Act 1995, s. 154(3).
[25] *Jaggers (trading as Shide Trees) v Ellis* [1997] STC 1417, *The Times*, December 10, 1997 (Christmas trees). And see Revenue Inspector's Manual IM 2870
[26] *Hopwood v CN Spencer Ltd* (1964) 42 T.C. 169.
[27] *Murray v Commissioners of Inland Revenue (IRC)* (1951) 32 T.C. 238; *Mohanlal Hargovind of Jubbulpore v ITC for Central Provinces and Berar* [1949] A.C. 521, 2 All E.R. 652, P.C.
[28] *Kauri Timber Co v New Zealand Commissioner of Taxes* [1913] A.C. 771, P.C.
[29] *IRC v Pilcher* [1949] 2 All E.R. 1097, 31 T.C. 314, CA.
[30] *Hood Barrs v IRC* [1957] 1 All E.R. 832, 37 T.C. 188, H.L.

Prior to 1988, where income from commercial woodlands was assessed to income or corporation tax under Schedule B,[31] any consideration relating to the disposal of trees or saleable underwood was excluded in computing the gain or loss arising on a disposal of the woodlands.[32] This meant that woodlands were effectively exempt from capital gains tax. Where an election had been made for assessment of income from woodlands under Schedule D, Case I, that exemption did not apply; but roll-over relief (see below) was available for the replacement of assets used for the purposes of the commercial occupation of woodlands.[33]

Since 1988, when Schedule B was effectively abolished,[34] the exemption from capital gains tax has applied to woodlands generally.[35] Any woodlands that were at that time subject to a Schedule D election, which would have been exhausted by 1993, reverted to the same treatment as other commercially occupied woodlands.

The general exemption now applies, therefore, to all gains realised either:

- from the disposal of woodlands "where they are managed by the occupier on a commercial basis and with a view to the realisation of profit"; or

- from the receipt of capital sums under an insurance policy in respect of the destruction of or damage to trees or underwood by fire or other hazard.

The effect of this exemption is to ensure that the value of standing or felled timber (that would, of course, be free from any charge to income tax if it were sold by itself[36]) does not end up being caught by CGT where it forms art of a sale together with the underlying land.

It is also worth noting that the commercial occupation of woodlands remains a qualifying business for the purposes of roll-over relief.[37] This means that capital gains arising from the disposal of a qualifying business can be deferred by rolling them over to be offset against the cost of acquiring new commercial woodlands. The gain is only realised for tax purposes on the eventual disposal of the woodlands.

12.3 Value added tax

Generally, there is no exemption from value added tax (VAT) applying to transactions made in the course of a business relating to woodlands. However, transactions relating to land are usually exempt from VAT, and trees and other natural objects growing on the land are considered part of it and are exempt accordingly (although it is possible for the taxpayer to elect for land transactions to be chargeable).

Furthermore, VAT is not payable on receipts under the Woodland Grant Scheme (including the Community Woodland Contribution, and the Community Forest Premium) and the Farm Woodlands Premium Scheme.[38]

---

[31] See **12.2.2**.
[32] Capital Gains Tax Act 1979, s. 113(1), as originally enacted.
[33] Taxation of Chargeable Gains Act 1992, s. 158(1) (b).
[34] See **12.2.2**.
[35] Taxation of Chargeable Gains Act 1992, s. 250.
[36] See **12.2.2**.
[37] Taxation of Chargeable Gains Act 1992, s. 152 *et seq.*
[38] See **12.7**.

Sales of timber and other woodland products by a VAT-registered trader in the course of a business are subject to the payment of VAT at the standard rate. There are, however, special rules for those who choose to operate the *Flat-Rate Scheme for Farmers.*[39] Forestry is designated as a farming activity for the purposes of this scheme, and includes not only the sale of growing or felled trees but also certain basic derivatives, such as sawlogs, firewood and fencing materials. Under the scheme, a flat 4 per cent may be added by the "farmer" to all sales, and not included in the accounts submitted to the Customs and Excise.[40] On the other hand, no claim may be made in relation to VAT paid on expenditure relating to such sales.

It is also worth noting that registration for VAT is possible not just for a trader but also for someone intending to trade. This would allow someone intending to exploit woodlands commercially to register for VAT, and then to recover the VAT incurred on setting-up costs – even though it may be some years before any sales are made, realising income on which output tax would be payable.

12.4 Estate duty and inheritance tax (IHT)

12.4.1 Estate duty

Estate duty ("death duties") used to be chargeable at the death of a taxpayer on the value of his or her estate – although, unlike inheritance tax (IHT), not on the occasion of a lifetime transfer. Estate duty was abolished in 1975, but the relief available for the deferred payment of duty in respect of woodlands may have some continuing relevance.

Where the owner of woodlands died on or before March 12, 1975, there was a relief from estate duty in respect of growing timber. The duty payable on the death could be deferred until the timber was sold.[41] It then became payable if the timber was sold before the first subsequent transfer of value for IHT purposes (other than a transfer that was exempt as a gift to a spouse).[42] This potential liability ended as soon as there was such a transfer of value. However, where such a transfer (that is, the first transfer following the death of the original owner) took place after June 30, 1986, it could not be a potentially exempt transfer for IHT.

It follows that there may in some cases still be a potential liability to pay estate duty –for example, where an owner of woodlands died in 1970, and passed them on to his daughter, who still owns them. In such a situation, if the daughter sells the woodlands, estate duty will be payable. If, however, she either dies without having sold them, or transfers them to her husband during his lifetime, the liability to estate duty will cease.

12.4.2 Inheritance tax: general principles

Since the abolition of estate duty in 1975, inheritance tax (IHT[43]) is generally payable on any transfer from a person's estate following his or her death, and

---

[39] See Customs and Excise booklet.
[40] Rate current as at Easter 2002.
[41] Finance (1909–1910) Act 1910, s. 61(5), amended by Finance Act 1912, s. 9, and Finance Act 1969, s. 40, Sched. 17, para. 7.
[42] Finance Act 1975, s. 49(4), Sched. 6, para. 1.
[43] Formerly known as capital transfer tax, from 1975 to 1984.

also, at a reduced rate, on certain transfers during a person's lifetime. It may in addition apply to property held in trust (also known as "settled property"[44]) that is not subject to an interest in possession – that is, most commonly, discretionary trusts. The main body of legislation is contained in the Inheritance Tax Act 1984.

The basic rule is that IHT is payable, currently at 40 per cent, on the value of the estate or the transfer above a certain limit (below which there is a nil rate band). As would be expected, there are various exemptions and reliefs that qualify that rule, reducing either the amount of the estate or transfer that is chargeable to tax or the rate at which it is chargeable.

There are potentially four IHT reliefs affecting woodlands:

- Agricultural Property Relief (APR);
- Business Property Relief (BPR);
- the National Heritage Exemption; and
- Woodlands Relief.

In practice, Business Property Relief is the most commonly used of these concessions. However, when more than one is potentially applicable, they take precedence in the order listed above. So, for example, in the case of farm woodlands owned by a business, where both Agricultural Property Relief and Business Property Relief would apply, the former would take precedence – although, given that many, if not most, farms are now operated as businesses, there are suggestions that Business Property Relief may in due course replace Agricultural Property Relief altogether.

The specific Woodlands Relief is thus now of considerably less significance, since commercially operated woodlands will often qualify for 100 per cent Business Property Relief. And one notable difference between the Woodlands Relief and the other reliefs is that the former is available only on transfers at death, whereas the others are also available on lifetime transfers.

Each of the four reliefs is considered in turn.

12.4.3 Farm woodlands: agricultural property relief

"Agricultural property" means agricultural land or pasture, and includes woodland that is occupied along with such property if the occupation of the woodland is ancillary to that of the land or pasture.[45] As a result, where woodlands form part of a farm, they will be eligible for Agricultural Property Relief (APR) rather than either Business Property Relief or Woodlands Relief. Where woodland is occupied on its own, the former will not be available, and it will be the other two that should be considered.

The rules of Agricultural Property Relief, which has been available since 1981, are significantly more complex than those applying to Woodlands Relief, and a full discussion of them is beyond the scope of this book.[46] However, the general rule is that Agricultural Property Relief applies to the transfer of agricultural land that has been:

---

[44] See **2.4.3**.
[45] Inheritance Tax Act 1984, s. 115(2).
[46] The relevant provisions are in Inheritance Tax Act 1984, ss. 115 to 124 (introduced by Finance Act 1981, Sched. 14). For details and worked examples, see Simon's Direct Tax Service, Division 17.3.

- occupied by the transferor for agricultural purposes for two years immediately prior to transfer; or

- owned by the transferor for seven years prior to transfer and occupied for agricultural purposes either by the transferor or another.[47]

Ownership or occupation is considered to be continuous where property is transferred between spouses on the death of one of them.[48]

Agricultural Property Relief operates so as to reduce the value of the transfer, and so decreases the value of the property chargeable to IHT. The value potentially subject to the relief is the "agricultural value" of the property, which has a specific meaning in this context.[49] The relief will vary according to the transferor's interest in the land being transferred. It will be 100 per cent of the agricultural value where the transferor has:

- vacant possession of the property;

- a right to obtain vacant possession within 24 months of the transfer;[50]

- a leasehold interest that has a value broadly the same as the vacant possession value; or

- a leasehold interest granted on or after September 1, 1995.[51]

In other cases, the relief is allowed at 50 per cent of agricultural value, subject to a transitional 100 per cent relief in respect of land let on a tenancy before March 10, 1981. And the relief may also apply on the transfer of shares in companies whose assets include agricultural property.

The result of these provisions is that in many cases a transfer of agricultural property (including agricultural woodlands), either on the death of the transferor or during his or her lifetime, now attracts a 100 per cent relief from IHT. This is in most (but not all) respects equivalent to an exemption.

12.4.4 Business Property Relief

Where there is a transfer of "relevant business property" (other than agricultural property) Business Property Relief applies so as to reduce the value of the transfer, thus reducing the amount becoming chargeable to IHT.[52] A full discussion of the rules governing the application of Business Property Relief is obviously beyond the scope of this book; but "relevant business property" generally includes all assets employed in a business that exist to make profits or gains.

It follows that, where woodlands are run as a business, or form part of one, their transfer – either on the death of the transferor or during his or her lifetime – will be subject to Business Property Relief. The rate of the relief will depend on the basis of the transfer:

---

[47] Inheritance Tax Act 1984, s. 117.
[48] Inheritance Tax Act 1984, s. 120(1)(b).
[49] See Inheritance Tax Act 1984, s. 115(3).
[50] Finance (No. 2) Act 1992, Sched. 14, para. 4(a) (12 months); extended to 24 months by Inland Revenue Extra-Statutory Concession F17.
[51] Finance Act 1995, s. 155.
[52] The relevant provisions are in Inheritance Tax Act 1984, ss. 103 to 114.

- 100 per cent relief: transfer of business or of an interest in a business (including a business owned by a company in which the transferor owns a qualifying interest[53])

- 50 per cent relief: transfer of assets out of a business, where the business is retained.

For the relief to apply, the business or asset being transferred must have been owned by the transferor for the two years immediately prior to the transfer – where the transfer is between spouses on death, the two-year rule is deemed to have been met. In addition, where property is transferred within two years of an earlier transfer, the relief will still apply (notwithstanding the rule), provided that:

- the earlier transfer itself qualified for the relief; and

- at least one of the transfers was on death.

As would be expected, there are a number of restrictions and qualifications to the operation of the relief. In particular, it only applies where the asset being transferred is used wholly or mainly for business purposes.[54] Consequently, any land used to a significant extent for non-business purposes, such as amenity or sporting woodlands surrounding a mansion house, would not qualify for the relief. A parcel of land, part of which is used for business purposes and part of which is not, may be split so that the relief is applied only to the qualifying area.

12.4.5 The National Heritage Exemption

A special exemption applies on the transfer of land (which could include woodlands) that has, in the opinion of the Board of the Inland Revenue, outstanding scenic, historic or scientific interest, such that it may be treated as "heritage property".[55] This might include, for example, an area of "ancient woodland".[56] In addition, land that is essential for the preservation of the character and amenities of a building that is itself designated as heritage property may also be granted heritage status – such as in the case of a parkland (including woods) associated with a country house.[57] Special rules apply in the case of such associated land, to ensure that it is not alienated from the building itself.[58]

Where woodlands qualify as heritage property, they can benefit from conditional exemption from IHT on transfer, provided that the new owner undertakes that their character and appearance will be maintained and that reasonable public access will be provided. Such undertakings are reviewed by the Inland Revenue every five years; and failure to comply with their conditions may lead to the loss of the exemption, with the value of the woodlands consequently coming into charge to IHT.[59]

---

[53] See Inland Revenue booklet IHT 17.
[54] Inheritance Tax Act 1984, s. 112.
[55] Inheritance Tax Act 1984, s. 31.
[56] See 15.2.
[57] And see 15.3.
[58] Inheritance Tax Act 1984, s. 32A, inserted by Finance Act 1985, Sched. 26.
[59] Inheritance Tax Act 1984, s. 32.

Further exemptions apply to funds set up for the maintenance of such land,[60] and to its transfer to certain heritage bodies.[61]

12.4.6 Woodlands Relief

Where none of the above reliefs or exemptions apply, there is a further specific concession available in relation to inheritance tax on the transfer of woodlands on death – similar to, but slightly less generous than, the concession which used to apply in relation to estate duty.[62] The relevant provisions are in sections 125 to 130 of the Inheritance Tax Act 1984.[63]

If a person's assets immediately before his or her death include land on which trees or saleable underwood are growing, other than agricultural land[64]:

- the value of the trees and underwood may be left out in determining the value of the estate transferred on death; and

- IHT then becomes chargeable on any later disposal of the trees and underwood.[65]

The amount left out in computing the value of the estate at death is the value of the land with the standing trees or underwood, less the value of the land on its own.

To be entitled to this relief, the woodlands in question must either have been owned by the deceased for the whole of the five years before his or her death or have been transferred to the deceased by inheritance or as a gift. In addition, in either case, the land must not have been subject to a contract for sale at the date of death. And Woodlands Relief is not available where woodlands are held in a discretionary trust.

To take advantage of this relief, an election must be made in writing to the Inland Revenue within two years of the death.[66]

Where the relief has been given, IHT is chargeable if the whole or any part of the trees or underwood is disposed of (other than to a spouse), either for money or as a gift, before the land is again part of a disposal on death. This applies whether or not the trees or underwood are disposed of together with the land on which they were or are growing.[67] The tax is payable by the person who is entitled to the proceeds of the sale (or who would be so entitled if the disposal were in fact by gift), who should make a return within six months from the end of the month in which the disposal takes place.

The tax is then chargeable on the net value of the trees or underwood sold or otherwise disposed of. The net value for this purpose is the proceeds of any sale, or (if the disposal is by gift or at an under-value) the market value, less any allowable expenses. The latter include, in particular, the expenses incurred in disposing of the trees or underwood – such as the cost of felling and drawing out

---

[60] Inheritance Tax Act 1984, Sched. 4.
[61] Inheritance Tax Act 1984, s. 26A, inserted by Finance Act 1986, Sched. 19.
[62] As to which, see **12.4.1**.
[63] Originally in Finance Act 1975, Sched. 9.
[64] For woodlands on agricultural land, see **12.4.3**.
[65] Inheritance Tax Act (CTT Act) 1984, s. 125 (1),(2).
[66] Inheritance Tax Act 1984, s. 125(3); the time may be extended at the discretion of the Revenue.
[67] Inheritance Tax Act 1984, s. 126.

timber, including restoration of property injured in the process; and the expenses
of sale, including commission. Also included would be the expenses incurred in
planting, within three years of a disposal, trees to replace those disposed of.[68]
That 3-year period may be extended at the discretion of the Inland Revenue.[69]
And any replacement planting costs not so allowed may be carried forward to be
offset against future disposals.

The rate of tax payable is in principle that which would have been payable if the
value (as thus calculated) of the trees or underwood had been included in the
estate at the date of the relevant death, and if that value had formed the highest
slice of the value of the estate.[70] If, however, the scale of rates of tax payable
generally has increased since the date of the relevant death, the appropriate scale
is the one applying at the date of the actual transfer.[71]

Finally, where the transfer following the original death is itself a chargeable
transfer, the tax in respect of the second transfer is calculated by reference to the
amount transferred reduced by the amount of the (deferred) tax payable.[72] And
where in those circumstances the timer or underwood would have been eligible for
Business Property Relief[73] at the date of the death, a 50 per cent reduction in the
value of the timber transferred is allowable at the time of the subsequent transfer.

12.4.7 Inheritance tax on non-agricultural woodlands: an example

It may be helpful to demonstrate the principles explained above by way of an
example.

Suppose A died in December 1987, leaving a net estate of £760,000, which
included woodlands worth £120,000; the land on which they stood would have
been worth £20,000 on its own. A left all his estate to his daughter B, having made
no chargeable transfers in his lifetime. B elected to have Woodlands Relief. In
October 1997, B made a gift to her nephew, C, of felled trees worth £200,000, in
the process incurring felling costs of £32,000 and replanting expenses of £8,000.
This was not the first potentially exempt transfer made by B, as she had already
made a gift of £180,000 to her nephew in 1995, and had always used her annual
exemptions. B died in 2001 (and thus within seven years of the gift of the timber to
C).

At A's death, in 1987, IHT would have been chargeable on £660,000, calculated
as follows:

Total value of estate:		£ 760,000
Deduct: Value of woodlands:	£ 120,000	
Less bare value of land	20,000	100,000
Net value of estate		£ 660,000

[68] Inheritance Tax Act 1984, s. 130.
[69] Inheritance Tax Act 1984, s. 130(2).
[70] Inheritance Tax Act 1984, s. 128.
[71] Inheritance Tax Act 1984, Sched. 2, para. 4.
[72] Inheritance Tax Act 1984, s. 129.
[73] See **12.4.4**.

If the election for woodland relief had not been made, IHT would have been payable on the full £760,000; and the tax payable on the extra £100,000 would have been at the top rate of 60 per cent.

When B gives the timber to C, in 1997, IHT would be payable by reference to A's death on £160,000, calculated as follows:

Gross value of trees disposed of		£ 200,000
Deduct: Cost of disposal:		
Felling costs	£ 32,000	
Replanting expenses	8,000	40,000
Net value of trees disposed of		£ 160,000

IHT on £160,000 would be chargeable at the rate applicable in 1997, that is, 40 per cent, leading to a demand for £64,000. If the timber had been relevant business property at the date of A's death, the 50 per cent business relief would have meant that tax would be chargeable on £80,000.

Since the gift from B to C is itself a chargeable transfer, IHT is payable on £96,000 – that is, the net value of the gift (£160,000) less the tax already payable by reference to A's death (£64,000).

12.5 Rating of woodlands

12.5.1 Woodlands

The general rule is that woodlands other than those associated with dwellings are exempt from local taxation.

Under Schedule 5 to the Local Government Finance Act 1988, land is exempt from local non-domestic rating to the extent that it consists of agricultural land or agricultural buildings. Agricultural land includes, amongst other things, "land used for a plantation or a wood or for the growth of saleable underwood", and orchards[74]; but it does not include:

"(a) land occupied together with a house as a park,
 (b) gardens (other than market gardens),
 (c) pleasure grounds,
 (d) land used mainly or exclusively for sport or recreation . . . ".[75]

This continues the exemption found previously, in precisely the same terms, in section 26 of the General Rate Act 1967. It means that any land used as a wood or an orchard, as opposed to merely a few trees, would in principle be exempt – regardless of whether the woodland is operated on a commercial basis or, for example, merely as an amenity or a shelter belt.

It should be noted, incidentally, that for these purposes "agricultural land" includes *any* woodlands (subject to the above exclusions), and not just woodlands

[74] Local Government Finance Act 1988, s. 51; Sched. 5, para. 2(1).
[75] Local Government Finance Act 1988, s. 51; Sched. 5, para. 2(2).

occupied along with other agricultural land. The position in respect of local taxation is thus different from that in respect of national taxation, and in particular the reliefs from inheritance tax.[76]

Woodland is not exempt from rating by virtue of this provision if it is either a "garden" (or, presumably, part of one) or if it is occupied together with a house as a park. However, if (as is likely) the garden or the house is in domestic use, its occupation will give rise to a liability to council tax, not rating; and its existence, and characteristics, will be taken into account in assessing the value of the hereditament, and thus the extent of such liability.[77] As to the meaning of "garden", see *McInerney v Portland Port Ltd*.[78] Woodland constituting a public park or pleasure grounds would be exempt in any event.[79] Problems could arise where the principle function of a woodland is as cover for game birds, as this might lead to liability for rating.

As for saleable underwood, this includes any wood that is so treated as to produce periodical profits from the same stools and roots.[80]

12.5.2 Forestry buildings

It has already been noted that agricultural buildings are exempt form rating.

An "agricultural building" is defined to include a building (other than a dwelling) which is "occupied together with agricultural land and used solely in connection with agricultural operations on the land".[81] Therefore, this would presumably include a building other than a dwelling used for forestry – for example, for the storage of implements and machinery.

As to the extent of this exemption, the Lands Valuation Appeal Court in *Midlothian Assessor v Buccleuch Estates*[82] held as follows:

"It was argued that the expression 'land used as woodlands' was habile to include all buildings devoted to the growing, harvesting and preparing for disposal of timber. I would agree that agriculture and pasturage do not cease when the crops are grown or beasts raised, but may properly include operations reasonably necessary to make the product marketable or disposable to profit. Similarly forestry, use of land as woodlands, does not cease when the timber is grown, but may well include operations necessary to render the timber marketable as timber or disposable to profitable use as timber. The buildings where such uses are carried on, if otherwise satisfying the requirements of the definition of agricultural buildings, would be entitled to be excluded from the roll."[83]

The Court also held:

"Occupation of the woodlands of an estate involves more than planting trees in a plantation and letting them grow. There is the crop to be handled, which may take the form of thinnings, or windfalls, or fellings."[84]

---

[76]   See **12.4**.
[77]   Local Government Finance Act 1988, s. 42.
[78]   [2001] 1 PLR 104.
[79]   *Lambeth Overseers v London County Council* [1897] A.C. 625, H.L.
[80]   *Lord Fitzhardinge v Pritchett* (1867) L.R. 2 Q.B. 135, 36 L.J.M.C. 49.
[81]   Local Government Finance Act 1988, s. 51; Sched. 5, paras 2, 4, 7.
[82]   1962 S.C. 453, [1962] RVR 799.
[83]   1962 S.C. 453, per Lord Patrick at p. 463, upheld in *W &JB Eastwood v Herrod (VO)* [1971] A.C. 160, H.L., per Lord Reid at p. 169F.
[84]   Per Lord Sorn at p. 462.

That seems eminently sensible, and would mean that the exemption would extend to any building used in connection with the forestry operation, including a sawmill (which was the building being considered in that case).

However, the court went on to argue (by a majority) that a building, such as a sawmill, if it is to enjoy the exemption, must actually be located on the same land as the forestry operations, so that the sawmill in that case, which was used solely to process timber grown on land which was both nearby and in the same ownership, might in principle be exempt from rates because it was used in association with the woodlands, but it was not in that instance because it was not on the land actually used as woodlands. That seems, with respect, to be fallacious, as the wording of the statutory provision[85] requires one first to identify the land on which agricultural operations (including forestry) are being carried out, and then to consider whether the building in question is both occupied together with that land and used for a purpose that relates solely to the agricultural operations being carried out on that land. There does not seem to be any requirement that the building must be "on the land"; it is the operations that are there being referred to.

An alternative approach is that adopted by Lord Sorn, in a dissenting judgment in *Midlothian*. He held that, where a woodland holding consists of several portions, it is necessary to see what is the use of each portion. The ground on which the sawmill was standing was one of those portions, and one on which an operation critical to the forestry use of the whole was being carried out.

12.6 Forestry dedication covenants and agreements

12.6.1 Entering into agreements

Since 1947, the Forestry Acts have included a provision whereby land can be devoted to forestry, by means of the landowner and the Forestry Commission entering into an agreement to the effect that "the land shall not be used otherwise than for the growing of timber or other forest products in accordance with the rules or practice of good forestry or for purposes connected therewith".[86] Such an agreement is called a "forestry dedication covenant" in relation to land in England or Wales.[87]

Associated with a dedication covenant would be a plan of operations, approved by the Commission. A felling licence was required (after 1951) for any felling involved, but it could not be refused for felling in accordance with the plan other than in consequence of an act of God or other emergency.[88] In exchange for these restrictions, the owner would then receive financial support, on the basis current at the time.[89]

A "forestry dedication covenant" bound, and still binds, not only the landowner who originally made it but also his or her successors in title and

---

[85] The statutory provision considered in *Midlothian* was s. 7 of the Valuation and Rating (Scotland) Act 1956, which was in broadly similar terms to the provision in the 1988 Act, save that it contained the word "thereon" instead of "on the land".

[86] FA 1967, s. 5(1).

[87] FA 1967, s. 5(1)(a).

[88] FA 1951, s. 10(2); see now FA 1967, s. 14(2). In practice, no licence was needed for felling on dedicated estates after 1958; although the legal basis for that exemption is not clear. See now **14.2.9**.

[89] See **12.7.2**.

anyone deriving title under him, her or them (such as purchasers of part only of the land, and leaseholders) – provided that it did not contain any provision purporting to negate that principle.[90] If it were to be subsequently enforceable, it would have to have been registered under the Land Registration Act 1925 in the case of registered land,[91] or as a Class D land charge in the case of unregistered land.[92] A dedication covenant is not a local land charge.[93]

Where land was the subject of a settlement under the Settled Land Act 1925,[94] the tenant for life could enter into a dedication covenant; and doing so counted as a disposal of the land for the purposes of that Act.[95] A university or college could also enter into a covenant.[96] As to land owned by the Church of England, a covenant could be entered into by the incumbent or, in the case of glebe land, the diocesan board of finance.[97] In all these cases, the covenant could be entered into either for consideration or gratuitously.

Dedication covenants were not needed for land owned by the Crown, Government departments, or the Church Commissioners. And a special version of the covenant was drawn up for use by the National Trust.

The equivalent of a "forestry dedication covenant" in Scotland is a "forestry dedication agreement". Such an agreement should have been recorded in the General Register of Sasines, and was thereafter enforceable against the successors in title to the original covenantor.[98]

As already mentioned, the Forestry Commission has not entered into new dedication covenants for some years now, but existing covenants remain in force until terminated.

12.6.2 Enforcement of covenants

Once land has been made the subject to a forestry dedication covenant, it must not be used other than in the manner specified, unless the Forestry Commission gives its prior consent in writing or, in the event of such consent not being forthcoming, the Minister gives a direction to the same effect.[99] However, where a licence is required for felling trees on land subject to a forestry dedication covenant, and is not forthcoming, that will not constitute a breach of the covenant.[1]

If the current owner of the land uses it in some manner that is in breach of the covenant, the Commission may in principle enforce it as though it were the owner of adjacent land, and the covenant had been expressed to be for the benefit of that land.[2] This makes it clear that the covenant itself can be enforced against successors in title, but only in so far as it is negative in character – which is no doubt why the Act phrases its purpose negatively ("not to use the land otherwise . . . .", etc.).

[90] FA 1967, s. 5(2)(a).
[91] Land Registration Act 1925, ss. 50, 52, 59(6).
[92] Land Charges Act 1972, ss. 2(5)(ii), 4(6).
[93] Local Land Charges Act 1975, s. 2(g).
[94] See 2.4.3.
[95] FA 1967, Sched. 2, para. 1.
[96] FA 1967, Sched. 2, para. 2.
[97] FA 1967, Sched. 2, para. 3; Endowments and Glebe Measure 1976, s. 20.
[98] FA 1967, s. 5(1)(b), (3); Sched. 2, para. 4.
[99] FA 1967, s. 5(1).
[1] FA 1967, s. 10(7).
[2] FA 1967, s. 5(2)(a).

As for enforcing a plan of operations, the ability for the Commission to enforce a dedication covenant as if it were a standard restrictive covenant is unlikely to assist, since the plan of operations will contain positive obligations on the part of the landowner – for example, to employ skilled supervision, to protect the woodlands from fire, and to (for Basis I schemes only[3]) keep accounts. That effectively means that it will not be enforceable against owners of the land other than the original covenantor; and in practice covenants will usually terminate on a change of ownership.

The only formal provision for resolving any dispute as to whether a plan of operations is being complied with is in the context of a proposal by the Minister to acquire compulsorily the land in question[4] – which will not often arise.

It is unlikely that enforcement of dedication covenants will be a major issue, now that the Forestry Commission no longer operates the dedication scheme. And, of course, in practice the real enforcement mechanism has always been the ability of the Forestry Commission to withhold any grants payable under the covenant.

12.6.3 Termination of dedication schemes

Even though a dedication covenant is basically similar to a restrictive covenant, it is not possible to apply to the Lands Tribunal to have an existing covenant modified or discharged.[5] Instead, the Forestry Commission has since 1974 been willing for either party to terminate a Basis III Agreement[6] where land is to be clear-felled. Alternatively, it may agree to terminate a scheme in the context of agreeing a new arrangement under the Woodland Grant Scheme,[7] or where the owner of the land is unable to continue the dedication due to circumstances beyond his or her control.

In addition, dedication schemes generally terminate when land changes hands. The view of the Commission is that a new owner may continue the dedication, but only until the expiry of the current plan of operations.

Release from a dedication covenant is normally by means of a dead of release; here, too, the Forestry Commission should be consulted as to the appropriate procedure to be followed and the details to be supplied.

12.7 Forestry Commission grant schemes

12.7.1 Introduction

Financial assistance for forestry is largely outside the law, being governed simply by the general powers of the Forestry Commission to give grants and loans. This used to be restricted to the giving of grants and loans to the owners of land in respect of afforestation.[8] Since the enactment of the Forestry Act 1979, however, the powers of the Commission are now somewhat wider, in that it is free to make grants and loans as it sees fit to owners and lessees of land "for and in connection

---

[3] See **12.7.2**.
[4] FA 1967, s. 40(3); see **11.2.3**.
[5] FA 1967, s. 5(2)(b).
[6] See **12.7.2**.
[7] See **12.7.3**.
[8] Originally under FA 1919, s. 3(3)(d), later FA 1967, s. 4.

with the use and management of the land for forestry purposes",[9] which includes the subsequent maintenance of woodlands as well as the initial planting.

Payment of grants and loans by the Commission comes from money provided by Parliament (or by the Scottish Consolidated Fund), and requires the approval of the Treasury (or that of the Scottish Ministers north of the border).[10]

It will be noted that the mechanisms for grant aid have periodically changed. Since, however, the essence of forestry (and indeed the whole justification for Government assistance) is that it is a very long term business, grants will continue to be payable under the arrangement as it was when first entered into, even though that may no longer be available to new applicants. And although the relevant statutory provisions make reference to the giving of either grants or loans, in practice loans are rarely if ever offered.

The remainder of this section of the Chapter, inevitably, concentrates on the legal structures underpinning the giving of financial assistance by the Forestry Commission to private forestry owners and operators. For guidance as to the way in which the various schemes operate in practice, enquiries should be made to the local office of the Commission or to the Grants and Licences Section at its headquarters in Edinburgh.

12.7.2 The grant schemes associated with dedication covenants

Where an owner of land entered into an agreement with the Forestry Commission under the dedication scheme,[11] in exchange for the restrictions on the use of the land, the Commission would give financial support in the form of a grant equal to 25 per cent of net approved expenditure until the woodland was self-supporting (Basis I) or a planting grant plus an annual management grant (Basis II). In 1951, the Small Woodlands Planting Grant scheme was introduced, under which a formal plan of operations was not required.

The Dedication Basis I and Basis II schemes and the Small Woodlands Planting Grant schemes were closed to new applicants in 1972, but those already subject to Basis I and Basis II could switch to the new Basis III, introduced in 1974. The Basis III scheme was a grant for planting, with a supplement for broadleaf trees; a fixed rate of management grant was added in 1977. Also in 1977, Basis III was extended to cover unproductive land which could be brought up to a productive stage by selective planting and natural regeneration without clear felling; and special measures were introduced to encourage the planting of Caledonian Pine in Scotland. In addition, a new Small Woods scheme replaced Basis III for grant aid in relation to areas of land of less than 10 hectares.

In 1979, the statutory basis for grant aid was slightly altered, in that the purposes for which grants and loans could be given by the Commission was widened from afforestation to forestry purposes generally.[12] And in the following year a review of all the grant schemes was carried out.[13] As a result, the Dedication and Small Woods Schemes were closed to new applicants in 1981. The new Forestry Grant Scheme was introduced, designed to be simpler to administer. Woodlands could continue to be managed under existing dedication covenants,

[9] FA 1979, s. 1.
[10] FA 1967, s. 41; see 11.3.3.
[11] See 12.6.1.
[12] FA 1979, s. 1.
[13] By Mr Derek (later Lord) Rayner.

but the covenants would terminate if the land changed ownership after August 1, 1981.

The basis of the Forestry Grant Scheme (and the remaining Basis III dedication schemes) was as follows:

- the production of utilisable timber;

- good land use, including integration of woodlands with agriculture;

- the securing of environmental benefits; and

- the provision of recreation and public access as appropriate.

The Broadleaved Woodland Grant Scheme was introduced in 1985, along with management guidelines, to encourage the planting of broadleaf trees.

Finally, the Forestry Grant Scheme and the Broadleaved Woodland Grant Scheme were both ended in 1988, and replaced by the Woodland Grant Scheme[14] and (on a trial basis) the Farm Woodland Scheme.[15]

The details of the entitlement to grant aid under each of these schemes, and the mechanism for claiming payment, are beyond the scope of this book; for further information, the Grants and Licences Section of the Forestry Commission should be consulted.

12.7.3 The Woodland Grant Scheme

The various schemes under which grants were available in the past, briefly described above, are no longer available; instead, the current arrangement for administering financial assistance is the Woodland Grant Scheme (WGS), which has been in existence since 1988. The various farm woodland schemes, described below, are linked to the WGS, since a farm woodland premium can only be paid where a woodland grant has also been approved.[16-17]

Grants are paid under the WGS to help with the creation of new woodlands and to encourage the good management and regeneration of existing woodlands. The stated aims of the Scheme are:

- to encourage people to create new woodlands and forests which increase the production of wood, improve the landscape, provide new habitats for wildlife and offer opportunities for recreation and sports;

- to encourage good management of forests and woodlands, including their well-timed regeneration, particularly looking after the needs of ancient and semi-natural woodlands;

- to provide jobs and improve the economy of rural areas, and other areas with few alternative sources of economic activity; and

- to provide a use for land in place of agriculture.[18]

[14] See **12.7.3**.
[15] See **12.7.4**.
[16-17] Farm Woodland Premium Scheme 1997 (S.I. 1997 No. 829), para. 3(1)(a).
[18] *A Guide to the Woodland Grant Scheme*, Forestry Commission, October 2000.

Normally a woodland would have to be at least 0.25 hectares in extent and 15 metres wide to be eligible for grant aid, but smaller woods may be considered if the aims of the Scheme are met.

12.7.4 The Farm Woodlands Premium Schemes

Studies of changes taking place in the rural landscape have for many years concluded that one worthwhile improvement would be to encourage the planting of woods in marginal areas on farms, which would benefit both the appearance of the area and the quality of habitat for wildlife.[19] The desirability of such a move has increased with the realisation that Britain does not need all the agricultural land it has, and that conversion to woodland may be one of the most appropriate alternative uses.

In order to provide an incentive for farmers to plant woodlands on farms, the Farm Land and Rural Development Act 1988 provided that grants may be paid by the relevant Minister – that is, in principle, the minister responsible for agriculture[20] – under the terms of a scheme made under the Act. Such a grant may be made:

- towards expenditure incurred for the purposes of, or in connection with, the conversion of land from agricultural use to use for woodlands or the management of land; and

- to abate any financial loss suffered in consequence of the conversion of land from agricultural use to woodlands.[21]

Under those powers, the Farm Woodland Scheme 1988[22] was made on a 3-year trial basis, to encourage the planting of some 36,000 hectares of agricultural land. The initial arrangement was that the Forestry Commission would pay the planting grant, and the relevant Government Department would make an annual payment to compensate for agricultural revenue foregone. That Scheme was slightly varied in 1991 and 1997[23] (not least by an increase in the amount payable per annum). It was replaced a year later by the Farm Woodland Premium Scheme 1992.[24] The new Scheme was broadly similar, but tightened up some of the details, and made explicit the link with the Woodland Grant Scheme. The 1992 Scheme was in turn amended in 1997.[25]

Neither of those two Schemes is available to new applicants, but grants already approved will continue to be paid at the rates current for the time being.

The 1992 Scheme was replaced by the Farm Woodland Premium Scheme 1997,[26] which applied to all proposals submitted for approval on or after April 1, 1997. It is thus the 1997 Scheme that currently applies to all applications. It is funded by the relevant agriculture ministry, but administered by the Forestry Commission. Its objectives are:

[19] See, for example, *New Agricultural Landscapes*, Countryside Commission, 1974.
[20] See **11.2.1**.
[21] Farm Land and Rural Development Act 1988, s. 2(1).
[22] S.I. 1988 No. 1291.
[23] By S.I. 1991 No. 1631 and S.I. 1997 No. 828.
[24] S.I. 1992 No. 905; the Scheme was in compliance with Title VIII of Council Regulation (EEC) No. 2328/91, on improving the efficiency of agricultural structures (OJ L218, August 6, 1991, p. 1).
[25] S.I. 1997 No. 829, Schedule 3.
[26] S.I. 1997 No. 829.

- to enhance the environment through the planting of farm woodlands;

- in particular, to improve the landscape, provide new habitats and increase biodiversity; and

- to encourage land managers to realise the productive potential of woodland as a sustainable land use.

The annual payments under the Scheme are made to compensate farmers for agricultural revenue foregone.

An application may only be made in relation to an area of agricultural land of less than 1 hectare, or more than 200 hectares (40 hectares in the case of unimproved land).[27]

12.7.5 Procedure

An application may be made under either the WGS alone or under both the WGS and the FWPS. It should be made to the local Forestry Commission office, either by the owner of the land or by the leaseholder with the agreement of the owner.[28] Details of the material to be submitted, and of the terms and conditions of the Schemes, are in the *Applicant's Pack*, which contains a booklet describing each scheme, a set of *Guidance Notes*, and all the relevant forms. The *Pack* is available from Forestry Commission local conservancy offices or may be downloaded from the Commission's website.[29]

Once they have been given a preliminary assessment, applications under the WGS that contain new planting and felling are publicised on the website; and where an application is also made under the FWPS, the details will at the same time be considered by the local office of the relevant Agriculture Department. Once an application has been approved, the Commission will issue a draft contract under the WGS, and (where relevant) approval under the FWPS. The applicant then signs the WGS contract and FWPS declarations and undertakings, and returns them to the Commission for countersigning. No work may be carried out until the paperwork has been completed.

The basis of the support under the WGS is a contract between the owner and the Forestry Commission. Any subsequent changes to the proposed work must, therefore, be notified to the Commission, to enable it to issue an amended contract.

WGS grants for new planting are paid in two instalments – 70 per cent once the planting is complete, and the remainder after five years – at the appropriate rate per hectare.[30] Discretionary grants are also available for creating new woodlands by natural regeneration; and other grants for short rotation coppice. Additional contributions to the planting grant are payable for new woodlands close to towns and cities (Community Woodland Contribution), and in specially targeted areas (Community Forest Premium). Where the land to be planted is currently higher quality agricultural land, an additional Better Land Contribution.

---

[27] S.I. 1997 No. 829, para. 7.

[28] FA 1979, s. 1; Farm Land and Rural Development Act 1988, s. 2(1); S.I. 1997 No. 829, para. 5(1)(c).

[29] www.forestry.gov.uk.

[30] Currently (since 1997) £700 for conifers; £1,350 for broad-leaves in woodlands of less than 10 hectares, £1,050 for broad-leaves in larger woodlands; special rates apply for woodlands over 300 hectares.

In addition, grants are available under the WGS for existing woodlands – annual management grants towards the cost of maintenance and improvement; and grants for restocking and natural regeneration.

Grants under the Farm Woodland Scheme 1988 are paid annually for a period of between 10 and 40 years, depending on the type of woodland to be created[31]; those under either of the Farm Woodland Premium Schemes for 15 years where more than 50 per cent of the planting is broadleaved trees,[32] and for ten years in other cases. The amount of grant payable per hectare varies under each of the schemes according to the type of agricultural land being converted.[33]

12.7.6 Challenges to grant decisions

It is possible for those objecting to an award of a grant to mount a challenge to it by way of an application for judicial review. There have been at least two reported cases of this being done, albeit that in both instances the challenge was unsuccessful.[34] In each case the ostensible basis for the complaint was the failure to insist on an environmental assessment being produced in connection with a grant application; but it was the grant application which provided the trigger for the challenge:

". . . it is obvious that there is an intimate connection between the payment of the grant and the carrying out of a project of afforestation, and even counsel for the respondents [the Forestry Commission] conceded that the availability of the grant would make it much more likely that the trees would be planted. That seems to me to be sufficient to constitute a reasonable connection between the decision and the maters in which the petitioners [the local authority] have an interest."[35]

Such a challenge would require immediate action, since an application for permission must be made to the High Court "promptly, and in any event within three months" of the date of the decision being challenged.

12.8 Other grants

There are various other statutory grant schemes relating to forestry in addition to the schemes administered by the Forestry Commission, considered above.

In particular, there are one or two schemes originating in European legislation that may benefit forestry in general (along with agriculture). The England Rural Development Programme thus provides for the Minister (of Agriculture) to pay grants towards the provision of vocational training for those involved in forestry activities.[36] And assistance may be paid from the European Agricultural

---

[31] S.I. 1988 No. 1291, Sched. 2.

[32] Or Scot Pine in certain areas of Scotland, where it once occurred naturally; see FWPS 1997, para. 2(1).

[33] For the 1988 Scheme, see S.I. 1997 No. 828, Sched. 1 (between £30 and £230); for the 1992 Scheme, see S.I. 1997 No. 829, Sched. 1 (between £60 and £300); for the 1997 Scheme, see S.I. 1997 No. 829, Sched. 3, para. 8 (from £60 to £160).

[34] *Kincardine and Deeside District Council v Forestry Commission* 1991 SLT 1180; and *Swan v Secretary of State for Scotland* (IH) 1998 S.C.L.R. 763, (OH) Court of Sessions [1999] Env. L.R. 60.

[35] *Kincardine* (above) at p. 1184D.

[36] Vocational Training Grants (Agriculture and Forestry) Regulations 2000 (S.I. 2000 No. 3045); England Rural Development Programme (Enforcement) Regulations 2000 (S.I. 2000 No. 3044).

Guidance and Guarantee Fund towards operations (including forestry) which facilitate the development and structural adjustment of certain rural areas – in England, these are Cornwall and the Isles of Scilly, Merseyside and South Yorkshire.[37]

For details of schemes current at any time, it is worth contacting the relevant Section of DEFRA.

---

[37] Rural Development Grants (Agriculture and Forestry) Regulations 2000 (S.I. 2000 No. 2907).

Chapter 13

Environmental Impact of Forestry

13.1 Introduction

Planting a woodland, obviously, changes the appearance and ecology of the land concerned – and if it is carried out on a major scale, so as to amount to afforestation, that change may be both very far-reaching and long lasting. The same is true of clear felling on any scale. The normal response to the problems posed by a significant land use change is for Parliament to require that it may not take place until planning permission has been obtained. However, for political reasons relevant at the time when the planning system was introduced (but probably not now), the use of land for forestry or agriculture has always been specifically excluded from the definition of development requiring permission.

Forestry buildings and roads were also, in effect, similarly excluded from the planning system by being automatically granted permission under successive General Development Orders. However, this freedom from control has in recent years been significantly trimmed by the requirement to afford the planning authority a chance to control the details of such proposals.

This exemption from planning control (considered here at **13.2**) seems to have generated surprisingly little controversy, although one academic commentator questioned more than twenty years ago whether forestry should be assimilated along with agriculture and exempted from control, since the practice of foresting unspoilt hill areas raised its own problems.[1] And the Royal Commission on Environmental Pollution, in its review of environmental planning, is looking carefully at whether forestry, and in particular afforestation, should be brought within the ambit of the planning system.

However, the issue has come to a head with the adoption in 1985 of the European directive on the assessment of certain public and private projects on the environment.[2] That required that an impact assessment should be made of "public and private projects which are likely to have significant effects on the environment", and "project" was for this purpose defined as "intervention in the natural surroundings and landscape".[3] Unsurprisingly, amongst the types of project for which assessment might in some cases be required was "initial afforestation where this may lead to adverse ecological changes and land

---

[1] *Development Control*, John Alder, Sweet and Maxwell, first edn, 1979.
[2] Directive 85/337/EEC (OJ L175/40, July 5, 1985), subsequently amended by 97/11.
[3] Directive 85/337/EEC, art. 1.

reclamation for the purposes of conversion to another type of land use".[4]

As a result, a new procedure was introduced requiring an environmental assessment to be submitted along with an application for a Forestry Commission grant where it was considered that the proposal would have a significant effect on the environment.[5] It was subsequently recognised that not all afforestation projects were the subject of such applications, so that a privately funded project could slip through the net. As a result, revised regulations were introduced in 1998,[6] which were themselves replaced the following year in the light of revisions to the 1985 Directive,[7] which introduced a number of changes designed to tighten up the whole procedure.[8] It also made it clear that the words "land reclamation" in the description of projects highlighted above referred to "deforestation".

The current rules are accordingly to be found in the Environmental Impact Assessment (Forestry) (England and Wales) Regulations 1999,[9] which came into force on September 6, 1999. Very similar regulations apply in Scotland and Northern Ireland.[10]

The system is, in essence, that the consent of the Forestry Commission is needed for any forestry project that is likely to have a significant effect on the environment by virtue of factors such as its nature, size or location (see **13.3**). Where such consent is required, the procedure is not dissimilar to that which applies to seeking planning permission for a development project which has to be the subject of an environmental impact assessment (EIA). It is considered here at **13.4**. And, if consent is not obtained, the Commission may serve an enforcement notice on those responsible (see **13.5**). Reference may also be made to a helpful Forestry Commission booklet, entitled *Environmental Impact Assessment of Forestry Projects*.[11]

The system is still in its infancy, at least in its current form, and only some 260 or so assessments have been required to date. But if forestry continues to remain outside the planning system, it may well be that this parallel system, administered by the Forestry Commission, of EIA for forestry proposals becomes of increasing significance.

13.2 Forestry and the planning system

13.2.1 Use of land for forestry

It has already been noted that planning permission is not required to carry out works to an existing tree, or to fell it.[12] Nor will it be required to plant a new one.[13] That applies whether the number of trees involved is one or a thousand.

The only possible requirement for planning permission might arise if the use of land is to be changed – if, for example, an area of open land, previously used as a

---

[4]   Directive 85/337/EEC, Annex II, (1)(d).
[5]   Environmental Assessment (Forestry) Regulations 1988 (S.I. 1988 No. 1207).
[6]   Environmental Assessment (Afforestation) Regulations 1998 (S.I. 1998 No. 1731)
[7]   By Council Directive 97/11/EC (OJ No. L73, March 14, 1997, p. 5).
[8]   Helpfully summarised at para. 2A-043/1 of the *Encyclopedia of Planning Law and Practice*.
[9]   S.I. 1999 No. 2228 ("1999 Regulations").
[10] For Scotland, see now EIA (Forestry) (Scotland) Regulations 1999 (S.I. 1999 No. 43), and for Northern Ireland, EIA (Forestry) Regulations (Northern Ireland) 2000 (S.I. 2000 No. 84).
[11] January 2001; available from Forestry Commission offices.
[12] See **9.4.5**.
[13] See **10.1.3**.

military training centre, is planted with trees; or if a woodland is clear felled and the land used for grazing horses. In either case, although planning permission would not have been required for the works involved in the planting or the felling, there has taken place a material change in the use of the land concerned; and that change itself would normally amount to "development", which requires planning permission.

However, the significance of this is not great in practice. This is because section 55(2) of the Town and Country Planning Act 1990 provides that:

"The following . . . uses of land shall not be taken for the purposes of this Act to involve development of land –

. . .

(e) the use of any land for the purposes of agriculture or forestry (including afforestation) and the use for any of those purposes of any building occupied together with land so used; . . ."

This means, firstly, that planning permission cannot be required where the use of land is changed to forestry from some other use. This is so even where the afforestation of a large tract of land may have very considerable effects on the appearance and ecology of a wide area. The problems which may arise have now been dealt with by means of a new environmental assessment regime, considered in detail later in this Chapter[14]; but this does not affect the basic exemption of forestry from planning control, which has been a feature of all planning Acts since 1947 and remains in place now.

The term "forestry" is not defined in the 1990 Act, other than by the reference to afforestation.[15] It was, however, considered in the decision of the Inner House in *Farleyer v Secretary of State for Scotland*,[16] in the context of the corresponding provision in the Scottish legislation.[17] In that case, Lord Ross cited the dictionary definition of "forestry" – namely, "the science and art of forming and cultivating forests, management of growing timber" – and expressed the view that this must include both the felling of timber and the extraction of the timber, once felled, from the plantation. Further, he cited the decision in *Midlothian Assessor v Buccleuch Estates*, a rating case,[18] and concluded that the use of land for activities such as stockpiling timber or loading it onto lorries may properly be classified as "forestry", provided that those activities are indeed essential to the operation of a commercial plantation. And it may, in some cases, not matter that the land used for such activities is physically separated from the plantation – even by as much as 1.5 kilometres, as in the *Farleyer* case itself; what is important is not proximity to woodlands, but the use to which the land is put.[19]

Further, the use of land for woodlands where that use is ancillary to the farming of land for other agricultural purposes is included within the definition of "agriculture" in the 1990 Act.[20]

---

[14] See **13.3 to 13.5**.
[15] TCPA 1990, s. 55(2)(e); also TCP (General Permitted Development) Order 1995, Sched. 2, Pt. 7, para. A; and see **10.1.3**.
[16] [1992] 2 PLR 123
[17] TCP (Scotland) Act 1972, s. 19(2)(e); see now TCP (Scotland) Act 1997, s. 26(2)(e).
[18] 1962 SC 453, approved of in *W & JB Eastwood v Herrod (VO)*, [1971] A.C. 160, H.L.; see **12.3.2**.
[19] *Farleyer* at p. 127.
[20] TCPA 1990, s. 336(1).

And once it is established that the proposed use of land is forestry or agriculture, not only is planning permission not required, but it is not even "development", so that the planning authority cannot in any particular case impose an Article 4 direction requiring planning permission to be obtained.

The second consequence of section 55(2)(e) of the 1990 Act is that a change in the use of land from forestry to agriculture does not amount to development. This means that where former woodland is to be used for some new purpose following clear felling, planning permission will not be required where that new use is agriculture, but will be required where the new use is something other than agriculture – or, of course, where it involves the carrying out of building or engineering operations, which would themselves require permission.

Finally, planning permission is granted automatically by the General Permitted Development Order[21] for the stationing, on land used for forestry, of caravans to house forestry workers during a particular season (that is, not permanently). Nor does the stationing of such caravans require a site licence under the Caravan Sites and Control of Development Act 1960.[22]

13.2.2 Use of existing buildings for forestry

Planning permission is not required for the change of use of any building for the purpose of forestry, provided that it is used together with land for that purpose.[23]

There have been a series of decisions considering the extent of the corresponding exemption applying to buildings used for agriculture.[24] The question of how much "imported" produce may be sold in a farm shop has thus been considered in various cases, of which the first was *Williams v MOHLG*, in which it was held:

"In my judgement . . . there is, clearly, from a planning point of view, a significant difference in character between a use which involves selling the produce of the land itself and, and a use which involves importing goods from elsewhere for sale. All sorts of planning considerations may arise which render one activity appropriate and desirable in a neighbourhood and the other activity quite unsuitable."[25]

In that case, and in those that followed it,[26] it has generally been considered that the sale of imported produce has led to the use being unacceptable in terms of planning policy.

In *Warnock v Secretary of State*,[27] part of a farm was used as lairage – that is, for the housing of cattle from various farms in the area prior to export outside the United Kingdom. There the Divisional Court upheld the decision of an inspector that the part of a farm so used constituted a physically separate and distinct unit from the remainder, and thus a separate planning unit[28]; further, lairage was not

---

[21] TCP (General Permitted Development) Order 1995 (S.I. 1995 No. 418), Sched. 2, Pt 5, Class A.
[22] Caravan Sites and Control of Development Act 1960, Sched. 1, para. 8.
[23] TCPA 1990, s. 55(2)(e).
[24] Including, of course, the series of cases relating to egg-vending machines [sic], starting with *Hidderley v Warwickshire County Council* (1963) 14 P&CR 134 – not, mercifully, directly relevant to forestry!
[25] (1967) 65 L.G.R. 495, per Widgery J. at p. 500 (18 P. & C.R. 514).
[26] See, for example, *Lloyd-Jones v MOHLG* (1967) 204 E.G. 1200, and *Bromley v Hoeltschi (George) Ltd* (1977) 244 E.G. 49.
[27] [1980] J.P.L. 590.
[28] See *Burdle v Secretary of State* (1972) 24 P. & C.R. 174.

included within the definition of "agriculture" within the Act. It followed that the
introduction of the lairage use constituted a material change in the use of the land
and buildings involved. Here too, planning permission was refused on policy
grounds.

The application of this to forestry is that the use of buildings and associated
land for purposes ancillary to forestry (timber drying and storage, processing, saw
mills, and so on) is definitely included within the forestry use as long as the timber
involved arises on the same unit of land (which can of course include parcels of
land which are not all contiguous – see *Farleyer* above). But where the timber
arises from other land, it will be a matter of fact and degree as to whether that
constitutes a material change in the use of the land concerned, amounting to
development for which planning permission would be required – and indeed
whether the land concerned becomes in law a separate planning unit. If by one
analysis or the other the new operation does amount to development, it is likely
that permission may be difficult to obtain, particularly if it involves the use of
large commercial vehicles in what will almost inevitably be a rural area.

13.2.3 *Building and engineering works associated with forestry*

The forestry exemption in the Act itself, considered above, applies only to the use
for forestry purposes of open land or existing buildings associated with such land.
There is in addition a provision in the General Permitted Development Order,[29]
which provides further limited exemption from the need for planning permission
to be sought for the carrying out of certain building or engineering works.

Planning permission is thus granted automatically for the erection of a new
building, other than a dwellinghouse, and for the extension or alteration of an
existing one, provided that the works are on land being used for the purposes of
forestry and that they are reasonably necessary for those purposes.[30] However, in
response to concerns expressed as to the poor appearance and siting of some
agricultural and forestry buildings erected under this provision, a new procedure
was introduced in 1991 to give a chance for the planning authority[31] to approve
the details of proposed works.

Accordingly, before any significant works are carried out in reliance on the
permission granted by the Order, the authority must be notified and given a
description of them, a plan showing their location, and details of the materials to
be used, together with the appropriate fee (currently £30).[32] The authority then
has 28 days from receipt of that notification in which to decide whether it wishes
to require the detailed siting, design and external appearance of the building to be
approved before the start of the works. "Significant" works are those that increase
the height of the original building, or which increase its volume by more than 10
per cent.[33]

If either the authority states within the 28-day period that it does not require to
approve the details of the proposed works, or the period elapses without the
authority having made any determination, the works may then proceed without

---

[29] TCP (General Permitted Development) Order 1995 (S.I. 1995 No. 418), Sched. 2, Pt 7.
[30] S.I. 1995 No. 418, Sched. 2, Pt 7, paras A(a), A1(a).
[31] Generally the unitary authority or, where one exists, the district or borough council.
[32] S.I. 1995 No. 418, Sched. 2, Pt 7, para. A2(1)(a), (b), (3); TCP (Fees for Applications and Deemed
      Applications) Regulations 1989 (S.I. 1989 No. 193), reg. 11A, inserted by S.I. 1991 No. 2735,
      substituted by S.I. 1992 No. 1817, current figure substituted by S.I. 1997 No. 37.
[33] S.I. 1995 No. 418, Sched. 2, Pt 7, para. A3.

further ado, in accordance with the details submitted and within five years of the date of that submission.[34] If, on the other hand, the authority does require prior approval of the details, the applicant is to display a notice at the site for at least 21 days, taking reasonable steps to protect it and, if need be, to display a replacement if the original is removed or defaced. Once that approval has been given, the works may then proceed, in accordance with the details approved and within five years of the date of that approval.[35] If the approval is not forthcoming, there is a right of appeal to the Secretary of State.[36]

A building may be only significantly extended or altered once in reliance on this exemption; thereafter, further significant works require planning permission in the normal way.[37] Where the land is within or near a national park or the Broads, the authority must be notified in advance of any building works, significant or otherwise.[38]

The same procedure applies to the formation, alteration and maintenance of private roads, needed for forestry. This provision may be of some significance in more remote rural areas, where forestry tracks may stretch for miles, and may create obtrusive scars on prominent hillsides. Notice must be given to the authority, which then has 28 days to decide whether it wishes to require prior approval of the siting and means of construction of the proposed works.[39] Works to obtain the materials for such roadworks may be undertaken without needing either to obtain formal planning permission or to notify the authority, as may other minor building works.[40]

None of the exemptions noted above apply to any works which are within 25 metres of a trunk road or classified road, or more than 3 metres in height within 3 kilometres of an airfield.[41] Those therefore require planning permission in the normal way.

13.2.4 Government guidance on forestry and the planning system

Policy guidance on the operation of these provisions is contained in:

- Planning Policy Guidance note (PPG) 7, *The Countryside: Environmental Quality and Economic and Social Development*[42] (England); and

- Technical Advice Note (Wales) 6, *Agricultural and Rural Development*.[43]

---

[34] S.I. 1995 No. 418, Sched. 2, Pt 7, para. A2(1)(c)(i),(iii), (e)(ii), (f)(ii).
[35] S.I. 1995 No. 418, Sched. 2, Pt 7, para. A2(1)(c)(ii), (e)(i), (f)(i). For the procedure as to site notices, see para. A3.
[36] TCPA 1990, s. 78(1)(c).
[37] S.I. 1995 No. 418, Sched. 2, Pt 7, para. A2(2).
[38] S.I. 1995 No. 418, art. 1(6); Sched. 1, Pt 3; Sched. 2, Pt 7, para. A2(3).
[39] S.I. 1995 No. 418, Sched. 2, Pt 7, paras A(b), A2(1); see the Forestry Commission booklet *Forest Road Guidelines*.
[40] S.I. 1995 No. 418, Sched. 2, Pt 7, paras A(c), (d).
[41] S.I. 1995 No. 418, Sched. 2, Pt 7, para. A1(b), (c).
[42] PPG 7, 1997, paras 3.1 to 3.7; Annexes C (para. C23, farm woodlands), E (permitted development rights) and I (forestry dwellings).
[43] See in particular paras 26, 7, 40, 52.

13.3 The need for environmental assessment

13.3.1 Introduction

The basic requirement under the Environmental Impact Assessment (Forestry) (England and Wales) Regulations 1999[44] is that consent will be required for the carrying out of any "relevant" project, as defined in the Regulations. An application for such consent is to be made to the Forestry Commission, accompanied by an EIA, and determined by it (subject to a right of appeal).[45] The current Regulations came into force on September 6, 1999, but outstanding applications made under previous regulations are treated as though they had been made under the 1999 Regulations.[46]

A "project" for this purpose means the execution of construction works or of other installations or schemes or other intervention in the natural surroundings or landscape, including those involving the extraction of mineral resources.[47] It thus in principle includes the planting and felling of trees, both of which are normally outside the definition of development for the planning Acts. And a "relevant project" is any project which is likely to have a significant effect on the environment by virtue of factors such as its nature, size or location, and which consists of:

- afforestation;

- deforestation;

- forestry road works; or

- forestry quarry works.[48]

"Afforestation" means initial afforestation (that is, not replacement planting following felling) by direct seeding or natural regeneration, including planting Christmas trees and short rotation coppice; and "deforestation" means deforestation for the purposes of conversion to another type of land use, such as heathland (not clear felling prior to such planting).[49] "Forestry road works" means the formation, alteration or maintenance of private ways on land used or to be used for the purposes of forestry; and "forestry quarry works" are operations on such land, or on land held or occupied with it, to obtain the material (such as rock, sand and gravel) for forestry road works. All, in other words, are projects that in any sensible system would require planning permission.

The Forestry Commission may direct that a particular project (note, not a particular category of projects) is exempt from the need for environmental assessment; such a direction is to be in writing, and state the reasons why it was made.[50] This power is said in the Regulations to be in accordance with article 2(3) of the Directive. But that provision makes it clear that such an exemption should

[44]   S.I. 1999 No. 2228 ("EIA Regulations 1999").
[45]   EIA Regulations 1999, reg. 4(1).
[46]   EIA Regulations 1999, reg. 25; and 1998 Regulations (S.I. 1999 No. 1731), reg. 20.
[47]   EIA Regulations 1999, reg. 2, echoing the definitions in art. 1(2) of the 1985 Directive, as amended.
[48]   EIA Regulations 1999, reg. 3.
[49]   EIA Regulations 1999, reg. 2, echoing the definitions in para. 1(d) of Annex II to the 1985 Directive, as amended.
[50]   EIA Regulations 1999, reg. 4(2)–(4).

only be granted in exceptional circumstances, and that information as to why it was granted should be made available to the public and to the European Commission, which should then forward the information to all other member states. It is difficult to imagine in what circumstances this power would ever be used in the context of forestry projects.

Finally, it should be noted that the Regulations, and thus the text of this Chapter, refer to "the appropriate Authority". This is defined as the Secretary of State, in relation to England, and the National Assembly for Wales.[51] In practice, this means respectively the Department for the Environment, Food and Rural Affairs (DEFRA) and the Agricultural Department of the Assembly (NAWAD).

13.3.2 Thresholds

As with all systems of control, thresholds have been introduced to define those projects of little significance that will not normally require consent. Paragraph 2 of Schedule 2 to the Regulations thus provides in effect that a project will always require the Forestry Commission to make a determination as to whether consent under the Regulations will be required if it comes within any of the following categories:

- where any part of the land comes within a site of special scientific interest,[52] a European site under the Conservation (Natural Habitats, etc.) Regulations 1994,[53] a world heritage site under the UNESCO convention,[54] a scheduled monument,[55] or the Norfolk and Suffolk Broads[56]:

  - all projects;

- in other cases, where any part of the land comes within a national park or an area of outstanding natural beauty (AONB):

  - afforestation projects affecting more than 2 hectares,
  - deforestation projects affecting more than 0.5 hectares, and
  - all projects involving forestry road works and quarry works.

- in all other cases:

  - afforestation projects affecting more than 5 hectares,
  - deforestation projects affecting more than 1 hectares, and
  - projects involving forestry road works and quarry works affecting more than 1 hectare.

Where a proposed project is to be on land adjacent to land on which another project has been carried out since September 6, 1999 and within the previous five

---

[51] EIA Regulations 1999, reg. 2, interpreted in accordance with the Ministry of Agriculture, Fisheries and Food (Dissolution) Order 2002 (S.I. 2002 No. 794).
[52] Under WCA 1981, ss. 28 to 28R, substituted by the Countryside and Rights of Way Act 2000, Sched. 9; see **9.3.8**. The 1999 Regulations as originally made also referred to land subject to nature conservancy orders under WCA 1981, s. 29; but that s. was repealed by the 2000 Act, Sched. 16, Pt III.
[53] S.I. 1994 No. 2716, reg. 10; see **9.3.9**.
[54] Under the Convention concerning the Protection of the World Cultural and Natural Heritage, 1972.
[55] Under Ancient Monuments and Archaeological Areas Act 1979; see **9.4.2**.
[56] As defined in the Norfolk and Suffolk Broads Act 1988, s. 2.

years, a determination will be required if the total land area of the two (or more) projects, added together, exceed the relevant threshold.[57]

Even where a project is below these thresholds, however, the Commission (or, on appeal, the appropriate Authority[57a]) may decide that there are exceptional circumstances – notably the proximity of a proposed project to another project nearby – which mean that a project will have significant effects on the environment, such that environmental assessment will be required.[58] Such a decision should only be made in the light of the criteria set out in Schedule 3, considered below.[59]

13.3.3 Overlap with other legislation

The need for consent under these provisions is wholly independent of any requirement for a felling licence.[60] It is almost inevitable that any deforestation project that is on such a scale as to require consent under the Regulations would also require a licence, but a project falling below the relevant threshold may well still require one.

Secondly, the EIA (Forestry) Regulations 1999 ("the Forestry Regulations") and the Town and Country Planning (EIA) Regulations 1999[61] ("the Planning Regulations") have been carefully constructed to ensure that there is in no circumstances a requirement for environmental assessment under both systems.[62]

Where a forestry project constitutes development, other than development permitted under Part 7 of Schedule 2 to the General Development Order,[63] the question of whether it requires assessment should be considered first in relation to the Planning Regulations. Where such consideration indicates that assessment is required (for example, where a forestry project forms part of a larger development which requires planning permission), the matter will be dealt with by the local planning authority as with any other such development project. Where, on the other hand, the Planning Regulations indicate that assessment is not required, the matter must then be considered in relation to the Forestry Regulations; and where they indicate that assessment is required, the matter will be dealt with by the Forestry Commission. Finally, where a project is development, but permitted under Part 7, the need for assessment is considered by the Commission under the Forestry Regulations.[64]

13.3.4 The need for consent

It will readily be appreciated that, in considering whether a project is a "relevant project" in the terms of the 1999 Regulations, so that it requires to be the subject of an environmental assessment and an application for consent from the Commission, the only issue which may cause problems in practice is whether it is a

[57] EIA Regulations 1999, Sched. 2, para. 3.
[57a] See **13.3.1**.
[58] EIA Regulations 1999, regs. 6(3),(6), 7(6),(9); Sched. 2, para. 4.
[59] See **13.3.5**.
[60] See **Chapter 14**.
[61] S.I. 1999 No. 293.
[62] EIA Regulations 1999, reg. 3(1)(c).
[63] Forestry buildings and operations; see **13.2.3**.
[64] The application of article 3(10) of the General Development Order (which overrides the permission given by the Order where development is such that it requires assessment under the Directive) is excluded by article 3(12) in the case of Part 7 development (forestry buildings and operations).

project which is "likely to have a significant effect on the environment by virtue of factors such as its nature, size or location." This, on the face of it, is a very subjective matter; what is significant will depend on who is asked.

The proper approach to the interpretation of this phrase has been considered by the Outer House of the Court of Session in *Swan v Secretary of State for Scotland*.[65] That decision needs to be considered with care, as it was decided initially in relation to the 1988 Regulations, and later the 1998 Regulations (which came into force while the litigation was under way) – both of which applied throughout Great Britain. It related to an application by a landowner to the Forestry Commission for a grant for afforestation on his farm, on land that was subject to a number of special designations under the relevant environmental legislation. The Commission had decided, after consultation with a number of relevant bodies, that there need not be an environmental assessment; and the Minister[66] had then decided, in effect, not to overrule that decision. During the course of the consideration of the project by the Commission, it had been the subject of various amendments which had been made to take account of objections received; and the final decision of the Minister had been made in relation to the project in the form in which it was following those amendments.

In a letter to an objector, the Minister had stated that his task had been "to determine whether such an assessment would reveal information that had not already been taken into account by the Forestry Commission", and that he had concluded he had no reason to believe that a formal assessment would give the Commission cause to take a different view of the proposals; although he hoped that further knowledge would be gained in relation to one relevant technical matter. In a subsequent letter, he stated his conclusion that he "would not have allowed the scheme to be approved if he had believed that it would be likely to cause significant harm".

The court accepted that the terms of the Minister's letters were far from satisfactory, particularly in relation to what he perceived to be the task before him. It was also true that the correct test was to consider the significant effects of a project, not just the significant harm; but since all the representations before him centred on the alleged harmful effects resulting from the project, it was difficult to state that he did not have that in mind. Nor was it fair to argue that the reference to obtaining further information vitiated the Minister's decision; after all, it was to be hoped that most environmental statements will advance the body of technical knowledge. And it certainly made no sense to insist on the Minister ignoring the amendments that had been made to the project. Nor could it be said that the Minister's decision had been "unreasonable", even in the light of all the relevant Government policy material, since the existence of the various protective designations had been clearly before him. The court accordingly dismissed the challenge.

It is open to question whether *Swan* would be decided the same way today, other than in relation to the amendment point, particularly in light of the subsequent decisions of the Court of Appeal and the House of Lords emphasising the importance of the requirement for assessment. Thus in *Berkeley v Secretary of State for the Environment*,[67] Lord Hoffman emphasised that nothing less than substantial compliance with the terms of the Directive (or with those of the

---

[65] [2000] Env.L.R. 60.
[66] It was at that time the Minister, rather than the Secretary of State, who made the relevant decision.
[67] (2001) 81 P. & C.R. 35, H.L.

Regulations in so far as they accurately reflect the Directive) would suffice; and that there would seem to be little room for discretion by the court in considering whether to quash a decision which was not in compliance. Further, the mere fact that the decision maker had available to it all or most of the material which would be included in a formal assessment was irrelevant; the Directive required that material be readily available to the public.

13.3.5 Criteria determining the need for assessment

In deciding whether a project is one which requires the submission of a formal environmental assessment, the relevant criteria are those listed in Schedule 3 to the 1999 Regulations, since they are the criteria which are to be taken into account by the Forestry Commission (or by the appropriate Authority on appeal[67a]) if asked for an opinion as to whether a project is a relevant project.[68]

The wording of these criteria follows precisely that in Annex III to the Directive,[69] which is a general instrument referring to a very wide range of projects. It is therefore not surprising that the criteria are only moderately relevant to forestry projects in particular. However, the key provisions are that it is necessary to have regard to:

● the characteristics of the project (including, in particular, its size, and its relationship to other projects);

● the location of the project; and

● in the light of the characteristics and location of the project, its potential impact (including the extent, magnitude, complexity, probability, duration, frequency and reversibility of any impact).

In the context of forestry, it is likely to be the location that will be of greatest significance. In that regard, the Schedule provides[70] as follows:

"The environmental sensitivity of geographical areas likely to be affected by projects must be considered, having regard, in particular, to:

● the existing land use;
● the relative abundance, quality and regenerative capacity of natural resources in the area; and
● the absorption capacity of the natural environment, paying particular attention to the following areas:
    (a) wetlands;
    (b) coastal zones;
    (c) mountain and forest areas;
    (d) nature reserves and parks;
    (e) [European sites under the Habitats Regulations[71]];
    (f) areas in which the environmental quality standards laid down in Community legislation have already been exceeded;

[67a] See **13.3.1**.
[68] EIA Regulations 1999, regulation 6(2).
[69] Directive 85/337/EEC, Annex III, substituted by Council Directive 97/11/EC, Annex.
[70] EIA Regulations 1999, Sched. 3, para. 2.
[71] S.I. 1994 No. 2716, reg. 10; see **9.3.9**.

(g) densely populated areas; and

(h) landscapes of historical, cultural or archaeological significance."

As already noted, these criteria should be taken into account in determining the need for assessment, whether or not a project comes above the threshold in Schedule 2.[72]

13.3.6 Opinion as to need for consent

The Forestry Commission may be asked to give an opinion as to whether consent will be required for a particular project. There is no requirement for such an opinion to be sought. It thus seems that is perfectly open for someone proposing to carry out a project (referred to in the Regulations as "the proposer") either to decide that it clearly does require an assessment, and so to submit one anyway; or to decide that no assessment is required, and to risk enforcement. On the other hand, the Commission is entitled to decide that an assessment is not required even if a project comes above the relevant threshold, or (exceptionally) that one is required even if a project comes below the threshold, so it is almost always safer to seek a formal opinion.

An application for an opinion is made to the local office of the Forestry Commission,[73] and should be accompanied by:

- a map identifying the location and extent of the proposed project (usually a clear Ordnance Survey map at a scale of 1:10,000 or 1:2,500);

- a brief description of what is proposed, and an indication of any possible significant environmental impact; and

- any other relevant information (species maps, plans, photographs, etc.).[74]

In the majority of instances, this information will be provided as part of an application under the Woodland Grant Scheme (in the case of initial afforestation) or of an application for a felling licence (in the case of deforestation). Where, in the course of processing such an application, the Commission forms the view that consent for the project will be required, and an environmental statement prepared, it will automatically require this to be done before going any further.

The Commission may, if it wishes, require the proposer to supply further information.[75] It is to reach an opinion within 28 days of receiving the application, or within 28 days of receiving any further information sought, unless a longer time has been agreed with the proposer.[76]

The opinion of the Commission is to be made in the light of the criteria set out in Schedule 3; and, where the opinion is that a project is not a relevant project, that is binding – but only for five years (or such shorter period as may be specified in the opinion) if the relevant work has not by then been completed.[77] Where, on

---

[72] EIA Regulations 1999, regs. 6(2),(3), 7(5),(6); see **13.3.2**.

[73] Listed in most Forestry Commission publications, including the booklet *Environmental Assessment of Forestry Projects*.

[74] EIA Regulations 1999, regulation 5(2); *Environmental Assessment of Forestry Projects*, p. 5.

[75] EIA Regulations 1999, reg. 5(3).

[76] EIA Regulations 1999, reg. 6(1).

[77] EIA Regulations 1999, reg. 8(1),(2).

the other hand, the Commission forms the opinion that a project is a relevant project, it must provide a statement of the reasons why.[78]

In the latter case, or where the Commission fails to reach any decision within the agreed timescale, the proposer may apply to the appropriate Authority[79] for a direction. Curiously, there appears to be no time limit for lodging such an application. There is no specified form either, but the application must be accompanied by any documents and other material sent by the proposer to the Commission, and (where it exists) the opinion and reasoning of the Commission. If the appropriate Authority wants more information, he or she is to notify the proposer, and may seek it from the Commission (although there is obviously nothing to prevent the proposer supplying it where appropriate).[80] As with the initial application to the Commission, the appropriate Authority is to give a direction (note, not just an opinion) within 28 days of receiving the appeal, or within 28 days of receiving any further information sought. That time limit may be extended, but not unreasonably.[81]

The direction of the appropriate Authority is to be made in the light of the criteria set out in Schedule 3; and, again, where the direction is that a project is a relevant project, it must contain a statement of the reasons why.[82] And the same five-year time limit applies to a direction by the appropriate Authority as to an opinion of the Commission.[83]

If the Commission forms the view that an opinion or direction should have been sought as to the need for an assessment, it can volunteer one without being asked, and send it in writing to the person who seems to be the proposer; as can the Secretary of State.[84]

13.3.7 Register of projects

The Forestry Commission maintains an EIA Public Register, of which copies are available at its local offices and on the web.[85] This shows information about the opinion of the Commission as to whether the project is a relevant project, its decision as to any application for consent, details of any directions made by the appropriate Authority, and the decision on any appeal.

13.3.8 Challenge to decision on need for consent

There is no statutory right to challenge a decision of the Forestry Commission or the appropriate Authority that consent is not needed. The only course of action open to an aggrieved third party (either a member of the public or an interested body such as a local authority) is, therefore, to apply to the High Court for judicial review of the decision. Such an application would need to be made promptly, and in any event within three months of the decision being challenged.

It may be noted that this is in marked distinction to the position relating to

---

[78] EIA Regulations 1999, reg. 6(2)–(4); see **13.3.4**.
[79] See **13.3.1**.
[80] EIA Regulations 1999, reg. 7(2),(3).
[81] EIA Regulations 1999, reg. 7(4).
[82] EIA Regulations 1999, reg. 7(5)-(7); see **13.3.4**.
[83] EIA Regulations 1999, reg. 8(1),(2).
[84] EIA Regulations 1999, regs. 6(5), 7(8).
[85] At www.forestry.gov.uk (the Register will probably be available in mid-2002). See 1999 Regulations, reg. 24.

disputes as to the need for environmental assessment of proposed development projects. In most, if not all, of the reported cases, such challenges have taken the form of a statutory application to quash the grant of planning permission – since there was no dispute that planning permission was required. In that situation, objectors to a proposal can await the outcome of the normal planning process, and need only mount a court challenge if and when permission is granted. In the case of forestry projects, by contrast, it has already been noted that the general rule is that planning permission is not required. If, therefore, the Commission decides that an environmental assessment is not required either (or if it fails to address its mind to the issue), there is nothing to stop the project going ahead without further ado. It is thus vital for any potential challenger to move quickly.[85a]

13.4 Applications for consent

13.4.1 Material to be included with application

Once the proposer of a forestry project has decided that it requires consent from the Forestry Commission – either as a result of being told so by the Commission[86] or having reached that decision unaided – he or she must then submit an application (at which point, in the language of the Regulations, a "proposer" becomes the "applicant").

An application consists of the following:

- a map identifying the land involved and showing the extent of the project;
- a description of the nature of the project;
- an environmental statement in respect of the project; and
- a copy of the press notice.[87]

The first and second of these are straightforward (and will in any event presumably be included within the environmental statement). The Commission suggests that the description should include a brief description of the proposed work and of the possible significant effects on the environment, as well as any other information which might be relevant (such as species maps, plans, photographs, etc.).[88] The contents of an environmental statement and the requirements as to publicity are considered below.[89]

There is no standard application form, but it may be wise to consult the local office of the Commission before starting to prepare the material for an application, to make sure of what is required (and see below on the preparation of the environmental statement). Where the Commission considers that more information is required, and that the applicant is able to supply it, it may notify

[85a] See also **13.4.7**.
[86] See **13.3**.
[87] EIA Regulations 1999, reg. 10(1).
[88] *Environmental Assessment of Forestry Projects*, p. 6.
[89] See **13.4.2** and **13.4.4** respectively.

the applicant in writing of what it requires, and the applicant is then to provide it.[90] However, there is a limit to the extent of information that can be required and if an applicant declines to submit as much as is being sought, it is possible to appeal without waiting for a formal decision from the Commission.[91] As to how many copies are required of the material constituting the application, the Regulations state that this can, within reason, be specified by the Commission[92]; in practice, the number sought depends on the type of case.

Where, as will often be the case, an application is being submitted to the Commission under the Woodland Grant Scheme, it will not be necessary to submit an additional application for consent under the EIA Regulations as well – the amount and type of information required for a grant application is sufficient to satisfy the requirements of the Regulations. Where, on the other hand, an application is made for a licence for clear felling, not followed by replanting, a separate application will also need to be made under the environmental assessment procedures.

13.4.2 Contents of environmental statements

The key requirement in these provisions is that is that an application for consent under the 1999 Regulations must be accompanied by an environmental statement. As to what such a statement should contain, the guidance from the Forestry Commission is as follows:

"There is no set format for an ES [environmental statement], but it must contain the standard information contained in Appendix 2 [which reproduces Schedule 1 to the 1999 Regulations]. Your Statement must include everything from the list that relates to your application, placing the emphasis on the significant environmental effects."[93]

The Regulations state that an environmental statement must contain:

"(a) . . . such of the information in Part I of Schedule 1 as is reasonably required to assess the environmental effects of the project and which the applicant can, having regard in particular to current knowledge and methods of assessment, reasonably be required to compile, but
(b) . . . at least the information referred to in Part II of Schedule 1".[94]

As for Part I of the Schedule, the problem is that it simply reproduces word for word the text of Annex IV to the Directive[95]; and, as already noted, the Directive applies to all sorts of projects. Unfortunately, in imposing the requirement for environmental assessment onto the forestry regime, no one took the trouble to refine the list of items to be considered in the course of the assessment, to eliminate those which are irrelevant (such as the emission of radiation) and to modify those which are only relevant to a very limited extent (such as the emission of pollutants). The principal items likely to be relevant in the case of forestry would thus seem to be as follows:

---

90 EIA Regulations 1999, reg. 11.
91 *R v Secretary of State for the Environment Transport and the Regions, ex p. Bath and North East Somerset District Council* [1999] 2 PLR 120, CA.
92 EIA Regulations 1999, reg. 10(2).
93 *Environmental Assessment of Forestry Projects*, p. 6.
94 EIA Regulations 1999, reg. 2.
95 Directive 85/337/EEC, Annex IV, substituted by Council Directive 97/11/EC, Annex.

"PART I.

. . . 3. A description of the aspects of the environment likely to be significantly affected by the proposed project, including, in particular, population, fauna, flora, soil, water, air, climatic factors, material assets including the architectural and archaeological heritage, landscape and the interrelationship between the above factors.

4. A description of the likely significant effects of the proposed project on the environment, which should cover the direct effects and any indirect, secondary, cumulative, short, medium and long-term, permanent and temporary, positive and negative effects of the project, resulting from –

(a)   the existence of the project;
(b)   the use of natural resources;
(c)   [. . .]

and the description by the applicant of the forecasting methods used to assess the effects on the environment.

5. A description of the measures envisaged to prevent, reduce and, where possible, offset any significant adverse effects on the environment.

6. A non-technical summary of the information provided under paragraphs 1 to 5 above.

7. An indication of any difficulties (technical deficiencies or lack of know-how) encountered by the applicant in compiling the required information."

It must be emphasised however that it is the full list of criteria in Annex IV to the Directive, reproduced in both the Regulations and in the Forestry Commission guidance, which is definitive.

As for the material in Part II of Schedule 1, which must be included, this reproduces article 5(3) of the Directive,[96] and is as follows:

"PART II.

1. A description of the project comprising information on the site, design and size of the project.

2. A description of the measures envisaged in order to avoid, reduce and, if possible, remedy significant adverse effects.

3. The data required to identify and assess the main effects which the project is likely to have on the environment.

4. An outline of the main alternatives studied by the applicant and an indication of the main reasons for his choice, taking into account the environmental effects.

5. A non-technical summary of the information provided under paragraphs 1 to 4 above."

As to what is required in practice, see below.

13.4.3 Preparing the environmental statement

In order to establish what information should be included in an environmental statement in any particular case, it is possible for the person proposing a project to seek an opinion from the Forestry Commission (a procedure generally referred to as "scoping"). This can be done either before the Commission has decided that the project is a relevant project,[97] in which case the Commission will prepare the scoping opinion on the assumption that it is a relevant project, or once that decision has been reached.[98]

---

[96]   Substituted by Council Directive 97/11/EC, art. 1(7).
[97]   See **13.3.2**.
[98]   EIA Regulations 1999, reg. 9.

The Commission is to give its opinion as to what should be included in a statement within five weeks of receiving the request for it, or within such longer period as may be agreed. Before the Commission gives an opinion, it is to consult:

- the proposer of the project;

- the relevant countryside bodies (that is, in England, the Countryside Agency and English Nature; in Wales, the Countryside Council for Wales; and in either case the Environment Agency[99]); and

- any relevant local authority.[1]

The Commission sensibly suggests that a person proposing a project consults it, and the countryside bodies, at an early stage. And a scoping meeting can be held at which all concerned can provide advice and information.[2] Indeed, if any of the above bodies have any relevant information, it is under an obligation to provide a copy of it to the proposer at a reasonable charge (except, obviously, where it is confidential).[3] The Commission also suggests that it is supplied with a draft copy of an environmental statement before the final version is prepared.

Finally, further advice can be obtained from the Commission's publication *Environmental Impact Assessment in Forestry and Preparing an Environmental Statement*, which is available on its website.[4]

If no scoping opinion is received from the Commission within the 5-week period (subject to any extension agreed), the proposer of the project may seek a direction from the appropriate Authority,[5] and the appropriate Authority must then make a direction within a similar period, having gone through a similar consultation exercise.[6]

13.4.4 Publicity for applications

A person who makes an application for consent, or who supplies further information in response to a request from the Commission to do so, is to place a notice in two or more newspapers (the Commission has the right to choose which). Such a notice must state:

- that an application has been made, or that further information has been supplied;

- where the application or the further information can be inspected, free of charge, for at least 28 days at all reasonable hours (this will usually be an office of the Commission, but may be another location nominated by it);

- where a copy of the application or the information can be obtained from the applicant (on payment of copying charges); and

---

[99] In Scotland, Scottish Natural Heritage and the Scottish Environmental Protection Agency.
[1] EIA Regulations 1999, reg. 9(3),(6),(8).
[2] *Environmental Assessment of Forestry Projects*, p. 6.
[3] EIA Regulations 1999, reg. 12; Environmental Information Regulations 1992, reg. 4.
[4] www.forestry.gov.uk.
[5] See **13.3.1**.
[6] EIA Regulations 1999, reg. 9(4),(5),(7).

- that anyone wanting to make representations should send them in writing to the Commission within the 28-day period.[7]

It will be clear from the above that in practice the Commission will have to be consulted before the press notice is finalised, as it has the right to nominate where it is to appear, where the application is to be available for inspection, and the address to which comments should be sent.

Once the Commission has received a completed application, or supplementary information, it is to send a copy to the relevant countryside bodies (see above) and any local authority or public body which appears to have an interest in the application (note, not an interest in the land to which it relates). The Commission should also send all of the bodies thus consulted a notice stating that they too have only 28 days in which to respond – which is a somewhat optimistic timetable for a sensible response from a public body with a committee structure.[8]

There is an elaborate procedure whereby the Commission must notify the appropriate Authority of any project that it considers likely to affect another EEA member state, so that the Authority may in turn pass the relevant information to that state.[9] However, here too it is difficult to imagine this being relevant in the case of a forestry project.[10]

13.4.5 Determination of application

Once the 28-day period for making representations has expired, the Forestry Commission may grant conditional consent, or it may refuse to do so.[11] In reaching its decision, it must take into account the information in the environmental statement, any representations made in response to the publicity or the consultation, and any other material considerations. The latter will include its assessment as to the direct and indirect affects of the project on:

- human beings, fauna and flora;
- soil, water, air, climate and the landscape;
- material assets and the cultural heritage; and
- the interaction between the above factors.[12]

Where consent is granted, it is to be subject to conditions that the project is to be started within a specified time scale (not longer than five years), and is to be finished within a specified time scale (not longer than ten years).[13] It may also be subject to any other appropriate conditions.

Whatever the decision, the Commission is to give notice of it to the proposer of

---

[7] EIA Regulations 1999, reg. 13(1),(2).
[8] EIA Regulations 1999, reg. 13(3).
[9] EIA Regulations 1999, reg. 14. An "EEA state" is a state that is a contracting party to the Agreement on the European Economic Area (resolution 2).
[10] Other than, possibly, in the case of a project in Northern Ireland near the border with the Irish Republic.
[11] In the very rare case where a project is notified to another EEA member state under reg. 14, the period for consultation under that procedure must expire before a decision is made by the Commission.
[12] EIA Regulations 1999, reg. 15, Sched. 4.
[13] EIA Regulations 1999, reg. 18.

the project, and to all those who made representations in response to the application; and that notice is to state the reasons and considerations on which its decision is based. Note that, unlike decisions on planning applications, reasons must be given for a grant of consent, and not just for a refusal. It is not clear what is meant by "considerations", as opposed to reasons. The Commission must also publish a notice of the decision in the same paper as was used to publicise the application, stating where and when the public may inspect the details of the decision (including any conditions), the reasons and considerations on which it was based, and a description of the main measures to deal with any adverse effects of the proposal.[14]

13.4.6 Appeals against decisions of the Commission

There is a right of appeal to the appropriate Authority[15] against any decision by the Forestry Commission to refuse consent or to impose non-standard conditions – that is, any conditions other than those imposing 5-year and 10-year time limits for starting and finishing the work.[16]

Such an appeal must be made by the applicant within 28 days of receiving notice of the decision – experience with other types of appeal suggests that a late appeal will only be allowed in the most exceptional circumstances. The appeal is made simply "by notice" – that is, there is no prescribed form. And it should be accompanied by:

- the original application, together with any supporting documentation;
- the decision by the Commission; and
- any further representations by the applicant.

On receipt of the appeal, the appropriate Authority is to supply to the Commission a copy of the further representations; and the Commission is then to supply to the Authority any representations made to it in relation to the application. Curiously, there is no provision for the Commission itself to make representations in response to the further representations by the applicant, but there would be no reason why it should not do so.

The appropriate Authority is then to reach a decision, taking into account the same matters as applied in relation to the original application – together with, obviously, any further representations made in relation to the appeal. There is no formal right for either the applicant or the Commission to request, let alone require, the holding of an inquiry; but it might be prudent to hold one on a non-statutory basis, if only to minimise the risk of a challenge under the Human Rights Act 1998.[17] The decision of the Authority is to be notified and publicised in the same way as the original decision of the Commission.

13.4.7 High Court challenge

Anyone aggrieved by a decision to grant consent has a statutory right to apply to

---

14 1999 Regulations, reg. 16.
15 See 13.3.1.
16 1999 Regulations, reg. 17.
17 Human Rights Act 1998, Sched. 1, art. 6(1) (right to a public hearing).

the High Court for an order quashing it, within six weeks of the date of its being published.[18] The grounds are either:

- that the decision was not made on the basis of the matters specified in the Regulations[19]; or

- that the Regulations have not been complied with, and the interests of the aggrieved person have been substantially prejudiced.

This right would benefit an objector (either a member of the public or a relevant public body), in relation to a grant of consent either by the Forestry Commission or by the appropriate Authority, or the Commission itself in relation to a grant of consent by the Authority. It is noteworthy that a local authority has been held to have sufficient interest to challenge a decision of the Commission.[20] Statutory time limits of this sort must be strictly complied with; there is no possibility of any extension.[21]

Where the applicant is refused consent by the Commission, the remedy is to appeal to the appropriate Authority. If that appeal fails, the only possibility for further remedy would be an application to the High Court for judicial review of the Authority's decision.

The only two challenges known to have been made to decisions relating to the environmental assessment provisions as they relate to forestry[22] were both in the form of an application for judicial review rather than a statutory challenge, as there was no provision under the 1988 or 1998 Regulations corresponding to regulation 19 of the 1999 Regulations.

13.5 Works carried out without consent

13.5.1 Enforcement notices

The requirement to obtain the consent of the Forestry Commission for the carrying out of any relevant project, and to carry out the project only in accordance with the conditions attached to such consent, is similar to the requirement to obtain planning permission for the carrying out of (almost) any development. That is, non-compliance does not of itself automatically amount to a criminal offence.

However, where it appears that work is being carried out in relation to a relevant project without the required consent, or in breach of any condition which has been imposed on any consent, any person duly authorised in writing by the Commission may enter the land to ascertain the true position[23]; and the Commission may serve an enforcement notice on the person doing the work.[24]

[18] 1999 Regulations, reg. 19.
[19] That is, the information in the environmental statement, any representations made in response to the publicity or the consultation, an assessment as to the direct and indirect affects of the project, and any other material considerations (regulations 15(3), 17(7)). See **13.4.2**.
[20] *Kincardine and Deeside District Council v Forestry Commission* 1991 S.L.T. 1180.
[21] *R v Secretary of State for the Environment, ex p Ostler* [1977] Q.B. 122.
[22] *Kincardine* (note 20 above), and *Swan v Secretary of State for Scotland* (IH) 1998 S.C.L.R. 763; (OH) Court of Sessions [1999] Env. L.R. 60; see **13.3.4**.
[23] EIA Regulations 1999, reg. 23(1).
[24] EIA Regulations 1999, reg. 20(1).

The power to take such action was only introduced in 1998 and no notices have yet been issued; but it would clearly be unsatisfactory to have an elaborate consent system with no mechanism to enforce it.

An enforcement notice may thus require the recipient:

(a) to apply to the Commission for consent;

(b) to discontinue work;

(c) to restore the land to its former state; or

(d) to carry out works which are reasonably necessary:

- to secure compliance with the conditions attached to any consent granted, or
- to remove or alleviate any damage to the environment caused by the works already carried out.

The notice must state the time within which consent is to be sought or the specified works are to be done.[25]

A notice should, in general, explain the right of the recipient to appeal against it, and, where consent has not been obtained, why the Commission considers that it was needed. However, in either case, the Commission may in an emergency serve a notice without these details, and supply the missing material as soon as practicable afterwards.[26] It is perfectly possible to imagine why the need for consent may take a while to specify accurately – where, for example, it relates to detailed scientific measurements or data – but it difficult to see why it would not always be possible to explain the right of appeal at the outset.

The usual provisions apply as to the service of notices; and a notice, once served, may be varied by a subsequent notice, or withdrawn.[27]

13.5.2 Appeals against enforcement notices

As might be expected, there is a right of appeal against such a notice. An appeal must be made to the appropriate Authority[28] within 28 days of receiving the enforcement notice, unless the Authority allows an extension of time – experience with other types of appeal suggests that a late appeal will only be allowed in the most exceptional circumstances. It should be accompanied by:

- the enforcement notice;
- any relevant consent; and
- any further representations by the applicant.[29]

The procedure thereafter is exactly as for an appeal against the refusal of consent, save that the decision does not have to be publicised in the press.[30] The appropriate Authority may allow or dismiss the appeal, or vary the notice; but, if

[25] EIA Regulations 1999, reg. 20(2),(3).
[26] EIA Regulations 1999, reg. 20(4),(5).
[27] EIA Regulations 1999, reg. 20(6)–(8).
[28] See **13.3.1**.
[29] EIA Regulations 1999, reg. 21(1)–(3).
[30] EIA Regulations 1999, reg. 21(4), (6)–(8) See **13.4.4**.

he or she forms the view that consent is required, an appeal must not be allowed against a notice requiring consent to be obtained (requirement (a) above).[31] The purpose of the latter provision is presumably to ensure that it is not possible to avoid the burden of producing an environmental statement simply by carrying out the project and appealing against any enforcement notice served – and thus, in effect, asking for consent retrospectively without supplying the full information that would otherwise be required.

The making of an appeal generally has the effect of suspending the operation of the enforcement notice until the appeal is either determined by the appropriate Authority or withdrawn. Note that, technically, if there is a further appeal on a point of law against the decision of the Authority, the notice has to be complied with in the meanwhile. However, where a notice requires work to cease (requirement (b)), that must be complied with while awaiting the outcome of the appeal.

There is no statutory right of appeal against the decision of the appropriate Authority; so a challenge would have to be by way of an application for judicial review.[32]

13.5.3 Consequences of non-compliance

Once an enforcement notice has come into effect, non-compliance with a requirement to discontinue work is a serious offence, triable either way. On conviction in the magistrates court, the maximum penalty is a fine not exceeding the statutory maximum; on conviction in the Crown Court, the penalty is an unlimited fine. Non-compliance with any other requirement of a notice is a lesser offence, attracting a fine of up to level 5 on conviction in the magistrates' court.[33] Where the offence has been committed by a company, any senior officer may be charged and convicted as well as the company.[34]

Where an enforcement notice requires work to be carried out, and it seems that those works have not been carried out, any person duly authorised by the Commission may enter the land to carry out the works in default; and the Commission may then recover the cost of so doing.[35]

---

[31] EIA Regulations 1999, reg. 21(5), (9).
[32] See **13.4.7**.
[33] See **Appendix C**.
[34] EIA Regulations 1999, reg. 22.
[35] EIA Regulations 1999, reg. 23(2).

Chapter 14

Felling Licences and Directions

14.1 Introduction

The control of felling was first introduced during the Second World War as a means of ensuring a strategic reserve of standing timber – which was of course vital for the war effort. The 1943 report on post-war forest policy[1] recommended that a licensing system be continued after the end of the war, and the Forestry Act 1951 accordingly introduced the requirement for a felling licence to be obtained from the Forestry Commission before trees could be felled in any quantity. The provisions of the 1951 Act were carried across more or less unchanged into Part II of the Forestry Act 1967, which was a consolidating measure, and which is still in force today. Apart from the introduction of restocking notices in 1986,[2] and minor changes from time to time to reflect the changing grant regimes,[3] the legislation has remained virtually unaltered over the half century since it was first enacted.

The policy behind the operation of that legislation, on the other hand, has changed dramatically over that period. In 1958, the Government made it clear that a reserve of trees was no longer an end in itself, but that economic and other criteria must also affect a decision to grant a licence.[4] A further review of forestry policy in 1972 stressed that amenity considerations were of primary importance in reaching decisions.[5] The relevant Minister then required, in a direction of April 12, 1984, that the Forestry Commission must consult with central Government agriculture departments, local authorities and other interested bodies to ensure that land use, amenity, recreation and nature conservation were taken into account. In addition, the Commission stated publicly that amenity would be the principal factor taken into account when considering applications for licences.[6]

The net result of all this is that, whereas the tree preservation order system (considered in the following Part of this book) is aimed at preserving the amenity provided by individual trees, the felling licence regime described in this Chapter is now aimed at preserving and enhancing the amenity provided by woodlands and

---

[1] Cmd 6447.
[2] Under the Forestry Act 1986; see **14.7.6 to 14.7.8**.
[3] See **14.2.9**.
[4] Report of Zuckerman Committee, 1957.
[5] Treasury cost/benefit study. Also see Ministerial statement of July 5, 1974 .
[6] See Forestry Commission annual report.

forests. It is partly for that reason that the former controls the felling, topping and lopping of a tree – in other words, more or less any works to it – and the latter controls only its felling. And the felling licence system also excludes works on a small scale, which are controlled more appropriately (if at all) by preservation orders.

This Chapter, therefore, first considers (in **14.2**) the circumstances in which it is necessary to obtain a felling licence, and more especially those in which it is not. It then looks at the procedure for applying for a licence where one is required, and the basis on which such applications are determined (**14.3**). There are special provisions, described at **14.4**, to deal with the overlap between the felling controls described in this Chapter and the controls under planning legislation described in **Part IV**; but it should not be forgotten that the controls described in this Chapter are also additional to those described in **Chapter 9** – notably those relating to wildlife and habitats[7] and health and safety.[8]

The following sections examine the remedies available in the event that a felling license is not forthcoming (**14.5**), how conditions attached to licences are enforced (**14.6**) and what happens if works are carried out without a felling licence (**14.7**). The final section (**14.8**) looks at felling directions.

These provisions are also the subject of a Forestry Commission booklet entitled *Tree Felling: Getting Permission.*[9]

14.2 Need for a felling licence

14.2.1 General rule

The essential provision, in section 9 of the Forestry Act 1967, is that a felling licence must be obtained from the Forestry Commission to fell growing trees in any quantity. "Felling" a tree includes wilfully destroying it by any means.[10] A licence is not required, on the other hand, for lopping, topping or pruning operations, or for the trimming or laying of hedges,[11] or to fell trees which are dead or dying. It was established many years ago that "lopping" means cutting off the branches of a tree, and "topping" is cutting off its top.[12]

There are a number of exceptions to this general rule – some contained in the Act itself, and others (noted at **14.3**) prescribed in regulations made under the Act. The Regulations currently in force are the Forestry (Exceptions from Restriction of Felling) Regulations 1979.[13] They have been amended, slightly, by the Forestry (Exceptions from Restriction of Felling) (Amendment) Regulations of 1981, 1985, 1988 and 1998[14] – of which only the last is currently in force.

The provisions of the Act relating to felling licences do not apply within Inner

---

[7] See **9.3**.
[8] See **9.5**.
[9] November 2000; available from Forestry Commission offices.
[10] FA 1967, s. 35.
[11] FA 1967, s. 9(2)(c).
[12] *Unwin v Hanson* [1891] 2 Q.B. 115, CA, per Lord Esher M.R. at p. 119; see **6.4.3** for a fuller extract.
[13] S.I. 1979 No. 792.
[14] S.I. 1981 No. 1476; S.I. 1985 No. 1572; S.I. 1988 No. 970; and S.I. 1998 No. 603: see **14.2.9**.

London.[15] Given the existence of the other exemptions discussed below, this is of little significance in practice.

It should be noted that felling without a licence is a criminal offence, under section 17 of the Act, but only where a licence is required; and that in the event of a prosecution it is up to the person carrying out the felling to show that one of the various exemptions can be relied on, rather than for the prosecution to show that it none of them applies.[16] Any necessary evidence to substantiate reliance on an exemption – such as estimates of the quantity of timber felled, or reasons why a tree is considered to be dangerous – should therefore be obtained at the time the felling is carried out, to avoid having to rely on mere assertion many months later.

Finally, it has already been noted that the provisions of Part II of the Act relating to felling licences do not apply to felling proposals by the Commission itself (in its guise as Forest Enterprise).[17] Such proposals, known as forest design plans, do still have to be approved by the Forestry Commission, however, following publicity on the public register.[18]

14.2.2 Felling on a small scale

Perhaps the most significant exemption is that a felling licence is not required for the removal of small trees or of small numbers of larger ones. That is, authorisation is not needed for the felling of:

- a tree with a diameter of 8 cm or less;

- a tree with a diameter of 10 cm or less, where the work is carried out to improve the growth of other trees; or

- a tree with a diameter of 15 cm or less if coppice (that is, a tree managed by cutting to promote multi-stemmed growth arising at or near ground level) or underwood.[19]

The second of these (thinning) applies only where the work is carried out by the freeholder or leaseholder of the land on which they are growing. All of the measurements are to be taken as the diameter, measured over the bark, at a height of 1.3 m above ground level.[20]

Nor is a licence needed for felling of trees where:

- the total volume of timber felled in any calendar quarter by that person does not exceed 5 cubic metres; and

- the total volume sold in any calendar quarter by that person (before or after felling) does not exceed 2 cubic metres.

[15] FA 1967, s. 36; "Inner London" consists of the London Boroughs of Camden, Greenwich, Hackney, Hammersmith and Fulham, Islington, Kensington and Chelsea, Lambeth, Lewisham, Southwark, Tower Hamlets, and Wandsworth, the Cities of London and Westminster, and the Temple: London Government Act 1963, s. 1(1).
[16] R v Alath Construction Ltd [1990] 1 W.L.R. 1255; [1991] 1 EGLR 285, CA (applied in the context of the Forestry Act by the Crown Court in Forestry Commission v Grace [1992] 1 EGLR 28). See **14.7.1**.
[17] FA 1967, s. 33; see **11.3.4**.
[18] See **14.3.2**.
[19] FA 1967, s. 9(2)(a), (3)(a).
[20] FA 1967, s. 9(6); metric measurements were substituted by FA 1979, s. 2, Sched. 1.

These limits were substantially reduced (from 30 and 5 cubic metres respectively) in 1985.[21] In calculating the amount that may be felled in reliance in this exemption, it is necessary to exclude trees felled without a licence in reliance on any other exemption. So, for example, if a landowner fells 6 cubic metres of trees in his garden, and a further 3 cubic metres in neighbouring woodland, and sells 2 cubic metres of each, he does not need a licence.

The calendar quarters referred to are the periods of three months starting January 1, April 1, July 1, and October 1.[22]

14.2.3 Felling of trees in orchards, gardens, churchyards and open spaces

A licence is not needed for the felling of "fruit trees or trees standing or growing on land comprised in an orchard, garden, churchyard or public open space".[23] It is not clear whether this exempts all fruit trees, or only those standing or growing in an orchard, garden, etc. Nor is it obvious what is intended by the inclusion of the word "standing", as the requirement to obtain a felling licence only applies to "growing trees". But note that this exemption applies regardless of the quantity or size of the trees being felled.

This provision has been recently considered by the Divisional Court in *McInerney v Portland Port Ltd.*[24] Latham L.J. noted that there was no definition in the Forestry Act 1967 of any of the words "orchard, garden, churchyard or public open space", and held that each of those words must accordingly be given its ordinary meaning. An orchard is thus defined in the dictionary as "a piece of enclosed land planted with fruit trees",[25] which tends to suggest a walled or fenced domestic orchard. But the exemption presumably applies equally to fruit trees growing in a commercial orchard. The meaning of "garden" was considered in *Portland* itself:

"The ordinary meaning of the word 'garden', it seems to me, is accurately reflected in the definition of a garden in the Oxford English dictionary, namely, 'an enclosed piece of ground devoted to the cultivation of flowers, fruit or vegetables'. The definition may be said to be deficient in detail, in that one can readily accept that an enclosed area which is mainly or perhaps entirely filled with a lawn might be considered to be a garden. Equally, there may well be circumstances in which an area which is wild in its nature is nonetheless, by reason of the use that is made of it, clearly intended as a garden."[26]

It is also noteworthy that the definition of 'garden' in at least one other dictionary omits the reference to enclosure, but inserts the words "adjoining a house". So dictionary definitions must be used only with caution.

The court in *Portland* also made it clear that, in deciding whether a piece of land is or is not an orchard or garden, what needs to be considered is primarily the state of the land at the time its description is called into question, and, only secondarily, its history:

". . . where, as in this case, land which had been a garden has been disused for two and a

[21] By the Forestry (Modification of Felling Restrictions) 1985 (S.I. 1985 No. 1958).
[22] FA 1967, s. 9(6)
[23] 1967 Act, s. 9(2)(b).
[24] [2001] 1 PLR 104.
[25] *New Oxford Dictionary of English*, first edn, 1998.
[26] [2001] 1 PLR 104, per Latham L.J. at p. 106E (para. 8).

half years, so as to be, in effect, overgrown, [it] is no longer to be considered a garden unless there is some evidence which suggests that there is an intention in relation to the use of that land which could enable the court to conclude that the historical categorisation of it as a garden could properly be said to continue".[27]

In other words, land that was an orchard or garden may, if it has been allowed to grow wild, lose that status. That contrasts with the position in planning law, whereby vacant land and buildings are generally categorised according to their most recent use. In addition, a use of land may only be said to have been abandoned (other than by change to a wholly new use) if there is evidence of that abandonment by reference to the physical condition of the land, the length of time it has been disused, and the owner's intentions.[28]

This incidentally means that a developer purchasing a large garden with the intention of eventually carrying out some form of development on it would be well advised to carry out any necessary tree-felling promptly, while the land may still properly be described as a garden. If the land is allowed to degenerate into overgrown scrub, the exemption will no longer apply, so that a felling licence would be required.

A churchyard is not defined in the 1967 Act. The Faculty Jurisdiction Rules 2000 define a churchyard solely by the inclusion of a consecrated burial ground not adjacent to a church,[29] but the requirement as to consecration would not seem to be relevant in the present context. It must therefore remain an open question whether a felling licence would be required, other things being equal, for the felling of trees in a municipal cemetery.

"Public open space" is defined in the Act[30] to mean:

- land laid out as a public garden;
- land used for the purposes of public recreation other than:
  - metropolitan commons, and other land subject to public rights of air and exercise under section 193 of the Law of Property Act 1925;
  - land subject to access agreements under Part V of the National Parks and Access to the Countryside Act 1949; and
  - land subject to a right to roam under Part I of the Countryside and Rights of Way Act 2000; and
- land being as a disused burial ground.[31]

It also excludes country parks provided under section 7 of the Countryside Act 1968, and parks within the Lee Valley Regional Park.[32]

The net result of these various provisions is, broadly, to exclude from the need for a felling licence the felling of any trees on small areas of open space, which are more appropriately protected by the imposition of tree preservation orders where justified in particular cases.

---

[27] [2001] 1 PLR 104, per Latham L.J. at p. 106F (para. 10).
[28] *Hughes v Secretary of State* [2000] 1 PLR 76, CA, at p. 77H.
[29] S.I. 2000 No. 2047, r. 2(1).
[30] Despite the suggestion in *Portland*, noted above, that there was no such definition.
[31] FA 1967, s. 9(6), amended by Countryside and Rights of Way Act 2000, Sched. 4.
[32] Countryside Act 1968, s. 24(4).

14.2.4 *Felling to prevent a danger*

A felling licence is not required for any felling which is "for the prevention of danger".[33] The wording of this exemption is slightly different to that of the corresponding exemption from the requirement for consent under a tree preservation order, discussed in **Chapter 17**,[34] since that applies only where the tree itself "has become dangerous". However, the distinction may be minimal in practice since where the condition, location or size of a tree is such that its felling is required for the prevention of danger, it would usually, if not always, be reasonable to categorise the tree as dangerous.

The subject of hazardous trees in general has already been explored in full.[35] In short, a tree may be dangerous, by virtue of both its condition and its location, such that the owner would be liable in negligence or under the Occupier's Liability Acts if it were to fall and cause harm to persons, animals or property. In such circumstances, it would be reasonable for it to be felled without a licence, in reliance on this exemption. But it would probably not be possible to rely on the exemption to justify felling a tree merely because its owner fears that it might fall over. In addition, a danger might arise not because of the condition of the tree but by virtue of its size and location – so that, for example, a tree close to a highway might obstruct the visibility of a warning sign, and thus endanger motorists or pedestrians.

It is thus necessary to produce strong evidence as to the existence of an appreciable or practical danger,[36] rather than indication of mere anxiety, however genuinely felt. For further details, see **5.8.1**. It is also clear that, in the event of a query as to whether a tree was justifiably felled in reliance on this exemption, the burden is on the person carrying out the felling to prove that the tree was dangerous, rather than on the Forestry Commission to prove that it was not. This emerges from the decision of the Court of Appeal in *R v Alath Construction Ltd*,[37] in relation to the corresponding exemption under the tree preservation order legislation, considered in more detail at **17.3**. The same approach would seem to apply equally in relation to this exemption from the need for a felling licence.[38]

14.2.5 *Felling to prevent or abate a nuisance*

A felling licence is not required for any felling which is "for the prevention or abatement of a nuisance".[39]

The meaning of the word "nuisance" and the phrase "abatement of a nuisance", in the context of trees, has already been considered at length,[40] but it may be summarised as follows:

- any encroachment by roots or branches onto neighbouring land is a nuisance;

---

[33] FA 1967, s. 9(4)(a).
[34] See **17.5**.
[35] See **Chapter 5**.
[36] *Wandsworth Board of Works v United Telephone Company* (1884) 13 Q.B.D. 904.
[37] [1990] 1 W.L.R. 1255, CA.
[38] The principle of *R v Alath* was applied to prosecutions under the FA 1967 in one reported Crown Court decision, *Forestry Commission v Grace* [1992] 1 EGLR 28.
[39] FA 1967, s. 9(4)(a).
[40] See **Chapter 3**, and in particular **3.3.4** and **3.6**.

- if damage has been caused, an action may be brought for the recovery of damages;

- if future damage is imminent, an action may be brought for an injunction; and

- in any other case, the owner of the neighbouring land may rely on the self-help remedy of abatement – that is, he or she may cut back the roots or branches to the boundary.

The phrase "the abatement of a nuisance" thus had a clear meaning stretching back at least half a century before its appearance in the Town and Country Planning Act 1947,[40a] in the context of tree preservation orders, and in the Forestry Act 1951,[40b] in the context of felling licences. It referred then, and still refers, to the self-help remedy available to anyone who owns or occupies land over or under which grows a branch or a root of a tree that is growing on a tree on neighbouring land.

The remedy of abatement will thus usually take the form of lopping a tree – that is, severing all or (more often) part of a branch from the remainder of the tree – or removing some of the roots from the remainder. Such works may need consent under a tree preservation order, where one exists; and the meaning of the phrase "prevention or abatement of a nuisance" is thus an important issue in that context, and is accordingly considered fully in **Chapter 17**. The conclusion tentatively reached there is that the exemption applies where there is any encroachment, regardless of whether that encroachment is actually causing harm.[41] If the same approach were to be applied in the present context, the result would be that lopping a tree or severing its roots (which in principle only requires a felling licence where they lead to the loss of the tree[42]) will not require a licence where the branches or roots in question are encroaching from other land so as to constitute a nuisance.

It may also occasionally occur that to remove only the parts of a tree crossing the boundary would lead to the remaining portion of the tree being dangerous, in which case the only way to abate the nuisance would be for the owner of the land onto which the tree is encroaching to fell the whole tree – subject to the owner's consent in relation to that part of the tree which is not encroaching. The same work if carried out by the tree owner rather than by the neighbour would probably be classified as preventing a nuisance.[43] In those situations, the exemption from the need for a felling licence would apply.

14.2.6 Felling authorised under other procedures

A felling licence is not required for felling which is in compliance with any obligation imposed by or under an Act of Parliament.[44] This means that the requirements of any public or private Act, and of any secondary legislation, would override the need for a felling licence. This exemption is in identical terms

---

[40a] TCPA 1947, s. 28(5).
[40b] FA 1951, s. 2(2)(d).
[41] See, in particular, **17.5**.
[42] See **14.2.1**.
[43] See **17.5.8**.
[44] FA 1967, s. 9(4)(b).

to that applying in relation to tree preservation orders, considered in **Chapter 17**.[45]

Nor is a felling licence required for "felling which is immediately required for the purpose of carrying out development authorised by planning permission granted or deemed to be granted under the Town and Country Planning Act 1990".[46] This obviously includes felling required to carry out development authorised by a permission granted in response to an application submitted to a local planning authority and determined by that authority or by the Secretary of State. However, the wording of the exemption is slightly different to that used in relation to the tree preservation order legislation, in that it does not specify "planning permission granted *on an application*".[47] The omission of the italicised words means that the exemption extends also to felling required to carry out development authorised by permission granted under the Act itself, such as those granted by a development order, an enterprise zone scheme or a simplified planning zone scheme. This means that where, for example, an agricultural or forestry building is to be erected in reliance upon permitted development rights under the TCP General Permitted Development Order, the removal of any trees currently growing on the site to be occupied by the building would not require a felling licence.

The reference to planning permission "deemed to be granted" under the 1990 Act refers to the authorisation of the carrying out of development by departments of central Government, the retention of development where steps are taken in response to an enforcement notice, and the display of advertisements complying with the Control of Advertisements Regulations.[48] Only the first of these is likely to be relevant in the present context.

Note, however, that the exemption only applies to felling which is "immediately" required for the carrying out of the relevant development. That is, it does not authorise felling of trees near to, but not actually on, the site of a new building; nor does it allow felling of trees which are on the site of a building which has been authorised only by an outline planning permission subject to the approval of reserved matters.

14.2.7 Felling by statutory undertakers and other public bodies

In relation to land owned by a statutory undertaker, a licence is not required for felling trees which are impeding the construction of any works (presumably buildings or plant) needed for the purposes of the undertaker, or which interfere with the maintenance or operation of such works.[49] For these purposes, "statutory undertakers" are defined as:

". . . persons authorised by any enactment to carry on any railway, light railway, tramway, road transport, water transport, canal, inland navigation, dock, harbour, [pier] or

---

[45] See **17.4**.
[46] FA 1967, s. 9(4)(d).
[47] The reference to an application occurs in para. (3)(c) of Schedule 2 to the 1969 Model Order: see **17.8.1**.
[48] Under TCPA 1990, ss. 90, 173 and 222 respectively.
[49] Forestry (Exception from Restriction of Felling) Regulations 1979 (S.I. 1979 No. 792), reg. 4(2).

lighthouse undertaking, or any undertaking for the supply of hydraulic power or water, and public gas transporters within the meaning of Part I of the Gas Act 1986".[50]

It should be noted that this element of the exemption thus applies only to trees growing actually on the undertaker's own land – it does not extend to the felling of trees which hinder the functions of the undertaker on other land.

The most notable example of such a hindrance is where trees are in conflict with electricity cables or other equipment, either above or below ground. The Electricity Act 1989 accordingly provides a procedure, described in **Chapter 7**, to enable an electricity operator (that is, the holder of a licence under the 1989 Act) to take appropriate action to remove the problem[51]; and the 1967 Act provides that any felling involved will not require a licence. [52] It should be noted that the provisions of the 1989 Act themselves afford at least some degree of protection for trees in such circumstances.

Nor is a felling licence required where the Secretary of State certifies that a tree has to be removed because it is obstructing aircraft approaching or departing from an aerodrome, or hindering the safe and efficient use of air navigational equipment.[53] Certification may be by either the Secretary of State for Defence (presumably in the case of military airfields) or the Secretary of State for Trade and Industry (in other cases). This appears to be entirely independent of any order made under the Civil Aviation Act 1982, or any direction made under any such order.[54]

Finally, a licence is not required for the felling of a tree by (or at the request of) the Environment Agency or an internal drainage board, where the tree is interfering with any of the exercise of any functions of the Agency or board.[55]

14.2.8 Felling of trees subject to disease

A felling licence is not needed to fell an elm tree which is affected by the disease caused by the fungus *Ceratocystis ulmi* (commonly known as Dutch elm disease) to such an extent that the greater part of the crown of the tree is dead.[56]

14.2.9 Felling in accordance with a plan agreed with the Commission

There are a number of other mechanisms, considered already, whereby the Forestry Commission approves the carrying out of felling and restocking operations (usually in the context of approving an application for grant aid[57]). Therefore, in the past there have been exceptions from the general requirement for a felling licence, to ensure that the Commission does not in effect have to go through the approval process twice.

---

[50] Forestry (Exception from Restriction of Felling) Regulations 1979 (S.I. 1979 No. 792), reg. 3, amended by S.I. 1986 No. 1356, S.I. 1990 No. 526, S.I. 1996 No. 252. In the printed text, the word "power" appears instead of "pier".
[51] Electricity Act 1989, Sched. 4, para. 9; see **7.2.1**.
[52] FA 1967, s. 9(4)(c), (6).
[53] Forestry (Exception from Restriction of Felling) Regulations 1979 (S.I. 1979 No. 792), regulation 4(1).
[54] Civil Aviation Act 1982, s. 46, Sched. 9; see **7.3.2**.
[55] Forestry (Exception from Restriction of Felling) Regulations 1979 (S.I. 1979 No. 792), regulation 4(3).
[56] Forestry (Exception from Restriction of Felling) Regulations 1979 (S.I. 1979 No. 792), regulation 4(4).
[57] See **12.7**.

Since 1958, a felling licence has thus not been required for the felling of trees in dedicated woodlands – that is, woodlands subject to a forestry dedication covenant.[58] However, this exception, now in the 1979 Regulations,[59] is limited. It has already been noted that a covenant will have been linked to a plan of operations agreed with the Forestry Commission, and will contain positive obligations on the part of the owner which will be unenforceable against a successor in title to the original covenantor. Accordingly, a licence is not required where:

- the land is still owned by that original covenantor, or where the positive obligations are otherwise binding on the current owner of the land; and

- proposed felling is in line with the agreed plan of operations.

In other circumstances, a licence will be required – but will normally be granted (see below[60]).

Similarly, a licence was not required from 1981 for the felling of trees in accordance with a plan of operations approved by the Commission as part of an agreement with a landowner under the Forestry Grant Scheme where the felling was carried out by a person who was bound by the terms of that agreement. That arrangement was extended in 1985 to approved felling under the Broadleaved Woodland Grant Scheme and, in 1988, to approved felling under the Woodland Grant Scheme (WGS).[61]

Plans approved under these various schemes almost invariably required the land to be restocked on completion of the felling. However, where the land was sold before the restocking had taken had place, the requirement was effectively unenforceable; and a small number of unscrupulous owners were taking advantage of this loophole to avoid the expense of having to replant. The exemption was accordingly ended with effect from April 1, 1998, in respect of felling in accordance with agreements entered into after that date.[62] It does still apply, however, in relation to felling carried out in accordance with agreements under the Woodland Grant Scheme (but not any of the other schemes) entered into before that date.[63]

In practice, where an application is made for a grant under the Woodland Grant Scheme, there is no need to make a separate application for a felling licence. The approved Grant Scheme contract will describe the restocking and maintenance required, and will be accompanied by a felling licence authorising any felling involved.

---

[58] See **12.6**.

[59] Forestry (Exception from Restriction of Felling) Regulations 1979 (S.I. 1979 No. 792), reg. 4(5).

[60] See **14.3.2**.

[61] Forestry (Exception from Restriction of Felling) Regulations 1979 (S.I. 1979 No. 792), regulation 4(6), inserted by S.I. 1981 No. 1476, and substituted by S.I. 1985 No. 1572 and in turn by S.I. 1988 No. 970.

[62] Forestry (Exceptions from Restrictions of Felling) (Amendment) Regulations 1998 (S.I. 1998 No. 603), regs. 2,4.

[63] 1998 Regulations, reg. 3.

14.3 Applications for felling licences

14.3.1 Submission of applications to Forestry Commission

Where a felling licence is needed, it should be sought from the Forestry Commission by the owner of the land on which the trees are growing.

Where there is more than one owner (for example, in the case of land subject to a lease or a settlement), or where the right to fell timber is vested in someone other than the owner of the land on which it is standing, the application should be made by whoever has such an estate or interest in the land as entitles him or her to carry out the work without any further consent from anyone else.[64] Where someone other than such a person (for example, a forestry contractor) makes an application for a licence, it must be as agent for the owner, whose name and other details must be supplied, as any licence issued will be in the name of the owner.

This may be crucial, in that the Act provides that it is a criminal offence for "anyone" to fell a tree without a felling licence. The Divisional Court in *Forestry Commission v Frost and Thompson*[65] considered that the word "anyone" meant precisely that – it was not restricted to those (owners) who could have obtained a felling licence. It follows that a person who has a licence to occupy land, or a forestry contractor, is liable to prosecution if he or she carries out felling without a felling licence having been issued to the freehold or leasehold owner of the land in question.

An application may not be made by a prospective owner of land.

The application must be made in the manner prescribed by regulations under the Act. The current regulations are the Forestry (Felling of Trees) Regulations 1979,[66] which were amended in 1987 so as to prescribe a form to be used for licence applications.[67] More recently, however, the 1979 Regulations were amended again, to avoid the need for a specific form to be used. Regulation 4 now requires that an application is to be in writing or in electronic form, and must include the information specified in Schedule 2 and an Ordnance Survey map.[68]

Unsurprisingly, the information to be supplied includes details of the applicant, the trees to be felled, the operations proposed, any restocking envisaged, and any tree preservation orders and conservation areas applicable.[69] Oddly, the new provisions do not require (as did the old prescribed form) details of the proposed treatment of the land after felling, or of any other designation such as a site of special scientific interest, although it would be wise to give details of any such designation which may be applicable. Once complete, the application is to be sent to the local Forestry Commission office.

The trees which form the subject of the application should be marked in some appropriate way – either each tree to be felled, or those on the boundary of a large area to be felled. But permanent marking (for example, by blaze) should be avoided where the trees are of high amenity value or are a habitat for wildlife.

---

[64] FA 1967, s. 10(1); see **2.4** as to land held under a trust, and **2.5** as to land held under a lease or licence.
[65] [1989] E.G.C.S. 96, [1990] 154 J.P. 14.
[66] S.I. 1979 No. 791.
[67] Regulations 1979, amended by S.I. 1987 No. 632.
[68] Regulations 1979, reg. 4, substituted by S.I. 2002 No. 226, reg. 2(4).
[69] Regulations 1979, Sched. 2, substituted by S.I. 2002 no. 226, reg. 2(5).

As already noted,[70] there is no need to submit an application for a felling licence where felling forms part of an application under the Woodland Grant Scheme.

These provisions are also the subject of a Forestry Commission booklet entitled *Tree Felling: Getting Permission*,[71] already mentioned; also relevant is the Commission's pamphlet *Tree Felling: Charter Standard Statement for Felling Licensing*.

14.3.2 Determination of applications

On receipt of an application for a felling licence, the Forestry Commission will acknowledge the application – it aims to do so within three working days. It will return promptly any application which it considers cannot be dealt with – together with a statement as to why (for example, because the application contains insufficient information to enable it to be sure precisely what is envisaged). In any other case, the Commission will then contact the applicant within three weeks to arrange a site visit if one is considered necessary, and carry out any such visit within six weeks.

Once an officer of the Commission has visited the site, and discussed with the applicant any changes felt to be necessary, the application will be placed on the Public Register of New Planting and Felling, except where the application is only for thinning, with no other felling. The Register is available for inspection at Forestry Commission offices, and on the web[72]; and details of an application will remain there for four weeks. The Commission will also at this stage carry out any necessary consultation with the local authority and other organisations as appropriate, to ensure that it is aware of land use and other relevant environmental issues. Larger applications, which need an environmental statement, will be notified to the national countryside bodies anyway.[73]

If the Commission is considering attaching conditions to a licence, it must discuss them with the applicant.[74] It will also discuss whether the applicant is willing to make any amendment to the proposal, if it considers that a licence would otherwise have to be refused. Such discussions are likely to take place at the site visit.

The Commission is under a statutory duty to grant an unconditional licence, except where it appears to be expedient either to impose conditions on a licence or to refuse an application altogether in the interests of any of the following:

- good forestry;

- agriculture;

- the amenities of the district; or

- the establishment and maintenance of adequate reserves of growing timber.[75]

---

[70] See **14.2.9**.
[71] November 2000; available from Forestry Commission offices.
[72] www.forestry.gov.uk.
[73] See **13.4.3**.
[74] FA 1967, s. 12(1).
[75] FA 1967, s. 10(2).

If a proposal is to clear fell an area and not restock with trees, the Commission is required to consider the application for a felling licence, but will be guided by the Government's general policy against the loss of woodland. In particular, it normally does not agree to land clearance for agricultural use, although it will consult the relevant Government agriculture department to assess the contribution that the extra land would make to the economy of an existing land holding.[76] As for the amenities of the district, these are likely to include landscape, nature conservation, recreation opportunities and archaeology.

Section 14 of the Act provides that, where the proposed felling is in accordance with a plan of operations or other working plan approved by the Commission (either under a forestry dedication covenant[77] or otherwise) a licence is generally not to be refused. The only exception is where the Minister certifies that, by reason of an act of God or other emergency which has arisen since the approval of the plan, the grant of a licence would be detrimental to the national interest – which is unlikely to occur often.[78] However, this provision is somewhat academic, as explained by the Divisional Court in *Forestry Commission v Frost and Thompson*:

"Strictly, the section seems to me to require a formal application for a licence which cannot be refused, save in exceptional circumstances. It seems that the Forestry Commissioners accept that if they approve the variation of a working plan, so as to provide for the felling of trees, that in effect is the grant of a licence for the felling of trees in accordance with the amended working plan. That is no doubt a sensible and practical approach."[79]

14.3.3 The UK Forestry Standard

There is no statutory provision as to the matters to be taken into account by the Forestry Commission when deciding whether or not to grant a felling licence in any particular case.

In practice, such decisions are based on the principles set out in the Forestry Commission publication *The UK Forestry Standard: the Government's Approach to Sustainable Forestry*.[80] The *Standard* contains, as well as useful general guidance, a set of Standard Notes, the purpose of which is described as follows:

"The Standard Notes are based on the principle that each situation is unique and demands individual attention in order to develop appropriate plans and working practices. Provided forestry is practised within the framework of the standard and its supporting publications, owners are encouraged to adopt the methods most appropriate to their objectives.

"The Standard Notes are a reference for identifying acceptable options for management. They are a synthesis of the most important guidance contained within the Guidelines and other publications. The Keyword Index (Appendix 5) links the practice described in the Standard Notes to these supporting publications. New or revised guidance published after this edition of the Standard must be given precedence."[81]

---

[76] *Tree Felling: Getting Permission*, November 2000, pp. 4,5. The Government departments responsible for agriculture are listed at **11.2.1**.

[77] As to forestry dedication covenants (agreements in Scotland), see **12.6**.

[78] FA 1967, s. 14(2).

[79] *Forestry Commission v Frost and Thompson* [1990] 154 JP 14, per Glidewell L.J. at p. 17B.

[80] Published in January 1998 (complete with foreword by and picture of the Prime Minister) by the Forestry Commission and the Department of Agriculture Northern Ireland; available from either, at £5.00.

[81] *UK Forestry Standard*, p. 25.

The Notes in the first edition of the *Standard* are as follows:

SN1   *General Forestry Practice*

SN2   *Creating New Woodland*

SN3   *Creating 'New Native Woodland'*

SN4   *Felling and Restocking Planted Woodland*

SN5   *Managing Semi-Natural Woodland*

SN6   *Planting and Managing Small Woods*

No new editions of any of the notes are currently planned.

In addition, as already noted, the Commission has publicly stated that amenity is the principal factor taken into account when considering applications.[81a] The meaning of "amenity" is considered later.[82]

14.3.4 Grant or refusal of licence

It has already been noted that the Commission is under a duty to grant an unconditional licence, unless there are good reasons to indicate otherwise.[82a] In practice, the great majority of applications are granted but subject to conditions. The Act provides that conditions may, in particular, be imposed to secure:

"(a)   the restocking of stocking with trees of the land on which the felling is to take place, or of such other land as may be agree between the Commissioners and the applicant; and

  (b)   the maintenance of those trees in accordance with the rules and practice of good forestry for a period not exceeding ten years".[83]

Thus, conditions may not be imposed as to the manner in which the felling is carried out, or to secure amenity. And conditions may not be imposed on a felling licence relating to land subject to a dedication covenant, provided that the felling is in accordance with a plan of operations or other working plan approved by the Commission that is in force under the covenant.[83a] Surprisingly, where the Commission does impose conditions when granting a licence, it is not required to give reasons for them – although it would be good practice for it to do so. It is, in some cases, possible to appeal against conditions.[84]

In practice, most licences are issued subject to a condition relating to restocking, usually discussed with the applicant; and to assist in drafting this, the material to be submitted with an application include details of any proposal for restocking each area where felling is to take place.[85] It may well be sensible to show such proposals on a map of suitable scale, and to describe what is proposed by a more extensive schedule, or even a full report. As to the enforcement of

---

[81a] See **14.1**.
[82]   See **15.6.2**.
[82a] See **14.3.2**.
[83]   FA 1967, s. 12(1).
[83a] FA 1967, s. 12(2), amended by Trees Act 1970, s. 2.
[84]   FA 1967, s. 16; see **14.5.4**.
[85]   Forestry (Felling of Trees) Regulations (S.I. 1979 No. 791), Sched. 2, substituted by S.I. 2002 No. 226, reg. 2(5).

restocking conditions, this is considered in detail below.[86]

A felling licence, once granted, continues in force for such period (of at least a year) as may be specified in it – there is no maximum period imposed by law. As a matter of practice, a licence should allow a reasonable period for completing the programme of work envisaged; and this will usually not exceed five years.

Where a licence is refused, written notice of the decision, together with reasons for it, is to be given to the applicant.[87] Compensation or other financial assistance may then be available,[88] and it may be possible to appeal.[89]

The Commission is required to make a decision on a felling licence application within three months of receiving it, unless the applicant agrees to a longer period; or at least if it makes no decision at all within that period, the applicant may proceed as if the application had been refused.[90] In practice, it aims to issue a decision in most cases within ten weeks – although it will take longer where a case raises sensitive or complex issues. Where the Commission is willing to grant a licence subject to conditions, but considers that the applicant will not be in a position to comply with them (for example, because the applicant owns the timber but not the land), it may postpone dealing with the application until the person who is in a position to comply with the conditions is a party to it.[91] In such a case, the three-month period for determining the application starts only when that person is joined.

Where an application raises serious objections, which cannot be resolved by informal negotiation, the Commission will seek the advice of the Regional Advisory Committee.[92] The Committee will make its advice public, by issuing a press release; and the Commission is required to consider such advice in reaching its decision.[93] If the Commission decides to refuse an application, it will immediately inform the applicant.[94] If, on the other hand, the Commission disagrees with the views of a consultee, and wishes to grant a licence, it will normally first consult the Minister.

Once a decision has been reached, the Commission may identify on site the relevant trees – either those for which a licence has been granted or those for which it has been refused.[95]

There is no provision for a licence to be granted retrospectively; it follows that, if felling is carried out before a licence has actually been issued, the person responsible is (at least in theory) liable to prosecution even if one is indeed issued subsequently.

14.3.5 Premature applications

It may happen that the Forestry Commission considers that an application for a felling licence is premature – that is, felling will, in principle, be acceptable, but not yet. In such a case, it will refuse to grant a licence in response to the

---

[86] See **14.6**.
[87] FA 1967, s. 10(6).
[88] FA 1967, s. 10(4); see **14.5.1**.
[89] FA 1967, s. 16; see **14.5.4**.
[90] FA 1967, s. 13(1).
[91] FA 1967, s. 13(2).
[92] See **11.3.2**.
[93] FA 1967, s. 37(3).
[94] See **14.5** for options open to the applicant following an adverse decision.
[95] FA 1967, s. 28.

application; but it may at any time after that decision, if it thinks fit, notify the owner of the trees that it now considers that a licence should be issued, either unconditionally or subject to specified conditions.

The owner then still has to apply for the licence, but it must be granted – subject to the joinder of any person whose co-operation is necessary to ensure compliance with the conditions, and to any constraints arising from a tree preservation order.[96]

14.4 Felling of protected trees

14.4.1 Trees subject to tree preservation orders

Where a proposal relates to the felling of a number of trees which are subject to a tree preservation order, it may, in principle, require both a felling licence and consent under the order. There is therefore a complex procedure (contained in section 15 of the Forestry Act 1967) which applies to ensure that such a proposal is considered both by the Forestry Commission and by the relevant local planning authority.

In the first instance, an application should be submitted to the Commission, with the same details as are required in other cases; those include a statement as to whether any of the trees concerned are subject to a tree preservation order.[97] When there was a standard application form for felling licences, it sensibly suggested that where only some of the trees concerned were subject to an order, two separate applications should be made – one for those which are protected and one for the remainder. The former could then be processed by the special procedure described below, and the latter could be considered like any other felling licence application. That would seem still to be good advice.

The Forestry Commission, on receipt of an application for a licence which refers to protected trees, has three options:

- it may decide in principle that it is not willing to grant a licence;

- it may decide in principle that it is willing to grant a licence; or

- it may decide not to form a view one way or the other as to the felling licence application, but instead to allow the matter to be determined by the local planning authority.

Where it is in principle not willing to grant a licence, it can simply refuse the application without further ado, and without involving the local planning authority. In that situation, the question of consent under the tree preservation order does not arise, since in the absence of a licence any felling would be unlawful anyway.

In either of the other situations, the procedure is slightly more complex.

---

[96] FA 1967, s. 10(5).
[97] Forestry (Felling of Trees) Regulations (S.I. 1979 No. 791), Sched. 2, substituted by S.I. 2002 No. 226, reg. 2(5); see **14.3.1**.

14.4.2 Referral to the planning authority for comment

Where the Forestry Commission decides that it is in principle willing to grant a felling licence for the felling of trees which are subject to a tree preservation order, it must not do so without first notifying the planning authority that made the order (or its successor authority).[98]

That authority then has one month to respond.[99] If it fails to make any objection within one month of being notified, the Commission can simply proceed to grant the licence in the usual way, subject to conditions where appropriate. The trees may then, in due course, be felled without further ado, and no separate consent under the tree preservation order will be required.[1]

If, on the other hand, the authority does object to the granting of a licence, presumably because it wishes to prevent the felling of the trees, it should object to the Commission, which will then refer the matter to the Secretary of State. The Secretary of State will then deal with it as if it had been an application for consent under the tree preservation order which had been called in for his or her own decision.[2] Tree preservation orders made before 1999 will contain provisions as to the calling in of applications for consent (based on those relating to the calling in of planning applications, although orders made under the 1999 Regulations will not.[3] However, where the relevant order does not itself contain such provisions, it is to be assumed for these purposes that it does – save that the Secretary of State is entitled to modify the call-in provisions as appropriate.[4]

If the Secretary of State refuses consent for the felling, that is an end to the matter. However, if he or she grants consent, that will be sufficient to authorise the felling, so that a licence will not be required.[5]

Where an authority wishes to prevent the felling of only some of the trees in a licence application, it can, of course, make representations to the Forestry Commission to that effect. The Commission may then invite the owner to submit a further application for a licence just in respect of those trees, so that it can grant a licence in respect of the remainder with no objections from the authority. The second (opposed) licence application may then be referred to the Secretary of State for determination.

The "Secretary of State" in this context refers (in relation to England) to ODPM[6] and not to DEFRA.[7]

14.4.3 Referral to the planning authority for its decision

The third possibility is that the Commission may decline to form a view one way or the other as to the felling licence application, but simply leave it to the planning authority to decide.

---

[98] FA 1967, s. 15(1)(a).
[99] Regulations 1979, reg. 7.
[1] FA 1967, s. 15(6).
[2] FA 1967, Sched. 3, para. 2; see **18.3.2**.
[3] As to pre-1999 orders, see note 26 to **18.3.2**; as to post-1999 orders, 1999 Model Order does not apply s. 77 of the TCPA 1990.
[4] FA 1967, Sched. 3, para. 2(b).
[5] FA 1967, s. 15(2).
[6] The Office of the Deputy Prime Minister – the (current) successor to the Department of the Environment, responsible for the planning system. See **16.2.8**.
[7] FA 1967, s. 15(8), Sched. 3, para. 4; S.I. 1970 No. 1681.

This might have occurred where, for example, a landowner proposed to fell four large specimen trees growing on land in an urban area which was not a garden, such that (because of the volume of timber to be felled) a felling licence would have been, albeit perhaps only just, required. Since the only objection to such a proposal would have been on amenity grounds, it used to be considered more appropriate for the matter to be determined by the planning authority rather than by the Forestry Commission.

In this type of situation, the authority would simply deal with the application as if it had been made under a tree preservation order, and would grant or refuse consent as it saw fit, subject to a right of appeal to the Secretary of State.[8]

Although the legislation still exists to allow this procedure to operate, it has, in practice, not been used since August 1999, as the Government considered that it was more appropriate to have a single procedure for applications involving both felling licences and tree preservation orders. The procedure now, therefore, is that the Forestry Commission always makes the decision, albeit subject to consultation with the planning authority.

However, it may be noted that, once an application for a felling licence has been referred to the planning authority for its decision, no felling licence will be required for any felling of the trees in question for as long as the tree preservation order remains in force.[9]

14.4.4 Trees in conservation areas

Where an application for a felling licence relates to the felling of trees that are within a conservation area, there is no formal requirement for the Forestry Commission to notify the local planning authority. And once a licence has been granted, there is no requirement for the person carrying out the works to notify the authority either.[10] In practice, however, where the Commission is aware that an application for a licence relates to a conservation area, it will consult the authority on a non-statutory basis – and an authority would in theory be able to impose a tree preservation order on some or all of the trees concerned, so as to give it a right to require the Secretary of State to determine the application.

In order to enable such consultation to take place, the details required with a felling licence application include a statement as to whether any of the trees concerned are in a conservation area. As with trees subject to a preservation order, where only some of the trees affected by a felling proposal are within a conservation area, it is probably sensible for two separate applications to be made, one for those which are protected and one for the remainder.

14.5 Action following adverse decision

14.5.1 Compensation

Where a felling licence is refused, this will generally give rise to entitlement to compensation under section 11.[11] The measure of the compensation is:

---

[8] FA 1967, s. 15(1)(b),(3)(a), Sched. 3, para. 3; as to the procedure for consent under a tree preservation order, see **18.3**, **18.5**.
[9] FA 1967, s. 15(3)(b).
[10] TCP (Trees) Regulations 1999, reg. 10(1)(b).
[11] FA 1967, s. 10(4)(a).

". . . any depreciation in the value of the trees which is attributable to deterioration in the quality of the timber comprised therein in consequence of the refusal of a felling licence for them".[12]

The amount payable is thus the difference between the value of the trees at the date of the claim and their value at the date of the refusal (based on prices current at the date of the claim). If, however, the trees have been neglected following the refusal of a licence, any depreciation due to that neglect is to be ignored – that is, it is to be assumed that they had been properly managed.[13]

Suppose, for example, that in 1994 a licence was refused for the felling of some trees, which were valued as timber (on the basis of prices then current) at £100,000. A claim for compensation is submitted some eight years later, by which time prices for good quality timber generally have risen by 25 per cent. Following the refusal of the licence, the trees in question were in fact neglected, so that their value as timber fell by the date of the claim to £80,000; but even if they had been properly managed, their value would only have risen slightly, to £105,000. The compensation would be calculated as follows:

Value of woodlands in 1994 (at prices current then)		£100,000
Value of woodlands in 1994 (at prices current in 2002)	x 1.25	£125,000
Deduct Value of woodlands in 2002 (at prices current in 2002), ignoring neglect		105,000
Compensation payable		£20,000

If, following the initial refusal of a licence, the Commission gives a notice indicating that it is willing to grant a licence for the trees to be felled, no account is to be taken of any further deterioration in the quality of the timber (and consequent depreciation in the value of the trees) following the date of the notice.[14] And if a subsequent application for a felling licence is made, but is referred either to the Secretary of State or to the local planning authority because the trees are now subject to a tree preservation order, no account is to be taken of any deterioration following the date of the referral.[15]

A claim for compensation may normally be made in respect of any deterioration that takes place after an application for a felling licence has been refused, save that no claim may be made in respect of any deterioration that took place more than ten years before the date of the claim. Indeed, if the quality of the timber continues to deteriorate following one such claim, a further claim may be made. If a felling licence is subsequently granted (presumably in response to a fresh application), and the trees are felled in accordance with that licence, a claim may be made in respect of any deterioration occurring between the original refusal and the subsequent grant. Such a claim must be submitted within one year from the date of the felling.[16]

[12] FA 1967, s. 11(1).
[13] FA 1967, s. 11(4)
[14] FA 1967, s. 11(5).
[15] FA 1967, s. 15(4).
[16] FA 1967, s. 11(3).

Any claim is to be made to the local conservancy of the Forestry Commission on the form prescribed in the Regulations, generally by the owner of the trees (note, not the owner of the land where the two are distinct).[17] Special rules apply where the interest of that owner is subject to a mortgage, or where the trees are comprised within a settlement and their owner is a tenant for life impeachable for waste[18] – essentially, in either case, the compensation is to be treated as if it were arising from the sale of the trees.[19]

Any dispute as to compensation is to be resolved by the Lands Tribunal.[20]

14.5.2 Loan from the Commission

As an alternative to a claim for compensation, the Forestry Commission may make a loan to anyone with an interest in the land on which the trees are growing – provided that it is satisfied that the land will be properly managed.[21] Such a loan is to be approved by the Treasury.

14.5.3 Works in accordance with approved plan

Neither compensation nor loan is available where a decision by the Forestry Commission to refuse a licence relates to felling in accordance with a plan that it has earlier approved.[22] Instead, following such a decision, the applicant may serve on the Commission within three months a notice requiring it to purchase all or some of the trees.[23] Where a notice to purchase is served, the Commission is deemed to have contracted with the applicant to buy the trees at such price as may be determined by agreement or, in default, by the Lands Tribunal.[24]

14.5.4 Appeal against decisions of the Forestry Commission

Where the Forestry Commission decides to refuse a licence, or to impose conditions on one, there is not an automatic right to appeal. However, an applicant who is unhappy about the decision may contact the Minister,[24a] who may ask the Commission to reconsider its decision. Further, where a licence is refused, and after a period of three years is refused again or only granted subject to conditions, it is possible to make a formal appeal to the Minister against the subsequent decision, under section 16 of the 1967 Act. Where such an appeal has been made, it is not possible to make another one until at least a further three years have elapsed.[25]

The appeal is to be within three months of the decision of the Commission or, where no decision has been made, within three months of the expiry of the period

---

[17] FA 1967, ss. 10(4)(a), 11(2); S.I. 1979 No. 791, reg. 5; Sched. 1, Form 1 (England or Wales), Form 2 (Scotland).
[18] See **2.5.4**.
[19] FA 1967, s. 29.
[20] FA 1967, s. 11(6), 31.
[21] FA 1967, s. 10(4)(b).
[22] FA 1967, s. 14(4)(a), (5). This will not occur often; see **14.3.4**.
[23] FA 1967, s. 14(3); S.I. 1979 No. 791, regulation 6; for the form of notice, see Sched. 1, Form 3.
[24] FA 1967, ss. 14(4)(b), 31.
[24a] That is, in practice, the Department for the Environment, Food and Rural Affairs (DEFRA), the National Assembly of Wales Agriculture Department (NAWAD) or the Rural Affairs Department of the Scottish Executive (SERAD): see **11.2.1**.
[25] FA 1967, s. 16(1), (4).

within which it should have made a decision (usually three months from the date of the application, unless a longer period has been agreed.)[26] The relevant forms are in the regulations.[27]

On receipt of such an appeal, the Minister is to refer the matter to a special reference committee.[28] The committee is to consist of a chairman and two other members selected from a panel of persons appointed for the conservancy following consultation with the regional advisory committee[29] and appropriate specialist bodies. No member of the committee is to be either a Forestry Commissioner or an employee of the Commission. The committee will then give the appellant an opportunity to make representations at an oral hearing, and will also consider any representations made by the Commission; and it will if it wishes to, or is requested to do so by the appellant, inspect the trees in question.[30]

The committee will then make a report to the Minister, who will then either confirm the Commission's decision, or reverse or modify it.[31]

14.6 Enforcement of conditions

14.6.1 Notice requiring compliance

One of the key features of the felling licence procedure is the ability of the Forestry Commission to impose a condition on a felling licence requiring the land to be restocked. As already noted, almost every felling licence granted is subject to such a condition.

There is little point in imposing such a condition, however, if it cannot be enforced. Section 24 of the 1967 Act accordingly provides that, where a restocking condition is not complied with, the Commission may issue a notice to the owner of the land requiring the default to be remedied by the taking of such steps as may be specified in the notice. Those steps must be taken within the period specified in the notice, which must be at least three months.[32] It is likely that, in practice, the steps required would in essence be simply to carry out the planting required by the condition in the first place.

Where such a notice has been served, the recipient may comply with it even if to do so would conflict with the requirements of any lease, covenant or contract relating to the land or the trees.[33]

Not surprisingly, there is a right to appeal to the Minister against a notice under section 24. Such an appeal must be made within three months after the receipt of the notice, and may be on either of two grounds:

(a) that the required works have been carried out; or

(b) that the steps required by the notice were not required by the original condition.[34]

---

[26] FA 1967, s. 13(1).
[27] S.I. 1979 No. 791, reg. 6; for the forms, see Sched. 1, Forms 4 to 6.
[28] FA 1967, s. 16(2)(a).
[29] See **11.3.2**.
[30] FA 1967, s. 27. Members of the committee are paid.
[31] FA 1967, s. 16(2)(b), (3).
[32] FA 1967, s. 24(1)(a), (2)(a); S.I. 1979 No. 791, reg. 13, substituted by S.I. 1987 No. 632, reg. 2(3).
[33] FA 1967, s. 24(5).
[34] FA 1967, s. 25(1); S.I. 1979 No. 791, reg. 14, substituted by S.I. 1987 No. 632, reg. 2(3); for the form of appeal, see S.I. 1979 No. 791, reg. 9, substituted by S.I. 1987 No. 632, reg. 2(6).

Such an appeal is dealt with by a special committee, as with an appeal against a felling licence (see above[35]); and the effect of the notice is suspended until the appeal has been finally disposed of.[36]

14.6.2 Non-compliance with section 24 notice

Where the requirements of a notice under section 24 are not complied with, the person responsible is liable to prosecution in the magistrates' court – proceedings would normally be instituted by the Commission. As with failure to obtain a felling licence (see below[37]), a prosecution may be instituted at any time within six months after the offence has been discovered, subject to an upper limit of two years after its commission.[38]

It is a defence to a charge under this provision to show a reasonable excuse as to why the notice has not been complied with – and for this defence to succeed it is for the person charged to show the existence of a reasonable excuse on the balance of probabilities. Otherwise, the relevant procedure to be followed in connection with such a prosecution would be broadly similar to that applying following a failure to comply with a replanting notice under the Town and Country Planning Act 1990.[39]

The penalty following conviction for non-compliance with a section 24 notice without reasonable excuse is a fine of up to Level 3 on the standard scale.[40]

Probably of greater significance in practice is that, whether or not a prosecution is brought, the Commission may enter the land and carry out the steps required by a section 24 notice, where it has not been complied with by the specified date.[41] If it does so, it may recover its expenses from the person on whom the notice was first served – if necessary, by an action for a simple contract debt.[42] Special provisions relate to the recovery of such expenses where the land is subject to a mortgage or is held under a settlement.[43]

14.7 Unauthorised felling

14.7.1 The elements of the offence

Once trees have been felled, they cannot be brought back to life. They can, of course, be replaced, but that will not restore the loss of amenity value for many years. Logically, therefore, the only ultimate sanction against unauthorised felling can be to make it a criminal offence. Section 17 of the Forestry Act 1967[44] accordingly provides as follows:

[35] See **14.5.4**.
[36] FA 1967, s. 25(2).
[37] See **14.7.1**.
[38] FA 1967, s. 17(2).
[39] As to which, see **20.5**.
[40] FA 1967, s. 24(4); see **Appendix C** for the current penalties.
[41] FA 1967, s. 24(3).
[42] FA 1967, s. 26(1), (4).
[43] FA 1967, s. 29; and see **14.5.1**.
[44] The reference to the standard scale was substituted by virtue of Criminal Justice Act 1982, s. 46. The maximum fine under the 1967 Act as originally passed (and indeed under s. 12 of the Forestry Act 1951) was £10, increased to £250 by the Civic Amenities Act 1967, s. 15(2). See **Appendix C** for the current penalties.

"Anyone who fells a tree without the authority of a felling licence, the case being one in which section 9(1) applies so as to require such a licence, shall be guilty of an offence and liable on summary conviction to a fine not exceeding level 4 on the standard scale or twice the sum which appears to the court to be the value of the tree, whichever is the higher."

And section 9(1) provides:

"A felling licence granted by the Commissioners shall be required for the felling of growing trees, except in a case where by or under the following provisions of this Part of this Act this subsection is expressed not to apply."

The combined effect of these two provisions is that the elements of an offence under section 17 are as follows:

- a tree has been felled by the defendant;
- the tree was, immediately prior to its felling, a growing tree;
- the case was not such as to be subject to one of the exemptions to section 9(1); and
- a felling licence had not been obtained.

As to the first two elements, they should be straightforward matters of fact, readily capable of being proved by the prosecution. The meaning of "felling" has already been considered.[45] The second could cause problems if it is claimed by the defence that a tree was felled because it was dead, since it would be difficult, if not impossible, for the prosecution to prove otherwise if there were no evidence as to the condition of the tree prior to felling, and the stump has been grubbed up or ground out. However, where (as is more likely in the case of prosecutions under the 1967 Act, as opposed to breaches of tree preservation orders) a number of trees have been felled, it would be unusual for there to be no evidence as to the condition of any of them.

As to the third and fourth elements, these constitute an exception or defence created by statute; they are, therefore, in principle for the defence to prove rather than for the prosecution to disprove.[46] It follows that, in order to avoid conviction, someone charged under section 17 must succeed in proving (on the balance of probabilities[47]) either that a felling licence had been obtained before the carrying out of the works in question, or that one was not required. The latter will entail careful examination of the various exemptions provided in the Act and the Regulations, considered in detail above.[48]

The corresponding exemptions under the planning Acts (in particular relating to a tree claimed after the event to have been dangerous) were scrutinised by the Court of Appeal in *R v Alath Construction Ltd*.[49] The application of the decision in that case in the context of the Forestry Act has been considered (albeit only by the Crown Court) in *Forestry Commission v Grace*,[50] in which it was held:

---

[45] See **14.2.1**.
[46] Magistrates' Courts Act 1980, s. 101; *R v Edwards* [1975] Q.B. 27, CA.
[47] *R v Carr-Briant* [1943] K.B. 607, CA.
[48] See **14.2**.
[49] [1990] 1 W.L.R. 1255, [1991] 1 EGLR 285, CA; see **17.3.5** and **19.4.2**.
[50] [1992] 1 EGLR 28.

". . . we are satisfied that this case falls within one of the very rare exceptions to the general rule relating to the burden of proof in criminal cases, and that it is for the appellants [who had been convicted of an offence under section 17 of the 1967 Act of felling growing trees without the authority of a felling licence] to establish, if they can, upon the balance of probabilities, that they fall within one or other of the exceptions set out in section 9 of the Forestry Act 1967".

14.7.2 Liability

Section 17 of the 1967 Act states that criminal liability attaches to "anyone" who fells a tree without a licence. This may appear to cause a problem in that a felling licence can only be sought by, and granted to, a person with an estate or interest in the land on which the trees are growing.[51] Accordingly, where felling is carried out by a person with only a licence to use and occupy the land (as opposed to a freehold or leasehold interest), he or she cannot obtain a felling licence. However, the Divisional Court in *Forestry Commission v Frost and Thompson*[52] considered that the word "anyone" meant precisely that – it was not restricted to those who could have obtained a felling licence.

The Act only refers to the person who actually fells the tree. It follows that where (as will normally be the case) felling is carried out by a contractor, under the instructions of the owner of the land, on the face of it only the contractor is liable to prosecution. However, by virtue of the Magistrates' Courts Act 1980,[53] those who aid, abet, counsel or procure the commission of a summary offence may be prosecuted as if they had actually committed the offence themselves. A person who instructs someone else to fell a tree may, therefore, be prosecuted under section 17 just as if he or she had felled the tree him/herself.

It should also be noted that the power of the Forestry Commission to serve a restocking notice following unauthorised felling applies only where the owner of land has been convicted under section 17.[54] If, therefore, it is intended that such a notice should in due course be served, it is essential that the landowner be prosecuted in addition to anyone else who may be involved. Where there is more than one owner (for example, in the case of land subject to a lease or a settlement), or where the right to fell timber is vested in someone other than the owner of the land on which it is standing, the "owner" for these purposes is the person who has such an estate or interest in the land as entitles him or her to carry out the work without any further consent from anyone else.[55]

14.7.3 Prosecution: procedure

A prosecution under section 17 may be brought by anyone, but in practice it is always the Forestry Commission that takes the necessary action. Oddly, the Commission has no explicit power to institute a prosecution. Nevertheless, it is to be assumed that it has an inherent power to do so, if necessary through the good

---

[51] FA 1967, s. 10(1); see **14.3.1**.
[52] [1989] E.G.C.S. 96, [1990] 154 J.P. 14.
[53] MCA 1980, s. 44.
[54] FA 1967, s. 17A(1), inserted by FA 1986; see **14.7.5**.
[55] FA 1967, s. 10(1); s. 17A(1), inserted by FA 1986; see **2.4** as to land held under a trust, and **2.5** as to land held under a lease or licence.

offices of the relevant Government department (DEFRA or its Welsh equivalent), acting on its behalf.[56]

Unlawful felling is a summary offence – that is, a prosecution may only be brought in the appropriate magistrates' court.[57] Summary offences may generally not be the subject of a prosecution more than six months after being committed. In this case, however, because felling on a remote hillside may not come to light for some while, the Act provides that a prosecution may be instituted at any time within six months after the offence has been discovered, subject to an upper limit of two years after its commission.[57a]

Where, owing to a mistaken view of the law, it is not appreciated that an offence has been committed, there is no discovery of the offence until it is realised that the view of the law which had been taken is erroneous.[58] This might be relevant where, for example, the Forestry Commission considers, wrongly, that a person who felled a tree was entitled to rely on one of the exemptions from the need for a licence, in section 9 of the Act and the Regulations made under that section.[59]

Where (as is likely) a number of trees have been felled, thought will need to be given by the prosecution as to whether the whole operation should form the subject of a single charge, or whether there should be several informations relating to different parts of the operation. The matter was considered by the Divisional Court in *Cullen v Jardine*,[60] which related to a conviction for felling 90 trees over the course of three days. It was held:

". . . it was not essential that the act should take place once and for all on a single day.[61] It was entirely possible for magistrates to decide which trees were cut down illegally and which were not, and to impose a penalty by reference to those findings. The mere fact that a number of issues may arise in the course of a trial does not turn one activity into two or more activities and thus render the information bad for duplicity."

However, this decision, which has been described as "the high-water mark of decisions on duplicity",[62] should be treated with caution. Other decisions have shown an almost complete lack of consistency on this issue; thus in one case[63] (cited by the court in *Cullen*) a single information for possessing five obscene video-tapes has been held valid, whereas three years later an information for possessing fifteen video-tapes in breach of copyright was held invalid.[64]

On balance, therefore, it seems that where a substantial felling operation has been carried out, it would generally be inappropriate to lay a separate information in respect of each tree felled. However, where the operation can be divided into

---

[56] See, for example, National Heritage Act 1983, s. 33(2A), which empowers English Heritage to prosecute certain offences. For a case where it was held that the Inland Revenue, which also has no explicit powers to prosecute, may nevertheless bring a prosecution in the Crown Court, see *R v Criminal Cases Review Commission* [2001] 2 W.L.R. 319.

[57] FA 1967, s. 17(1).

[57a] FA 1967, s. 17(2).

[58] *Cenlon Finance Co Ltd v Ellwood* [1962] A.C. 782, 1 All E.R. 854, H.L.

[59] See **14.2** and **14.7.1**.

[60] [1985] Crim. L.R. 668, DC; *The Times*, April 29, 1985.

[61] See *Hodgetts v Chiltern DC* [1983] 2 A.C. 120, H.L., per Lord Roskill.

[62] In *Ministry of Agriculture, Fisheries and Food v Nunn Corn (1987) Ltd* [1990] Crim. L.R. 268, DC; see *Archbold*, 2000 edn, para. 1-139.

[63] *R v Bristol Crown Court, ex p. Purnell*, reported as *R v Bristol Crown Court, ex p. Willetts* [1985] Crim. L.R. 219.

[64] *Ward* [1988] Crim. L.R. 57.

several separate parts – for example, where it relates to distinct geographical areas, or was carried out at different times, or by different contractors – each should form the subject of a separate information. Not the least important factor is to consider whether there could be separate defences in respect of each part, and whether different evidence may need to be called (either by the prosecution or by the defence) in respect of each.

14.7.4 Sentencing

The penalty following conviction would be a fine of up to Level 4 on the standard scale, or twice the value of the tree, whichever is the higher.[65] This may not seem a large penalty; where a large plantation is clear felled without a licence, the total maximum penalty could in principle be very significant.

There is, however, no explicit requirement to take into account any gain realised as a result of the offence – even though that might in some cases seem to be a relevant factor, such as where an area of trees at the edge of a town is clear-felled to allow development to take place. In any event, the maximum penalty (calculated as explained above) would usually be very much less than any development gain.

Other factors which would be relevant to determining the size of any fine are the seriousness of the offence, the culpability of the defendant and his or her financial circumstances.

14.7.5 Injunctions

It would appear that the Forestry Commission has no powers to seek an injunction preventing a breach of felling licence control, however much such powers might seem to be desirable. On the other hand, the Commission may seek to prevail upon the Secretary of State to do so on its behalf; in practice, such action would be taken by the Treasury Solicitor on behalf of DEFRA, or by the Solicitor to the National Assembly for Wales.[66]

14.7.6 Restocking of land following unauthorised felling

Where trees have been felled without a felling licence, it will often be at least as important to ensure their replacement as to punish the person responsible. But they will not be restored by a successful prosecution (however much that may discourage others from offending in the future). Nor can an enforcement notice be served under section 24, since that assumes the existence of a restocking condition; and if there was no licence, there cannot be a condition.

To deal with this problem, the Forestry Act 1986 was enacted, to enable the Forestry Commission to serve "restocking notices" following unauthorised felling. The 1986 Act inserted sections 17A to 17C into the Forestry Act 1967.

Now, therefore, where a person has been convicted of an offence under section 17, the Commission may within three months of the conviction serve on him or

---

[65] FA 1967, s. 17(1); see **Appendix C** for the current penalties.
[66] See **14.7.3**; and see *London Docklands Development Corpn v Rank Hovis McDougall Ltd* [1986] J.P.L. 826, where it was held that an urban development corporation had no power to seek an injunction.

her a restocking notice.[67] Although this only applies where the person is an "owner" of land – that is, the person who has such an estate or interest in the land as entitles him or her to carry out the work without any further consent from anyone else.[68]

A restocking notice is to require the recipient:

- to restock with trees the land on which the unauthorised felling took place; or

- to stock with trees such other land as may be agreed with the Commission; and

- in either case, to maintain those trees in accordance with the rules and practice of good forestry, for such period (of not more than ten years) as may be specified.

In deciding whether to serve a notice, the Commission may consult the relevant regional advisory committee; if it does so, it must take into account any advice tendered by the committee.[69] More importantly, it must take into account the following matters:

- good forestry;

- agriculture;

- the amenities of the district; and

- the establishment and maintenance of adequate reserves of growing timber.[70]

It is not possible to serve a restocking notice where the trees that were felled were the subject of a tree preservation order. In that case, it would instead be possible for the local planning authority to serve a replacement notice under section 206 of the Town and Country Planning Act.[71]

14.7.7 Appeal against restocking notice

There is an automatic right to appeal to the Minister against a restocking notice.[72] Such an appeal must be made within three months after the receipt of the notice; the relevant form is in the Regulations.[73]

On receipt of such an appeal, the Minister is to refer the matter to a special reference committee, as with felling licence appeals. The committee will then give the appellant an opportunity to make representations at an oral hearing, and will

[67] FA 1967, s. 17A(1), (2), inserted by FA 1986.
[68] FA 1967, s. 10(1); s. 17A(1), inserted by FA 1986; see **2.4** as to land held under a trust, and **2.5** as to land held under a lease or licence.
[69] FA 1967, s. 17A(3)(c), inserted by FA 1986; as to regional advisory committees, see **11.3.2**. In practice the Commission does not consult the regional advisory committees in connection with restocking notices.
[70] FA 1967, s. 17A(3)(a), (b), inserted by FA 1986.
[71] FA 1967, s. 17A(4), inserted by FA 1986; see **20.3**.
[72] FA 1967, s. 17B(1), inserted by FA 1986. As to "the Minister", see **11.2.1**.
[73] S.I. 1979 No. 791, reg. 8A, inserted by S.I. 1987 No. 632, reg. 2(2); for the forms, see Sched. 1, Form 6A, inserted by S.I. 1987 No. 632, reg. 2(5).

also consider any representations made by the Commission; and it will if it wishes to, or is requested to do so by the appellant, inspect the land in question.[74] The committee will make a report to the Minister, who will then either confirm the notice, or direct the Commission to withdraw or modify it.[75]

14.7.8 Enforcement of restocking notices

Where the recipient of a restocking notice fails to comply with it, the Commission may serve on the owner of the trees a notice under section 17C requiring him or her to take such steps as may be specified to achieve compliance. The procedure following the service of such a notice (including a further right of appeal) is exactly as with a notice requiring compliance with the conditions on a felling licence, considered above.[76]

14.8 Felling directions

14.8.1 Issue of felling directions

In general, the Forestry Commission will not interfere with the management of private forestry. Thus, subject to the need for a felling licence, already discussed, the owner of trees is entitled to fell them whenever it seems most appropriate. However, under powers in section 18 of the 1967 Act, the Commission may give a felling direction to the owner of land where it considers that trees on the land should be felled:

- to prevent deterioration or further deterioration in the quality of the trees as timber; or
- in order to improve the growth of other trees.

In deciding whether to issue a direction, the Commission may consult the relevant regional advisory committee; if it does so, it must take into account any advice tendered by the committee.[77]

In practice, the Commission has rarely, if ever, issued a felling direction; but the relevant statutory provisions are included here for completeness.

A felling direction may not be issued in relation to "fruit trees or trees standing or growing on land comprised in an orchard, garden, churchyard or public open space". This is the same formula as appears in one of the exemptions from the need for a felling licence; and the meanings of the various words used in it have already been considered.[78] In any other case, the Commission must have regard to:

- the interests of agriculture;
- the amenity and convenience of any farm or dwellinghouse, or park usually

---

[74] FA 1967, s. 27.
[75] FA 1967, s. 17B(2) , inserted by FA 1986.
[76] FA 1967, ss. 24 to 26, 29; see **14.6**.
[77] FA 1967, s. 37(3); as to regional advisory committees, see **11.3.2**.
[78] FA 1967, s. 19(1)(a); see **14.2.3**.

occupied with a dwellinghouse; and

- the amenity and convenience of land held by the National Trust.[79]

The first of these would mean, for example, that trees which are valued as shelter belts would probably not be appropriate to form the subject of a felling direction. The second and third give some degree of protection for landscape features.

Nor may a direction be given in relation to trees which are on land subject to a forestry dedication covenant or which are otherwise being managed in accordance with a plan of operations or working plan approved by the Commission.[80]

Where the Commission has issued a felling direction, this will be sufficient authority for the owner of the trees concerned to fell them, even where he or she would otherwise be constrained by the terms of a lease, covenant or contract not to carry out the felling.[81] In practice, it would be prudent (albeit not strictly necessary) for the recipient of a direction to fell trees affected by such a restriction to inform the person entitled to the benefit of it. If that leads to an objection, the owner can then appeal, in reliance on the support of that beneficiary.

14.8.2 Felling directions relating to protected trees

As might be expected, there are special provisions relating to trees that are protected by a tree preservation order.

Where an application for a licence to fell protected trees has in the past been referred to the relevant local planning authority under the procedure in section 15(1)(b) of the 1967 Act, so that any felling is under the control of the authority rather than that of the Forestry Commission, a felling direction may not be given for as long as the order remains in force.[82]

In any other case where the Commission proposes to make a felling direction relating to trees that are subject to a preservation order, it should first give written notice to the planning authority which made the order. If the authority objects within a month, the Commission should refer the matter to the Secretary of State,[83] who will consult with the authority; the direction may only be given once he or she has given consent.[84] And once the direction has been given after such consultation, no further consent is needed under the order to carry out the required works.[85]

14.8.3 Contents of felling directions

A felling direction will require the trees specified in it to be felled within the period stated – which should be at least two years.[86] It must also contain a statement of the reasons why it is being given.[87]

---

[79] FA 1967, s. 18(2).
[80] FA 1967, s. 19(1)(b),(c); see **12.6, 12.7**.
[81] FA 1967, s. 18(4).
[82] FA 1967, s. 19(2); see **14.4.3**.
[83] That is, in practice, to ODPM (see **16.2.8**), not to DEFRA: FA 1967, s. 19(4).
[84] FA 1967, s. 19(3); S.I. 1979 No. 791, reg. 9.
[85] FA 1967, s. 18(5).
[86] FA 1967, s. 18(1).
[87] FA 1967, s. 18(3).

14.8.4 Appeal against felling directions

Where the Commission gives a felling direction, there is under section 20 of the 1967 Act an automatic right to appeal to the Minister[87a] – unlike the position with regard to felling licences.[88]

The appeal is to be within three months of the receipt of the direction; the relevant form is in the regulations.[89] On receipt of such an appeal, the Minister is to refer the matter to a special reference committee, as with felling licence appeals. The committee will then give the appellant an opportunity to make representations at an oral hearing, and will also consider any representations made by the Commission; and it will, if it wishes to or is requested to do so by the appellant, inspect the land in question.[90] The committee will then make a report to the Commission, which will either confirm the direction, or reverse or modify it, in line with the committee's decision.[91]

Consideration of an appeal by the Minister may be postponed until the expiry of the three-month period, or until a purchase notice is served under section 21. Once both an appeal and a purchase notice have been served, they will then be considered together, and determined at the same time.[92]

14.8.5 Requiring the Commission to purchase trees following felling directions

Where the owner of an interest in land claims that compliance with a felling direction would lead to a net loss, he or she may serve a notice under section 21 of the 1967 Act on the Minister, requiring:

- the Forestry Commission to purchase the trees; or

- the Minister to purchase that interest in the land.

The former will apply only where the owner has the right to sell the trees for immediate felling (that is, it may not apply where the land is subject to a lease or settlement). If the notice requires the Minister to purchase an interest in land, it will automatically be assumed that the owner is willing to convey to the Secretary of State any necessary interests over adjoining land, such as rights of way to get to the land and to haul timber away from it.[93]

A purchase notice under section 21 must be served within three months of the receipt of the direction, and the relevant form to be used is in the Regulations.[94]

On receipt of the notice, the Minister must within three months either accept the notice, or revoke the direction, or refer the matter to a special reference committee[95] – save that a decision may be postponed until the expiry of the three-month period, or until an appeal has been made under section 20. Once both an

[87a] See **11.2.1**.
[88] FA 1967, s. 20(1).
[89] S.I. 1979 No. 791, reg. 10; for the forms, see Sched. 1, Form 7.
[90] FA 1967, s. 27.
[91] FA 1967, s. 20(2).
[92] FA 1967, s. 23; S.I. 1979 No. 791, reg. 12(1),(3).
[93] FA 1967, s. 21(2).
[94] S.I. 1979 No. 791, reg. 11(1); for the forms, see Sched. 1, Form 8.
[95] FA 1967, s. 21(3).

appeal and the purchase notice have been served, they will be considered together and determined at the same time.[96]

If the Minister refers the matter to a special committee, as with an appeal, the committee must then give the owner of the trees concerned an opportunity to make representations at an oral hearing, and will also consider any representations made by the Commission; and it will, if it wishes to or is requested to do so by the owner, inspect the trees in question.[97] The committee will then make a report to the Minister, which will state the views of the committee as to whether the felling required by the direction would, in fact, cause the owner of the trees to suffer a loss and, if so, whether any modification to it would help to mitigate that loss.[98]

In determining whether compliance with a felling direction would lead to the owner of the trees concerned suffering a loss, the committee will take into account any increase in the value of other trees not being felled[99] – after all, one of the reasons for giving a felling direction is to improve the growth, and hence possibly the value, of other trees. It is also required to take into account any compensation received under any tree preservation order applying to the trees in question.[1] Although, it is not quite clear to what that refers, since such compensation would only be payable in the event of a tree not being felled, and thus by definition would not be available in the event of compliance with a felling direction.

If the committee concludes that compliance with the direction would not in fact involve the owner in any loss, the notice is automatically quashed. If, on the other hand, it accepts that there may be a loss, the Minister has a further period of three months within which he or she must either accept the purchase notice, or else revoke the direction or modify it in accordance with the committee's report.

If the Minister accepts the notice, where it requires the Commission to buy trees, there is deemed to have come in to existence a contract for the Commission to buy the trees, and to fell and remove them – all details (including the price payable) to be determined by the Lands Tribunal in default of agreement.[2] If, on the other hand, the notice requires the Minister to purchase the owner's interest in land, the Minister is deemed to have been authorised to acquire that interest under compulsory powers[3]; and no doubt on acquisition of the land he or she will then place it at the disposal of the Commission.[4] Since, in either case, the Commission ends up with the ownership of the trees, with or without the land on which they are growing, there is no need for the felling direction to continue in existence, and it accordingly lapses.

Finally, if the Minister fails to make any decision within the prescribed period, either on initially receiving the notice or on subsequently receiving the committee's report, the direction will automatically cease to have effect at the end of that period[5] – although there seems to be no reason why the Commission should not simply serve another one.

---

[96] FA 1967, s. 23; S.I. 1979 No. 791, reg. 12(2),(3).
[97] FA 1967, s. 27.
[98] FA 1967, s. 21(4); S.I. 1979 No. 791, reg. 11(2).
[99] FA 1967, s. 21(2).
[1] FA 1967, s. 21(7).
[2] FA 1967, ss. 22(3), 31.
[3] FA 1967, s. 22(4), 39.
[4] See 11.2.3, 11.3.4.
[5] FA 1967, s. 21(6).

14.8.6 *Failure to comply with felling direction*

Where the recipient of a felling direction fails to comply with it, the Commission may serve on the owner of the trees a notice under section 24 requiring him or her to take such steps as may be specified to achieve compliance. The procedure following the service of such a notice (including a right of appeal) is exactly as with a notice requiring compliance with the conditions on a felling licence, considered above.[6]

Where such a notice is not complied with, and the Commission itself carries out the required felling, it may either retain or dispose of any trees felled; but it must pay to the owner of the trees any sums arising, less any expenses incurred in carrying out the felling and removal of the timber.[7]

---

[6] FA 1967, ss. 24 to 26, 29; see **14.6**.
[7] FA 1967, s. 26(2); reg. 15; for the forms to be used when requesting such payment, see Sched. 1, Forms 10 (England and Wales) and 11 (Scotland).

Part IV

Trees and Woodlands of Particular Value

"The indifference towards old trees makes a mockery of our supposed new respect for the environment. Consider the raw facts. The giants of our native species – oak, ash and beech – are the biggest living things on these islands: heavier than any land animal, taller than most buildings, older than many ancient monuments. If a big tree were not a living organism, it would still be a remarkable object. A big oak or beech can weigh 30 tons, cover 3,000 square yards, include ten miles of twigs and branches. Each year the tree pumps several tons of water about 100 feet into the air, produces a new crop of 100,000 leaves, and covers half an acre of trunk and branches with a new pelt. Yet the tree is alive. There is no mass production: every tree, sexually conceived, is built to a different design – as we see at first glance."

– Thomas Packenham, in *Meetings with Remarkable Trees* (1996).

"A tree's a tree. How many do you need to look at?"

– Ronald Reagan, on plans to expand California's Redwood National Park (1967).

Chapter 15

Protection for Significant Trees and Woodlands

15.1 Introduction

15.1.1 Trees and woodlands of particular value

The preceding Parts of this book have described the law as it applies to trees and woodlands in general – that is, to any tree, whether it be the most magnificent spreading oak tree or the most unimpressive self-sown hazel, and to any woodland, whether it be the ancient Burnham Beeches or the most recent Forestry Commission plantation of sitka spruce.

However, it is perfectly obvious that some trees, and some woodlands, are of greater value than others. This Part of the book accordingly describes the recognition given by the law to that fact, and explains the protective mechanisms (in most case fairly limited) that have arisen as a result.

15.1.2 Ancient woodlands, parks and trees

Several thousand years ago, most of Britain was covered with trees – sometimes called the "wildwood" – but since Neolithic times woodland has been steadily cleared, principally to provide land for agriculture and other forms of development. At the start of the twentieth century, woodland cover in England had been reduced to only 4 per cent of the total land area, but a hundred years later that figure had risen to 7.5 per cent. However, while woodland of more recent origin is still considered as important – not least as a recreation resource – it is obvious that not all woodland is of equal value, either ecologically or as an amenity.

Special attention is thus now, rightly, paid to the protection, improvement and (where appropriate) enlargement of surviving older woodlands – particularly those on land where there has been continuous woodland cover for many centuries, known as "ancient woodlands", as they are likely to be of most ecological interest. The legislation and policy measures available to achieve this are, as yet, not extensive; but, such as they are, they are described at **15.2**.

Historic landscapes, including parks and gardens, and the trees in them, also have a distinctive value. However, as with ancient woodlands, they have only a limited degree of special protection, explained at **15.3**.

Almost as significant as these collective designations, although only considered as such relatively recently, are the veteran trees, either individual specimens or in groups – sometimes as descendants of the wildwood, sometimes as remnants of planting now long forgotten. It is curious that Britain now has almost the sparsest level of tree cover in Europe (only Ireland has a smaller proportion of its land area covered with trees), yet has one of the highest populations of veteran trees (along with Greece and Spain). Here, too, the protection afforded by the law (described at **15.4**) is almost non-existent – other than in cases where a tree preservation order has been used.

The mechanism for protecting particular species of plants, as yet almost unused in connection with trees, is touched upon at **15.5**.

15.1.3 Protection systems

Ancient trees, and trees within ancient woodlands, clearly need special protection – not least from unsympathetic development.

And there are other trees, which may not be of such value, but which are still much appreciated as a local amenity. These will be particularly significant in urban areas, where trees are scarcer. In the words of the anonymous romantic employed to write the Ministry of Housing and Local Government Circular 36/56:

"How much trees can contribute to the grace and charm of cities. They improve the urban scene and enhance the dignity of architecture. Green foliage and blossoms bring cheerfulness into drab streets and do much to relieve the monotony and ugliness."[1]

The law has thus for many years contained provisions aimed at providing at least a limited degree of protection for selected trees – whether a magnificent veteran in the heart of an ancient forest, or an avenue of attractive specimen trees at the focal point of a 1930s housing estate.

The most obvious of these is the system of "tree preservation orders", misnamed though they are, since nothing can preserve a tree for ever. The selection of which trees and woodlands should be protected by a tree preservation order is accordingly considered at **15.6**. The following Chapters (**16 to 20**) set out in more detail the law relating to preservation orders – which is quite unnecessarily complex, as a result of the evolutionary process described in **16.1**. The related provisions applying to trees in conservation areas are considered in outline at **15.7** (and in more detail in **Chapter 21**).

One of the greatest threats to the continuing existence of trees is the carrying out of ill-sited new development. All the considerations discussed above are, therefore, capable of being a material consideration in the determination of planning applications and appeals; indeed the presence of trees and woodlands may play a significant and sometimes decisive role – as explained in **15.8**. And a moment's reflection will make it clear that trees are at greatest risk when building works are actually being carried out. This is partly because the presence of trees may impede large scale development, and thus lessen the value of land. It is also because the nature of building sites is such that, with the best will in the world, trees are likely to be damaged or destroyed as a result of negligence. The possible mechanisms available to protect trees in such situations are described at **15.9**.

Some of the oldest and most attractive trees are found in churchyards. These

---

[1] Quoted (and the author thus described) by Anthony Mellows, in *The Preservation and Felling of Trees*, Oyez, 1964, at p. 14.

are afforded a measure of special protection by the Church of England's faculty system, which has existed for many years but has recently attained increased significance in relation to trees. This is touched on at **15.10**, and explored fully in **Chapter 22**.

Finally, there are a number of pieces of legislation, in particular those setting up the new arrangements to replace the public utilities (gas, water, telecommunications and so on), which impose duties (noted at **15.11**) relating to the protection of, amongst other things, trees and woodlands.

15.2 Ancient woodlands

15.2.1 The ancient woodlands inventory

Ancient woodland is land that has had a continuous woodland cover since at least 1600. It may be in either of two categories:

- *ancient semi-natural woodland*, which retains a native tree and shrub cover that has not been planted, although it may have been managed by coppicing or felling and allowed to regenerate naturally (about 200,000 hectares in England as at the end of the twentieth century); or

- *ancient replanted woodland*, where the original tree cover has been felled and replaced by planting, often with conifers, and usually during the twentieth century (about 150,000 hectares).[2]

Ancient woodland thus covers around 350,000 hectares in England (2.6 per cent of its land area).

English Nature and the Countryside Commission for Wales (CCW) have prepared an ancient woodland inventory, recording ancient woodlands sites (in either category) of over 2 hectares. The information is held on a computerised database, and available on paper data sheets and maps. Copies of the county-based inventories should be held by local planning authorities, but further copies are available from local offices of English Nature and regional conservancies of the Forestry Commission.[3] Note, however, that the information in the inventory is constantly being refined and updated as new information comes to light; so it may be important to ensure that the inventory being consulted is up to date.

Categorisation of land as ancient woodland does not of itself provide any statutory protection. And whilst it would be possible to use preservation orders to give some protection to individual trees or small groups within an ancient woodland, that would be inappropriate as a mechanism to protect a whole woodland. For one thing, the making and enforcing of orders on such a scale would be administratively burdensome. But, possibly more significantly, the value of ancient woodland is as a habitat and eco-system, and a historical record, quite as much as a group of individual trees. And the imposition of a preservation order will not prevent a gradual deterioration in the quality of an ancient woodland due

---

[2] Definitions from *Help Notes for Planning Consultations on Ancient Woodland*, English Nature, 1999. The second category is sometimes referred to as "planting on ancient woodland site" (or PAWS).

[3] *Help Notes for Planning Consultations on Ancient Woodland*, English Nature, 1999; and see *Tree Preservation Orders: A Guide to the Law and Good Practice*, DETR, 2000, Chapter 5, note 58.

to over-use by the public for recreation, or overgrazing, or a decline in the diversity of species (of birds, animals and other types of plants).

In practice, what is required in order to preserve and gradually extend the ancient woodlands is, first, good management and, secondly, protection from development proposals. As to the first, owners of semi-natural woodland (including ancient woodlands) are encouraged by the Forestry Commission to manage them in accordance with *Standard Note 5* in the *UK Forestry Standard*[4]; and applications for felling licences for proposals involving ancient semi-natural woodlands will be considered by the Forestry Commission in the light of that guidance.

15.2.2 Development affecting ancient woodlands

Since the 1930s, it has been estimated that some 28,800 hectares of ancient woodland has been lost – principally by way of agricultural expansion (20,3000 hectares), but also to mineral extraction (about 2,000 hectares) and for urban development (6,500 hectares).[5]

A proposal to clear-fell ancient woodland to provide for agricultural expansion would not require planning permission,[6] but it would of course generally require a felling licence. And it is most unlikely that a licence would now be granted for such a proposal.[7]

As for other proposals, the effect of proposed development on an area of ancient woodland would almost certainly be a "material consideration", to be taken into account by the planning authority or the Secretary of State when determining an application for planning permission or an appeal.[8] Furthermore, all planning applications affecting ancient semi-natural or ancient replanted woodlands, as recorded in English Nature's Provisional Inventory of Ancient Woodlands, must now be notified to the Forestry Commission.[9] The types of proposal subject to the new consultation arrangements are as follows:

"The Forestry Commission wishes to be consulted on the following categories of development:

● proposals where any part of the development site consists of ancient semi-natural woodland or ancient replanted woodland recorded in the Provisional Inventory; or
● proposals where any part of the development site is within 500 metres of an ancient semi-natural woodland or ancient replanted woodland, and where the development would involve erecting new buildings or extending the footprint of existing buildings.

"The Forestry Commission's main concern in relation to the second of these categories relates to the effect the proposed development may have on the continuing viability and health of the woodland.

---

[4] See **14.3.3**.
[5] *English Woodland and Nature Conservation*, English Nature, 1998.
[6] See **13.2.1**.
[7] See **14.3.2**.
[8] Town and Country Planning Act 1990, s. 70(2).
[9] Circular 9/95, *General Development Order Consolidation 1995* (WO Circ 29/95), Appendix B, Table 2, amended by letter from DETR to Chief Planning Officers, March 15, 1999, *Addition of the Forestry Commission to the list of Non-Statutory Consultees* (ref 98DPL025, copies available from DETR Free Literature Unit) and similar letter from Welsh Office.

"Where the authority is unclear whether to consult on a particular proposal, it should seek the advice of the Forestry Commission."[10]

Consultation should be with the relevant local Forestry Commission conservatory.

And whether or not the Commission is consulted, the Woodland Trust have advised local planning authorities that the following factors should be borne in mind when assessing development proposals:

- "Ancient woodland may be adversely affected by the proposal even if the planning application does not impact directly on the site itself. Increasing ecological isolation, changes in adjacent land use and negative environmental effects which penetrate the woodland from outside the site may all take a significant toll.
- It is not just clearance of ancient woodland that should concern local authorities. Other activities can cause severe damage and permanent loss of the special features that make it important – even activities permitted under the General Development Orders, including recreational uses.
- Concern should not be restricted to semi-natural ancient woodland, but equally to ancient woodland sites which have been replanted with non-native species. Retaining many special characteristics of ancient woodland, including historical features and relict ground flora, they represent our only chance to increase the area of semi-natural ancient woodland habitat through removal of planted trees and regeneration with site-native species."[11]

It will thus in future become increasingly difficult to obtain planning permission for development leading to the loss of ancient woodlands.

15.2.3 Policy on development and woodlands

The Government's general policy on nature conservation in England is contained in Planning Policy Guidance note (PPG) 9, *Nature Conservation*. This sets out in its introduction a series of bland platitudes in support of habitat conservation and bio-diversity, and later makes a passing reference to ancient woodlands.[12] The corresponding document for Wales (Technical Advice Note (TAN) 5) contains no reference to woodlands.

PPG 2 states that the control of land-use in green belts should have the objective of, amongst other things, securing nature conservation interest, and retaining land in agricultural, forestry and related uses.[13] Similar sentiments in relation to the countryside generally are contained in PPG 7 (in relation to England)[14] and in Technical Advice Note (TAN) (Wales) 6.[15] And advice on maintaining a balance between the maintenance of woodlands and the pressures

---

[10] Letter from DETR to Chief Planning Officers, March 15, 1999, *Addition of the Forestry Commission to the list of Non-Statutory Consultees* (ref 98DPL025, copies available from DETR Free Literature Unit; similar letter issued by the Welsh Office); *Tree Preservation Orders: A Guide to the Law and Good Practice*, DETR, 2000, para. 5.15.

[11] *Ancient Woods and Planning Applications*, January 2000, Woodland Trust.

[12] See PGG9, para. 14.

[13] PPG 2, *Green Belts*, 1995, para. 1.6.

[14] PPG 7, *The Countryside: Environmental Quality and Economic and Social Development*, 1997, para. 2.8

[15] TAN 6, *Agricultural and Rural Development*, 2000, para. 4.

of recreation is given in PPG 17[16] – including newer leisure activities, such as war games, in ancient woodlands.[17]

Even the most recent policy advice on tree preservation orders, which contains a section on trees and development,[18] mentions the requirement for planning authorities to consult the Forestry Commission, but does not provide any policy advice.

More significantly, perhaps, given the paucity of national policy support for the protection of ancient woodlands, many local planning authorities are now including policies for the protection of ancient woodlands in their development plans.[19] This is important, given that applications for planning permission must be determined in accordance with the provisions of any relevant development plan, unless other material considerations indicate otherwise.[20]

15.3 Historic landscapes, parks and gardens

15.3.1 Register of historic parks and gardens in England

Ancient woodlands comprise trees and other plants growing, generally as a result of natural regeneration, in more or less "natural" habitats. Parks and gardens, by contrast, are the opposite – they consist of trees and other plants that have been planted or consciously retained as elements in artificial (or at least contrived) landscapes. They vary from the old and mature to the very recent, from the splendid to the ordinary, and from spacious gardens such as at Stourhead through to tiny urban patios.

Although parks and gardens are man-made, the principal elements in them are trees, shrubs and other plants. And it has already been noted that the planning system generally does not take account of plants.[21] There is thus only very limited scope for the protection of parks and gardens from the removal or maltreatment of existing plants (other than by the imposition of preservation orders on significant specimen trees or groups) or from the introduction of inappropriate new ones.

On the other hand, the basic layout may be capable of being protected, as may any man-made features within it. And it has been recognised that historic parks and gardens are a fragile and finite resource, which can easily be damaged beyond repair or lost forever. In order to recognise the existence of those sites that are of particular historic importance, English Heritage maintains, under powers introduced by the National Heritage Act 1983,[22] a register of parks and gardens of special historic interest in England. The parks and gardens included in the Register are chosen primarily on the basis of the age of their main layout and features, their rarity as examples of historic landscape design, and the quality of their landscaping:

---

[16] PPG 17, *Sport and Recreation*, 1991, paras. 38, 39.

[17] PPG 17, para. 53.

[18] *Tree Preservation Orders: A Guide to the Law and Good Practice*, Chapter 5; see para. 5.15.

[19] See *Conservation Issues in Local Plans*, published jointly by English Heritage, English Nature and the Countryside Commission, 1996, paras. 3.17–3.20.

[20] Town and Country Planning Act 1990, s. 54A, inserted by Planning and Compensation Act 1991.

[21] See **9.4.5** (works to existing trees and other plants) and **10.1.3** (introduction of new ones).

[22] Historic Buildings and Monuments Act 1953, s. 8C, inserted by National Heritage Act 1983.

". . . what makes a site of interest is the survival, quality and interest of its historic structure. For a garden, the structure will usually include the basic pattern of its layout which might, for example, be formal with terraces, straight walks and hedges, formal pools and canals, or informal with winding paths through lawns, rockwork, and informally planted trees and shrubberies. For a park it may include the historic boundary and entrances, the route of the approach drives and rides, the siting of the main buildings, the underlying landform, built features which provide structure and focal points in the design, lakes and rivers, and the planting of trees, clumps, shelter belts, and woodland." [23]

From this it will be appreciated that the trees and shrubs in a park or garden are only one factor amongst many. Indeed, it is noted that:

"Registered sites might also be of note for other reasons such as their amenity value, or for nature conservation. Although not relevant to an assessment of a site in terms of the *Register*, such features do need to be taken into account to ensure the sensitive management of the site's landscape."[24]

Any protection afforded to trees and woodlands at a site by its inclusion in the Register is thus to a large extent a by-product of a conservation regime that is primarily directed towards the protection of man-made structures and layouts.

The Register is currently being updated, and is expected to be complete by 2003; at the end of 2001 there were 1,450 sites included. Approximately 10 per cent of those were classified as Grade I, 28 per cent Grade II*, and 62 per cent Grade II.

A similar register is being prepared for the counties of Wales, albeit on a non-statutory basis, by Cadw (the agency of the National Assembly for Wales responsible for the built heritage), in conjunction with ICOMOS and the Countryside Council for Wales, as the first part of a Register of Historic Landscapes, Parks and Gardens.[25]

15.3.2 Development affecting historic parks and gardens

As with ancient woodlands, the effect of proposed development on a historic park of garden included in the Register is a "material consideration", to be taken into account by the planning authority or the Secretary of State when determining an application for planning permission or an appeal. Authorities have also been asked to include policies for the protection of registered parks and gardens in their development plans,[26] and many have indeed done so.

Furthermore, all planning applications affecting sites registered at Grade I and II* must now be notified to English Heritage[27] or (in Wales) to Cadw[28]; and all applications affecting registered parks and gardens (of whatever grade) should be notified to the Garden History Society.[29]

[23] *The Register of Parks and Gardens: an Introduction*, English Heritage leaflet, 1998; an updated version appears on the web at www.english-heritage.org.uk/knowledge/conservation.
[24] *The Register of Parks and Gardens: an Introduction*, English Heritage leaflet, 1998.
[25] Welsh Office Circular 61/96, *Historic Buildings and Conservation Areas*, para. 16 and Annex B. ICOMOS is the International Council on Monuments and Sites (responsible for world heritage sites).
[26] PPG 15, para. 2.24; Welsh Office Circular 61/96, para. 16.
[27] TCP (General Development Procedure) Order 1995, art. 10(1)(o).
[28] Welsh Office Circular 61/96, para. 16.
[29] TCP (Consultation with the Garden History Society) Direction, at Appendix C to Department of the Environment Circular 9/95 (England); and Welsh Office Circular 61/96, para. 16.

These requirements may provide at least a small measure of protection for the trees and woodlands within the best parks and gardens – although, that needs to be set aside the possibility that other parks and gardens (and the trees within them) may, by inference, be seen to be expendable.

15.3.3 The historic landscape generally

Whilst the most important historic parks and gardens have for some time been given at least some protection, awareness has grown in recent years as to the importance of the wider historic landscape. Some guidance is given in PPG 15, although it is sensibly pointed out that:

"Appraisals based on assessment of the historic character of the whole countryside will be more flexible, and more likely to be effectively integrated with the aims of the planning process, than an attempt to define selected areas for additional control. It is unlikely therefore to be feasible to prepare a definitive register at a national level of England's wider historic landscape. The whole of the landscape, to varying degrees and in different ways, is an archaeological and historic artefact, the product of complex historic processes and past land-use."[30]

At present, therefore, there is no particular mechanism in England for the protection of historic landscape as such, or for the trees and woodlands forming part of it, other than through the normal process of development control. Areas of particular significance and key landscape characteristics have accordingly been identified in some structure and local plans; details should be sought from local planning authorities.

In Wales, by contrast, a non-statutory register of historic landscape is being prepared on a trial basis by Cadw, as the second part of its Register of Landscapes, Parks and Gardens.[31]

15.4 Veteran trees

Veteran trees are "trees which, because of their great age, size or condition, are of exceptional value culturally, in the landscape, or for wildlife"; some trees are instantly recognisable as veterans, but many are less obvious.[32] They may be associated with ancient woodland or historic parks and gardens, but they may well not be. Many of those that survive are centuries old; arguably they are one of the truly distinctive features of Britain's wildlife, compared to that of continental Europe. And they are of course irreplaceable:

"The greatest threat to the trees is not death, but misunderstanding; many veteran trees have been cut down as they were thought of as dying, diseased and dangerous. Agricultural intensification resulted in the removal of many old hedgerows, along with their trees, and the ploughing up of old parklands. Surviving trees may suffer directly through

---

[30] PPG 15, *Planning and the Historic Environment*, paras. 2.26 and 6.40.
[31] Welsh Office Circular 61/96, para. 16.
[32] See, for example, *The Future for Veteran Trees*, and *Veteran Trees: a Guide to Risk and Responsibility* – two (free) leaflets published by English Nature in 2000 as a result of the Veteran Trees Initiative.

inappropriate tree surgery, damage by grazing animals or vandalism, as well as indirectly through unsympathetic management of the surrounding land."[33]

Awareness of the significance of veteran trees grew in the closing years of the twentieth century, with the formation of the Ancient Tree Forum and, subsequently, the setting up (and funding) by English Nature of the Veteran Tree Initiative.

As with ancient woodlands and registered parks and gardens, the mere fact that a tree is capable of being classified as a veteran tree does not, of itself, provide any formal protection. And there is no formal schedule, list or inventory of such trees.

It is, of course, possible for a local planning authority to impose a tree preservation order on a veteran; and indeed that may well be appropriate as recognition of its importance. But that will only provide limited protection; it will not, for example, prevent the soil around the base of the tree becoming trampled or poached, and it will only prevent to a limited extent over-grazing of the area around it by animals. In addition, there is a particular problem in that consent under a tree preservation order is not necessary for the cutting down, uprooting, topping or lopping of a tree which is "dying or dead or which has become dangerous".[34] The precise meaning of that exemption is considered later,[35] but some veteran trees may be dying or dead without needing to be removed, and it may be possible to remove the cause of a danger by relatively limited surgery; whereas in either case the mere existence of a tree preservation order would not necessarily prevent premature felling.

Veteran trees are also sometimes referred to as "ancient trees"[36]; the terms veteran trees and ancient trees are often used interchangeably, but the distinction between the two would seem to be as follows:

"Veteran trees are taken to be those trees beyond their normal economic life.[37] They are characterised by branches which are beginning to die-back from the tips, and by colonisation of the heartwood with fungi and other primary saproxylic organisms, that is – organisms that depend for part or all of their life cycle on dead and decaying wood. Ancient trees are those of greater antiquity. They are frequently hollow or their heartwood is colonised by a greater range of saproxylic organisms. They contain a high proportion of dead wood including large dead limbs. There is no single point at which a tree becomes veteran or ancient. Some, like birch, may become veteran or ancient at a relatively young age compared with longer living trees such as oak.

"Where concentrations of ancient or veteran trees occur in a woodland context these can form 'old growth' woodland. In the UK the term old growth woodland has been defined as 'stands with more than 200 years growth'[38] with a continuity of trees reaching back into the past[39] (Rose 1992). Old growth woodland is distinct from ancient woodland. The latter is defined as woodland which has existed continuously without disturbance for more than 400

---

[33] *The Future for Veteran Trees*, p. 3.

[34] Town and Country Planning Act 1990, s. 198(6)(a).

[35] See **17.3**.

[36] It appears that English Nature (and the Veteran Trees Initiative) favour the term "veteran tree", whereas the Woodland Trust (and the Ancient Tree Forum) favours "ancient tree". *cf. Romeo & Juliet*, Act II, sc II, line 43.

[37] N A Sanderson, V*eteran Trees in Highland Wood Pasture*, in *Scottish Woodland History Discussion Group Notes III*, ed. T C Smout, Institute of Environmental History, St Andrews, 1998.

[38] G F Peterken, *Natural Woodland*. Cambridge University Press, 1996.

[39] F Rose, *Temperate Forest Management: its effects on bryophyte and lichen floras and habitat*, in *Bryophytes and Lichens in a Changing Environment*, ed. J W Bates, A M Farmer, Oxford University Press, 1992.

years but individual trees or stands need not be more than 200 years old. These distinctions are subtle but are given here to focus on the longevity and continuity of individual trees rather than the continuity of overall woodland cover."

There appears to be no official central Government policy on veteran or ancient trees as such, as opposed to general support and enthusiasm from English Nature and the Woodland Trust. However, as with ancient woodlands, some development plans are including references to veteran and ancient trees.

15.5 Rare species

The provisions considered so far are aimed at protecting specific groups of trees or individual trees. It might also be desirable, in principle, to protect all trees (wherever located) of a particular species. There are, for example, eleven species of tree in Britain known to be in critical danger of extinction.[40]

The legislation specifically aimed at the protection of particular species of plants is the Wildlife and Countryside Act 1981 and the Conservation (Natural Habitats, etc) Regulations 1994 – the latter being the transposition into United Kingdom law of the EC Habitats Directive.[41] So far, however, only one species of tree (however that word is defined) has been included on the list of plants thus protected – the Plymouth pear (*Pyrus cordata*).[41a] Nevertheless, the protection of some other species of plants (such as various mosses and lichens), and of various species of birds and animals, may, by a side-wind, give protection to the trees which form their habitat – which may, in particular, afford a significant measure of protection to veteran trees.[42]

Sometimes it may be appropriate to protect trees of species that are rare, either nationally or locally, by the use of tree preservation orders. This is considered further below.[43]

15.6 Tree preservation orders

15.6.1 Need for protection

Although professional awareness of the value of ancient woodlands, historic parklands and veteran trees has only emerged relatively recently, it has been recognised since the start of the twentieth century that a measure of protection may be needed for at least some trees. As already noted, this will apply not just to ancient trees and woodlands but also to any trees that provide a useful amenity, particularly in built-up areas.

All planning Acts since 1909 have thus made provision for the securing of amenity, and since 1932 that has explicitly included the protection of trees – the process by which the legislation came to acquire its present, unsatisfactory state is

---

[40] All eleven species are members of the *Sorbus* family; the rarest, *Sorbus leyana* (Ley's whitebeam) has a population of only 16 at two sites in Powys. See *World List of Threatened Trees*, 1998, published by World Conservation Centre and World Conservation Union.
[41] See **9.3.1**.
[41a] See **9.3.4**.
[42] See **9.3**.
[43] See **15.6.4**.

considered in the following Chapter.[44] The key provision is now section 198 of the 1990 Act,[45] which provides as follows:

> "(1) If it appears to a local planning authority that it is expedient in the interests of amenity to make provision for the preservation of trees or woodlands in their area, they may for that purpose make an order with respect to such trees, groups of trees or woodlands as may be specified in the order.
>
> (2) An order under subsection (1) is in this Act referred to as a 'tree preservation order'."

An order may thus be made by a local planning authority where it appears to that authority that it is expedient to do so for the preservation of trees or woodlands in its area, in the interests of amenity.[46] The Secretary of State has similar powers.[47]

In the context of historic buildings, it has been held in the Court of Appeal and the House of Lords that "preserve" has its normal meaning, that is, "keep safe from harm".[48] There seems to be no reason why the same would not apply in this context too. The purpose of a tree preservation order is thus not to keep alive forever the tree or woodland in question – nothing can do that – but merely to keep it safe from harm.

In practice, among the most common situations in which an authority is likely to consider making a tree preservation order are the following:

- when notice is given to the authority of proposal to carry out works to a tree in a conservation area[49] or a churchyard,[49a] and the authority decides that it should be retained;

- when the authority becomes aware of a proposal to carry out development on land on which there are trees that it wishes to see retained[50];

- where an authority is alerted by a member of the public or an amenity group to work that is about to be carried out to a tree that is currently unprotected;

- when the authority carries out a survey of an area – either specifically in relation to trees or for some other reason – and becomes aware of the amenity value of trees; and

- where an authority reviews the trees and groups of trees currently protected by an area order.[51]

The questions which therefore arise are, what are the circumstances in which a tree preservation order may properly be made and, in particular, what is meant by "amenity", and when is it "expedient" to make an order? Each of these is here

---

[44] See **16.2**.
[45] TCPA 1947, s. 28(1), TCPA 1962, s. 29(1), and TCPA 1971, s. 60(1) were in similar terms.
[46] TCPA 1990, s. 198(1).
[47] TCPA 1990, s. 202; see **16.2.8** and **16.4.4**.
[48] *South Lakeland DC v Secretary of State* [1992] 2 W.L.R. 204, H.L., upholding [1991] 2 PLR 97, CA, overturning [1991] J.P.L. 144. The word occurred in the phrase "special attention shall be paid to the desirability of preserving or enhancing the character or appearance of the area" – see now Planning (Listed Buildings and Conservation Areas) Act 1990, s. 72.
[49] See **15.7** and **Chapter 21**.
[49a] See **15.10** and **Chapter 22**.
[50] See **15.8** and **15.9**.
[51] See **15.8.2** and **16.5.4** and **16.8**.

dealt with in turn. Nor, since a tree preservation order can only protect a tree or woodland, is it possible to ignore altogether the apparently difficult question of what is a "tree", and what is a "woodland"?

15.6.2 Protection in the interests of amenity

A local planning authority may only make a tree preservation order where it appears to the authority that it is expedient to do so in the interests of amenity.[52] It has been held in the Court of Appeal[53] that:

". . . the word 'amenity' still connotes in a statute what Scrutton L.J. thought it did[54] on its first appearance in the Housing and Town Planning, etc Act of 1909: 'pleasant circumstances or features, advantages' ".

In an Australian decision of 1955, it was held:

". . . the word may be taken to express that element in the appearance and layout of town and country which makes for a comfortable and pleasant life rather than a mere existence".[55]

And it has been held that the amenity of land may be defined as "[its] visual appearance and the pleasure of its enjoyment".[56]

A current Dictionary definition is "the pleasantness or attractiveness of a place".[57]

Current Government guidance on this issue provides a useful (but not exhaustive) checklist of factors which may be relevant:

"In the Secretary of State's view, tree preservation orders should be used to protect selected trees and woodlands if their removal would have a significant impact on the local environment and its enjoyment by the public. Local planning authorities should be able to show that a reasonable degree of public benefit would accrue before orders are made or confirmed. The trees, or at least part of them, should therefore normally be visible from a public place, such as a road or footpath, although, exceptionally, the inclusion of other trees may be justified.

- The benefit may be present or future;
- trees may be worthy of preservation for their intrinsic beauty or for their contribution to the landscape;
- [they may be worthy of preservation] because they serve to screen an eyesore or future development;
- the value of trees may be enhanced by their scarcity; and
- the value of a group of trees or woodland may be collective only.

Other factors, such as importance as a wildlife habitat, may be taken into account which alone would not be sufficient to warrant a TPO."[58]

---

[52] TCPA 1990, s. 198(1).
[53] *FFF Estates v Hackney LBC* [1981] Q.B. 503, CA.
[54] In *Re Ellis and Ruislip-Northwood UDC* [1920] 1 K.B. 343, at p. 370.
[55] *Re Parramatta City Council, ex p. Tooth & Co* (1955) 55 S.R. (N.S.W.) 282 at pp. 306, 308.
[56] *Cartwright v Post Office* [1968] 2 All E.R. 646, at p. 648.
[57] The New Oxford Dictionary of English, first edn, 1998.
[58] *Tree Preservation Orders: a Guide to the Law and Good Practice*, DETR (cited below as "*DETR Guide*": see **16.2.6**), 2000, para. 3.2 [bullet points added for clarity]; see also Technical Advice Note (TAN) 10, *Tree Preservation Orders* ("TAN 10"), 1997, para. 15.

This echoes similar advice since 1949.[59] It emphasises, in particular, that orders should in general only be made to protect trees which are publicly visible, and only rarely those in rear gardens – although, a tree at the centre of a large block of urban gardens may in fact be seen by more people, and give more pleasure, than one beside a remote country lane.

However, although such Government policy is "clearly relevant" to the decision as to whether making a particular order would be in the interests of amenity, that decision is ultimately a matter for the planning authority; and Government advice cannot reduce the wide discretion given to an authority by section 198.[60] On the other hand, in the event of unauthorised felling, a failure by the local authority to comply with policy might be relevant to any decision as to sentencing.[61]

Also relevant will be general statutory duties. In particular, a planning authority is required to have regard to the desirability of preserving or enhancing the character or appearance of a conservation area, in exercising in relation to land within the area any of its functions under the planning Acts[62] – which would undoubtedly include the making of tree preservation orders. Secondly, authorities are under a duty to consider making tree preservation orders in connection with determining planning applications.[63] And, thirdly, public bodies are under a general duty to have regard to the desirability of conserving the natural beauty of the countryside in the exercise of any of their functions relating to land[64] – which, again, would include the making of preservation orders.

15.6.3 Assessment of amenity

Government guidance suggests that local planning authorities should develop ways of assessing the amenity value of trees in a structured way.[65] This is obviously sensible, as judging the contribution made by a tree to the amenity of an area can reduce to a hopelessly unscientific exercise – especially where it is under threat from a development proposal.

One approach is to use the "Helliwell method", originally devised in 1967, and adopted by the Tree Council in 1974 and the Arboricultural Association in 1984.[66] This identifies seven factors to be taken into account in assessing the value of a tree in relation to visual amenity, as follows:

- size of tree (small, medium, large, very large);

- useful life expectancy (10–20 years, 20–40 years, 40–100 years, more than 100 years);

- importance of position in landscape (little, some, considerable, great);

- presence of other trees (many, some, few, none);

---

[59] *Memorandum on the Preservation of Trees and Woodlands*, 1949, paras. 4, 5; second edn, 1966, para. 5; Department of the Environment Circ 36/78 (WO 64/78), para. 40, 41.

[60] *Armitage v South Oxfordshire DC* [1998] 2 PLR 89; see **15.6.5**.

[61] See **19.6.3**.

[62] Planning (Listed Buildings and Conservation Areas) Act 1990, s. 72; see **15.7.3**.

[63] TCPA 1990, s. 197; see **15.8.3**

[64] Countryside Act 1968, s. 11; see **15.11.1**.

[65] *DETR Guide*, 2000, para. 3.3; see also TAN 10, 1997, para. 16.

[66] Based on proposals originally published in the *Aboricultural Journal*, 1967. See now *The Amenity Valuation of Trees and Woodlands*, D R Helliwell, Aboricultural Association, revised edn, 2000.

- relationship to the setting (barely suitable, fairly suitable, very suitable, especially suitable);

- form (poor, fair, good, especially good); and

- other, special factors (none, one, two, three).

Each of these factors is assessed on a scale of 1 to 4, and the scores multiplied to achieve an overall rating. So, for example, a medium-sized birch tree in a fairly secluded garden in a well-wooded residential area would be assessed as having a much lower value than a healthy plane tree about 50 years old in a prominent position in the centre of a small market town.

The Helliwell method is not without its critics; in particular, it takes little account of factors other than *visual* amenity. And no doubt there are other techniques. What is important is to adopt some reasonably systematic approach.[67]

15.6.4 Factors other than appearance

Current Government advice, noted above, concentrates principally on the extent to which a tree contributes to amenity by virtue of its appearance. It does, however, suggest, in common with guidance going back to 1978,[68] that "the value of trees may be enhanced by their scarcity". And the earliest guidance (in 1949) suggested that "woodland itself may be of value to amenity if it is of scientific or recreational interest".[69] These both hint that the "amenity" value of a tree or woodland may lie in factors other than simply visual ones. And there has in recent years been a noticeable trend towards greater awareness – both amongst informed professionals and among the general public – of wider environmental issues.

It must therefore be at least arguable that among the "pleasant circumstances or features [and] advantages"[70] of a piece of land, and amongst the items which contribute towards "the pleasure of its enjoyment",[71] and thus to its "amenity" value, would now be the ecological diversity of that land, its history, its value as a wildlife habitat, and its scientific and recreational interest. It would follow that it might be perfectly appropriate to make a tree preservation order on those grounds alone – such as where a veteran tree, which may not be particularly "beautiful", is an important habitat for various forms of wildlife. To suggest otherwise would be tantamount to valuing trees solely on visual grounds, which would be equivalent to valuing old buildings merely on the basis of whether or not they are "pretty".

There must, therefore, be some doubt as to the correctness of the Government guidance, quoted above, which states that "other factors (such as importance as a wildlife habitat) may be taken into account, [but] alone would not be sufficient to warrant a TPO".[72] Moreover, it must be questionable whether the 1994 Review of the legislation was right to reject the possibility of introducing new powers to

---

[67] See also **19.6.4**, on the use of this method in relation to sentencing for unauthorised works.

[68] Department of the Environment Circular 36/78 (WO 64/78), para. 40, quoted in *Tree Preservation Orders: a Guide to the Law and Good Practice*, DOE, 1994, at para. 3.2; second edn, DETR, 2000, para. 3.2.

[69] *Memorandum on the Preservation of Trees and Woodlands*, 1949, para. 5.

[70] *FFF Estates v Hackney LBC* [1981] Q.B. 503, CA.

[71] *Cartwright v Post Office* [1968] 2 All E.R. 646, at p. 648.

[72] Circular 36/78 (WO 64/78), para. 40, quoted in *Tree Preservation Orders: a Guide to the Law and Good Practice*, DOE, 1994, at para. 3.2.

enable authorities to place orders on trees which are of special importance for nature conservation, on the grounds that this was not in the interests of amenity.[73]

As with visual factors, it is important that any assessment of the contribution to amenity made by non-visual factors is systematic. Thus, it would be particularly relevant to consider factors such as whether the tree or woodland in question is included within an ancient woodland on the inventory maintained by English Nature or a historic park in the register maintained by English Heritage, and whether a tree is itself capable of being categorised as a veteran or ancient tree.[74]

15.6.5 Expediency of making an order

The other arm of the test as to whether a local planning authority should make a tree preservation order is whether it is "expedient" to do so.[75] There is no judicial authority directly considering the issue of expediency; but current Government advice on this point is as follows:

"Although a tree may merit protection on amenity grounds, it may not be expedient to make it the subject of a TPO. For example, it is unlikely to be expedient to make a TPO in respect of trees which are under good arboricultural or silvicultural management.

"It may be expedient to make a TPO if the authority believes that there is a risk of the tree being cut down or pruned in ways which would have a significant impact on the amenity of the area. It is not necessary for the risk to be immediate. In some cases, the authority may believe that certain trees are at risk generally from development pressures. The authority may have some other reason to believe that trees are at risk; changes in property ownership and intentions to fell trees are not always known in advance, and so the protection of selected trees by a precautionary TPO might sometimes be considered expedient."[76]

This advice suggests that it would not often be expedient to make an order in relation to land that is in the ownership of a body that is both well-informed and capable of implementing regular tree management – such as, for example, the Woodland Trust or the National Trust. The same principle would seem to apply to responsible private landowners with large holdings of trees and appropriately qualified and experienced staff to look after them.

The applicability of this advice was considered in *Armitage v South Oxfordshire DC*,[77] in which a tree preservation order had been made notwithstanding an objection made by the landowners that the trees in question were under good arboricultural management. That objection, and the policy quoted above, had not been drawn to the attention of the relevant Council sub-committee, and the court accepted that this was a significant and regrettable flaw in the decision-making process. Nevertheless, the sub-committee had its reasons for making the order, notably in relation to pressure on the woodland as a result of recent unsuitable development; and even though there was in existence an agreed plan of management under the Woodland Grant Scheme,[78] that did not guarantee protection at the end of the plan. Accordingly, given the wide discretion afforded to the authority by the Act, it could not be said that the sub-committee would or

---

[73] *Tree preservation orders: Review*, DOE, 1994, para. 2.64.
[74] See **15.2**, **15.3** and **15.4** respectively.
[75] TCPA 1990, s. 198(1).
[76] *DETR Guide*, 2000, paras. 3.4, 3.5; see also TAN 10, 1997, para. 16.
[77] [1998] 2 PLR 89.
[78] See **12.7.3**.

might have reached any different decision if it had taken into account the policy advice from Government. The court therefore declined to quash the order.

This makes it clear that a Council considering whether or not to make a tree preservation order should consider carefully all relevant Government advice; but it also emphasises that there is a wide discretion as to when an order may be suitable. On the other hand, the High Court has agreed that, in the light of the amendment made to the legislation in 1980, whereby there is no appeal to the Secretary of State against the making of an order but only against a subsequent refusal of consent, it is particularly important that the Council gives proper consideration to the making of the order in the first place.[79]

A tree preservation order should generally not be made solely in order to prevent or inhibit development, but only where the occurrence of a development proposal draws the attention of the authority to trees which are intrinsically worth preserving. This is considered in more detail below.[80]

Finally, there are certain special cases (land owned by the Crown or local authorities, or cases in which the Forestry Commission have an involvement) where different issues may arise when considering the issue of expediency. These are dealt with in the following Chapter.[81]

15.6.6 "Trees" and "woodlands": what may be protected

A tree preservation order may only be used to protect trees, groups of trees and woodlands. But there is no statutory definition of either "tree" or "woodland".

This problem seems to have been first considered, by the Court of Appeal, in *Kent County Council v Batchelor*,[82] in which Lord Denning M.R. held as follows:

"Furthermore, I must say that there is an ambiguity in this Act and in the order. We are not told what is a 'tree'. Many bushes and saplings are certainly not 'trees'. In woodland like this, it is often, from an agricultural point of view (especially on a derelict area like this) very important to get out the bushes, scrub and saplings and to replant – as indeed Mr Batchelor was doing. There is no definition of 'tree'. I should have thought that in woodland it ought to be something over seven or eight inches in diameter."[83]

A number of commentators at the time pointed out that this could not be right.[84] In the first place, what is a sapling, if not a small tree? Thus the 1990 Act itself provides that a tree preservation order may apply to a "tree" newly planted as a result of a planning condition or a replanting notice,[85] which is likely to be a sapling. Secondly, there is no basis for the size limitation suggested. The Forestry Act 1967, as originally enacted, refers to "the felling of trees with a diameter not exceeding three inches or, in the case of coppice or underwood, with a diameter not exceeding six inches",[86] which suggests that smaller plants can be trees. The TCP (Trees) Regulations 1999 refer to "a tree whose diameter does not exceed 75 millimetres".

Accordingly, when the matter next came before the courts, in *Bullock v*

---

[79] *Bellcross v Mid-Bedfordshire DC* [1988] 1 EGLR 200 at p. 202J.
[80] See **15.8.3**.
[81] See **16.4.7**.
[82] (1976) 33 P. & C.R. 185, 75 L.G.R. 151, CA, [1976] J.P.L. 484.
[83] (1976) 33 P. & C.R. 185, CA at p. 189. For further comment on this litigation, see **19.7**.
[84] See in particular the heavy sarcasm of the comment at [1977] J.P.L. 7.
[85] TCPA 1990, ss. 198(5), 206(4); see **10.4.1.**, **20.2.1**.
[86] FA 1967, s. 9(1); the two measurements are now, respectively, 8 and 15 centimetres. See **14.2.2**.

Secretary of State,[87] in the context of whether coppice could be covered by a tree preservation order, Phillips J. noted – possibly with some relief – that Lord Denning's remarks in *Batchelor* had been *obiter* (in that he had not based his judgment solely on that point), and that the other two members of the Court of Appeal had not touched upon the point. He also raised the points noted above, and therefore concluded that, whilst Lord Denning's observations were entitled to great respect, he ought not to follow them:

"Bushes and scrub nobody, I suppose, would call 'trees', nor, indeed, shrubs, but it seems to me that *anything that ordinarily one would call a tree is a 'tree' within this group of sections in the Act . . .* "[88]

The italicised words in that dictum seem to be as good a definition as there is likely to be.

One other judicial observation, which is occasionally relied on in this context,[89] is to be found in the pre-Victorian decision *Bullen v Denning*: "the word *trees,* generally speaking, means wood applicable to buildings, and does not include orchard trees."[90] However, that arose in a wholly different context,[91] and is of no relevance whatsoever to tree preservation orders, which undoubtedly can be made to protect fruit trees.[92]

It may be helpful at least to note a number of other possible definitions. Two typical definitions of "tree" in general dictionaries are as follows:

"A woody perennial plant, typically having a single stem or trunk growing to a considerable height and bearing lateral branches at some distance from the ground. Compare with SHRUB [a woody plant which is smaller than a tree and has several main stems arising at or near the ground]. ~ (in general use) any bush, shrub, or herbaceous plant with a tall erect stem, e.g. a banana plant."[93]

"A large plant with a single branched woody trunk (sometimes loosely applied)."[94]

Neither of these is particularly precise. But the editors of biological and botanical dictionaries also seem somewhat reluctant to define the word with any greater precision:

"A woody plant distinguished from a shrub in part by its larger size and in part from having a single, or at least only a few, main stems."[95]

"A tall, woody perennial plant having a well marked trunk with few or no branches persisting from the base."[96]

"A woody, perennial plant with a main axis or trunk which bears branches."[97]

[87] (1980) 40 P. & C.R. 246.
[88] (1980) 40 P. & C.R. 246 at p. 251 [emphasis added].
[89] Possibly because it appears, for example, in Stroud's *Judicial Dictionary.*
[90] (1826) 5 B. & C. 842, per Littledale J. at p. 851. The Denning referred to is, presumably, no relation.
[91] See **2.3.4**.
[92] See **17.9.1**.
[93] The New Oxford Dictionary of English, first edn, 1998.
[94] Chambers Dictionary, seventh edn, 1988.
[95] Gray's *Dictionary of Biological Sciences*. This and the two following definitions are quoted in the comment on the *Batchelor* decision at [1977] J.P.L. 7.
[96] George Usher's *Dictionary on Botany.*
[97] Edward Steen, *Dictionary of Biology.*

The definition apparently preferred by arboriculturists is that from Alan Mitchell's authoritative *Field Guide to Trees of Britain and North Europe*:

"A tree may be defined as a woody, perennial plant which can attain a stature of 6m or more on a single stem. The stem may divide low down, but it must do so above ground level. . . . the Hawthorn qualifies because there are a few specimens over 10m tall with a single bole, although this plant is seen almost everywhere as a low shrub with many stems. The Elderberry and Dogwood, however, do not qualify for inclusion. The Hazel has been given the benefit of the doubt."[98]

This seems both imprecise and unhelpful in the present context; and it seems a little hard on elderberries, which may surely in some cases qualify as trees. And there are some shrubs, such as a few older rhododendrons, which might qualify.

Generally, though, it is probably best to stick with the definition put forward in *Bullock*: "anything that ordinarily one would call a tree". And, on that basis, trees would include coppice.[99]

As for "woodland", there appears to be no definition either in legislation or judicial decision – it is noteworthy that, for example, the matter was not even canvassed in *Evans v Waverley Borough Council*,[1] which concerned the difference between orders affecting woodlands and others. It seems therefore that there is no reason to depart from the ordinary dictionary definition – "land covered with trees".[2]

Finally, it has been noted that section 198 of the 1990 Act, in common with all of its predecessors since 1932, provides that orders may be framed by reference to "trees, groups of trees or woodlands". And the model orders made under those Acts have since 1953 also referred to "areas". The significance of these is explored in the following Chapter.[3]

15.6.7 Hedgerows

There is no reason why a tree preservation order should not be made to protect a tree or group of trees in a hedge, or an old hedge that has become a line of trees of reasonable height, as recognised in Government advice.[4] However, a hedge is principally composed of woody plants, each of which, if allowed to do so, could grow into a mature tree; and it has already been noted that a tree preservation order can in principle be made in relation to trees that are small or immature. Tricky problems may therefore arise if an area order is made in relation to land on which there is a hedge.

More generally, important hedgerows (as opposed to the individual trees within them) should be protected by the requirement for consent to be obtained under the Hedgerows Regulations 1997, considered in Part V of this book, rather than by tree preservation orders.

---

[98] First edn, 1974.
[99] *Bullock v Secretary of State* (1980) 40 P. & C.R. 246 at p. 251.
[1] [1995] 2 PLR 46, upheld at [1995] 3 PLR, CA.
[2] The New Oxford Dictionary of English, first edn, 1998.
[3] See **16.5.2**.
[4] *DETR Guide*, 2000, para. 2.3; TAN 10, para. 7.

15.6.8 Information about tree preservation orders

A planning authority which has made a tree preservation order is required to keep it available for public inspection at its offices at all reasonable times. It follows that, to discover whether a particular tree is subject to a preservation order, it should only be necessary to ring the appropriate planning authority. Indeed, the Secretary of State has stated that authorities should be able to provide members of the public with such information over the telephone within 48 hours.[5] As to which authority should be contacted, in areas where there exists more than one, it is normally best to try the district or borough council.

15.7 Trees in conservation areas

15.7.1 The protection of trees on a more general basis

It is obvious that there are some areas in which there are numerous trees of value, such that it would be wholly unrealistic to expect the local authority to be able to protect all of them, even by the use of orders relating to "groups" or "areas" of trees. And the Secretary of State has, in any event, made it clear that he expects area orders to be used only exceptionally.[6]

To provide some sort of protection to trees on a more general basis, it would have been possible to impose a requirement for consent to be obtained for any works to any tree anywhere. That, after all, is in effect the method used to control building operations and changes of use (through the blanket requirement to obtain planning permission for all development). However, that would have brought within control a large number of works to trees which were wholly unexceptionable; it would have failed to highlight those areas where the tree cover was particularly important; there would have been considerable overlap with felling control; and the whole system would have been very burdensome to administer. And, for all those reasons, it would have probably have been widely ignored.

Alternatively, it would have been possible for Parliament to have introduced some form of control over works to trees in particular areas, chosen specially for the significance of the tree cover. That would have required such areas to be identified, and would have introduced yet another area designation, alongside conservation areas, sites of special scientific interest, areas of special control over advertising, and so on – not to mention the various areas identified in local development plans within which particular policies will operate – and those living or owning property within them would have to have been notified. Again, therefore, such a system would have been burdensome to administer, and might well have been largely ineffectual.

The mechanism actually adopted, therefore, albeit somewhat crude and still (probably) to a significant extent unknown or simply ignored, relies on the fact that the boundaries of the areas with the most important tree cover in amenity terms, at least in towns and villages, are often fairly similar to those of the areas which have been designated as conservation areas ("[areas] of special architectural or historic interest, the character or appearance of which it is desirable to preserve

[5] *DETR Guide*, 2000, para. 3.49.
[6] *DETR Guide*, 2000, para. 3.17; see also TAN 10, 1997, para. A5.

or enhance"[7]). And it recognises, too, that the trees in conservation areas constitute a significant element in that character, and are therefore worth protecting for that reason, whether or not they are worth protecting in their own right.[8]

There is accordingly a requirement, introduced by the Town and Country Amenities Act 1974, and now contained in sections 211 to 214 of the Town and Country Planning Act 1990, to notify the local planning authority of any proposal to carry out works of any consequence to any tree in a conservation area.[9] This enables the authority to have a chance to consider whether a tree preservation order should be placed on the tree in question (where one has not been made already), which in turn enables the authority to refuse consent for the works or, more positively, to grant consent but only subject to suitable conditions.

The detailed outworking of this is considered in **Chapter 21**.

15.7.2 Trees as a factor in the designation of conservation areas

Quite apart from the above considerations, trees are in many instances a significant element in the character and appearance of some localities, both urban and rural. In appropriate cases, therefore, the presence of trees (and other landscape features) may in part justify the designation of such area as conservation areas. This has been recognised by the High Court in *R v Canterbury CC, ex p. Halford*:

"Buildings are part of their surroundings. They are to be seen in their setting. Trees may do much to enhance the interest, and to make them special. Consider some of the great houses of England, Blickling for instance. Can one imagine making the house a conservation area without its hedges, its trees and its garden? Why should the old villages be treated differently? The charm of a village does not come from its houses and its church alone. What about its greens and paddocks, its trees and the fields that come closes to the houses? . . . So I reject the submission that section 69 [designation of conservation areas] required the meadows and woods, the trees and the views to be left out of account."[10]

In that case, the planning authority had explicitly recognised that the designation of land as a conservation area provided extra protection for trees and woodlands; and the report to the relevant committee also recognised the value of protecting the landscape setting for a village that was itself of architectural and historic interest. Its decision to designate that setting as part of the area was thus in principle upheld.

Indeed, the only reason why the court in that case quashed the decision to include the land in question within a conservation area was that the committee report had omitted to mention that some of the trees on the land had very recently been protected by the making of a tree preservation order:

"All three reports stressed the protection that would be given to trees were the proposed conservation area to be designated; yet in none of the reports was the attention of members drawn to the protection that could be given by tree preservation orders, let alone to the fact that the protection given to trees merely by being in a conservation area is less. None even

---

[7]   Planning (Listed Buildings and Conservation Areas) Act 1990, s. 69(1).
[8]   *R v Canterbury City Council, ex p. Halford* [1992] 2 PLR 137; see **15.7.2**.
[9]   TCPA 1990, ss. 211 to 214.
[10]   *R v Canterbury City Council, ex p. Halford* [1992] 2 PLR 137, per McCullough J. at p. 144B–C, F.

mentions the possibility of making such orders, let alone addresses the question of whether members might consider that the setting of a village could be sufficiently protected in that way, particularly when one remembers that Barham already had the benefit of being within both the Kent Downs Area of Outstanding Natural Beauty and the North Downs Special Landscape Area. . . . That was, in my judgment, a material factor which ought to have been drawn to the committee's attention and was not. That failure renders the decision to designate unlawful."[11]

It follows that the availability of the protection afforded to trees may perfectly properly be a consideration, and possibly an important one, in deciding whether to designate a conservation area, but that the legislative position, and the possible alternatives available, must be fully considered by the relevant committee.

On the other hand, it is unlikely – although perhaps not altogether impossible – for a tree or a group of trees to be the sole factor in the decision to designate a conservation area, since it is to be an area of "special architectural or historic interest". If the aim of an authority is to protect trees, it should use a tree preservation order, not designate a conservation area.

15.7.3 The protection of trees in conservation areas

Once a conservation area has been designated, for whatever reason, a planning authority is required to have regard to the desirability of preserving or enhancing its character or appearance, in exercising in relation to land within the area any of its functions under the planning Acts.[12] It has already been noted that trees constitute an important element in the character and appearance of many conservation areas.[13]

It follows that a planning authority should have particular regard to trees in carrying out in relation to the conservation area its functions under the planning Acts, which would in particular include:

- the response to notifications under section 211 of proposed works to trees[14];

- the making of tree preservation orders[15];

- the determination of applications for consent under such orders[16];

- the determination of applications for planning permission[17]; and

- the preparation of proposals for the preservation and enhancement of the area.[18]

The first four of these are considered elsewhere in the book, as noted.

---

[11] [1992] 2 PLR 137 at p. 145H–146B.
[12] Planning (Listed Buildings and Conservation Areas) Act 1990, s. 72.
[13] *R v Canterbury City Council, ex p. Halford* [1992] 2 PLR 137; see **15.7.2**.
[14] See **15.7.1**, **21.3.3**.
[15] See **15.6.2**.
[16] *Sherwood and Sherwood v Secretary of State and Islington LBC* [1996] J.P.L. 925; see **18.3.4**.
[17] See **15.8.3**.
[18] Planning (Listed Buildings and Conservation Areas) Act 1990, s. 71.

15.7.4 Information

A conservation area may be designated by any local planning authority[19]; although, in practice, the great majority are designated by district planning authorities (in areas where there is not a single tier of local authority). And county councils are under a duty to consult district councils before designating areas.[20]

It is therefore the district planning authority that should be consulted as to whether a particular piece of land, and thus the tree growing on it, is within a conservation area. Here, too, the Secretary of State has stated that authorities should be able to provide members of the public with such details over the telephone within 48 hours.[21] The existence of a conservation area designation is also a planning charge in Part 3 of the Local Land Charges Register.[22]

15.8 Woodlands and trees as a factor in planning decisions

15.8.1 Trees and woodlands and the development plan

One of the two times when trees and woodlands of particular value are most under threat is when the owner (or prospective owner) of the land on which they are growing is proposing to carry out development on it – that is, to change the use of the land or to carry out building, mining or engineering operations on it.[23]

When a local planning authority or a planning inspector is considering whether planning permission should be granted for proposed development and, if so, subject to what conditions, that decision should be taken "having regard to the provisions of the development plan, so far as material, and to any other material considerations".[24] Further, the decision is to be made "in accordance with the plan, unless material considerations dictate otherwise".[25] In other words, if an issue is to be considered seriously in the development control process, it has to be included in the development plan.

The Town and Country Planning Act 1990 provides that structure, local and unitary development plans must include policies in respect of the conservation of the natural beauty and amenity of the land,[26] and Government guidance suggests such policies should be designed also to secure the enhancement of the natural beauty and amenity of the land, and should in particular relate (amongst other things) to tree and hedgerow protection and planting.[27]

It is therefore not surprising that many, if not all, development plans contain policies seeking to protect trees and woodlands. The guidance produced by the national heritage bodies comments as follows:

"Trees and woodlands are one of the most widely valued parts of our environment in both

---

[19] Planning (Listed Buildings and Conservation Areas) Act 1990, s. 69(1).
[20] Planning (Listed Buildings and Conservation Areas) Act 1990, Sched. 4, para. 4(2), amended by Environment Act 1995, Sched. 20.
[21] DETR Guide, 2000, para. 3.49.
[22] Local Land Charges Rules 1977 (S.I. 1979 No. 985), r. 2(2), 3.
[23] The other time of particular threat is when property changes hands.
[24] TCPA 1990, s. 70(2).
[25] TCPA 1990, s. 54A, inserted by Planning and Compensation Act 1991, s. 26.
[26] TCPA 1990, s. 31(3) (structure plans); s. 36(2)(a) (local plans); s. 12(3A)(a) (Part I of unitary development plans).
[27] Planning Policy Guidance Note PPG 12, Development Plans, para. 4.4; DETR Guide, 2000, para. 5.4; see also TAN 10, 1997, para. 17.

town and country, with their cultural and historical associations, their importance for nature conservation, and their contribution to the landscape. Local plans should contain a strong commitment to protecting them from damaging change, if necessary by the use of tree preservation orders, especially where they are in one or more of the following categories:

- ancient woodland, identified by English Nature as woodlands which have existed from at least medieval times without ever having been cleared for uses other than wood or timber production.
- important tree and woodland features contributing to the character of open spaces in or near settlements, or in the wider landscape, including those associated with major road routes, with rivers, lakes and canals, or in highly visible positions."[28]

This seems to be a reasonable approach. However, since the management of trees and woodlands is often as important as their protection, many plans go further and contain policies that – however worthy in concept – seem somewhat inappropriate for inclusion in land use and development plans. Inappropriate policies in draft plans may (and arguably should) be challenged at the deposit stage.

In addition to general policies, it may in certain cases be appropriate for a planning authority to issue a site brief for the guidance of developers; for example, where it is known that a site will shortly be coming up for development or is about to change hands. The preparation of such a brief is likely to involve carrying out a survey of the site and the surrounding area, and making tree preservation orders on those trees and woodlands which the authority wishes to see retained. Such an approach, especially if carried out in conjunction with the owner of the site and relevant statutory undertakers, may save much time later on.

15.8.2 Trees as material consideration in determining planning applications

The presence of trees and woodlands has always been recognised as an important material consideration to be taken account of by planning authorities and inspectors when determining applications.[29]

This will be particularly so where proposed development affects ancient woodland, a registered park or garden, or a tree or woodland subject to a tree preservation order. But, as noted above, there are many other trees which are of amenity value, and which are not (yet) protected by tree preservation orders; and it is perfectly lawful (in principle) for a planning authority to refuse planning permission for a proposal on the grounds of its effect on trees and woodlands on, or close to, the site.

This is emphasised by section 197 of the 1990 Act, which provides that a local planning authority is under a duty:

"(a) to ensure, whenever it is appropriate, that in granting planning permission for any development, adequate provision is made, by the imposition of conditions, for the preservation or planting of trees; and

(b) to make such orders under section 198 [tree preservation orders] as appear to the authority to be necessary in connection with the grant of such permission, whether for giving effect to such conditions or otherwise."

[28] *Conservation Issue in Local Plans*, published by Countryside Commission, English Heritage and English Nature, 1996, para. 3.19.
[29] *DETR Guide*, 2000, para. 5.5; see also TAN 10, 1997, para. 18.

It would clearly be nonsensical if an authority were under a duty to make provision for the protection of trees at the stage of granting planning permission, but were not also able to take account of the existence of those same trees as a material consideration when deciding whether to give permission in the first place.

Much useful guidance on the whole topic is given in British Standard BS 5837:1991, *Trees in Relation to Construction*. This provides, in particular, advice on a general strategy to be adopted by those undertaking development, and on carrying out a pre-planning site assessment. A tree survey plan and schedule should be commissioned from an experienced arboricultural consultant, to identify every significant tree and shrub on or close to the site, and to estimate its species, its approximate age, height and spread, its condition and vigour, and any significant defects. That will help the developer and the authority to reach a sensible view as to what should be retained.

And once a development proposal of any consequence is first broached with a planning authority, the relevant officer of the authority should go and inspect the site and the neighbourhood, and see (amongst other things, no doubt) whether there is any tree or woodland which looks as if it might be of value in amenity terms. If there is, he or she should contact the officer dealing with tree matters to see whether a preservation order should be placed on the tree or woodland, to ensure its retention – or, if such an order is already in existence, whether the tree or woodland should still be retained. Any survey that has already been prepared will obviously greatly assist this assessment. Generally, no development should be allowed so close to any of the trees to be retained that to construct it would require intrusion within the protected zone[30] around those trees.

15.8.3 Tree preservation orders made in response to development proposals

There is a specific duty on planning authorities to consider making tree preservation orders in connection with the grant of planning permission.[31] In practice, of course, by the time permission is granted, it is sometimes far too late: some, at least, of the trees on the site may have long since gone. The time to make an order is thus as soon as the authority gets wind of a development proposal – possibly months before permission is even sought. This may not be enthusiastically received by the developer, but it will at least remove the uncertainty, and enable the development, and in particular the layout of the site, to be designed in the knowledge of which trees the authority wishes to see retained – and, indeed, if that seriously interferes with the proposal, to object to the order at the earliest stage.

In the absence of such pre-emptive action, where an application is submitted for outline planning permission, it is important for the planning authority to consider as soon as possible whether a tree preservation order needs to be placed on any trees or woodlands on the site. Again, this will enable the developer to work up the layout and the other reserved matters appropriately. And if outline permission has been granted, possibly on appeal, without an order having been considered, the matter should be addressed promptly, as problems may occur if the making of the order is left until the details have been submitted.[32]

Where, on the other hand, an application is submitted with a detailed layout

---

[30] See **15.9.4**.
[31] TCPA, s. 197(b).
[32] See, for example, *Bellcross v Mid-Bedfordshire DC* [1988] 1 EGLR 200.

plan – an application for full planning permission, or for the approval of reserved matters, or an outline application but accompanied by an illustrative layout, it should be possible to consider precisely which trees should be retained.

It may be, for example, that the trees on and near the site will rule out the possibility of any development, or will severely limit what can sensibly be achieved. In that case, if a tree preservation order does not already exist, one should be made promptly covering all the trees and woodlands to be retained. If the developer were then to apply for consent under that order to fell all or some of the trees, consent would presumably be refused, and the authority would have to pay compensation. But at least the trees will have been retained – albeit at a price. At the other extreme, some or all of the trees may be of no great value – or they may be inappropriate for the site, or diseased, or whatever, so that they can be removed without further ado. Or it may be that an existing tree preservation order was made many decades ago, and that this represents a good opportunity to review it – to allow consent to fell some and prune some, and to retain the remainder, which can in future be protected by a new order, more relevant to the new situation.

It should not be forgotten that no consent is required to fell any tree protected by a tree preservation order, where the felling is immediately required for the carrying out of development which has been authorised (provided that the tree preservation order was made in or after 1966).[33] Nor is there any need for a felling licence.[34] That emphasises the importance of identifying at the very outset which trees are to be kept, and which lost, long before permission is given. Thus, while it may well be useful to impose conditions and to make tree preservation orders at the stage of granting planning permission, as required under section 197 of the Act (see above),[35] that will often be too late. The protection of trees which are under threat needs to be put in place right at the outset.

There was, incidentally, no corresponding exemption from consent in the 1949 and 1953 Model Orders (or, therefore, in orders whose wording followed that of those Model Orders) for works to protected trees needed to implement a planning permission. Accordingly, where planning permission is granted for development which necessitates the carrying out of works to trees protected by an old (pre-1966) order, the planning authority should draw to the attention of the applicant the need to obtain consent under the order – although the processing of an application for such consent should be a mere formality.

Where there is a threat of pre-emptive felling, with no time to enable a proper survey to be carried out of the trees on a site, the authority may have to move very quickly, and impose an "area" order protecting all trees, of whatever species – using the procedure under section 201 to ensure that it comes into effect immediately.[36] This was the situation that led to a recent High Court challenge being made by the owner of trees on which an "area" order had been made in response to a planning application, in *Robinson v East Riding of Yorkshire*. Sullivan J. commented as follows:

"It is not in the least unusual for provisional tree preservation orders to be triggered by the making of a planning application. In an ideal world, the Council would have the resources

---

[33] 1966 Model Order, Sched. 2, para. (3)(f); 1969 Model Order, Sched. 2, para. (3)(c), 1999 Model Order, art. 5(1)(d); see **17.8**.

[34] FA 1967, s. 9(4)(b); see **14.2.6**.

[35] And see **15.9.5** below.

[36] See **16.6.2**.

and the time to survey its area to decide where it might be expedient in the interests of amenity to make tree preservation orders, regardless of whether or not there were any proposals for development. In reality, there are only 24 hours in the planning officer's day, ant if there is a threat to trees by reason of a development proposal, very often that will be the occasion when the making of a tree preservation order will first be considered. . . . That should not be equated with the Council seeking to bolster its position at a planning inquiry."[37]

However, the use of area orders on anything other than an emergency basis is, rightly, not encouraged by central Government[38]; and the authority, as soon as it has made the area order, should carry out a full survey (or commission the developer to do so) and replace the area order with a new one which only applies to protect the trees and groups which are actually of value.

15.8.4 Evidence of effect of development on trees

The desirability of preparing a thorough survey has already been stressed.[39] This will ideally be done by the developer prior to the submission of a planning application.

However, it may happen that there is a dispute as to the effect of a proposed development on the trees growing on a site, in which case it will be necessary for the matter to be resolved by way of an appeal to the Secretary of State – which will, in practice, almost always be determined by an inspector. It will then be necessary for the developer and the planning authority each to produce appropriate technical evidence; the inspector, however experienced or knowledgeable, must not simply rely on his or her own opinion without giving the parties an opportunity to comment.[40]

Such evidence will usually need to consider each tree, group of trees and bush on the site, in the light of the survey already produced – and if a survey has not already been produced, it should be by the time any appeal is determined. It would also be sensible to include all the new trees and other planting proposed. The evidence will then need to evaluate the likely effect on each tree of the development proposed and, if that effect will be negative, how it will be ameliorated – for example, by hand digging close to trees. It should not be forgotten that the effect will not just be caused by the finished buildings, but also by the construction of those buildings (which will undoubtedly cover a wider area), and the outbuildings, walls, roads, pipes, cables and open spaces associated with the development.

Nor should future effects be forgotten – in some cases, elaborate precautions are taken (including the imposition of a tree preservation order) to protect a valuable tree from the effect of constructing a new house nearby; but within a few years the occupiers of the house are seeking consent under the order for the removal of the tree, on the grounds that it has now grown to the point where it is overshadowing the garden, or causing the foundations to subside. In such a situation, it may be in practice very difficult for the planning authority to resist granting consent; but that should have been foreseen when it was originally considering whether to grant permission for the house.

---

[37] [2002] 06 E.G. 152 (CS), EWHC 63 Admin, at paras. 36, 37.
[38] DETR Guide, 2000, para. 3.18; see also TAN 10, 1997, para. A5.
[39] See 15.8.2 above.
[40] See, for example, Relayshine Ltd v Secretary of State [1994] E.G.C.S. 12.

On the other hand, it should not necessarily be assumed that every tree on a site must be kept. It may well be that a few could be lost, particularly if conditions are to be imposed requiring new ones to be planted. But here, too, evidence will need to be produced by those acting for the developer, to justify any allegation that there will be little or no loss overall to amenity. And sometimes the loss of just one or two trees may enable the construction of an access road, which in turn will unlock the future use of a whole site.

15.8.5 Planning applications following pre-emptive felling

It sometimes occurs that, in spite of alertness by the local planning authority (or possibly because of its lack of alertness), trees on a site are felled by a landowner or developer, prior to submitting a planning application for development. This may occur perfectly lawfully, where there is no tree preservation order or conservation area and no felling licence is required; or the felling may constitute a criminal offence. Either way, it is pertinent to ask, on what basis is any subsequent planning application to be considered?

This was the situation in *Rutland DC v Secretary of State*,[41] where a developer who hoped to build some houses on a wooded site in a village felled some eight trees before the local planning authority was able to impose a tree preservation order on the remaining 14. The authority subsequently refused planning permission for the houses, but the inspector considering the resulting appeal allowed it, on the basis that he was satisfied that there was enough space on the site to construct three houses, whilst retaining all the remaining protected trees, and to carry out further tree planting and landscaping. As he put it: "I can well understand the concern of the local people and the Council at the loss of mature trees on the site. However, I have to deal with the situation which now exists". The authority challenged that decision in the courts, on the basis that the inspector failed to consider the possibility of action being taken in the future to deal with the results of the felling. The court, on the other hand, considered that the approach adopted by the inspector had been the correct one.

In practice, there is a fundamental difference between pre-emptive demolition of listed buildings, which cannot be replaced, and felling protected trees, which can (albeit only with young trees). It would thus seem that the correct approach for an authority faced with this problem is for it to pursue vigorously all possible action to ensure that replacement trees are planted (as required either by the Forestry Act or under the Town and Country Planning Act) and, until that has been resolved, to reject any planning application as being premature. Alternatively, it can negotiate with the developer as to where the replacements should be planted so as both to repair the damage to amenity caused by the felling and to enable at least some development to proceed. The latter course is obviously more constructive, and should be pursued wherever possible.

15.8.6 Planning obligations

It may in some cases be possible to alleviate the harm caused by a proposed development, or to achieve some compensatory benefit, by the use of a planning obligation, under section 106 of the Town and Country Planning Act 1990.[42] Such

---

[41] [1990] J.P.L. 144.
[42] As substituted by Planning and Compensation Act 1991.

an obligation may be by way of an agreement between the developer and the local planning authority, or may take the form of a unilateral undertaking by the developer, which comes into effect once the development is implemented.

Current guidance from central Government on the use of planning obligations is as follows:

"Properly used, planning obligations can remedy genuine planning problems, and enhance the quality of development. They can help reconcile the aims and interests of developers with the need to safeguard the local environment. For example, where a site includes woodland or open space which would be lost if a development proposal went ahead, the LPA may wish to seek agreement form the developer to provide some form of replacement facility in the site or on other land over which the developer has control. It may not be essential to provide an exact substitute: a woodland walkway, for example, may in some cases be an acceptable replacement for a green space. But there should be some relationship between what is lost and what is replaced, in scale as well as in kind. DETR welcomes the use of planning obligations by some developers in creating nature reserves, planting trees, establishing wildlife ponds and providing other nature conservation benefits."[43]

More general advice on the use of planning obligations is contained in the Department of the Environment Circular 1/97.[44]

15.9 Conditions on planning permissions

15.9.1 The use of conditions generally

It has already been noted that section 197 of the 1990 Act requires a local planning authority "to ensure, whenever it is appropriate, that in granting planning permission for any development, adequate provision is made, by the imposition of conditions, for the preservation or planting of trees".

Such conditions may be designed to ensure either that existing trees on the site are retained or that new ones are planted – in either case, no doubt, so as to co-ordinate with any landscaping proposals associated with the proposal.

Appendix A contains some sample conditions, based on those in Circular 11/95.[45] Care should be used in selecting which is appropriate in each case and adapting it to suit the particular circumstances. That Circular should be consulted for more guidance on conditions generally.

It should be noted that several of the conditions are drafted by reference to what is referred to in the British Standard[46] as the protected zone round the trees in question, within which no building works should be carried out. As a general guide, the boundary of that zone will be below the outermost limit of the branch spread, or at a distance equal to half the height of the tree, whichever is the further from the tree.[47]

---

43 *DETR Guide*, 2000, para. 5.24.
44 *Planning Obligations*. WO Circular 13/97 is in identical terms.
45 Department of the Environment Circular 11/95, *The Use of Conditions in Planning Permission* (WO Circular 35/95); see particularly Annex Appendix A, conditions 71 to 74; 75(a),(b).
46 British Standard BS 5837:1991, *Trees in Relation to Construction*. See **15.8.2** above.
47 Or calculated in accordance with Table 1 in BS 5837:1991 (which usually leas to a smaller area); see s. 7.5.

15.9.2 Outline planning permissions

Where an application is made for outline planning permission, it is in the first instance for the developer to decide how much detail, if any, it wishes to supply of the proposed development; and it is for the planning authority to decide whether it is willing to accept an application with only that level of detail – and, if it is not, to seek further information as appropriate.[48] Where, for example, an outline application is received for the construction of one house on a very large wooded site, it might be appropriate for the authority to grant permission (assuming that there was no other reason for refusal) on the basis that probably one or two trees would be lost, but that there would be enough remaining to ensure no overall loss of amenity, and that the details of precisely which (if any) trees would be felled, how all the trees would be dealt with could be left until the stage of approval of reserved matters.

On the other hand, where an outline application is for a large number of houses on a small site with a few important trees, the planning authority may be genuinely unconvinced as to whether it is possible to fit everything on the site. In that situation, it might be appropriate for the authority to decide as rapidly as possible which trees it wishes to see retained in any event, and then either to seek full details of the layout and landscaping of the development, or else to grant permission subject to a condition that the chosen trees (specified) must be retained, and to place a tree preservation order on them. The latter approach means that the developer does not have to spend time and money supplying details at this stage, but is clearly on notice as to which trees are to be retained. It would, in such a case, be possible to place an area order on all the trees on the site, as a holding operation,[49] but it is better to put a more specific order as soon as possible on those trees which are genuinely of value, rather than to cloud the position.

The sample conditions in the first section of **Appendix A** are appropriate for use with outline planning permissions, to specify the details which the local planning authority wishes to be supplied at the stage of approval of reserved matters – again, both as to which existing trees are to be retained and which new ones are to be planted.

15.9.3 Full planning permissions: details to be approved

It will usually be appropriate to impose a condition on a full (detailed) planning permission requiring specified trees to be retained, and others to be planted.

Applicants not infrequently seek to omit full details of matters such as landscaping and planting, arguing that they can be approved later. And that may be perfectly appropriate in a particular case. However, where there are important trees or woodlands on or close to the site, it might be perfectly possible for an authority to say that it is not willing to consider an application without full details of the landscaping, including details of which trees are to be retained and how that is to be achieved, and which new trees are to be planted.

As for new planting, it may be best for it to be carried out at the end of the building operations, so that the new saplings are at no risk of being trampled to death or simply neglected. Alternatively, it may be best for some specimen trees

---

[48] TCP (General Development Procedure) Order 1995, art. 3(2).
[49] See **15.8.3**.

and structural planting to be planted at an early stage in the development programme, so that they will be reasonably established when the building is first occupied.

And it is important not to forget that, once the details of proposed planting have been approved, they must be implemented. To achieve this in practice may require some thought, to avoid problems of enforceability. With larger schemes, it may be appropriate to prohibit the occupation of a particular phase of the development, or the start of building works on a subsequent phase, until landscaping (including tree planting) has been completed.

Sample conditions are in the second section of **Appendix A**; and the sample conditions relating to outline permissions, in the first section, may also be adapted for use with full permissions.

15.9.4 Protection of trees during building works

The British Standard, noted above, points out that:

". . . damage to trees is frequently caused unwittingly, because of failure to appreciate the vulnerability of trees, particularly the root system, and how easily and often insidiously they can be damaged. Irreparable damage is frequently done to existing trees and other planting in the first few days of a contractor's occupation of a site." [50]

It goes on to place great emphasis on developers and planning authorities, once they have selected which trees are to be retained, then identifying a protected zone round them within which no building works should be carried out.[51] This should then be protected at all times by a robust fence erected right at the start of the building operations, before any demolition or development, including the erection of site huts, is started. A suitable specification for such a fence is in the Standard. And once erected, the fence should be regarded as sacrosanct, and should not be removed or altered until the works (including landscaping) are absolutely complete.

Guidance to the same effect, often with reference to the Standard, is issued by many local planning authorities in leaflet form.

Planning authorities are required to consider imposing conditions on planning permissions in order to ensure that this type of protection is actually implemented.[52] A suitable condition, in line with the model condition suggested in the relevant Government guidance,[53] is included as condition [A7] in **Appendix A**. This, in effect, requires the developer:

- to agree with local planning authority the precise location and constructional details of suitable protective fencing;

- to erect such fencing right at the beginning of the building works, before any equipment, machinery or materials is brought onto the site; and

- not to remove it until all the other works are complete.

Nothing is to take place within the area thus protected.

---

[50] British Standard BS 5837:1991, *Trees in Relation to Construction*.
[51] See **15.9.1** above.
[52] TCPA 1990, s. 197(a).
[53] DOE Circular 11/95, *The Use of Conditions in Planning Permissions*, Appendix A, model condition 75(c).

The importance of such a condition was illustrated in the recent decision of the High Court in *Leisure Great Britain PLC v Isle of Wight County Council*,[54] which concerned a similar condition to the same effect. As is normal, another condition had required the development[55] to be started within five years of the permission and, before that period had expired, a road was constructed in accordance with the details that had been approved. However, no fencing had been erected around the trees to be retained on the site, in accordance with the condition, either at the date the roadworks were begun, or by the expiry of the 5-year period. It was said by the developer that the trees could still be protected despite what had taken place by way of roadworks. However, the court considered that to be irrelevant. It followed that the works that had been carried out were in breach of the tree-protection condition, and were therefore unlawful; accordingly, the development had not been started with in the 5-year period, and the planning permission lapsed.

This emphasises that a condition requiring trees to be protected may appear trivial to a developer but, until it has been complied with, any development carried out – even if on a different part of the site – is unlawful and at risk of being the subject of enforcement action.

15.9.5 Protection of trees after the completion of development

It will usually be appropriate to impose a condition on the permission requiring specified trees to be retained, others to be planted, and both sets to be maintained and replaced if they die within the first year or two. It may be wise to require the owner to notify the authority of any trees that die or are removed, so as to enable the owner and the authority to decide whether a replacement is indeed necessary. A sample is at **Appendix A**.[56]

The advice from Government is that conditions should not be used to provide permanent protection; that is more effectively achieved using tree preservation orders – and, of course, a preservation order may be imposed either on a tree already on the site which is to be retained, or on a tree which is to be planted under the terms of a condition.[57]

15.9.6 Protection by contract

Given the importance of protecting trees during the course of building works, not least in the light of the ability of the planning authority to insist on suitable arrangements being made, and kept in place, it is important for the property owner or developer to take sufficient steps to ensure that the necessary protection is in fact implemented and maintained.

In practice, the best way to ensure this may be to make a suitable provision in the building contract, and to include a penalty clause to ensure that the builder is liable to make a suitable payment in the event of any damage caused. If such a provision is to be effective, the size of such a payment would presumably need to be significantly greater than just the cost of obtaining, planting and maintaining a new specimen tree of reasonable size.

---

[54] [2000] PLCR 88.
[55] A leisure club and holiday lodges – not that it matters. There were, in fact, two conditions requiring prior approval by the Council of certain matters; but the principle would have applied equally had there been just the one.
[56] See **Appendix A**, conditions [A9] and [A10].
[57] *DETR Guide*, 2000, para. 5.19; see also TAN 10, 1997, para. 19.

Such penalty clauses are not popular with contractors, and may lead to the contract sum being increased accordingly, but they do significantly increase the chances of the trees concerned still being alive and well at the end of the contract.

15.10 Trees in churchyards

In some towns and, more especially, in some villages, some of the finest trees are in the churchyards of Church of England churches.

The churchyard may be, and indeed in many cases is, within a conservation area, and the trees within it subject to a tree preservation order. But whether or not that is the case, a faculty is needed for any works in a consecrated churchyard, and this includes the planting pruning and felling of trees there. This requirement, which in the past may have been only somewhat cursorily complied with, has recently been given renewed emphasis by the redrafting of the relevant procedural rules.[58]

The current position is outlined in **Chapter 22**.

15.11 Statutory duties relevant to trees of particular value

15.11.1 General provisions

In addition to the various statutory duties relating specifically to trees and woodlands, already considered earlier in this Chapter, there are a number of other, more general environmental duties imposed by law that may also be relevant.

Most of these are phrased in the form of "having regard to the desirability of" certain matters. This would seem to mean that consideration must be given as to whether, and, if so, to what extent and by what means, those matters are desirable. In other words, it does not mean that the specified considerations are necessarily to take precedence over all others, but simply that they must at least be taken into account. And the courts will, on occasion, be willing to strike down a decision made which takes account of one statutory duty but ignores another.[59]

There is thus a general duty (under section 11 of the Countryside Act 1968) laid upon every Minister, Government department and public body in the exercise of any of their functions relating to land to have regard to the desirability of conserving the natural beauty of the countryside – that is, its flora, fauna and geological and physiographical features.[60] That would obviously include trees and woodland – and hedgerows – in the countryside.

Secondly, Ministers, Government departments and the National Assembly for Wales are also to have regard to the purpose of "conserving biological diversity" in accordance with the United Nations Environmental Programme Convention on Biological Diversity of 1992.[61] That would of course include the Secretary of State when determining planning appeals, and might be of particular relevance in relation to proposals affecting veteran trees and ancient woodlands. For an indication of what this is supposed to mean in practice, it is necessary to study

---

[58] See Faculty Jurisdiction Rules 2000 (S.I. 2000 No. 2047); see **22.2.5**.

[59] *Heatherington UK Ltd v Secretary of State and Westminster CC* [195] J.P.L. 228 (listed buildings v the development plan); *Kent County Council v Secretary of State* [1995] J.P.L. 610 (conservation areas v road safety).

[60] 1968 Act, s. 49(4).

[61] Countryside and Rights of Way Act 2000, s. 74.

statements of Government policy in this area, including *Biodiversity: the UK Action Plan*[62] and the more recent strategy for sustainable development, *A Better Quality of Life.*[63]

It remains to be seen whether these particular duties – general as they are – will be enforced by the courts in so far as they relate to trees and other plants (or at all), or whether they will simply remain well-meaning but slightly platitudinous aspirations.

And there are, in addition, various duties relating to particular industries and activities.

15.11.2 Water, pollution, land drainage and harbours

There is a general environmental duty laid upon the Secretary of State and the Environment Agency, [64] and upon internal drainage boards,[65] in exercising any functions relating to such matters as waste disposal, pollution control and land drainage:

- to do so in such a way as to further the conservation and enhancement of natural beauty and the conservation of flora of special interest;

- to have regard to the effect of proposals upon the beauty or amenity of any rural or urban area, or upon such flora; and

- to have regard to the desirability of preserving for the public any freedom of access to areas of woodland and other places of natural beauty.

This clearly imposes upon the industry a duty (amongst others) to have regard to trees, woodlands and hedgerows of special interest or beauty. It supersedes the duty, in similar terms, previously laid upon the National Rivers Authority.[66] There are further duties in relation to sites of special scientific interest.[67]

Duties in more or less identical terms are laid upon all those in the water industry – that is, in particular, the Secretary of State and the water companies.[68] And similar duties, although in slightly different terms, are laid upon harbour authorities when formulating or considering proposals.[69]

Of greater significance in practice will be the codes of practice noted in **Chapter 7.**[70]

15.11.3 Electricity and telecommunications

A similar, but less extensive, duty is imposed upon any body licensed to generate, transmit or supply electricity,[71] or exempt from the need for such a licence,[72]

---

[62] Cm 2428, January, 1994.
[63] Cm 4345, 1999.
[64] Environment Act 1995, s. 7(1), (2).
[65] Land Drainage Act 1991, s. 61A, inserted by Land Drainage Act 1994.
[66] Under s. 16 of the Water Resources Act 1991.
[67] Environment Act 1995, s. 8; Land Drainage Act 1991, s. 61C, inserted by Land Drainage Act 1994.
[68] Water Resources Act 191, s. 3. And see **7.2.3**.
[69] Harbours Act 1964, s. 48A, and Sched. 2, para. 16A, inserted by Transport and Works Act 1992.
[70] See **7.2.4**.
[71] Under Electricity Act 1989, s. 6.
[72] Under Electricity Act 1989, s. 7.

when formulating proposals for generating stations, transmission lines or other works. That duty is (amongst other things):

- to have regard to the desirability of preserving natural beauty and of conserving flora of special interest; and

- to do whatever can reasonably be done to mitigate any effect which proposals would have on the natural beauty of the countryside or on any such flora.[73]

These more general duties, which obviously may be relevant to trees, woodlands and hedgerows, are of course additional to the more specific provisions laid down in relation to cables interfering with trees.[74]

As to telecommunications, there appears to be no general duty laid down – other than, again, the specific provisions already considered in relation to cables and trees.[75]

And, again, in relation to both electricity and telecommunications, and to gas (as to which, perhaps surprisingly, there is no general statutory duty), reference should be made to the codes of practice noted in **Chapter 7**.[76]

15.11.4 Coal

As the coal industry is run down, the Coal Authority has to formulate proposals for dealing with land no longer required for mining operations. In doing so, it too is to have regard to the desirability of preserving natural beauty and of conserving flora of special interest. It must also take into account (but not necessarily mitigate) any effect which proposals would have on the natural beauty of any area or on any such flora.[77]

Secondly, anyone putting forward a proposal for new coal mining, or (perhaps now of more significance) for the restoration of land formerly used for mining, must have regard to those matters, and must also put forward measures to mitigate any adverse effects.[78] And planning authorities considering planning applications for such proposals must also take all these matters into account[79] – although it is difficult to imagine that they would not do so anyway.

15.11.5 Housing

Finally, housing authorities are required, when preparing any proposals for housing accommodation, or taking any other action under the Housing Act 1985, to have regard to the beauty of the landscape and the countryside, and the other amenities of the locality.[80] This would mean that, for example, it would probably not be appropriate for an authority to clear-fell woodland in order to construct a new housing estate on the edge of a town.

---

[73] Electricity Act 1989, Sched. 9, para. 1.
[74] See **7.2.1**.
[75] See **7.2.2**.
[76] See **7.2.4**.
[77] Coal Industry Act 1994, s. 3(7).
[78] Coal Industry Act 1994, s. 53(3).
[79] Coal Industry Act 1994, s. 53(2).
[80] Housing Act 1985, s. 607.

Chapter 16

Making a Tree Preservation Order

16.1 Introduction

The previous Chapter noted that there are various legal mechanisms for the protection of trees of special value, of which the making of tree preservation orders is only one. It also considered in detail the circumstances in which a tree preservation order might properly be made.[1] This and the following Chapters, by contrast, concentrate on the detailed mechanics of how a tree preservation order may be made, and the consequences of such an order.

First, however, there is (at **16.2**) a brief historical account of how the legislation came to acquire its present structure, and of the various proposals that were made during the 1990s for its reform. This is partly in order to enable a full understanding of some of its features that would otherwise seem to be illogical or incomprehensible (and to assist in appreciating the significance of past decisions of the courts). But an awareness of this somewhat obscure history is also helpful because there are many tree preservation orders – in one or two cases, made over half a century ago – which are still in existence and in force, even though made under earlier Acts and regulations which were subsequently amended and eventually, long since, repealed. Those orders would have followed the form of one of the various Model Orders issued by the Secretary of State, highlighted at **16.3**.

The powers to make a tree preservation order are considered at **16.4**, and the form of an order at **16.5**. The relevant procedures for making and challenging an order are outlined at **16.6** and **16.7**, and the power to revoke and modify one at **16.8**. The consequences of an order being made, which are the subject matter of the following four Chapters, are summarised briefly at **16.9**.

16.2 Historical background

16.2.1 Planning schemes and private Acts: pre-1947 legislation

Under the Housing and Town Planning, etc Act of 1909,[2] town planning schemes could be prepared by local councils for any land that was in the course of

---

[1] See **15.6**.
[2] Amended by the Town Planning Act 1919, and consolidated by the Town Planning Act 1925.

development or which appeared likely to be used for building. In the event, relatively few schemes were ever made under that legislation. However, the Model Clauses issued in 1923 by the Ministry of Health, by way of guidance as to the contents of such a scheme, included provisions whereby a scheme could control felling in woodlands (although it could not insist on replacement planting).

The Town and Country Planning Act 1932 then extended the scope of town planning so as to enable a council to prepare a scheme for any area, rural or urban (and in some cases to require it to do so). Section 46 of that Act provided that the provisions in such a scheme with respect to securing amenity could include provisions for the preservation of single trees, groups of trees, and areas of woodland. Where an area of woodland was specified in such a scheme, and was felled, the owner could be required by the owner to carry out replanting in accordance with the practice of good forestry, with any dispute as to such a requirement being resolved by the Forestry Commission.

But the 1932 Act was little more successful than its predecessors were in securing the preparation of schemes. Accordingly, several local authorities secured the passage of private legislation containing provisions under which the relevant Council maintained a register of trees and groups of trees that ought to be preserved in the interests of amenity. A typical example was section 144 of the Essex County Council Act 1933, by virtue of which the cutting down, topping, lopping or wilful destruction of any registered tree without consent was a criminal offence, attracting a penalty of £5. If the Council refused consent, there was a right of appeal to the magistrates' court, and a further right to compensation.

It is not known how many such Acts there were; nor whether any trees were in fact included in such registers. Presumably any that did exist expired (as indeed the Essex Act did[3]) under the terms of the Local Government Act 1972, since they would by then have been rendered superfluous by the general legislation considered below. Any tree that had been registered under a local Act would then have to be protected by a tree preservation order.

The provisions of a scheme under the 1925 or 1932 Act relating to tree preservation, provided they were in force on June 30, 1948, were kept alive by the Town and Country Planning Act 1947 and by all subsequent planning Acts[4]; with the result that they are still (in theory) in force today unless specifically repealed. In fact, of course, all schemes made under the pre-1947 Acts have presumably long since been repealed.

16.2.2 Interim preservation orders: the 1943 Act

The operation of the 1932 Act was in any event overtaken by the outbreak of war. The Town and Country Planning (Interim Development) Act 1943 was therefore passed to provide temporary protection for trees pending the coming into force of schemes under the 1932 Act. Section 8(1) of the new Act provided as follows:

"If it appears to any interim development authority that it is expedient, having regard to any provision proposed to be included in the scheme in accordance with section 46 of the [1932] Act, to make provision for the preservation of trees or woodlands during the period

---

[3]   Although, surprisingly, it had been amended at least twice – most recently by S.I. 1952 No. 196 and S.I. 1965 No. 510. The author would welcome being informed of other relevant private legislation of this kind.

[4]   TCPA 1947, Sched. 10, para. 7(b); TCPA 1962, Sched. 13, para. 1; TCPA 1971, Sched. 24, para. 87(1)(a); Planning (Consequential Provisions) Act 1990, Sched. 3, para. 3.

pending the coming into operation of that provision, they may for that purpose make an order (in this section referred to as an 'interim preservation order') with respect to such trees, groups of trees or woodland areas as may be specified in the order . . . and in particular provision may be made by any such order –

(a) for prohibiting (subject to any exemptions for which provision may be made by the order) the cutting down, topping, lopping or wilful destruction of trees except with the consent of the interim development authority, and for enabling that authority to give their consent subject to conditions;

(b) for securing the replanting of any part of a woodland area which is felled in the course of forestry operations permitted by or under this order; and

(c) for the imposition of pecuniary penalties, recoverable in a court of summary jurisdiction, in respect of contraventions of the order not exceeding the sum of fifty pounds and, in the case of a continuing offence, forty shillings for each day on which the offences continues after conviction."

The penalties have gone up a bit since then, and the "interim development authority" was replaced in 1948 by the "local planning authority"; but otherwise almost all the provisions quoted above are still in force, in more or less the same words, in the 1990 Act.[5]

That, as it turned out, was unfortunate – since the principle underlying the 1944 provisions was that preservation orders were clearly an interim measure, pending the coming into force of a "scheme" under the 1932 Act. And, of course, only a few years later the whole concept of schemes was swept away by the introduction of a nation-wide system of development control, under the Town and Country Planning Act 1947. But the clumsy system of preservation orders remains. Indeed, it is noteworthy that the parallel system of "building preservation orders", introduced in the Town and Country Planning Act 1944, was eventually swept away in favour of the modern system of listed building control (by the Town and Country Planning Act 1968). It is a pity that there was not also a similar reform of the law relating to tree preservation.

Regulations were to be produced under the 1943 Act regulating the making of a preservation order,[6] and the Town and Country Planning (Additional) Regulations 1944[7] were made accordingly. An order was itself to provide for the appealing against any refusal of consent and the payment of compensation for any loss suffered by tree owners.[8]

Interim preservation orders under the 1943 Act were kept alive by the Town and Country Planning Acts of 1947, 1962 and 1971.[9] They were then further continued in force by the Planning (Consequential Provisions) Act 1990,[10] with the result that they are still in force today unless revoked. Having said that, recent guidance from central Government stresses the desirability of reviewing orders,[11] and it must be doubtful whether a prosecution based on a pre-1948 order would be very fruitful.

---

[5] See, in particular, TCPA 1990, s. 198(1), (3).
[6] TCP (Interim Development) Act 1943, s. 8(3).
[7] S.I. 1944 No. 319, superseding the Provisional Regulations of 1943 which were "to like effect".
[8] TCP (Interim Development) Act 1943, s. 8(2).
[9] Town and Country Planning Act 1947, Sched. 10, para. 15; TCPA 1962, Sched. 13, para. 18, and Schedule 14, para. 1; TCPA 1971, Sched. 24, paras 1, 7
[10] Planning (Consequential Provisions) Act 1990, Sched. 3, para. 3.
[11] See *Tree Preservation Orders: a Guide to the Law and Good Practice*, DOE, 1994, para. 4.4; second edn, DETR, 2000, para. 4.4.

16.2.3 The present system introduced: the Town and Country Planning Act 1947

It was the Town and Country Planning Act 1947 which introduced the term "tree preservation order", in section 28. Otherwise, as already noted, the provisions of that section were surprisingly similar to those of section 8 of the 1943 Act. The principal innovations were:

- that an order was to apply to applications for consent under the order any of the provisions of the 1947 Act relating to planning permission, subject to such adaptations and modifications as may be specified in the order[12];

- that a tree preservation order was not to be made in relation to land subject to a forestry dedication covenant, or which had been the subject of a grant or loan from the Forestry Commission[13];

- that an order was not to prevent the carrying out of works to a tree which was dying, dead or dangerous, or works required by or under an Act of Parliament, or which were necessary for the prevention or abatement of a nuisance.[14]

All of these are still a feature of the legislation. The exemptions from the need for consent, interestingly, were in terms reflecting those of the private Acts passed in the 1930s.[15]

In pursuance of the 1947 Act, the TCP (Tree Preservation Order) Regulations 1948[16] were made. Both the Act and the Regulations came into force on July 1, 1948. Their commencement was accompanied by a brief Circular from the Ministry[17]; that was in turn followed by the reasonably comprehensive *Memorandum on the Preservation of Trees and Woodlands*, issued by the Ministry the following year.[18] The Regulations dealt with the procedure for making orders, but did not prescribe a model order; it was simply stated that "an order . . . shall be in such form as the local planning authority may determine".[19] Every order had to be confirmed by the Minister, however, and he made clear what he expected to be included, by the issue to local authorities of a Model Order, as Appendix A to the 1949 *Memorandum*.[20]

The 1948 Regulations were then replaced by the TCP (Tree Preservation Order) Regulations 1950,[21] which simplified the order making procedure – by relaxing the former requirement that every order should include a map, and by dispensing with the requirement to advertise the making and confirmation of the order (reforms which seem, with hindsight, somewhat surprising, as both requirements would appear to be useful). The enactment of the Forestry Act 1951, introducing

---

[12] TCPA 1947, s. 28(1)(c); see **Chapter 18**.
[13] TCPA 1947, s. 28(2); see **12.6, 12.7** and **16.4.7**.
[14] TCPA 1947, s. 28(5); see **17.3** to **17.5**.
[15] See **16.2.2**.
[16] S.I. 1948 No. 1436.
[17] Ministry of Town and Country Planning Circular 52, *The Town and Country Planning (Tree Preservation Order) Regulations 1948*.
[18] Issued to planning authorities along with Ministry of Town and Country Planning Circular 66.
[19] S.I. 1948 No. 1436, reg. 3(1).
[20] See **16.3.1**.
[21] S.I. 1950 No. 534, issued along with Ministry of Town and Country Planning Circular 85.

the system of felling licences granted by the Forestry Commission,[22] did not lead to any amendment of the 1947 Act, but it did give rise to a further Circular, explaining the interaction between the two control regimes.[23]

Further Circulars appeared in 1953 and 1956, the former containing a new Model Order, which included some revisions to the original model made in the light of experience and others reflecting the changes introduced by the 1951 Act.[24]

Orders made under the 1948 Act were kept in force by the transitional provisions in the Town and Country Planning Acts of 1962, 1971 and 1990.[25]

16.2.4 Town and Country Planning Act 1962

No amendments had been made to section 28 of the 1947 Act before it was replaced by the Town and Country Planning Act 1962. Most of the provisions relating to the protection of trees in the new Act were in section 29, which also incorporated cross-references to the Forestry Act 1951 and the Opencast Coal Act 1958.[26] But the provisions relating to unauthorised works and compensation were separated out as, respectively, sections 62 and 125 of the 1962 Act.

The enactment of the 1962 Act was followed by the making of the TCP General Regulations 1964,[27] Part III of which updated and replaced the 1950 Regulations relating to the order-making procedure. Those Regulations still did not prescribe a model order; but a revised Model Order was once again included as an Appendix to the second edition of the *Memorandum on the Preservation of Trees and Woodlands*, issued by the Ministry of Land and Natural Resources in 1966.

The 1962 Act was a consolidation measure, and so included no new provisions. The first change to primary legislation since 1947 was thus introduced by the Civic Amenities Act 1967, which tightened up the enforcement of the tree preservation order system. Section 15 increased the penalties (which had not been changed since 1943[28]) and sections 13 and 14 introduced a duty to plant replacement trees.[29] Perhaps most significantly, a new provision was introduced enabling a local planning authority to make a provisional order which came into effect immediately, to avoid the obvious loophole whereby trees could be lost while the Minister was considering whether to confirm an order.[30] The 1967 Act also introduced a new duty for local planning authorities to have regard to trees when determining planning applications.[31]

These changes were followed through into the secondary legislation, by means of the TCP General (Amendment) Regulations 1967,[32] which amended the 1964 General Regulations. And they in turn were replaced by the TCP (Tree Preservation Order) Regulations 1969,[33] which included (as a Schedule) a Model Order – which thus, for the first time, had statutory force.

[22] See **11.1.3**.
[23] Ministry of Housing and Local Government Circular 60/51.
[24] Ministry of Housing and Local Government Circular 27/53, and Circular 36/56, *Trees*.
[25] TCPA 1962, Sched. 13, para. 18, and Sched. 14, para. 1; TCPA 1971, Sched. 24, paras 1, 7; Planning (Consequential Provisions) Act 1990, Sched. 3, para. 3.
[26] See **17.10.1**.
[27] S.I. 1964 No. 1382.
[28] See **16.2.2**.
[29] See **Chapter 20**.
[30] Civic Amenities Act 1967, s. 16; see **16.6.2**.
[31] Civic Amenities Act 1967, s. 12, see now TCPA 1990, s. 197; and see **10.4.1** and **15.8.2**.
[32] S.I. 1967 No. 1241, reg. 2(c),(d). And see Ministry of Housing and Local Government Circular 53/67 (Welsh Office Circular 48/67).
[33] S.I. 1969 No. 17.

Orders made under the 1962 Act were kept in force by the transitional provisions in the Town and Country Planning Acts of 1971 and 1990.[34]

16.2.5 Town and Country Planning Act 1971

The 1962 Act was short-lived. It was replaced, along with the 1967 Act, by the Town and Country Planning Act 1971, another consolidating measure. The provisions relating to tree preservation orders were in sections 60 to 62 – save those relating to prosecution and enforcement of the replacement planting duty (sections 102 and 103) and compensation (sections 174 and 175).

These provisions of the 1971 Act were amended a number of times. First, the Town and Country Amenities Act 1974 extended the scope of new orders so as to cover uprooting of and wilful damage to trees as well as their felling, lopping, topping and destruction.[35] This change was duly carried through to the model order in the 1969 Regulations by the TCP (Tree Preservation Order) (Amendment) (etc) Regulations 1975[36] – although, note that this change did not apply to orders made prior to March 12, 1975. The 1974 Act increased the penalties for unauthorised works, and enabled prosecutions to be brought in the Crown Court in appropriate cases – regardless of when the order in question had been made.[37] And it was also the 1974 Act that introduced control over works to trees in conservation areas.[38]

Secondly, the Local Government, Planning and Land Act 1980 restricted the power of county councils to make orders, and (more significantly) amended the order-making procedure so that in future every order was to be confirmed by the authority that had initially made it.[39] The latter change was carried through to the 1969 Model Order by the TCP (Tree Preservation Order) (Amendment) Regulations 1981.[40] And, thirdly, the Town and Country Planning Act 1984 introduced a power for local authorities to make tree preservation orders in relation to Crown land in anticipation of its disposal.[41]

Finally, following the decision of the Court of Appeal in *Bell v Canterbury City Council*,[42] the provisions in the model order relating to compensation for the refusal of consent to fell trees in woodlands were amended by the TCP (Tree Preservation Order) (Amendment) Regulations 1988, so as to bring them in line with those relating to other trees.[43] Again, note that these changes apply only to orders made after June 30, 1988.

Central Government guidance was updated with the issue by the Department of the Environment of the important Circular 36/78, *Trees and Forestry*.[44] That

---

[34] TCPA 1971, Sched. 24, para. 1; Planning (Consequential Provisions) Act 1990, Sched. 3, para. 3.
[35] Town and Country Amenities Act 1974, s. 10(1), (2).
[36] S.I. 1975 No. 148, reg. 2.
[37] Town and Country Amenities Act 1974, s. 10(3)–(7).
[38] Town and Country Amenities Act 1974, s. 8; see **15.7** and **Chapter 21**.
[39] Local Government, Planning and Land Act 1980, Sched. 15, para. 13.
[40] S.I. 1981 No. 14, reg. 2.
[41] TCPA 1984, s. 2; see **16.4.6**.
[42] [1988] 2 PLR 69, CA, upholding [1986] 2 EGLR 209.
[43] S.I. 1988 No. 963; see **18.7**.
[44] WO Circular 64/78. Parts VI to X of the Circular (dealing with tree preservation orders) were finally cancelled in relation to England, by the second edn of *Tree Preservation Orders: a Guide to the Law and Good Practice*, DETR, 2000. The remaining Parts of the Circular, although not formally cancelled, are largely obsolete. The whole Circular remains (at least in theory) fully in force in Wales – see Technical Advice Note (TAN) 10, *Tree Preservation Orders* ("TAN 10"), 1997.

Circular contained a comprehensive *Memorandum on Trees and Forestry* which cancelled all previous guidance, and much of which is still in force today (even though officially admitted to be "largely out of date"[45]).

Tree preservation orders made under the 1971 Act were kept in force by the transitional provisions in the Planning (Consequential Provisions) Act 1990.[46]

16.2.6 The current legislation: the 1990 Act and the 1999 Regulations

As a result of this lengthy process of evolution, the current legislation is found in the Town and Country Planning Act 1990, which was a consolidating measure, replacing the 1971 Act and the numerous Acts which had amended it; the provisions relating to trees are in Chapter I of Part VIII. That was amended by section 23 of the Planning and Compensation Act 1991, which substantially increased the penalties for unauthorised felling,[47] and introduced new powers for planning authorities to seek injunctions[48] and to enter land.[49] The full list of relevant provisions is now as follows:

197	General duties of planning authorities as respects trees
198 to 202	Tree preservation orders
203 to 205	Compensation for loss or damage caused by tree preservation orders
206 to 209	Duty to plant replacement trees
210	Penalties for non-compliance with tree preservation orders
211 to 214	Trees in conservation areas
214A	Injunctions
214B to 214D	Rights of entry

This means that, for the first time since 1962, the statutory provisions relating to the protection of trees are all conveniently gathered together in one place.

The guidance in Circular 36/78 was "supplemented" – in reality, largely superseded – in relation to England, by the first edition of *Tree Preservation Orders: a Guide to the Law and Good Practice* (popularly referred to in some quarters as "the blue book"), issued by the Department of the Environment in 1994. New guidance for Wales (similar, but briefer than that applying in England[50]) was issued as Technical Advice Note (TAN) 10, *Tree Preservation Orders*, by the Welsh Office in 1997. The 1978 Circular remained officially in force, however, in both England and Wales.

The most recent development has been the introduction of the Town and Country Planning (Trees) Regulations 1999,[51] which came into force on August 2, 1999, and which are referred to in this and subsequent chapters as "the 1999 Regulations". The new Regulations finally replaced the 1969 Regulations, and

---

[45] See *England's Forestry Strategy: A New Focus for England's Woodlands*, Forestry Commission, 1998, p. 12.
[46] Planning (Consequential Provisions) Act 1990, Sched. 3, para. 3.
[47] See now **19.6.1**.
[48] See **19.7**.
[49] See **16.6.1** and **19.5.1**.
[50] Much briefer, and as a result nearly useless. Welsh readers are recommended to read the English guidance – if excuse is needed, it is more up-to-date (2000 as opposed to 1997).
[51] S.I. 1999 No. 1892.

implemented a number of the Government's proposed reforms to the tree preservation order system, and in particular:

- improved the order-making procedures[52];
- tightened up the exemption from consent for works to fruit trees[53];
- brought up to date the exemptions for works by statutory undertakers[54]; and
- defined more precisely the rights to compensation.[55]

These and the other changes introduced by the new Regulations are noted at appropriate points in the following Chapters of this book.

The 1999 Regulations also included (as the Schedule) the first new Model Order for thirty years. But it must be emphasised that the changes to the need for consent under an order, and the procedure for applying for that consent, only apply to orders made on or after August 2, 1999. The corresponding provisions in orders made before that date remain in force unaltered.[56]

A second edition of *Tree Preservation Orders: a Guide to the Law and Good Practice* was issued by the Department (by then the Department of the Environment, Transport and the Regions) in April 2000, to accompany the new Regulations.[57] That guidance (referred to in this book as "*DETR Guide*") relates to England only, and replaces the sections of Circular 36/78 dealing with tree preservation orders.[58] Guidance for Wales is still to be found in TAN 10 (see above), even though that has not been amended to take account of the 1999 Regulations; and the Circular (as Welsh Office Circular 64/78), at least in theory, remains in force.

16.2.7 Review of tree preservation order legislation

By the end of the 1980s, it had become obvious to many of those who came into contact with it that the system of tree preservation legislation and policy was far from perfect. The Government in 1989 accordingly appointed Mr James Batho, a former Under Secretary in the Department of the Environment, to undertake a comprehensive review, and to consider whether the system remained appropriate and whether it needed to be amended in any way. He submitted his report, which has been described as "a careful and useful study of numerous legal and administrative issues related to tree preservation",[59] in October 1990; and the

---

52 See **16.6**.
53 See **17.9.5**.
54 See **17.7.3**.
55 See **18.7.5**, **18.7.6**.
56 See **Chapter 17** as to the need for consent, and **Chapter 18** for the procedure for applying for it; each explains the position both in relation to orders following the 1999 Model Order and in relation to earlier orders.
57 See also **16.3.1**.
58 It is available on the web at www.regeneration.dtlr.gov.uk/info/env/treeshedges/tpo/guide/index.htm; presumably "dtlr" will soon be replaced with "odpm".
59 *Encyclopedia of Planning Law and Practice*, Monthly Bulletin, November 1990.

Government, in response, issued a consultation paper inviting views on the way forward.[59a]

Following that consultation exercise, the Government published in July 1994 its considered view as to the way forward, which recommended a number of reforms to policy and legislation.[60] It realised that the implementation of a number of the proposed reforms would require changes to primary legislation, for which there was no opportunity in the foreseeable future. In the meanwhile, however, the issue of *Tree Preservation Orders: a Guide to the Law and Good Practice* in 1994 (see above) meant that at least the policy was more or less up-to-date. In addition, the issue in 1999 of the new Regulations and the second edition of the *Guide* were further steps forward.

But that did not overcome one of the most tiresome features of the legislation, namely, that it is the order which itself provides the requirements as to when consent is required and how it is to be obtained. In the light of the above historical account, it can now be appreciated that the explanation for this feature is the origin of the modern order in the system of "interim preservation orders" (under the 1943 Act[61]) – which, as its name suggests, was never intended to be permanent. But it has two disadvantages. The first is that the order itself is far too cumbersome. The second is that changes to primary or secondary legislation after an order has been made cannot be taken account of, other than by the order in question being replaced.

There are thus a number of proposed changes to primary legislation, supported by the Government, which are still outstanding, of which the principal ones are as follows:

- changing the form of a tree preservation order[61a];

- limiting the use of area orders[62];

- ensuring that all orders come into effect immediately, on a provisional basis[62a];

- tightening up a number of the exemptions from the need for consent under tree preservation orders[63];

- tightening up the penalties for unauthorised works[64]; and

- improving the rules relating to the planting of replacement trees.[65]

These and the other changes promoted by the Government in 1994 are noted at appropriate points in this and the following Chapters.

[59a] *Review of Tree Preservation Policies and Legislation*, Department of the Environment and Welsh Office, undated but issued late December 1990.
[60] *Tree Preservation Orders: Review*, Department of the Environment, July 21, 1994.
[61] TCP (Interim Development) Act 1943, s. 8; see **16.2.2**.
[61a] See **16.5.7**.
[62] See **16.5.4**.
[62a] See **16.6.4**.
[63] See **17.3.1**, **17.3.4**, and **17.5.10**.
[64] See **19.3.6**.
[65] See **20.2.5**.

16.2.8 Central Government involvement in tree preservation orders

The identity of the section of central Government responsible for the tree preservation order system has changed over the years. Since existing orders, still in force, and much of the guidance referred to in this Part of the book, relates to departments now extinct, it may be as well to rehearse briefly how the present arrangements were arrived at.

Back in the 1940s, the Minister of Town and Country Planning was responsible, in both England and Wales for the implementation of the 1943 and 1947 Acts, and thus for the implementation of the system of tree preservation orders. He gave way in January 1951 to the Minister for Local Government and Planning;[65a] but on the return of a new government later that year, a new Ministry of Housing and Local Government (MOHLG) was created.[65b] That arrangement survived for somewhat longer (albeit replaced for a brief period by the Ministry of Land and Natural Resources).[65c]

A new Department for the Environment (DOE) then took over in England in 1970.[65d] That lasted for many years; but on the return of a new government in 1997, there was a steady stream of reorganisations. First, the DOE was replaced by the Department for the Environment, Transport and the Regions (DETR).[65e] That Department had responsibility for all matters relating to trees and hedgerows. However, following the election in 2001, that was split between two new departments: trees (including tree preservation orders) and high hedges went to the Department for Transport, Local Government and the Regions (DTLR), whereas responsibility for the new Hedgerows Regulations went to the Department for the Environment, Food and Rural Affairs (DEFRA).

The DTLR proved to be short-lived, and was in May 2002 split into two; planning matters, including trees and (high) hedges, went to the new Office of the Deputy Prime Minister (ODPM).[65f] The official title of the head of this new Department is "Deputy Prime Minister and First Secretary of State"; references in this Part of the Book to "the Secretary of State" should be read accordingly, at least in relation to England.

In Wales, the Secretary of State for Wales and the Welsh Office assumed responsibility for planning matters, including tree preservation orders, in 1965.[65g] On the coming into effect of devolution, under the Government of Wales Act 1998, the National Assembly for Wales took over the planning functions of the Secretary of State.[65h] In relation to Wales, therefore, references to "the Secretary

---

[65a] Transfer of Functions (Minister of Health and Minister of Local Government and Planning) (No.s 1 and 2) Orders 1951 (S.I.s 1951 No.s 142 and 753).

[65b] Minister of Local Government and Planning (Change of Style and Title) Order 1951 (S.I. 1951 No. 1900).

[65c] Secretary of State for Wales and Minister of Land and Natural Resources Order 1965 (S.I. 1965 No. 319) and Ministry of Land and Natural Resources (Dissolution) Order 1967 (S.I. 1967 No. 319).

[65d] Secretary of State for the Environment Order 1970 (S.I. 1970 No. 1681).

[65e] Secretary of State for the Environment, Transport and the Regions Order 1997 (S.I. 1997 No. 2971).

[65f] At the time of writing, there appears to be no statutory authority for this arrangement. A Statutory Instrument will doubtless appear in due course.

[65g] Secretary of State for Wales and Minister of Land and Natural Resources Order 1965 (S.I. 1965 No. 319).

[65h] National Assembly for Wales (Transfer of Functions) Order 1999 (S.I. 1999 No. 672).

of State" should be taken as references to the Assembly. Day to day administration is carried out by "Welsh Assembly Government" in Cardiff.

Appeals in both England and Wales are dealt with by the Planning Inspectorate, an Executive Agency of the ODPM and the National Assembly.

16.3 Model Orders

16.3.1 Model Orders since 1948

It has been noted in the course of the historical account that the Minister (and, later, the Secretary of State[66]) has issued over the years a series of "model orders" to guide local authorities in preparing draft orders, so that they could have some idea of what they would be willing to confirm. These were initially issued as part of "guidance", with no statutory authority – but the need for ministerial confirmation ensured that they were closely followed in practice. Since 1969, the model order has been prescribed in regulations, which was perhaps just as well since local authorities were able, from 1981, to confirm their own orders, and it was good for there to be some form of reasonably tight central supervision.

The complete list of the Model Orders issued since 1948 appears to be as follows:

1949	Issued as Appendix A to the *Memorandum on the Preservation on Trees and Woodlands*
1953	Issued as Appendix to Circular 27/53
1966	Issued as Appendix A to the second edition of the *Memorandum*.
1969	Schedule to the TCP (Tree Preservation Order) Regulations 1969[67]
1999	Schedule to the TCP (Trees) Regulations 1999[68]

References in this and the following Chapters to "1969 Model Order", and so on, should be interpreted accordingly.

The 1969 Model Order was amended several times – principally by the following Regulations:

- TCP (Tree Preservation Order) (Amendment) and (Trees in Conservation Areas) (Exempted Cases) Regulations 1975[69]; and

- TCP (Tree Preservation Order) (Amendment) Regulations 1988.[70]

The 1969 Regulations were themselves also amended in 1981,[71] but those amendments did not affect the Model Order.

---

[66] See **16.2.8**.
[67] S.I. 1969 No. 17.
[68] S.I. 1999 No. 1892.
[69] S.I. 1975 No. 148, reg. 2.
[70] S.I. 1988 No. 963, reg. 2. Other minor amendments were made by the Electricity Act 1989 (Consequential Modification of Subordinate Legislation) Order 1990 (S.I. 1990 No. 526).
[71] By TCP (Tree Preservation Order) (Amendment) Regulations 1981 (S.I. 1981 No. 14), reg. 2; see **16.2.5**.

So, for example, if an order was made in 1976, it should have been made under the provisions of the TCP (Tree Preservation Order) Regulations 1969, and its wording would have followed that of the model in the Schedule to those Regulations ("the 1969 Model Order"), as amended in 1975. The fact that those Regulations were amended again in 1981 and 1988, and that subsequent Regulations were made in 1999, is irrelevant; it is the provisions of the order itself that are relevant.

16.3.2 Earlier Model Orders

As for orders made under the TCP (Interim Development) Act 1943, which came into force on March 9, 1944,[72] these presumably also followed a model order – which was probably in a Memorandum or Circular to local authorities. The terms of that model can be deduced, from surviving orders which were made at that period, presumably in reliance on it; but it has not proved possible to locate the source of the model.[73] In any event, it is the wording of the actual order applicable in a particular case that is crucial, not that of the model on which it was based.

16.3.3 Current position

As noted at various points above,[74] orders made under earlier legislation have remained in force.

To obtain a rough indication of how many orders made under each of the model orders still lead to applications for consent, an analysis has been made of the 1,288 appeals processed by the DETR in London in the period from January 1998 to July 2001. As would be expected, they have arisen from applications for consent under tree preservation orders made at various dates since 1944. The number of appeals made in each group of years is as follows:

Year of origin	1944 to 1948	1949 to 1953	1954 to 1966	1967 to 1969	1970 to 1975	1976 to 1988	1982 to 1988	1989 to 1999	2000	All
Total number of appeals	4	10	142	75	194	142	196	503	22	1288
Average number per year	0.8	2.0	10.9	25.0	32.3	23.7	28.0	45.7	22.0	22.6

Unsurprisingly, four out of five of the orders leading to these appeals were made in the period 1970 to 1999 – that is, under the terms of the 1969 Model Order (either as originally drafted, or as altered in 1975, or as altered in both 1975 and 1988).

---

[72] See **16.2.2**.

[73] If any reader has access to a copy of the 1943 Model Order, or any other actual order based on it, the author would be grateful to see it!

[74] See **16.2.2** to **16.2.5**.

16.4 Powers to make tree preservation orders

16.4.1 Introduction

By virtue of section 198 of the Town and Country Planning Act 1990, a local planning authority may make a tree preservation order where it appears to the authority that it is expedient in the interests of amenity to make provision for the preservation of trees or woodlands in its area.[75] The Secretary of State has similar powers.[76] In the previous Chapter,[77] consideration has already been given to the questions of which trees are eligible for protection by tree preservation orders, when is it "expedient" to make an order, and what is meant by "amenity". The remainder of this Chapter looks at the details of how an order is made and challenged.

All new tree preservation orders will now (since August 2, 1999) be made under the powers contained in the 1990 Act, and following the procedures set out in the TCP (Trees) Regulations 1999, and will follow the form of the model contained in the Schedule to those Regulations. In practice, however, at least as important as the law (that is, the Act and the Regulations, and the judicial decisions interpreting them) will be the relevant guidance from central Government – in particular, *Tree Preservation Orders: a Guide to the Law and Good Practice*, issued by the Secretary of State[78] in 2000, and referred to here as "the *DETR Guide*".[79]

16.4.2 Orders made by the local planning authority

A tree preservation order may be made by "the local planning authority".[80] Unfortunately, as so often with functions under the Planning Acts, it is not altogether straightforward to determine precisely what this means in practice.

First, in any of the areas in which there is now a unitary system of local government – that is, all of Wales,[81] Greater London and the other major conurbations,[82] and some other areas of England[83] – the rule is (obviously) that an order may only be made by the sole local authority which exists (usually called a borough, district or county borough council).[84]

---

[75] TCPA 1990, s. 198(1).
[76] TCPA 1990, s. 202; see **16.4.4**.
[77] See **15.6**.
[78] That is, the Secretary of State for the Environment, Transport and the Regions (as he then was). See **16.2.8**.
[79] See **16.2.6**.
[80] TCPA 1990, s. 198(1).
[81] Including Monmouthshire (Gwent).
[82] That is, Greater Manchester, Merseyside, South Yorkshire, Tyne and Wear, West Midlands and West Yorkshire.
[83] All of the former (1974) counties of Avon, Berkshire, Cleveland, Herefordshire, Humberside, the Isle of Wight and Rutland; and the former districts of Blackburn, Blackpool, Bournemouth, Brighton and Hove, Darlington, Derby, Gillingham, Halton (Runcorn), Leicester, Luton, Milton Keynes, Nottingham, Peterborough, Plymouth, Poole, Portsmouth, Rochester, Southampton, Southend-on-Sea, Stoke-on-Trent, Thamesdown (Swindon), The Wrekin (Telford), Thurrock, Torbay, Warrington, York.
[84] Wales: TCPA 1990, s. 1(1B), inserted by Local Government (Wales) Act 1994. London and other metropolitan areas: TCPA 1990, s. 1(2). Other unitary authorities in England: Local Government Changes for England Regulations 1994 (S.I. 1994 No. 867), reg. 5(6), (7); TCPA 1990, s. 1(1), (3). Note that the Common Council of the City of London is treated as a Borough Council for this purpose (TCPA 1990, s. 336(1)).

In the remainder of England, the general rule is that an order may only be made by the district council. However, the county council may also make an order in the following cases:

- where it is granting planning permission subject to conditions designed to preserve existing trees or to achieve the planting of new trees, and the order is made (in accordance with section 197) to secure the preservation of those trees[85];

- where the order relates to land that is in the area of more than one district council; or

- where it relates to land in which the county council has an interest.[86]

In practice, the only planning applications determined by county councils are those relating to minerals and waste disposal and those for development on land straddling the boundary of a national park.[87] It follows that orders will only rarely be made by county councils – although there are still a number in force made by county councils under previous legislation (prior to the 1974 local government reorganisation).[88]

In each of the national parks, in England and Wales, the relevant national park authority is for almost all purposes the sole local planning authority.[89] However, functions relating to tree preservation orders are, for some reason, almost unique in that they may also be exercised by the district council, where there is one, or elsewhere by the metropolitan borough council or unitary authority.[90] In the Norfolk and Suffolk Broads, an order may be made either by the Broads Authority or by the relevant district council, save that a district council may not grant planning permission, and may therefore not make an order under section 197 (see above).[91] However, the relevant county councils still have concurrent powers, in the circumstances outlined above, just as county councils elsewhere.

The Secretary of State also has powers to appoint various other bodies as local planning authorities in special cases:

- an enterprise zone authority, in relation to an enterprise zone designated under the Local Government, Planning and Land Act 1980[92];

- a housing action trust, in relation to a housing action trust area set up under the Housing Act 1988[93]; and

- the Urban Regeneration Agency (also known as English Partnerships), in

---

[85] TCPA 1990, s. 197(b); see **15.8.3**.
[86] TCPA 1990, s. 1(1), (3), (5)(c), Sched. 1, para. 13(1).
[87] TCPA 1990, Sched. 1, paras 1, 3; S.I. 1980 No. 2010, reg. 2.
[88] See TCPA 1947, s. 4(1); TCPA 1962, s. 2(1); TCPA 1971, s. 1(1), as originally enacted prior to its replacement by Local Government Act 1972, Sched. 16.
[89] TCPA 1990, s. 4A(2), inserted by Environment Act 1995.
[90] TCPA 1990, s. 4A(4), (5), inserted by Environment Act 1995; Local Government Changes for England Regulations 1994 (S.I. 1994 No. 867), reg. 5(7). The only other such function is that of issuing notices under s. 215.
[91] TCPA 1990, s. 5.
[92] Local Government Planning and Land Act 1980, Sched. 32, para. 5; TCPA 1990, s. 6.
[93] Housing Act 1988, s. 67; TCPA 1990, s. 8.

relation to an urban area in England designated under the Leasehold Reform, Housing and Urban Development Act 1993.[94]

The powers of these bodies could, in theory, include those relating to tree preservation orders. In practice, it appears that no such appointment has yet been made or is in prospect.

Finally, in urban development areas, for as long as they lasted, tree preservation orders could be made by urban development corporations, and not by the relevant district or borough councils whose planning powers had been temporarily supplanted.[95] All the corporations have now been wound up; it is not known how many, if any, orders they made.

16.4.3 Local authority procedures

The form of a tree preservation order is considered in more detail below.[96] In theory at least, and sometimes in practice, an order will be made by the elected members of the local planning authority. In such a case, the relevant standing orders of the authority will need to be complied with as to the making and confirmation of a preservation order – in terms of which committee or sub-committee has authority to make the necessary decision, how that decision must be reached, whether the order needs to be sealed, and so on.[97]

More often, an order will be prepared by an officer of the local planning authority, and signed on behalf of the authority. Again, this will need to be done according to any relevant standing orders. In particular, it is likely in the scheme of things that an order will in many cases need to be made in a hurry – a tree can be felled in a surprisingly short time. It will therefore be important for every planning authority to ensure that there is in place a scheme of delegation,[98] which authorises one or more officers to make provisional orders without needing specific approval from either senior officers or committees – and for those officers to know what they are empowered to do and how practically it can be done. Arrangements must also be made to cope with evenings, weekends, public holidays and officers on leave.

It should not be forgotten that such delegation arrangements could involve other local authorities;[99] so it would be possible, for example, for two neighbouring councils to arrange to assist each other on a reciprocal basis.

16.4.4 Orders made by the Secretary of State

The Secretary of State also has power to make a tree preservation order, under section 202 of the 1990 Act, if it seems "expedient". These default powers have, in practice, rarely, if ever, been used[1]; but they might be appropriate where trees are growing on land owned by an uncooperative semi-public body, or a foreign government, or a local authority.

Before making an order, the Secretary of State (or, in practice, officers of the

---

[94] Leasehold Reform, Housing and Urban Development Act 1993, s. 171; TCPA 1990, s. 8A (inserted by 1993 Act, Sched. 21).
[95] Local Government Planning and Land Act 1980, s. 149. The only exception was Cardiff Bay.
[96] See **16.5**.
[97] *Bates v Secretary of State* [1975] 1 EGLR 127.
[98] Under Local Government Act 1972, s. 101(1)(a), (2).
[99] Local Government Act 1972, s. 101(1)(b).
[1] See *Tree Preservation Orders: Review*, DOE, 1994, para. 2.51.

Department) must first consult the relevant local planning authority. This will be the authority with power to make an order itself. Where that could be either the district council or the county council,[2] the Secretary of State is to consult with whichever council he or she thinks appropriate. Thereafter, the procedure for making an order is just as for an order by the authority.

Once an order has been made by the Secretary of State, it will have the same effect as if it had been made by a planning authority. It will name a planning authority by whom it will be enforced, and that authority then has the power to determine applications for consent made under the order, and to enforce requirements as to the planting of replacement trees.[3]

The Secretary of State may also revoke a tree preservation order.[4]

16.4.5 Crown land

Special rules, in Part XIII of the 1990 Act, apply to the making of tree preservation orders on Crown land – that is, land in which the Crown (usually in the form of a Government department or the Crown Estate) – has a freehold or leasehold interest.[5]

A tree preservation order under section 198 may only be made by a planning authority on trees or woodlands on Crown land with the consent of "the appropriate authority" – which will generally be the Crown Estate Commissioners or the relevant Government department.[6] The Government has stated that departments "have no objection in principle to the making of orders on Crown land; and their consent will not unreasonably be withheld".[7]

However, as with trees in the ownership of any other large and responsible landowner,[8] it must be questionable whether it will often be "expedient" to make such an order. Once it has been made, an order will not bind the Crown itself, of course, in that consent will not have to be obtained for works carried out by Government departments. But the Government has stated that departments will normally consult the local planning authority before carrying out works which would otherwise require consent.[9] On the other hand, such an order will require consent to be obtained for tree works carried out by any others, such as non-Crown tenants, who would otherwise have the right to do such works.

It follows that, whilst the preservation of trees on Crown land may frequently be desirable in the interests of amenity, it will – at least for the time being – generally be expedient to make an order for this purpose only where there is someone other than the Government department or Crown Estate who is entitled to carry out tree works, or where it is known that the land may, in due course, be disposed of to a private owner. A special procedure would normally be used in the latter case, described below.[10]

This may change, as the Government has stated on numerous occasions that its

---

[2]   In practice, in non-metropolitan areas in England (including the Broads); see **16.3.3**. TCPA 1990, Sched. 1, para. 20.

[3]   TCPA 1990, Sched. 1, para. 13(2).

[4]   TCPA 1990, s. 202(1).

[5]   TCPA 1990, s. 293(1). It also relates to land owned by the Duchy of Cornwall or the Duchy of Lancaster.

[6]   TCPA 1990, ss. 296(2)(a), 293(2); and see *DETR Guide*, 2000, para. 2.5.

[7]   *DETR Guide*, 2000, para. 2.5; see also TAN 10, 1997, para. 8.

[8]   See **15.6.5**.

[9]   *DETR Guide*, 2000, para. 2.5; see also TAN 10, 1997, para. 9; see **18.3.11**.

[10] See **16.4.6**.

intention is to remove Crown immunity from planning control (including tree preservation order controls) when a suitable legislative opportunity arises.[11] When such a change is imminent, it may then be appropriate for authorities to consider more actively the desirability of making orders in relation to Crown land – especially in the light of the statement by the Government that "Crown bodies [must] continue to be able to meet their statutory obligations".[12]

Finally, it may be noted that land owned by the Secretary of State for Health is Crown land, including land transferred to the Secretary of State from regional health authorities in 1996[13]; whereas land owned by NHS trusts is not.[14]

16.4.6 Land about to be disposed of by the Crown

As explained above, it is unlikely to be expedient for an authority to make a tree preservation order where land is currently wholly owned by the Crown (that is, where there is no leasehold or other interest owned by any other person or body). However, where an interest in Crown land is to be granted to a non-Crown person or body, or the land is to be altogether disposed of by the Crown, so that (in either case) someone other than the Crown will then have the right to carry out works to trees on it, it might then be expedient to make an order which comes into effect immediately on the change of ownership.

To deal with this situation, there is a special procedure, introduced in 1984,[15] whereby an order may be made (under section 300 of the 1990 Act) which has no effect until the transfer of ownership, but then comes into effect on a provisional basis immediately.[16] Such an order is to be made, prior to the transfer, with the consent of the appropriate authority (the Government department or the Crown Estate)[17]; and that authority is then to notify the planning authority as soon as practicable that the transfer has taken place, and to inform it of the name and address of the new owner.[18] Once the planning authority has thus been notified, it is then to go through the normal process of notifying the new owner and others, publicising the order, and dealing with objections, as in any other case.[19]

Thereafter the position is exactly as with an order made with a direction under section 201.[20] An order made under section 300 thus remains effective only for six months after the transfer, unless it has been confirmed during that period. If it has not been confirmed by then, it ceases to have effect; but it may be subsequently confirmed.[21]

16.4.7 Land in which the Forestry Commission has an involvement

As explained earlier, land which is managed by Forest Enterprise (the land-

---

[11] See, for example, *DETR Guide*, 2000, para. 2.6.
[12] *DETR Guide*, 2000, para. 2.6.
[13] Under Health Authorities Act 1995.
[14] National Health Service and Community Care Act 1990, s. 6.
[15] As s. 2 of the TCPA 1984.
[16] TCPA 1990, s. 300(3).
[17] TCPA 1990, s. 300(2); for the meaning of "appropriate authority", see TCPA 1990, s. 293(2).
[18] TCPA 1990, s. 300(6).
[19] TCPA 1990, s. 300(7); see **16.6.3**.
[20] See **16.6.2**.
[21] TCPA 1990, s. 300(5); see **16.6.6**.

owning arm of the Forestry Commission[22]) is also technically "Crown land".[23] The law and principles outlined above in relation to any other Crown land therefore apply here too; and it would only be expedient to make a tree preservation order where land is about to be disposed of.

Where land in private ownership is subject to a forestry dedication covenant,[24] or has been the subject of a grant or loan from the Forestry Commission,[25] a preservation order may only be made with the consent of the Commission; and no order may be made where there is in force a plan operations under a dedication covenant.[26] For the outworking of this in practice, see *Armitage v South Oxfordshire DC*,[27] in which it was held that a failure to obtain the formal consent of the Commission was not fatal to the validity of the order in that case, as there was clear evidence that the Commission had been fully aware of the position and would undoubtedly have given its consent had it been sought.

In practice, local planning authorities are in any event encouraged to liase closely with the Commission.[28] The Commission will thus always consult the relevant planning authority where it receives an application for assistance under the Woodland Grant Scheme in relation to trees which are already protected by a tree preservation order (or which are in a conservation area). And special arrangements apply where proposed works to a tree require both a felling licence and consent under a tree preservation order.[29]

When Crown immunity from planning control is withdrawn, arrangements will be made to ensure that Forest Enterprise is treated on the same basis as any other landowner managing its land in accordance with an approved plan of operations.[30]

16.4.8 *Local authority land*

A local planning authority may make a tree preservation order in relation to land that it owns, or that is owned by another Council.

As to the first, this would require the authority to grant itself consent for any proposed tree works – which might be relevant where those works are proposed by a department of the Council other than that responsible for tree preservation orders. A special procedure is now in place for applications made in such circumstances.[31] But it must be questionable how often it could be said to be "expedient" to place an order on the authority's own land, except (as with Crown land) where works are likely to be carried out by a tenant, or where it knows that the land is, or may be, about to be disposed of.

As to making a tree preservation order on land owned by another local authority (such as a district council making an order on land owned by a county council), the Government's view is that this would "very rarely be appropriate".[32]

---

[22] See **11.3.2**.
[23] See **11.2.3**.
[24] See **12.6**.
[25] See **12.7**.
[26] TCPA 1990, s. 200(1).
[27] [1998] 2 PLR 89; see **15.6.5**.
[28] *DETR Guide*, 2000, para. 2.10.
[29] See **14.4**.
[30] *DETR Guide*, 2000, para. 2.6.
[31] TCP General Regulations 1992, reg. 11A, inserted by TCP(T) Regulations 1999, reg. 17; see **18.3.10**.
[32] *DETR Guide*, 2000, para. 2.12; see also TAN 10, 1997, para. 10.

16.5 Form of a tree preservation order

16.5.1 General structure of an order

The structure of a tree preservation order following the 1999 Model Order – subject to one exception[33] – will be somewhat simpler than that of orders made following earlier Models.[34] The order is divided into "articles", as follows:

Article 1	states the name of the order, for example, the "Barchester City Council Tree Preservation Order No. 3 of 1999" or the "Acacaia Avenue and Walnut Gardens Tree Preservation Order 1999".
Article 2	states the name of the authority which is making the order, and by which it will (if necessary) be enforced.
Article 3	*[omitted where not applicable]* states that the order will come into effect on a provisional basis on the date stated, without being confirmed.
Article 4	states which categories of works are in principle prohibited in relation to the trees, groups of trees or woodlands described in Schedule 1 to the order.
Article 5	lists the various exemptions to that general rule.
Article 6	explains how an application is made for consent to carry out works that would otherwise be prohibited.
Article 7	refers to Schedule 2 to the order.
Article 8	*[presumably may be omitted where not applicable]* explains that a replanting direction may be given where consent is granted to fell a woodland.
Article 9	explains the entitlement to compensation in the event of an adverse decision in response to an application for consent.
Article 10	*[only inserted where appropriate]* explains how the order takes effect in relation to a tree planted as a result of a condition attached to a grant of planning permission.
Article 11	*[only inserted where appropriate]* states that the order is made in relation to Crown land, in anticipation of its disposal.
Schedule 1	specifies the trees that are protected by the order, with reference to individual trees, groups of trees, areas and woodlands.
Schedule 2	sets out detailed provisions of the Town and Country Planning Act 1990, modified so as to apply to:

- applications for consent under the order; and
- appeals in the event of an adverse decision in response to such an application (consent refused or granted subject to adverse conditions).

Also, a map will form an essential part of an order will be a map.

In other words, the order explains which trees it protects (Schedule 1 and map), when it comes into force (articles 3, 10 and 11),[35] which works to those trees need

---

[33] See **16.5.6**.
[34] See **16.3**.
[35] See **16.6**.

consent (articles 4 and 5),[36] how that consent may be applied for, what happens if it is refused, including rights of appeals, and when replanting may be required (articles 5 to 9, and Schedule 2).[37]

The order must state clearly the date on which it was made, which will, in most cases, also be the date on which it comes into force.

16.5.2 Which trees are protected: Schedule 1 and map

The 1990 Act states that a tree preservation order may be made "with respect to such trees, groups of trees or woodlands as may be specified in the order".[38] In the 1999 Model Order, as in all the Model Orders that preceded it, this "specification" is achieved by means of a map and a Schedule – the first Schedule to the Model Order.

An order is thus to contain, or have annexed to it, a map indicating the position of the trees, groups of trees and woodlands to which the order relates. No scale or type of map is prescribed, but the map is to be "to a scale sufficient to give a clear indication of the position of the trees . . . [, etc.]".[39] What that scale will be depends on the circumstances. And it should be borne in mind that an order may need to be used as evidence in a criminal prosecution many years after it is made, by which time the appearance of the trees and of the surrounding area may have changed, possibly out of all recognition. It will also be used in the event of any protected tree being lost in certain circumstances, to specify the location of the replacement.[40]

The High Court recently considered this matter in *Robinson v East Riding of Yorkshire*, concluding that:

"No doubt it is desirable that an up-to-date plan should be used if possible, but what the Regulations require is that the map 'shall indicate the position of the trees'. Provided that the plans attached to the order are sufficient to achieve that objective, it is of no consequence whatsoever that they may be outdated and/or inaccurate in other respects."[41]

Where the map and the schedule are inconsistent, there is no provision in the 1999 Model Order that either should take precedence over the other as there was in earlier Model Orders.[42] Clearly it is highly desirable that no such inconsistency shall arise.

The trees to be protected are to be marked in different ways on the map (although it does not matter if the wrong type of line is used, so long as the result is clear[43]), and listed in the Schedule under relevant headings, according to whether they are specified individually, or by reference to an area, or in groups, or as woodlands. Any combination of these categories may be used in a single order. Each is now considered in turn.

---

[36] See **Chapter 17**
[37] See **16.5.6** and **Chapter 18**.
[38] TCPA 1990, s. 198(1); TCP(T) Regulations 1999, reg. 2(1)(a).
[39] TCP(T) Regulations 1999, reg. 2(1)(c), (2), (3).
[40] *Bush v Secretary of State* [1988] J.P.L. 108.
[41] [2002] 06 E.G. 152 (CS), EWHC 63 Admin, at paras 31, 32.
[42] See **19.3.1**.
[43] *Robinson v East Riding of Yorkshire* [2002] 06 E.G. 152 (CS), EWHC 63 Admin, at para. 33.

16.5.3 Trees specified individually or in groups

The most straightforward situation is where trees are protected individually or as a group. As to the use of each classification, the *DETR Guide* advises as follows:

" If trees merit protection in their own right, they should be specified as **individual** trees in the TPO. The **group** category should in general terms be used for trees whose *overall* impact and quality merit protection. The intention of the group classification is not simply to protect trees which have individual merit and happen to be standing close to one another, but for their merit as a group. The number of trees in the group and their species should be specified in the First Schedule if the TPO, and if each tree's location can be indicated within the broken line on the map, so much the better."[44]

That may be the intention of the group classification, and the advice seems perfectly sensible in policy terms, but there would appear to be no reason in law why the classification should not be used to protect a group of "trees which have individual merit and happen to be standing close to one another".

The First Schedule to the order is to list each individual tree to be protected; and, as well as its number, its species is to be given and, where appropriate, its location. Thought should be given as to how to specify the location most helpfully – for example, if there are two poplar trees within a front garden, of which one is to be protected, it is no good stating "the taller one"; once (either) one has been felled, it may not be possible to prove with any certainty which was protected by the order. As to groups, the number of trees in each group must be recorded in the Schedule.[45] The Model Order seems to indicate that the species of each constituent tree needs to be recorded, which suggests that there will, in a number of cases, be little practical advantage to using the group classification. And, indeed, the more trees are specified individually, the better.

As to the depiction on the map of individual trees and groups, the main requirement – whether as to the choice of the scale of the map or as to the depiction of the groups on it – is simply to ensure that there can be no possible ambiguity. It may in some cases be appropriate to include, as well as a plan covering the whole land affected by an order, an enlarged plan of a small area with a number of protected trees close together, to assist identification. Trees specified individually are each to be indicated by a black circle on the map forming part of the order, and marked "T1", "T2" and so on. Those to be protected as a group are to be indicated by a broken line on the map around the perimeter of the group, and each group marked "G1", "G2".

Where the order relates to, for example, the only tree growing within a small urban garden, it may be sufficient for the Schedule to the order simply to record the reference number of the tree (presumably T1), its species and the address of the property concerned. There would then need to be within the order (probably before or after Schedule 1), or attached as a separate sheet at the end of it, a copy of the relevant Ordnance Survey 1:1250 map, possibly enlarged to 1:1,000 or even 1:500, of an area sufficient to indicate the location of the property, showing the garden and its immediate neighbours, and highlighting the tree with a circle. Even in such a simple case, it is important to specify correctly the species of the tree in the First Schedule to the order, so as to avoid potential problems later.

---

[44] *DETR Guide*, 2000, para. 3.14; see also TAN 10, 1997, Annex A, para. A.4. Emphasis in original.
[45] TCP(T) Regulations 1999, reg. 2(1)(b).

On the other hand, where there are several trees, more care will be required, particularly where the order is not protecting all of the trees growing on a particular piece of land. The *DETR Guide* gives the following example:

"A TPO is made in respect of T2, specified in the first Schedule to be an ash tree standing in the front garden of 22 Amenity Drive, and a circle is shown on the map. As it happens, there are three ash trees in the front garden of 22 Amenity Drive. If the first Schedule does not describe the tree in a way that clearly distinguishes it from the rest, the ambiguity should be settled by reference to the position of the tree shown on the map. But if the encircling line is too loosely drawn, it may not be possible to ascertain with certainty which of the ash trees is protected."[46]

The same approach would apply to specifying groups.

And where an order relates to, say, a number of individual trees and groups scattered all over a large golf course, it would be more appropriate for a map to be prepared on a separate sheet – possibly at scale 1:2,500, and on whatever size of paper is necessary.

16.5.4 Trees specified by reference to an area

A slight oddity of the legislation is that the 1990 Act provides that a tree preservation order may be made to protect "trees, groups of trees or woodlands"[47]; whereas the 1999 Model Order – in common with all its predecessors back to 1953 – also allows trees to be specified by reference to "an area". The 1949 Model Order had referred only to "trees, groups of trees or woodland area"; but the notes on the revised (1953) Model Order explained that:

". . . for convenience, the Schedule provides for trees to be specified by reference to an area, *e.g.*, where the trees do not stand in well-defined groups and are so numerous that individual enumeration and marking on the map would be irksome."[48]

All subsequent Model Orders allowed for the "area" category of specification; and the 1999 Model Order provides that trees specified in this way (numbered "A1", "A2" and so on) should be indicated on the map attached to the order by a dotted black line around the perimeter of the relevant area. Further, in the first Schedule to the order, it is not necessary to specify the species of the trees concerned – although, it is no doubt helpful to have an indication of the predominant or noteworthy species. On the other hand, an order protecting "trees", including trees specified by reference to an area, as opposed to one protecting "woodlands", only applies to those trees which existed at the time the order was made; and the use of an area order may therefore cause difficulties in the event of allegedly unauthorised felling. And there may also be problems when it comes to the requirement to plant replacement trees, as highlighted in *Bush v Secretary of State*.[49]

However, an area order is not without its uses, as recently explained by Sullivan J. in *Robinson v East Riding of Yorkshire*:

[46] *DETR Guide*, 2000, para. 3.13(2).
[47] TCPA 1990, s. 198(1).
[48] Ministry of Housing and Local Government Circular 27/53.
[49] [1988] J.P.L. 108; see **20.2.2**.

"Merely because more than one tree is included within an order, it does not follow that the trees must be described either as a group or as a woodland. For example, scattered trees in a parkland surrounding a listed building may not comprise a group or be fairly described as a woodland, but in such circumstances it may very well be sensible, rather than specifying each tree, to specify the parkland area within which they are located . . . [T]here may be practical reasons for specifying trees in that way. If, for example, an area contains a number of trees which are not part of a group and do not comprise a woodland, and there is an imminent threat of their removal, there may simply not be the time available to carry out a survey to enable each tree to be specified individually. So in those circumstances it may well be appropriate to specify the trees as trees within a particular area."[50]

Thus an area order may be particularly useful where the owner of land threatens to clear-fell all the trees on it, so as to increase its development potential; but the authority should survey the land as soon as possible after making the order, and modify it so as to relate only to trees specified individually or by reference to groups.[50a] Note that it is not possible to modify an "area" order so as to refer to woodland, since a woodland order is "a different animal" altogether.[51]

The use of area orders has thus been broadly discouraged by the Department, for the above reasons and because it may lead to trees of little merit being preserved.[52] The current guidance is that "the area classification should only be used in emergencies, and then only as a temporary measure until the trees in the area can be assessed properly and reclassified".[53] However, that is only guidance, and not law; and area orders may thus be made, confirmed and left in place indefinitely.[54] The Government accordingly proposes to continue to allow area orders to be made, but in due course to introduce a new provision requiring that, by the time they come to be confirmed, they are converted to orders specifying the trees to be protected either individually or by reference to groups.[55] This seems sensible.

It should also be noted that the Government has indicated that, when it introduces that change, it will also introduce a five-year limit on the future life of existing area orders.[56] That suggests that it would be prudent for any planning authority which has not already done so to start now reviewing and updating all its area orders, so as to spread out the administrative process over as long a period as possible. Useful advice as to the way in which this may be done is provided in the *DETR Guide*.[57]

16.5.5 Woodlands

A tree preservation order may be made for the preservation of "trees or woodlands".[58] The use of the word "or" suggests that that the preservation of

---

[50] [200] EWHC 63 Admin, 06 E.G. 152 (CS), at para. 25.
[50a] See **16.8** for procedure.
[51] *Evans v Waverley Borough Council* [1995] 3 PLR 81, CA, per Hutchinson L.J. at p. 93D – following the language of Jowitt J. in *R v Secretary of State, ex p. Lancashire County Council* [1994] 4 All E.R. 165 at p. 173; see **16.6.8**.
[52] See Department of the Environment Circular 36/78, Memorandum, para. 43.
[53] *DETR Guide*, 2000, para. 3.18; see also TAN 10, 1997, Annex A, para. A.5.
[54] Indeed, in Liverpool, there are apparently some 380 TPOs, all of which are area orders, and the largest of which covers some 5 square miles!
[55] *Tree Preservation Orders: Review*, DOE, 1994, paras 2.16 to 2.19.
[56] *Tree Preservation Orders: Review*, DOE, 1994, para. 2.20.
[57] *DETR Guide*, 2000, paras 4.15 to 4.18.
[58] TCPA 1990, s. 198(1).

woodlands implies something other than simply the preservation of trees which happen to be growing in a group large enough to justify being classified as a "woodland". And, indeed, it has already been noted that a woodland order is a different animal to an area order.[59]

The principal differences between a woodland order and any other are thus as follows:

- it seems to apply to all trees within the woodland specified, regardless of whether they were planted before or after the order was made;

- there is, arguably, a presumption in favour of consent being granted under a woodland order, rather than (as in other cases) the reverse[60];

- there are special provisions as to the imposition of a requirement to replant woodlands felled in the course of forestry operations,[61] and as to the compensation which may be claimed following such a requirement[62]; and

- the duties as to the replacement of trees are slightly less onerous, in that they do not apply to trees felled because they are dying, dead or dangerous.[63]

As to the first of these, it has been universally assumed to be correct – for example, by the Court of Appeal in *Evans v Waverley Borough Council*[64] and by the Secretary of State in the *DETR Guide*.[65] But it is not immediately apparent why. Article 4 of the Model Order, for example, refers to it being an offence "to cut down [, etc] any tree specified in Schedule 1 to this Order or comprised in a group of trees or in a woodland so specified"; there is no difference between the language used to refer to "a group of trees" and that used in relation to "a woodland". If, therefore, the area and group classifications apply only so as to protect the trees actually growing at the time of the making of the order, why does the same not apply to woodlands? It is, incidentally, noteworthy that this assumption is not mentioned in departmental guidance prior to 1994. The point was not mentioned in the 1994 Review of the legislation, but it should be clarified when any other changes are being made.

It is sensible to ensure that the boundaries of any woodland to be protected by a preservation order are clear on the ground – for example, marked by a fence, a road or a stream. This will avoid the difficulties which occurred in *Kent County Council v Batchelor*,[66] where a tree preservation order sought to protect part of a woodland, demarcated from the remainder by an arbitrary line not following any feature of the landscape.

Woodlands are to be shown on the map accompanying a tree preservation order bounded by a solid line, marked "W1", "W2", and so on. A woodland might perfectly appropriately be shown on a less detailed map than would be suitable for individual trees or groups, provided that its boundaries were clear on

---

[59] *Evans v Waverley Borough Council* [1995] 3 PLR 81, CA, per Hutchinson L.J. at p. 93D; see **16.5.4**.
[60] See **18.3.8**.
[61] 1999 Model Order, art. 8.
[62] TCPA 1990, s. 204; see **18.7.8**.
[63] TCPA 1990, s. 206(1)(b); see **20.2.1**.
[64] [1995] 3 PLR 81, CA, at pp. 87B, 93C.
[65] *DETR Guide*, 2000, para. 3.17.
[66] (1976) 33 P. & C.R. 185, 75 L.G.R. 151, [1976] J.P.L. 484, CA.

the ground. Where its boundaries are not obvious, a larger map may be required, or a clear specification ("woodland to the north and east of a straight line drawn between the south-east corner of field 1 and the north-west corner of field 20").

More generally, there is clearly a potential overlap between control of felling in woodlands under a tree preservation order and felling licence control by the Forestry Commission. Authorities are thus sensibly advised to liase with the Commission, before making a woodland order, as to the best way in which the future management of woodlands can be controlled in the interests of amenity; and to encourage owners to bring woodlands into proper management under the grant schemes run by the Commission.[67] In practice, woodland orders may not often be appropriate, bearing in mind that all applications for felling licences are these days determined in the light of the impact on amenity of the proposed works[68]; and the administrative arrangements for dealing with such applications have been streamlined so that any proposal which potentially requires both forms of consent must be first notified to the Commission.[69]

16.5.6 Applications for consent: Schedule 2

Article 6 of the 1999 Model Order provides for the making of applications for consent under an order; and article 7 and Schedule 2 for the processing of those applications and the making of appeals. The effect of these is considered in **Chapter 18**; but it may be worth highlighting a particularly tiresome feature of the way in which the 1999 Order has been drafted.

Thus, although the majority of the 1999 Order is considerably clearer than its predecessors, Schedule 2 is at first glance much less clear. This is because it is in two parts, and the first Part lists not only those provisions of the 1990 Act that apply to applications for consent under an order, but also (in full detail) the modifications to those provisions that are necessary to make them applicable to such applications. So, for example, Part I contains the following entry:

"*Section 75 (effect of planning permission)*	(a) In subsection (1), substitute –
	    (i) "Any" for the words from "Without" to "any";
	    (ii) "consent under a tree preservation order" for "planning permission to develop land";
	    (iii) "the consent" for "the permission"; and
	    (iv) "the land to which the order relates" for "the land".
	
	 (b) Omit subsections (2) and (3)."

Which, of course, makes no sense at all to anyone not intimately familiar with the precise wording of section 75. Part II of the Schedule accordingly sets out section 75 as modified, as follows:

"*Section 75*

Any grant of consent under a tree preservation order shall (except insofar as the consent

---

[67] *DETR Guide*, 2000, paras 3.15, 3.16; see also *Tree Preservation Orders: Review*, DOE, 1994, paras 2.56 to 2.61.
[68] See **14.1** and **14.3.3**.
[69] See **14.4**.

otherwise provides) enure for the benefit of the land to which the order relates and of all persons for the time being interested in it."

Which is a good deal more straightforward.[70] Unfortunately, section 75 is much the simplest of the five sections involved, and the same technique has been used in relation to all of them.

The reason for this cumbersome two-part approach, which was not adopted in any of the pre-1999 Model Orders, lies in the unhappy wording of the 1990 Act, which provides that:

"(3) A tree preservation order may, in particular, make provision . . . (c) for applying, in relation to any consent under the order, and to applications for consent under the order, any of the provisions of the Act mentioned in subsection (4), subject to *such adaptations and modifications as may be specified in the order*."[71]

That is, the modifications to the Act must themselves be set out in full in every order made.

In the light of the drafting of the Act, which will hopefully be amended at the earliest opportunity, the approach adopted by the drafters of the 1999 Order is probably correct, and Part I of Schedule 2 must therefore be included in every tree preservation order based on the Model – preferably in the smallest type available. But it is Part II of the Schedule which is important, and which (in effect) sets out all the relevant procedural rules; and Part I, provided that it is actually included, may safely be altogether ignored for all purposes.

16.5.7 Possible future changes to the form of order

As already noted, the 1999 Model Order is a considerable improvement on its predecessors – other than its inclusion of the clumsy Part I of Schedule 2.[72] If that were to be omitted, and the substance of Part II of that Schedule incorporated into the body of the Model Order, it would be considerably shorter than it is at present, but would still provide the recipient of an order with a complete guide to his or her rights, without the need to refer to any other document, Act or Regulations.

Alternatively, if the process of simplification were to be taken a step further, it would be possible to put much of the material currently in the Model Order into a free-standing set of regulations.[73] That would have the advantage of making every tree preservation order even shorter, but would mean that the procedural provisions would need to be sought elsewhere. And should the exemptions from the need for control be in the Act, in the order itself, or in the Regulations? Indeed, it is from some points of view unfortunate that some exemptions are in the Act, and some in the order. It is thus not entirely clear how far the simplification should go.

It is, in any event, likely that the shape of the Model Order will undergo further

---

[70] Always providing, of course, that the reader knows the meaning of the word "enure" (OED: "belong or be available to").
[71] Emphasis added. See also TCPA 1947, s. 28(1)(c); TCPA 1962, s. 29(1)(c); TCPA 1971, s. 60(1)(c), which are in similar terms.
[72] See **16.5.1** and **16.5.6**.
[73] As suggested in *Tree Preservation Orders: Review*, DOE, 1994, paras 2.6, 2.7.

changes, possibly in the relatively near future, but that will require primary legislation.[74]

16.6 Procedure for making orders

16.6.1 Preliminary procedure

The 1999 Regulations do not deal with the actual making of a tree preservation order; they simply prescribe the form of the order, and the procedure after one has been made.[75] The *DETR Guide*,[76] on the other hand, provides much sensible guidance – albeit aimed almost entirely at planning authorities, rather than landowners, tree surgeons and others who may be affected by tree preservation orders.

The circumstances when it may be appropriate to make an order have already been explored.[77] The first thing for an authority to do is thus to decide whether it is expedient in a particular case to make an order. This will, in practice, almost always involve a site visit by an officer of the planning authority or, possibly, a consultant on its behalf (where, for example, the relevant officer is on leave). There is obviously a risk of the tree in question being felled once it is known that a preservation order is in prospect, so it may be best to make a provisional order without a full survey; but this does not outweigh the duty of an authority not to act unreasonably.[78] There must, therefore, be at least some basis for supposing that the making of an order is expedient.

For the same reason, it may be best for the authority's officer not to enter actually onto the land in question – after all, it is likely that a tree that is suitable to be the subject of a tree preservation order will be visible from a public place.[79] However, if it is considered that going onto the site is appropriate, any person duly authorised by the authority may enter any land (including any building) at any reasonable hour to survey it in order to decide whether or not an order should be made or confirmed.[80] It will thus be important for the appropriate officer to have some form of authorisation which can be relied upon at all times. A person exercising a right of entry under these provisions may also take samples from any tree or from the soil, and may take an assistant; they must produce evidence of their authority if required to do so; they must leave the land as effectively secured against trespassers as they found it; and if they cause any damage, the authority is liable to pay compensation.[81] Anyone who wilfully obstructs a person exercising such a right is liable to prosecution, and to a fine of up to level 3 on the standard scale.[82]

Where it is anticipated that admission onto the land will be refused, or where it already has been, a warrant may be obtained from a magistrate, which authorises

---

[74] Or possibly an order under the Regulatory Reform Act 2000.
[75] As prescribed by TCPA 1990, s. 199(2), (3).
[76] See **16.2** and **16.3**.
[77] See **15.6**.
[78] *Associated Picture House v Wednesbury Corporation* [1948] 1 K.B. 223, CA, at p. 230.
[79] See **15.6.2**.
[80] TCPA 1990, s. 214B(1)(a), (3), (8), inserted by Planning and Compensation Act 1991.
[81] TCPA 1990, s. 214D(1), (2), (4), inserted by 1991 Act.
[82] TCPA 1990, s. 214D(3), inserted by 1991 Act; see **Appendix C**.

a named person to enter the land on one occasion only within the following month.[83] However, this right to enter land under warrant only applies where an authority is considering making or confirming a tree preservation order "with respect to" the land being entered.[84] It is not clear whether this would authorise the seeking of a warrant to enter, for example, land from which it is possible to see a tree under consideration, even though some distance from it.

Whether or not the site is entered, it is important for the positions and species of the relevant trees, and for the boundaries of any areas of trees and woodlands, to be recorded with sufficient accuracy for the order, once made, to be valid. This has already been considered.[85] It is also helpful to take photographs of the site and of the trees concerned, although it should be borne in mind that a photograph of a tree taken at this stage, before an order is made, does not prove that it was in existence at any later time. It may, therefore, be necessary to return to take a further photograph (timed and dated) immediately after the order has been made, if it is feared that a tree is about to be felled.[86] Other relevant information may be useful, such as details as to the ownership and use of any land involved, and a brief assessment of the amenity value of the trees.

However, whilst it is clearly desirable that a proper survey should be carried out, a claim that a survey was perfunctory or inadequate, even if established, would not lead a court to the conclusion that the resulting order was invalid as a matter of law. The merits of the order, and the value of the trees protected by it, can be tested by those affected through the making of an application for consent under the order.[87]

16.6.2 Coming into effect of an order

In theory, a tree preservation order does not come into force immediately, but only (by virtue of section 199) when it has been confirmed by the planning authority, following notification and a chance for objections to be heard.[88] There is no time limit within which a "draft order" must be confirmed. But it would clearly be undesirable for the delay to be too great, since the amenity value of the tree, and thus the expediency of protecting it by the making of an order, might have changed – as might the identity of the owners and occupiers of the land, or even the boundaries of the site. Until such an order has been confirmed, it is not an offence to carry out any works to any trees that are to be protected by it.

In practice, however, because of the obvious risk that at least some of the trees involved will be felled, the great majority of tree preservation orders contain a direction (under powers contained in section 201 of the 1990 Act[89]) that it should come into effect immediately. Where such a direction is included in the order (as article 3, under the 1999 Model Order), the order will take effect as a "provisional order" on the date stated in it, which will presumably be the date on which the order is made. It is, however, vital for the existence of the order to be notified to everyone who may be involved, including tenants, licensees and any other occupiers. Failure by an authority to do this may invalidate any prosecution in

---

[83] TCPA 1990, s. 214C, inserted by 1991 Act.
[84] TCPA 1990, s. 214B(1)(a), inserted by 1991 Act.
[85] See **16.5.2**.
[86] See **19.3.1**.
[87] *Robinson v East Riding of Yorkshire* [2002] 06 E.G. 152 (CS), EWHC 63 Admin, at para. 29.
[88] TCPA 1990, s. 199(1).
[89] Introduced in the Civic Amenities Act 1967.

relation to works carried out after the order was made but before it was notified to the person responsible.[90]

Once a provisional order under section 201 has come into force, it will then remain in force by virtue of section 201 for a maximum of six months. The normal practice is that the order will be confirmed by the authority within that six-month period, possibly with modifications.[91] It will then have effect as a full order, just as an order made under section 199. If, on the other hand, the authority decides to drop the order, it will lapse; although, that would not (at least in theory) affect any criminal liability for works carried out while the provisional order was in force. And if by the end of the six months no decision has been reached either way, the order will no longer be in force by virtue of section 201,[92] but it may subsequently be confirmed just as any other order – although anyone carrying out works after the end of the six months but before the eventual confirmation will not be liable to prosecution.

As to confirmation of orders generally, see below.[93]

16.6.3 Notification and publicity

Once an order has been made – either a draft order under section 199 of the 1990 Act or a provisional order under section 201 – its existence must be notified "as soon as practicable" to all "the persons interested in land affected by the order".[94] This is to be achieved by sending to each such person a copy of the order itself, along with a notice which must provide a statement of the reasons for making the order, and details of how, and by when, to make objections to it (or any other representations[95]). If it is a provisional order made under section 201, that too must be made clear.[96] The time for making objections and representations must be at least 28 days from the date of receipt of the notice.

The *DETR Guide* includes a model notice at Annex 2; it also sensibly suggests that every order be accompanied by a copy of the Department's explanatory leaflet *Protected Trees: a Guide to Tree Preservation Procedures*. It also suggests that the authority should provide the name and telephone number of the officer who will deal with the confirmation of the order, and who can (or should be able to) answer any questions.

As to how far the notification should extend, the land affected by an order clearly includes the land on which are growing any of the trees or woodland protected by it. It also includes (but is not necessarily limited to) the land adjoining that land.[97] Note that this requirement applies whether or not the trees involved overhang any boundaries. In practice, the precise extent of the land affected – over and above the immediately adjoining properties – would need to be determined by the authority in each case on a common sense basis, depending on the precise geography of the various parcels of land in the immediate vicinity of the tree. Thus, in the case of an order protecting a tree at the bottom of an urban

---

[90] *Knowles v Secretary of State and Chorley Borough Council* [1998] J.P.L. 593 – it is not clear why the Secretary of State was involved in this action at all. See **16.6.3**.
[91] See **16.6.6**.
[92] See TCPA 1990, s. 201(b)(i).
[93] See **16.6.6**.
[94] TCP(T) Regulations 1999, reg. 3(1).
[95] See **16.6.5**.
[96] TCP(T) Regulations 1999, reg. 3(1)(a), (2).
[97] TCP(T) Regulations 1999, reg. 1(2).

garden, there may be many other plots of land which could properly be said to be "affected".

The persons interested in such land are:

- the owners and occupiers of the land affected by the order;

- every other person whom the authority knows to be entitled to fell any of the trees to which the order relates; and

- every other person whom the authority knows to be entitled to carry out surface mineral extraction on or under the land.[98]

Particular care must be exercised in the case of land owned by companies, to ensure that a copy of the order and the accompanying notice does reach those who need to know of it – and, in particular, that it reaches those likely to be instructing contractors to remove the trees concerned, as well as the contractors themselves. Care is also needed where land has just changed hands, or is about to do so – again, it must reach those who need to know about it. *Knowles v Secretary of State and Chorley Borough Council*[99] is an example of a case involving both of those problems, and the failure by the Council to notify the correct owner meant that the owner was able to escape conviction. This means that where there is a significant delay before an order is confirmed, it may be sensible for the authority to carry out a further round of publicity.

There used to be a requirement for the authority to notify the local conservatory of the Forestry Commission and the District Valuer of the making and confirmation of an order.[1] That no longer applies, but authorities are asked to notify the Forestry Commission informally of any woodland orders they make[2] (and, indeed, in some cases they will have had to obtain the consent of the Commission before making the order anyway[3]).

There is no formal requirement for the authority to notify anyone else, but it may be wise in some cases to bring the order to the attention of the parish council[4] (where there is one) and any concerned local amenity group. The authority must also have at its offices a copy of the order available (free) for public inspection at all reasonable hours.[5] It may also be appropriate to display a notice on a nearby notice board or in the local press, although there is no formal requirement to do so.

16.6.4 *Service of documents*

The copy of the tree preservation order and the accompanying notice are to be served in the same way as any other document under the Town and Country Planning Act 1990, as prescribed in section 329 of the Act. The three principal methods are as follows:

- by delivering them into the hands of the owner or occupier; or

---

[98]   TCP(T) Regulations 1999, reg. 1(2).
[99]   [1998] J.P.L. 593.
[1]   TCP (TPO) Regulations 1969, regs. 5(b), 6(2), 9.
[2]   *DETR Guide*, 2000, para. 3.22.
[3]   See **16.4.7**.
[4]   Or town council or (in Wales) community council.
[5]   TCP(T) Regulations 1999, reg. 3(1)(b), (3).

- by leaving them at their usual or last known address, clearly marked "Important – this communication affects your property"; or

- by sending them to that address by registered letter or recorded delivery.[6]

In the case of an incorporated company or body, the first and third of the above methods may be used to serve the documents on the company's secretary or clerk at its registered or principal office.[7]

Before serving any documents, the authority may first serve a notice on the occupier of land to ascertain what his or her interest is in the land, and who else has any interest in the land. Such a request for information must be complied with – a failure to do so attracts a fine of up to level 3 on summary conviction, and supplying false information attracts even higher penalties.[8] That should reveal the names of the owners and occupiers, but not necessarily those of others entitled to carry out works to trees.

Where the owner of land cannot be found after reasonable enquiry, the documents may be simply addressed to "the owner", and then served:

- in any of the three ways noted above; or

- by being clearly marked "Important – this communication affects your property", and sent to the premises by registered letter or recorded delivery; or

- by being so marked, and delivered to someone on the land, or fixed conspicuously to some object on the land – presumably one obvious possibility being the tree itself.[9]

And any of these methods may be used to serve the documents on the occupier of the land, simply addressed to "the occupier" – that is, there is no need to identify his or her name; although the documents are more likely to be taken notice of if they are addressed to the occupier by name.

Where the land appears to be unoccupied, the notice may be duly served by being marked "to the owners and any occupiers", and fixed conspicuously to some object on the land (although if the only object to which it can be fixed is the tree itself, it should be done in a way which does not damage it).

Finally, where a tree preservation order relates to ecclesiastical land, notice is also to be given to the Church Commissioners, as well as to the owner and occupier (the incumbent).[10] This applies, in particular, to churchyards, parsonage houses and diocesan glebe land.

16.6.5 Objections and representations in response to an order

Anyone who wishes to may object to a tree preservation order – whether it is a "draft order" under section 199 or a "provisional order" under section 201.[11] Any

---

[6] TCPA 1990, s. 329(1)(a)–(c); TCP General Regulations 1992 (S.I. 1992 No. 1492), reg. 13.
[7] TCPA 1990, s. 329(1)(d).
[8] TCPA 1990, s. 330.
[9] TCPA 1990, s. 329(2).
[10] TCPA 1990, ss. 318(1), 318(6), as amended by Planning and Compensation Act 1991, see **2.1.7** and **Chapter 22**.
[11] See **16.6.2**.

objection should be in writing, and should either be delivered by hand to the authority by the date specified in the notice sent out with the order, [12] or sent in the post so that in the ordinary course of post it would arrive by that date.

There is no prescribed form for making an objection, so a simple letter will suffice. However, any objection should specify the details of the order to which it relates, and the particular trees, groups of trees or woodlands in respect of which the objection is being made, and the reason for the objection.[13] On the other hand, it may be appropriate, for example, in the context of an order covering a large number of trees on a development site, for an objector to submit a substantial report.

There is no limitation as to what those reasons can be, but typically they might include some of the following:

- the preservation of the tree in question is not expedient in the interests of amenity;

- the tree or woodland is under proper management;

- the tree is dying or dead;

- the tree is dangerous, either by virtue of a disease or defect taken together with its location;

- the tree is causing (or is likely to cause) damage to property, such as foundations;

- the tree is overshadowing nearby land (either in the same ownership as the tree or otherwise).

In every case, full details must be given – and photographs may be helpful.

Given the general tendency of people to write to the local authority only when objecting to something, and never in support of anything, it is refreshing to note that the Regulations also provide for the making of "representations" other than objections.[14] These could take the form of letters in support of the order – for example, from those in neighbouring properties whose gardens benefit from the presence of the trees concerned. Or they may be neither against nor in support of the order, but making useful comments as to the its factual accuracy (perhaps as to species), or as to the procedure followed in its making (for example, a failure to notify certain neighbours or tenants). Or the tree owner or a neighbour may wish to support the order in principle, but nevertheless to point out disease or defects in a tree which may not be apparent to the authority. It may also be helpful to draw the attention of the planning authority to any value the trees or woodland may have as habitat for wildlife – such as birds, fungi or lichen. Here too, full details must be given.

And, of course, given that many orders include more than one tree, it is perfectly possible to object to the order in respect of one tree or group, but to support the remainder of it.

Finally, one type of objection, which may well be particularly worthwhile, is to object to the making of an area order, on the grounds that it would be more appropriate to specify the trees to be protected individually or by reference to

---

[12] See **16.6.3**.
[13] TCP(T) Regulations 1999, reg. 4(1).
[14] TCP(T) Regulations 1999, reg. 4(1).

groups. In some cases, it may be appropriate for the property owner to contact the authority and to arrange for a detailed survey to be carried out, either by the authority's tree officer or by an independent consultant, to establish which trees are really of sufficient amenity value to justify long-term protection. And where an area order has been made in advance of a development proposal being received by the planning authority, it may be helpful for the authority to be given, as early as possible, a plan showing the eventual planting and landscaping scheme, or to be involved in the preparation of such a plan, so that the order can then be restricted to those trees which are to remain.

The authority is entitled to take into account objections and representations if they do not comply with the strict requirements of the Regulations – for example, as to time limits – if there is a good reason for the non-compliance.[15] If, therefore, someone only discovers the existence of a draft or provisional tree preservation order towards (or after) the end of the period for making objections, he or she should still send in any objection or other representation as soon as possible – or, if necessary, telephone the relevant officer. And if a neighbour wishes to make a representation, either in favour of or against an order, but does not wish it to be on file in case it sours relations with the tree owner, an authority may nevertheless be willing to take into account the substance of an oral representation.

16.6.6 Confirmation of orders

Before deciding whether or not to confirm a tree preservation order, the local planning authority must "consider" any objections and other representations duly made.[16] And the Secretary of State has sensibly encouraged the relevant local planning authority officers to meet objectors, as this often clarifies the issues at stake.[17]

As to whether an order should be confirmed, the relevant issues will presumably be those which determine whether it is expedient in the interests of amenity to make an order in the first place, which have already been considered.[18]

And as to the procedure by which that decision is reached, it is a noteworthy feature of the process that an order is confirmed by the same authority which made it in the first place. The authority is thus, of course, wide open to the criticism that it has only paid lip service to any objections and has in reality simply rubber-stamped its original decision. One apparent answer to this problem, adopted by many authorities, is to ensure that objections are considered by someone who did not make the order. So, for example, where objections have been raised to a provisional order made by an officer, the decision as to whether or not it should be confirmed is made by a sub-committee or committee of elected members. And where (unusually) a provisional order was made by the sub-committee or committee, or with the authority of its chairman, the decision to confirm it should be given to a specially constituted committee with non-overlapping membership. Where, on the other hand, there are no objections to a provisional order, the officer can confirm it without further ado. Other useful advice as to procedure is given in the *DETR Guide*.[19]

---

[15] TCP(T) Regulations 1999, reg. 4(2).
[16] TCP(T) Regulations 1999, reg. 5(1).
[17] *DETR Guide*, 2000, para. 3.37; TAN 10, 1997, Annex A, para. A.12.
[18] See **15.6**.
[19] *DETR Guide*, 2000, paras 3.33–3.38.

However, sensible as such procedures may be to reduce any appearance of bias, there is ultimately no way round this problem. If there is in existence a proper scheme of delegation,[20] a decision taken by the appropriate officer, sub-committee or committee will still be, in law, that of the authority; and there will be no basis on which to refute the claim that the confirmation is not by a tribunal independent of the body which made the order in the first place.

Perhaps surprisingly, there seems to have been no reported case of a challenge to a tree preservation order having been made on the basis that the procedure leading up to its adoption was unfair. There have however been a whole string of cases relating to the adoption of local plans by planning authorities in the face of objections. The key principle which emerges of the local plan decisions (such as, notably, those of the Court of Appeal in *Stirk v Bridgnorth DC*[21] and *Miller v Wycombe DC*[22]) is that a local authority is in a special position as both proposer and decision maker, and is accordingly under an enhanced obligation to deal thoroughly, conscientiously and fairly with any objection to its plan. The same would apply to an authority confirming a tree preservation order; and indeed the duty on the authority is even greater than in relation to local plans, since in the latter case at least there is the safeguard of objections being considered at an inquiry conducted by an independent inspector, which does not apply in the case of trees. It may therefore be worth an authority considering appointing an independent inspector, perhaps a tree consultant from another part of the country, to conduct a (non-statutory) inquiry in particularly controversial cases and to advise the authority what to do.

That an authority is seen to have in place a meticulously fair procedure to deal with objections (in so far as that can be achieved) is particularly important following the coming into force of the Human Rights Act 1998. That provides that public authorities must now act in a manner that is compliant with the terms of the European Convention on Human Rights, article 6 of which provides that a person's civil rights should be determined by "an independent and impartial tribunal". If the making of a tree preservation order constitutes such a determination, it would seem to be difficult to sustain a claim that an authority that made an order is a suitable tribunal to consider complaints as to its merits. Such a challenge could be met by the argument that the ability to seek consent under the order rectifies any defects in the procedure leading to its making. Alternatively, it could be argued that the ability to challenge the confirmation of an order in the High Court[22a] constitutes a sufficient safeguard of the rights of landowners. Only time will tell whether that (or any other argument) will succeed.

The duty on an authority to consider fairly all objections and representations applies particularly strongly where it has made an emergency order to stop immediate felling – including area orders made to stop a site being clear-felled prior to development. In particular, there will often in such cases have been a fairly limited site inspection when the order was first made; it is thus all the more important to ensure that the committee or other decision-taker inspects the trees and woodlands thoroughly at the confirmation stage.

There is no time limit by which an order must be confirmed. In the case of a draft order, made under section 199, it does not come into effect until it is

[20] See **16.4.3**.
[21] (1996) 73 P. & C.R. 439, CA.
[22] [1997] J.P.L. 951, CA.
[22a] See **16.7**.

confirmed, so the sooner the confirmation process can be completed, the better. In the (much more usual) case of a provisional order, made under section 201, the order will have come into effect immediately, but if by the end of six months it has not been confirmed, it will then lapse until it is finally confirmed.[23] Again, therefore, the authority should confirm the order as soon as it can, and if at all possible within the six months. In any event, if too much time is allowed to lapse before the order is confirmed, it will then be arguable that the value of the tree (in amenity terms) will have changed.

Once an order has been confirmed, it must be clearly endorsed to that effect; and the endorsement must state the date on which it was confirmed.[24]

16.6.7 Subsequent notification and publicity

Once an order has been confirmed, the authority that confirmed it is to send to all the persons interested in the land affected by the order a letter:

- stating that the order had been confirmed, and the date on which that occurred; and

- notifying them of their right to challenge the validity of the order in the High Court (the date by which any challenge must be made, and the grounds on which a challenge may be based).[25]

A sample letter is contained at Annex 3 to the *DETR Guide*.

Note that those who are to be thus notified are those who are interested in the land at the time the order is confirmed – which may, of course, be some while after it was first made. It follows that some of those who were initially notified of the order may have moved. It is probably best, therefore, to notify those who were initially involved,[26] but to ask them to notify the current owners if appropriate. It may also be appropriate in some cases to send (or deliver) a letter addressed to "the occupier" of the land concerned, where there is genuine uncertainty over the position as to ownership.

The Regulations require that notice of confirmation be given "as soon as possible". Given that any challenge has to be mounted within six weeks, and that that deadline may not be extended for any reason whatsoever, the *DETR Guide* rightly stresses that it is "of the utmost importance" that the notice is indeed sent out without delay.[27] There is, in fact, no reason for the authority to supply any reasons for its decision, but the *Guide* sensibly suggests that it do so.

It is also necessary to make a copy of the order, as confirmed, including the map which forms a very important part of it, available for public inspection at all reasonable hours, at the offices of the authority which made it (in place of the draft or provisional order which was previously available).[28] The order and the map must then remain available until it is revoked. It will be crucial for an

---

[23] See **16.6.2**.
[24] TCP(T) Regulations 1999, reg. 5(3).
[25] TCP(T) Regulations 1999, reg. 6(a); for High Court challenges, see **16.7**.
[26] As to which, see **16.6.3**.
[27] *DETR Guide*, 2000, para. 3.44.
[28] TCP(T) Regulations 1999, regs. 6(c), 3(3).

authority to be able to prove that this has been done, if it is to be able to rely on it when mounting a prosecution in due course for unauthorised works.[29]

And the existence of a confirmed order, as a "prohibition or restriction on the use of land", will be a local land charge.[30] It will be a "planning charge", and thus must be registered under Part 3.[31]

Perhaps most significantly in practice, the *DETR Guide* sensibly observes that "in the Secretary of State's view, local planning authorities should also be able to let members of the public know, over the telephone, whether or not particular trees are the subject of a tree preservation order or situated in a conservation area within 48 hours."[32]

Finally, where an authority has notified the Forestry Commission informally of a draft or provisional woodland order having been made,[33] it would obviously be sensible for it also to notify the Commission once the order has been confirmed. And the same would apply where an authority has informed a parish council[34] or local amenity group of a draft or provisional order, or has advertised it on a nearby notice board or in the press.

16.6.8 Confirmation of an order subject to modifications

A draft order or provisional order will normally be confirmed in the same form as it was made; but it is possible for the local planning authority to confirm it subject to "such modifications as [it considers] expedient".[35]

The question of what "modifications" would be permissible under this power was considered by the courts in *Evans v Waverley Borough Council*.[36] In that case, a provisional order had been made under section 201, specifying the trees to be protected by reference to an "area", and describing them as "mixed broad-leaved trees (including willow and alder) and conifer"; when the order was confirmed, it had been modified so as to refer to "woodland comprising mixed broad-leaved trees (including willow, alder, ash and sycamore) and pine".

At first instance, the deputy judge held that there was no reason why the word "modification" should be limited to "restrictive changes"[37]; and the Court of Appeal agreed that the power to modify should not be narrowly or strictly construed and, in particular, it confers a right to enlarge as well as to restrict the ambit of that which is modified.[38] However, it was accepted by both counsel that a woodland order is more extensive than an area order, because it protects trees planted or self-seeded after the date on which the order is made[39]; and on that basis it was held in the Court of Appeal that to change a woodland order into an area order was to produce "a different animal",[40] which was therefore outside the power to modify the order.

---

[29] *Vale of Glamorgan Borough Council v Palmer and Bowles* [1983] J.P.L. 334; see **19.3.2**.
[30] Local Land Charges Act 1975, s. 1(1)(b).
[31] Local Land Charges Rules 1977 (S.I. 1977 No. 985), r. 2(1), Sched. 2.
[32] *DETR Guide*, 2000, para. 3.49.
[33] See **16.4.7**.
[34] Or town council or (in Wales) community council.
[35] TCPA 1990, s. 199(1); TCP(T) Regulations 1999, reg. 5(2).
[36] [1995] 3 PLR 80, CA, overturning [1995] 2 PLR 46.
[37] [1995] 2 PLR 46, per Nigel Macleod QC (sitting as deputy judge).
[38] *Evans* at [1995] 3 PLR 80, CA, per Hutchinson L.J. at p. 89B, and Neill L.J. at p. 94F.
[39] As to whether that concession was rightly made, see **16.5.5** above.
[40] The phrase originated in the judgment of Jowitt J. in *R v Secretary of State, ex p. Lancashire County Council* [1994] 4 All E.R. 165, at p. 173; see *Evans v Waverley Borough Council* at [1995] 3 PLR 80, CA, at p. 89E.

It would seem from *Evans* that it would almost certainly be in order, for example, to amend the species of a tree in a provisional or draft order (although, not if that had the effect of making the order refer to a completely different tree) or to miss out one or two. It might well be in order to alter a group order to an individual order (although the court explicitly left that point open[41]), or an area order into a collection of individual and group orders. There is much to be said for the approach advocated by counsel for the applicant in *Evans*, when he suggested that the correct approach was that identified in *Bernard Wheatcroft v Secretary of State*, in the context of the related issue of how much can a development proposal be altered by the Secretary of State in considering a planning appeal:

"The true test is, I feel sure, that accepted by both counsel: is the effect of the conditional planning permission to allow development that is in substance not that which was applied for? Of course, in deciding whether or not there is a substantial difference, the local planning authority or the Secretary of State will be exercising a judgment, and a judgment with which the courts will not ordinarily interfere unless it is manifestly unreasonably exercised. The main, but not the only, criterion on which that judgment should be exercised is whether the development is so changed that to rant it would be to deprive those who should have been consulted of the opportunity of such consultation . . ."[42]

It should also be noted that there is no requirement for the authority to carry out any consultations in relation to any modifications it proposes to make.[43]

Once the order has been confirmed, subject to modifications, it must be endorsed to the effect, and the modifications indicated in the order "by distinctive type or other means".[44] And those who are to be notified of the confirmation of the order – that is, all those interested in the land affected[45] – are to be sent, along with the notice telling them that it has been confirmed, a copy of the order as modified.[46]

16.6.9 *Decision not to confirm order*

If the authority decides not to confirm a provisional or draft order – either as a result of objections received or for any other reason – it must endorse the order accordingly, with a note of the date on which the decision was reached, and notify every person interested in the land affected by the order.[47] If any of those who were originally notified of the draft or provisional order have moved away, they do not have to be notified, but it may be good practice to do so, where their new address is known. And it would also be wise to notify all those who objected, where they do not need to be notified for any other reason.

The copy of the original draft or provisional order which was on public display must be removed, so as to avoid confusion[48]; but again, it may be good practice to have a copy of the order publicly available for a few months, clearly endorsed with the authority's decision not to confirm it.

[41] *Evans* at [1995] 3 PLR 80, CA, at p. 93A.
[42] (1980) 43 P. & C.R. 233, per Forbes J. at p. 241.
[43] *Evans v Waverley Borough Council* [1995] 2 PLR 46, at p. 54E.
[44] TCP(T) Regulations 1999, reg. 5(3)(a), (4).
[45] See **16.6.3**.
[46] TCP(T) Regulations 1999, reg. 6(b).
[47] TCP(T) Regulations 1999, reg. 7(a), (b).
[48] TCP(T) Regulations 1999, reg. 7(c).

It may be noted that this procedure was introduced for the first time in 1999.

16.6.10 Compensation

Compensation is not payable for the making of a tree preservation order, but only for the refusal of any consent that may be required as a result of it. This is considered further in a later chapter.[49]

16.6.11 Possible future changes to order-making procedure

Since almost all orders are now made with a direction under section 201, so as to come into effect immediately, and since every order is confirmed by the authority which made it, rather than by the Secretary of State, it is arguable that the whole confirmation process is a waste of time, and every order should simply come fully into effect immediately without further ado.

The Government is fully aware of this problem, but has resisted introducing a provision whereby orders would never need to be confirmed. Rather, it considers that the need for an order to be confirmed provides an opportunity for mistakes and anomalies in the provisional order to be rectified. And as to procedural problems, the practice adopted by some authorities, and noted above, whereby orders are generally made by officers and confirmed by members, could be adopted by all.[50] It will, however, amend the legislation so that all orders come into effect provisionally – that is, there would be no need for the order to include a special direction to that effect.[51]

16.7 High Court challenges to tree preservation orders

16.7.1 Basis of a challenge

It has already been noted that there is a chance to object to a draft or provisional tree preservation order when it is first made.[52] Once it has been confirmed, however, there is no further right of appeal, either to the local planning authority or to the Secretary of State. But it is possible to apply to the High court for a tree preservation order to be quashed, albeit only on very limited grounds.

Section 284 of the Town and Country Planning Act 1990 thus provides that the validity of a tree preservation order, whether before or after it has been confirmed, "shall not be questioned in any legal proceedings whatsoever", except by means of a challenge under section 288.[53] Such a challenge may be made where any person is aggrieved by an order and wishes to challenge its validity on the grounds:

"(i) that the order is not within the powers of [the] Act; or
(ii) that any of the [requirements of the Act or the Regulations] have not been complied with in relation to that order".[54]

---

[49] See **18.7**.
[50] See *Tree Preservation Orders: Review*, DOE, 1994, paras 2.8 to 2.10.
[51] See *Tree Preservation Orders: Review*, DOE, 1994, para. 2.11.
[52] See **16.6.5**.
[53] TCPA 1990, ss. 284(1)(e), (2)(c), 288(4).
[54] TCPA 1990, s. 288(1)(a),(9).

In other words, a challenge may only be based on a point of law, not on the merits of the trees in question or any other factual issues. Thus it was emphasised in *Bates v Secretary of State*[55] that an application to the High Court was not a rehearing of the matters which were for decision by the Minister (who in those days had the job of confirming orders) – a point that unfortunately seems, to their cost, to elude a number of eager would-be litigants.

The distinction between the two grounds is that the court may quash the order if it is satisfied that either ground is made out; and the use of the word "may" indicates that the decision to quash is always a matter of discretion[56] – even in relation to ground (i).[57] But the Act provides in relation to ground (ii) that the order may only be quashed if the court is satisfied that the failure to comply with the relevant requirements has substantially prejudiced the interests of the applicant.[58] In other words, many administrative requirements are imperfectly complied with, but that is usually not sufficient to justify the order being quashed. Thus, in one case, it was argued (to be fair, along with other many grounds) that an order was invalid because it showed a woodland edged in a dotted line, rather than a continuous line as required by the terms of the relevant Model Order; the deputy judge at first instance rightly found this to be "a minor matter of no significance".[59] Before mounting a challenge, therefore, it is worth considering carefully whether there has in fact been any substantial prejudice.

The general law relating to High Court challenges of this kind are beyond the scope of this book. It may be sufficient, perhaps, to paraphrase the decision in *Ashbridge Investment Ltd v MOHLG*: the court can interfere with an authority's decision to make a tree preservation order if it has acted on no evidence; or if it has come to a conclusion to which on the evidence it could not reasonably have come; or if it has given a wrong interpretation to the words of the statute; or if it has taken into consideration matters which it ought not to have taken into account, or vice versa.[60]

And there are, in fact, relatively few reported cases of challenges to tree preservation orders having been attempted.[61]

16.7.2 Procedure

It is of crucial importance to realise that a challenge under section 288 must be mounted within six weeks of the tree preservation order being confirmed (either in the form it was originally made, or with modifications).[62] This time limit is calculated on the basis that a challenge to an order made on, for example, a Monday must be challenged by an application made to the court before midnight

---

[55] [1975] 1 EGLR 127
[56] For the principles determining the exercise of that discretion, see *Bolton MBC v Secretary of State* (1990) 61 P. & C.R. 343, [1991] J.P.L. 241, CA.
[57] See, for example, *Miller v Weymouth and Melcombe Regis Corpn* (1974) 27 P. & C.R. 468.
[58] TCPA 1990, s. 288(5)(b).
[59] *Evans v Waverley BC* [1995] 2 PLR 46, per Nigel Macleod Q.C. at p. 55H.
[60] [1965] 1 W.L.R. 1320, CA, per Lord Denning MR at p. 1326.
[61] They include *Bates v Secretary of State and Essex CC* [1975] 1 EGLR 127; *Bellcross v Mid-Bedfordshire DC* [1988] 1 EGLR 200; *Evans v Waverley BC* [1995] 3 PLR 80, CA, overturning [1995] 2 PLR 46; *Knowles v Secretary of State and Chorley BC* [1998] J.P.L. 593; *Armitage v South Oxfordshire DC* [1998] 2 PLR 89; and *Robinson v East Riding of Yorkshire* [2002] 06 E.G. 152 (CS), EWHC 63 Admin. If any reader has the transcript of any unreported case (or a report that has been missed!), the author would be grateful for a copy.
[62] TCPA 1990, s. 284(3), (8).

on Monday six weeks later[63]; and it may not be extended for any reason whatsoever.[64] This means that anyone contemplating making a challenge to an order must take legal advice as soon as possible.

An application is made by the filing of a Part 8 claim form with the Administrative Court (formerly the Crown Office) within the High Court, and serving it on the authority that made the order.[65] Evidence will normally be by witness statement.[66]

Where a challenge is successful, the court may quash the order in whole or in part.[67] It may also suspend the operation of the order, although it is not immediately obvious when that would be appropriate. Unlike other types of challenges under section 288, the court has no power to suspend the operation of a tree preservation order on an interim basis while the substantive action is proceeding through the courts[68] – so the order remains in force, valid or not, until the litigation is finally disposed of.

An appeal may be made to the Court of Appeal from a decision of the High Court, but since 1999 permission is always required – either from the High Court, or from the Court of Appeal itself.[69] And then on to the House of Lords, although again only with leave.[70]

16.8 Review, variation and revocation of orders

16.8.1 Review of existing orders

The Secretary of State has sensibly advised local planning authorities to keep under review the tree preservation orders they (and their predecessors) have made. This is principally for two reasons.

First, the law governing the need for consent under a tree preservation order, and the procedure for applying for it, is governed by the wording of the order itself. And that, in turn, will be determined by the wording of the Model Order that was in force when the order in question was made or confirmed. Since the precise wording of the Model Orders has changed over the years, it follows that the requirements under an old order will become progressively more and more out of tune with modern legislation.

This is particularly significant with regard to the need for consent – the analysis in the following chapters notes a number of places where earlier Model Orders differ from the 1999 Order. For example, orders made prior to 1975 contained no

---

[63] *Okolo v Secretary of State* [1997] 4 All E.R. 242; bank holidays are ignored for this purpose (*Stainer v Secretary of State* [1992] E.G.C.S. 130).

[64] See, for example, *R v Cornwall County Council, ex p. Huntingdon* [1992] 3 All E.R. 566 (right of way order unchallengeable, even though a nullity); *R v Secretary of State, ex p. Kent* [1990] 1 PLR 128, CA (planning permission unchallengeable, even though applicant could not possibly have known of it within 6-week period).

[65] Civil Procedure Rules (CPR) 1998 (S.I. 1998 No. 3132), Sched. 1, RSC Order 94, r. 2. Note that it is likely that a new Part of the CPR will in due course appear to replace the provisions of the RSC in Sched. 1.

[66] RSC Order 94, r. 3.

[67] TCPA 1990, s. 284(5)(b), (7).

[68] TCPA 1990, s. 284(6).

[69] See now Civil Procedure Rules (CPR) 1998 (S.I. 1998 No. 3132), Pt 52.

[70] Administration of Justice (Appeals) Act 1934, s. 1. As far as is known, no tree preservation order challenge has ever reached the Lords.

prohibition against the "uprooting" of protected trees or "wilful damage" to them – they only sought to prevent the cutting down, topping, lopping or wilful destruction of trees.[71] Orders made before 1966 contained no exemption relating to works to fruit trees; those made between then and 1999 exempted a wide variety of such works; and the 1999 Model Order significantly tightened up that exemption.[72] There are a number of, relatively minor, changes relating to tree works by statutory undertakers as between the various Model Orders. And so on. As for the procedures relating to consent under an order, to take but one example, the provisions as to the award of compensation for a refusal changed significantly in 1988 and 1999.[73]

It may, therefore, be helpful to replace old orders with ones made under current legislation, so as to bring their requirements up to date. On the other hand, it is not unlikely that, when the relevant primary legislation is eventually reformed, it will be amended so that the provisions now only in the 1999 Model Order will automatically apply also to earlier orders. So it may not be a clever use of resources at this stage to replace old orders solely to update the applicable legislation.

The second reason for reviewing tree preservation orders is thus likely to be rather more significant in practice. This is simply the purely practical difficulties arising from the passage of time since an order was first made. The *DETR Guide* puts it thus:

"Some tree preservation orders which are still in force were made as long ago as the 1940s and 1950s. In many cases the use of land might have changed; the land might have been developed; trees standing at the time the order was made might have been removed (with or without the consent of the local planning authority); some of the trees still standing, perhaps, no longer merit the protection of the order; new trees might have been planted which do merit protection; the map attached to the original order might bear little comparison with a modern map of the area. . . . If it is no longer possible, by reference to the order and the map, to ascertain with certainty which trees on the site are protected, it may well be time to vary or revoke the order.

"These difficulties are not necessarily reserved for older orders. Tree preservation orders are often made on land which is developed shortly afterwards. When the development is complete, it may well be desirable to vary or revoke the order."[74]

When orders have been reviewed, the authority may decide to vary them, either by adding new trees or otherwise, or to revoke them. There was apparently some uncertainty on the part of some local authorities as to whether there they had power to do this, and as to the procedure to be adopted, since the Regulations contained no explicit provision prior to 1999. In fact, however, section 333(7) of the 1990 Act has always provided that a power conferred by any of the provisions of the Act to make an order shall include power to vary or revoke any such order by a subsequent order; and the procedure has now been codified in the 1999 Regulations. The details of that procedure depend on what is to be the effect of the proposed variation.

---

[71] See **17.2**.
[72] See **17.9.5**.
[73] See **18.7.5**.
[74] *DETR Guide*, 2000, paras 4.4 to 4.6.

16.8.2 Variation of orders: new trees added

Where an authority proposes to vary a tree preservation order so as to include new trees, groups of trees, areas or woodlands not hitherto protected, the procedure is (unsurprisingly) very similar to that for making a new preservation order.[75] That is, the authority must make a variation order, and serve a copy of it on all those affected, together with a notice explaining the effect of the proposed variation and the reason for it, and setting out how and by when objections and representations must be made. A copy of the variation order must also be available for public inspection.[76]

The procedure for objecting to a variation order, and for the processing of such objections, is exactly as for a new order.[77] If the variation is confirmed, the original order must be endorsed to indicate the variation; the copy of that order which had been hitherto kept publicly available must be replaced with a copy of the order as varied (and of course, in theory, the variation order may itself be modified[78]); and all those involved must be notified. And if the variation is not confirmed, that too must be notified.[79] It is not altogether clear whether a variation order may contain a direction under section 201, so that it comes into effect immediately[80]; both the Regulations and the *DETR Guide* are silent on the point, but it probably could.

It is difficult to see much point in varying a tree preservation order to add trees; the procedure is effectively the same as making a new tree preservation order, save that the paperwork is more complex, and as a result both more conducive to errors being made and less comprehensible to the public. It would seem to be more sensible for an authority to make a new order – either one just containing the trees to be added, or one containing both those and the trees currently protected – and, either way, containing a direction under section 201 if appropriate. If the second course is adopted, the existing order can then be revoked once the new order has been confirmed.[81]

It should not be forgotten that the making and confirmation of the variation order should be notified to the local land charges section of the authority.

16.8.3 Variation of orders: no new trees added

Where an authority proposes to vary a tree preservation order so as to remove from it trees, groups of trees, areas or woodlands which have been hitherto protected, the procedure is (also unsurprisingly) somewhat simpler.

Again, a variation order must be made, and a copy served on all concerned, together with a notice explaining the effect of the variation; and the public copy of the original order must be replaced with a copy of the order as varied.[82] However, there is in this case no need for confirmation – or at least there is in the Regulations, oddly, no reference to any need for confirmation; and it is just assumed by the *DETR Guide* that a variation order comes into force immediately

---

[75] See **16.6**.
[76] TCP(T) Regulations 1999, reg. 8(1).
[77] TCP(T) Regulations 1999, reg. 8(2).
[78] See **16.6.6**.
[79] See **16.6.9**.
[80] See **16.6.2**.
[81] See **16.8.4**.
[82] TCP(T) Regulations 1999, reg. 8(1).

it is made.[83] That is entirely sensible, but the point should be clarified when the primary legislation is next amended.

16.8.4 Revocation of orders

Where a tree preservation order is to be revoked, a revocation order must be made (to include the date on which it was made) and a copy served on all concerned; and the public copy of the original order must be withdrawn.[84]

A revocation order, too, appears to come into effect on the date on which it was made. The *DETR Guide* sensibly points out that it is important to ensure that an order is not revoked until all unfinished business has been dealt with in relation to it – such as appeals against refusal of consent, prosecutions for unauthorised works, or requirements as to replacement planting.[85] This will be the case even where, as will not infrequently be the case, a tree preservation order is revoked because it is being replaced by a one or more new ones; they will obviously need to be brought into force at the same time as or before the old order is revoked, if there is not to be any discontinuity of protection.

16.9 Consequences of a tree preservation order being made

Once an order has been made, and until it is revoked, anyone wishing to carry out works to any of the trees protected by it needs to obtain consent from the relevant planning authority – a requirement that is subject to numerous important exceptions, explored in **Chapter 17**.

If consent is needed, it must be applied for. If the application is not successful, an appeal may be made to the Secretary of State. And if all else fails, it is sometimes possible to obtain compensation (see **Chapter 18**). If works are carried out without consent, that is a criminal offence (**Chapter 19**). And once a tree has gone, it is not possible to get it back; in a number of situations, therefore, there is a requirement for a replacement tree to be planted following the felling of a protected tree. The occasions where that arises, and the way in which the requirement can be enforced, are set out at **Chapter 20**.

On the other hand, the making of an order imposes no duty on the owners of the trees and woodlands affected to carry out pruning or other maintenance, either to any particular standard or at all. That must be a matter for the owner's decision, subject to the duties laid upon him or her by the common law as discussed in Part II of this book; and if a local authority wishes to encourage such works to be carried out, it must do so by persuasion, through the offer of grants or (possibly) by the imposition of conditions on consents. The Government was encouraged by some to introduce, as part of the 1994 Review of the legislation, a system of tree management orders, whereby formal plans of maintenance would be agreed between authorities and owners at the time an order was made; but it rejected such a system as being too burdensome on all concerned.[86]

---

[83] *DETR Guide*, 2000, para. 4.11.
[84] TCP(T) Regulations 1999, reg. 9.
[85] *DETR Guide*, 2000, para. 4.16.
[86] See *Tree Preservation Orders: Review*, DOE, 1994, paras 2.2 to 2.4.

Chapter 17

Works to Protected Trees: the Need for Consent

17.1 Introduction

17.1.1 Consent required by tree preservation order

The basic rule is that consent must be obtained before almost any works are carried out to a protected tree (for brevity, the phrase "protected tree" is used in this and the following Chapters as a shorthand for "tree that is the subject of a tree preservation order that is currently in force"). As to precisely what works are included in this requirement, this is considered at **17.2**.

There are, however, a number of significant exceptions to the general requirement for consent to be obtained.

First, the Town and Country Planning Act 1990 itself provides (in section 198(6)) that no order shall apply to the cutting down, topping or lopping of a tree:

- where the tree is dying or dead or has become dangerous;

- in compliance with a statutory obligation; or

- so far as may be necessary for the prevention or abatement of a nuisance.

These three exemptions are dealt with here at **17.3** to **17.5**. It should be noted that, because they arise from the wording of the Act rather than from that of the relevant order, the meaning and extent of these exemptions does not vary according to when the order was made.

Secondly, there is a complex statutory scheme that operates where works are carried out to a tree protected by a preservation order as part of forestry operations. The 1990 Act thus provides that no consent is necessary for works to trees in accordance with a forestry dedication covenant or a plan approved by the Forestry Commission.[1] And no consent under a tree preservation order will be needed for works that are the subject of a felling licence.[2] These provisions are the subject of **17.6**.

Thirdly, the preservation order itself will prescribe a series of exemptions. These fall principally into three categories:

---

[1] 1990 Act, s. 200(3); also 1969 Model Order, Sched. 2, paras (1), (2); see **12.6**.
[2] 1990 Act, s. 198(7)(b), Forestry Act 1967, s. 15(6); see **14.4**.

- some works by, or at the request of, statutory undertakers and other public bodies – largely in circumstances where works to trees are necessary to ensure the safe and efficient operation of their undertakings;

- works required to carry out development for which planning permission has been granted; and

- some works to fruit trees.

These exemptions, each of which is subject to various conditions and limitations, are dealt with at **17.7 to 17.9**.

Finally, by virtue of section 198(7) of the Act, consent is not required for certain works to trees required in connection with opencast coal mining; see **17.10**.

Unfortunately, the more detailed provisions as to precisely what types of work require consent, and as to what exemptions there are to that requirement under the third group of exemptions noted above, will be contained in the order which applies to the particular tree or group of trees in question. That remains so even if the general primary or secondary legislation changed from time to time after that order was made. It is therefore vital in any particular case to refer to a copy of the actual order to see what provisions it contains.

It has already been noted that the Minister (or, later, the Secretary of State) issued over the years a series of "model orders" to guide local authorities in preparing draft orders; and a list of the Model Orders has been given at **16.3.1**. The text below accordingly relates, where appropriate, to the exemptions that were prescribed in each of these model orders, on the grounds that every actual order made will have followed the model that was current at the time. So, for example, as noted there, if an order was made in 1976, it should have been under the provisions of the TCP (Tree Preservation Order) Regulations 1969, and, if so, its wording would have followed that of the model in the Schedule to those Regulations ("the 1969 Model Order"), as amended in 1975.

In practice, the great majority of orders actually made did follow the relevant Model Order in force at the time; but occasionally there were some deviations. It is essential, therefore, to look at the actual wording of the order concerned in any particular case. This is particularly so with very early orders, which sometimes contained idiosyncratic provisions, and more recent ones made without the benefit of ministerial checking and approval.

17.1.2 *Application to carry out works to other trees in conservation areas*

It may be noted that all of the exemptions outlined above apply (with the exception of that relating to opencast mining) equally in relation to the requirement to notify the planning authority of works to a tree in a conservation area.[3] In relation to such a tree, the extent of the exemptions equivalent to those in the order itself (the third group referred to above) follows that in article 5 of the 1999 Model Order.

17.2 Works requiring consent

The wording of article 2 of the 1969 Model Order is as follows:

---

[3] TCPA 1990, s. 211, TCP(T) Regulations 1999, reg. 10(1)(a)–(c); see **21.2.2**.

"Subject to the provisions of this Order, and to the exemptions specified in the Second Schedule hereto, no person shall, except with the consent of the authority and in accordance with the conditions if any imposed on such consent, cut down, top, lop, *uproot, wilfully damage,* or wilfully destroy or cause or permit the cutting down, topping, lopping, *uprooting, wilful damage,* or wilful destruction of any tree specified in [the order]."

The references to uprooting and wilful damage were added in 1975.[4] The wording of the Model Orders prior to 1969 is the same as the original wording of the 1969 Order, omitting the italicised words[5]; and that of the 1999 Model Order is essentially the same as the amended 1969 wording.[6]

The first group of works requiring consent is thus the cutting down, topping or lopping of a protected tree, or (in relation to post-1975 orders) its uprooting. Usually there will be no need to determine which of the various terms best describes any particular proposed works, but it may be necessary to determine that they fall into at least one of the prescribed categories.

The "cutting down" of a tree presumably means the making of a horizontal cut through the base of the principal stem or stems, causing the fall to the ground of the whole of the tree above ground, but leaving the stump and the roots. "Felling" is more or less synonymous. The "uprooting" of a tree means the removal from the ground of the whole tree, including its root system. Either operation may be, and indeed frequently will be, carried out in more than one stage; but it is the operation as a whole that needs consent. These terms are considered further in the context of unauthorised works.[6a]

As for "topping" and "lopping", these have been fully considered by the Court of Appeal in *Unwin v Hanson*,[7] which concerned the interpretation of what is now section 154 of the Highways Act 1980.[8] Lord Esher M.R. made it clear that "lopping" means cutting off the branches of a tree, and "topping" is the cutting off of its top. In the present context, the distinction between the two terms is not of any great consequence, since consent is needed for either; but the decision in *Unwin* also by implication made it clear that "lopping" was distinct from "pruning", since the Act under consideration in that case referred to both terms. Moreover, the 1990 Act does not authorise the making of preservation orders so as to require consent to be obtained for pruning; nor do any of the Model Orders purport to do so.

It follows that consent is required for "lopping", that is, for cutting off a branch, but not for "pruning". Where the line is to be drawn between the two must inevitably be a matter of judgment, depending on the particular facts of the case.

It was suggested in the Batho review[9] that some term other than "lopping or topping" should be used, as those are forestry terms. The Government, however, considered that the use of these terms seemed to cause few problems in practice; and no change is currently proposed.[10] This may be sensible, since there is a wide variety of terms used in the tree surgery business, and promoted by the relevant

---

4   TCP (TPO) (Amendment) and (Trees in Conservation Areas) (Exempted Cases) Regulations 1975 (S.I. 1975 No. 148), reg. 2.
5   1949 Model Order, art. 2; 1953 Order, art. 2; 1966 Model Order, art. 2.
6   1999 Model Order, art. 4.
6a   See **19.3.4**.
7   [1891] 2 Q.B. 115, CA.
8   For a fuller extract from the judgment, see **6.4.3**.
9   See **6.2.7**.
10   See *Tree Preservation Orders: Review*, DOE, 1974 ("*1974 Review*"), para. 2.39.

British Standard[11] – in particular cleaning out (or deadwooding), crown reduction, crown lifting (or raising), pollarding; also thinning or balancing. In reality, each of these consists of a combination of lopping and topping, and no further specification seems necessary or wise.

The second group of works requiring consent is the carrying out of works for the wilful damage or wilful destruction of a protected tree. These are of relevance primarily in the context of prosecution for unauthorised works.

Finally, the Model Orders make no difference between carrying out any of the various types of work and causing or permitting someone else to do so.[12] It is true that the Act itself does not refer to orders prohibiting the causing or permitting of works, but the Divisional Court in *R v Bournemouth Justices ex parte Bournemouth Corporation* held that:

"It is quite clear that an enabling provision with regard to the prohibition of certain matters permits an order being made to cover all aspects of the prohibition – the prohibition of cutting, of causing cutting or of permitting cutting."[13]

Thus, consent is in principle required, other things being equal, by both the tree surgeon actually doing the work to the protected tree, and by the landowner paying him; by the householder who asks her son-in-law to lop off a branch, and by the son-in-law.

This is all considered further in relation to prosecutions for unauthorised works.[14]

17.3 Works to dying, dead and dangerous trees

17.3.1 Dead or dying trees

By virtue of section 198(6)(a) of the 1990 Act, consent is not needed for the cutting down, uprooting, topping or lopping of protected trees which are "dying or dead". This is not quite as simple as it might at first sight appear, since it is not always a straightforward matter to determine when a tree can first truly said to be dying; nor when it is dead.

The first point to note is that, for the exemption to apply, it is a tree – that is, the entire tree – which must be dying or dead, and not just part of it. There is no provision in the Act defining "tree" to include "part of a tree" – as there is, for example, with "building".[15] It commonly occurs that a branch or a part of a branch dies, and in veteran trees it is not unusual for a substantial proportion of the heartwood, or a branch, or indeed almost (but not quite) the entire tree, to be dead; but in neither case is the tree necessarily dying, let alone dead. Secondly, as a tree gets older, parts of it may gradually cease to function in the way they used to – for example, the crown may diminish in volume (the phenomenon which used to be known as "crown die-back"). But that, too, does not amount to "dying". Moreover, of course, it can be argued that any organism, whether plant or animal,

---

[11]   BS 3998: 1989, *British Standard Recommendations for Tree Work*; see also **9.5.1**.
[12]   1949, 1953, 1966 and 1969 Model Orders, art. 2; 1999 Order, art. 4(b).
[13]   (1970) 21 P. & C.R. 163, per Lord Parker C.J. at p. 165.
[14]   See **Chapter 19**, and in particular **19.3**.
[15]   TCPA 1990, s. 336.

is dying from the day it is born – but that too cannot be what was in the mind of Parliament when enacting this provision.

In the case of a young tree, death may occur relatively swiftly – because of lack of water, or vehicle impact, or a trench being dug (perhaps for pipes or cables) so close to a tree as to kill a significant number of its roots,[16] or the ground being raised or lowered close to the tree, or some other catastrophic intervention with the tree's life support mechanisms. In such cases it will usually be relatively straightforward to decide that a tree is dead, or is in terminal decline.

In older trees, on the other hand, problems are just as likely to arise as a result of pests, diseases and disorders, which will not normally be fatal and which, even when they are, may take a long time to cause the ultimate death of the tree. The question of whether, in such cases, a tree can be truly said to be dying or dead may be a matter of opinion, depending very much on the species concerned and the syndrome or disease from which it is suffering. An old man may lose the ability to function fully, and may be blind or incontinent, or lose one or more limbs, but that does not (necessarily) mean that he is "dying". In the same way a tree may lose branches, and, in due course, some or all of its heartwood, but still be far from "dead". But care should be taken not to press too far any analogy between a human being and a tree; they are very different organisms. And trees are much more tolerant than people, being able to lose a greater proportion of their body before ceasing to function.

Perhaps one useful test in borderline cases is thus to consider whether the problem affecting the tree is chronic or acute, and whether the death of the whole tree is, as far as can be predicted, both certain and imminent. And it may be difficult to say with certainty that a whole tree is actually "dead" until at least a year, or possibly longer, has elapsed with no signs of continuing life (and, in particular, no new leaves or foliage). It is also worth noting that the phrase used in the Act is "dying or dead", so that it does not matter which of those two adjectives best describes a particular tree, provided that it is at least in one category or the other.

Finally, it appears that there is as yet no reported decision of the higher courts as to the meaning of the phrase "dying or dead", but it is likely that the conclusion in *Smith v Oliver* (considered below), that the issue of whether a tree is dangerous is "a question of fact for the justices",[17] would apply equally to whether or not a tree is dying or dead.

The procedure to be followed where works are to be carried out in reliance upon this exemption is considered below.[18]

As to the removal of deadwood, this would not be covered by the exemption (unless, of course, the tree as a whole was dying). But it would probably not be necessary to seek consent for the works, unless carried out on a substantial scale, as they would be regarded as "de minimis", and thus outside the scope of control.[18a]

The Government has stated that it intends, in due course, to extend this exemption (which incidentally applies equally in relation to the requirement to notify the planning authority of works to a tree in a conservation area[19]) so that in

---

[16] As in *Barnet LBC v Eastern Elecricity Board* [1973] 1 W.L.R. 430, 2 All E.R. 319; (1973) 117 S.J. 245.

[17] [1989] 2 PLR 1, per Farquharson J. at p. 3E.

[18] See **17.3.5**.

[18a] *De minimis non curat lex*: the law takes no account of trifles.

[19] TCPA 1990, s. 211, TCP(T) Regulations 1999, reg. 10(1)(a); see **21.2.2**.

future it would also apply to allow the removal without consent of parts of a tree (such as branches) which are dead, but to repeal the exemption relating to "dying" trees .[20]

17.3.2 Dangerous trees

Section 198(6)(a) also provides that consent is not needed for the cutting down, uprooting, topping or lopping of protected trees which "have become dangerous".[21] This, too, is not straightforward. This section considers the general principles, and the following sections consider the particular case of trees which are alleged to be dangerous because they are likely to cause damage to buildings or other property, the extent of works which may be carried out in reliance upon this exemption, and the procedure to be followed.[22] Again, this exemption applies equally in relation to giving notice of proposed works to a tree in a conservation area.[23]

The "dangerous trees" exemption has been considered by the Divisional Court in *Smith v Oliver*,[24] a decision relating to the requirement to notify the authority of works to a tree in a conservation area – which is subject to the same exemption as that now in section 198(6) relating to dangerous trees.[25] The decision, which is commonly cited by those seeking to justify the felling of trees claimed to be dangerous, should, however, be treated with considerable caution, because the underlying logic seems to be not entirely clear. It is therefore worth quoting at length.

In the principal judgment, Farquharson J. held as follows [emphasis added]:

"The phrase at the very beginning of that subsection[26] removes the prohibition made by section 60 and section 61A in relation to the cutting down, topping or lopping of trees 'which are dying or dead or which have become dangerous'. In my judgment, that must be a question of fact for the justices. The approach which they should make is the everyday sensible approach of a prudent citizen looking at the trees in question, and deciding in his own mind whether he can properly say those trees are dangerous. The existence of the danger must be a present danger. He must be able to say that the existing condition of the tree is one of danger in relation to the tree or trees he is examining. *Of course that does not mean that the danger which has been threatened has actually occurred.* It is not necessary to show that the tree has fallen or that its roots have disturbed the foundation of the house, fence or pavement nearby. The justices must be in a position to say to themselves that 'having regard to the state of the tree, its size, its position, and such effect as any of those factors have so far had, we can properly come to the conclusion that the tree has now become dangerous'. *It may be that the condition of the tree itself is perfectly healthy, but because of those other factors the magistrates may be able nonetheless to say that the tree is in the condition described by the subsection, that is to say that it has become dangerous.*

"In deciding that question, the magistrates are entitled to look at what is likely to happen. If the tree has already shown signs of disturbing a fence or a pavement or indeed the house itself, it does not need the justices or indeed anyone actually concerned with the treatment of the tree to wait for those events actually to occur, namely for the fence to fall

---

[20] *1994 Review*, paras 2.23, 2.24.
[21] TCPA, s. 198(6)(a).
[22] See **17.3.4, 17.3.5**.
[23] TCPA 1990, s. 211, TCP(T) Regulations 1999, reg. 10(1)(a); see **21.2.2**.
[24] [1989] 2 PLR 1.
[25] See **21.2.2**.
[26] TCPA 60(6) (applied to trees in conservation areas by TCPA 1990, s. 61A); the corresponding ss. in the TCPA 1990 are 198(6) and 212.

down on some passing pedestrian or the pavement to be such that somebody falls and is injured or that the house begins to subside. The present danger is one that is constituted by the conditions at the time the tree is being examined, and the fact that these other matters may shortly arise is something that can be properly be taken into account when the justices come to their decision.

"Of course it does not mean that any individual who owns trees and wishes to remove them can say to himself: 'having regard to their position, the way they have been planted and their unsuitability, I can see that in a number of years they are going to constitute a danger' and then cut them down. One has to look at the position at the time. If such damage is far off, remote and not immediate in the sense I have just described, the trees to not come within the meaning of the expression."[27]

The general approach adopted here seems correct – that is, the question of whether a tree is dangerous is a matter of fact, to be decided by the magistrates or jury (after, if appropriate, holding a site inspection). And the test propounded, "the everyday sensible approach of a prudent citizen looking at the trees in question, and deciding in his own mind whether he can properly say those trees are dangerous", echoes the dicta in judgments, considered earlier in this book, as to when an owner should inspect a tree, and how thorough that inspection should be. See, in particular, the extracts from the leading case of *Caminer v Northern & London Investment Trust*,[28] referring to "a person with general knowledge and experience of trees" and "a reasonable and prudent landlord".[29]

However, there seems to be confusion as to the meaning of what constitutes a "danger". The first of the two italicised sentences in the extract above thus refers "the danger which has been threatened" actually occurring, whereas what was presumably meant was actually "the harm which has been threatened"; since "danger" means the threat of harm.[30]

The more serious problem is that the learned judge states that "it may be that the condition of the tree itself is perfectly healthy, but because of those other factors [its size, its position, and such effect as any of those factors have so far had], the magistrates may be able nonetheless to say that the tree . . . has become dangerous". This tends to suggest that "danger" may arise due to a tree being subject to ill health or other defects, but that equally it may arise due solely to its position or size. That is almost never right, in that a danger only arises as the result of the existence of a tree (which is a more precise way of expressing the matter than "a tree is dangerous") where all or part of it is likely to cause damage to persons, animals or property. And that will in most cases only occur either:

- where the tree has an inherently dangerous feature (such as thorns or poisonous fruit) and it is in close proximity to those likely to be harmed as a result; or

- where a characteristic of the tree – perhaps disease, defective form, vehicle impact or whatever – means that it is likely to fall and shed branches in a location where they are likely to cause harm.

The first of these situations is unlikely to be often used as a justification for felling

---

[27]   [1989] 2 PLR 1, at p. 3E to 4A.
[28]   [1951] A.C. 88, H.L., per Lord Normand at pp. 99-100, Lord Reid at p. 108, and Lord Radcliffe at p. 111.
[29]   See **5.5.1**.
[30]   See **1.3.2**.

a protected tree – although, it might be where, for example, a young family move into a house with a laburnum tree in the garden, and are concerned that a child might eat the pods.[31] The second would only apply where the condition and location of the tree were both such that there was a problem. A tree with advanced butt rot, liable to fall at any minute, is not dangerous if it is in the middle of an impenetrable forest, because no one will be hit if it falls. A tree overhanging a main road is not dangerous if it is in perfect health, because it will not fall.

Of course, it is true that a tree may, in fact, be in a location where a fall would be harmful, and suffering from a disease which is such that a fall is likely but which is invisible to external inspection – as in the *Caminer* case.[32] Such a tree would be correctly categorised as "dangerous", but there is no way in which anyone could guess (let alone know) that; and it cannot be right that all protected trees could be felled just in case they had such a hidden defect.

A further difficulty is that the Act refers to "a tree" becoming dangerous – not "all or part of a tree". Assuming that the phrase, as suggested above, refers to the existence of a state of affairs in which a danger exists as a result of the condition and location of a tree, can it be said that this occurs where the danger exists only due to the condition and location of a part of a tree – such as, notably, a branch? Arguably, if a tree has, for example, butt rot, and as a result is liable to fall onto a path, the danger relates to the whole tree. But where the problem is a fungus at the junction between a branch and the main trunk, the danger arises only due to the likelihood of the branch falling, not the remainder of the tree. It is at least arguable that it cannot be said in the latter case that "the tree" is dangerous.

Finally, almost the only possible exception to this general approach, where a danger arises not because of the condition of the tree but by virtue of its size and location, is where, for example, a tree close to a highway is allowed to grow to a size and shape such that it obstructs the visibility of a warning sign or the light coming from a street lamp, and thus endangers motorists or pedestrians. It is arguable that in such a case the tree, although not dangerous in itself, is dangerous to the extent to which it causes those motorists or pedestrians to be in danger. It is, of course, true that the highway authority has powers to deal with this type of situation, described earlier,[32a] but that does not mean that consent is required where private landowners chose to carry out such works by themselves.

The conclusion would thus seem to be that only very rarely will the size of a tree or its location – or indeed those two factors in combination – *on their own* make a tree dangerous; there must usually be a further factor, objectively ascertainable, to justify that judgment. The second italicised sentence in Farquharson J's judgment in *Smith v Oliver* is thus, it is submitted with respect, only correct in that very limited sense.

Another way of looking at the problem might be to say that, where a protected tree is hazardous to an extent which would justify a court holding its owner liable either in negligence or under the Occupier's Liability Acts in the event of it causing harm, it may be removed without consent in reliance upon the exemption in section 198(6). The test in determining that liability would be those factors – the condition of the tree and the existence of a potential target – which have been touched upon briefly above and at greater length in **Chapter 5**. That approach, for

---

[31]   See **1.3.4**.
[32]   [1951] A.C. 88, H.L., per Lord Oakley at p. 104; see **5.10.1**.
[32a]   See **6.4**.

which it must be said there is no case law authority, has the merit of ensuring that where a tree is sufficiently hazardous that its owner is under a civil obligation to take some action, he or she is not incurring a penalty under the criminal law.

As for the other judgment in *Smith v Oliver* (that of Tudor Price J.), this has already been considered earlier in this book, with somewhat similar conclusions.[33]

17.3.3 Damage to foundations

Clearly, where a tree is likely to cause harm to persons or animals, that may constitute a danger. But the position is less certain where the only likely damage is to property – through either a branch or a whole tree falling onto a building or the moisture uptake through roots causing subsidence and foundation damage.

Thus, in *Smith v Oliver*[34] itself, the damage, being caused by the tree was a fence being pushed over by it as it grew, and roots pushing up the pavement. Both judges in their judgments referred to a tree falling and roots disturbing foundations as though they were in the same category.[35] However, it is at least arguable that the label "dangerous" can properly be ascribed to a tree which is liable to shed a branch, causing injury to persons or animals, but not to one which is only threatening to cause foundation damage through subsidence. As a matter of language, the distinction is probably between harm (either to persons or to property) that is both sudden and unavoidable, and harm that is gradual and readily remediable.

A tree might thus be categorised as dangerous if it is likely to fall onto a building, or to cause damage to foundations which, due to the design of a building, might in turn cause injury or death – because of a sudden collapse of masonry, for example, or the fracture of a gas pipe. But the not uncommon situation where roots cause subsidence damage to foundations, resulting only in minor cracks which lead to discovery of a problem in time for it to be cured, is, no doubt, a nuisance (in the non-legal sense of that term), and expensive – if not dealt with promptly, possibly very expensive – but it is not, normally, dangerous. It is, for example, noteworthy that in hardly any of the numerous cases involving trees and foundations, cited in **Chapter 3**, is there any mention of the word "danger"; indeed the only exception appears to be one case where Lord Evershed MR refers to there being "no imminence of danger" in a context where it seems that he means "no imminence of harm"[36] (the same error as noted in relation to *Smith v Oliver* above). Here, too, it is unfortunate that the Act refers to the tree "becoming dangerous", rather than "leading to the existence of a danger".

And in *Edgeborough Building Co v Woking Urban District Council*,[37] a case of a protected tree being removed without consent due to impending damage from its roots, there was much discussion as to whether the felling had been necessary to abate a nuisance, but no one suggested that the tree had been dangerous.

17.3.4 Extent of works which may be carried out

A further question is, what works may be carried out without consent if a tree is

[33] See **5.10.1**.
[34] [1989] 2 PLR 1.
[35] [1989] 2 PLR 1; Farquahrson J. at p. 3F, Tudor Price J. at p. 4G
[36] *Lemos v Kennedy Leigh Development Co* (1961) 105 S.J. 178, CA.
[37] (1966) 198 E.G. 581; see **17.5.2** below.

indeed dangerous? That is, if it is agreed that, for example, a branch is diseased and liable to fall in the near future onto a well-used path, but that the remainder of the tree is entirely healthy, may the whole tree be removed in reliance upon the relevant exemption, or only the branch?

It was contended by counsel for the defendant in *Smith v Oliver*[38] that the exemption, now in section 198(6)(a), relating to "dangerous" trees entitled the owner or the person concerned with the treatment of the trees only to reduce them to the extent that the danger is removed. That was described by Farquaharson J as "an attractive argument", but he rightly rejected it on the basis that there was nothing to that effect indicating that interpretation; further, section 198(6)(a) should be contrasted with section 198(6)(b), which refers to "works so far as may be necessary for the prevention or abatement of a nuisance". The works "so far as may be necessary" are introduced by the draftsman in relation to the question of nuisance, but not when referring to the trees being dangerous. It follows that, once a tree has "become dangerous", any of the types of work referred to – cutting down, uprooting, topping or lopping – may be carried out with impunity.

However, it should again be noted that it is "the tree" which must have become dangerous for the exemption to apply. As discussed above, where a large branch is liable to fall, it must be open to argument as to whether "the tree has become dangerous" or merely the branch. Clearly, where a twig is about to fall, that does not make the whole tree dangerous. The true rule may be that a tree is dangerous where any significant part of it can be so described; after all, if it is just a twig which is about to flutter to the ground, that does not make the twig "dangerous", any more than a leaf is dangerous in the autumn. And if this exemption does not apply where only the branch is dangerous, there is no other exemption that would allow the dangerous branch to be removed without consent – which would be a strange result.

Clearly, this whole area needs to be clarified – possibly by the adoption into the 1990 Act of the wording of the corresponding exemption under the Forestry Act, which provides that a felling licence is not needed for any felling which is "for the prevention of danger"[39] – which might be a more appropriate phrase. It is noteworthy that the Government has stated, sensibly, that it proposes to limit the "dangerous trees" exemption so that in future it would apply to allow only the minimum works necessary to remove the cause of any danger – and, where only part of a tree is dangerous, only that part could be removed.[40]

17.3.5 Procedure

Where works are to be carried out to a protected tree in reliance on any of the exemptions in section 198(6)(a) of the Act, relating to dying, dead or dangerous trees, it is prudent for the person responsible to obtain evidence of the fact that it is dying or dead, or has become dangerous – if possible, before the works are carried out. This could become of crucial importance if the condition of the tree, and thus the lawfulness of the works, should be questioned afterwards by the local planning authority.

The Court of Appeal has considered this in the context of dangerous trees in *R v Alath Construction Ltd*, and held as follows:

---

[38]   [1989] 2 PLR 1, at p. 4E.
[39]   FA 1967, s. 9(4)(a); see **14.2.4**.
[40]   *1994 Review*, paras 2.25, 2.26.

"Having considered *Hunt's* case,[41] the recorder in the instant case [K H Zucker QC] towards the end of his ruling said:

'. . . This being an exemption or exception, the burden of proof, in my judgment, lies on the person who asserts it, who in this case is the defendant. I am reinforced in that view because from a practical viewpoint I have no doubt that it is far easier for the owner of the land, or the person responsible for the cutting down of a tree, to prove its condition at the time such action was taken than the local authority. It is to be noted in particular that section 60(6)[42] provides for a tree becoming dangerous after an order has been made, and . . . it would place an impossible burden on a local authority to check every tree which is to be the subject of a tree preservation order to determine what is its condition is and to continue to check it after an order has been made to determine whether it has become dangerous or not. I accept . . . that the defendant responsible for the cutting down of a tree or otherwise dealing with it, contrary to the terms of a tree preservation order, is in a unique position to know the true condition of the tree at the time of the act . . .'

"With respect, we simply cannot improve upon those observations, which are clear and to the point and in our judgment accurately analyse the legal position in this appeal."[43]

Precisely the same principles would apply in the case of a tree which was claimed to have been dead or dying at the time works were carried out to it.

The question of the burden of proof principally arises in the context of a prosecution for unauthorised works, and is accordingly considered further elsewhere.[43a] However, the practical consequences need to be taken into account right at the outset, when the works are first contemplated.

Secondly, where a tree is removed (as opposed to merely lopped or topped) in reliance on the exemption, there is a duty to plant a replacement tree unless the planning authority agrees to dispense with the requirement.[44] The question of replacement planting is considered further in **Chapter 20**.

The "Notice" at the end of the 1969 Model Order required that, except in an emergency, "not less than five days previous notice of the carrying out of the removal, etc., should be given to the authority, to enable it to decide whether to dispense with the requirement". It is doubtful whether this is a mandatory requirement, as opposed to simply a statement of good practice. Since the exemption applies whether or not the authority wants a replacement, and since it would in practice probably be easier to assess whether or not a replacement was desirable once the existing tree is felled, it is difficult to avoid the suspicion that the main value of the requirement to give notice was to enable the authority to check whether the tree was in fact dying, dead or dangerous.

Neither the 1999 Model Order nor any of the Model Orders prior to 1969 contain any requirement to notify the authority.

17.4 Works to comply with a statutory obligation

Consent is not required for the carrying out of any works to a protected tree in compliance with any obligation imposed by or under an Act of Parliament.[45] This means that the requirements of any public or private Act, and of any secondary legislation, would override the terms of any tree preservation order. However, for

[41] *R v Hunt (Richard)* [1987] A.C. 352, H.L.
[42] Of the TCPA 1971 (the predecessor to s. 198(6) of the TCPA 1990).
[43] *R v Alath Construction Ltd; R v Brightman* [1990] 1 W.L.R. 1255, CA.
[43a] See **19.4.2**.
[44] TCPA 1990, ss. 206; 211(1)(b): see **20.2.1**.
[45] TCPA 1990, s. 198(6)(b).

this exemption to apply, the legislation in question must impose an obligation, not merely authorise something to be carried out.

This exemption also authorises the carrying out of works necessary to comply with a notice under section 23 of the Local Government (Miscellaneous Provisions) Act 1976 (dangerous trees[45a]), section 154 of the Highways Act 1980 (trees obstructing the highway)[45b]), or Schedule 4 to the Electricity Act 1989 or Schedule 2 to the Telecommunications Act 1984 (trees interfering with cables[45c]).

It is not clear whether this exemption would extend to the requirements of a condition imposed on any form of licence or permission granted under statutory powers (such as a waste management licence or a planning permission), or on an order under the Transport and Works Act 1992. The licence or order is in itself merely permissive; but once it is acted on, the conditions must be complied with. If they require works to be carried out to protected trees, that is arguably an obligation under an Act. The point remains to be litigated.

As for works required to carry out development for which planning permission has been granted, see below.[46]

Where a tree is removed in reliance upon this exemption, there is no requirement to plant a replacement – unless that is stated as a condition in the statute or other instrument imposing the obligation.

This exemption also applies in relation to the requirement to notify the planning authority of works to a tree in a conservation area,[47] but in this case, oddly, there is a requirement to plant a replacement.[48]

17.5 Works to prevent or abate a nuisance

17.5.1 Purpose of exemption

Section 198(6)(b) of the 1990 Act provides that "no tree preservation order shall apply to the cutting down, uprooting, topping or lopping of any trees . . . so far as may be necessary for the prevention or abatement of a nuisance". This form of words has been adopted in each Town and Country Planning Act since 1947, where exactly the same words appeared in section 28(5).

There is, however, considerable uncertainty as to the correct interpretation of the phrase "prevention or abatement of a nuisance" – in particular, as to whether it entitles a landowner (A) to carry out works without consent under a tree preservation order:

- where a protected tree growing on A's land causes damage or inconvenience to buildings or structures on that same land;
- wherever a protected tree growing on the land of B (a neighbour) encroaches onto A's land; or
- only where the encroachment of B's tree onto A's land actually causes

---

[45a] See **5.10.2**.
[45b] See **6.4.3**.
[45c] See **7.2**.
[46] See **17.8**.
[47] TCPA 1990, s. 211, TCP(T) Regulations 1999, reg. 10(1)(a); see **21.2.2**.
[48] TCPA 1990, s. 213(1)(b), TCP(T) Regulations 1999, reg. 10(1)(a); see **21.5.2**.

damage – such as overhanging branches shading A's crops or encroaching roots damaging the foundations of A's house.

There seems to be little support for the first of those three views – for example, the Secretary of State, in one widely cited appeal decision, stated that he had been advised that "a tree standing on a person's own property cannot be a legal nuisance to the owner or occupier of that property".[49] That must be right. Unfortunately, however, immediately before that, he had stated that he had also been advised that "nuisance", as referred to in what is now section 198(6)(b) of the 1990 Act, meant "the tort of nuisance actionable at law". That view, although influential, is of no binding authority; and in any event, that decision related to a set of facts which fell within the first of the three categories above. Thus the Secretary of State (and his advisors) did not have to grapple with the key question, namely, does the phrase "a nuisance" mean "any nuisance" (the second category above) or merely "any actionable nuisance" (the third)? The traditional view is that the latter is the correct interpretation, but this must be open to very considerable doubt.

17.5.2 The meaning of "nuisance" in the 1990 Act

The term "nuisance" is neither defined nor qualified in the either the 1947 Act or the 1990 Act. Nor has it been definitively considered in the courts. Indeed, it appears that there are only two cases in which the point has been considered at all, of which one is unreported and of no binding authority; both are somewhat unsatisfactory.

The first decision is that of the Divisional Court in *Edgeborough Building Co v Woking Urban District Council*,[50] which related to the cutting down by a development company, without consent, of a tree that, it was said, was likely to cause damage to a nearby house on land in the same ownership. The company relied on the exemption in section 29(6) of the Town and Country Planning Act 1962 (now section 198(6)(b) of the 1990 Act). Lord Parker C.J. held as follows:

"[Counsel for the appellants] had said that the appellants had to satisfy the justices that they were honestly doing what they did for the purpose of preventing or abating as nuisance, whether or not that nuisance was in fact in existence or imminent. Counsel also contended that 'nuisance' was used in a general colloquial sense, and did not mean actionable nuisance. He said that that a danger of damage to property, namely damage to the house through the shrinkage of soil underneath the house caused by the roots of the tree, would amount to such a nuisance.

"It was argued before the justices, and would have been argued for the respondents in the present hearing, if necessary, that there was no reason for departing from the ordinary meaning of nuisance in the legal sense. He (his Lordship) considered that there was much to be said for that view, but there was no need to decide the matter, since Mr Reece had conceded that 'nuisance' at any rate meant something more than inconvenience, and in this context meant at least a risk of damage to property which seriously interfered with the enjoyment of that property.

"Counsel had gone on to say that the magistrates, on the evidence before them, could not have properly to any other conclusion than that there was risk of damage to property. In fact, the magistrates showed that they were not satisfied that there was such a risk. In the

---

[49] Appeal relating to the Vicarage, Nassington, ref. EMP2815/147/2, noted at [1992] J.P.L. 389.
[50] (1966) 198 E.G. 581.

stated case, they said that they found that on certain soils such roots could cause shrinkage in the soil beneath a house, and that such shrinkage could result in damage to the premises. But they also said it was not inevitable or probable that such damage, or any damage, would result to this house because of the proximity of the tree."

Lord Parker is there saying that there is much to be said for the view that "nuisance" should bear "its ordinary meaning . . . in the legal sense", but explicitly refrains from deciding the matter. Nor does he consider what that ordinary meaning is. He instead relies on a concession by counsel that "nuisance" at any rate "means something more than inconvenience, and in this context meant at least a risk of damage to property which seriously interfered with the enjoyment of that property". Lord Parker was correct, in that there is no reason to depart from the ordinary meaning of the term – that is, in its legal sense. It follows that, with all due respect to counsel for the appellants in that case, it would seem that his concession was wrong, since – for reasons explained below – "nuisance" sometimes means more than mere inconvenience, but sometimes means less.

17.5.3 The decision in the Sun Timber case

Counsel for the defendant in *Edgeborough* submitted that "nuisance" did not mean "actionable nuisance". Unfortunately, however, Lord Parker did not explicitly deal with that submission. This point, and indeed the decision in *Edgeborough* generally, was considered in what is apparently the only other known relevant decision, that of Mrs Recorder Norrie in 1980 in the Leeds Crown Court, *Ayres and Sun Timber Company v Leeds City Council*. That case related to works carried out without consent to the branches of a tree overhanging a boundary between two properties.

It should first be noted that the decision was not the subject of an appeal, and therefore – as a decision of the Crown Court – it has no binding authority. On the other hand, it is the only known decision, binding or otherwise, to have dealt with the point, and is widely relied upon by those seeking perfectly properly to protect trees from undesirable works. It is therefore worth examining in some detail.

In a preliminary judgment, the Recorder considered the meaning of "nuisance" in the predecessor to section 198(6) of the 1990 Act.[51] She held as follows:

"The contention, on behalf of the appellants, is that the expression 'nuisance' should be interpreted widely, and that, if the overhanging parts of the tree were an annoyance or irritation, the Appellant Mr Ayres was entitled to remove them. In other words, that mere encroachment by the branches over his land constituted a nuisance and he was, therefore, allowed under the terms of the sub-section to abate that nuisance by lopping the overhanging and encroaching branches.

"For the respondents [the planning authority], it is argued that the meaning of the word 'nuisance' in sub-section (6) can only mean 'actionable nuisance' – that is, nuisance from which damage flowed, and anything less than an actionable nuisance cannot be freely abated without contravening the provisions of section 60(1) [now section 198(3)].

"We have been referred to a number of cases and to the 17th edition of Salmond on the *Law of Torts* and to the 14th edition of Clerk and Lindsell on *Torts*. None of the cases or books referred to the specific issue which is before the case today; but rather as to what may or may not cause a nuisance, and indeed, as Everleigh J. said, in the case of *King v Taylor*,[52] "the word 'nuisance' has many different shades of meaning.

[51] TCPA 1971, s. 60(6).
[52] [1976] 1 EGLR 132, at p. 132H.

"Having given these arguments which were advanced before us consideration, we are driven to the clear conclusion that the expression 'nuisance' in sub-section (6) must mean 'actionable nuisance'. We say this for the following reasons.

"Firstly, if the expression were to mean anything less than actionable nuisance, it would seem to us to render the whole effect of sections 60 and 61 [now sections 198 to 201] nugatory. Consider the context of sub-section (6). Exemptions are made for trees which are dying or dead or have become dangerous. These are all extreme cases and circumstances.

"The intention of sections 60 and 61 is to preserve trees which are valuable in the sense of their amenity value. Old trees, by their nature, have widely outspreading branches, and if it were to be possible for anyone affected by the branches to cut them down at will, so altering the shape of the tree and possibly causing irretrievable harm to the tree, then the whole effect of a TPO would be negated.

"Secondly, we were referred in the course of argument to the judgment of Lord Parker C.J. in *Edgeborough*. . . . In that case, it was unnecessary for Lord Parker to decide the meaning of 'nuisance' because it was conceded that the word 'nuisance' meant more than 'inconvenience', but Lord Parker did say that the contention that there was no reason for departing from the ordinary meaning of the word 'nuisance' in the legal sense as an actionable nuisance had a great deal to be said for it. We find those words of Lord Parker to be of powerful persuasive authority.

"Furthermore, in the penultimate paragraph of his judgment, Lord Parker clearly has the necessity of damage as a result of 'nuisance' in his mind. He says that the appellants in that case before him must prove on the balance of probability that there was either a nuisance or immediate risk of a nuisance causing damage to the property, and that if there was no immediate risk of damage, then the appellants could not bring themselves within the Schedule which allowed topping or lopping of a tree to prevent a nuisance."

A lengthy extract has been given from the judgment, since the decision was (unsurprisingly) not reported.

However, it must be very questionable whether the conclusion of the learned Recorder was in fact correct. As to her second argument, she purported to rely upon the words of Lord Parker in *Edgeborough*. However, looking at his actual words, quoted above[53] – at least in the form in which they have been reported – it will be seen that he did not say that "the contention that there was no reason for departing from the ordinary meaning of the word 'nuisance' in the legal sense *as an actionable nuisance* had a great deal to be said for it". The desirability of including the italicised words may have been urged upon him by counsel for the respondent local authority, but it was rejected in submissions by counsel for the appellants; and Lord Parker explicitly declined to decide the matter. What he actually said was thus simply that "the contention that there was no reason for departing from the ordinary meaning of the word 'nuisance' in the legal sense had a great deal to be said for it".

It is also noticeable that the quotation by the learned Recorder from the judgment of Eveleigh J. in *King v Taylor* was somewhat selective. To put it in context, that case related to damage caused or threatened by the roots of a tree growing on a neighbouring property. The judge found that damage had indeed been caused to drains, a path and a garage (for which he awarded damages), but that no damage had yet been caused to the bungalow itself. He went on as follows:

"Although no damage had been done to the bungalow, the plaintiff sought an injunction to restrain further encroachment from the roots. The defence argued that if there was no damage, there was no nuisance, but this was a misconception. The word 'nuisance' has

---

[53] At **17.5.2**.

many different shades of meaning. It could accurately be said that there could be no claim for damages unless it was established that damage had been caused, but his Lordship thought it was sufficient to establish damage that the tree roots were shown to be abstracting water from the soil and making the soil less suitable than it was before they encroached . . . There was nothing to justify the defence in its claim that the plaintiffs had forfeited their protection through the law of nuisance. There was nothing unreasonable in granting an injunction if the threat to the stability of the bungalow was a real one."

This seemed to make it clear that, in relation to the path, etc. in that case, an action in nuisance would succeed and result in damages, since actual physical damage had been caused. In relation to the bungalow, on the other hand, an action in nuisance should also succeed, but should result in an injunction, since damage was only threatened, and had not yet occurred. The injunction that was granted restrained the defendant from causing or permitting roots from any tree on the defendant's land to encroach on to the plaintiff's land so as to cause a nuisance. In particular, however, the judge explicitly rejected as a "misconception" the view that if there was no damage, there was no nuisance.

As to the first argument relied on by the Recorder in *Ayres*, the starting point in attempting to understand the meaning of the word "nuisance" in section 198(6) is that, if a word or phrase has a technical meaning in a certain branch of law, and is used in a context dealing with that branch, it is to be given that meaning unless the contrary intention appears.[54-55] Before seeing whether a contrary intention appears, it is therefore necessary to see whether "nuisance" has a specific technical meaning in the context of trees.

Further, and at least as important, it should not be forgotten that the phrase under review is that in section 198(6) of the 1990 Act, which is not simply "nuisance" *simpliciter* but "prevention or abatement of a nuisance".

17.5.4 Trees as a nuisance at common law

The common law doctrine of nuisance as it applies to trees has been considered in some detail earlier in this book,[56] but it may be as well to revisit the topic, briefly, here. In summary, the House of Lords has confirmed that the tort of private nuisance takes three forms: encroachment on a neighbour's land; direct physical injury to the land; or interference with the enjoyment of the land.[57] The encroachment of the branches or roots of trees over or under a neighbour's land is always cited as the only example of the first of these.[58]

One distinction between an encroaching tree and other sources of nuisance (noise, smell and so on) is that the latter can only be rectified by entry onto the land on which they occur, so that, in practice, intervention by the court is felt to be necessary. In the case of a tree, by contrast, it will be possible for the owner of the affected land to abate the nuisance without going off that land, so that a court action is not required. But the encroachment of branches or roots may still interfere with the enjoyment of the neighbouring land, just as much as any other source of nuisance.

The encroachment of a tree over neighbouring land is also different to the encroachment over neighbouring air space by part of a building (such as a

---

[54-55] See, for example, Bennion, *Statutory Interpretation*, third edn, s. 366.
[56] See **Chapter 3**, and particularly **3.3.4**.
[57] *Hunter v Canary Wharf Ltd* [1997] 2 W.L.R. 684 per Lord Lloyd at p. 698.
[58] See, for example, Winfield & Jolowicz on *Tort*, fifteenth edn, p. 494.

cornice), which is a trespass. The distinction appears to arise because the latter will have been unlawful when the building was first erected, and will only become lawful after the passage of time allows its owner to claim a right of prescription. The planting of a tree, by contrast, is not unlawful, and its subsequent encroachment over or under neighbouring land cannot, of itself, make the tree unlawful; nor can a right of prescription arise.[59]

The position was considered most thoroughly by the Court of Appeal in *Lemmon v Webb*[60] which, after considering at length the various authorities going back to the eighteenth century, concluded thus:

"The result of the authorities seems to be this: –
The encroachment of the boughs and roots over and within the land of an adjoining owner is not a trespass or occupation of that land which by lapse of time could become a right. It is a nuisance.
For any damage occasioned by this, an action on the case would lie.
Also, the person whose land is so affected may abate the nuisance if the owner of the tree after notice neglects to do so."[61]

This conclusion was not doubted in the House of Lords. It echoes the formulation of Eveleigh J. some years later in *King v Taylor* (see above[62]).

Since *Lemmon v Webb*, there seem to have been only two reported cases relating to branches[63]; *Lemmon* was, unsurprisingly, followed in both. As for roots, the law was said by the Court of Appeal in *Lemmon* to be the same as that relating to branches.[64] That conclusion must strictly be *obiter*, since *Lemmon* was a branches case, and the point was not considered in the House of Lords; but it has been followed in many cases subsequently.

The first case directly relating to roots was *Middleton v Humphries*[65]. That was an Irish case, in which the law was not considered by the court, although *Lemmon* and other previous English cases had been cited by counsel. It was, however, followed by Lewis J. a generation later in the first English case, *Butler v Standard Telephone and Cables Ltd.*[66] *Butler* established the right of a plaintiff to cut the roots of an offending tree, and to recover damages if those roots have caused damage. That suggests, although the point is not entirely clear (since in *Butler* there had been actual damage), that the right to cut roots would apply even if there was mere encroachment without damage.

There seems to have been no other reported case, relating to either roots or branches, prior to 1947, the year in which the first Town and Country Planning Act was enacted containing the "nuisance" exemption.

There have, of course, been many cases relating to roots since then.[67] Thus, the decision in *Butler* was cited with approval in *McCombe v Read*.[68] That decision, too, was slightly unclear, as the judge (Harman J.) noted that the plaintiff was not

---

[59] See *Lemmon v Webb* [1895] A.C. 1, H.L., per Lord Herschell at p. 6
[60] See **3.3.4**.
[61] [1894] 3 Ch., 1, per Kay L.J. at p. 24.
[62] At **17.5.3**.
[63] *Smith v Giddy* [1904] 2 K.B. 448; *Mills v Brooker* [1919] 1 K.B. 555.
[64] See, for example, Lindley L.J. at [1894] 3 Ch. 1 at p. 14, as well as the passage in the judgment of Kay L.J. quoted in the previous paragraph.
[65] (1912) 47 ILT 160.
[66] [1940] 1 All E.R. 121.
[67] See **3.5**.
[68] [1955] 1 W.L.R. 635.

entitled to an unqualified injunction, for he had no remedy unless a nuisance was caused. An injunction was therefore granted to prevent the encroachment of roots onto the plaintiff's land so as to cause a nuisance. It is not clear whether that prevented any encroaching roots, or simply roots that were actually causing damage to foundations. However, it would be perverse if it were simply the latter, since that would mean that roots could only be prevented once damage was being caused, whereas what was required was presumably to remove them before they reached the foundations. That would seem to be the logic behind decisions preventing any encroaching roots.

A number of other first instance decisions in the 1950s did not consider the law explicitly, but simply awarded damages in relation to damage caused to structures (usually foundations). Then, in *Davey v Harrow Corporation*,[69] the matter came again before the Court of Appeal. Counsel for the defendant landowner submitted that the section of the judgment of Kay L.J. in *Lemmon* (quoted above) was *obiter*, and invited the court to depart from it, at least in part, but the court declined to do so, confirming that the encroachment of a tree, whether by branches or roots, onto neighbouring land, is a nuisance. It went on to find that an action would lie if damage were caused; but that did not mean that there was not a right to abate a nuisance in other cases. That conclusion was not disturbed in the various subsequent cases, again almost all at first instance, the dispute usually centring rather on whether the particular tree had in fact caused the damage alleged. It is perhaps significant that the most recent decisions of the High Court are largely unreported; the law is no longer in any dispute.

17.5.5 Conclusion

The conclusion from the 30 or so cases dealing with damage caused by the roots and branches of trees is that the position has not moved on far from the judgment of Kay L.J. in *Lemmon v Webb*, quoted above. His *obiter* pronouncements (on roots) have been supported by the Court of Appeal in *Davey*; and the availability of injunctive relief has been clarified. But there seems to be little doubt that the position in 1947 was, and is still, as follows:

- any encroachment by roots or branches onto neighbouring land is a nuisance;

- if damage has been caused, an action may be brought for the recovery of damages;

- if future damage is imminent, an action may be brought for an injunction; and

- in any other case, the owner of the neighbouring land may rely on the self-help remedy of abatement – that is, he or she may cut back the roots or branches to the boundary.

It will be appreciated from the above analysis that the phrase "the abatement of a nuisance" had a clear meaning stretching back at least half a century before its first appearance in the context of tree preservation orders, in the Town and

[69] [1958] 1 Q.B. 60.

Country Planning Act 1947 (and relevant local legislation some years earlier; see below[70]). It referred then, and still refers, to the self-help remedy available to anyone who owns or occupies land over or under which grows a branch or a root of a tree that is growing on neighbouring land.

On the face of it, therefore, it would be odd if the phrase as used in the 1947 Act, and thus in the 1990 Act, had any other meaning. Nor does any contrary intention appear in either Act, to suggest that some other meaning should be preferred.

Is there, however, some inherent absurdity or other difficulty which would suggest, as held by the Recorder in *Sun Timber*, that some other meaning should be preferred? She considered, it will be recalled, that: "If ["nuisance"] were to mean anything less than actionable nuisance, it would seem to render the whole effect of sections 60 and 61 [now sections 198 to 201] nugatory".

If, however, the phrase "abatement of a nuisance" had the meaning outlined above, particularly in the social and political climate of 1947, this would have simply made clear what was to occur where the common law right of someone affected by an encroaching tree was in conflict with the "new" statutory control – that is, it made it clear that he or she could not be prevented from exercising that right. This makes sense if it is remembered that the intention was that tree preservation orders were to be used only, or at any rate principally, in relation to trees whose removal "would have a significant impact on the environment and its enjoyment by the public" (see, for example, paragraph 5 of the 1949 *Memorandum on the Preservation of Trees and Woodlands* and, more recently, paragraph 40 of Circular 36/78[71]). Thus, trees in front gardens might be protected, but the removal of branches overhanging the highway could be carried out by the highway authority in reliance on its powers under section 130 of the Highways Act 1980. Consent under the tree preservation order would then not be required by virtue of the first limb of section 198(6)(b), regardless of the effect on amenity of such work. Preservation orders would not, in general, be used on rear garden trees, however; but, if they were, they were not to over-ride common law rights.

It should also be borne in mind that it was recognised over a century ago by the House of Lords that the widespread reliance upon the common-law rights of abatement would be very undesirable:

"It might be very reasonable that there should be some law regulating the rights of neighbours in respect of trees, which, if planted near the boundary, necessarily tend to overhang the soil of a neighbour. It may be, and probably is, generally a very unneighbourly act to cut down the branches of overhanging trees unless they are really doing some substantial harm. The case is a common one; such trees constantly do overhang, and it certainly might call for the intervention of the Legislature if it became at all a common practice for neighbours to exercise what may be their legal rights in thus cutting off what would frequently be a considerable proportion of the trees which grow on the other side of their boundary."[72]

However, in spite of that comment, there has been apparently no suggestion that there should be legislation to restrict the exercise of the common law right of abatement. Similarly, therefore, if the exercise of that common law right became at all frequent in relation to trees that are the subject of a tree preservation order,

[70] See **17.5.6**.
[71] See **15.6.2**.
[72] *Lemmon v Webb* [1895] A.C. 1, per Lord Herschel L.C. at p. 4.

the case for intervention by the Legislature would become correspondingly greater. In fact, however, the right is, in general, only exercised where roots and branches are "really doing some substantial harm" (or occasionally, no doubt, in pursuance of a dispute between neighbours arising for quite other reasons). It follows that it is not altogether unreasonable that such remedial works should not be impeded by a tree preservation order.

Whilst the sentiment behind the comment of the Recorder in *Ayres* that "old trees, by their nature, have widely outspreading branches, and if it were to be possible for anyone affected by the branches to cut them down at will, so altering the shape of the tree and possibly causing irretrievable harm to the tree, then the whole effect of a TPO would be negated" is understandable, the answer is that, in practice, it simply does not happen like that – most people prefer to keep the tree, unless it is genuinely causing harm.

It thus does not seem that the obvious meaning of "abatement of a nuisance" leads to an absurdity. It follows that the exemption in section 198(6)(b) of the 1990 Act allows a landowner to cut back roots in his soil, or branches over it, that are part of a tree growing on neighbouring land. The extent of the work that may be carried out is considered below.[72a]

17.5.6 Other early protective legislation

It is also perhaps noteworthy that, although the "nuisance" exemption did not appear in provisions in general legislation dealing with the protection of trees prior to 1947,[73] some local legislation prior to 1947 did contain a somewhat similar provision. Thus, for example, section 144 of the Essex County Council Act 1933 provided as follows:

"(2) No person shall cut down lop, top or wilfully destroy any tree registered by the Council under this section except –

. . .

    (c)   to such an extent as may be necessary to prevent its constituting a nuisance to the owner or occupier of neighbouring lands; or
    (d)   to such an extent as may be necessary in pursuance of a right to abate a nuisance;
. . ."

No doubt, there were other local Acts from around that period with similar provisions.[74]

That form of words, even more than the shorter version appearing in the planning Acts of 1947 and onwards, seems to support the above analysis, in that it more clearly refers to the general position at common law, without any need for "actionable" nuisance to be proved.

17.5.7 Abatement: the need for consent in a particular case

It follows from the above analysis, if it is correct, that no consent is needed to remove the roots in, or branches overhanging, the land of someone other than the owner of the tree.

[72a] See **17.5.7**.
[73] Such as TCP (Interim Development) Act 1943, s. 8; see **16.2.1**.
[74] See **16.2.1**.

However, the wording of section 198(6)(b) is that consent is not needed for the carrying out of works "so far as may be necessary for the prevention or abatement of a nuisance" – the key word here being "necessary", so that the exemption applies only to the minimum works actually necessary to achieve the specified result. If, for example, a large tree is located such that a few centimetres at the end of one branch overhang a neighbouring garden, that part of that branch could be lopped without consent; but that would not justify the removal of the whole branch, let alone the whole tree. On the other hand, if a large section of branch or root is encroaching and if (but only if) there is no way in which anything less can be retained without leading to the creation of a danger, then it might be that the whole branch or even the whole tree could be felled without consent in reliance upon the exemption – subject, of course, to the consent of its owner.

The first question to be answered, therefore, is whether it is possible, sensibly, to remove anything less than the whole tree, in order to enable the branches or roots growing across the boundary to be removed. If it is, then only that amount may be removed without consent. The second question is, of course, whether that would lead to a resulting form for the tree that would be worth keeping in terms of its amenity value – but that does not affect the need for consent.

In addition, it should not be forgotten that simply to abate a nuisance by cutting an overhanging branch or root might lead to a resulting form for the tree that would mean that it was unstable, and thus potentially dangerous. That would mean that the owner of the tree would be in breach of his or her common law duty of care to those (possibly including the neighbouring owner) who might be affected by that instability,[75] such that he or she would be liable to them in negligence if it failed to remove some or all of the remainder of the tree. As to whether consent under the tree preservation order would be required for that further work, that would need to be the subject of careful thought – and would depend on whether the instability was such as to render the tree dangerous.

17.5.8 Prevention of a nuisance

Finally, it will be recalled that the wording of the exemption in section 198(6)(b) of the 1990 Act is "prevention or abatement of a nuisance". The discussion above has considered the meaning of "abatement of a nuisance"; but what is meant by "prevention of a nuisance"?

It could be argued that it means the carrying out of works to stop the re-occurrence of the nuisance – thus, if half a branch overhangs a neighbouring garden, to cut off that half would be abatement; but to cut the other half, back to the trunk, would prevent the nuisance arising again. However, there is no right at common law for B to cut down more than the part of the branch or root of A's tree that is actually encroaching into B's airspace or soil; and it would be surprising if Parliament thought it appropriate or necessary to sanction the carrying out of work that was not authorised at common law (other than, of course, with the explicit consent of the owner of the tree).

Alternatively, it could be that the removal by B of encroaching branches or roots of A's tree is abatement, whereas the removal of those same branches or roots by A, the owner of the tree, is prevention. After all, since a tree cannot be a nuisance (in the legal sense of the word) to its owner, there cannot be a right to carry out work to one's own tree without consent, on the grounds that one is

---

[75] See **3.6.3**.

"abating a nuisance". Nevertheless, it would be absurd if the owner of neighbouring land was able to take action both at common law and in reliance on the statutory exemption, whereas the owner of the tree – who, of course, also owns the overhanging branch – was not able to prevent the nuisance arising.

It seems, therefore, that "prevention of a nuisance" means the carrying out of works for the removal of branches and roots of one's own tree that are encroaching over or into the land of a neighbour.

This view is also supported by consideration of the wording of the provisions of local Acts such as the Essex County Council Act 1933 considered above.[76]

17.5.9 Overall conclusion

It seems, therefore, that the exemption applies where a protected tree is encroaching into or over neighbouring land, and entitles either the owner of the tree or the owner of that land to remove the encroaching portions without the need for consent under any tree preservation order.

Finally, however, it must be noted that the view of the relevant department of central Government, of many local authorities, and of many practitioners – in reliance on *Sun Timber* – is that "nuisance" means "actionable nuisance". Whilst that view would seem, for the reasons given above, to be in error, it must be recognised that it might be correct, and that the position will undoubtedly have to be resolved one day by litigation in the higher courts. In the meanwhile, therefore, those who carry out works to protected trees solely in reliance on the view reached here (that is, that "nuisance" includes situation where there are overhanging branches or roots) should be aware that they are treading on dangerous ground.

Where a tree is removed in reliance upon this exemption, there is no requirement to plant a replacement. This may be regarded by some as unfortunate, but it is perhaps not surprising – if the tree being removed encroached onto a neighbour's airspace, it is likely that any other tree at or near the same spot will also, in due course, become a nuisance, and so itself become capable of being felled without consent. In a conservation area, on the other hand, where this exemption also applies in relation to the requirement to notify the planning authority of proposed tree works,[77] there is, for some reason, a requirement to plant a replacement.[78]

17.5.10 Proposed reform

The Government has, unsurprisingly, proposed to clarify the scope of this exemption, which is clearly sensible.

It also proposes to introduce a revised arrangement whereby works to prevent or abate an *actionable* nuisance could be carried out without consent, but subject to a requirement to give prior notice to the authority. This seems very cumbersome. It would seem to be more sensible simply to scrap the exemption altogether, so that a landowner who claimed that, for example, a neighbour's encroaching tree was spoiling his foundations or shading her lawn, would have a common law right to remove the offending root or branch, but would have to apply for consent from the authority under any tree preservation order (or notify

---

[76] See **17.5.6**.
[77] TCPA 1990, s. 211, TCP(T) Regulations 1999, reg. 10(1)(a); see **21.2.2**.
[78] TCPA 1990, s. 213(1)(b), TCP(T) Regulations 1999, reg. 10(1)(a); see **21.5.2**.

it, if within a conservation area). Such an application could presumably be dealt with on precisely the same basis as where a tree is causing problems on the land on which it is growing – no doubt the authority (or, on appeal, the Secretary of State) would give those problems appropriate weight, and balance them against any effect on amenity that would be caused by the proposed remedial works.

17.6 Forestry operations

17.6.1 Works on land subject to a Forestry Commission involvement

It has already been noted[79] that a tree preservation order will not normally be made in relation to land in respect of which either there is in existence a forestry dedication covenant[80] or the Forestry Commission has entered into a grant loan under one of the schemes devised under the Forestry Act 1979 (currently the Woodland Grant Scheme).[81]

However, where a preservation order has been made in relation to such land, section 200(3) of the Act then provides that consent is not required for felling in accordance with a plan of operations or working plan which has been approved by the Commission and is currently in force either:

- as part of a forestry dedication covenant; or
- under the conditions of a grant or loan.

Theoretically, consent is still required for topping or lopping in such circumstances, but that is presumably somewhat unrealistic. Otherwise this exemption was both straightforward and logical – there was no need to obtain the consent of the planning authority if that of the Forestry Commission had already been obtained.

In addition, the 1969 Model Order provided that, where land was subject to a forestry dedication covenant, trees protected by a preservation order may be cut down without consent, provided that:

- any covenants relating to the management of the land were being complied with by the owner of the land, in so far as they were binding on him or her at the time of the felling; and
- the works were in accordance with a plan of operations approved by the Forestry Commission as part of the dedication covenant.[82]

Again, the logic of this was that the exemption would generally apply where the works were in accordance with a plan approved by the Commission. However, covenants relating to management, which would have been contained in the dedication covenant, were likely to have been predominantly positive in form, and would therefore have only bound the original covenantor. It was thus unreasonable to penalise the current owner for not complying with covenants

---

[79] TCPA 1990, s. 200(1),(2); see **16.4.7**.
[80] See **12.6**.
[81] See **12.7**.
[82] 1969 Model Order, Sched. 2, para. (1).

by which he or she was not bound. The second of these two provisos duplicated exactly the provision of the Act; and the second purported to impose control that was rendered pointless by the wider exemption contained in the Act. Not surprisingly, therefore, the exemption was not reproduced in the 1999 Model Order.

Similarly, the felling of protected trees in accordance with a plan approved by the Forestry Commissioners in connection with a grant application under the approved woodland grant scheme, or under any other grant scheme approved under the Forestry Act 1979,[83] is exempt from consent under the 1969 Model Order[84]; and, again, there is (for the same reason) no corresponding exemption in the 1999 Order.

Whatever the date of an order, therefore, it is the exemption in section 200(3) which is important in relation to any land in which the Forestry Commission has had some form of involvement, not any exemption which may be in the Schedule to the order (if made in line with the 1969 Model Order).

17.6.2 Works requiring a felling licence

Where a tree protected by a tree preservation order is to be felled in circumstances such that a felling licence is required, the felling does not also require consent under the order; the felling licence once granted is sufficient authority to fell the tree.[85] In practice, it is the Forestry Commission that takes the leading role in such cases, although it does always consult the relevant local planning authority. The procedure is accordingly considered in **Chapter 14**.[86]

17.7 Works by statutory undertakers and other public bodies

17.7.1 Introduction

Each of the Model Orders provides that consent is not required under a tree preservation order for the cutting down, uprooting, topping or lopping of a tree by, or at the request of, a range of public bodies, in various circumstances specified in the Order. Here, in particular, because the precise wording of the applicable Model Order has changed over the years, the wording of the order actually applying in a particular case must be carefully checked to ascertain the extent of the exemption.

The underlying justification for these exemptions is, presumably, that a statutory undertaker or other public body would not exercise its powers irresponsibly. Thus, it does not extend to the wilful damage or destruction of a tree by such a body – as occurred in *Barnet LBC v Eastern Electricity Board*,[87] in which the Board was prosecuted for destroying six trees by laying a cable so close to them that the roots had been severed, reducing their life expectancy: digging a trench somewhere may have been necessary, but not at that precise location.

Probably more important than any exemptions under any tree preservation

---

[83] See **12.7**.
[84] 1969 Model Order, Sched. 2, para. (2); amended by S.I. 1975 No. 148, reg. 2(iii).
[85] FA 1967, s. 15(5),(6).
[86] See **14.4**.
[87] [1973] 1 W.L.R. 430.

orders are the provisions of the various codes of practice issued under the New Roads and Street Works Act 1991 and the voluntary guidelines produced by the National Joint Utilities Group (NJUG).[88]

17.7.2 Trees on operational land of statutory undertakers: pre-1999 Model Orders

In relation to trees on the operational land of a statutory undertaker, the 1969 Model Order provides that consent is not required for the cutting down, etc. of a protected tree:

- "where works on such land cannot otherwise be carried out", or
- "where the cutting down, topping or lopping is for the purpose of securing safety in the operation of the undertaking".[89]

It is not entirely clear what works are being referred to – presumably building or engineering operations. The same wording is used in the 1949, 1953 and 1966 Model Orders.[90]

The difficulty with this provision is in trying to determine what is a "statutory undertaker". There is no definition in the Model Order itself; but in the Town and Country Planning Acts of 1962, 1971 and 1990, and thus (in principle[91]) in the 1969 Model Order, the basic definition of "statutory undertakers" included:

- bodies authorised by any enactment to carry on any railway, light railway, tramway, road transport, water transport, canal, inland navigation, dock, harbour, pier or lighthouse undertaking; and
- any undertaking for the supply of hydraulic power.[92]

Electricity suppliers were statutory undertakers until March 31, 1990. After that date, the 1969 Model Order was amended to include a reference to the holders of licences under section 6(1) of the Electricity Act 1989, so that they were thereafter treated on the same basis as statutory undertakers.

In addition, the British Airports Authority was a statutory undertaker until 1986,[93] since then only the operators of airports subject to Part V of the Airports Act 1986 are statutory undertakers.[94]

Suppliers of gas and water used to be statutory undertakers until 1986 and 1989 respectively; after those dates, public gas transporters within the meaning of Part I of the Gas Act 1986, and water and sewerage undertakers under the Water Act 1989, were statutory undertakers for some provisions of the planning Act, but not for those relating to trees. Other bodies which are not statutory undertakers for these purposes include the Environment Agency, the Post Office, British Telecommunications, the Civil Aviation Authority and British Coal – although

---

[88] See **7.2.4**.
[89] Model Order, Sched. 2, para. (3)(b)(i).
[90] 1949 Model Order, Sched. 2, para. (2)(e); 1953 Order, Sched. 2, para. (2)(e); 1966 Model Order, Sched. 2, para. (3)(e)(i).
[91] See Interpretation Act 1889, s. 31; Interpretation Act 1978, s. 11.
[92] TCPA 1962, s. 221; TCPA 1971, s. 290; TCPA 1990, s. 262.
[93] Airports Authority Act 1975, s. 19(1).
[94] Airports Act 1986, s. 58, Sched. 2; see now TCPA 1990, s. 262(1).

special arrangements, considered below,[95] exist in relation to opencast coal mining.

"Operational land" is land owned by the undertaker and used for the day-to-day operation of its business – it thus excludes, for example, land on which there happens to be an item of the undertaker's plant, and land held by the undertaker as an investment.[96]

17.7.3 Trees on operational land of statutory undertakers: the 1999 Model Order

The exemption in the 1999 Model Order relating to works on the operational land of statutory undertakers (which applies also to the need to notify authorities of proposed tree works in caas[97]) is in somewhat different terms from those used in earlier Orders. It thus exempts from the need for consent:

". . . the cutting down, topping, lopping or uprooting of a tree by or at the request of a statutory undertaker, where the land on which the tree is situated is operational land of the statutory undertaker and the work is necessary:

(i)   in the interests of the safe operation of the undertaking;
(ii) in connection with the inspection, repair or renewal of any sewers, mains, pipes, cables or other apparatus of the statutory undertaker; or
(iii) to enable the statutory undertaker to carry out development permitted by or under the TCP (General Permitted Development) Order 1995".[98]

The effect of this is broadly similar to the 1969 exemption, save that the extent of development permitted by the General Development Order[99] is less than the extent of all "works" referred to in the earlier provision.

On the other hand, the new provision is also significantly more extensive than its predecessor, in that "statutory undertaker" is defined more widely than in the Act, to include the following:

- "a person authorised by any enactment to carry on any railway, light railway, tramway, road transport, water transport, canal, inland navigation, dock, harbour, pier or lighthouse undertaking, or any undertaking for the supply of hydraulic power;
- a relevant airport operator (within the meaning of Part V of the Airports Act 1986);
- the holder of a licence under section 6 of the Electricity Act 1989;
- a public gas transporters;
- the holder of a licence under section 7 of the Telecommunications Act 1984 to whom the telecommunications code (within the meaning of that Act) is applied;
- the Civil Aviation Authority or a body acting on behalf of that Authority; and
- the Post Office."[1]

This covers more or less everyone. It also has the advantage that, by including the definition within the Model Order itself, and thus within any actual order that is made in accordance with it, it makes absolutely clear who is affected. Not least

---

[95] See **17.10**.
[96] TCPA 1962, s. 221; TCPA 1971, s. 222; TCPA 1990, s. 263.
[97] TCPA 1990, s. 211, TCP(T) Regulations 1999, reg. 10(1)(a); see **21.2.2**.
[98] 1999 Model Order, art. 5(1)(a).
[99] See TCP (General Permitted Development) Order 1995, Sched. 2, Pts 17, 18.
[1] 1999 Model Order, art. 5(2).

since the Model Order will no doubt be amended in the future in the light of changing political imperatives as to the organisation of public services, and those changes will be reflected in the orders made.

"Operational land" is not defined, and again, therefore, the definition in the 1990 Act applies.[2]

17.7.4 Trees interfering with cables, railways and aircraft

Trees may have to be felled, or, more commonly, lopped or topped, from time to time because they are in conflict with electricity cables or plant, either above or below ground. The Electricity Act 1989 accordingly provides a procedure, described in **Chapter 7**, to enable an electricity operator (that is, the holder of a licence under the 1989 Act) to take appropriate action[3]; and the 1999 Model Order provides that, where that involves a protected tree, consent will not be required.[4] It should be noted that the provisions of the 1989 Act themselves afford at least some degree of protection for trees in such circumstances.

The 1969 Model Order does not refer explicitly to the procedure under the 1989 Act, but only to works needed where a protected tree will obstruct the construction, maintenance and working of an electricity line. However, the net effect is the same. The 1949 Model Order makes no explicit reference to any equivalent provision, but the 1953 and 1966 Orders both refer to the relevant statutory provisions relating to trees interfering with the maintenance or working of electric cables.[5]

The pre-1999 Orders also exempt from the need for consent works carried out by the Postmaster General under section 5 of the Telegraph (Construction) Act 1908, necessary to ensure the safety of telephone cables.[6] The provisions of the 1908 Act were, in effect, superseded by the Code of the Telecommunications Act 1984.[7]

The 1949 and 1953 Model Orders also contained a specific exemption[8] for works required to be carried out by a court under powers in the Regulation of Railways Act 1868, relating to trees in danger of falling onto railways so as to obstruct rail traffic.[9] Nor is consent required under the 1969 Model Order where the relevant authority is of the opinion that a protected tree is obstructing aircraft approaching or departing from an aerodrome, or hindering the safe and efficient use of air navigational equipment.[10] This is entirely independent of any order made under the Civil Aviation Act 1982, or any direction made under any such order.[11]

The 1999 Model Order had no such provisions relating to telephone cables or aircraft; nor did any of the post-1953 Model Orders make any specific reference to railways. This is presumably because a tree that would have been the subject of any of those exemptions could be removed without consent anyway, in reliance on

[2] TCPA 1990, s. 263; see **17.7.2**.
[3] Electricity Act 1989, Sched. 4, para. 9; see **7.2.1**.
[4] 1999 Model Order, art. 5(1)(g).
[5] 1953 Model Order, Sched. 2, para. (2)(f); 1966 Model Order, Sched. 2, para. (3)(e)(ii).
[6] 1949 Model Order, Sched. 2, para. (2)(b); 1953 Order, Sched. 2, para. (2)(b); 1966 Model Order, Sched. 2, para. (3)(d); 1969 Model Order, Sched. 2, para. (4)(a) (after 1975, para. (3)(a)).
[7] See **7.2.2**.
[8] 1949 Model Order, Sched. 2, para. (2)(c); 1953 Order, Sched. 2, para. (2)(c).
[9] See **7.3.1**.
[10] 1969 Model Order, Sched. 2, para. (4)(b)(iv) (after 1975, para. (3)(b)(iv)).
[11] Civil Aviation Act 1982, s. 46, Sched. 9; see **7.3.2**.

the "dangerous tree" exemption in the Act.[12] However, if works are carried out without consent solely in reliance on that general exemption, it will usually be necessary to plant a replacement tree.[13]

17.7.5 Trees affected by works to watercourses

It may be necessary to cut back or remove a tree where it is interfering with a watercourse or drainage works. In such a case, under the 1969 Model Order, consent is not required if the work is done by, or at the request of, the Environment Agency, an internal drainage board, the Thames Conservators or the Lee Valley Conservancy Catchment Board.[14] There was a similar exemption in the 1966 Model Order.[15] Under the 1999 Order, the exemption applies to works carried out by a drainage body under the Land Drainage Act 1991, where a tree interferes (or is likely to interfere) with the exercise of any of the functions of that body in relation to the maintenance, improvement or construction of water-courses or drainage works.[16]

In addition, consent is not required under the 1999 Model Order for works to protected trees in connection with the carrying out by the Environment Agency of development permitted under the TCP (General Permitted Development) Order 1995.[17] Such development consists largely of land drainage improvement works and works to implement drought orders; and in the case of larger schemes may be subject to a requirement for environmental impact assessment similar to that applying to forestry projects.[18] This exemption applies also to proposed tree works in conservation areas[19]; but there is no corresponding exemption under previous Model Orders.

17.8 Works required to carry out development

17.8.1 Exemption under 1966 and 1969 Model Orders

The 1966 and 1969 Model Orders exempt from the need for consent the cutting down, uprooting, topping or lopping of a tree:

" . . . where immediately required for the purpose of carrying out development authorised by planning permission granted on an application made under Part III of the [1990] Act or deemed to have been so granted for any of the purposes of that Part".[20]

This obviously includes felling required to carry out development authorised by a permission granted in response to an application submitted to a local planning

---

[12] TCPA, s. 198(6)(a); see **17.3.2**.
[13] TCPA 1990, s. 206(1)(b); see **20.2.1**.
[14] 1969 Model Order, Sched. 2, para. (4)(b)(iii), (e) (after 1975, para. (3)(b)(iii), (e)).
[15] 1966 Model Order, Sched. 2, para. (3)(e)(iii), (h).
[16] 1999 Model Order, art. 5(1)(f).
[17] 1999 Model Order, art. 5(1)(e).
[18] TCP (General Permitted Development) Order 1995, Sched. 2, Pt 15; Environment Assessment (Land Drainage Improvement Works) Regulations 1999 (S.I. 1999 No. 1783); for the similar provisions relating to forestry, see **13.3**.
[19] TCPA 1990, s. 211, TCP(T) Regulations 1999, reg. 10(1)(a); see **21.2.2**.
[20] 1966 Model Order, Sched. 2, para. (3)(f); 1969 Model Order, Sched. 2, para. (4)(c) (after 1975, para. (3)(c)); for the corresponding exemption under the felling licence regime, see **14.2.6**.

authority and determined by that authority or by the Secretary of State. However, it does not include felling required to carry out development authorised by permission granted by a development order, an enterprise zone scheme or a simplified planning zone scheme – since those permissions are actually granted under the Act, not merely deemed to be granted.

This means that where, for example, a householder wishes to lay a patio or construct a shed in his or her garden, in reliance upon permitted development rights under the TCP General Permitted Development Order, if there is on the site of the proposed building works a tree protected by a tree preservation order, consent would be required for its removal before the works can proceed. The reference to planning permission "deemed to be granted" under the 1990 Act thus refers only to the authorisation of the carrying out of development by departments of central Government, the retention of development where steps are taken in response to an enforcement notice, and the display of advertisements complying with the Control of Advertisements Regulations.[21] Only the first of these is likely to be relevant in the present context.

Note, however, that the exemption only applies to tree work that is "immediately" required for the carrying out of the relevant development. That is, it does not authorise the carrying out of works to trees which are near to, but not actually on, the site of a new building. Nor does it allow such works on the site of a building which has been authorised only by an outline planning permission subject to the approval of reserved matters. Moreover, see *Bellcross v Mid-Bedfordshire DC*[22] on the effect of making a tree preservation order after outline planning permission has been granted but before reserved matters have been approved.

One important consequence of this exemption is that planning authorities (and the Secretary of State), in considering whether to granting planning permission for development, should have careful regard to whether the implementation of such a permission would require any works to be carried out to protected trees – either because they are actually on the site of a proposed building, or because they are in the way of the service runs (drains, pipes, cables, etc.) or hard surfaced areas (drives, patios, etc.), or the area used by those constructing the building or laying the services. Nor should it be forgotten that building works may require branches to be lopped from trees whose trunks are some distance away from the proposed building. If tree works will be required, and are considered undesirable, that would be a material consideration in considering whether planning permission should be withheld. More positively, it may suggest that the location of the proposed building should be adjusted so as to allow the retention of the trees.[22a]

17.8.2 Exemption under 1949 and 1953 Model Orders

There was no corresponding exemption from consent in the 1949 and 1953 Model Orders. Consent is thus needed to carry out works to trees protected by pre-1966 orders which are necessary in order to implement a planning permission. However, the determination of an application for consent in such circumstances should (presumably) be a mere formality.

On the other hand, both of those early Model Orders allowed for the insertion

---

[21] Under TCPA 1990, ss. 90, 173 and 222 respectively.
[22] [1988] 1 EGLR 200.
[22a] See **15.8** and **15.9**.

by the planning authority of other general or specific exemptions; so it may be that some orders included exemptions for works necessary to carry out development. Once again, the key is to check the wording of the actual order.

17.8.3 Exemption under the 1999 Model Order

The 1999 Model Order exempts from the need for consent:

". . . the cutting down, uprooting, topping or lopping of a tree where that work is required to enable a person to implement a planning permission (other than an outline planning permission or, without prejudice to paragraph (a)(iii) [development by statutory undertakers], a permission granted by or under the TCP (General Permitted Development) Order 1995)

- granted on an application under Part III of the [1990] Act, or
- deemed to have been granted (whether for the purposes of that Part or otherwise)".[23]

The wording of this is different from, and slightly more convoluted than, that of the exemption in the 1969 Model Order; but the result is the same.

The exemption from the need to notify authorities of proposed tree works in conservation areas follows that contained in the 1999 Model Order.[24]

17.9 Works to fruit trees

17.9.1 Exemption under the 1966 and 1969 Model Orders: fruit trees

Works to fruit trees are the one topic where, perhaps more than with any other of these exemptions, it is important to check carefully the wording of the particular order in issue – the wording of the exemption is identical in the 1966 and 1969 Model Orders, but significantly different in the 1999 Model Order,[25] and there was no corresponding exemption in the 1949 and 1953 Model Orders. Here too, the exemption from the need to notify authorities of works in conservation areas follows that contained in the 1999 Model Order.[26]

Under the 1966 and 1999 Orders, consent is not required for the cutting down, uprooting (post-1975 only), topping, or lopping of a "a tree which is a fruit tree cultivated for fruit production growing or standing on land comprised in an orchard or garden".[27] The meaning of these words was recently considered by the Court of Appeal (Criminal Division) in *R v Clearbrook Group PLC*, which concerned the cutting down of a pear tree and two cherry trees protected by a tree preservation order made under the 1969 Model Order. Rose L.J. considered that:

". . . the words which appear at paragraph (3)(d) of the Second Schedule to the Regulations are perfectly normal, simple, straightforward English words. They are susceptible to a perfectly straightforward, simple interpretation, namely [that] a tree which

---

[23] 1999 Model Order, art. 5(1)(d); bullet points added for clarity.
[24] TCPA 1990, s. 211, TCP(T) Regulations 1999, reg. 10(1)(a); see **21.2.2**.
[25] See **17.9.5**.
[26] TCPA 1990, s. 211, TCP(T) Regulations 1999, reg. 10(1)(a); see **21.2.2**.
[27] 1966 Model Order, Sched. 2, para. (3)(g); 1969 Model Order, Sched. 2, para. (4)(d) (after 1975, para. (3)(d)).

is a fruit tree and which is cultivated for fruit production – provided, of course, it is on land comprised in an orchard or garden – is a tree within the exemption. How it is demonstrated by evidence in a particular case that a particular tree is properly characterised as being cultivated for fruit production, will depend on the circumstances of each case."[28]

He went on to say that, for a person to rely on the exemption, four matters must be proved:

- the tree in question is a fruit tree;

- it is cultivated;

- the purpose of the cultivation is for fruit production; and

- the tree is growing or standing on land comprised in an orchard or garden.

As to the first, there is no definition of "fruit" or "fruit tree" in either the 1990 Act or the 1969 Regulations. The view of the Secretary of State, in the 1994 edition of *Tree Preservation Orders: a Guide to the Law and Good Practice*, is that:

". . . the exemption could apply to most varieties of apple, pear, plums and cherries which are normally pruned to encourage fruit production, but not to ornamental varieties of these species or such trees as mulberry and walnut".[29]

It is perhaps significant that that definition was not repeated in the 1999 revision of the guidance. The Oxford Dictionary[30] defines "fruit" principally as "the sweet and fleshy product of a tree or other plant that contains seed and can be eaten as food"; but goes on to include the specialised botanical definition "the seed-bearing structure, *e.g.* an acorn". A "fruit tree" is "a tree grown for its edible fruit"; a "nut" is "a fruit consisting of a hard or tough shell around an edible kernel".

It was noted in *Bullen v Denning*[31] that, "the term *fruit* in legal acceptation is not confined to the produce of those trees which in popular language are called fruit trees, but applies also to the produce of oak, elm and walnut trees". That tends to suggest that the wider, botanical definition of "fruit" should be followed – but that clearly does not mean that every tree which bears fruit, in that sense, is a fruit tree. The dictum in *Bullen* itself distinguishes "those trees which in popular language are called fruit trees" from, for example, walnut trees (let alone oaks and elms). And in the same case it was noted that a grant of "timber trees and other trees" would not operate so as to grant fruit trees.

The phrase in the Model Order is "fruit tree", and not "a tree which bears fruit". The straightforward, simple interpretation of these words is that they refer to a tree that in popular language is called a fruit tree – which probably does not include a nut tree. It is therefore difficult to avoid the conclusion that the view of the Secretary of State, quoted above, was wrong as to mulberry trees, since mulberries are clearly "fruit" in the straightforward or popular sense of that term (as are also, for example, crab apples, even though rarely consumed these days); but that he may well have been right as to nut trees. The reference to "fruit" in the definition of "nut", noted above, would thus seem to have been using the former

---

[28] [2001] EWCA Crim 1654, [2001] 4 PLR 78, para. 12 at p. 81. This decision is also reported at [2002] J.P.L., sub nom *R v Havering LBC*.
[29] *Tree Preservation Orders: a Guide to the Law and Good Practice*, DETR, 1994, para. 6.16.
[30] *New Oxford Dictionary of English*, first edn, 1998.
[31] (1826) 5 B. & C. 842, per Bayley J. at p. 847.

word in its narrower, botanical sense.[32] And trees that grow no edible fruit, such as certain ornamental pears and cherries, are presumably not "fruit trees" for the purposes of the Regulations.

17.9.2 Cultivation for fruit production

Even if a tree is a fruit tree, however, it must be one "cultivated for fruit production". In *R v Clearbrook Group PLC*,[33] Rose L.J. held, in effect, that this phrase means "which is being cultivated for fruit production at the time of the works in question", and not "which has at some time in the past been cultivated for fruit production". It is therefore the character of the tree at the time of those works that is crucial, not its character at some earlier (or later) time. To determine what that character is may involve considering the position over a period of many years, from which its state of cultivation or non-cultivation at the crucial time may properly be determined.

Thus, for example, an apple tree which has been regularly pruned for a number of years and from which apples have regularly been picked for eating, does not cease instantly to be cultivated for fruit production merely because, following a change of ownership, the tree is neglected for a year. On the other hand, a tree which was actively cultivated in the 1930s but which has been completely ignored ever since then would probably not now be properly characterised as "cultivated for fruit production".

It is thus necessary to show that the purpose, or at least a purpose, of the cultivation is fruit production:

"If it is the case that a particular tree is cultivated for fruit production, then it is, on the face of it, within the exemption, even if, in addition, the tree has, for example, decorative qualities which its owner enjoys."[34]

This makes it clear that a decorative or ornamental tree is not necessarily excluded from the definition of "fruit tree", but that there must be some element of fruit production (presumably at or around the time the works are carried out) if it is to be included. For example, some trees that grow cherries which are picked regularly (for eating) may be decorative, but that does not mean that they cease to be fruit trees. But many flowering cherries in suburban gardens are chosen or cultivated, not for fruit, but for their blossom, and in practice they produce no fruit which is remotely edible. They would probably not be fruit trees within the scope of the exemption, but, even if they were, they could not be said to be "cultivated for fruit production".

It is perhaps noteworthy that the corresponding exemption under the Forestry Act 1967 ("fruit trees or trees standing or growing on land comprised in an orchard, garden, churchyard or public open space"[35]) makes no reference to cultivation. This is not surprising, since that same exemption applies equally to trees other than fruit trees. But it means that an elderly plum tree, which has not been actively cultivated for many decades, would still be within the exemption under the 1967 Act, because it is undoubtedly a "tree", but it might well not be under the exemption under the Model Order.

---

[32]   And see phrases such as "fruit *and* nut chocolate".
[33]   [2001] EWCA Crim 1654, [2001] 4 PLR 78, (as *R v Havering LBC*) [2002] J.P.L. 567.
[34]   *R v Clearbrook Group plc* [2001] 4 PLR 78, per Rose J. at p. 81 (para. 10).
[35]   FA 1967, s. 9(2)(b); see **14.2.3**.

The wording of the exemption does not refer, incidentally, to the cultivation having to be either domestic or institutional. Thus, it would apply equally to an apple tree which is the only tree in a small domestic garden or an apple tree which is one of a thousand in a large commercial orchard. In this respect, the position is different from the corresponding exemption under the 1999 Model Order.[36]

17.9.3 Growing in an orchard or garden

The fourth point which has to be proved if this exemption is to be relied on is that the tree in question is "growing or standing on land comprised in an orchard or garden".

This wording is similar to that which is found in the corresponding exemption (under the Forestry Act 1967[37]) from the need for a felling licence to be obtained. That exemption was recently considered by the Divisional Court in *McInerney v Portland Port*,[38] which emphasised that it is primarily the state of the land at the time when its description is called into question, and only secondarily its history. That approach accords with the view taken by the Court of Appeal in *Clearbrook* that, in considering whether a tree is "cultivated", it is its character "at the crucial time" which should be considered, and its history is only relevant as to that.[39]

The decision in the *Portland* case, which also looked at the meaning of the word "garden", has already been considered in more detail in the context of felling licences.[40]

17.9.4 Exemption under 1949 and 1953 Model Orders

There was no corresponding exemption from consent in the 1949 and 1953 Model Orders relating to fruit trees. Consent is thus needed to carry out works to fruit trees protected by pre-1966 orders. One possible approach for a planning authority faced with an application for such consent would be to grant it more or less automatically in circumstances where consent would not be required under the 1999 Model Order,[41] as that accords with current Government thinking; but that cannot be assumed by those contemplating works. In any event, the scope of the 1999 order is very limited.

However, as already noted, both of the early Model Orders allowed for the inclusion of other general or specific exemptions; so it may be that some orders from that period included exemptions for works to fruit trees. Here, too, it is essential to check the wording of the actual order.

17.9.5 Tightened-up exemption for fruit trees: the 1999 Model Order

The exemption in the 1999 Model Order relating to fruit trees provides that consent is not required for:

"(b) the cutting down, topping, lopping or uprooting of a tree cultivated for the

---

[36] See **17.9.5**.
[37] FA 1967, s. 9(2)(b); see **17.9.2**.
[38] [2001] 1 PLR 104.
[39] [2001] EWCA Crim 1654, [2001] 4 PLR 78, per Rose L.J. at para. 8 (pp. 80-81).
[40] See **14.2.3**.
[41] See **17.9.5**.

>   production of fruit in the course of a business or trade where such work is in the
>   interests of that business or trade;
>
> (c) the pruning, in accordance with good horticultural practice, of any tree cultivated
>   for the production of fruit."[42]

The first of these two provisions clearly applies only to commercial fruit growers, and allows felling and up-rooting as well as pruning. It is difficult to imagine why it would ever now be appropriate to make a tree preservation order in relation to fruit trees cultivated commercially.

The second exemption relates to any tree if it is cultivated for fruit production – the meaning of the latter phrase has already been considered[43] – but only allows pruning, not lopping or topping, let alone felling or uprooting. Arguably, consent under a tree preservation order is not required for pruning anyway,[44] but this puts the matter beyond doubt; and it does make it clear that tree work of any consequence does need consent.

Here, too, the exemption from the need to notify authorities of proposed works in conservation areas follows the 1999 Model Order.[45]

17.10 Works required by opencast coal mining

17.10.1 Opencast mining authorised before 1987

Opencast mining used to be outside the normal planning system, but instead the Minister (later the Secretary of State) authorised proposals under a special procedure laid down in the Opencast Coal Act 1958.[46] Once an operation had thus been authorised, it was deemed to have been granted planning permission.[47] The National Coal Board, when formulating proposals for opencast operations, and the Minister, when authorising them, were under a duty to have regard to the desirability of (amongst other things) preserving natural beauty, and conserving flora, fauna and geological or physiographical features of special interest, and to take into account any effect which the proposals would have on the natural beauty of the countryside or on any such flora, fauna or features (including, obviously, trees).[48]

The significance of this in the present context is that an authorisation under the 1958 Act effectively overrode any tree preservation order that was in force with respect to the land affected by the authorisation, so that consent was not required under the order for any felling or other works necessary to carry out the mining operations. However, the Minister was able to designate which protected trees should be excepted from this exemption – so that, in other words, they could not be felled. Further, in relation to those protected trees that were going to be felled, he was required to consider whether other trees should be planted to replace them and, if so, to give directions accordingly.[49]

---

[42] 1999 Model Order, art. 5(1)(c), (d).
[43] See **17.9.2**.
[44] See **17.2**.
[45] TCPA 1990, s. 211, TCP(T) Regulations 1999, reg. 10(1)(a); see **21.2.2**.
[46] Opencast Coal Act 1958, s. 1, Sched. 1.
[47] Opencast Coal Act 1958, s. 2(1).
[48] Opencast Coal Act 1958, s. 3.
[49] Opencast Coal Act 1958, s. 2(4).

The special authorisation procedure was abolished by section 39 of the Housing and Planning Act 1986, with effect from December 4, 1987.[50] But this did not affect any authorisations already given prior to that date. Therefore, where a protected tree is on land affected by an opencast operation which was authorised under section 1 of the 1958 Act prior to its repeal, it may still be felled without further consent under the preservation order, unless the Minister directed otherwise at the time of authorising the mining.[51] This is regardless of the date of the order in question.

17.10.2 Opencast mining permitted after 1987

Since December 4, 1987, opencast mining proposals have to be approved through the planning system just like any other development proposal – and the Coal Authority (the successor to the National Coal Board[52] and the British Coal Corporation) is under a similar general environmental duty as that which used to apply under the Opencast Coal Act 1958.[53]

Once an opencast mining operation has been granted planning permission, of course, any necessary felling or other works to protected trees will be exempt from consent by virtue of the provisions of the relevant preservation order.[54]

---

[50] S.I. 1987 No. 1939.
[51] Town and Country Planning Act 1990, s. 198(7)(a).
[52] Coal Industry Act 1987.
[53] See now Coal Industry Act 1994, s. 53.
[54] See **17.8**.

Chapter 18

Works to Protected Trees: Seeking Consent

18.1 Introduction

18.1.1 Consent under a tree preservation order

Before any works can lawfully be carried out to a tree that is subject to a tree preservation order (referred to in this Chapter as a "protected tree"), consent must usually be obtained from the local planning authority. That requirement is subject to a number of exceptions, which have been considered in the previous Chapter. If consent is needed, and works are carried out without it, a criminal offence will have been committed (the consequences of which could be a substantial fine[1]) and a replacement tree will generally have to be planted; these are the subjects of the two following Chapters.

An application for such consent should be made to the planning authority, and will be processed much in the same way as a planning application (see **18.2** and **18.3**). One distinctive feature of decisions on tree applications, which does not exist in relation to the most recent orders, is the power to make certificates (under article 5 of the order[2]) and as to the necessity of the works in the interests of good forestry, as to the amenity value of the tree in question (see **18.4**). Where consent is refused or granted subject to adverse conditions, including as to replanting, or where no decision is made, an appeal may be made to the Secretary of State (see **18.5**); and there is a limited right to make a challenge in the High Court to decisions of planning authorities and of the Secretary of State (**18.6**). Further, if any loss is suffered in consequence of a decision relating to an application for consent, compensation may sometimes be payable (see **18.7**). Finally, planning authorities may[3] revoke or modify consents they have granted (**18.8**).

It should be borne in mind that the precise procedure governing an application for consent under a tree preservation order will be determined by the wording of the order in question. As noted in **Chapter 16**, the order will have been made so as to follow the relevant Model Order in force at the time; Model Orders were made in 1943, 1949, 1953, 1966, 1969 and 1999.[4] There is therefore, unfortunately, no one procedure universally applicable to all applications. The principal differences

---

[1]   Or, in theory, a prison sentence. But only in theory.
[2]   Article 6 of the 1949 Model Order.
[3]   And even, occasionally, do: see *Mills v Secretary of State* [1998] 3 PLR 12.
[4]   See **16.3**.

between the various Model Orders relate to the powers to issue an article 5 certificate (non-existent after 1999), and the rules as to compensation, which changed in 1988 and again in 1999. But there are other minor divergences, most of which are noted here. As always, the one vitally important rule is to look at the actual order involved.

Much useful guidance on the matters considered in this Chapter is contained in Chapters 6 to 9 of *Tree Preservation Orders: a Guide to the Law and Good Practice*, published by the DETR in April 2000 (also referred to colloquially as "the blue book"; referred to here simply as the *DETR Guide*).

18.1.2 Overlap with need for felling licence

In some cases, proposed works to trees – particularly, but not only, those in woodlands – will be such that they require both consent under a tree preservation order and a felling licence. In those cases, the person responsible should apply only to the Forestry Commission for a felling licence, and the Commission will liase with the planning authority as appropriate.[5]

Where an application is received by a planning authority for consent under a tree preservation order in such circumstances, the authority should decline to accept it, and direct the applicant to the Forestry Commission instead.[6]

18.2 Applications for consent under a tree preservation order

18.2.1 Initial discussions

The *DETR Guide* sensibly recommends[7] that those contemplating carrying out works to protected trees should consider first seeking the advice of the planning authority – in practice, the authority's arboricultural officer. As it points out, the officer will (or at any rate should) visit the site anyway once an application is received, so providing an opportunity for an early visit can only save time – particularly if it leads to the conclusion that a felling licence is required, so that the Forestry Commission needs to be involved, or indeed that no consent is needed at all, so that works may proceed without further ado.

The applicant will be able, at such a meeting, to obtain information as to the planning authority's procedures; and if the authority officer brings with him or her a copy of the application form (where one exists), it can be filled in there and then. That may also avoid problems arising later as to the specification of what works are required.[8]

The officer may also in some cases be able to offer useful general advice, based on relevant experience, to suggest how the work may best be carried out, or other ways in which perceived problems may be overcome. But there is a limit to the amount of time which an officer can properly spend on any particular proposal, and such informal guidance will not take the place of proper advice from an appropriately qualified tree surgeon or arboricultural consultant.

Applicants may also wish to obtain a copy of the current edition of the free

---

[5] See **14.4**.
[6] FA 1967, s. 15(5); and note to 1969 Model Order.
[7] *DETR Guide*, 2000, para. 6.33.
[8] See **18.2.4**.

leaflet produced by the DTLR entitled *Protected Trees: a Guide to Tree Preservation Procedure*; most local authorities have a stock of them, or a copy can be obtained from the Department.[9]

18.2.2 Submission of applications

An application for consent to carry out works to a tree that is subject to a tree preservation order is, in principle, to be made to the planning authority that made the order.[10]

Where the order was made some years ago, and particularly if prior to 1974, it may well have been made by an authority which no longer exists, or by an authority (such as the county council) which still exists but which is no longer the relevant authority for dealing with tree preservation orders. In areas where there is now only one local authority,[11] that will obviously be the local planning authority, and an application for consent should be made to it regardless of which authority made the order. Elsewhere, it is probably best to make the application to the district or borough council – which will redirect it to the county council if appropriate.

An application for consent may be made by anyone.[12] There is no requirement to submit a certificate as to ownership, as there is with many other types of application under the planning Acts. If consent is granted, it is up to the person carrying out the works to obtain the consent of the owner (or owners) of the tree, where necessary.[13] Where works are to be carried out by a landowner to remove branches of a neighbour's overhanging tree, consent may not be required anyway.[14] However, even if the permission of a neighbour is not strictly required, it is always prudent for anyone carrying out works to a tree close to a property boundary to notify owners of any nearby land.

The application must be in writing (it is not sufficient simply to ring up the local authority officer and ask if it would be in order to carry out the works). All that is required is to supply details of:

- the tree or trees involved (if necessary, by reference to a plan);
- the works to be carried out; and
- the reasons for those works.[15]

Many authorities have their own application form – where one exists, there is no obligation to use it, although doing so assists the authority to obtain the required information in a standard way. A model form is at Annex 5 to the *DETR Guide*. However, until the use of a form is made compulsory, there is nothing to stop an application being made in the form of a simple letter, provided the three matters listed above are adequately covered. As to what is "adequate", this is considered in more detail below.

There is no need to submit more than one copy of any information, and the

---

[9] See **Appendix D** for contact details.
[10] 1949 to 1969 Model Orders, art. 3; 1999 Model Order, art. 6.
[11] See **16.4.2**.
[12] Unlike the position with regard to an application for a felling licence: see **14.3.1**.
[13] See **Chapter 2** as to ownership generally, and **3.2** as to ownership of trees on boundaries.
[14] See **17.5**. And see *DETR Guide*, 2000, para. 6.36.
[15] 1949 to 1969 Model Orders, art. 3; 1999 Model Order, art. 6.

authority has no right to insist on more – although, again, it may in some cases be helpful to have several copies, to assist in the publicity and consultation process. And of course, whether or not a form is used, it is prudent to keep a copy of everything that is sent to the authority.

There is no fee payable in respect of an application for consent under a tree preservation order.

It seems that there is no reason why an application should not include a number of different operations to a single tree (for example, to reduce some branches and to lift the crown) or works to a number of trees protected by a single order (such as to reduce the crowns of a line of trees) – certainly the *DETR Guide* (albeit without giving any authority) supports such an approach.[16] A single application for works to a number of trees may lead to complications where different issues are involved in relation to different trees, such as different reasons for the works. It is worth discussing with the authority how the matter can best be dealt with.

Finally, where there are a number of possible options as to the way in which the works might be done, or as to the extent of the works, adequate details must be given of each possible option that the planning authority is intended to consider, and sufficient justification for it. Thus, in one extreme case, where an application was submitted for consent to clear-fell 7,000 trees, there was some discussion as to the possibility of felling only 20 per cent of the trees. By the time the matter reached the Secretary of State on appeal, the only evidence before the inspector related to the clear-felling; he therefore declined to deal with the proposal for partial felling.[17] Whether relying on a range of possible works is considered as one application with several options or as several applications does not seem to matter greatly. The important thing is that the authority considering what should be allowed, and those whom it may choose to consult, should be clear as to what works are being proposed to which trees and why.

18.2.3 Identification of the trees involved

As to the first item required, the identification of the tree or trees involved, this should be straightforward.

Problems may arise, however, particularly where an application relates to one of a number of similar trees or to only some of the trees within a woodland. A plan will usually be helpful, to put the matter beyond doubt. In the *Richmond* case (see below[18]), there was no uncertainty as to which tree was involved; the difficulty related solely to precisely what works were proposed. But the same difficulty could occur if it was not even certain which tree was being referred to.

However, a plan may not always be required, provided the description is entirely clear – "the tree in the front garden of 22 Acacia Avenue" is quite sufficient if there is only one tree in the garden. A photograph (or, perhaps, one in summer and one in winter to assist identification) may, however, be of assistance.

18.2.4 Specification of the proposed works

The specification of the proposed works will also be straightforward, if the works

---

[16]   *DETR Guide*, 2000, para. 6.41.
[17]   *Batchelor v Secretary of State* [1993] 1 EGLR 207, at p. 210E; see also **18.5.8**.
[18]   *Richmond-upon-Thames LBC v Secretary of State* [2001] EWHC Admin 205, unreported, March 5, 2001; see **18.2.4**.

are simply felling the tree concerned, although, the application should make it clear whether the root system is proposed to be ground out or otherwise removed.

Where works other than felling are proposed (such as pruning, crown lifting or removal of only some branches), it is best for the person actually carrying them out to specify precisely what is intended. It is important in such cases that quantities are stated – either as percentages or otherwise. The authority will, in any event, have to be certain that it understands precisely what is intended, since otherwise it cannot grant a consent in clear terms and, if it refuses consent, nor can the Secretary of State on appeal. A graphic illustration of the problems that may occur was given recently in *Richmond-upon-Thames LBC v Secretary of State*,[19] in which an application was made for consent:

" . . . for the tree to be cut back or pruned sufficiently to alleviate a danger, nuisance and damage to our property".

The grounds of appeal referred in more general terms to the Council's refusal to grant consent:

" . . . to have the larch tree sympathetically and sufficiently pruned to alleviate some of the nuisance at least, caused by falling pine needles, cones and branch debris collecting on our conservatory roof".

Consent was eventually granted by the Secretary of State:

" . . . to remove the two longest branches that overhang [the property in question]".

The court was not impressed. After analysing the possible interpretations of the consent, Richards J. commented:

"The fact is that, on the material before me, I cannot be sure which branches are being referred to. Equally, I doubt whether the Secretary of State can have known which were the two branches being referred to. One cannot be sure from the photographs which they are. . . . Thus the Secretary of State relies on a description which is not itself a clear-cut description and the practical application of which he cannot even now confirm.

"It is, in my view, no answer to say that the parties could establish on-site, with a tape measure, which are the two longest branches. It appears that Richmond, notwithstanding that its officers know the site, does not know with certainty which they are. I have no reason to doubt its evidence on this. In any event, the position should be clear from the documents, without having to depend on further steps on-site which are liable themselves to be the subject of contention. In this respect, one is concerned not only with the position of the parties, but also with the position of those inspecting the register upon which such consents have to be entered. They are entitled to a sufficiently clear description in the documents to enable them to know what has and had not been authorised."[20]

That case related (primarily) to a decision by the Secretary of State, but exactly the same principles apply to the specification of works in the initial application to the authority; indeed, if that is absolutely clear, there should be no problems of identification at any subsequent stage. In the case of applications by householders acting without professional advice, or only with the assistance of a tree surgeon who is not willing to deal with the paperwork, it may sometimes be appropriate

---

[19] [2001] EWHC Admin 205, unreported, March 5, 2001.
[20] [2001] EWHC Admin 205, unreported, March 5, 2001, at paras 25 to 27.

for the relevant officer of the planning authority to assist the applicant with this element of the application.[21] Where, on the other hand, there is a written quotation for the works, this can simply be copied and submitted along with the application.

18.2.5 The reasons for the works

The third matter to be addressed in any application for consent is the reasons for the proposed works. Since preservation orders are made in the interests of amenity, it is likely that many works to protected trees will be inherently undesirable from an amenity point of view, but may be perfectly justifiable where there is some reason for them – but that reason must be fully substantiated. It may be noted that this contrasts with an application for planning permission, where there is no requirement to give any reasons for proposed development.

If, for example, it is alleged that tree roots are causing damage to the foundations of a nearby building, it may be necessary to produce a report from an engineer or a surveyor to substantiate the claim (unless, of course, it is blindingly obvious). And this will be even more important where the damage is expected, rather than present.

18.3 Decisions on applications for consent

18.3.1 Action by planning authority on receipt of application

The first action by the planning authority on receipt of an application for consent is to consider whether it is clear precisely which trees are affected, what works are proposed and why they are said to be necessary. Where either of the first two matters is in any doubt, the authority cannot reach any decision on the application; if it purports to do so anyway, there may be problems later if works are carried out which are alleged not to comply with what has been permitted. Where the third item (the justification for the work) is not clear, the authority cannot balance any harm caused by the works against the need for them; and others involved – such as neighbours and amenity groups – may also find it difficult to make sensible comments.

To avoid such difficulties, the authority should, where necessary, seek clarification promptly from the applicant.

The second step is to consider whether a felling licence is necessary, and, if so, to advise the applicant as soon as possible to submit the proposal to the Forestry Commission instead. And, thirdly, in the light of the various exemptions in the Act and in the order itself, it may well be that consent is not needed under the order. Again, if so, the applicant should be informed and told if there is any need for a replacement – as there would be, for example, where a tree can be felled without consent because it is dead.[22]

It is necessary for every planning authority to maintain a register of applications, and every application is to be registered on receipt – together with, in due course, the decision on it and the result of any appeal. In the case of an application made under the terms of a pre-1999 order, the register will also need

---

[21] See also **18.2.1**.
[22] See **17.3.1**.

to contain details of any compensation awarded, and any direction as to replanting (in the case of woodlands being felled).[23] Such details need not be registered in the case of applications under post-1999 orders, but it would probably be good practice to continue to do so on a non-statutory basis.

There is, for some reason, no requirement to acknowledge receipt of an application for consent under a tree preservation order, as there is with other types of application under the 1990 Act, but the *DETR Guide* rightly suggests that to do so would be a matter of good administrative practice.[24] And the *Guide* provides (at Annex 6) a model acknowledgement letter. Similarly, it encourages authorities to consider displaying a site notice or notifying the residents, authorities or groups affected.[25] This could be especially valuable in the case of trees in exposed or publicly visible locations. In particular, where the application is by someone other than the owner of the tree concerned (or an agent on behalf of the owner), the tree owner should be contacted and given a chance to comment. Again, however, such publicity is not mandatory, and may in some cases be superfluous.

18.3.2 Call-in of applications by the Secretary of State

The Secretary of State has a power in relation to applications for consent under pre-1999 orders to call them in for his or her own consideration.[26] In practice, this power has been rarely, if ever, exercised, but it is still theoretically available; and it could be useful where a proposal is linked to an application for planning permission which is also being called in for some other reason. It might also be appropriate where a local planning authority is proposing to carry out works to its own preserved trees that are the subject of much local controversy. And it could be relied on where an application for a felling licence is approved by the Forestry Commission, but leads to objections from the planning authority.[26a]

Where an application is called-in, there is a right for either the applicant or the authority to insist on a hearing or an inquiry.[27]

18.3.3 Matters to be taken into account

In reaching their decision on applications for consent to carry out works to protected trees, the current advice of the Secretary of State to authorities is as follows:

"(1) to assess the amenity value of the tree or woodland, and the likely impact of the proposal on the amenity of the area, and

"(2) in the light of their assessment at (1) above, to consider whether or not the proposal is justified, having regard to the reason put forward in support of it.

---

[23] 1949 Model Order, art. 4(3); 1953, 1966 and 1969 Model Orders, art. 4(2); TCPA 1990, s. 69, applied by 1999 Model Order, Sched. 2.

[24] *DETR Guide*, 2000, para. 6.42.

[25] *DETR Guide,* 2000, para. 6.43.

[26] TCPA 1947, s. 15, applied by 1949 and 1953 Model Orders, Sched. 3; TCPA 1962, s. 22, applied by 1966 and 1969 Model Orders, Sched. 3. s. 22 of the TCPA 1962 was replaced by s. 35 of the TCPA 1971 and, in due course, by s. 77 of the TCPA 1990.

[26a] See **14.4.2**.

[27] TCPA 1947, s. 15(2), applied by 1949 and 1953 Model Orders, Sched. 3; TCPA 1962, s. 22(5), applied by 1966 and 1969 Model Orders, Sched. 3.

"They are advised also to consider whether any loss or damage is likely to arise if consent is refused or granted subject to conditions . . . In general terms, it follows that the higher the amenity value of the tree or woodland, and the greater the impact of the application on the amenity of the area, the stronger the reasons needed before consent is granted. On the other hand, if the amenity value of the tree or woodland is low, and the impact of the application in amenity terms is likely to be negligible, consent might be granted even if the local planning authority believe that there is no particular arboricultural need for the work."[28]

Although it has now been formally cancelled, at least in relation to England,[29] the advice in Circular 36/78 is also still relevant:

"It must be recognised that the mere preservation of existing trees would lead to their decay and ultimate loss. There are occasional examples where preservation far beyond maturity for timber may be justified (for example, the old oak on the village green) but, even in such cases, the need for felling and replanting will arise sooner or later."[30]

That advice needs to be treated with considerable caution in the case of veteran trees,[31] since it may well be appropriate to seek to preserve them for as long as possible.

In addition, authorities should not forget the duties laid upon them by other statutes:

- where the tree or woodland in question is in a conservation area, to pay special attention to the desirability of preserving or enhancing the character and appearance of that area[32]; and

- where it is in the countryside, to have regard to the desirability of preserving the natural beauty of the countryside.[33]

On the other hand, there is no formal requirement to have regard or pay any attention to the provisions of the development plan, as there is with some other decisions under the 1990 Act.[34] Notwithstanding that, many local plans and even some structure plans do contain policies purporting to govern the determination of applications for consent under tree preservation orders; and the objectives of such policies are highly likely to be perfectly appropriate for authorities to pursue in any event.[35]

Finally, the authority should be aware of the matters that may give rise to a compensation claim if consent is refused or if conditions are imposed on a grant of consent. This is partly because the authority may wish to avoid paying such compensation; but also because they represent the true "cost" of keeping the tree, to be offset against the loss of amenity that would result from it being felled.[36] In

---

[28] *DETR Guide*, 2000, para. 6.47.
[29] See *DETR Guide*, 1999, Preface.
[30] Department of the Environment Circular 36/78 (Welsh Office 64/78), *Trees and Forestry*, Memorandum, para. 58.
[31] See **15.4**.
[32] Planning (Listed Buildings and Conservation Areas) Act 1990, s. 72; *Sherwood and Sherwood v Secretary of State and Islington LBC* [1996] J.P.L. 925; and see **15.7.3**.
[33] Countryside Act 1968, s. 11; and see **15.11.1**.
[34] See, for example, TCPA 1990, ss. 70(2) and 54A (planning applications).
[35] See *Sherwood and Sherwood v Secretary of State and Islington LBC* [1996] J.P.L. 925, considered at **18.3.4**.
[36] See *DETR Guide*, 2000, para. 14.7.

addition, if the order in question was made on or before August 1, 1999, it may be sensible for the authority to revoke it after making a new one following the 1999 Model order, if there is a possible claim in relation to:

- the cost of making an appeal;

- loss of development value; or

- the cost of works which could have been avoided by the appellant.

This is because compensation is not payable under a post-1999 order in respect of those items.[37]

18.3.4 The Sherwood case

A good indication of the correct approach to be taken, in the light of these various considerations, was given by the High Court (Robin Purchas Q.C,. sitting as Deputy Judge) in *Sherwood and Sherwood v Secretary of State and Islington LBC*.[38] The case concerned a decision by the Secretary of State on an appeal against the refusal of consent, but it would, in principle, apply equally to the decision of an authority at first instance. It related to a proposal to fell a sycamore tree in north London, around 12 metres high, a healthy specimen in early maturity, about a metre from a short return wall leading from the road to a garage. The wall had suffered damage from the tree, and it was agreed that it would need to be replaced. As the tree was in a conservation area, notice of the works had been given to the planning authority, which had responded by making a tree preservation order to protect the tree.

Once the order had been confirmed, the owners of the tree had sought consent to remove it; and when the authority, unsurprisingly, declined to grant consent, they appealed to the Secretary of State. He upheld the conclusion of his inspector, who had carried out a balancing exercise of the kind indicated above, and had formed the view that the proposed felling would be both harmful to amenity and unnecessary. His decision, to refuse consent, was challenged on various grounds.

First, it was said that he had paid too much weight to a policy in the development plan which committed the Council to making tree preservation orders, with the objective of ensuring that trees thus protected were not felled to the detriment of the environment unless it was necessary, in which case they should be replaced. The Deputy Judge, on the other hand, considered that the inspector had been fully entitled to bear that objective in mind. In other words, there may be no formal duty to consider the development plan, but the relevant policy is in most cases so framed that it is perfectly reasonable to have regard to its objectives – and most, if not all, development plans contain policies in similar terms to the one in this case.[39]

Secondly, given that the site was in a conservation area, the Deputy Judge held that the approach to applications for consent under a preservation order should be guided by section 72, in accordance with the approach outlined by the House of Lords in *South Lakeland DC v Secretary of State*:

---

[37] See **18.7.5**.
[38] [1996] J.P.L. 925.
[39] See **15.8.1** on development plan policies generally.

". . . planning decisions in respect of development proposed to be carried out in a conservation area must give a high priority to the objective of preserving or enhancing the character or appearance of the area. If any proposed development would conflict with that objective, there will be a strong presumption against the grant of planning permission, though, no doubt, in exceptional cases the presumption may be overridden in favour of development which is desirable on the ground of some other public interest."[40]

The Deputy Judge accepted that there was a difference between the subject matter of decisions granting planning permission for development and those giving consent for the felling of a tree. In any particular case, the application of section 72 would accordingly reflect that difference. However, if a tree made a significant contribution to the character or appearance of an area, so that its removal, albeit to be replaced, caused harm to that character or appearance, that was a matter to which special attention must be paid. In this case, the inspector had decided that the tree was "clearly visible" and made "a significant positive contribution to the street scene in view of its size, location and general appearance". That analysis was sufficient to justify the conclusion that its removal would harm the character and appearance of the conservation area.

Thirdly, the court commended the approach adopted by the inspector in considering whether the tree was worthy of continuing protection by a tree preservation order. The inspector had properly taken into account ministerial advice (then in Circular 36/78[41]) as to the criteria for making an order; that was capable of being a material consideration in deciding whether or not he should recommended consent being granted for felling the tree.

Fourthly, as to the cost of remedial works made necessary by the tree, the inspector had categorised this as not being "excessive" or "prohibitive". The Deputy Judge held:

"In context, by 'not excessive' the inspector meant that the additional costs would not have exceeded what was reasonable when balanced against the detriment that would flow from the tree's removal. Similarly 'not prohibitive' was used in the sense that it would not be an unreasonable cost to be incurred in all the circumstances. Save for exceptional cases, the question of reasonableness would be expected to be approached on an objective basis without regard to the personal means of a particular applicant."[42]

Personal circumstances may thus be relevant, but only in exceptional cases.

18.3.5 The decision

Authorities may grant consent, either unconditionally or subject to conditions, or may refuse it.[43] The great majority of applications result in a grant of consent, albeit in many cases subject to conditions (which are considered below[44]).

Consent need not be granted for all the works applied for – so, for example, it would be possible to grant consent for a 20 per cent crown reduction rather than the 50 per cent asked for, or for the felling of some, rather than all, of the trees in a group.[45] This would be achieved by the imposition of an appropriately drafted

---

[40] [1992] 2 A.C. 141, per Lord Bridge at p. 146E.
[41] At para. 40.
[42] [1996] J.P.L. 925, at p. 929.
[43] 1949 to 1969 Model Orders, art. 4(1); TCPA 1990, s. 70(1), applied by 1999 Model Order, Sched. 2.
[44] See **18.3.7**.
[45] *DETR Guide*, 2000, paras 6.50–6.51.

condition.[46] It would then be open to the applicant to appeal against the refusal of consent for the remainder of the works originally proposed. But the precise extent of what is being permitted must, of course, be made crystal clear, if subsequent enforcement problems are to be avoided.[47]

Where consent is granted, it has effect for the benefit of the land and anyone interested in it.[48] Strictly speaking, that applies only to consents under orders made after February 10, 1969, since the earlier Model Orders did not contain an equivalent provision; but it is likely that a court would imply such a provision in relation to consents under earlier orders. The result of this is that a consent is not normally personal to the particular applicant, so that if the land changes ownership before the works have been carried out, they may be carried out by the new owner without the need for a new consent. It would be theoretically possible to impose a condition limiting the consent to a particular person, but it is difficult to see in what circumstances that would be justifiable, since the purpose of the tree preservation order system is the protection of trees in the interests of amenity, and specified works will have the same effect regardless of who carries them out.

Where consent is granted subject to conditions, or is refused, there is no formal requirement to give reasons for the conditions or for the refusal of consent, other than as a matter of fairness, and a failure to do so would not invalidate the decision.[49] However, it is good administrative practice to provide reasons – in the case of a grant of consent subject to conditions, a separate one for each condition. In the case of a refusal, the *DETR Guide* suggests that the stated reason should deal with each of the justifications for the works put forward with the application.[50] This may not be straightforward in practice – it is, for example, easy to state, in a situation such as the one in the *Sherwood* case considered above,[51] that the planning authority considers that the loss of amenity that would result from the felling of the tree outweighs the cost of repairing the wall; but it might be difficult to state with any precision why.

Similarly, it is highly desirable, although not explicitly required, for an authority to supply along with the decision a statement of the applicant's right to appeal to the Secretary of State against any conditions or refusal (along with the time limit and the address of the Government office to which such an appeal should be made[52]), and rights to compensation for any resulting loss or damage.

Annex 7 to the *DETR Guide* contains a sample refusal notice, which could be adapted for use in relation to a grant of consent subject to conditions.

It will also be sensible for an authority, when granting consent, to draw the attention of the applicant to any other relevant matters, such as where to obtain professional advice and what other consents may be required. As to the former, useful guidance is given in the *Guide*.[53] As to the latter, this can be quite significant, in that (for example) most applicants should be aware of the desirability of notifying neighbours of proposed works close to property

---

[46] See conditions [B1] to [B5] in **Appendix B**.
[47] See *Richmond-upon-Thames LBC v Secretary of State* [2001] EWHC Admin 205, unreported, March 5, 2001; see **18.2.4**.
[48] TCPA 1962, s. 21, applied by 1969 Model Order, Sched. 3; TCPA 1990, s. 75, 1999 Model Order, Sched. 2.
[49] *Beyers v Secretary of State and Uttlesford District Council* [2001] J.P.L. 586, at paras 44 to 46; see also *Brayhead (Ascot) v Berkshire County Council* [1964] 2 Q.B. 303, (1964) 15 P. & C.R. 423.
[50] *DETR Guide, 2000*, para. 6.61.
[51] [1996] J.P.L. 925; see **18.3.4**.
[52] See **18.5.5**.
[53] *DETR Guide*, 2000, paras 6.62 to 6.63.

boundaries, but many may be less aware of the statutory provisions discussed in **Chapter 9** – such as the restrictions on disturbing birds' nests at certain times of year. It may be easiest to have at least some of the relevant information in a standard booklet (possibly prepared in conjunction with neighbouring authorities).

18.3.6 Timetable for decision making

Planning authorities should aim to reach a decision on all applications within two months of receipt (eight weeks in the case of orders made under the 1999 Model Order); but they may seek an extension of time from the applicant.[54] An applicant is entitled to appeal if a decision has not been forthcoming by that time, on the basis that the application is deemed to have been refused.

Where an application is made under an order made between 1966 and 1999, and an authority considers that it is likely to refuse it and issue an article 5 certificate, it should try, if at all possible, to do so within the two-month period. This is because it may be that there is no power for the Secretary of State to issue a certificate when determining an appeal[55-56]; if the applicant appeals against non-determination, therefore, the authority may be liable to pay compensation even if it wins the appeal.

Conversely, from the appellant's point of view, once it seems likely that an application for consent is going to fail, there is no incentive to agree an extension of the two-month period; it may be best to appeal promptly to the Secretary of State. Then there is a chance of either winning consent or, failing which, at least being able to claim compensation.

18.3.7 Conditions

As to conditions to be imposed on consents under tree preservation orders, much of the general guidance by the Department of the Environment as to conditions on planning permissions[57] would be relevant. In particular, conditions must be precisely worded, so that the applicant is left in no doubt as to what is required. Some examples of possible conditions are included as **Appendix B**.[58]

Conditions on tree consents may be used for a number of purposes, but the most common ones are:

- to define accurately the scope of the permitted works;

- to control the manner in which (and the time by when) the permitted works are to be carried out; and

- to require replacement trees to be approved, planted and subsequently protected.

---

[54] See **18.5.4**.

[55-56] See **18.5.9**.

[57] Currently Department of the Environment Circular 11/95 (Welsh Office 35/95); see also *Pyx Granite v MOHLG* [1958] 1 Q.B. 554 ; *Newbury DC v Secretary of State* [1981] A.C. 578, H.L.

[58] The author would be pleased to receive details of other specimen conditions (and examples of ones to avoid!).

The use of conditions to define or limit the scope of the works has already been considered.[59]

In most cases, a condition will be imposed restricting the period within which the works may be carried out. There is at present no automatic time limit on a consent, but in practice many authorities impose a condition limiting consent so as to expire if the works have not been completed within two years – or perhaps longer in the case of a programme of works to woodland. The possibility of such a condition was explicitly mentioned for the first time in the 1999 Model Order,[60] although there is no reason why one should not be imposed on consents under earlier orders. And the Government has indicated that it intends to make this a default condition when the legislation is next reviewed (similar to the automatic five-year limit on the life of a planning permission).[61]

It is worth noting that it is particularly important to impose a time-limit condition on a consent granted under a post-1999 order, since there is no mechanism to modify or revoke a consent in the 1999 Model Order.[62] Such a consent would, therefore, in the absence of a time-limit condition, be capable of being implemented many years after being granted, by which time the amenity value of the tree may have changed significantly.

Secondly, where there is a concern as to precisely how works are done, for example, in the case of works other than felling, the correct course is for the planning authority – possibly in collaboration with the applicant – to specify accurately precisely what is being permitted, possibly by reference to the relevant British Standard,[63] so that (at least in theory) any contractor can then implement the consent with the same result. This is preferable to imposing a condition restricting the consent so as to require works to be carried out by a named contractor or tree surgeon, which would rarely, if ever, be lawful.

Note that where a condition requires works to be carried out by a specialist contractor, there may be a compensation liability if a particular applicant is able to show that he or she would have been able to carry them out on his or her own, or using a less qualified (and thus cheaper) contractor.[64] It follows that such a condition should not be imposed unless it is really necessary.

As to the third type of condition, this will often be appropriate to ensure that the harm to amenity caused by the felling of a tree is (at least to some extent) mitigated by the planting of a suitable tree or trees to replace it. This is indeed the only type of condition explicitly mentioned in the Model Orders.[65] And, indeed, in some cases the new tree can be of a more appropriate species, or at a more appropriate location, than the one being felled. Helpful advice as to the wording of conditions to secure the planting of replacement trees is contained in the *DETR Guide*.[66] It is, in particular, sensible to ensure that the condition specifies the preferred species, size, location and timing of the replacement tree or trees, or refers to documents where such details may be found, so as to avoid further unnecessary negotiation.

---

[59] See **18.3.5**.
[60] TCPA 1990, s. 70(1)(a), applied by 1999 Model Order, Sched. 2.
[61] *Tree Preservation Orders: Review*, DOE, 1994; para. 2.21.
[62] See **18.8.4**.
[63] BS 3998: 1989, amended December 1990; see **9.5.1**.
[64] *Deane v Bromley LBC* [1992] J.P.L. 279, LT.
[65] As explicitly provided for by 1949 to 1969 Model Orders, art. 4(1); and TCPA 1990, s. 70(1), applied by 1999 Model Order, Sched. 2.
[66] *DETR Guide*, 2000, para. 6.56.

It will also be necessary to ensure that a further tree is planted if the replacement itself dies or is destroyed, since a replacement tree will not normally be covered by the order that protected the tree it replaced. But there would seem to be no reason why the order should not be varied appropriately to provide such protection. Alternatively, a new order could be made to cover the new tree once it has been planted.

It may also be sensible for a condition to require the details of the replacement trees to be agreed before the existing ones are felled – there is little incentive to agree details once felling has taken place. More generally, as to the enforcement of replacement planting conditions, see **Chapter 20**. It may also be noted that the Government is committed to introduce a power to enable planning authorities to require replacement trees to be planted before the existing protected trees are felled.[67]

Finally, if the planting of a new tree is likely to require the consent of some other person or body,[68] this should be pointed out to the applicant.

18.3.8 Woodlands

Slightly different considerations apply where an application relates to trees that are subject to protection by a tree preservation order as part of a "woodland". In practice, of course, such applications will not often be required, since consent under a tree preservation order is not required where work is carried out in accordance with a scheme approved by the Forestry Commission.[69] And in other cases, a felling licence is likely to be needed if the works are on any scale, in which case the application will need to be sent in the first instance to the Commission, rather than to the authority.[70]

Where such an application is required, however, the local planning authority is under a duty to grant consent for any works to woodland trees, provided that those works are in accordance with the principles of good forestry. The only exception is where the authority considers it necessary "to maintain the special character of the woodland or the woodland character of the area".[71] No specific advice is given in the *DETR Guide*, but here, too, the advice in the old Circular 36/78 may still be relevant:

"Management is important in all woodlands – not only productive ones – and, unless there are nature conservation reasons for leaving a completely undisturbed unit, trees must be felled from time to time and replaced. A tree preservation order should be used to ensure that these operations take place in an orderly fashion so as to maintain the amenity of the woodland as far as possible. The principles of good forestry do not generally conflict with the long term aim of an order."[72]

The wording of the order arguably indicates a presumption in favour of allowing felling in the case of a woodland order, whereas the consideration of amenity is

---

[67] *Tree Preservation Orders: Review*, DOE, 1994; para. 2.5.
[68] See **10.1.2**; and 1966 and 1969 Model Order, art. 7 (there is no corresponding provision in the earlier Model Orders).
[69] See **17.6.1**.
[70] See **18.1.2**.
[71] 1949 to 1969 Model Orders, art. 4(1), proviso; TCPA 1990, s. 70(1A), as inserted and applied by 1999 Model Order, Sched. 2.
[72] Department of the Environment Circular 36/78 (Welsh Office 64/78), *Trees and Forestry*, Memorandum, para. 58.

likely to indicate a refusal of consent in other cases, except where the applicant can show strong reasons to justify proposed works.

Secondly, where an authority grants consent for felling of woodland trees, it must not impose conditions requiring replacement or replanting.[73] Instead, it must normally direct the owner of the land on which the woodland is growing to replant the land; and such a direction may include requirements as to:

- the preparation and drainage of the ground;

- the erection and maintenance of protective fencing;

- the species of the trees to be planted, and the number per hectare;

- the removal of brushwood, lop and top; and

- protective measures against fire.[74]

The distinction between a condition requiring replanting and a direction to the same effect is not immediately obvious; although it does enable more elaborate provisions to be included than might be appropriate in a condition.

It appears that, under a pre-1999 order, the authority is under a duty to give a replanting direction except where the Secretary of State dispenses with the requirement, or where the felling is necessary to permit the carrying out of development. The latter presumably relates to a wider scheme of felling than that which is "immediately required" for the carrying out of the development, as that does not require consent anyway (at least under orders made in or after 1966[75]). Under a post-1999 order, the authority may give a direction, but does not have to. However, the Court of Appeal has held that the power to issue a replanting direction applies as a result of section 198(3)(b) of the Act, and therefore applies only where consent is being granted for the felling of trees "in the course of forestry operations". It thus does not apply where consent is granted to fell woodlands for some other purpose – notably, in order to convert the land to agriculture.[76]

When an authority makes a replanting direction under these procedures, it should, as a matter of good practice, inform the applicant that there is a right of appeal to the Secretary of State against the direction.

Once a direction has been given, if the permitted felling is then carried out, the landowner is under a duty to comply with it, subject to payment of compensation where appropriate.[77]

The Government has accepted that the present system can, in some cases, be cumbersome, and that ways need to be found to streamline the management of protected woodlands.[78]

---

[73] 1953 to 1969 Model Orders, art. 4(1), proviso; TCPA 1990, s. 70(1B), as inserted and applied by 1999 Model Order, Sched. 2. There is no corresponding provision in the 1949 Model Order.

[74] 1949 Model Order, art. 7; 1953 to 1969 Model Orders, art. 6; 1999 Model Order, art. 8.

[75] 1966 Model Order, Sched. 2, para. (3)(f); 1969 Model Order, Sched. 2, para. (4)(c); see **17.8.1**; for the position under earlier orders, see **17.8.2**.

[76] *Bell v Canterbury City Council* [1988] 2 PLR 69, CA, at p. 72G.

[77] See **18.7.8**.

[78] *Tree Preservation Orders: Review*, DOE, 1974, paras 2.56–2.61.

18.3.9 Certificates issued with consents

Where an authority decides to refuse consent or issue it subject to conditions, it may, along with the notification of that decision, issue a certificate to the effect that the refusal or condition is in the interests of good forestry, or that the tree is of outstanding or special amenity value.[79] The significance of such a certificate, which may only be issued where the tree preservation order in question predates August 1999, is explained in the following section of this Chapter.

In addition, where an application for consent is under an order following the 1949 Model Order, an authority may issue a certificate if it is satisfied that "other more suitable consents could be granted, and would be so granted under this order if application were made for the purpose".[80] Such a certificate is rarely, if ever, found in practice; in the unlikely event that this situation arises in relation to such an order, it would probably be best for the authority to deal with it by negotiation, rather than through the formal issue of a certificate.

18.3.10 Local authority works

As already noted, it will not often be expedient for a planning authority to place a tree preservation order on trees growing on its own land.[81] However, an authority may do so; and, more often, it may acquire land on which there is already a preservation order.

Where a protected tree is on land owned by a local authority that is a local planning authority, the rule used to be that any works to it required the consent of the Secretary of State.[82] However, the 1999 Regulations changed that, and enabled the authority to grant itself consent, but only subject to procedural safeguards.[83]

The authority is first to register the application, as with any other. It must then publicise the application by posting for not less than 21 days at least one notice on or near the land in question, "sited and displayed in such a way as to be easily visible and legible by members of the public", and the notice is to be preserved and, if necessary, replaced. The notice is to specify the trees concerned, the proposed works and the reasons for them; and it must state where the application can be inspected, where representations can be sent, and by when (which must be at least 21 days after the notice is first displayed).[84]

Members of the public may then make representations, which must be taken into account by the authority in reaching its decision; and those who make representations must be informed of the outcome.[85]

Perhaps most importantly, the decision is to be made by a committee, sub-committee or officer of the authority other than the one with responsibilities for

---

[79] 1949 Model Order, art. 6(b)–(e); 1953 to 1969 Model Orders, art. 5.
[80] 1949 Model Order, art. 6(a).
[81] See **16.4.8**.
[82] TCP General Regulations 1992 (S.I. 1992 No. 1492), reg. 11, as originally made.
[83] TCP (T) Regulations 1999, reg. 17.
[84] TCP General Regulations 1992 (S.I. 1992 No. 1492), reg. 11A(1)–(3), as inserted by TCP (T) Regulations 1999, reg. 17.
[85] TCP General Regulations 1992 (S.I. 1992 No. 1492), reg. 11A(4), (5), as inserted by TCP (T) Regulations 1999, reg. 17.

the management of the land concerned.[86] This enshrines in law the principles of Chinese walls, so that there is at least some distance between those in the authority who want the tree removed (the education committee, for example, where a tree is impeding the provision of a new facility at a school) and those who are making the decision as to whether that is desirable.

The Government originally intended to require applications to be determined by the Secretary of State where objections were received, but that proposal was dropped without explanation.[87]

18.3.11 Crown land

As already noted, tree preservation orders are rarely made in relation to Crown land.[88] However, where an order has been made, it does not formally bind either the Crown itself – or, of course, an agent of the Crown, such as a tree contractor carrying out works on behalf of a Government department. The Government has, however, stated that Government departments will normally consult the local planning authority before carrying out any work which would otherwise require consent, and take into consideration any comments the authority wishes to make.[89]

18.3.12 Diplomatic premises

Where a foreign government owns land (for example, an embassy or high commission) on which there is a tree subject to a tree preservation order, works to the tree need to be authorised by the local planning authority just as in any other case. However, where an authority wishes to refuse consent, it will refer the application to the ODPM, which will deal with it (where appropriate, in conjunction with the Foreign and Commonwealth Office) as if it were a called-in application.

18.4 Article 5 certificates

18.4.1 The effect of a certificate

As explained below,[90] compensation may be payable for any loss or damage arising from a decision on an application for consent under a tree preservation order. But no liability arises where the authority, in refusing consent or imposing conditions, issues a certificate to the effect:

- that the refusal or condition is in the interests of good forestry; or
- that the tree is of outstanding or special amenity value.[91]

---

[86] TCP General Regulations 1992 (S.I. 1992 No. 1492), reg. 11(3), as inserted by TCP (T) Regulations 1999, reg. 17.
[87] *Tree Preservation Orders: Review*, DOE, 1974, para. 2.66; no explanation in the 1998 consultation paper on the draft Regulations (see Chapter 5).
[88] See **16.4.5**.
[89] *DETR Guide*, 2000, para. 2.5; see also TAN 10, 1997, para. 9.
[90] See **18.7**.
[91] 1949 Model Order, art. 9, proviso (b); 1953 Model Order, art. 8, proviso; 1966 Model Order, art. 9, proviso; 1969 Model Order, art. 9, proviso.

All the Model Orders prior to 1999 have contained the power to issue such a certificate – in article 6 of the 1949 Order, and in article 5 of the 1953, 1966 and 1969 Orders (which is why they are generally known as "Article 5 certificates") – although the precise wording of the second limb has changed over the years (see below). There is no corresponding provision in the 1999 Model Order. It follows that in any particular case it is important to consult the actual order involved to see the wording of the relevant provision (if any).

Recent Government guidance has stressed that planning authorities have been advised to use Article 5 certificates with discretion, and not simply as a means of avoiding the potential liability to pay compensation.[92] To back that up, there is a right of appeal against a certificate; and applicants should be reminded of this when one is issued. On the other hand, this goes against one of the original principles underlying the entitlement to compensation, and the issue of certificates, namely:

"Woodlands are primarily a timber crop from which the owner is entitled to benefit, but

"(a)   the national interest demands that they should be managed in accordance with the principles of good forestry;
"(b)   where they are of amenity value, the owner has a public duty to act with reasonable regard for amenity aspects.

"Thus a refusal of permission for, or the imposing of conditions on, operations which would be contrary to the principles of good forestry or would amount to vandalism, ought not to carry compensation rights.

". . . [N]o question of compensation arises until consent to fell is refused or conditions are imposed in respect of the felling. In such event compensation is ordinarily payable, but a woodland owner has a public duty to manage his woodlands in the national interest, and in accordance with principle (2) above, it would be reasonable to exclude from right to compensation, if, and to the extent to which the felling proposal would offend against the principles of good forestry or be so detrimental to amenity as to amount to vandalism."[93]

Authorities were then invited to issue certificates where they were satisfied as to any of the above.

It is also important that an authority makes it clear that it has formally issued a certificate – rather than (for example) simply stating, in the form of a reason for the refusal of consent, that the tree in question is of special amenity value. Thus in *Henriques v Swale Borough Council*, the Lands Tribunal considered that a certificate was valid where it took the form of merely an extra sentence following the reason for the refusal of consent:

"Furthermore, for the purposes of Para 5 of the Tree Preservation Order, the Borough Council is satisfied that this refusal is in the interests of good forestry."[94]

Alternatively, and probably preferably, the certificate may take the form of a separate document: a model is at Annex 8 of the *DETR Guide*.

It is also crucial that the certificate is issued at the same time as the decision to which it relates. That is, the committee or officer which makes the substantive decision on the application for consent must at the same time also decide that the

---

[92]   *DETR Guide*, 2000, para. 6.67.
[93]   *Memorandum on the Preservation of Trees and Woodlands*, Ministry of Town and Country Planning, 1949, paras 42, 45.
[94]   [1997] 1 PLR 1, LT, at pp. 3B, 7D.

refusal is in the interests of good forestry or whatever; and both decisions must be promptly communicated to the applicant.[95] A failure to comply with this requirement is not simply procedural (as with many administrative oversights), but goes to jurisdiction. It therefore prevents the authority declining to pay compensation. As to whether a committee of the authority may make the critical decision, or whether it can be done by an officer, that will depend on the relevant standing orders of the authority.[96]

The authority should also, as a matter of good practice, make clear to the applicant the effect of a certificate, and state why it has considered it right to issue one in this particular case, to enable the applicant to decide whether it is appropriate to make an appeal.

The Secretary of State may also issue a certificate in connection with a decision made on a called-in application.[97] He or she may also, in theory, issue a certificate in connection with a decision on an appeal under an order made prior to 1966, and possibly in connection with an appeal under an order made between 1966 and 1999.[98] The absence of a corresponding power in relation to later orders suggests that the power, where it exists, is not likely to be exercised in practice.

Where a felling licence is required for proposed works to a protected tree or group of trees, the matter may be referred by the Forestry Commission to the planning authority for its comments, under the provisions of section 15 of the Forestry Act 1967.[99] And in the event of a disagreement between the Commission and the authority, the matter will be referred to the Secretary of State. Any resulting decision by the Secretary of State is deemed to be in response to a called-in application for consent under the preservation order.[99a] It follows that an Article 5 certificate may be used in connection with such a decision.

Finally, it was held in *Beyers v Secretary of State and Uttlesford DC* that, once issued, a certificate is effective to remove the right to compensation in respect of subsequent decisions concerning the tree in question.[1] That seems highly questionable, and is out of line with the conclusion in the same case that the decision to issue a certificate must be made at the time at which the substantive decision is made. It also defies common sense, in that the amenity value of a tree is likely to change over the years, as will the interests of good forestry. To be on the safe side, it would be prudent for an authority to reconsider at the time of each and every application whether it wishes to issue a certificate.

18.4.2 Decision in the interests of good forestry

The first type of certificate is issued by an authority where it considers that "the refusal or condition is in the interests of good forestry" – the wording is identical in all the Model Orders.[2] It would probably be prudent to issue such a certificate only after consultation with the Forestry Commission.

95 *Henriques v Swale Borough Council* [1997] 1 PLR 1, LT, at p. 7B; *Beyers v Secretary of State and Uttlesford District Council* [2001] J.P.L. 586, at paras 35 to 38.
96 *Henriques v Swale Borough Council* [1997] 1 PLR 1, LT, at p. 7C–G.
97 TCPA 1947, s. 15(2), as applied by 1949 and 1953 Model Orders, Sched. 3; TCPA 1962, s. 22(4), as applied by 1966 and 1969 Model Orders, Sched. 3.
98 See **18.5.9**, notes 84 and 84a.
99 See **14.4.2**.
99a FA 1967, Sched. 3, para. 2.
1 [2001] J.P.L. 586, at para. 50 – although that part of the judgment was strictly *obiter* – that is, it was not a necessary part of the decision reached by the court in relation to the actual facts of that case.
2 1949 Model Order, art. 6(b); 1953 to 1969 Model Orders, art. 5(a).

Such a certificate may be issued where an application is made for consent for felling that the authority (or the Commission) feels is premature. Logically, however, even if it is desirable at a particular date to retain a tree or trees in the interests of good forestry, there will come a time when it is desirable for them to be felled and replaced. It cannot be in the interests of forestry, as opposed to nature conservation or general amenity, for trees to remain long past their economic maturity. Alternatively, a "forestry" certificate may be issued where consent is granted for felling but subject to a condition requiring a replacement tree to be planted; in such a case, the condition may be said to be in the interests of good forestry.

For an example of a forestry certificate, see *Henriques v Swale Borough Council*,[3] a decision on by the Lands Tribunal on a preliminary point of law in the course of a claim for compensation for the refusal of consent to clear-fell a woodland. Unfortunately, the basis of the decision by the authority in that case to issue a certificate is far from clear from the report of the decision by the Tribunal.

Occasionally such a certificate is issued by an authority on the basis that all the trees in a particular urban area together constitute an "urban forest", and those who tend them are urban foresters. There is no known decision of the courts relating to such a situation, but the views of the Secretary of State are as follows:

"Before issuing a certificate that their decision is in the interests of good forestry, the LPA are advised to satisfy themselves that there is a 'forestry context' to justify it. In the Secretary of State's view, it is unlikely to be appropriate to issue a 'good forestry' certificate in cases where there is no such context but where the LPA believe their decision is in the interests of 'good arboriculture'."[4]

Thus, for example, where an authority grants consent for the removal of a tree but subject to a replacement condition, it cannot issue a certificate on the basis of special amenity value, since that can only relate to the tree that is the subject of the application; and the authority can scarcely state that it is of special value and at the same time allow it to be felled. If, however, it were able to issue a good forestry certificate in relation to the condition, it would be able to escape paying compensation. The guidance suggests that such a course of action would scarcely, if ever, be appropriate, other than in the context of "forestry" as a genuine activity.

This can be contrasted with the decision of the Court of Appeal in *Davis v Secretary of State for Social Security*[5] which suggested that "forestry" meant "the management of growing timber" – regardless of whether that growing timber is in a forest, parkland or elsewhere, or for what purpose it is being grown. However, that case was in a very different statutory context,[6] and would probably not be of great influence here.

18.4.3 Trees of outstanding or special amenity value

Possibly more common than a forestry certificate is a certificate accompanying a refusal of consent under a tree preservation order or a conditional consent, to the effect that the tree or woodland in question is of special value. The precise

---

3   [1997] 1 PLR 1, LT.
4   *DETR Guide*, 2000, para. 6.68.
5   [2001] EWCA Civ 105, para. 26.
6   See **9.5.6**.

wording depends on the date of the order in question, and on which Model Order it is based. Thus, the 1949 Model Order (which governed orders made between 1949 and April 1953) required that a certificate should state that:

"(c) in the case of a woodland area, it has an outstanding amenity value in relation to the woodland character of the area; or

(d) in the case of trees or groups of trees, the trees have an outstanding amenity value; or

(e) there is a special amenity served by the trees and woodlands other than amenity in relation to the woodland character of the neighbourhood."[7]

The 1953 Model Order simplified this somewhat, so that a certificate is to state simply that "the trees have an outstanding or special amenity value"; but such a certificate could no longer be issued in respect of trees comprised in woodlands.[8] The relevant provision in the 1966 Model Order[9] was in identical terms, as was that in the 1969 Model Order[10] as originally made. That form of words would thus apply to a certificate issued under any order made between April 29, 1953 and June 29, 1988, and thus an "amenity" certificate cannot be issued in relation to a woodland order made during that period.

That led to a major compensation claim when consent was refused (on appeal) for the felling of an area of ancient woodland near Canterbury, in respect of which the planning authority was unable to issue a certificate.[11] As a result of the widespread concern which ensued,[12] the 1969 Model Order was amended in 1988, so that a certificate under an order made between June 30, 1988 and August 1, 1999 is to state either:

● in the case of trees, other than trees comprised in a group of trees or in woodland, that the trees have an outstanding or special amenity value; or

● in the case of trees which are comprised in a group of trees or in woodland, that the group of trees or woodland, as the case may be, has an outstanding or special amenity value.[13]

Thus, it is possible to issue a certificate concerning woodland trees in relation to orders made during that period. Note that, in the case of an application for consent relating to a single tree within a group or woodland, it is the amenity value of the group that needs to be considered, not that of the tree immediately concerned.

In considering whether to issue a certificate under any of these provisions, an authority should consider carefully the amenity value of the tree, and whether it is really "special" or "outstanding". After all, a tree preservation order should only be made in the interests of amenity in the first place, so every protected tree should be of at least *some* amenity value; thus the issue of a certificate should only be to

---

[7]   1949 Model Order, art. 6.
[8]   1953 Model Order, art. 5(b).
[9]   1966 Model Order, art. 5(b).
[10] 1969 Model Order, art. 5(b), as originally drafted.
[11] *Bell v Canterbury City Council* [1988] 2 PLR 69, CA; and see article in *Chartered Surveyor Weekly*, August 7, 1986. See also **18.7.4**.
[12] See Hansard, H.L., June 21, 1988.
[13] 1969 Model Order, art. 5(b), as substituted by TCP (Tree Preservation Order) (Amendment) Regulations 1988 (S.I. 1988 No. 963), reg. 3.

recognise something out of the ordinary. The guidance of the Secretary of State is as follows:

"The LPA may in some cases consider that the trees have both a 'special' and an 'outstanding' amenity value, but in most cases they would normally be expected to choose just one of these terms. For example, the term 'outstanding' may be used in relation to dominant features of the landscape, whereas the term 'special' may be attributed to trees that perform a specific function in their setting, such as screening development operations.

"... In deciding whether to uphold a certificate [on appeal], the Secretary of State will consider whether or not there are 'special' or 'outstanding' features that distinguish the trees from other *protected* trees, rather than trees generally."[14]

Further, it is the existing state of the tree in question that is relevant, not its state following the carrying out of any works for which consent may be granted.[15]

18.5 Appeals

18.5.1 Response to adverse decision

There are several options open to an applicant following the receipt of an adverse decision – that is, the grant of consent subject to adverse decisions (such as requiring replacement planting or limiting in some way the works which can be carried out) or the refusal of consent.

First, it may be worth discussing with the relevant officer of the local authority the reasons why the authority reached the decision it did, and whether there is any way round the problem. If the proposal was to fell a tree to create more light, would it be possible simply to raise the canopy, or remove some branches? Or was the problem the way in which the works were to be carried out? Alternatively, it may be necessary to provide the authority with more evidence in order to persuade it to grant consent, in which case it would be sensible to find out what information the authority would find helpful. And such negotiations may suggest that it would be of assistance to engage an appropriate consultant.

Secondly, it is possible to appeal to the Secretary of State against the decision. This is considered in more detail below, but it is important to remember that any appeal must be submitted within 28 days of the decision being received, unless the limit is extended.[16] It is also worth remembering that if compensation is to be claimed, there is a duty on a claimant to mitigate his or her loss, so that it may be appropriate to submit an appeal if there is a reasonable chance of success.[17]

And, thirdly, it may be possible to claim compensation. This too is considered below.[18]

18.5.2 Right to appeal

An applicant for consent under a tree preservation order to carry out works to a protected tree is entitled to appeal to the Secretary of State if he or she receives an adverse decision (or no decision at all) from the planning authority.

[14]   *DETR Guide*, 2000, paras 6.69 and 6.70.
[15]   *Beyers v Secretary of State and Uttlesford District Council* [2001] J.P.L. 586, at para. 50.
[16]   See **18.5.3**.
[17]   See **18.7.3**.
[18]   See **18.7**.

The entitlement is contained not in the Act, nor on the current Regulations, but in the relevant order itself – where it will be found in a schedule to the order, prescribed by way of a modified version of the relevant provisions of the Town and Country Planning Act which was in force at the date the order was made; and if the order in question was made on or after August 2, 1999, that schedule will be even more complex.[19] This is one of the least helpful features of the whole legislative scheme, and is crying out for simplification.

The 1949 and 1953 Model Orders thus set out, in the Third Schedule to each Order, a modified version of section 16 of the Town and Country Planning Act 1947, which provided the right of appeal against:

- any refusal, condition, certificate or direction given by the local planning authority; and

- a failure by the authority to make any decision within two months (or such longer time as may have been agreed with the applicant).

That section then applied section 15 of the 1947 Act, which provided the right for the appellant and the authority to be heard (that is, to make oral representations to the Secretary of State) if either wishes. Sections 15 and 16 were replaced by corresponding provisions in the subsequent Town and Country Planning Acts (of 1962, 1971 and 1990).

The 1966 and 1969 Model Orders similarly set out (again in the Third Schedule) a modified version of section 23 of the Town and Country Planning Act 1962, which provided both the right of appeal any refusal, condition, certificate or direction given by the local planning authority and the right to be heard; and section 24 which provided the right to appeal against a failure by the authority to make any decision within two months (or such longer time as may have been agreed). Again, those sections were replaced by corresponding provisions in subsequent planning Acts.

The 1999 Model Order sets out (in Part II of Schedule 3) a modified version of section 78 of the Town and Country Planning Act 1990, which provides the right of appeal against:

- any refusal, condition or direction given by the local planning authority;

- the refusal (or grant subject to conditions) of any application required by any condition or direction; and

- a failure by the authority to make any decision within eight weeks.

It then sets out a modified version of section 79, which prescribes the ways in which the Secretary of State may determine such an appeal, and affords the right to be heard.

The 1999 Regulations also prescribe, for the first time, a procedure to be followed for appeals dealt with on the basis of written representations.[20] However, they appear to have been defectively drafted, so that the same procedure also applies to appeals dealt with by informal hearings or inquiries. The outworking of that is considered below.[21]

[19] See **16.5.6**.
[20] TCP(T) Regulations, Pt IV.
[21] See **18.5.7** and **18.5.8**.

18.5.3 Appeals against decisions, directions and certificates

As a result of the statutory mess described above, the position is now as follows.

The simplest situation is where a planning authority makes a decision refusing to grant consent under a tree preservation order, or granting consent but subject to an adverse condition (such as one requiring a replacement tree to be planted in a location which is undesirable to the applicant). In that case, whatever the date of the order in question, an appeal may be made to the Secretary of State, normally within 28 days of receiving notification of the decision.[22]

The same applies where an authority makes a replanting direction in relation to a woodland[23] or (in the case of pre-1999 orders) issues an Article 5 certificate.[24] Again, the appeal must normally be submitted within 28 days of receiving the certificate or direction.[25]

It should be noted that the 28-day period within which an appeal must be submitted is significantly shorter than the 6-month period allowed for appeals against planning decisions. On the other hand, it starts on the date on which the notice of the decision is received by the applicant, rather than, as with planning appeals, the date of the notice itself.

An appeal may be submitted so as to arrive after the expiry of the 28 days if the Secretary of State allows an extension of time.[26] In relation to the corresponding provision as to planning appeals he has stated that "late appeals will only be accepted in extraordinary circumstances", and he gives as examples of extraordinary circumstances "where representations are delayed because of a postal strike, or by the ill-health of an appellant".[27] Experience suggests that the position is somewhat more relaxed in relation to tree preservation order appeals. This may be because of the relatively short time limit. Or it may be because, where the deadline has been missed, all that has to be done by the applicant is to submit a further application, which of course would cost virtually nothing, since no fee is payable. The authority would presumably make the same decision again, so that an appeal could then be submitted against the second decision.

On the other hand, if the reason for delay by the applicant in submitting an appeal is due to the need to obtain more information (for example, to substantiate a claim that the roots of a tree are damaging the foundations of a nearby building, so as to justify its felling), the extra material, once it has been obtained, may be sufficient to persuade the authority to change its mind and grant consent, without the need to pursue an appeal.

Finally, in some cases a condition or a replanting direction may itself require a further consent to be obtained from the planning authority – for example, a condition requiring the planting of a replacement tree may require its species and location to be agreed. In the absence of such consent or agreement being

---

[22] TCPA 1947, s. 16(1), applied by 1949 and 1953 Model Orders, Sched. 3; TCPA 1962, s. 23(2), applied by 1966 and 1969 Model Orders, Sched. 3; TCPA 1990, s. 78(3), applied by 1999 Model Order, Sched. 2.

[23] See **18.3.8**.

[24] See **18.4** above.

[25] TCPA 1947, s. 16(1), applied by 1949 and 1953 Model Orders, Sched. 3; TCPA 1962, s. 23(2), applied by 1966 and 1969 Model Orders, Sched. 3; TCPA 1990, s. 78(3), applied by 1999 Model Order, Sched. 2.

[26] TCPA 1947, s. 16(1), applied by 1949 and 1953 Model Orders, Sched. 3; TCPA 1962, s. 23(2), applied by 1966 and 1969 Model Orders, Sched. 3; TCPA 1990, s. 78(3), applied by 1999 Model Order, Sched. 2; see *DETR Guide, 2000*, para. 7.5.

[27] DETR Circular 05/2000, *Planning Appeals: Procedure, [etc.]*, paras 20, 14.

forthcoming, an appeal may be made to the Secretary of State within 28 days of receiving the decision. It is not altogether clear whether such a right exists in relation to pre-1999 orders, since in each case the relevant provision refers merely to "an application for consent under the order",[28] which might or might not extend to include an application for consent or agreement required as a result of a condition. However, the matter has been put beyond doubt, at least in relation to post-1999 orders, by a new, explicit right of appeal introduced by the 1999 Regulations.[29]

18.5.4 Appeals against failure to reach a decision

It is also possible, in relation to an application for consent under a pre-1999 tree preservation order, to make an appeal to the Secretary of State if the authority fails to make any decision within two months of an application having been submitted (or within such longer time as it may have agreed with the applicant), unless it has within that time notified the applicant that the Secretary of State has called in the application for his or her own decision.[30] Such an appeal is made on the basis that it is to be assumed that the application was refused at the end of the 2-month period (as extended, where appropriate), so that the appeal then has to be made within 28 days of that deemed refusal.

In relation to a post-1999 order, the provision is slightly different. The time within which the authority must make a decision on the application is eight weeks, not two months, and an appeal may be made at any time from then until the application is eventually determined. Once it has been determined, any appeal would have to be against the decision actually made, not against the deemed refusal.[31]

The comments above as to extending the time for lodging an appeal would apply here too; and here, again, it would be possible to make a second application if the time for appealing had passed.

18.5.5 Submission of an appeal

The appeal is to be submitted in writing to the relevant regional Government office (or to the office of the National Assembly for Wales). This will usually take the form of a letter informing it of the decision to appeal – and it is the receipt of this letter that must be before the expiry of the relevant time limit. If the appeal is out of time, the reasons for the delay must be stated. There is no fee for making an appeal.

In response to that initial letter, the regional office will then send the appellant a simple appeal form to be completed. This will ask for the details of the appellant, and his or her status in relation to the land on which the tree in question is growing – that is, owner (freeholder), tenant, neighbour, prospective purchaser, or whatever. As with the initial application, no formal ownership certificate is required. The form will also require the appellant to state the grounds of the

---

[28] TCPA 1947, s. 16(1), applied by 1949 and 1953 Model Orders, Sched. 3; TCPA 1962, s. 23(1), applied by 1966 and 1969 Model Orders, Sched. 3.

[29] TCPA 1990, s. 78(1)(b),(c), (3)(a), applied by 1999 Model Order, Sched. 2.

[30] TCPA 1947, s. 16(3), applied by 1949 and 1953 Model Orders, Sched. 3; TCPA 1962, s. 24, applied by 1966 and 1969 Model Orders, Sched. 3.

[31] TCPA 1990, s. 78(1)(d), (3)(b), applied by 1999 Model Order, Sched. 2.

appeal, and whether he or she is willing to have the appeal determined on the basis of written representations.

All tree preservation orders provide for a right for appellants and authorities to be heard if they wish.[32] This means either an informal hearing or a public inquiry. However, in practice most cases are dealt with on the basis of written representations – that is, without the need for either a hearing or a public inquiry. The written procedure has the merit of being quicker and cheaper, but the other methods enable any contentious evidence to be examined more carefully. An inquiry is also more appropriate if there are to be any legal submissions, or if there is substantial interest from members of the public, or third parties. A hearing may be a sensible middle course in relatively straightforward cases.

An application may be made by either party at an informal hearing or at an inquiry for his or her costs to be paid by the opposing party,[33] but no such award is possible in the case of an appeal determined following written representations.

The appellant must choose whether or not to be heard, and may indicate a preference for an informal hearing or an inquiry, either when initially making his or her appeal, or when completing the appeal form; the planning authority will make its choice when responding to that form with the completed appeals questionnaire.[34] Once one or other party (or both) have chosen to be heard in connection with a particular appeal, the Government regional office will then decide which form of hearing would be more appropriate, following consultation with both parties.

And, of course, it should not be forgotten that, whatever procedure has been chosen for the appeal, negotiations can still continue. The *DETR Guide* thus sensibly observes that:

". . . appeals are expensive for the Government to administer, and time-consuming for all concerned. The parties should not rule out further discussions after the appeal has been made; difficulties or misunderstandings can sometimes be resolved even at this stage, leading to the eventual withdrawal of the appeal and a saving of public resources."[35]

18.5.6 Determination of appeal on the basis of written representations

The procedure governing the determination of appeals on the basis of written representations used to be entirely non-statutory; but it is now governed by Part IV of the TCP (Trees) Regulations 1999.[36] The new rules apply to any appeal made on or after August 2, 1999 – regardless of when the tree preservation order in question was made.

Where an appellant states on the appeal form a preference for the appeal to be determined on this basis, the Government regional office will send the planning authority an "appeals questionnaire", seeking all relevant information in a standardised order. The date of the letter to the authority accompanying the questionnaire will usually be the "starting date" for the purposes of the

---

[32] TCPA 1947, s. 15(2), applied by s. 16 and 1949 and 1953 Model Orders, Sched. 3; TCPA 1962, s. 23(5) and 24, applied by 1966 and 1969 Model Orders, Sched. 3; TCPA 1990, s. 79(2), applied by 1999 Model Order, Sched. 2.

[33] See DOE Circular 8/93 (WO Circular 29/93), *Award of Costs Incurred in Planning and Other (including Compulsory Purchase Order) Proceedings.*

[34] See **18.5.6**.

[35] *DETR Guide*, 2000, para. 7.5.

[36] S.I. 1999 No. 1892, reg. 11.

Regulations; and that date will also be notified to the appellant.[37] Within two weeks of that date, the authority must return the questionnaire, duly completed, together with a copy of each of the documents referred to in it.[38] The *DETR Guide* suggests that the planning authority should send a copy of the questionnaire and supporting documents to the appellant.[39]

The appellant and the planning authority may then submit any additional representations they wish, so as to be received by the regional office not later than six weeks after the starting date. The regional office will copy these to the other side.[40] Sensible advice on the preparation of such representations is given in the *DETR Guide* to planning authorities,[41] although it is equally applicable to appellants – the advice could be simply summarised as "keep representations short and to the point". A so-called "model appeal statement" is at Annex 9 to the *Guide*, but it adds little.

The appellant and the authority are then both entitled to make further representations in response, and those must be sent to the regional office so as to arrive not later than two weeks after receipt of the representations to which they are responding. The applicant's further representations may also, obviously, deal with the documents accompanying the questionnaire.[42] On this the *Guide* comments (no doubt based on bitter experience):

"Late and repetitious representations are discouraged. Whether intended to reinforce points already made, have the last word, or save the best arguments to the end, such tactics confer no advantage and only prolong the appeal process."[43]

The Secretary of State (in practice, the relevant officer within the regional office) may extend the above time limits in a particular case.[44] It remains to be seen whether in practice the approach to the exercise of this power will be as relaxed as the extension of the time limit for the initial appeal, or as strict as the approach towards corresponding time limits for planning appeals.[45] Certainly if the regional office accepts from one party representations which are submitted late, the other party will still be given (at least) two weeks in which to respond.

Planning authorities have also been advised to notify any third parties (such as neighbours) of the appeal, at an early stage, so that they have a chance to submit representations within the six-week period[46] – although there is no statutory basis for this.

Finally, the regional office will arrange a site inspection by an officer of the Department[47] or an arboriculturist appointed by the Department. The inspection will usually be accompanied by representatives of the appellant and the authority, to identify the trees in question and to clarify the work for which consent is being

---

[37] S.I. 1999 No. 1892, reg. 12.
[38] S.I. 1999 No. 1892, reg. 13.
[39] *DETR Guide*, 2000, para. 7.7.
[40] S.I. 1999 No. 1892, reg. 14(1).
[41] *DETR Guide*, 2000, para. 7.9.
[42] S.I. 1999 No. 1892, reg. 14(2), (3).
[43] *DETR Guide*, 2000, para. 7.10.
[44] S.I. 1999 No. 1892, reg. 15.
[45] Under the TCP (Appeals) (Written Representations Procedure) (England) Regulations 2000 (S.I. 2000 No. 1628), which do not apply to tree preservation order appeals.
[46] *DETR Guide*, 2000, para. 7.8.
[47] That is, the Office of the Deputy Prime Minister (ODPM) or, as appropriate, the National Assembly for Wales.

sought. No discussion of the merits of the case will be allowed at this stage. Alternatively, where there is no difficulty with access, the site visit may be unaccompanied (which obviously saves time).

18.5.7 Informal hearings

There are no formal rules governing the procedure to be followed.

The rules which govern the conduct of informal hearings in England relating to planning appeals, the TCP (Hearings Procedure) (England) Rules 2000,[48] explicitly do not apply to appeals under section 78 of the TCPA 1990 as applied by any other enactment.[49] Thus, they do not apply to tree preservation order consent appeals. Those Rules do not apply in Wales even in relation to normal planning appeals; but nor do any other – they are, in practice, the subject of the non-statutory Code of Practice which operated in England prior to 2000.[50]

Unfortunately, regulation 11(1)(b) of the 1999 Trees Regulations explicitly states that Part IV of those Regulations – which was clearly intended to apply only to written representations appeals – applies:

" . . . to every appeal . . . which is to be disposed of without a hearing or an inquiry to which rules under section 9 (procedure in connection with statutory inquiries) of the Tribunals and Inquiries Act 1992 apply".

Since there appear to be no rules under the 1992 Act applying to tree consent appeals, it would therefore seem that Part IV of the 1999 Regulations applies also to such appeals dealt with by way of hearings and inquiries.

The Government is aware of this anomaly, and is currently considering what to do to rectify the formal position. In the meanwhile, the rules governing hearings held in connection with normal planning appeals (already noted) will be followed as far as possible, on a non-statutory basis, so far as they are not inconsistent with the 1999 Regulations. Government guidance relating to the Hearings Rules 2000 is at Annex 2 to Circular 05/2000.[51]

Once it has been decided that an appeal will be determined on the basis of an informal hearing, the Government regional office will notify the Planning Inspectorate, which will then appoint an inspector, and fix a place and time for the hearing (after consultation with the parties).

The authority must submit the questionnaire to the Government regional office within two weeks of the starting date.[52] The authority and the appellant must submit hearing statements (together with supporting documents) within six weeks of that date,[53] and comments on those statements within eight or nine weeks.[54]

On the assumption that the Hearings Rules 2000 will be applied, albeit on a non-statutory basis, the actual hearing will be, if at all possible, held within 12 weeks of the starting date[55]; and the procedure at the hearing, which will be in the

---

[48] S.I. 2000 No. 1626 ("Hearings Rules 2000").
[49] Hearings Rules 2000, r. 3(1).
[50] Set out at Annex 2 to DOE Circular 15/96 (which, ironically, did not apply in Wales).
[51] DETR Circular 05/2000, *Planning Appeals: Procedure, etc.*
[52] TCP (T) Regulations 1999, reg. 13; Hearings Rules 2000, r. 4(2); for "the starting date", see **18.5.6**.
[53] TCP (T) Regulations 1999, reg. 14(1); Hearings Rules 2000, r. 6(1).
[54] TCP (T) Regulations 1999, reg. 14(1) (8 weeks); Hearings Rules 2000, r. 6(1) (9 weeks).
[55] Hearings Rules 2000, r. 7.

form of an informal discussion, generally without any cross-examination, will be almost entirely at the discretion of the inspector.[56] It may well be appropriate in cases relating to trees for the hearing to be held partly at the site; and this is provided for in the Rules.[57] Advice on the format of a hearing statement is at Annex 2(i) to the Circular, and details of the procedure at a hearing is at Annex 2(ii).

18.5.8 *Inquiries*

Just as with hearings, there are no procedural rules applying to inquiries into tree consent appeals; the rules governing normal planning inquiries – the TCP Appeals (Inquiries Procedure) (England) Rules 2000[58] and, for Wales, the TCP (Inquiries Procedure) Rules 1992[59] – do not apply to tree preservation order consent appeals.[60] It may be noted that the rules governing inquiries where appeals are to be determined by inspectors do not apply, since there is (as yet) no power for inspectors to determine tree preservation order appeals.[61]

Unfortunately, for the reasons explored above in relation to hearings,[62] it seems that Part IV of the 1999 Trees Regulations applies also to tree consent appeals dealt with by way of inquiries. Until steps have been taken to rectify this anomaly, the rules (of 2000 and 1992) governing appeals held in connection with normal planning appeals will be followed wherever possible, on a non-statutory basis, so far as they are not inconsistent with the 1999 Regulations. Government guidance relating to the Inquiries Rules 2000 is at Annex 3 to Circular 05/2000.[63] It would seem likely that new rules will soon be produced for Wales, to bring it into line with England.

Once it has been decided that an appeal will be determined on the basis of an inquiry, the Government regional office will notify the Planning Inspectorate, which will then appoint an inspector, and fix a place and time for the inquiry (again, after consultation with the parties). Occasionally the inspector may be assisted by a technical assessor; for a bizarre example of a challenge to the competence of such an assessor, see *Batchelor v Secretary of State.*[64]

Under the Inquiries Rules 2000, each party must submit within six weeks of the starting date a brief statement setting out its case (often known as a "rule 6 statement").[65] This is designed to assist each party to know what its opponent's case is; but it can also be a valuable means of enabling each party to think through carefully, possibly for the first time, what its own case actually is. Once a date for the inquiry has been arranged, each party must submit no less than four weeks in advance a written proof for each witness to be called, together with a summary where the proof is longer than 1,500 words.[66] Useful guidance on the preparation

---

[56] Hearings Rules 2000, r. 11.
[57] Hearings Rules 2000, r. 12(1).
[58] S.I. 2000 No. 1624 ("Inquiries Rules 2000").
[59] S.I. 1992 No. 2038 ("Inquiries Rules 1992").
[60] Inquiries Rules 2000, r. 3(1); Inquiries Rules 1992, r. 3(1).
[61] See **18.5.9**.
[62] See **18.5.7**.
[63] DETR Circular 05/2000, *Planning Appeals: Procedure, etc.*
[64] [1993] 1 EGLR 207.
[65] Inquiries Rules 2000, r. 6(1), (3).
[66] Inquiries Rules 2000, r. 13.

of proofs is at Annex 3(i) to the Circular. Note that the time limits under the 1992 Rules, which apply in Wales, are slightly different.[67]

In addition, in England, the appellant must submit by the same date a statement of common ground agreed with the planning authority.[68] The preparation of this could start at an early stage in preparing for the inquiry, as it may save everyone's time by avoiding the need for material to be produced in evidence. Matters which might be suitable for inclusion in such a statement include:

- the age and species of the tree or trees concerned;
- when they were first protected by a tree preservation order;
- the points from which they are visible;
- the relevant planning history;
- the precise details of what is proposed;
- all relevant policies;
- other documents (such as consultants' reports).

All of the above matters, and there may well be others, need not be particularly controversial; and the production of such a statement does not prevent inferences being drawn in support of one side or the other. But at least the preparation of a common bundle will save everyone time and effort.

The procedure at an inquiry into a tree preservation order consent will be as for a normal planning inquiry – that is, after brief opening submissions by both parties, the planning authority will call evidence, followed by the appellant, and then any third parties[69] (the appellant still goes first in Wales[70]). The inspector will carry out a site inspection, usually after the end of the inquiry. The *Batchelor* case,[71-72] mentioned above, provides a vivid example of how not to win friends or influence the inspector at an inquiry, including the appellant declining to turn up or give evidence, and the inspector not being allowed to visit the site. Hopefully the lessons arising from that case will not be of general application.

18.5.9 The decision

Following the exchange of written representations, the hearing or the inquiry, the officer (in written representations cases) or the inspector will then write a report to the Secretary of State, who will reach a decision on the appeal.

By virtue of the 1999 Regulations, the Secretary of State is entitled to make a decision, in written representations cases, on the basis of (only) "such representations and supporting documents as have been submitted within the relevant time limits",[73] and indeed to decide the appeal even if no material has been submitted, provided that warning has been given to both parties.[74]

---

[67] See Inquiries Rules 1992, rr. 6, 13.
[68] Inquiries Rules 2000, r. 14; Circular 05/2000, Annex 3, para. 40, and Annex 3(ii).
[69] Inquiries Rules 2000, r. 15(4); Circular 05/2000, Annex 3, para. 41.
[70] Inquiries Rules 1992, r. 14(2).
[71-72] *Batchelor v Secretary of State* [1993] 1 EGLR 207.
[73] TCP(T) Regulations 1999, reg. 16(1).
[74] TCP(T) Regulations 1999, reg. 16(2).

In cases decided following an informal hearing or an inquiry, the Secretary of State is entitled to disregard new evidence arising after the close of the hearing or inquiry.[75] Even though (at least in theory) the 1999 Regulations seem to apply also to appeals determined following hearings or inquiries, it is inconceivable that the Secretary of State in such cases would not take full account of the evidence presented at the inquiry, albeit only on a non-statutory basis.

Unfortunately, there is no power in relation to appeals arising from pre-1999 orders for the Secretary of State to delegate decisions on tree preservation order consent appeals to inspectors – even though such appeals would be eminently suitable for this approach. This omission arises because the power to delegate was only introduced in relation to ordinary planning appeals in 1968, and was initially exercised only in relation to very few appeals. The pattern of all appeals being determined by the Secretary of State was, therefore, unsurprisingly followed in all of the Model Orders up to and including 1969.[76] As a result, the Secretary of State (that is, in practice, an officer of the Department) determines all tree appeals.

The problems that can result from this were graphically illustrated in *Richmond-upon-Thames v Secretary of State*,[77] which related to a tree preservation order consent appeal determined on the basis of written representations. It has already been noted that this case partially concerned the inability of anyone to be certain as to precisely what works were proposed to the tree in question.[78] The officer considering the representations and carrying out the site inspection realised that, and accordingly dealt with all possible types of works which could be carried out to the tree, and concluded that all of them were unjustifiable. The Secretary of State, on the other hand, decided that some work was justified. The Council challenged that decision, and the court found as follows:

"It is all very well for the Secretary of State to reach a different judgment as to the balance between alleviation of the problem and protection of amenity but, in my view, the Secretary of State went further than striking a different balance. By holding that the works, whatever precisely they were, would have a minimal impact to the amenity value of the tree to the area, he was necessarily disagreeing with the Inspecting Officer's assessment of the harm to amenity that the works would cause. If the Secretary of State wishes to disagree with the views of the Inspecting Officer, it seems to me that he had to give some reasons in support. There are none. Indeed I doubt whether there is any evidence upon which the Secretary of State could properly disagree with those views. But it is sufficient for me to state my conclusion that, at the very least, the reasoning in support of the conclusion is wholly inadequate.

" . . . This case seems to me to illustrate the dangers of reaching a judgment [as to] effects on amenity, including here the effect of measures on the overall form or shape of a tree, as a purely paper exercise, even with the benefit of photographs and plans. That is the kind of judgment best made by an experienced inspecting officer on a site visit. In this case, I regret to say that I get the strong impression that an ill-informed judgment has been made by a decision-maker lacking the benefit of a proper assessment of the situation on site."[79]

It is noteworthy that the 1999 Model Order contains a power to delegate the

---

[75] Hearings Rules 2000, r. 13; Inquiries Rules 2000, r. 17; Inquiries Rules 1992, r. 17.
[76] TCPA 1968, s. 21; see now TCPA 1990, Sched. 6.
[77] *Richmond-upon-Thames LBC v Secretary of State* [2001] EWHC Admin 205, unreported, March 5, 2001.
[78] See **18.2.4**.
[79] [2001] EWHC Admin 205, unreported, March 5, 2001, per Richards J. at paras 39, 41.

determination of appeals to inspectors,[80] but that power has not yet been exercised.

The Secretary of State on determining the appeal may allow it in whole or in part, or may dismiss it, and may reverse or vary any part of the authority's decision.

The Secretary of State is, in particular, entitled to grant consent for part of the works for which consent was sought; but he or she is not bound to do so. If the carrying out of lesser works results in a significantly different proposal, it would probably be right not to reach a final decision until all parties concerned, including those (neighbours, parish councils, and so on) who were consulted on the initial application, have had a chance to express a view on the revised proposal.[81]

As for what the decision should be, the correct approach to be adopted by the Secretary of State has already been considered, in the context of decisions by local authorities.[82] And if he or she allows the appeal and grants consent, it may be subject to conditions, including of course conditions requiring replacement trees to be planted.[83] He or she may also issue (in theory) an Article 5 certificate where refusing to grant consent under a pre-1966 order,[84] and possibly in relation to an order made between 1966 and 1989.[84a]

The Secretary of State may also cancel or vary any replanting direction, and may cancel any certificate issued by the authority; the policy adopted in relation to the latter has also been considered already.[85]

18.6 High Court challenges

18.6.1 Challenges to decisions by local authorities

It is possible to seek judicial review of any decision by a public body, except where statute provides an alternative remedy that is stated to be exclusive. On the other hand, permission is always required to make a claim for judicial review; and the courts are unlikely to grant permission where there exists a right of appeal to a specialist tribunal.

The result of these principles is that an applicant for consent under a tree preservation order who is aggrieved by the decision of the local authority – a refusal of consent, a condition attached to a grant of consent, a replanting direction or an Article 5 certificate – should first exercise his or her right of appeal to the Secretary of State,[86] and only contemplate court proceedings if the Secretary of State's decision is also perceived to be defective.[87]

On the other hand, there is no such right of appeal by aggrieved third parties – such as neighbours. If, therefore, consent is granted by a local planning authority

---

80   TCPA 1990, s. 79(7), applied by 1999 Model Order, Sched. 2.
81   *Batchelor v Secretary of State* [1993] 1 EGLR 207, at p. 210E.
82   See **18.3.3** to **18.3.5**.
83   See **18.3.7**.
84   TCPA 1947, s. 16(2), as applied by 1949 s. 15(2) and Model Order, Sched. 3 explicitly apply art. 6 of the Order to a decision of the Secretary of State on appeal. The 1953 Model Order is similar.
84a TCPA 1962, s. 23(4), as applied by 1966 and 1969 Model Orders, Sched. 3 simply state that the Secretary of State may deal with the application as if it had been made to him in the first instance.
85   See **18.4**.
86   See **18.5.3**.
87   See **18.6.3**.

for the carrying out of works to a tree, the only possible remedy (other than persuading the successful applicant not to implement the consent) open to anyone else affected by the decision is to apply to the High Court for permission to seek judicial review of the decision. However, three matters need to be borne firmly in mind by anyone contemplating such a move:

- the court will only review the decision of the authority to see whether it was wrong in law; it will not revisit the matter from first principles and make a new decision on the facts;

- even if there is found to have been an error of law, the court is not bound to quash the decision; and

- mounting a claim for judicial review is not at all straightforward, and there are tight time limits to be observed,[88] so that speed is of the essence.

In addition, if the consent relates to the felling of a single tree, it may be necessary to seek an injunction within hours if the felling is to be prevented – there is little point in proving that a consent was unlawful once the tree has gone. In practice, therefore, a claim for judicial review may be of use principally where the consent relates to the felling or thinning of a woodland over a longer period.

It should also be noted that – although there are, for example, a growing number of examples of successful challenges to decisions by planning authorities to grant planning permission – there appears to no reported instance of a challenge (successful or otherwise) having been made to a decision of a local planning authority on an application for tree preservation order consent.[89]

It follows that it is essential for anyone in this position to seek specialist legal advice promptly.

18.6.2 Judicial review: procedure

The procedure for seeking judicial review has since October 2, 2000 been governed by Part 54 of the Civil Procedure Rules 1998.[90] It should be noted that this altered some of the terminology, but otherwise left the old rules largely unchanged. All claims under Part 54 are now heard in the Administrative Court.

A person seeking permission to bring a claim for judicial review must file a Part 8 claim – promptly, and in any event within three months from the date of the decision being challenged.[91] This requirement has been the subject of much litigation[92]; but in practice a claim should be issued not later than six weeks after the decision to which it relates. A later application is likely to be rejected, although it is theoretically possible to seek permission to apply out of time, even once the 3-month limit has passed.

The Practice Direction issued along with the new Part 54 should be consulted

---

[88] See **18.6.2**.
[89] Any reader who knows that this statement is incorrect is invited to send a transcript or report to the author.
[90] S.I. 1998 No. 3132: Part 54 added by S.I. 2000 No. 221. The procedure was previously governed by Order 53 of the Rules of the Supreme Court.
[91] Civil Procedure Rules 1998, r. 54.5.
[92] See, for example, *R v Ceredigion District Council* [1997] COD 463; *R v Cotswold DC, ex p. Barrington Parish Council* (1997) 75 P. & C.R. 524; and *Re Burkett's application*, December 13, 2000, CA, unreported.

for details as to procedure; and, in particular, for a list of what needs to be served on whom. And if a claim is unsuccessful, it may of course be pursued on to the Court of Appeal or even the House of Lords – but only with leave.

As to the substance of a claim, that is beyond the scope of this book; although the principles touched upon in connection with challenges to tree preservation orders will also be relevant here.[93]

18.6.3 Challenges to decisions by Secretary of State

In general, a decision of the Secretary of State on an appeal against a refusal of consent under a tree preservation order is final.[94] The same applies to a decision on any other appeal in relation to an order, such as against a condition imposed on a consent, a replanting direction or an Article 5 certificate.

There is, however, a specific right under section 284 of the Town and Country Planning Act 1990 to challenge any such decision of the Secretary of State.[95] Such a challenge is essentially similar to a challenge to the validity of a tree preservation order, which has already been considered[96] – that is, it can only be based on points of law, and may not be used as a re-hearing of an appeal on its facts or policy merits. And the same, strict 6-week time limit applies to filing claims.

Examples of challenges made under this provision (or its predecessors) have already been cited earlier in this Chapter.[97]

18.7 Compensation

18.7.1 Entitlement to compensation

The general rule is that, since 1991, no compensation has been payable for the refusal of planning permission or listed building consent, and even prior to that the right to compensation was extremely limited. It is therefore perhaps slightly surprising that there is any right to compensation in relation to the refusal or conditional grant of consent under a tree preservation order. But there is. The principles underlying the entitlement to compensation were set out in Part VII of the first edition of the *Memorandum on the Preservation of Trees and Woodlands*[98] – interestingly, the one section of that guidance which was quietly dropped in subsequent editions.

Section 203 of the Town and Country Planning Act 1990, in common with each of the preceding planning Acts, simply provides that a tree preservation order may make provision for the payment of compensation in respect of loss and damage caused by a refusal of consent under the order or the grant of consent subject to conditions.[99] The courts and the Lands Tribunal have then made clear

[93] See **16.7.1**.
[94] TCPA 1947, s. 15(3), applied by s. 16 and 1949 and 1953 Model Orders, Sched. 3; TCPA 1962, s. 23(7) and 24, applied by 1966 and 1969 Model Orders, Sched. 3; TCPA 1990, s. 79(5), applied by 1999 Model Order, Sched. 2.
[95] TCPA 1990, s. 284(3)(b); Planning (Consequential Provisions) Act 1990, s. 2(3).
[96] See **16.7**.
[97] *Batchelor v Secretary of State* [1993] 1 EGLR 207; *Sherwood and Sherwood v Secretary of State* [1996] J.P.L. 925; *Beyers v Secretary of State* [2001] J.P.L. 586; *Richmond-upon-Thames LBC v Secretary of State* [2001] EWHC Admin 205, March 5, 2001, unreported; as always, the author would welcome receiving a transcript or report of any other such challenges.
[98] Ministry of Town and Country Planning, 1949; see **18.4.1**.
[99] See now TCPA 1990, s. 203.

the general principle that, for compensation to be payable in respect of a particular item, that item must be:

- the natural or probable consequence of the relevant decision;
- within the contemplation of the authority or the Secretary of State at the time of making that decision;
- quantifiable in money terms; and
- not too remote.[1]

The Lands Tribunal has over the years considered a number of cases in which various items of expenditure have been successfully claimed, which are considered below.

However, as well as that general principle, the entitlement to compensation is limited by the terms of the relevant provision in the order that led to the need for consent. Each of the Model Orders has thus contained relevant provisions as to the extent of the eligibility to claim payment, and the procedure for seeking it; but the actual order should always be consulted to see what provisions it contains. The references below to "pre-1999 orders" is to orders made in accordance with the 1949, 1953, 1966 or 1969 Model Orders. In relation to pre-1949 orders,[2] there appears to have generally been a power, as opposed to a duty, for authorities to contribute towards expenses arising as a result of decisions on applications for consent.

Orders made on or after August 2, 1999 are significantly different to those made earlier. They are accordingly considered separately.

18.7.2 Claims relating to pre-1999 orders

In principle, any person who suffers loss or damage in consequence of any refusal of consent under a pre-1999 tree preservation order, or due to the imposition of a condition on a grant of such consent, is entitled to recover compensation from the authority that made the order.[3]

As already noted, the entitlement to compensation does not apply in any case where the planning authority has issued an Article 5 certificate.[4] In the case of orders made between 1949 and 1953, the entitlement was also excluded in relation to any tree contained in the Fourth Schedule to the order, which was to include individual trees of significant amenity value[5] (there is no equivalent in post-1953 orders[6]).

The amount of compensation will generally be equal to the amount of the loss incurred by the person making the claim. However, not surprisingly, account will be taken of any compensation already paid in respect of the same trees or

---

[1] *Bell v Canterbury City Council* [1988] 2 PLR, CA, per Russell L.J. at p. 74C; *Fletcher v Chelmsford BC* [1991] 2 EGLR 213, L.T., at p. 214L, following *Bollans v Surrey CC* (1968) 209 E.G. 69 and *The Liesbosch* [1933] A.C. 449, H.L. See also *Hadley v Baxendale* (1854) 9 Exch 341.

[2] See **16.3.2**.

[3] 1949 Model Order, art. 9; 1953 Model Order, art. 8; 1966 and 1969 Model Orders, art. 9.

[4] 1949 Model Order, art. 9, proviso (b); 1953 Model Order, art. 8, proviso; 1966 and 1969 Model Orders, art. 9, proviso. As to Article 5 certificates, see **18.4**.

[5] *Memorandum on the Preservation of Trees and Woodlands*, Ministry of Town and Country Planning, 1949, para. 44.

[6] See MOHLG Circular 27/53, *Tree Preservation Orders*, Note on Article 8 of Revised Model Order.

woodlands – under the same or any other order – thus avoiding the possibility of an owner making a string of applications for consent and claiming compensation for each refusal.[7] Also to be excluded is any element of injurious affection that would have arisen if consent had been granted (or if the condition in question had not been imposed).[8] So, for example, if consent is refused for the felling of a woodland, on the grounds that it is premature, compensation is payable in respect of the value of the felled timber foregone, but against that is to be set any loss in the value of the land which would have occurred if consent had been granted.

18.7.3 *The cost of an appeal against the refusal or conditions*

Logically, the first item to be considered is the cost of attempting to overturn the decision that gave rise to the claim.

Thus, where an applicant receives from a planning authority an adverse decision (either a grant of consent subject to a condition, such as one requiring replacement planting, or a refusal), rather than simply accepting the decision and claiming compensation, it may be appropriate to make an appeal to the Secretary of State. It was put this way by the Tribunal in *Buckle v Holderness BC*[9]:

"On the basis of the submitted documents, the decision upon the application to fell appears to have been notified to the claimant by a single sentence contained in a letter from the Council . . . following a committee . . . I think that there is force in the submissions by [counsel for the claimant] that it was reasonable and foreseeable the claimant would pursue an appeal and that, had it been successful, the amount of the present claim would have been reduced if not eliminated. To that extent the appeal was an attempt by the claimant to mitigate his loss and accordingly the costs involved should be recoverable."

It should be noted from this that the costs of an appeal will not always be recoverable. If the refusal had been in circumstances such that an appeal would be doomed to fail, there would probably be no entitlement to compensation, and thus no need actually to go through the process of appealing.

Of course, an appeal may succeed, so that the works may proceed – but only some while after the initial application. The question which then arises is whether compensation is payable in respect of the extra cost arising as a result of the delay. The answer appears to be that it is not. This is because a decision following an application for consent under a tree preservation order is a "planning decision" within the meaning of section 336(1) of the Town and Country Planning Act 1990; and a reference in that Act to a planning decision altered on appeal (by the reversal or variation of all or part of it) is to be construed as being a reference to the decision as it is after having been so altered.[10] It follows that the entitlement to compensation under section 203 of the Act, which is stated to apply only following the refusal, etc. of consent required under an order, does not apply where consent is refused by the planning authority but granted on appeal by the Secretary of State.

This situation was considered by the Lands Tribunal in *Factorset Ltd v Selby DC*,[11] which concerned a claim for compensation in respect of the costs of

---

[7]   1949 Model Order, art. 10(a); 1953 Model Order, art. 9(a); 1966 and 1969 Model Orders, art. 10(a).
[8]   1949 Model Order, art. 10(b); 1953 Model Order, art. 9(b); 1966 and 1969 Model Orders, art. 10(b).
[9]   [1996] 1 PLR 66, L.T.
[10]   TCPA 1990, s. 336(5).
[11]   [1995] 2 PLR 11, L.T.

mounting a successful appeal against the refusal of tree consent, and the interest on borrowing to fund the costs of development that could not be carried out until the tree had been lopped. The Tribunal in that case held that compensation was properly allowable, and went on to consider in detail which items of claim should be allowed, but it did not consider the basic question of whether there was any entitlement in principle; and the point appears not to have been argued by the solicitors appearing as advocates for the parties. It would seem, therefore, that *Factorset* was wrongly decided on that point of principle – although it does provide useful guidance as to the items that may be claimed where the costs of an appeal are allowable in principle. In particular, fees relating to work carried out prior to the decision in question may not be claimed.

It may be noted that there is no entitlement to the costs of making an appeal in relation to a post-1999 order.[12]

18.7.4 Other items which may be claimed in relation to decisions under pre-1999 orders

The largest item that may potentially be claimed in relation to a pre-1999 order will be any loss in the value of land resulting from the decision. This was established by the Court of Appeal in *Bell v Canterbury City Council*,[13] in which the compensating authority sought unsuccessfully to argue that land value was not capable of forming the subject matter of a claim. The Lands Tribunal in that case had confirmed that the compensation was to be calculated on the basis of the capital value of the land following felling and reclamation, less the cost of reclamation and the capital value of the land in its existing state (under trees); the first two of those three items would need to be appropriately deferred. The Tribunal had also established that the appropriate date of valuation was the date of the relevant decision by the planning authority or the Secretary of State.[14] Loss in land value is likely to arise either as a result of it being less valuable in its present state (due to the overshadowing of a terrace, for example) or because of a loss in development value.

Another item is likely to be any loss in the value of the trees as timber – where, for example, woodland trees have to be retained beyond the age where they would otherwise normally be felled.

Thirdly, the inability to carry out works to trees may lead to damage to buildings affected by them, in particular as a result of damage to foundations. It is not possible to claim the cost of carrying out work after the date of the decision for the purpose of remedying damage occurring before that date, since the need for that work does not arise as a result of the decision. However, it is possible to claim the cost of works necessary to prevent future damage, as well as the associated professional fees. Thus in *Fletcher v Chelmsford BC*,[15] consent was refused for the felling of a mature lime tree that was likely, according to specialist advice received by the owner, to damage the foundations of the house. The owner then commissioned a second report, which included a programme of monitoring, to investigate the position fully. His insurance had paid for the cost of the initial

---

[12] 1999 Model Order, art. 9(4)(d); see **18.7.5**.
[13] [1988] 2 PLR, CA.
[14] [1986] 2 EGLR 209, L.T., following *Birmingham Corpn v West Midlands Baptist (Trust) Association* [1968] 3 All E.R. 172, H.L.; see also *Chartered Surveyor Weekly*, August 7, 1986.
[15] [1991] 2 EGLR 213, L.T., [1992] J.P.L. 279.

advice and the remedial works carried out as a result of that second report, but he successfully claimed the cost of the report itself from the local authority. The Lands Tribunal considered that it had been perfectly reasonable to obtain further advice following the refusal, and the need for it was not too remote to attract compensation liability.

In calculating the amount of any award, allowance must be made for the cost of the works that would have to have been carried out if the tree works had been allowed. It was accepted in *Buckle v Holderness BC*[16] that if the tree in question had been felled, the ground would not simply have returned unaided to its natural level, and that some underpinning would still have been required to prevent "heave". The cost of that should, therefore, be deducted from the cost of the much more substantial underpinning that had in fact been carried out in order to allow the tree to remain without causing harm to the dwelling.

Fourthly, compensation may be claimed for the additional cost of carrying out permitted works in a particular way to satisfy a condition. Thus in *Deane v Bromley LBC*,[17] the Lands Tribunal was persuaded that the landowner in question had the necessary skill and experience to have carried out himself the pruning works for which consent had been granted, at a cost of, say, £400 plus VAT for hiring additional equipment and the wear and tear of his own; whereas the condition required them to be carried out by a contractor approved by the Arboricultural Association ("in the interests of good arboricultural practice"), at a cost of £1,437.50 plus VAT. The difference between the two amounts was accordingly awarded as compensation.

Other items that have been the subject of awards have included depreciation on a bulldozer that had been purchased to carry out the grubbing up of trees and the loss of a grant that would have been available for the conversion of land to agriculture.[18]

The above principles are, in the main, those that have emerged following disputed cases decided by the Lands Tribunal; but they do not in any way represent an exclusive list. Thus the cost of any item is capable of forming the basis of a compensation claim in relation to a pre-1999 order, provided that it meets the four general criteria outlined at the start of this section.[19]

Finally, it is also possible that a landowner might be able to claim compensation if the value of his or her land was reduced following the grant of consent for works to a tree on neighbouring land. So, for example, where a tree on A's land is causing serious damage to the foundations of A's house, but blocks out the view from B's land across to an ugly factory, it is likely that the grant of consent to fell it would be sensible from A's point of view, but would be opposed strongly by B. If consent were granted, any loss suffered by B would be in consequence of the grant, and would thus seem to be within the strict terms of the Act and the pre-1999 orders. Having said that, there can be little doubt that this was not the intention of the legislation; and no claim is known to have been made, far less succeeded, under this head.

Where consent is granted under a tree preservation order for felling trees in a

---

[16] [1996] 1 PLR 66, L.T.
[17] [1992] 1 EGLR 251, L.T., per T Hoyes FRICS at p. 75F.
[18] *Bell v Canterbury City Council* [1986] 2 EGLR 209, L.T.
[19] See **18.7.1**.

woodland, and a replanting direction is made,[20] compensation for the direction may be available under section 204 of the Act, rather than section 203.[21]

18.7.5 Entitlement to compensation: post-1999 orders

The extent of the entitlement to compensation constitutes the most significant difference between tree preservation orders made following the 1999 Model Order and those made earlier. The broad principle underlying the change is that under post-1999 orders there is no longer any entitlement for the authority to serve an Article 5 certificate when making a decision on an application under a tree preservation order; instead, the entitlement to claim compensation is significantly more limited.

It should be stressed that the general rule remains that, in principle, any person who suffers loss or damage in consequence of any refusal of consent under a tree preservation order, or due to the imposition of a condition on a grant of such consent, is entitled to recover compensation from the authority that made the order.[22] It follows that the four general criteria outlined above still apply.[23] However, a post-1999 order will itself impose a number of limitations on this. And note that different rules apply in the case of refusal of consent for felling in the course of forestry operations: see below.[24]

First, no claim may be made for less than £500.[25]

Secondly, no claim may be made under a post-1999 order for the loss of development value or any other diminution in the value of land,[26] reversing the rule in *Bell v Canterbury CC*.[27]

Nor may any claim be made in relation to any item that was not reasonably foreseeable on the basis of the documents submitted with the application for consent (it will be recalled that a statement of reasons must be submitted as part of the application).[28] The effect of this exclusion is that the authority should know the extent of its liability when it is deciding whether to grant consent. So, for example, if a householder seeks consent to fell a fine specimen tree, and states that the felling is required because the tree is causing damage to the foundations of his house, the authority is able to balance the loss of amenity that would follow from the felling of the tree against the compensation that would be payable if the tree were to remain. This effectively formalises the rule that an item must be within the contemplation of the decision-making authority if it is to found a claim for compensation.[29]

Fourthly, no compensation is payable to a person in respect of a loss caused as a result of his or her failure to take reasonable steps to avert or mitigate the problem.[30] It is not clear what would be regarded as "reasonable" for this purpose. If, for example, the roots of a tree are causing damage to a patio, is it reasonable for the householder simply to move the patio?

---

[20] See **18.3.8**.
[21] See **18.7.8**.
[22] 1999 Model Order, art. 9(1).
[23] See **18.7.1**.
[24] See **18.7.6**.
[25] 1999 Model Order, art. 9(2)(b).
[26] 1999 Model Order, art. 9(4)(a).
[27] [1988] 2 PLR 69, CA; see **18.7.4**.
[28] 1999 Model Order, art. 9(4)(b).
[29] See **18.7.1**.
[30] 1999 Model Order, art. 9(4)(c).

Finally, no compensation is payable in respect of the costs of appealing against the decision in question.[31] This reverses the rule in *Buckle v Holderness BC*.[32]

18.7.6 Post-1999 orders: entitlement to compensation for forestry operations

As already noted, different rules apply in the case of a refusal of consent for felling of trees in a woodland in the course of forestry operations. "Felling in the course of forestry operations" is not defined in the order; but it does not include clear-felling to convert land for grazing or other agriculture.[33]

Generally, the rules are precisely the same as those relating to compensation from the Forestry Commission for the refusal of a felling licence.[34] That is, compensation is payable by the local planning authority, but otherwise the provisions of section 11 of the Forestry Act 1967 apply. A claim may be made only by the owner of the land, as defined in section 34 of the Forestry Act 1967 – generally the person in whom is vested the freehold, except where all concerned enter into an agreement whereby someone else is treated as being the owner.[35] And the compensation payable is limited to the deterioration in the quality of the timber resulting from the refusal (again, subject to a minimum of £500).[36]

The result of these provisions is that forestry operations are subject to one compensation regime, whether they are (as will normally be the case) subject to the requirement for a felling licence or whether they need consent under a tree preservation order. The latter would apply where, for example, the trees involved are too small for a felling licence to be required, as in the case of the removal of coppice stools that are subject to a woodland order.

Compensation is not available for the imposition of conditions relating to forestry; in practice, any consent for such operations is likely to be subject to the imposition of a replanting direction, which is subject to a separate compensation regime under section 204 of the Act.[37]

18.7.7 Procedure

A claim for compensation under section 203 must be made in writing, to the local authority. There is no prescribed form; that is, a simple letter will suffice. But the claim should contain a statement of the grounds on which it is based, and the amount claimed. It must generally be made within 12 months of the decision in respect of which it arises – either that of the authority or, where appropriate, that of the Secretary of State on appeal.[38] The time limit for claims under orders made between 1949 and 1953 is six months[39]; there appears to be no time limit in

---

[31] 1999 Model Order, art. 9(4)(d).
[32] [1996] 1 PLR 66, L.T.; see **18.7.4**.
[33] *Bell v Canterbury CC* [1988] 2 PLR 69, CA, at p. 72H.
[34] See **14.5.1**.
[35] 1999 Model Order, art. 9(6).
[36] 1999 Model Order, art. 9(2)(b), (3).
[37] See **18.7.8**.
[38] 1953 Model Order, art. 10(2); 1966 and 1969 Model Orders, art. 11(2); 1999 Model Order, art. 9(2)(a).
[39] 1949 Model Order, art. 11.

relation to claims under pre-1949 orders. Once a claim has been made within the relevant time limit, it may be subsequently amended.[40]

Disputes as to compensation are to be determined by the Lands Tribunal.[41] As to the procedure in the Tribunal and the payment of costs, the normal rules apply.[42]

Where compensation is payable, interest is payable from the date of the decision which gives rise to the claim, at the rate prescribed by regulations made under section 32 of the Land Compensation Act 1961.[43] That rate is determined in accordance with the formula prescribed by the Acquisition of Land (Rate of Interest after Entry) Regulations 1995.[44]

18.7.8 Compensation for replanting directions

Where consent is granted under a tree preservation order for felling trees in woodland, it is likely to be subject to a replanting direction.[45] In such a situation, a grant or a loan will often be available form the Forestry Commission under one of its grant schemes.[46] Where a replanting direction is made, the person who is required to comply with it is entitled to ask the Commission for a grant or a loan and, if one is not forthcoming, to ask why.[47]

If the Commission refuses to give financial assistance, on the ground that "replanting would frustrate the use of the woodland area for the growing of timber or other forest products for commercial purposes and in accordance with the rules or practice of good forestry", the applicant may claim compensation under section 204 of the Act (rather than section 203).[48] Note that this applies whatever the date of the order in question. The claim may be made in respect of any loss or damage arising as a result of complying with the direction.

A claim under this provision must be made within 12 months of the date on which the direction was given by the planning authority or, where an appeal has been made against it, within 12 months of the decision of the Secretary of State on the appeal.[49] Oddly, the authority may, if it wishes, extend the period for claiming under section 204, even though it may not do so in relation to claims under section 203.

As with claims for compensation under section 203, disputes relating to claims under section 204 are dealt with by the Lands Tribunal.[50]

18.7.9 Purchase notices

Where planning permission is refused, so as to lead to land becoming incapable of

[40] *Factorset Ltd v Selby DC* [1995] 2 PLR 11, L.T., at p. 22G-H.
[41] TCPA 1990, s. 205(1).
[42] TCPA 1990, s. 205(2), Land Compensation Act 1961, ss. 2, 4; see also the Lands Tribunal Rules 1996 (S.I. 1996 No. 1022).
[43] Planning and Compensation Act 1991, s. 80 and Schedule 18, Pt I.
[44] S.I. 1995 No. 2262. For the calculation of interest, see the table at Part C2 of the *Encyclopedia of Compulsory Purchase and Compensation.*
[45] See **18.3.8**.
[46] See **12.7**.
[47] TCPA 1990, s. 204(3).
[48] TCPA 1990, s. 204(1), (2).
[49] TCPA 1990, s. 204(4).
[50] TCPA 1990, s. 205; Land Compensation Act 1961, ss. 2, 4; Lands Tribunal Rules 1996 (S.I. 1996 No. 1022); Planning and Compensation Act 1991, s. 80 and Schedule 18, Pt I; see **18.7.7**.

reasonably beneficial use, the owner of that land may serve a purchase notice under Part VI of the Act on the local planning authority, requiring it to purchase the land.[51]

The list of provisions in the Town and Country Planning Act 1990 that may be adapted and applied to consent under a tree preservation order[52] include those relating to purchase notices. So far, however, no Model Order has in fact been framed so as to include those provisions, so that there is no right to serve a purchase notice on an authority following an adverse decision on an application for consent under an order, even if the result of the decision is to leave the land with no beneficial use.

18.8 Modification or revocation of consent

18.8.1 Power to revoke or modify consent

A planning authority may revoke or modify a consent previously granted under a tree preservation order made on or before August 1, 1999, wherever it appears to the authority to be expedient to do so. This is done by the authority making an order revoking the consent, which in most cases needs to be confirmed by the Secretary of State.

The extent of the discretion available to the Secretary of State in confirming a revocation order was considered by the High Court in *Mills v Secretary of State*.[53] In that case, consent had been granted in 1984 to fell and, arguably, to grub out a coppice. Not much work had been done by 1995, and the authority then decided to make an order revoking it. The Secretary of State confirmed the order, principally in reliance upon the report produced by his inspector, who summarised his views as follows:

". . . there has been a greater awareness of the importance of the environment and visual amenity since the original consent was granted, and the removal of the renewing coppiced areas would detract from the amenities of the area".

That situation is probably very typical of those which give rise to a decision to revoke a consent.

The deputy judge adopted the approach of the Court of Appeal in *de Rothschild v Secretary of State*,[54] a case concerning the power to confirm a compulsory purchase order, and held that the Secretary of State should have "good and sufficient cause" to confirm a revocation order, and should base his decision on "the right legal principles, adequate evidence and proper consideration of the factor which sways his mind into confirmation of the order sought"; and that "justification on the merits" is required.[55] However, said the deputy judge, there was ample evidence in the present case on which the Secretary of State could justify his decision – not least the conclusion of the inspector quoted above.

It is probable that the same approach would be taken in relation to a challenge to the discretion available to the authority in making a revocation order in a case

[51] TCPA 1990, s. 137.
[52] See TCPA 1990, s. 198(4)(b).
[53] [1998] 3 PLR 12.
[54] [1989] 1 E.G.L.R., CA.
[55] [1998] 3 PLR 12, at p. 18.

where confirmation is not required; "expediency" is a very wide concept.

The power to revoke a consent may be exercised at any time before the completion of the works authorised by the consent; and the revocation of the consent does not affect the lawfulness of the operations already carried out.[56]

Finally, although the text here refers, for simplicity, to the revocation of consent, precisely the same principles and procedures apply where consent is to be simply modified, rather than revoked outright. For example, where consent was granted some while ago to fell two trees, and only one was felled, it might be appropriate to modify the consent so as to remove the consent relating to the remaining tree.

As to the procedure to be adopted, that depends on the date of the tree preservation order under which the consent in question was granted (not that of the consent being revoked).

18.8.2 Consents granted under an order made before 1969

A planning authority wishing to revoke a consent granted under a tree preservation order made between 1949 and 1969 must make a draft revocation order. It must then serve on the Secretary of State (in practice the Government regional office) a copy of the draft order and its reasons for making it. It must also serve on the owner of the land concerned, and on anyone else involved, a notice informing them of the making of the draft order.[57]

Anyone receiving such a notice then has a period of 28 days (in the case of a tree preservation order made after 1953) in which to require an inquiry or hearing to be held before the draft revocation order is confirmed.[58] In the case of a consent granted under an earlier tree preservation order, the time-limit is only 14 days, which seems exceptionally short; and it is highly likely that the Government regional office would be willing to arrange for an inquiry to be held if an application was received within 28 days of the applicant being served with the notice.[59] Once the making of the draft order has been notified, no further works may lawfully be carried out in reliance on the original consent until the matter has been resolved by the Secretary of State.[60]

The Secretary of State will then hold an inquiry if one has been requested, and may confirm the revocation order, or may modify it as seems expedient.[61]

18.8.3 Consents granted under an order made between 1969 and 1999

The procedure where the consent being revoked was granted under a tree preservation order made between 1969 and 1999 will normally be exactly as for a consent granted under an order made before 1969.[62]

---

[56] TCPA 1947, s. 21(3), applied by 1949 and 1953 Model Orders, Sched. 3; TCPA 1962, s. 27(4), applied by 1966 and 1969 Model Orders, Sched. 3.
[57] TCPA 1947, s. 21(1), (2), applied by 1949 and 1953 Model Orders, Sched. 3; TCPA 1962, s. 27(1), (3), applied by 1966 Model Order, Sched. 3.
[58] TCPA 1947, s. 21(2), applied by 1953 Model Order, Sched. 3; TCPA 1962, s. 27(3), applied by 1966 Model Order, Sched. 3.
[59] TCPA 1947, s. 21(2), applied by 1949 Model Order, Sched. 3.
[60] TCPA 1947, s. 21(4), applied by 1949 and 1953 Model Orders, Sched. 3; TCPA 1962, s. 27(5), applied by 1966 Model Order, Sched. 3.
[61] TCPA 1947, s. 21(1), applied by 1949 and 1953 Model Orders, Sched. 3; TCPA 1962, s. 27(1), applied by 1966 Model Order, Sched. 3; *Mills v Secretary of State* [1998] 3 PLR 12 (see **18.8.1**).
[62] TCPA 1962, s. 27, applied by 1969 Model Order, Sched. 3.

In 1969, however, a new procedure was introduced to enable a consent to be revoked without the need for any involvement by the Secretary of State, where all those likely to be affected have notified the planning authority in writing that they have no objection.[63]

The authority in such a case is to advertise in the local newspaper the making of the draft revocation order. There is no prescribed form for the advertisement, but Schedule 3 to the TCP General Regulations 1992 prescribes a form for the unopposed revocation of planning permission, and that could, no doubt, be simply adapted for use in connection with a tree consent.[64] In any event, the advertisement must specify:

- the period within which anyone may object to the proposed revocation of consent (which must be of at least 28 days), and may request an inquiry; and

- the period (of at least 14 days) following that after which the revocation will take effect if no objection has been received by the Secretary of State.[65]

The authority must send the Government regional office a copy of the advertisement within three days of it being published, and must also send a copy to everyone likely to be involved.[66]

If no objection has been made to the revocation order within the 28-day period, and if the Secretary of State has not required the order to be submitted to him or her for confirmation, it will simply come into effect without further ado on the expiry of the 14-day period.[67]

This expedited procedure cannot be used to revoke or modify a consent that was initially granted by the Secretary of State (for example, following an appeal).[68]

18.8.4 Consents granted under an order made after 1999

The 1999 Model Order, for some reason, makes no provision for the modification or revocation of consent.

One consequence of this is that there is, in principle, no way in which an authority is able to avoid a consent under a post-1999 order being implemented possibly many years after it was granted. By that time, the amenity value of the tree concerned (or the policies of the authority) may have changed significantly. For that reason, it will, in most cases, be particularly important to impose a time-limit condition on the consent when it is granted.[69]

18.8.5 Compensation for the modification or revocation of consent

Compensation is generally payable in respect of any loss or damage arising out of:

---

[63] TCPA 1968, s. 80(1), applied by 1969 Model Order, Sched. 3.
[64] See *DETR Guide*, 2000, para. 8.7.
[65] TCPA 1968, s. 80(2), applied by 1969 Model Order, Sched. 3.
[66] TCPA 1968, s. 80(3), (4), applied by 1969 Model Order, Sched. 3.
[67] TCPA 1968, s. 80(5), applied by 1969 Model Order, Sched. 3.
[68] TCPA 1968, s. 80(6), applied by 1969 Model Order, Sched. 3.
[69] See **18.3.7**.

- the confirmation by the Secretary of State of an order revoking or modifying tree consent; or

- a notice by a planning authority that it has made such an order, which is subsequently not confirmed by the Secretary of State.[70]

The principles are broadly the same (and in the case of a tree preservation order made between 1969 and 1999, precisely the same) as those applying to compensation for the refusal of consent.

The only slight oddity is that there seems to be no right to compensation where an authority revokes or modifies a consent granted under a tree preservation order made between 1966 and 1969.[71]

---

[70] TCPA 1947, s. 22, applied by 1949 and 1953 Model Orders, Sched. 3; 1969 Model Order, art. 9.
[71] Neither Schedule 3 to the 1966 Order, nor article 9, contains a relevant provison.

Chapter 19

Unauthorised Works to Protected Trees

19.1 Introduction

19.1.1 Prosecution

If a building is erected without planning permission, it can always be demolished; if the use of a building is changed, it can always be changed back again. Even in the case of a historic building, whilst it cannot be restored following demolition, it may be possible to undo certain forms of alteration (if only in facsimile). With a tree, however, once it has been felled, it cannot be put back; true, a replacement can be planted, but it will not have the same amenity value as the original tree – indeed, for some years it may have very little if any amenity value. And if the tree was felled in order to facilitate development, there may be little point in requiring a replacement to be planted, merely to block the proposal, if other new trees could be planted to provide equal amenity value but in locations more convenient for the developer.

It follows that, if the system of tree preservation orders is to have any teeth at all, it is necessary for the contravention of an order to be an offence. The basic rule, therefore, is that it is a criminal offence to carry out any unauthorised works to a tree that is protected by a tree preservation order. That is the effect of section 210 of the Town and Country Planning Act 1990, which provides for two offences, as follows:

- to cut down, uproot or wilfully destroy a protected tree, or to damage, top or lop it wilfully in such a manner as to be likely to destroy it, without consent; and

- to carry out any other works to a protected tree without consent.

The first – effectively, the destruction of a tree – is an offence under section 210(1); the second is an offence under section 210(4), which carries a lower maximum penalty. The difference between the two is thus whether or not the tree will effectively be lost.

This Chapter considers first the elements of each of the two offences (see **19.2**) – looking at what has to be proved by the prosecution (**19.3**) and what defences are available (**19.4**). It then examines the relevant procedure (**19.5**), and the principles underlying sentencing in the event of a conviction (**19.6**).

Finally, where works are threatened to a protected tree, it may be necessary for the planning authority to seek an injunction (see **19.7**).

19.1.2 Requirement to plant replacement tree

It has already been noted that the planting of a replacement tree may (if only after a while) go some way to restoring the loss of amenity caused by unauthorised felling. The law therefore required that if a tree subject to a tree preservation order is removed without consent, the owner of the land must plant a replacement.[1] This requirement applies whether or not a prosecution is being undertaken or contemplated, unless the planning authority agrees in writing to dispense with it.

If the owner fails to comply with such a requirement, the authority may serve a notice requiring compliance, against which there is a right of appeal to the Secretary of State; and if that notice is itself not complied with, the authority may enter the land, carry out the replanting and recover its costs.[2]

This is all considered in more detail in the following Chapter.[2a]

19.1.3 Consent to retain works already carried out

Unlike the position with relation to planning permission and listed building consent, there is no provision for consent under a tree preservation order to be sought retrospectively.

This is perhaps because the only reason for such consent to be granted is to enable suitable conditions to be imposed – which does not apply in this case, since there is a duty to plant a replacement tree anyway,[3] and the other types of conditions which might be imposed[4] are largely irrelevant.

19.2 The offences under section 210

19.2.1 Two offences

Section 210 of the Town and Country Planning Act 1990[5] provides as follows:

"(1) If any person, in contravention of a tree preservation order –

(a) cuts down, uproots or wilfully destroys a tree, or
(b) wilfully damages, tops or lops a tree in such a manner as to be likely to destroy it,

he shall be guilty of an offence.

(2) A person guilty of an offence under subsection (1) shall be liable –

(a) on summary conviction to a fine not exceeding £20,000; or
(b) on conviction on indictment, to a fine.

(3) In determining the amount of any fine to be imposed on a person convicted of an offence under subsection (1), the court shall in particular have regard to the financial benefit which has accrued or appears likely to accrue to him in consequence of the offence.

---

[1]   TCPA 1990, s. 206(1)(a).
[2]   TCPA 1990, ss. 207 to 209.
[2a] See in particular **20.2.3**.
[3]   TCPA 1990, s. 206(1)(a); see **19.1.2**.
[4]   See **18.3.7**.
[5]   As amended by Planning and Compensation Act 1991, s. 23(6).

(4) If any person contravenes the provisions of a tree preservation order otherwise than as mentioned in subsection (1), he shall be guilty of an offence and liable on summary conviction to a fine not exceeding level 4 on the standard scale."

From this it is clear that there are two separate offences. The first, under subsection (1), relates to more serious works, may be tried either by magistrates or in the Crown Court, and carries a much higher penalty. The second, under subsection (4), relates to less serious works, may only be tried by magistrates, and carries a smaller maximum penalty (Level 4 is currently £2,500).

The distinction between the two offences was introduced in the Civic Amenities Act 1967. The original Civic Amenities Bill (a private member's Bill) simply proposed increasing the maximum penalty for any contravention of a tree preservation order (from £50 to £250). The Government, in response, proposed an amendment that was subsequently enacted:

"The heavy penalty which is more appropriately confined to the offence of cutting down – or destruction such as poisoning – ought to be left, but as for other infringements like lopping . . . could we really ask that a fine of up to £250 be imposed?"[6]

The intention was thus to differentiate between actions that resulted in the destruction of a tree, and those that damaged or defaced a tree in a manner falling short of destruction.[7] The fines have, of course, subsequently been very substantially increased.

19.2.2 The elements of the offence under section 210(1)

In order for a prosecution of a criminal offence to succeed, it is necessary for the prosecution to prove each of its constituent elements. Conversely, if a defence against such a charge is to succeed, it is necessary either to show that at least one of those elements cannot be proved, or to rely on a defence provided for in statute. The predecessor to section 210 has been analysed by the Court of Appeal in these terms:

"As it seems to us, that section creating the offence has within it the following ingredients. First, there has to be a tree preservation order. Secondly, it has to be proved that the appellants cut down the tree, or carried out the other activities referred to in the section. And, thirdly, it has to be shown that whatever was done by the appellants in the way of cutting down or engaging in other activities relative to the tree was done without the permission of the planning authority. No more than this is apparent from the section."[8]

The second and third of those ingredients may perhaps usefully be broken down into their constituent parts, so that the elements of the offence created by section 210(1) are as follows:

(1) the tree in question was covered by a tree preservation order at the time of the works;

(2) works were carried out to the tree consisting of:

---

[6]   Dr Mabon, proposing the amendment, in Standing Committee C, February 8, 1967, col. 123.
[7]   See *A Weak Branch of the Law on Trees?*, art. by C Crawford and p. Schofield, at [1981] J.P.L. 316.
[8]   *R v Alath Construction Ltd; R v Brightman* [1990] 1 W.L.R. 1255, CA, per Russell L.J. at p. 1257C; [1991] 1 PLR 25, at p. 27B.

- the tree being cut down or wilfully destroyed;
- (in the case of a post-1975 order) the tree being uprooted;
- the tree being topped or lopped in such a manner that it was likely to be destroyed; or
- (in the case of a post-1975 order) the tree being wilfully damaged in such a manner that it was likely to be destroyed;

(3) the works were executed, caused or permitted by the defendant;

(4) the works were not subject to any exemption from the need for consent under the relevant tree preservation order; and

(5) such consent had not been granted.

Each of these is considered in turn.

The normal rule is that every element of a criminal offence must be proved by the prosecution, to the criminal standard of proof – that is, beyond reasonable doubt.[9] That would apply to the first three of the above list, considered in **19.3**. As to the fourth and fifth, considered in **19.4**, the existence of any relevant exemption or of any consent is to be proved by the defence, to the civil standard (on the balance of probabilities), not disproved by the prosecution.[10]

19.2.3 The elements of the offence under section 210(4)

The five elements of the less serious offence, under section 210(4), are identical to those of the subsection (1) offence, save for the second, which is as follows:

(2) works were carried out to the tree consisting of:

- the tree being topped or lopped, but in such a manner that it was not likely to be destroyed; or
- (in the case of a post-1975 order) the tree being wilfully damaged, but in such a manner that it was not likely to be destroyed.

Otherwise, the matters to be proved, and the burden and standard of proof in relation to each matter, remain as for the more serious offence.[11]

19.2.4 Causing or permitting unauthorised works

An issue that sometimes causes difficulties in practice is the extent to which the causing or permitting of works carried out in contravention of a tree preservation order is an offence and, if it is, whether it should be charged as an offence under section 210(1) (the more serious offence), rather than under section 210(4) ("any other contravention").

The uncertainty presumably arises because the Act itself does not refer to orders prohibiting the causing or permitting of works – either in specifying what may be prohibited by an order[12] or in defining the offence of contravening one.[13]

---

9   *Woolmington v DPP* [1935] A.C. 462.
10   See **19.4**.
11   See **19.2.2**.
12   TCP (Interim Development) Act 1943, s. 8(1)(a), TCPA 1947, s. 28(1)(a), TCPA 1962, s. 29(1)(a), TCPA 1971, s. 60(1)(a), TCPA 1990, s. 198(3)(a).
13   TCPA 1990, s. 210(1), (4).

All of the Model Orders, on the other hand, have purported to prohibit not only the carrying out any of the various types of works, but also causing or permitting someone else to do so.[14]

It has been held by the Divisional Court (in *R v Bournemouth Justices ex p. Bournemouth Corporation*[15]) that causing or permitting any of the various categories of operations is just as much an offence as actually doing them (to suggest otherwise is "yet another of those submissions which are really doomed to failure and to put the clients to added expense"[16]). An offence is thus committed both by the tree surgeon actually doing the work to the protected tree, and by the landowner paying him; by the householder who asks her son-in-law to lop off a branch, and by the son-in-law. It would seem, by extension, that causing or permitting works that are likely to destroy the tree would properly be chargeable as an offence under subsection (1) (the more serious offence), rather than under section (4).[17]

An alternative approach open to a prosecuting authority would be to rely upon the powers in the Accessories and Abettors Act 1861[18] (in relation to offences under section 210(1)) and the Magistrates Court Act 1980[19] (for section 210(4)). That would then enable the landowner who hires a tree-surgeon to carry out works to a protected tree, without consent under the order, to be charged with aiding, abetting, counselling or procuring an offence under the relevant subsection of section 210 (depending on the nature of the works carried out). The offence may be charged as simply "cutting down, etc. the tree", even though the evidence suggests that the accused may have actually caused another to do the work. That means that there should be no problem if it is not clear precisely whose hand was on the chain saw (for example, as between: a landowner, a neighbour, and a contractor; or two brothers; or a landowner and a contractor who has conveniently vanished).

There are potential difficulties, however, with relying on the 1861 and 1980 Acts. Thus, although section 210 creates an offence which is one of strict liability, conviction for an offence of aiding and abetting requires evidence that the accused knew all the material facts constituting the principal offence, or was reckless (that is, consciously taking a risk as to whether or not a tree preservation order would be contravened).[20] Reliance on "causing or permitting" being implied by the Act (the approach adopted in *Bournemouth*) has the same requirement as to knowledge.[21] That may, in some cases, defeat the clear policy of the courts in holding that an offence under section 210 requires no element of knowledge.

Possibly in the light of the above arguments, and notwithstanding the robust judgment in *Bournemouth*, the Government has (probably sensibly) proposed to put the matter beyond doubt by referring explicitly to "causing or permitting" on the face of the statute itself.[22]

---

[14] 1949, 1953, 1966 and 1969 Model Orders, art. 2; 1999 Order, art. 4(b).
[15] (1970) 21 P. & C.R. 163.
[16] (1970) 21 P. & C.R. 163, per Lord Parker C.J. at p. 164; see also **17.2**.
[17] A submission to the contrary was rejected b the Crown Court at Snaresbrook in *Havering LBC v Clearbrook Group PLC*, March 16, 2001, unreported.
[18] Accessories and Abettors Act 1861, s. 8, as amended by Criminal Law Act 1977, Sched. 12.
[19] Magistrates' Court Act 1980, s. 44.
[20] *Johnson v Youden* [1950] 1 K.B. 544; *Carter v Richardson* [1974] RTR 314; see art. at [1981] J.P.L. 316.
[21] *Ross Hillman Ltd v Bond* [1974] 2 All E.R. 287.
[22] *Tree Preservation Orders: Review*, DOE, 1994, paras 2.42.

19.3 The matters to be proved by the prosecution

19.3.1 The existence of the tree preservation order

The first matter to be proved, obviously, is that the tree in question was actually covered by a tree preservation order that was in force at the relevant time – that is, when the works to it were carried out.

This will in many cases be straightforward. If the relevant order was made some years ago, covering an oak tree in the front garden of 22 Acacia Avenue, and everyone accepts that there was only one tree in the front garden, and that it was oak, and that it has been felled, there is clearly no problem. However, a number of difficulties may arise in practice.

First, where a tree has been felled on a piece of land on which were growing a number of trees, it is important to be sure that the order did cover the one that has gone. This will usually be a matter of carefully surveying the relevant land, and plotting the location and species of all the trees now growing on it – and, where known, of any which have been felled. That can then be compared with the schedule and plan forming part of the tree preservation order, to deduce which trees were protected at the date of the incident. This may call for particular care in the case of orders protecting trees specified by reference to "groups".

Where there is an inconsistency between the specification of trees in the schedule to an order and the map attached to it, in the case of pre-1999 orders, the map is to prevail.[22a] In relation to post-1999 orders, there is no such provision, so that it must be a matter of judgment in each case as to whether either should take precedence over the other – or whether the discrepancy is sufficient to render the order a nullity.

Secondly, where a tree preservation order is made protecting trees by reference to an "area", it will only apply to the trees that were actually growing at the date on which the order was made. This will need to be the subject of expert evidence – often in the form of photographs and a report by a qualified arboriculturist, no doubt based either on counting the number of rings on the stump (where it has not been ground out), or, as a matter of opinion, based on photographs of the tree before it fell. Where such evidence is missing, it will not be sufficient for the court (magistrates' or jury) simply to substitute its own opinion of the age of the trees in question based on such photographs. Thus, in *Carter v Eastbourne BC*,[23] a case which related to an area order made four years prior to the felling of the trees in question, it was held by the Divisional Court that the magistrates had not been entitled to form their own view of the age of the trees in question, even though the court agreed that they were "obviously" more than four years old.

The same principle would, it is submitted, be applicable to the felling of trees protected by a woodland order – that is, it would be necessary to show that the trees that have been felled were in existence at the date on which the order was made.[24-25] It must be pointed out, however, that conventional wisdom and Government advice are that a woodland order also protects trees that were planted or self-seeded subsequent to the date of the order.

Where felling operations have been undertaken on a substantial scale both on land protected by an area order and elsewhere, it may also be necessary to show

[22a] 1949, 1953, 1966, 1969 Model Orders, art. 2.
[23] [2000] 2 PLR 60.
[24-25] See **16.5.5**.

that the trees that form the subject of the charges were actually growing on the order land, and were not simply uprooted from elsewhere and pushed onto that land – as was (unsuccessfully) alleged to have taken place in *Carter*.

Thirdly, where a tree preservation order was made on a provisional basis, subject to confirmation by the authority,[26] it only remains in force for six months, unless it is confirmed within that period. Alternatively, it can be confirmed more than six months after being made, but in that case it will not be in force from the expiry of the 6-month period until the date of the confirmation. If works are carried out to a tree subject to such an order, it is therefore necessary to ensure that they were carried out either:

- within six months of the making of the order; or

- after the order had been confirmed by the authority.

So, for example, if the planning authority makes an order on February 1, protecting several trees, one of those is felled on August 15, and the authority purports to confirm the order on September 1, the order will have no effect in relation to the tree that has been felled, so that no offence has been committed, and no replacement needs to be planted.

19.3.2 Knowledge of the tree preservation order

Although it is necessary to show that the trees in question were in fact subject to a tree preservation order at the relevant date, it is not necessary to show that the accused actually knew of its existence. This was confirmed by the decision of the Divisional Court in *Maidstone BC v Mortimer*,[27] where Park J. held as follows:

"In my judgment, therefore, these sections demonstrate that Parliament intended that no tree the subject of a tree preservation order should be cut down . . . without the consent of the local authority. Plainly it is of the utmost public importance that such trees should be preserved. The risk to their continued existence in these days of extensive building operations, which encroach further and further into rural areas, is very great. It is not a difficult task for any member of the public wishing to interfere with the shape, size or continued existence of a tree to obtain from the local authority reliable information on the question whether the tree is subject to a preservation order and, if so, to seek the authority's consent to the operations proposed. (Mrs Twydell appears to have made a most perfunctory inquiry of the wrong department of the local authority and to have misunderstood or misinterpreted whatever it was she was told.)"[28]

The judge accordingly concluded that an offence under what is now section 210 fell within the category of "acts which are not criminal in any real sense, but are acts which in the public interest are prohibited under a penalty",[29] and was thus an offence of strict liability, not requiring proof by the prosecution of knowledge on the part of the accused.

However, it has been held that there is one exception to this principle. All of the Regulations relating to the making of tree preservation orders have stated – albeit

---

[26] See **16.6.2**.
[27] [1980] 3 All E.R. 552; [1981] J.P.L. 319.
[28] [1980] 3 All E.R. 552, per Park J. at p. 554e–g.
[29] See *Sherras v De Rutzen* [1895] 1 Q.B. 918 at pp. 921–922, [1895–9] All E.R. Rep 1167 at 1169; and *Sweet v Parsley* [1970] A.C. 132, H.L. at p. 149, [1969] 1 All E.R. 347, at p. 350.

in slightly differing terms – that the order, once made, is to be available for public inspection, along with the map identifying the trees to be protected.[30] The Divisional Court has held (in *Vale of Glamorgan BC v Palmer and Bowles*[31]) that this requirement is mandatory, not merely directory, so that where an authority could not establish that a copy of the order and the map had been deposited for inspection, as was the position in that case, the order could not be relied upon to found a prosecution. It further noted the passage in *Mortimer* (in the extract quoted above) stating that "it is not a difficult task for any member of the public ... to obtain from the local authority reliable information on the question whether the tree is subject to a preservation order"; but that presupposed that the order was available for inspection.[32]

In spite of a suggestion in *Palmer* to the contrary, to mount a defence to a prosecution on the basis that an order has not been available for public inspection is not to question the validity of the order itself, since that can only be done by an application to the High Court within the appropriate (short) time period after the order is first made.[33] Nor is it merely a claim that the particular defendant did not know of the existence of the order, since that defence was ruled out in *Mortimer*. It appears to be a new category of defence, namely, that nobody could possibly have known of the existence of the order.

19.3.3 Defects in the tree preservation order

It is commonly claimed, by way of an objection to a prosecution for unauthorised works to protected trees, that the tree preservation order in question should not have been made in the first place. This may be because the tree is said to be of little, if any, amenity value; sometimes it is alleged that the authority only imposed the order to prevent development, which is an improper use of the procedure; sometimes the qualifications or experience of the local authority officer who made the order are called into question. Alternatively, attention may be drawn to some error in the order-making procedure.

Unfortunately, all of these objections are of no relevance in determining guilt or innocence, since they are all, in essence, challenges to the validity of the order. And the Act is quite clear that the validity of a tree preservation order, whether before or after it has been confirmed, cannot be questioned, except by means of a challenge under section 288, "in any legal proceedings whatsoever"[34] – which would obviously include a criminal prosecution. In practice, the raising of such an objection is likely to be met with the response that, if the order was indeed so defective, the proper approach would have been to seek consent for the removal of the tree, if necessary from the Secretary of State on appeal, not simply to cut it down without any authorisation at all.

If, however, the order has only been very recently made, it may still be possible to challenge its validity in the High Court, with the criminal proceedings

---

[30] TCP Additional Regulations 1944 (S.I. 1944 No. 319), reg. 6(3); TCP (TPO) Regulations 1948 (S.I. 1948 No. 1436), reg. 4(b); TCP (TPO) Regulations 1950, reg. 2(2); TCP General Regulations 1964 (S.I. 1964 No. 1382), reg. 12(a); TCP (TPO) Regulations 1969 (S.I. 1969 No. 17), reg. 5(a); TCP(T) Regulations 1999, reg. 3(1)(b).

[31] (1983) 81 L.G.R. 678, [1982] J.P.L. 334.

[32] [1982] J.P.L. 334, at p. 336.

[33] See **16.7.2**.

[34] TCPA 1990, ss. 284(1)(e), (2)(c), 288(4).

pending[35] – but it must be remembered that there is a 6-week time limit for bringing such a challenge, which cannot be extended for any reason.[36]

19.3.4 The works carried out: cutting down, uprooting and wilful destruction of a tree

The second matter to be proved by the prosecution relates to the works that were carried out.

The 1990 Act states that it is an offence under section 210(1) to contravene a tree preservation order:

(a) by cutting down [, uprooting] or wilfully destroying a protected tree; or

(b) by [wilfully damaging,] topping or lopping a protected tree in such a manner as to be likely to destroy it.

It should, however, be noted that "uprooting" and "wilfully damaging" a tree were only mentioned explicitly in tree preservation orders made on or after March 12, 1975.[37] It follows that actions which come within those two categories will not be an offence if carried out in relation to trees protected by orders made before that date (or, indeed, by later orders if they followed the earlier wording), unless they can also be brought within one of the other categories.

The acts in the first of the two groups above are those which are intended to have the effect of destroying the tree, and which do in fact have that effect. "Cutting down" refers to the making of a single horizontal cut through the trunk of a tree near the base, so as to sever the whole (or very nearly the whole) of the tree above the ground from the portion below the ground. It also refers to the practice, which is much more common, at least in urban areas, of felling a tree in stages.

The meaning of "wilfully destroying" a tree was considered by the Divisional Court in *Barnet LBC v Eastern Electricity Board*,[38] which concerned six trees whose roots were damaged in the course of laying electricity cables. The damage was such that the life expectancy of the trees had been reduced from more than 20 years to perhaps as little as two to five years, and they had been rendered less stable and a possible danger. As a result, four had been felled, and the other two lopped. After some hesitation, May J. held as follows:

". . . in our judgment one must bear in mind in this case that the underlying purpose of the relevant legislation is the preservation of trees and woodlands as amenities, as living creatures providing pleasure, protection and shade; it is their use as such that is sought to be preserved, and a tree the subject of a tree preservation order is destroyed in the present context when, as a result of that which is done to it, it ceases to have any use as an amenity, as something worth preserving. For example, if a person intentionally inflicts on a tree so radical an injury that in all the circumstances any reasonably competent forester would in consequence decide that it ought to be felled, then in our opinion that person wilfully destroys the tree within the meaning of that word in the relevant legislation and order.

"Further, having regard to the way in which the trees are identified and described in Schedule 1 to the order and to the annexed map, and indeed to general considerations as to

---

[35] As occurred in *Knowles v Secretary of State* [1998] J.P.L. 593.
[36] See **16.7.2**.
[37] TCP (TPO) (Amendment) [, etc.] Regulations 1975 (S.I. 1975 No. 148), reg. 2(i).
[38] [1973] 1 W.L.R. 430.

what is or is not an amenity, we think that one of the relevant circumstances which a forester could or should take into account in deciding whether a given injured tree should be felled is its situation: a tree adjoining the highway, for instance, needs greater stability and more vigorous life than a similar tree in a country field, and the former may thus, by reason of its position alone, be destroyed in contravention of the order by a lesser injury than would be needed to destroy the latter."[39]

The court, therefore, remitted the matter back to the magistrates to continue to hear the information, on the basis of the approach it had outlined.

It follows from that analysis that the "wilful destruction" of a tree refers to any of various ways used to kill it, such as ring-barking, making strategic cuts near the base designed to kill it or at least make it unstable, pouring creosote over the ground next to its trunk, or severing its roots – provided that, "as a result of that which is done to it, it ceases to have any use as an amenity". Oddly, in the *Barnet* case the court did not make any comment on the meaning of the word "wilful", even though it seems that on that occasion the actions of the Electricity Board and its contractors may well have been negligent, rather than deliberate.

"Uprooting" refers to the lifting of a whole tree from the ground, which arguably does not come within the definition of either felling or destruction, since the tree itself is not interfered with at all, but (at least in theory) merely moved intact from one place to another. Thus, to transplant a sapling from a nursery to its permanent location could in some cases be categorised as uprooting, but could hardly be properly described as destruction. As noted above, the uprooting of a tree is not an offence in relation to pre-1975 orders, unless, on the facts, it could also be categorised as the wilful destruction.

19.3.5 The works carried out: other operations likely to lead to the loss of a tree

The acts in the second of the two groups above[40] are those which may or may not be intended to have the effect of destroying the tree, but which are, in fact, likely to have that effect.

"Lopping" and "topping" refer respectively to the making of a horizontal cut through the vertical stem of a tree, and a vertical cut through a horizontal limb[41]; together they thus presumably refer to the making of any cut through any branch, at whatever angle. They will only be an offence if carried out in such a manner as to be likely to destroy the tree. This covers the situation where a tree owner removes a substantial number of branches, in such a way that the remaining tree is an eyesore – or possibly much more liable to fall. Such an operation could not be described as felling the tree; but if the result is to lead to a tree that has to be felled, it is just as serious as felling it in the first place.

"Wilful damage" was added to the categories of works prohibited by orders in 1975, no doubt in the light of the *Barnet* decision.[42] It would catch works which are, arguably, not quite serious enough to merit the description "wilful destruction", even in the light of the broad definition of that term adopted in *Barnet*. It also ensures that it is an offence to cut roots in such a way as to lead to the loss of the tree – which would definitely not be included within the scope of

---

[39] [1973] 1 W.L.R. 430, per May J. at pp. 434H–435C.
[40] See **19.3.4**.
[41] *Unwin v Hanson* [1891] 2 Q.B. 115, CA; and see **17.2**.
[42] *Barnet LBC v Eastern Electricity Board* [1973] 1 W.L.R. 430; see **19.3.4**.

lopping and topping. The government is minded to amend the legislation to make clear that damage may be caused by root cutting.[43]

Indeed, it would not really be necessary for any of the second group to be included post-*Barnet*, since presumably any actions (however categorised) carried out to a tree in such a manner as to be likely to destroy it would cause the tree to cease having any use as an amenity, and would thus amount to "destroying" the tree in May J.'s definition (quoted above). However, their inclusion on the face of the statute lessens the scope for unfruitful litigation.

One remaining difficulty, however, is that the subsection (1) offence only relates to the carrying out of damage that is "wilful". Thus, it probably does not extend to damage to trees that is caused as a result of acts which are carried out reckless as to whether or not they will have that effect. Examples would be interfering with the water table, the use of harmful chemicals, the raising or lowering of soil levels (particularly during development) or the grazing of animals in woodlands. All of those might well have the effect of killing trees, even if only gradually, but it might be difficult to prove that that result was consciously intended. The Government is mindful of this problem, and has proposed to extend the scope of the operations prohibited by a tree preservation order to include damage caused negligently or indirectly.[44]

Finally, for reasons explained below, where there is any doubt as to whether works will, in fact, lead to the loss of a tree, those responsible should be charged under subsection (4)[45] rather than subsection (1).

19.3.6 The nature of the works carried out: operations not likely to lead to the loss of a tree: (subsection (4))

It will be recalled that tree preservation orders made prior to March 12, 1975 provide that:

"Subject to the provisions of this Order, and to the exemptions specified in the Second Schedule hereto, no person shall, except with the consent of the authority and in accordance with the conditions if any imposed on such consent, cut down, top, lop, or wilfully destroy or cause or permit the cutting down, topping, lopping, or wilful destruction of any tree specified in [the order]."[46]

The corresponding provision in orders made on or since that date also refers to the uprooting and wilful damage of protected trees.[47]

The cutting down, uprooting or wilful destruction of a tree, if unauthorised, must inevitably be an offence under subsection (1).[48] Works for the topping or lopping of a tree, or wilful damage to it, on the other hand, may or may not lead to its destruction. If they seem likely to have that result, they will constitute an offence under subsection (1); but otherwise they will constitute an offence under subsection (4). The result is that, to secure a conviction under subsection (4), the prosecution must prove that works were carried out to the tree consisting of:

---

[43] *Tree Preservation Orders: Review*, DOE, 1994, para. 2.67.
[44] *Tree Preservation Orders: Review*, DOE, 1994, paras 2.40, 2.41.
[45] See **19.3.6**.
[46] 1949, 1953 and 1966 Model Orders, art. 2; 1969 Model Order (as originally drafted), art. 2.
[47] 1969 Model Order, as amended by TCP (TPO) (Amendment), etc. Regulations 1975 (S.I. 1975 No. 148), reg. 2(i); 1999 Model Order, art. 4.
[48] See **19.3.4**.

- the tree being topped or lopped in such a manner that it was not likely to be destroyed; or

- (in the case of a post-1975 order) the tree being wilfully damaged in such a manner that it was not likely to be destroyed.

Problems can arise where works (other than cutting down, uprooting or destruction) have been carried out in circumstances such that, at the time of mounting a prosecution, it is not clear whether or not they will lead to the destruction of the tree. Following the *Barnet* case, there is a wide scope for charging those responsible for works to trees under subsection (1), but, even so, there must be a borderline. If a person is charged under subsection (1), the evidence adduced may be sufficient to prove that he or she carried out works to a tree, and thus to justify conviction under subsection (4), but not to prove "beyond reasonable doubt" that those works were likely to destroy the tree.

If the trial is in the magistrates' court, the bench can simply find the accused guilty of the lesser offence, but only if there is a separate count in the indictment referring to subsection (4).[49] However, if the accused has opted for jury trial, that course is not open, since the offence under subsection (4) is only triable summarily; whilst a jury may find an accused person guilty of a lesser offence, it may only do so if that lesser offence is itself triable either way.[50] It follows that an accused person who has been charged with the more serious offence, whether or not in conjunction with a charge on the lesser offence, if he or she considers that the evidence may only support conviction on the latter, should opt for jury trial and then submit that there is no case to answer on the former.

To avoid this problem, a prosecuting authority should always charge only the lesser offence if there is any doubt about the seriousness of the consequences of what has occurred. Of course, the converse situation is not a problem – if, following a charge under subsection (4), evidence emerges which would have justified a subsection (1) charge, it should still be possible to secure a conviction on the lesser charge, since the unlawful destruction or felling of a tree will almost always involve a number of actions which individually would not have been fatal, and which, therefore, would on their own have been sufficient to justify a lesser charge.

A more fundamental solution to this problem would be to replace the two charges with a single offence, triable either way, and to leave it to the court to determine a suitable sentence in the light of all the circumstances – as is the case with works to listed buildings. Such a change would, however, require primary legislation.

19.3.7 Liability for carrying out the works

The third matter to be proved by the prosecution is that the accused was actually responsible for the works that were carried out to the tree.

This may be straightforward where, for example, a landowner or a tree contractor was actually seen and photographed on site with the chainsaw in his hands. But it may be less so where the planning authority only becomes aware of the works some while after they have taken place.

---

[49] *Lawrence v Ridsdale* [1968] 2 Q.B. 93.
[50] Criminal Law Act 1967, s. 6(3).

The liability to conviction may take one of several forms. Thus, a person commits an offence under section 210 of the 1990 Act if:

- he or she actually does any of the prohibited acts, regardless of whether he or she knows of the existence of the tree preservation order[51]; or

- he or she causes or permits someone else to do so, either with knowledge of the order or reckless as to whether one exists.[52]

An offence is also committed, under the Accessories and Abettors Act 1861 or the Magistrates Court Act 1980, if a person aids, abets, counsels or procures someone else to do so, again either with knowledge of the order or reckless as to whether one exists.[53]

Another way of looking at this is to say that a landowner who instructs a contractor is vicariously liable for the actions of the contractor, and thus for any unauthorised works to protected trees carried out by the contractor.

However, that does not extend to the situation where a landowner hires a contractor to carry out works but specifically tells the contractor not to touch a preserved tree, and the contractor nevertheless does so. In that situation, although the contractor is clearly liable for the breach of the order, it has gone beyond its authority in carrying out the works, and the landowner is not also liable.[54]

Where, as will not infrequently occur, the actual act is carried out by an employee of a company, or indeed an individual trading as a company, the company will be liable as well as the individual – and that may apply even if the company can show that the employee was acting outside the scope of his or her authority.[55]

Conversely, where the offence is committed by a company – for example, a firm of tree surgeons carrying out the works, or a corporate landowner employing a tree-surgeon to do so – it is possible to prosecute not only the company concerned, but also the any officer of the company who consented to, or connived in, the commission of the offence, or whose negligence contributed to it.[56] This may help to ensure non-recurrence, especially by developers who are habitually dealing with sites on which protected trees are growing. So, for example, in *R v Alath Construction Ltd; R v Brightman*,[57] a development company (A) was fined £500 for felling a protected tree, and the managing director of the company (B), a further £500 – and each had to pay £1,000 towards the costs of the prosecution.

For a prosecution to succeed against the officer of a company, however, it will be necessary to show that the officer concerned was a decision-maker within the company with the power and responsibility to decide corporate policy and strategy.[58]

---

[51] See **19.3.2**.
[52] See **19.2.4**.
[53] See **19.2.4**.
[54] *Groveside Homes v Elmbridge BC* [1987] 2 EGLR 199; (1987) 284 E.G. 940.
[55] See, for example, *Green v Burnett* [1955] 1 Q.B. 78; [1954] 3 All E.R. 273.
[56] TCPA 1990, s. 331.
[57] [1990] 1 W.L.R. 1255, CA; [1991] 1 PLR 25.
[58] *Woodhouse v Walsall MBC* [1994] Env. L.R. 30.

19.4 The matters to be proved by the accused

19.4.1 Exemptions from the need for consent

Liability to criminal prosecution only arises where works are carried out in contravention of a tree preservation order. It has already been noted that, although orders require consent to be obtained (either from the local planning authority or from the Secretary of State), that requirement is subject to numerous exemptions. These can be summarised as follows:

(a) the cutting down, topping, lopping of a tree:

- where the tree is dying or dead or has become dangerous[59];
- in compliance with a statutory obligation[60]; or
- so far as may be necessary for the prevention or abatement of a nuisance[61];

(b) works to trees in accordance with a forestry dedication covenant or a plan approved by the Forestry Commission[62];

(c) works which are the subject of a felling licence[63];

(d) some works by, or at the request of, statutory undertakers and other public bodies – largely in circumstances where works to trees are necessary to ensure the safe and efficient operation of their undertakings[64];

(e) works required to carry out development for which planning permission has been granted[65];

(f) some works to fruit trees[66]; and

(g) certain works to trees required in connection with opencast coal mining.[67]

Exemptions (a) to (c) and (g) arise from primary legislation, and therefore apply regardless of the date of the tree preservation order in question. Exemptions (d) to (f), on the other hand, arise from the actual order, and their precise scope will therefore fall to be considered in the light of its actual wording.

If one or more of these is to be relied on by way of a defence to a criminal prosecution, careful thought will obviously need to be given to its meaning and extent; the relevant section of **Chapter 17** should be consulted accordingly.

19.4.2 The burden and standard of proof

There appears to be some confusion as to who has the burden of proof where one of the exemptions is being relied on. Thus, in one unreported case in the Crown Court at Isleworth in 1988, the judge apparently said in his concluding direction

---

59   TCPA 1990, s. 198(6)(a); see **17.3**.
60   TCPA 1990, s. 198(6)(b); see **17.4**.
61   TCPA 1990, s. 198(6)(b); see **17.5**.
62   TCPA 1990, s. 200(3); also 1969 Model Order, Sched. 2, para. (1), (2); see **12.6**, **12.7** and **17.6.1**.
63   TCPA 1990, s. 198(7)(b), Forestry Act 1967, s. 15(6); see **14.4** and **17.6.2**.
64   Model Order; see **17.7**.
65   Model Order; see **17.8**.
66   Model Order; see **17.9**.
67   TCPA 1990, s. 198(7)(a); see **17.10**.

to the jury that the prosecution has to prove their case, namely that the tree (which had been felled following the 1987 storm) was not dangerous, for a guilty verdict to be returned.[68] This is not correct.

In the earlier decision of the Divisional Court in *Edgeborough Building Co v Woking UDC*[69], which related to the "nuisance" exemption,[70] it had simply been conceded by counsel that, once the prosecution had proved that the tree in question was subject to a tree preservation order and that it had been cut down without the council's consent, the burden then shifted to the accused to show that they came within one or other of the exemptions to the application of the order. The matter was considered more fully, however, by the Court of Appeal in *R v Alath Construction Ltd; R v Brightman*,[71] which related to the "dangerous" exemption. The court in *Alath* adopted the ruling of the Recorder trying the case at first instance, who had concluded that:

". . . the burden of proving the matters which come within [what is now section 198(6) of the 1990 Act] lies upon the defendant, . . . to prove them on the balance of probabilities".[72]

The same would be true of any of the other exemptions.

Thus, it is for the defendant to prove that the tree in question had become dangerous, or was a fruit tree cultivated for fruit production, or that its felling was necessary to implement a planning permission, or to abate a nuisance, or whatever. It is not for the prosecution to prove the converse. And the defendant must prove this to the Civil Standard (that is, on the balance of probabilities).

19.4.3 The existence of consent

The last matter to be proved is that the acts complained of constituted a contravention of the order.[73] The order provides as follows:

"Subject to the provisions of this Order, and to the exemptions specified in the Second Schedule hereto, no person shall, except with the consent of the authority and in accordance with the conditions if any imposed on such consent, cut down . . . [, etc.] . . . any tree specified in [the order]."[74]

That is, a person carrying out any of the specified operations will be contravening the order unless he or she has obtained the consent of the local planning authority or the Secretary of State, and carries out the operations in accordance with the conditions attached to such consent.

Here, too, the burden is on the accused to prove that consent has been obtained, and that any conditions have been complied with. It is not on the prosecution to prove the converse (which is in any event logically impossible):

"In *R v Edwards*,[75] the Court of Appeal expressed their conclusion in the form of an

---

[68] Arboricultural Journal 1989, Vol. 13, p. 318.
[69] (1966) 198 E.G. 581.
[70] See **17.5**.
[71] [1990] 1 W.L.R. 1255, CA; [1991] 1 PLR 25.
[72] [1990] 1 W.L.R. 1255, CA, per Russell L.J. at p. 1259H, quoting Mr Recorder Zucker QC. See **17.3.5** for a fuller extract.
[73] TCPA 1990, s. 210(1), (4); see **19.2.1**.
[74] 1949, 1953, 1966 and 1969 Model Orders, art. 2; 1999 Model Order, art. 4.
[75] [1975] Q.B. 27, at pp. 39–40.

exception to what they said was the fundamental rule of our criminal law, that the prosecution must prove every element of the offence charged. They said that the exception 'is limited to offences arising under enactments which prohibit the doing of an act save in specified circumstances or by persons of specified classes or with specified qualifications or with the licence of specified authorities'."[76]

It is important, if prosecution is to be avoided, that the consent in question does cover precisely the works that have been carried out. Conversely, problems may occur where the scope of the works permitted is not clear: see *Richmond-upon-Thames v Secretary of State*[77] for an example of the type of consent ("to remove the two longest branches overhanging [the neighbouring property]") which could lead to serious difficulties for an authority attempting to enforce it against unauthorised works to the tree concerned.

19.4.4 Trees considered to be dangerous: "duress of circumstances"

Where works are carried out because a tree is dangerous, there is no need for consent to be obtained, as a result of the exemption under section 198(6) of the Act.[78] However, that does not apply where the tree is not dangerous, but where the owner thought it was, and took action to avoid the perceived harm. This may happen where, for example, an owner considers that a tree is dangerous following damage as a result of lightning or vehicle impact, and fells it. Once the tree has gone, it will usually be impossible for the authority to prove conclusively that it had not been dangerous at the time it was felled – but equally difficult for the owner or contractor prove the contrary.

There is, or at least may be, a further possibility open to the owner, if the authority persists in prosecuting in such circumstances: to rely on what is known as the defence of "duress of circumstances". The principles governing this defence were set out by the Court of Appeal in *R v Martin*:

". . . the defence is available only if, from an objective standpoint, the accused can be said to be acting reasonably and proportionately in order to avoid a threat of death or serious injury.

". . . assuming the defence to be open to the accused on his account of the facts, the issue should be left to the jury, who should be directed to determine these two questions:

- First, was the accused, or may he have been, impelled to act as he did because, as a result of what he reasonably believed to be the situation, he had good cause to fear that otherwise death or serious physical injury would result?
- Second, if so, may a sober person of reasonable firmness, sharing the characteristics of the accused, have responded to that situation by acting as he acted?

If the answer to both those questions was yes, then the jury would acquit: the defence of necessity would have been established."[79]

---

[76] *R v Hunt* [1987] A.C. 352, H.L., per Lord Griffiths at p. 375; quoted in *R v Alath Construction Ltd*; *R v Brightman* [1990] 1 W.L.R. 1255, CA at p. 1259C.
[77] [2001] EWHC ADMIN 205, March 5, 2001, unreported; see **18.2.4**.
[78] See **17.3.2**.
[79] (1989) 88 Cr.App.R. 343, per Simon Brown J. at p. 346 (following the earlier decision in *Conway* (1988) 88 Cr.App.R. 159, [1988] 3 All E.R. 1025, CA; see also *R v Pommell* [1995] 2 Cr.App.R. 607, and Archbold at 17–132.

In other words, if the owner of a tree genuinely believes that it is likely to cause death or serious injury – perhaps, for example, by falling or shedding a branch onto a path – he or she may remove the cause of the danger.

Note, however, that in order to avoid conviction on this basis, the accused must first be able to show that the defence is available on his or her account of the facts; that is, assuming that the factual evidence called by the defence is accurate, might the tree have caused death or serious physical injury? Secondly, it must be proved that the response by the accused to the perceived threat was both reasonable and proportionate. As discussed already, there may be several ways in which to deal with a possibly dangerous tree, such as preventing access to the land on which it is likely to fall until a specialist opinion can be obtained as to its state. It is therefore important, if this defence is to be relied on in any subsequent prosecution, for the owner of the tree or the contractor carrying out the works to assemble as much evidence as possible before the works are done.

It would, of course, be possible for this defence to be relied upon inappropriately. To minimise the risk of this, an authority that is notified of a potentially dangerous tree should send an officer as soon as possible to inspect it, take photographs and gather any other evidence. If the officer forms the view either that it is not dangerous, or that there are other ways of dealing with it, written advice to that effect should be given to the owner, who should sign a note acknowledging that the advice has been received. It would then be difficult for the owner to prove subsequently that it was reasonable to act in some way other than as recommended.

19.5 Procedure

19.5.1 Initial investigation

The planning authority is likely to become aware of the carrying out of apparently unauthorised works as a result of a complaint by a neighbouring resident, passer-by, tree warden or amenity group; or it may be one of its own officers or councillors who makes the discovery.

Sometimes the informer (or council officer) will actually see the works taking place, and who is carrying them out. In that case, he or she should take photographs if at all possible, and prepare and sign a written statement promptly (within a few days), before the recollection of what was seen has faded. If there is eventually a prosecution, it will then be possible for the maker of such a statement to use it in court to refresh his or her memory. Any photographs taken should be retained by the authority, along with a note of who took them, and when, and who processed them. Clearly the evidence of someone who was present and saw what occurred will be invaluable if the authority is to secure a conviction.

The usual practice is for a full record of events to be made contemporaneously in a notebook (referred to as a "memory refreshing document"). A signed statement[80] can then be prepared if and when a prosecution is instituted.

Where possible, anyone who seems to be responsible for the carrying out the works, or associated with them in any way – such as the owner and/or occupier of the land, and any contractors involved – should be briefly interviewed to establish what is going on. This will assist the authority to decide subsequently whether to mount a prosecution, but it will also enable the person responsible to point to any

---

[80] Under Criminal Justice Act 1967, s. 9.

defence which seems to be relevant – such as, that the tree was dangerous or dying. Thus, it may well be that it quickly becomes clear that no offence has been committed, and the matter can be allowed to drop without further ado. Alternatively, such an interview may enable the authority officer to take photographs and other evidence, such as samples of the allegedly rotten branch, which, in turn, will enable the branch or tree to be removed and the site cleared.

However, care must be used in talking to people who may have committed a criminal offence. Those likely to be in the position of conducting such interviews should read the code issued by the Home Secretary under the Police and Criminal Evidence Act (PACE) 1984, entitled *Code C: The Detention, Treatment and Questioning of Persons by Police Officers*[81] – before the problem arises, since there may be no time to read it once it does. In spite of its name, the Code applies to officers of local authorities investigating possible offences just as much as it does to police officers[82]; and a copy of the Code should be readily available at the authority's offices, for consultation by all concerned.[83] In particular, persons under suspicion must be cautioned that they do not have to say anything, but that anything that is said may later be used in court[84]; further, they must be given a chance to obtain legal advice if they wish.

In practice, if a prosecution does take place, a conversation at the site may provide useful evidence, but it should have been recorded in a notebook, signed both by the suspect and by the officer and, of course, it must have been under caution. From the point of view of the suspect, such a conversation bypasses the safeguards provided by a taped interview, and is therefore discouraged by the Code. After a relatively brief interview at the site, any further conversations are likely to take place at the authority's premises.

In some cases, the incident will only come to light after the works have been completed. The same principles still apply – as much information as possible must be gathered as soon as possible, and recorded accurately. In some such cases, the person who carried out the works may be willing to admit having done so, possibly with qualifications ("I cut it down because I was told it was unsafe"). In the event of subsequent court proceedings, such a statement, referred to as a "confession" under the terms of PACE, may be the best evidence available to the prosecuting authority. It follows that it is vital that the caution must be administered right at the start of any interview, otherwise the confession will be inadmissible.

Others willing to give evidence (neighbours and so on) should also be interviewed as soon as possible, so as to enable the authority to make an informed decision as to whether to prosecute. Such people should also be kept informed of the progress of the prosecution.

Finally, it may be noted that the 1990 Act provides rights for officers of the local planning authority to enter land to ascertain whether an offence under section 210 has been committed. These are identical to the rights that exist where an authority is making a tree preservation order in the first place.[85]

---

[81] Available in the Home Office publication *Police and Criminal Evidence Act 1984 (s. 66): Codes of Practice*, which is available from the Stationery Office.

[82] Police and Criminal Evidence Act 1984, s. 67(9).

[83] Code C, para. 1.2.

[84] See s. 10 of the Code on cautions generally, and in particular para. 10.4 as to the wording of the caution to be given.

[85] TCPA 1990, ss. 214B to 214D (especially s. 214B(1)(b)), as inserted by Planning and Compensation Act 1991, s. 23(7); see **16.6.1**.

19.5.2 Decision to prosecute

In principle, the first question to be asked is whether, in relation to a particular act or series of acts carried out to a protected tree or woodland, it appears that all of the ingredients of one of the offences under section 210 can be proved.[86] If they can, and if none of the exemptions seem to apply,[87-88] it is in principle possible to mount a prosecution of those responsible. However, merely because works have taken place to a protected tree in contravention of a tree preservation order does not of course mean that those responsible must inevitably be prosecuted.

For example, it may well be inappropriate for a planning authority to prosecute where consent would have been readily forthcoming had it been sought. That would apply where the tree concerned was of little amenity value, particularly if it was only protected by an area or woodland order, or where there was some other reason for allowing the works, such as that the tree was causing serious building settlement. In such a case, it is true that consent could readily have been obtained, and should therefore have been sought; but the failure to have done so would not be a major wrong, and would only rarely deserve a criminal penalty.

And it may not be appropriate to prosecute a householder who was genuinely ignorant of the existence of the need for consent, or someone who believed, perhaps wrongly, that one of the exemptions applied.

Nor should it be forgotten that, where works have been carried out in breach of a tree preservation order, there is a duty on the landowner to plant a replacement tree, unless the authority dispense with the requirement.[89] This applies whether or not those responsible are prosecuted or convicted. In some cases, to insist on this duty being complied with will be a sufficient response to the unauthorised act – and may negate any gain achieved by those who committed it. On the other hand, where a beautiful tree has been cynically felled in order to facilitate a development scheme, there may be no point in seeking a replacement, and prosecution may be more appropriate.

The Code for Crown Prosecutors, issued by the Director of Public Prosecutions under section 10 of the Prosecution of Offences Act 1985, sets out a two stage test in considering whether to mount a prosecution. The first question to be asked is whether there is sufficient evidence available to provide a "realistic prospect of conviction".[90] If there is, the prosecutor must then go on to ask whether a prosecution would be in the public interest. Among the factors listed, militating against prosecution, are the following:

"(a) the likelihood that the court will impose a very small or nominal penalty; . . .
(c) the offence was committed as a result of a genuine mistake or misunderstanding;
(d) the loss or harm can be described as minor and was the result of a single incident;
(e) there has been a long delay between the offence taking place and the date of the trial; . . .
(h) the defendant has put right the loss or harm that was caused."[91]

The same principles would apply to a prosecution by a local authority. And it should be borne in mind that, whereas a well-publicised successful prosecution

---

[86] See **19.3**.
[87-88] See **19.4**.
[89] See **20.2.3**.
[90] Code for Crown Prosecutors, s. 5.
[91] Code for Crown Prosecutors, para. 6.5.

may be useful to deter others from breaching orders, equally a well-publicised acquittal may be distinctly unhelpful. Thus, in some cases, it may be best for the authority simply to caution those responsible for apparently unauthorised works.

Thought needs to be given as to who should be prosecuted. Bearing in mind the position already explained as to prosecuting those who aid and abet the commission of an offence,[92] it may be appropriate for an authority to prosecute the owner and occupier of the land involved, or the contractor or sub-contractor who actually did the work (where different).

Finally, note that, where the works concerned are possibly better categorised as forestry, the planning authority should liase with the Forestry Commission, to ensure that any prosecution is brought under the correct legislation.

19.5.3 Procedure: offences under section 210(1)

An offence under section 210(1) (works likely to lead to the loss of the tree) may be tried either by the magistrates or by a jury in the Crown Court. The procedure will generally be as for any other criminal trial brought by a local authority in relation to an either-way offence.

The first stage of the prosecution will be that an information will be laid before the relevant magistrates. Normally the information will be drafted somewhat along the following lines:

"JOHN SMITH on or about 1st January 2002 did cut down a tree, namely the oak tree specified as tree T4 in the City of Barchester Tree Preservation Order number 23 of 1997, without consent under that order, contrary to section 210(1) of the Town and Country Planning Act 1990."

"JOHN SMITH on or about 1st January 2002 wilfully damaged a tree, namely the beech tree specified as tree T5 in the City of Barchester Tree Preservation Order number 23 of 1997, in such a manner as to be likely to destroy it, without consent under that order, contrary to section 210(1) of the Town and Country Planning Act 1990."

Difficulties may arise where works were carried out to more than one tree. It may or may not be appropriate to charge them all together as one offence, depending on the circumstances. The general rule was explained as follows in *DPP v Merriman*:

"When two or more acts of a similar nature committed by one defendant are connected with one another in the time or place of their commission, or by their common purpose, in such a way that they can be fairly be regarded as forming part of the same transaction or criminal enterprise, they can be charged as one offence in a single indictment."[93]

For example, in *Cullen v Jardine*,[94] it was held that an information charging the unlawful felling of 90 trees (in contravention of the Forestry Act 1967) was not bad for duplicity even though the felling had occurred over three days. Generally, however, more than one count will be preferable except where a homogenous group of trees was felled as a single operation on a single day.[95]

There will then be a "plea before venue" hearing at the magistrates' court, at

---

[92] See **19.2.4**.
[93] [1973] A.C. 584, H.L., at p. 607.
[94] [1985] Crim.LR., 668, *The Times*, April 29, 1985. See **14.7.3**.
[95] And see *R v Wilson* (1979) 69 Cr.App.R. 83.

which the accused will be asked to indicate his or her likely plea. If the accused pleads guilty, the magistrates proceed as they would following a guilty plea at a summary trial; and in practice they will proceed to sentencing unless they feel that their powers of sentence are inadequate.

If the accused pleads not guilty, the prosecution and the defence will be invited to make representations as to the appropriate mode of trial – by magistrates or in the Crown Court – and the magistrates will then state their opinion. In reaching their decision, they will be guided by the general principles laid down in the *Mode of Trial Guidelines*, issued in 1995,[96] which include the following:

> ". . . (d) where cases involve complex questions of fact or difficult questions of law, the court should consider [transfer] for trial; . . .
>
> (f) in general, except where otherwise stated, either-way offences should be tried summarily unless the court considers that the particular case has one or more of the features set out in the following pages and that its sentencing powers are insufficient;
>
> (g) the court should also consider its powers to commit an offender for sentence,[97] if information emerges during the course of the hearing which leads them to conclude that the offence is so serious . . . that their powers to sentence him are inadequate."

The first of these is likely to be relevant where, as will sometimes be the case, the magistrates are unfamiliar with offences of this kind. As to the second and third, an offence under section 210(1) carries a maximum sentence of £20,000 on summary conviction, but an unlimited fine in the Crown Court.

The general tenor of the advice is, nevertheless, that either-way offences should be tried in the magistrates' court; and experience suggests that that approach is right in relation to offences of this kind. There is, in any event, a right of appeal from the decision of the magistrates to the Crown Court, against a guilty verdict or sentence.

If all concerned agree to a summary trial, that will then take place in the normal way.

However, the accused is always entitled to a jury trial if he or she wishes it.[98] If that is the choice, or if the magistrates decide that it is most appropriate, the authority will then prefer a bill of indictment (on similar lines to the information), and the matter will proceed to the Crown Court. There will then be a brief plea and directions hearing (PDH)[99]; and, where appropriate, any preliminary points of law can be dealt with at a separate pre-trial hearing.[1] Thereafter, the trial will proceed as any other jury trial.

There is a right of appeal to the Court of Appeal (Criminal Division), with leave, against a guilty verdict or sentence.

For further details of procedure, standard works should be consulted.

---

[96] Unreported, but quoted at Blackstone, *Criminal Practice*, D3.7, and Archbold, 2000, para. 1–40; similar (although by no means identical) to those issued five years earlier, reported at [1990] 1 W.L.R. 216.

[97] Now under Powers of the Criminal Court (Sentencing) Act 2000, s. 3.

[98] At least for the moment.

[99] See the rules in *Practice Direction: Crown Court (Plea and Directions Hearings)* [1995] 1 W.L.R. 1318; and the judge's questionnaire annexed to them.

[1] Under the Criminal Procedure and Investigations Act 1996, s. 40.

19.5.4 Procedure: offences under section 210(4)

Where the offence is charged under section 210(4) (works not likely to destroy the tree), it can only be charged in a magistrates' court. The information[2] must therefore be laid within six months of the date on which the offence was committed.

The trial will generally be as for any other summary trial, with an automatic right of appeal to the Crown Court or, by way of case stated, to the Divisional Court.

19.5.5 Evidence

Evidence will need to be obtained to support all the various matters that need to be proved or, as the case may be, disproved – which have been considered in some detail already.[3]

In a trial of an offence of this kind, it is worthwhile for the parties to agree as much as possible in advance, by way of "formal admissions"[4] – it makes life easier for them, and also pleases magistrates and judges by expediting the progress of the trial. This may apply to, for example, details such as the identity of the owner and occupier of the land in question.

The first matter is that the prosecution must prove that the tree in question was indeed protected by a tree preservation order at the time of the acts complained of.[5] This will usually be straightforward, although care must be taken where the order relates to land on which there is, or was, more than one tree. This may well form the subject of formal admission. A further problem may occur in the case of trees protected by an area order, in that it only covers trees that were in existence at the date on which the order was made. An appropriately qualified expert must therefore be available to testify as to the age of the tree – it is not sufficient to rely on the court forming its own view.[6] However, in some cases it may be possible to produce a formal admission in relation to some or all of the trees in question. The same problem may apply in the case of a woodland order.[7]

Note that, because offences under section 210 of the 1990 Act are strict liability, there is no need for the prosecution to prove that the accused knew of the existence of the tree preservation order.[8] Further, if evidence is produced that shows that the accused did know of the order, or evidence is produced as to motive, it may be held to be not only irrelevant but also prejudicial to the accused, and thus fatal to the prosecution. In *R v Sandhu*,[9] a case where the owner of a listed building was being prosecuted for carrying out unauthorised works to it, the prosecution adduced evidence which showed that he knew it was listed, and had been warned of the consequences of carrying out the works. The Court of Appeal held that such evidence was both irrelevant and prejudicial, and quashed the conviction.

The second matter to be proved by the prosecution is that the relevant works

---

2   See **19.5.3**.
3   See **19.3**, **19.4**.
4   See Criminal Evidence Act 1965, s. 10.
5   See **19.3.1**.
6   *Carter v Eastbourne BC* [2000] 2 PLR 60; see **19.3.1**.
7   See **16.5.5**.
8   See **19.3.2**.
9   [1997] J.P.L. 853.

were carried out. This, too, should not be a problem – although in the absence of any eyewitnesses it may be difficult to prove when. But it may be possible to find local residents who can testify that the tree in question was present at a particular date, but not a few days later. Where works (other than outright felling) are alleged to be likely to lead to the loss of the tree, so as to justify a charge under section 210(1), rather than section 210(4), expert evidence will be required.[10]

The third matter is who carried out the works, under whose orders.[11] Again, this may be straightforward where there were eyewitnesses, or where someone has made a formal confession under caution; but otherwise problems may occur. It may be necessary sometimes to rely on circumstantial evidence – such as, where a protected tree is felled in a back garden, the owner of the garden must have either carried out the works or given his or her consent to someone else, and therefore will be guilty of breaching the order, or aiding or abetting a breach.

The fourth issue is whether consent was required for the works – or, in practice, whether the defence can prove that one or more of the exemptions from the need for consent apply in the particular circumstances of the case.[12] In appropriate cases, thought will need to be given as to who should provide evidence – for example, where a tree was felled ostensibly because it was dangerous, it will probably be necessary to instruct arboricultural consultants to consider and make deductions from such evidence as may exist (photographs, samples, any remaining part of the stump).

Finally, the defence need to consider whether they are able to show that consent has been granted.[13] In practice, this will only be an issue where there exists a consent that is unclear as to the extent of the works to which it relates, or where there is a dispute as to whether all of the conditions of the consent have been complied with. Again, appropriate expert evidence may be required.

The burden and standard of proof have already been considered.[14]

19.6 Sentencing

19.6.1 General principles

In relation to the offence (under section 210(1)) of carrying out works which lead to the destruction of a protected tree, the 1990 Act provides as follows:

"(2) A person guilty of an offence under subsection (1) shall be liable –

(a) on summary conviction to a fine not exceeding £20,000; or
(b) on conviction on indictment, to a fine.

(3) In determining the amount of any fine to be imposed on a person convicted of an offence under subsection (1), the court shall in particular have regard to any financial benefit which has accrued or appears likely to accrue or appears likely to accrue to him in consequence of the offence."

This applies to any offence committed since January 2, 1992, before which the

---

[10] See **19.3.5**.
[11] See **19.3.7**.
[12] See **19.4.1** and **Chapter 17**.
[13] See **19.4.3**.
[14] See **19.2.2**, **19.4.2**.

maximum fine on summary conviction was the statutory maximum (£2,000) or twice the value of the tree, with no explicit requirement to take account of the benefit accruing from the offence.[15]

That establishes the maximum fine that may be imposed, and one matter that is to be taken into account, but it gives no indication of the likely sentence in practice. Thus, in two cases in 2001 on broadly similar facts – trees felled allegedly to facilitate the development of the land, with a guilty plea offered at an early stage and significant extenuating circumstances – the Crown Court at Snaresbrook imposed a fine of £7,500 in respect of each of three trees, whereas the Aldershot Magistrates' Court imposed a fine of £1,000 for each of two.

It seems that the three principal matters to be taken into account by a court when arriving at an appropriate sentence are:

- the degree of financial gain that the defendant has attempted to achieve;

- the degree of culpability of the defendant; and

- the degree of damage that has been done.[16]

Each of these is considered in turn. They are, of course, in addition to the factors which will be potentially relevant in all criminal cases, such as the means of the defendant,[17] his or her previous record (so far as relevant), any guilty plea and the extent of the defence's co-operation with the prosecution.

In relation to the lesser offence (under section 210(4)) of carrying out works to a protected tree that are not likely to lead to its destruction, the 1990 Act provides simply that the maximum fine is Level 4 on the standard scale.[18] Although the discussion below is framed principally by reference to offences under section 210(1), it is submitted that the same principles would apply to the section 210(4) offence.

19.6.2 The benefit accruing from the offence

The Act makes it clear that the one matter that must at least be considered is "any financial benefit which has accrued or appears likely to accrue to him in consequence of the offence."

This was considered by the Criminal Division of the Court of Appeal in *R v Palmer*[19] – which appears to be only reported sentencing decision relating to a breach of a tree preservation order. The head note of the report summarises the facts and the decision of the Crown Court as follows:

"The appellant was convicted of cutting down a tree which was subject to a tree preservation order, contrary to [the predecessor to TCPA 1990, section 210(1)]. The appellant became the owner of a property on which a number of trees subject to preservation orders were situated. The appellant applied for and obtained for and obtained permission to cut down four of the trees, and made an application to install a root barrier

---

[15] Present wording of s. 210, introduced by Planning and Compensation Act 1991, s. 23(6); S.I. 1991 No. 2905.

[16] *R v Duckworth*, (1995) 16 Cr.App.R. (S) 529, at p. 531; see **19.6.3**.

[17] Powers of the Criminal Court (Sentencing) Act 2000, s. 128; *R v Duckworth*, (1995) 16 Cr.App.R. (S) 529, at p. 531; *R v Browning* [1996] 1 PLR 61, CA.

[18] See **Appendix C** for the current levels.

[19] (1989) 11 Cr.App.R. (S) 407.

between the tree in question and his house. Before this application had been decided, the appellant cut the tree down: he claimed in his defence that the tree had become dangerous as a result of wind damage caused by an exceptional storm, but this defence was rejected by the jury. Sentenced to a fine of £6,000, and ordered to pay £1,000 towards the costs of the prosecution."

On appeal, the Court of Appeal indicated that the proper approach to sentencing was as follows:

"To our minds there is one sure figure which is helpful in arriving at a starting point and that is the sum if a little under £1,000 which the appellant has been saved in the way of the cost of a retaining wall to guard his house from the tree roots. We consider that this gives some indication of the financial implications of what was done, and we consider that it is at any rate a starting point to approach the penalty which should be imposed. The penalty, and here we agree entirely with the learned assistant recorder, should be of an amount which will reflect the deliberate defiance by the appellant of an order made by the council, for purposes which can only be assumed in the light of the jury's verdict to serve his personal advantage.

"We give him credit for the fact that he is in other respects a man of excellent character and, in the particular context of tree orders such as this, has on other occasions co-operated in every way with the council. None the less we think that a substantial fine is called for to mark the importance of the offence, and to deter others from thinking that they can follow suit without paying heavily for doing so.

"Having, as we have said, concluded that the learned assistant recorder was wrong to take replacement value at all, and in particular wrong to take the figure for two trees as the measure of the penalty, and considering (as we do) that the better approach is to work up from the figure of approximately £1,000 which the appellant has saved, and to deduce from that the appropriate penalty, the figure at which we arrive is one of £3,000."[20]

This will be relevant in the not uncommon situation where the planning authority wants a protected tree to be retained, in circumstances where it is said to be causing damage to nearby structures, so that an alternative remedy has to be employed to avoid future damage – for example, underpinning or a root barrier. The cost of that remedy will be saved if the tree is removed – although there may then be further complications if the recovery of the moisture levels in the ground causes heave.

Equally, the same principle would be relevant where a developer seeks to remove one obstacle to the development of an otherwise ripe site by felling some or all of the trees on it. The removal of the trees may increase the value of the site by a very substantial amount; and a fine of anything less than that amount would still leave the developer with a profit. The Sentencing Advisory Panel,[21] in its recent advice to the Court of Appeal on sentencing for environmental offences, summarised the position as follows:

"As a general principle, individuals and companies should not profit from their offences. It is important that the sentence takes account of any economic gain achieved by the offender to take appropriate precautions; it should not be cheaper to offend than to prevent the commission of an offence."[22]

[20] Per Nolan J. at p. 409.
[21] Under Crime and Disorder Act 1998, s. 81(3). See www.sentencing-advisory-panel.gov.uk.
[22] *Environmental Offences: The Sentencing Advisory Panel's Advice to the Court of Appeal*, March 1, 2000, para. 16.

The offences being considered by the Panel, such as air or water pollution, are perhaps generally more serious than the illegal felling of trees; but the underlying approach would seem to be equally valid in relation to offences relating to trees.

It will be important to establish in any case whether the planning authority will be requiring a replacement to be planted, and whether any such requirement will be challenged. If a tree has been felled, and is not going to be replaced, with the result that access can now be obtained to a development site which is worth many hundreds of thousands of pounds, that should lead to a very substantial fine. If, on the other hand, a replacement will be required, and perhaps has already been planted, there may well be no benefit accruing at all.

19.6.3 The culpability of the defendant

It has already been noted, in the above extract from the judgment of the Court of Appeal in *R v Palmer*,[23] that the motives and conduct of the defendant are relevant to sentence.

Although there seems to have been no other guideline case in the Court of Appeal directly relating to trees, there have been several relating to the unlawful demolition of a listed building, under similar provisions in the Planning (Listed Buildings and Conservation Areas) Act 1990. In the most recent of these cases, *R v Duckworth*,[24] the ground floor of a historic building was demolished without listed building consent. The court reviewed its most recent previous decisions[25] and considered that the matters to be taken into account were the degree of damage that has been done to the historic structure, the degree of financial gain that the defendant has attempted to achieve and the degree of culpability of the defendant.[26] It considered the third of these to be "in many respects the most important", commenting as follows:

"These offences can be committed in a number of circumstances. They are sometimes described as offences of strict liability, whether or not that term is strictly accurate. But the offence may be committed though a lack of care on the part of the defendant or indeed through ignorance of his proper responsibilities in the relevant matter. On the other hand, it may be a case where the defendant has acted wilfully, in disregard of the need to obtain consent, or he has even acted wilfully, with an intent to destroy an historic structure.
". . . This man is a chartered surveyor. He is experienced in the relevant matters, and to suggest that he acted in any way other than in a wilful disregard of a necessity to obtain consents is, in our judgment, fanciful." [27]

The court accordingly held that the fine of £15,000 imposed in the Crown Court was, in the circumstances, not inappropriate or wrong in principle (although it did reduce it because of the appellant's financial circumstances). However, given that the offence resulted in a gain of £150,000, that still leaves a worrying net gain of £135,000, which seems to go against the approach adopted in *Palmer* of increasing the amount of the gain to arrive at the fine.

[23] (1989) 11 Cr.App.R. (S) 407; see **19.6.2**.
[24] (1995) 16 Cr.App.R. (S) 529.
[25] In particular, *R v Sims Ltd* (1993) 14 Cr.App.R. (S) 213, and *R v Simpson* (1993) 14 Cr.App.R. (S) 602 (both decisions under the ancient monuments legislation). See also *R v M and G Contractors* (1986) 8 Cr.App.R. (S) 474, and *R v Seymour* [1988] 1 PLR 19, (1988) 9 Cr.App.R. (S) 395.
[26] At p. 531.
[27] Per Hobhouse L.J. at pp. 531, 532.

Similarly, in *R v Sandhu*,[28] another listed buildings case, Bingham L.J. held that it was relevant to sentence that the appellant, before carrying out the unauthorised works, had been warned and advised of the dangers, chose an incompetent builder, and was generally happy to ride roughshod over the regulations.

The same principles would presumably apply to contraventions of tree preservation orders. In particular, although there is no need for the authority to prove that the accused knew of the existence of the tree preservation order in order to secure a conviction, the presence or absence of such knowledge may be highly relevant to the penalty imposed. Thus, in *Maidstone BC v Mortimer*,[29] the accused was a tree-feller by occupation, and had been told by the landowner (incorrectly, as it turned out) that she had obtained consent from the Council. The Divisional Court held that his lack of knowledge was insufficient for him to escape conviction, but "that fact can be reflected in the penalty imposed on him".[30]

Similarly, although a challenge to the validity of the order cannot be raised as a defence to a prosecution, it may be raised as a mitigating factor to secure a lower sentence. On the other hand, the court might take the view that even if, for example, an authority had made an order improperly (for example, protecting a poor quality self-sown sapling of no amenity value merit as a device to prevent development), the right course of action by the landowner would have been to seek consent under the order, if necessary from the Secretary of State on appeal, rather than simply to fell the tree in breach of the order. A reduction in sentence may therefore not be appropriate.

Finally, the advice given to the Court of Appeal by the Sentencing Advisory Panel[31] on sentencing for environmental offences emphasised the culpability of a defendant as a factor in assessing an appropriate sentence – either aggravating or reducing the seriousness of an offence.[32]

19.6.4 The extent of the damage

It has already been noted that the old formula prescribing the maximum sentence in the magistrates' court was calculated by reference to the value of the tree.[33] That no longer applies explicitly, but it is clear that some protected trees are more important than others, and it would be odd if the felling of an avenue of 300-year old veteran oaks resulted in a similar fine to the uprooting of a single ornamental cherry, preserved as part of an area order.

Both the Court of Appeal in *Duckworth*[34] and the Sentencing Advisory Panel[35] have accepted that the extent of the damage will be a relevant factor. In the case of an offence under section 210(1) of the 1990 Act, the damage will always be the total loss of the tree concerned, so the key factor will be the value of the tree that is lost. And that value will be the value of the tree as an amenity, since that is the focus of the Act[36] – rather than its value as timber or even firewood, or its

[28] [1997] J.P.L. 853.
[29] [1980] 3 All E.R. 552; [1981] J.P.L. 319.
[30] [1980] 3 All E.R. 552, per Park J. at p. 555f.
[31] See **19.6.2**.
[32] See *Environmental Offences: The Panel's Advice to the Court of Appeal*, March 1, 2000, paras 6, 12.
[33] See **19.6.1**.
[34] (1995) 16 Cr.App.R. (S) 529.
[35] See **19.6.2**.
[36] See the extract from *Barnet LBC v Eastern Electircity Board* quoted above at **19.3.4**.

replacement value (to the extent to which that could be calculated).[37]

In calculating the value of a tree as an amenity, one technique is to use the Helliwell method, explained in a guidance note produced by the Arboricultural Association.[38] This has already been explained in the context of making tree preservation orders.[39] It is, inevitably, not a perfect tool,[40] although its use has occasionally been approved by magistrates.

Clearly, in the case of an offence under section 210(4), where the unauthorised works have been less than total felling or destruction of the tree, it will be relevant to consider not just the amenity value of the tree but also the extent of the damage inflicted by the unauthorised act – was it simply the removal of a branch or wholesale butchery?

19.6.5 Procedure

Sentencing is in some cases a key element in a trial for unauthorised works to trees. If the defendant has pleaded guilty, no evidence at all will have been called prior to conviction, so that matters relevant to sentencing (such as, notably, the culpability of the defendant and the amenity value of the tree) may need to be explored following conviction prior to sentencing. Where there is a substantial difference between the two sides on such matters, there may have to be a hearing to determine the basis on which the court should arrive at its sentence. The procedure by which this is achieved is known as a *Newton* hearing.[41]

The same procedure may also be required, however, where there is a conviction following a not-guilty plea. In some cases, evidence relating to matters such as the culpability of the defendant and the amenity value of the tree would be both irrelevant and, possibly, highly prejudicial if admitted during the main trial. Such evidence must therefore be rigorously excluded at that stage,[42] but may be introduced following conviction. The Court of Appeal has advocated that in such cases a procedure similar to the *Newton* hearing be adopted.[43] The trial thus effectively splits into two parts.

It should be noted that, whilst the duty of those appearing for the defendant is to achieve the lowest possible sentence, it does not follow that the duty of the prosecution is to achieve the maximum possible; rather, it is to assist the court to achieve a level of penalty that is fair in all the circumstances.[44]

Where the magistrates, after a summary trial, convict a defendant of an offence under section 210(1), they may decide in the light of all the evidence they have heard that the case should be committed to the Crown Court for sentencing, because it deserves a greater fine than they have power to impose. Before doing so, however, they may seek further details of the means and previous convictions of the defendant. Note that this procedure is, for some reason, not available in the case of offences committed by companies.[45]

---

[37] *R v Palmer* (1989) 11 Cr.App.R. (S) 407, at p. 408.
[38] *The Amenity Valuation of Trees and Woodlands*, DR Helliwell, Arboricultural Assn, revised edn 2000; based on proposals originally published in the Arboricultural Journal, 1967.
[39] See **15.6.3**.
[40] The author would welcome details of any other methods that have been used in practice.
[41] After *R v Newton* (1882) 77 Cr.App.R. 13. See the note on *R v Hill* at [1997] Crim. L.R. 459.
[42] *R v Sandhu* [1997] J.P.L. 853., CA
[43] *R v Robinson* (1968) 53 Cr.App.R. 314; *R v Finch* (1992) 14 Cr.App.R. (S) 226.
[44] See *R v Banks* [1916] 2 K.B. 621.
[45] Magistrates' Courts Act 1952, s. 29, Sched. 2.

19.6.6 Costs

Finally, in the event of a conviction in a case of this kind, the prosecution will usually seek to recover all or part of its costs from the defendant; indeed, the amount of costs recovered can (exceptionally) exceed the amount of the fine, although it should never be "grossly disproportionate" to it.[46]

The computation of allowable costs is beyond the scope of this book; but in broad terms, the court may order the defendant to pay to the prosecution such costs as it considers just and reasonable.[47] This may include the costs of any investigation carried out by the prosecuting authority in preparation for a trial that eventually results in a conviction – even if the prosecution eventually modified its case.[48] The prosecution should produce as early as possible a statement of its costs, and serve it on the defence; and the defence should have a chance to object to them where appropriate.

In practice, having considered the means of the defendant and all the circumstances, the court will often order the defendant to pay some, rather than all, of the prosecution costs.

If the defendant is acquitted, his or her costs will be met from central funds, not by the prosecution; and there is no special rule as to costs in proceedings brought in the public interest.[49]

19.7 Injunctions

19.7.1 Introduction

There will inevitably be a few cases where urgent action is required to stop a protected tree or woodland being felled in the very near future – possibly in the next 24 hours – or to halt unauthorised works which are actually in progress. In such situations, it will be of limited use to institute criminal proceedings: even if those responsible for the works are convicted, the trees will have gone. And although it is possible for an authority to require replacement trees to be replanted, they will not, for many years, have the same amenity value as those which have been felled.

The only remedy available to a planning authority in such circumstances is to seek an injunction from the courts restraining the owner or occupier of the land, or the contractors involved, from carrying out, or continuing, any unauthorised works to any protected trees. If such an injunction is granted and its terms are then flouted, an action can be brought for contempt of court.

The power to grant such an injunction has since 1991 been explicit, in section 214A of the 1990 Act.[50] Prior to that, planning authorities had to rely on their inherent powers to bring proceedings under section 222 of the Local Government Act 1972[51]; and before that the Attorney-General would be invited to bring an

---

[46] R v Northallerton Magistrates' Court, ex p. Dove (1999) 163 J.P. 657.
[47] Prosecution of Offences Act 1985, s. 18.
[48] R v Associated Octel Ltd [1997] 1 Cr.App.R. (S) 435; see also [1997] Crim. L.R. 144.
[49] Re Southbourne Ltd [1993] 1 W.L.R. 244 at 250G.
[50] Introduced by PCA 1991, s. 23(7).
[51] As in Kent CC v Batchelor (1976) 75 L.G.R. 151, 33 P. & C.R. 185, CA; Kent CC v Batchelor (No. 2) [1979] 1 W.L.R. 213; Newport BC v Khan [1990] 1 W.L.R. 1185, CA.

action on behalf of the authority concerned.[52] It was thus recognised by the House of Lords that "an injunction may be granted in an emergency to restrain an infringement of the law, for example, the cutting down of a tree in breach of a tree preservation order."[53]

The existence of the new statutory provision means that the earlier case law, to the extent that it focussed on the jurisdiction of the court to grant injunctive relief, may now be ignored. Further, the provision makes it clear that the jurisdiction may be exercised either by the High Court or by the county court.[54] However, the remedy remains a discretionary one, and the earlier decisions will thus still be relevant in determining whether a court should grant an injunction in a particular case.

19.7.2 Principles governing the court's discretion

The basis on which the court should exercise its discretion whether or not to grant an injunction to enforce a tree preservation order was considered by the Court of Appeal in *Newport BC v Khan*.[55] Beldam L.J. held that the correct principles were those set out by Bingham L.J. in *City of London Corporation v Bovis*:

"The guiding principles must, I think, be –

(1) that the jurisdiction is to be invoked and exercised exceptionally and with great caution[56];
(2) that there must certainly be something more than mere infringement of the criminal law before the assistance of civil proceedings can be invoked and accorded for the protection or promotion of the interests of the inhabitants of the area[57]; and
(3) that the essential foundation for the exercise for the court's exercise to grant an injunction is not that the offender is deliberately and flagrantly flouting the law, but the need to draw the inference that the defendant's unlawful operations will continue unless and until effectively restrained by the law, and that nothing short of an injunction will be effective to restrain them."[58]

Lloyd L.J. was, essentially, of the same view.[59] He also dealt with the argument that a tree is irreplaceable:

"Finally there is the argument which Mr Bush, on behalf of the Council, put at the forefront of his case, although it is not reflected in the evidence, that the harm done by Mr Khan if he fails to comply with the order would be irreparable. In one sense this is of course true. A tree, once felled, cannot be restored. It can only be replaced by another tree. But irreparability on its own does not necessarily justify an injunction. One must also have regard to the gravity of the harm likely to be done, and the scale of the operations as a whole.[60] . . . I am not saying that there may not be a case where, exceptionally, an

---

[52]   As in *Attorney-General v Melville Construction Co Ltd* (1968) 20 P. & C.R. 131.
[53]   *Kirklees MBC v Wickes Building Supplies Ltd* [1992] 3 W.L.R. 170 at p. 178H, following *Newport BC v Khan* [1990] 1 W.L.R. 1185, CA.
[54]   TCPA 1990, s. 187B(4) (inserted by PCA 1991, s. 3), applied by s. 214A(2).
[55]   [1990] 1 W.L.R. 1185, CA.
[56]   See *Gouriet v Union of Post Office Workers* [1978] A.C. 435.
[57]   See *Stoke-upon-Trent City Council v B&Q (Retail) Ltd* [1984] A.C. 754, H.L., at pp. 767, 776; and *Wychavon DC v Midland Enterprises (Special Events) Ltd* (1987) 86 L.G.R. 83, at p. 87.
[58]   (1988) 86 L.G.R. 660 at p. 682; [1988] J.P.L. 263, cited in *Newport* at p. 1193G.
[59]   [1990] 1 W.L.R. 1185, CA, at pp. 1191F–1193A.
[60]   See per Ackner L.J. in *Stoke-upon-Trent City Council v B&Q (Retail) Ltd* in the Court of Appeal at [1984] Ch. 30.

injunction may not be justified in support of a tree preservation order. *Kent County Council v Batchelor*[61] was just such a case. But the facts of the present case fall far short of the gravity and persistence of the conduct of the farmer in that case. Accordingly, I would reject Mr Bush's argument based on the irreversible nature of a tree-cutting operation."[62]

The facts in *Newport* were that the Council had on April 19, 1989 made a tree preservation order in relation to the Khans' land in the centre of Newport. Mr Khan had applied to the Council the following day to remove fifteen trees that he considered dangerous, in particular a yew and a redwood as to which he had received specialist advice indicating that they were an obvious danger to passers-by. He was told that he would hear from the Council in six weeks; but when he had heard nothing for nearly six months he wrote to the Council on September 5, saying that unless he heard something within five days, he would have no alternative but to cut the yew for the sake of public safety. The yew was felled early on the morning of Sunday September 10.

The Court of Appeal considered that such conduct seemed to be the very reverse of "a deliberate flouting of the law". Nor was there any evidence that Khan ever intended to cut down any of the trees other than the yew and the redwood. It followed that there was no reason to infer that he would commit further breaches of the order. The injunction that had been granted was accordingly discharged.

This should be contrasted with the facts in the *Batchelor* litigation. When the matter initially came before the High Court, it was in the light of a tree preservation order that had been made on 80 hectares or so of beautiful countryside, which covered a great deal of land that had just been bought by a farmer, one Mr Batchelor.[63] As Lord Denning later put it:

"I am afraid that Mr Batchelor did not take much notice of the order with regard to some yew trees. . . . [H]e is said to have cut down large numbers of trees. There was considerable conflict between him and the Council. We are told that he has been served with some 54 summonses with regard to the trees which he has already cut down."[64]

Chapman J. accordingly granted an injunction restraining Batchelor from "cutting down, uprooting, topping, lopping or otherwise in any way damaging or destroying any tree on land owned or occupied by him which tree is subject of a tree preservation order".

These two cases make it clear that the court will grant an injunction, but that a good case will need to be made out by the planning authority as to both:

- deliberate breaches of a tree preservation order; and

- a clear inference that the unlawful operations will continue unless and until effectively restrained by the law, and that nothing short of an injunction will be effective to restrain them.

---

[61] (1976) 75 L.G.R. 151, 33 P. & C.R. 985, CA.
[62] [1990] 1 W.L.R. 1185, CA, at pp. 1192G–1193A.
[63] See also *Batchelor v Secretary of State* [1993] 1 EGLR 207 (noted at **18.5.8**).
[64] *Kent CC v Batchelor* (1976) 75 L.G.R. 151, 33 P. & C.R. 185, CA, at p. 186.

19.7.3 Procedure

An application for an injunction is best brought in the Chancery Division of the High Court, under the procedure set out in Part 25 of the Civil Procedure Rules. The first step, if time permits, is for the planning authority to file with the court an application notice, with supporting evidence (in the form of a witness statement) and a draft order (also on disk). The authority will not usually be required to give an undertaking in damages.[65] There will then be a hearing in open court without notice[66] and, if granted, an interim injunction will take effect immediately. Where a hearing cannot be arranged, an application can be made by telephone. Where a claim form has not already been issued, on can be issued later.

If an injunction is to be effective, copies should clearly be issued without delay on all involved – including, principally, the contractors carrying out the work.

There will then be a hearing on notice, at which the defendants (usually the owner and occupier of the land) are entitled to be represented, and an interlocutory injunction may be granted that will have effect until further order. Alternatively, the defendants may be willing to give an undertaking not to carry out further works without consent – breach of such an undertaking is equivalent to breach of an injunction.

19.7.4 Breach of an injunction

Where an injunction is breached, the authority may return to the court to seek the committal of those responsible, for contempt. Thus the *Batchelor* case came (back) to the courts because there was alleged to have been "wilful and intentional disobedience of [the injunction] by Mr Batchelor, who did not appeal to him as a witness 'in the slightest'."[67] However, because breach of an injunction is taken extremely seriously by the courts, it must be proved to the criminal standard – that is, beyond reasonable doubt.

Lord Denning noted that:

"There is nothing so important as that, in areas of natural beauty, the trees and the woodland should be preserved. If there was any deliberate and proved offence against the tree preservation order, the county council would be justified in taking steps to enforce it. It may well be that breach of [an injunction restraining breach of] such an order would justify a sentence of imprisonment. It is only because it seems to me that such a breach has not been proved in this case that I would allow the appeal and quash the [committal] order made by the judge."[68]

The other members of the court concurred in holding that, had the contempt been proved, they would not have interfered with the sentence that had been imposed – one month in prison.[69]

---

[65] *Kirklees MBC v Wickes Building Supplies Ltd* [1992] 3 W.L.R. 170 at p. 182G.
[66] The term "without notice" is the modern equivalent of *ex parte*.
[67] *Kent CC v Batchelor* (1976) 75 L.G.R. 151, 33 P. & C.R. 185, CA, per Stephenson L.J. at p. 190, quoting Caulfield J. at first instance.
[68] (1976) 33 P. & C.R. 185, CA, at p. 189.
[69] In that case, there were further breaches of the injunction following the appearance in the Court of Appeal; and B was indeed committed to prison: see *Kent CC v Batchelor (No. 2)* [1979] 1 W.L.R. 213 at p. 221.

Chapter 20

Requirement to Plant Replacement Trees

20.1 Introduction

There are several occasions on which a landowner may be required to plant a replacement for a protected tree,[1] as follows:

- where the protected tree was felled without consent, because it was dying, dead or dangerous[2];

- where it was felled in contravention of the order[3]; or

- where it was felled with a consent that was granted subject to a condition requiring the planting of one or more trees by way of replacement.[4]

In the first two cases, the duty that arises automatically (by virtue of section 206 of the Town and Country Planning Act 1990) is to plant a replacement of appropriate size and species, at the same place, unless the planning authority agrees to dispense with it. In the third case, the duty that arises is by virtue of the wording of the condition itself, which may require the planting of one or more trees at particular locations. The outworking of these requirements is considered in more detail in **20.2**.

A failure to comply with the duty to plant a new tree is not (at present) a criminal offence; instead, it is open to the planning authority in the event of non-compliance to serve a notice on the landowner, requiring him or her to take action (see **20.3**). The recipient of the notice may appeal against it to the Secretary of State (**20.4**). Once a notice has come into effect, if all else fails, the authority may enter the land and take the necessary action itself (**20.5**).

It may be noted that the procedures described in this Chapter apply also in relation to trees in conservation areas (see **21.5**).

---

[1] As in previous chapters, the term "protected tree" is used to refer to a tree that is subject to a tree preservation order.
[2] See **17.3**.
[3] See **19.1.2**.
[4] See **18.3.7**.

20.2 The duty to plant replacement trees

20.2.1 Replacement of a dying, dead or dangerous tree

It has already been noted that consent is not needed under a tree preservation order for the felling of a tree that is dying or dead, or that has become dangerous.[5] Because in each of these cases it is almost always the actual tree itself that was the problem, rather than its location, there is no particular reason why another tree should not be planted in the same place. The new tree will not, of course, be a full replacement, for it will not for many years attain the size of the one that has been removed – although, other things being equal, it will provide an amenity for a great deal longer than the old one would have done.

Section 206 of the 1990 Act, therefore, generally requires that, wherever a protected tree is removed, uprooted or destroyed because it is dying or dead, or has become dangerous, a replacement tree of appropriate size and species must be planted at the same place as soon as reasonably possible.[6] The duty is on the owner of the land (that is, broadly speaking, the freeholder or, sometimes, head leaseholder[7]) for the time being.[8] And once the replacement tree has been planted, it is automatically subject to the tree preservation order that protected the tree it replaces.[9]

The requirement to replace a dying, dead or dangerous tree does not apply, however, in the case of a tree that is subject to a tree preservation order as part of woodland. This is presumably because it is unlikely that it would arise in relation to more than one or two trees at a time, and the loss of a few trees within woodland is generally not a significant loss of amenity. Further, to plant one or two new trees in the middle of established woodland would usually not be in accordance with good forestry practice.

Nor does the duty to plant a replacement apply where the planning authority agrees to dispense with it.[10]

20.2.2 The extent of the replacement duty

It has already been noted that a new tree required to be planted to replace one that was dying, dead or dangerous must be:

- of an appropriate size;
- of an appropriate species; and
- at the same place as the one it replaces.

The first of these stipulations arises because it would clearly be unreasonable to require the new tree to be the same size as the one it is replacing. Indeed, in some cases, particularly in urban areas, there may be severe limitations on the size of tree that can be brought to the site (quite apart from the cost). Careful thought

---

5   TCPA 1990, s. 198(6)(a); see **17.3**.
6   TCPA 1990, s. 206(1)(b); see **20.2.2**.
7   TCPA 1990, s. 336.
8   TCPA 1990, s. 206(5).
9   TCPA 1990, s. 206(4).
10   TCPA 1990, s. 206(2); see **20.2.2**.

should therefore be given as to what is the appropriate size for the replacement, and as to whether it is necessary to insist on a large specimen. Usually it will be appropriate for the authority to simply specify either advanced nursery stock or heavy standard.

As to the second requirement, many a protected tree is of an inappropriate species in relation to the buildings and gardens now surrounding it. It would normally be sensible to choose a replacement tree that was appropriate to the current position, rather than to a pattern of land use that has possibly long since disappeared. And in this respect, the general constraints on planting trees, discussed earlier,[11] would be relevant.

The third stipulation, as to the location of the new tree, is less straightforward. For one thing, the stump of a tree is usually only removed (by grinding out) down to a depth of 30 cm or so, and it may therefore be impracticable to plant a new tree, particularly if it is of any size, at precisely the same location. That difficulty may be more apparent than real, in that the root system of a tree is sometimes surprisingly shallow immediately beneath the base of the trunk. However, it is still true that planting at exactly the same spot may require a considerable engineering exercise, which an authority should not insist on unless the precise location is critical (for example, as a focal point of a designed landscape, or to hide a particular view).

The High Court considered the meaning of the phrase "at the same place" in *Bush v Secretary of State and Redditch BC*,[12] and concluded that it should not be read as including the qualification "or as near as reasonably practicable". It pointed out that a tree preservation order is to be drawn up in the first place specifying the trees to be protected by reference to a map showing the location of each tree, area or group[13]; the replacement should therefore be planted at that same location. That would seem to mean that, where protected trees are specified by reference to an area or a group, the replacement tree must be planted at a site that is within the parcel of land shown on the map as being the location of the area or group in question.

The Government has accepted in principle that it would be sensible to relax this provision slightly, by enabling a replacement tree to be planted at or near the site of the original tree, rather than at the exact same place.[14] For the moment, however, the law remains that the new tree must (at least in theory) be at the same place as the one it replaces.

Note that, whereas a condition of consent may require (subject to a right of appeal) any number of trees to be planted in replacement of one being felled, the duty in relation to dying, dead or dangerous trees only requires one to be planted for each one lost.

Finally, the new planting should be carried out by the landowner "as soon as he or she reasonably can". The *DETR Guide* sensibly points out that this may well involve the owner waiting until the next planting season.

See below[15] as to how this requirement may operate in practice.

---

[11] See **10.1**.
[12] [1988] J.P.L. 108.
[13] See **16.5.2**.
[14] *Tree Preservation Orders: Review*, DOE, 1994, paras 2.44, 2.45.
[15] See **20.3.2**.

20.2.3 Replacement planting following unauthorised works

Most of the requirements of planning law are enforced not directly through the processes of the criminal law, but by the mechanism of requiring the wrongdoer to undo the effect of his or her wrongdoing (through the service of an enforcement notice). In the case of historic buildings and trees, however, there is power to prosecute those responsible for breaches of control without the need to serve an enforcement notice first. This is because it is not possible to put back a building that has been demolished or a tree that has been felled, and prosecution may therefore be the only effective deterrent.[16] But in the case of trees, the planting of a new one in the place of a tree that has been felled, although not a true "replacement", may go some way to mitigating the loss of amenity caused by the felling.

Section 206, therefore, also requires that when a tree that was subject to a tree preservation order (other than as part of a woodland) is "removed, uprooted or destroyed" in contravention of the order, the owner of the land must plant another tree of appropriate size and species at the same place as soon as he or she reasonably can.[17-18] This duty is in addition to any criminal liability, and applies whether or not a prosecution has been started or is in contemplation.

The general comments above relating to the replacement of a protected tree that was felled because it was dying, dead or dangerous[19] apply equally to the replacement of trees that have been unlawfully felled, save that the duty in relation to unlawful felling applies also in relation to woodland trees. Following the unlawful removal of trees that were subject to a tree preservation order by forming part of a woodland, the replacement duty is to plant the same number of trees "on or near" the land on which the trees used to stand, or on such other land as may be agreed between the owner and the authority – and in either case at locations designated by the authority.[20] There is thus significantly greater flexibility in relation to woodlands than in other cases.

This duty applies in every case following unauthorised works, except where the planning authority dispenses with it. Again, the duty attaches to whoever is the current owner of the land, even if the tree was felled by a previous owner, a tenant or licensee, or even a trespasser.[21] An owner wishing to avoid the need to plant a new tree should apply to the authority by letter for a dispensation. Here, too, once the replacement tree has been planted, it is automatically subject to the order that protected the original tree.[22]

The existence of the power for planning authorities to insist on a replacement for trees unlawfully felled should minimise the incentive for developers and others to breach the tree preservation order in the first place. However, once a tree has been felled, it may not be appropriate to insist on its replacement.

20.2.4 Replacement following windblow

There would seem to be no duty on a landowner to plant a new tree to replace one which has been blown over in a storm, since no person has removed, uprooted or

---

[16] See **Chapter 19**.
[17-18] TCPA 1990, s. 206(1)(a).
[19] See **20.2.1, 20.2.2**.
[20] TCPA 1990, s. 206(3).
[21] TCPA 1990, s. 206(5).
[22] TCPA 1990, s. 206(4).

destroyed the tree in contravention of the order. The *DETR Guide* suggests otherwise, although without giving any reasons.[23]

20.2.5 *Replacement required as a condition of consent under a tree preservation order*

It has already been noted that consent may be granted for the felling of a protected tree subject to a condition that one or more trees are planted by way of replacement.[24]

This duty arises not under section 206, but as a result of the wording of the condition itself. And indeed the condition should, if it has been properly drafted, require a further replacement to be planted if the original replacement fails. However, a replacement planting condition is enforced in exactly the same way as a requirement to plant a tree under section 206.

However, the requirement to plant a tree under a condition is unlike the position in relation to the replacement of trees that were felled because they were dead or in contravention of the order, because:

- it is permissible (subject to the right of appeal) for a condition to require more new trees to be planted than were felled; and

- the tree preservation order which protected the tree that was lawfully felled does not apply to the replacement tree.

As to the second of these, the Government appears to be sympathetic to the idea that it should be possible for a planning authority simply to vary the original order to include the new tree, rather than having to make a new order.[25] In the meanwhile, it may be appropriate for the authority to make a fresh order to protect the newly planted trees.

20.2.6 *Replanting woodlands*

Special arrangements exist to ensure the replanting of protected woodlands felled with consent under a tree preservation order, through the mechanism of replanting directions.

These have already been dealt with.[26]

20.3 Enforcing the replacement duty

20.3.1 *Service of a replacement notice*

If a landowner fails to comply with the duty to plant a replacement tree arising as a result of either section 206 of the 1990 Act, or with a condition on a tree preservation order consent, the planning authority is able to serve a tree replacement notice under section 207.

A tree replacement notice is to specify:

---

[23] *DETR Guide*, 2000, para. 11.8.
[24] See **18.3.7**; and **Appendix B**.
[25] *Tree Preservation Orders: Review*, DOE, 1994, para. 2.22.
[26] See **18.3.8**.

- the period (of at least 28 days) at the end of which the notice is to come into effect[27];

- the period after that within which the tree or trees are to be planted; and

- the size and species of the tree or trees which are to be planted.[28]

If the notice relates to more than one tree, it should, obviously, say how many trees must be planted. And it should state why the authority considers that there exists a duty to plant a new tree in the particular case.

The classic test applying to the validity of a planning enforcement notice[29] does not apply in terms to a notice under section 207, since the existence of the replacement duty does not necessarily imply that the recipient of the notice has done anything wrong. But the general approach would still seem to be valid, so that the test becomes, "does the notice tell the person on whom it is served what he or she must do, and why?"

Oddly, there is no requirement to specify the place where the trees are to be planted, but to do so would undoubtedly be good practice. Nor is there any duty to mention the existence of a right of appeal against the notice and the grounds on which such an appeal may be made (unlike the position in relation to planning enforcement notices[30]), but that too would be desirable, as would an indication of what will happen if the notice comes into effect but is not complied with, and details of who to contact for further information.[31] A model tree replacement notice is at Annex 11 to the *DETR Guide*.

The notice is to be served on the owner of the land in question – that is, generally, the freeholder or long leaseholder. It would be prudent also to serve a copy on the occupier(s) of the land, if not the owner.

It must be served within four years of the failure to comply with the requirements of section 206 or of the condition – that is, four years from the date when the replacement tree should have been planted. It will be recalled that section 206 requires the owner to plant a replacement as soon as he or she reasonably can[32] – which, in practice, may not be for some while after the requirement arises. Thus, if a tree is felled unlawfully in, say, January in year 1, and there is then a period of negotiation as to whether a replacement is required, it may be unreasonable to expect the owner to plant a new tree before September in year 1. If best practice of planting between November and March is observed, this may be delayed until the spring of year 2. If that planting does not take place, the replacement notice could, therefore, be served at any time before September in year 5 or spring in year 6.

There is no requirement for the owner to look after the new tree, once planted. However, if the new tree was planted to replace one that was dying, dead or dangerous, or that had been felled unlawfully, the original tree preservation order will protect the new tree. If it, too, fails to survive, the owner can be required to plant a further replacement – since the removal of the first new tree would be on the basis that it was dead, and the replacement duty under section 206 would apply all over again.

---

[27]   TCPA 1990, s. 207(3), (4).
[28]   TCPA 1990, s. 207(1).
[29]   *Miller-Mead v MOHLG* [1963] 2 Q.B. 196.
[30]   TCP (Enforcement Notices and Appeals) Regulations 1992 (S.I. 1992 No. 1904), reg. 4.
[31]   *DETR Guide*, 2000, para. 11.22.
[32]   TCPA 1990, s. 207(2); see **20.2.2**.

20.3.2 *Requiring tree replacement in practice*

It should be realised that the above discussion is all somewhat theoretical, as the power of the planning authority to dispense with the replacement duty means that the details of precisely what is to be planted where will, in practice, be the subject of negotiation between the landowner and the planning authority – if, indeed, the authority is involved at all. In any event, if the replacement tree is to have a chance of surviving, the goodwill of the landowner is crucial; it is unlikely to be forthcoming if the authority has been unreasonable as to the choice and location of the tree.

Thus, once a tree has been felled in reliance upon the exemption for dying, dead and dangerous trees, the owner may, if he or she wishes to do so, simply proceed with planting a replacement (of a size and species and at a location which seems sensible to him or her) and, as a matter of good practice, notify the authority of what has been done – although the duty is to plant the tree, not to notify the authority. Once the authority becomes aware (by whatever means) that a replacement has been planted, it is unlikely to insist on a tree of a different species being planted, or a different location being chosen. But it would be possible for it to serve a section 207 notice.

Alternatively, if the owner is only willing to plant a tree some way from the site of the one that has been removed, or does not want to plant a replacement tree at all, a letter should be written to the authority explaining the reasons for that preference and seeking a dispensation from, or variation of, the requirement under section 206. If the authority is willing to agree, possibly after negotiation, it should say so in a letter, making clear the agreed size, species and location of any tree that is to be planted, so there can be no doubt in future. If, on the other hand, it is not willing to vary the requirement, or not in the way desired by the landowner, it will have to serve a replacement notice,[33] against which the landowner is entitled to appeal.[34] Either way, the *DETR Guide* suggests that the authority should give reasons for its decision.[35]

The *Guide* also rightly points out that the authority should consider both the loss of amenity caused by the removal of the original trees and whether it is reasonable in all the circumstances to insist on the planting of a replacement. Thus, even if the original tree was removed in contravention of the order, that does not of itself justify the service of a replacement notice. And, similarly, even if a condition on a tree preservation order consent required a new tree to be planted, it will still be necessary for the authority to consider whether, if the landowner is not willing to comply, it is still desirable to insist on one being planted. After all, it is often only possible to assess the need for replacement once the original tree has gone – and indeed perhaps some while after that, once the surrounding area has been re-landscaped.

And if the authority does decide to serve a replacement notice, discussion with the owner is still vital:

"If the LPA believe, in the circumstances, that replacement trees should be planted, they should first try to persuade the landowner to comply with the duty voluntarily. The landowner may not fully appreciate that there is a statutory duty to replace the trees in

---

[33] See **20.3.1**.
[34] See **20.4**.
[35] *DETR Guide*, 2000, para. 11.18.

question. They should discuss the issue with the landowner, who may in turn appreciate the LPA's advice on a range of matters such as the choice of species, their size and location, the best time to plant, and good practice generally. If persuasion, discussion and advice fail, the LPA should then consider taking enforcement action."[36]

20.3.3 Variation of replacement notice

The view of the Secretary of State is that there is at present no power for a planning authority too waive or relax a replacement notice. However, the court has held that an authority may enforce only some of the requirements of a planning enforcement notice[37]; and there seems to be no reason why on the same basis it should not vary a tree replacement notice – although obviously not in such a way as to extend its scope.

An explicit power to vary a replacement notice may be introduced in due course.[38]

20.3.4 Tree planting required as a condition of planning permission

Where the planting of one or more trees is required as a condition of a planning permission,[39] the enforcement mechanism is not by the service of a section 207 notice but by the normal methods used in connection with any planning condition, considered earlier.[40]

20.4 Challenging the requirement to plant replacement

20.4.1 Appealing against replacement notice

A person served with a tree replacement notice is entitled to appeal against it to the Secretary of State under section 208 of the 1990 Act, at any time before the notice comes into effect.[41] Unlike the position in relation to appeals against refusal of consent, this time limit cannot be extended in any circumstances, and a notice may come into effect as little as 28 days from the date of its service. It is therefore important for anyone considering appealing to take advice immediately.

The only grounds of appeal are as follows:

"(a)   that the provisions of section 206 or, as the case may be, the conditions mentioned in section 207(1)(b) [requiring the replacement of trees] are not applicable or have been complied with;

(aa)   that in all the circumstances of the case the duty imposed by section 206(1) should be dispensed with in relation to any tree;

(b)   that the requirements of the notice are unreasonable in respect of the period or the size or species of tree specified in it;

(c)   that the planting of a tree or trees in accordance with the notice is not required in the interests of amenity or would be contrary to the interests of good forestry;

---

[36]   DETR Guide, 2000, para. 11.19.
[37]   Arcam v Worcestershire CC [1964] 1 W.L.R. 661.
[38]   Tree Preservation Orders: Review, DOE, 1994, para. 2.47.
[39]   See **10.4.1**.
[40]   See **10.4.2**.
[41]   TCPA 1990, s. 208(2).

(d)   that the place on which the tree is or trees are required to be planted is unsuitable for that purpose."[42]

These grounds are largely self-explanatory, and an appeal based on any of these grounds should be supported by appropriate evidence. Oddly, there is no ground of appeal that the notice is out of time – that is, that it was served more than four years after the time when the tree was due to be planted[43]; an omission which is likely to be remedied in due course.[44]

Where an appeal is made against a section 207 notice, the notice is of no effect until the matter has been finally determined – that is, broadly, until the Secretary of State has issued a decision, or an appeal to the courts has been dismissed, or the appeal to the Secretary of State has been withdrawn.[45]

The detailed statutory provisions relating to appeals under section 208 of the 1990 Act were significantly amended by the Planning and Compensation Act 1991, along with appeals against enforcement notices generally. Indeed, the law relating to such appeals, which has been the subject of a great deal of technical litigation over the years, broadly applies also to appeals against tree replacement notices. For further details of the resulting, complex law, a standard planning law textbook should be consulted; the notes below are only a brief summary of the principal points.

20.4.2 Procedure

An appeal is made in writing to the appropriate Government regional office, indicating the grounds of appeal relied on, and accompanied by a statement setting out any relevant facts. It must arrive by the relevant date, or be posted so that it would do so in normal circumstances.[46] There is no special form to be used.

Most appeals against tree replacement notices are dealt with on the basis of written representations; but either the appellant or the local planning authority may insist on a hearing or inquiry.[47] Whichever procedure is used, it is not governed either by the new rules in the TCP (Trees) Regulations 1999 or any of the other sets of procedural rules. It would, however, seem to be sensible for all concerned to follow the rules in Part IV of the 1999 Rules in the case of written representations appeals as if they applied; these have already been considered in connection with appeals against tree preservation order consent.[48]

There are no rules applying to hearings into appeals against enforcement notices; presumably the procedure is likely to follow the informal 1996 Code of Practice.[49] Inquiries would perhaps best be conducted on the basis of the TCP (Enforcement) (Inquiries Procedure) Rules 1992.[50]

Appeals against tree replacement notices are all determined by the Secretary of State – that is, not by inspectors. In determining an appeal, the Secretary of State may correct any defect in the notice, or vary its requirements – provided that such

---

[42]   TCPA 1990, s. 208(1); ground (aa) inserted by PCA 1991, s. 23.
[43]   See **20.3.1**.
[44]   *Tree Preservation Orders: Review*, DOE, 1994, para. 2.48.
[45]   TCPA 1990, ss. 208(6), 289(4B); *R v Kuxhaus* [1988] 2 PLR 59, CA.
[46]   TCPA 1990, s. 208(2), (4).
[47]   TCPA 1990, s. 208(5).
[48]   See **18.5.6**.
[49]   At Annex 2 to Circular 15/96, *Planning Appeal Procedures*.
[50]   S.I. 1992 No. 1903.

a correction or variation would not cause injustice to either party – or may quash it altogether.[51] Whichever procedure is chosen, an application may be made by either party for its costs to be paid by the opposing party.[52]

20.4.3 Appeal to the High Court

There is a limited, further right of appeal against the decision of the Secretary of State on an appeal against a tree replacement notice, under section 289(2) of the 190 Act. Such an appeal may only be on the basis of a point of law. It is thus not possible to reopen the debates as to the facts and merits of the case.

An appeal under this procedure may only be made with the permission of the High Court,[53] which must be sought within 28 days of the date of the Secretary of State's decision – although that time limit may be extended where there is good cause.[54] Again, the law on the corresponding provisions relating to enforcement appeals should be consulted for further details.

There appears to be no reported case of an appeal having been made under section 289 against a tree replacement notice.

20.5 Non-compliance with replacement notice

20.5.1 Required planting carried out by local authority

If it appears that a replacement notice is not going to be complied with, the authority should first consider once again whether it really wishes to take any further action. If it does, it should then, as a matter of good practice, remind the landowner of his or her obligation. If the work is still not done, the authority may then enter the land (it does not even have to give notice, although to do so may be prudent), plant the trees and recover the cost of the works from the landowner.[55]

Section 209 of the 1990 Act, which empowers planning authorities to take such action, is modelled on the corresponding provision of the Act relating to the carrying out of works required by an enforcement notice. Where the owner has to spend money complying with a replacement notice served because of the removal of trees by a third party (such as a previous owner), or has to reimburse the authority for its expenses in relation to such a notice, the expenditure is deemed to have been incurred on behalf of that other person[56] – thus leaving the way open to the owner recovering it as a civil debt. And if someone (such as a lessee or licensee) prevents the owner from complying with the notice, the court may order that person to desist.[57]

Anyone obstructing the authority in the exercise of these powers is liable on summary conviction to a fine of up to Level 3.[58]

There is a provision in the Act enabling the Secretary of State to make

---

[51] TCPA 1990, s. 208(7), (8), substituted by PCA 1991, s. 23.
[52] See DETR Guide, 2000, para. 12.8.
[53] TCPA 1990, s. 289(6).
[54] Civil Procedure Rules 1998 (S.I. 1998 No. 3132), Sched. 1, Order 94, r. 12(1), (2).
[55] TCPA 1990, s. 209(1).
[56] TCPA 1990, s. 209(2).
[57] Public Health Act 1936, s. 289, applied by TCPA 1990, s. 209(3), (4); TCP General Regulations 1992 (S.I. 1992 No. 1492), reg. 14.
[58] See Appendix C.

regulations under which expenses incurred by a local authority under these provisions (including a reasonable sum in respect of overheads[59]) may be registered as a charge on the land, binding subsequent purchasers[60]; but it appears that the power has not been exercised in relation to replacement notices.[61]

20.5.2 Prosecution for non-compliance

Corresponding provisions relating to planning enforcement notices and listed building enforcement notices enable the planning authority to carry out the required works and reclaim the cost from the owners; but they also make it an offence to fail to comply with a notice which has come into effect. There is no corresponding offence in relation to tree replacement notices, but the Government has agreed that this should be rectified.[62]

---

[59] Local Government Act 1974, s. 36.
[60] TCPA 1990, s. 209(5).
[61] Compare TCP General Regulations 1992 (S.I. 1992 1492), reg. 14(2) (enforcement notices); regulation 14(3) (waste land notices).
[62] *Tree Preservation Orders: Review*, DOE, 1994, paras 2.49, 2.50.

Chapter 21

Trees in Conservation Areas

21.1 Introduction

21.1.1 Conservation areas

Conservation areas are areas of special architectural or historic interest, the character or appearance of which it is desirable to preserve or enhance.[1] They were first introduced in the Civic Amenities Act 1967, but the only control mechanisms at that stage were a requirement for planning authorities to publicise planning applications in a conservation area, and to have regard to the character and appearance of the area in carrying out any of their planning functions. Although in some cases trees might well be a significant element in that character and appearance, there was no explicit mention of trees in the legislation as first introduced.

It was not until the Town and Country Amenities Act 1974 that some control was introduced over works to trees in conservation areas. The possible rationale behind such control has already been considered[2]; but, essentially, it not only recognises that trees may be an element in the character of conservation areas,[3] but also provides (albeit on a somewhat clumsy basis) a mechanism to control works to trees which are collectively of value, even if not of sufficient worth to justify individual tree preservation orders. It also enables planning authorities to have a chance to make orders on specific trees and groups of trees at the time when works are proposed, rather than having to survey all the trees in their area and make orders on a precautionary basis.

The broad principle underlying the legislation as it is now is thus that anyone proposing to carry out any works to a tree in a conservation area is required to give six weeks' written notice to the planning authority. That requirement is, inevitably, subject to numerous exceptions, considered in **21.2**. The procedure for giving notice, and the options open to the authority on receiving such notification, are considered at **21.3**. As with trees protected by tree preservation orders, carrying out works to trees in conservation areas without the necessary notice having been given is a criminal offence (see **21.4**); and there is a duty to plant replacement trees in certain circumstances (**21.5**).

---

[1]   Planning (Listed Buildings and Conservation Areas) Act 1990, s. 69(1).
[2]   See **15.7.1**.
[3]   *R v Canterbury City Council, ex p. Halford* [1992] 2 PLR 137; see **15.7.2**.

The protective control mechanism applying to trees in conservation areas is thus significantly different from that which applies to trees under tree preservation orders; and it is designed to operate less onerously to landowners and tree surgeons. It follows that trees in conservation areas are not, as is sometimes claimed, subject to "blanket tree preservation orders"; as the judge in one case put it: "being in a conservation area gives trees a measure of protection. But being the subject of a tree preservation order is better."[4] However, whether the distinction is more apparent than real must be open to question.[5]

21.2 Need to notify tree works to local authority

21.2.1 General requirement

The basic requirement, imposed by section 211 of the Town and Country Planning Act 1990, is that anyone proposing to carry out any works of any consequence to a tree in a conservation area, other than one which is protected by a tree preservation order, must give written notice to the appropriate local planning authority. Works to a tree that is protected by an order obviously need actual consent from the authority, under the terms of the order, in a conservation area just as anywhere else.

The works to which this applies in principle are "any act which might be prohibited by a tree preservation order"[6] – that is, "the cutting down, topping, lopping, uprooting, wilful damage or wilful destruction of trees".[7] The meaning of those terms has already been considered,[8] but broadly speaking they cover between them any works to a tree other than mere pruning. The requirement must logically also apply to the causing or permitting of others (such as tree surgeons) to carry out such works.[9]

There are, however, a number of exceptions to this requirement, which are set out in regulations made under section 212 of the 1990 Act. The current exceptions are listed in regulation 10 of the TCP (Trees) Regulations 1999,[10] and effectively mean that no notice needs to be given in the following cases:

- works to a tree in a conservation area in circumstances where consent would not be required if that tree were subject to a tree preservation order;

- works carried out as part of approved forestry operations;

- works by, or on behalf of, a local planning authority; and

- works to small trees.

Each of these is explored below.

---

[4] *R v Canterbury City Council, ex p. Halford* [1992] 2 PLR 137, per McCullough J. at p. 145F.
[5] And see *Tree Preservation Orders: Review*, DOE, 1994, para. 2.54.
[6] TCPA 1990, s. 211(1).
[7] TCPA 1990, s. 198(3)(a).
[8] See **17.2**.
[9] *R v Bournemouth Justices, ex p. Bournemouth Corporation* (1970) 21 P. & C.R. 163; see **19.2**.
[10] S.I. 1999 No. 1892.

21.2.2 *Works exempt from the need for consent under a tree preservation order*

The first group of exemptions mean, in effect, that the planning authority does not need to be notified of works to a tree in a conservation area in circumstances where consent would not be required if that tree were subject to a tree preservation order. This is no more than common sense, since it would be odd if some trees that were not subject to an order were subject to greater protection than those trees which were.

Regulation 10(1)(a) of the 1999 Regulations thus provides that no notice needs to be given to the authority of the following categories of works:

". . . the cutting down, uprooting, topping or lopping of a tree in the circumstances mentioned in section 198(6) or in article 5 of the prescribed form of tree preservation order set out in the Schedule to these Regulations".

The circumstances there referred to have been discussed already, in the context of works to trees protected by preservation orders. There is no point in repeating that discussion, save to note where it may be found.

First, then, section 198(6) of the 1990 Act provides that no order shall apply to the cutting down, topping or lopping of a tree:

- where the tree is dying or dead (see **17.3.1**) or has become dangerous (**17.3.2** to **17.3.4**);

- in compliance with a statutory obligation (**17.4**); or

- so far as may be necessary for the prevention or abatement of a nuisance (**17.5**).

Precisely the same exemptions apply to the need to notify the planning authority of tree works in conservation areas. It may be noted, for example, that the case of *Smith v Oliver*,[11] already explored in some detail,[12] arose as a result of a failure to notify the planning authority of works to be carried out to a tree in a conservation area that was alleged to have been dangerous.

Where a tree in a conservation area is removed without notice having been given to the authority, solely in reliance upon any of the exemptions in section 198(6), noted above, the person responsible is required to plant a replacement unless the authority agree that a replacement is not necessary.[13]

Secondly, article 5 of the 1999 Model Order prescribes a series of exemptions from the need for consent under the order – and thus from the need to notify the authority in relation to works in a conservation area. These fall principally into three categories:

- some works by, or at the request of, statutory undertakers and other public bodies – largely in circumstances where works to trees are necessary to ensure the safe and efficient operation of their undertakings (see **17.7.1**, **17.7.3** and **17.7.5**);

[11] [1989] 2 PLR 1.
[12] See **5.10.1** and **17.3.2**.
[13] TCPA 1990, s. 213(1)(b), (2); and see **21.5.2**.

- works required to carry out development for which planning permission has been granted (**17.8.3**); and

- some works to fruit trees (**17.9.5**).

These exemptions, each of which is subject to various conditions and limitations, have been explored as noted above. It should also be noted, however, that where the Model Orders are differently worded, it is the provisions of the 1999 Model Order which are applied to the need for notification of works in conservation areas. That is principally of significance in relation to fruit trees, where the extent of the exemption in the 1999 Order is very much narrower than that of the corresponding exemptions in earlier orders.

21.2.3 Works carried out as part of approved forestry operations

The next group of exemptions relates to forestry operations approved by the Forestry Commission. Just as there is no point in obtaining both a felling licence and consent under a tree preservation order, so too there is no need notify the planning authority of works which have been approved by the Commission.

Regulation 10(1)(b),(c) of the 1999 Regulations thus provides that no notice needs to be given to the authority of the following categories of works:

> ". . . (b)   the cutting down of a tree in accordance with a felling licence granted by the Forestry Commissioners under Part II (Commissioners' power to control felling of trees) of the Forestry Act 1967;
>
> (c)   the cutting down of a tree in accordance with a plan of operations or other working plan approved by the Forestry Commissioners, and for the time being in force, under a forestry dedication covenant entered into under section 5 (forestry dedication covenants and agreements) of the Forestry Act 1967 or under the conditions of a grant or loan made under section 1 (finance for forestry) of the Forestry Act 1979."

This is much more straightforward than the complex statutory scheme which operates where works are carried out to a tree protected by a preservation order, as part of forestry operations.[14] In essence, once the Commission has considered works to trees which happen to be within a conservation area, and has given its approval – in the form of either a felling licence or a grant or loan – there is no need for any involvement by the local planning authority.

In practice, however, where an applicant for a felling licence or a grant indicates on the relevant form that the proposed works include the felling of trees in a conservation area, the Forestry Commission will always consult the planning authority on the proposal.[15]

21.2.4 Works by or on behalf of a local planning authority

Where tree works are to be carried out by, or on behalf of, the local planning authority which would normally have to be notified if the works were being carried out by anyone else, the authority obviously does not have to notify itself.

---

[14]   para. (b) of regulation 10(1) is equivalent to s. 15(6) of the FA 1967 (see **14.4.2**); para. (c) is equivalent to s. 200(3) of the TCPA 1990 (see **17.6.1**).

[15]   See **14.4.4**.

Equally, however, no notice has to be given where the works are to be carried out by another local planning authority – so that, for example, works to be carried out by the county council do not have to be notified to the district council.[16]

This also means that no notice has to be given where works are to be carried out by a department of the planning authority (such as the housing or highways department) other than that which has responsibility for trees. It is therefore important that a good working relationship is maintained between the various departments, to ensure that all concerned are aware of best practice, as to whether and, if so, how works should be carried out.

21.2.5 Works to small trees

The final group of exemptions relates to work to small trees. By virtue of regulation 10(1) of the 1999 Regulations, notice does not have to be given to the planning authority of the following:

". . . (e)   the cutting down or uprooting –

        (i)   of a tree whose diameter does not exceed 75 millimetres; or

        (ii)   where carried out for the sole purpose of improving the growth of other trees, of a tree whose diameter does not exceed 100 millimetres; or

(f)   the topping or lopping of a tree whose diameter does not exceed 75 millimetres."

This is relatively straightforward, save that regulation 10(2) provides that the diameter is to be measured over its bark at a point 1.5 metres (about chest height) above the natural ground level. A multi-stemmed tree only comes within the exemption if all of its stems are smaller than the relevant size.

Where a tree is cut down or uprooted in reliance upon this exemption, it would be wise for evidence to be retained as to its size, as the burden will be on the person responsible to prove that it was within the exemption in the event of any future challenge (or even prosecution) by the planning authority.[17]

21.3 Notification procedure

21.3.1 Initial notification

The notification of works to be carried out to a tree in a conservation area is to be made in writing to "the local planning authority".[18]

The relevant local planning authority will obviously be the only local authority (usually called a borough, district or county borough council) in any of the areas in which there is now a unitary system of local government – that is, Greater London and the other major conurbations,[19] all parts of Wales,[20] and some areas

---

[16]   TCP (T) Regulations 1999, reg. 10(1)(d).
[17]   See **21.4.2**.
[18]   TCPA 1990, s. 198(1).
[19]   TCPA 1990, s. 1(2). The Common Council of the City of London is treated as a Borough Council for this purpose (TCPA 1990, s. 336(1)).
[20]   TCPA 1990, s. 1(1B), inserted by Local Government (Wales) Act 1994.

of England.[21] In the remainder of England, the relevant authority will generally be the district council[22] (or the Broads Authority in the Norfolk and Suffolk Broads[23]).

In national parks, in England or Wales, the relevant national park authorities have concurrent powers with the district councils, where they exist, or unitary authorities.[24] It is thus not entirely clear to whom notification should in fact be given; but it would be prudent before carrying out any works to telephone the appropriate district council or unitary authority, to see whether the park authority may wish to be notified as well.

There is no prescribed form on which the notification is to be given; some authorities have a standard form, but their use cannot be compulsory. Oddly, there appears to be no requirement that notice under section 211 should even be written, rather than oral – although it will obviously be a great deal easier for the person carrying out the works to avoid subsequent problems (and possible prosecution) if the notice is in writing. The notification must, in any event, clearly specify precisely which trees are involved, and what works are proposed[25]; a copy of the relevant Ordnance Survey map would be helpful, as would photographs of the trees, but, again, neither can be insisted upon.

The advice from the Secretary of State is as follows:

"It is vitally important that the section 211 notice sets out clearly what work is proposed. This should be straightforward if the proposal is to fell a tree, as long as it is clearly identified. But if the proposal is to prune a tree, the section 211 notice should clarify exactly what work is envisaged. A proposal simply to 'top' the tree or to 'lop' or 'cut back' some branches is too vague, because it fails to describe the extent of the work. People are advised not to submit a section 211 notice until they are in a position to present a clear proposal. They should consider first discussing their ideas with an arboriculturist or the tree officer of the local planning authority."[26]

It is also prudent for the person giving notice to retain a copy of whatever has been sent to the authority.

21.3.2 Action by local authority following receipt of Section 211 notice

A planning authority will normally acknowledge receipt of the Section 211 notice, although there is no requirement for it to do so.[27]

In doing so, the authority should check that the works are not exempt from the need for notification, and that a felling licence is not required (if it is, the person submitting the notice should be invited to contact the Forestry Commission instead). If it discovers that the tree in question is already subject to a tree preservation order, it should point this out to the person proposing the works; if

---

[21] Local Government Changes for England Regulations 1994 (S.I. 1994 No. 867), reg. 5(6), (7); TCPA 1990, s. 1(1), (3). See list at **16.4.2**, n. 83.

[22] TCPA 1990, Sched. 1, para. 14.

[23] TCPA 1990, s. 5(2), (3).

[24] TCPA 1990, s. 4A(4), (5), inserted by Environment Act 1995; Local Government Changes for England Regulations 1994 (S.I. 1994 No. 867), reg. 5(7).

[25] TCPA 1990, s. 211(3)(a).

[26] *DETR Guide*, 2000, para. 9.5.

[27] See *Tree Preservation Orders: Review*, DOE, 1994, para. 2.55.

both parties are content, the Section 211 notice can then simply be treated as if it were an application under the order, and processed accordingly.[28]

Otherwise, the authority should tell the person submitting the notice that the works in question may not lawfully be carried out until either:

- it has indicated in writing that it has no objection to the works; or

- six weeks have elapsed from the date of the notice with no tree preservation order having been made.

The authority's letter should also specify the date marking the end of the six-week period.

A model acknowledgement letter is at Annex 10 to the *DETR Guide*.

The authority may, if it considers it appropriate, publicise the receipt of a Section 211 notice; advice is given as to this in the *DETR Guide*.[29] Whilst, in principle, that may in many cases be sensible, an authority should not forget that the tree owner is entitled to carry out the works if he or she has received no adverse response in the six-week period, and that period may not be extended. It follows that tight deadlines need to be imposed at all stages in the process.

In addition to any such publicity carried out on a discretionary basis, the planning authority is also required (by section 214 of the Act) to maintain a public register of Section 211 notices. Such register must contain the following particulars:

"(1) the address of the land on which the tree stands, and sufficient information to identify the tree and the work proposed;
(2) the date of the section 211 notice, and who served it;
(3) the decision of the LPA (if they make one) and the date of the decision; and
(4) an index for tracing entries."[30]

The register must be publicly available at all reasonable hours.

21.3.3 Possible responses to Section 211 notice

In practical terms, the most important action by the planning authority on receipt of a Section 211 notice is for the appropriate officer (or consultant) to go out and inspect the tree, promptly, in order to consider whether the authority should make a tree preservation order. The rights of entry available to such a person have already been considered, in the context of making tree preservation orders generally.[31]

The decision as to whether an order should be made will involve the same considerations as in any other case, namely:

- is it desirable to make an order in the interests of amenity?

- is the making of an order expedient?[32]

---

[28] See **18.2**. This is possible because no special form is prescribed for an application for consent a tree preservation order.
[29] *DETR Guide*, 2000, para. 9.9.
[30] TCPA 1990, s. 214; *DETR Guide*, 2000, para. 9.10.
[31] See **16.6.1**.
[32] TCPA 1990, s. 198(1).

The matters to be considered under each heading have already been considered generally.[33]

As to amenity, the trees concerned will, by definition, be within a conservation area; it follows that the authority should give particular attention to whether their preservation would be desirable in the interests of preserving or enhancing the character of the area as a whole.[34]

However, even if the planning authority forms the view that the tree concerned is of sufficient merit to justify the making of a tree preservation order, it must then go on to decide whether such an order would be expedient, given the nature of the works proposed. Thus, if the authority considers that, were the tree to be already subject to a preservation order, consent would be given for the works (perhaps because, for example, the roots of the tree are damaging nearby foundations), then it may not be expedient to make a tree preservation order. This would particularly apply where the proposal is to fell the tree.

Where the proposed works are less substantial than outright felling, the authority may consider that the tree in itself merits being protected by a preservation order, but that the works are justifiable. Alternatively, the authority may consider that the works currently proposed may not be acceptable, but that other works having the same or a similar effect would be. In either case, an order should be made, promptly, and the owner informed, first, that the tree is now protected, but secondly, that no objection would be raised were an application to be made for consent under the order to carry out the works in question.

Note that an authority is not entitled to "grant consent subject to conditions", since there is no power for it to do so. If, therefore, it wishes to ensure that works are carried out in a particular way, it will have to make a tree preservation order. It may then notify the person who served the notice that, were an application to be made for consent under the order, consent would probably be granted, but only subject to conditions. If, then, an application is made, and consent is indeed granted subject to those conditions, the applicant has a right of appeal to the Secretary of State.[35] Precisely the same would apply if the authority were willing to see the tree removed, but only if a replacement was planted; it would have to make an order, and grant consent under the order subject to a replacement condition.

Where an authority considers that the tree is of sufficient amenity value to justify the making of an order, and that neither the works proposed nor any others, are acceptable, it should simply make an order without further ado, and inform the owner of the existence of the order and that consent is not likely to be given for the works. For an example of how this works in practice, see *Sherwood and Sherwood v Islington LBC*, already explored in an earlier Chapter.[35a]

A tree preservation order may be made at any time, before or after a formal Section 211 notice is received.[36] But if an order is made after more than six weeks have elapsed since the date of the notice, the tree will be unprotected from the expiry of the 6-week period until the date of the order. There is no provision for the 6-week period to be extended, either by agreement or otherwise.

Where an authority considers that a tree in a conservation area is not worthy of

---

[33] See **15.6.2** to **15.6.4** (amenity) and **15.6.5** (expediency).
[34] Planning (Listed Buildings and Conservation Areas) Act 1990, s. 72; see **15.7.3**.
[35] See **18.5.2**.
[35a] [1996] J.P.L. 925; see **18.3.4**.
[36] *R v North Hertfordshire District Council, ex p. Hyde* [1989] 3 PLR 89.

a tree preservation order, it cannot exercise any control over the carrying out of works to it even where it disapproves of those works. In that situation, its only option is to give advice – either at a meeting or, probably, by sending a suitable leaflet to the person responsible.

Finally, where the local planning authority has no objection to the proposed works specified in the notice, and does not wish to see a replacement tree planted, it may simply do nothing; and the person serving the notice may carry out the works without further ado as soon as the 6-week period has elapsed.[37] The only exception is where two years have gone by since the date of the notice, in which case the whole process has to start all over again, with a new notice being served on the authority. But, clearly, it would be good administrative practice for the authority to notify the person who served the notice that it has no objections, so that the position is clear in the event of any future dispute.

21.3.4 Right of appeal

Where an order is made in response to a Section 211 notice, those affected will have the same rights to object to it as in any other case[38] – and if appropriate to challenge it all the way to the High Court.[39]

Where the authority raises no objection to the proposed works, those adversely affected (such as neighbours) have no right of appeal against the decision, but may seek permission from the High Court for it to be quashed by way of an application for judicial review.

21.4 Unauthorised works to trees in a conservation area

21.4.1 The elements of the offence

It is an offence under section 211 of the 1990 Act to carry out works to a tree in a conservation area without notice having been given to the planning authority, in circumstances where such notice is required.

The scheme of the legislation is to apply section 210 of the Act to offences under section 211 as it applies to breaches of a tree preservation order.[40] As noted in **Chapter 19**, section 210 creates two offences – a more serious offence, under subsection (1), that applies where the tree is lost altogether, and a less serious one, under subsection (4), that applies in other cases.

The elements of the two offences created by section 211 are thus as follows:

(1) the tree in question was in a conservation area at the time of the works;

(2) either [for an offence under section 210(1), as applied by section 211(4)] works were carried out to the tree consisting of:

- the tree being cut down, wilfully destroyed or uprooted; or
- the tree being topped, lopped or wilfully damaged in such a manner that it was likely to be destroyed;

---

[37] TCPA 1990, s. 211(3)(b)(ii).
[38] See **16.6.5**.
[39] See **16.7**.
[40] TCPA 1990, s. 211(4).

or [for an offence under section 210(4), as applied by section 211(4)] works were carried out to the tree consisting of the tree being topped, lopped or wilfully damaged in such a manner that it was not likely to be destroyed; and

(3) the works were executed by the defendant, or he or she aided and abetted, counselled or procured their execution.

To obtain a conviction, each of these must be proved by the prosecution to the criminal standard – that is, beyond reasonable doubt.[41]

The first matter to be proved, obviously, is thus that the tree in question was actually in a conservation area at the time the works to it were carried out.

It has already been pointed out that, in the case of works to a tree protected by a tree preservation order, it is not necessary for the prosecution to show that the person responsible knew of the existence of the order[42]; and it has also been held by the courts that it is not possible for a person to escape conviction for unauthorised works to a listed building by proving that he or she was ignorant of the listing.[43] It is therefore reasonable to assume that the same approach would apply to an offence under section 211; in other words, that it is an offence of strict liability, so that it does not matter whether the accused knew that the tree was in a conservation area.

On the other hand, the Divisional Court has also held, in the case of a breach of a tree preservation order, that the planning authority must be able to show that the relevant order was kept available for public inspection, as required by the relevant Regulations.[44] There is – perhaps surprisingly – no equivalent requirement that the details of every conservation area should be permanently available for public inspection. However, the authority is required to advertise in the local press and the *London Gazette* the initial designation of a conservation area,[45] and to register the existence of the area as a local land charge,[46] which means that at least subsequent purchasers of property will be aware of it.

It would seem, therefore, that to obtain a conviction under section 211, the planning authority would have to:

• produce a copy of the advertisements published at the time the relevant area was designated; and

• show that the designation of the area has indeed been registered as a local land charge.

Alternatively, it may be sufficient for the authority to prove that it had made publicly available details of the conservation area, or even simply that the accused was aware of the existence of the area.

It must be a matter for speculation, as to whether it would be possible in an appropriate case for an owner of land to escape conviction by proving that he or she had no knowledge of the existence of the area, and that the land had not

[41] See **19.2.2**.
[42] *Maidstone BC v Mortimer* [1980] 3 All E.R. 552, [1981] J.P.L. 319; see **19.3.2**.
[43] *R v Wells Street Stipendiary Magistrate ex p. Westminster CC* [1986] 1 W.L.R. 1046, 3 All E.R. 4.
[44] *Vale of Glamorgan BC v Palmer and Bowels* (1983) 81 L.G.R. 678, [1982] J.P.L. 334; see **19.3.2**.
[45] Planning (Listed Buildings and Conservation Areas) Act 1990, s. 70(8).
[46] 1990 Act, s. 69(4).

changed ownership since the area was first designated (so that the registration of the area as a local land charge was irrelevant).

The second and third matters to be proved by the prosecution are that the works in question were actually carried out, and that they were carried out by, or at the behest of, the accused. This will be as for works to a tree protected by a tree preservation order.[47]

21.4.2 Defences to a charge under section 211

The accused will, of course, be able to escape conviction if he or she is able to prove that there was, in fact, no need to have notified the authority in any event. The various exemptions to the requirement to notify an authority under section 211 have been considered already; it will be for an accused to see whether any of them apply in the particular circumstances of the particular case – not for the authority to prove that none of them do.

Secondly, if none of the exemptions apply, the accused will still be able to avoid conviction if he or she can prove that notice of the proposed works was given to the local planning authority, and either:

- that consent had been granted by the authority before the carrying out of the works; or

- that the works were carried out more than six weeks and less than two years after the date of the notice.

This assumes, obviously, that the authority did not impose a tree preservation order on the tree prior to the carrying out of the works. If an order was imposed, then an offence will have been committed, but under section 210 (breach of tree preservation order), rather than section 211 (failure to notify works in a conservation area).

As to the existence of consent, this raises the same issues as those that arise where consent is alleged to have been granted under a tree preservation order.[48]

And if it is alleged that no response has been received from the planning authority, it will obviously be important to have evidence of precisely when the works were carried out.

21.4.3 Decision to prosecute

Finally, careful consideration needs to be given by an authority to the decision whether to institute a prosecution for a failure to notify proposed works to a tree in a conservation area.

It may well be that the authority decides that the tree in question was such that it would not have imposed a tree preservation order on it, even if notice had been given – either because the tree was inherently of insufficient amenity value, or because the works would have been given consent if an order was in existence.[49] Such a conclusion may be reached on the basis of information (photographs and so on) already in the possession of the authority. Or the person responsible for the works may provide such information on being challenged by the authority. In

---

[47] See **19.3.4** to **19.3.7**.
[48] See **19.4.3**.
[49] See **21.3.3**.

those circumstances, a prosecution – although technically possible – would serve little purpose, and would, therefore, probably not be in the public interest.[50]

Alternatively, it may be that the authority forms the conclusion that it definitely would have imposed a tree preservation order on the tree had it been given the opportunity – again, on the basis of information in its possession or supplied by others (such as by neighbours complaining of the loss of the tree). In those circumstances, a prosecution might well be justified – subject to the need to be sure that the evidence available was sufficient.

More difficult will be the case where it is uncertain, on the basis of information available after the event, whether or not a tree preservation order would have been imposed. It is true that an offence will have been committed, and that it should therefore be possible (subject to the availability of evidence) to secure a conviction; but it is likely that the penalty will be small. An authority may well decide in such a case simply to caution those responsible, rather than incur the not insubstantial costs of mounting a prosecution. One exception to this might be in the case of a flagrant breach – where, for example, a developer fells a number of trees in a conservation area in order to obtain a clear site for building, without giving notice.

And even where an offence has occurred, it may well be more appropriate in some cases to seek the planting of replacement trees,[51] rather than to mount a prosecution, as that will, at least in the long term, do more for the character and appearance of the conservation area.

21.4.4 Procedure and evidence

The procedural and evidential matters already considered in relation to prosecutions under section 210 (contravention of tree preservation orders)[52] apply, unsurprisingly, with equal force to prosecutions under that section as applied by section 211 (conservation area trees).

21.5 Duty to plant replacement trees

21.5.1 Replacement of trees in conservation areas removed without notice having been given

Where a tree in a conservation area is removed, uprooted or destroyed without notice having been given to the planning authority as required by section 211, the owner of the land is under a duty "to plant another tree of an appropriate size and species at the same place as soon as he reasonably can".[53] That duty does not apply where the authority has agreed to dispense with it.[54]

This duty is generally the same as that which applies where a tree subject to a tree preservation order has been felled without consent, which has already been considered,[55] – save that there are no special rules in relation to trees in woodlands. And the duty to replant trees in conservation areas is enforced in the

---

[50] See **19.5.2**.
[51] See **21.5.1**.
[52] See **19.5.3 to 19.5.5**.
[53] TCPA 1990, s. 213(1)(a).
[54] TCPA 1990, s. 213(2).
[55] See **20.2.2, 20.2.3**.

same way – that is, by means of the planning authority serving a notice under section 207 of the 1990 Act.[56]

21.5.2 Replacement of conservation area trees in other circumstances

A similar duty, to plant another tree of an appropriate size and species at the same place as soon as reasonably possible, applies where a tree in a conservation area is removed, uprooted or destroyed, or dies, when its cutting down is only authorised – that is, exempt from the need to notify the authority – because it is in one of the cases referred to in section 198(6) of the 1990 Act.[57] Those cases are as follows:

- Section 198(6)(a): the tree is dying or dead or has become dangerous[58];

- Section 198(6)(b): the works are necessary:

  (i) to comply with an obligation imposed by an Act of Parliament[59]; or
  (ii) to prevent or abate a nuisance.[60]

The duty to replace dying, dead and dangerous trees in conservation areas is, in principle, the same as the duty to replace such trees where they are protected by a tree preservation order; that duty has already been considered.[61] Here, too, the duty may be waived by the planning authority on the application of the owner of the tree; otherwise it is enforced by the service of a notice under section 207.[62]

However, whether due to defective drafting or for some other reason, the duty in relation to conservation area trees is more extensive than that which applies to trees protected by preservation orders, even though the latter will, by definition, be of greater value. This arises because section 206(1)(b) (the provision relating to the replacement of trees protected by a tree preservation order) refers only to section 198(6)(a), whereas section 213(1)(b) of the Act (relating to trees in conservation areas) unfortunately refers, albeit indirectly, to the whole of section 198(6). It follows that it will not normally be appropriate for the authority to insist on the planting of replacement trees in either of the cases specified in section 198(6)(b).

---

[56] TCPA 1990, s. 213(3); see **20.3**.
[57] TCPA 1990, ss. 213(1)(b), 212(4).
[58] See **17.3**.
[59] See **17.4**.
[60] See **17.5**.
[61] See **20.2.1, 20.2.2**.
[62] TCPA 1990, s. 213(3); see **20.3**.

Chapter 22

Trees in Churchyards

22.1 Introduction

22.1.1 The significance of churchyard trees

Many fine trees – including, of course, some of the finest specimen yews – are to be found in the churchyards surrounding Church of England churches. The law applies in general to trees in churchyards as to those elsewhere; but there are some additional provisions that may need to be borne in mind.

It has already been noted that the care and maintenance of a churchyard, and thus the upkeep of the trees within it, has for many years been the responsibility of the parochial church council (the PCC).[1] This applies equally to churchyards that are in active use and to those which have been closed for burials by Order in Council under the Burial Acts.[2] However, where a closed churchyard has been transferred to a local authority, under the provisions of the Local Government Act 1972,[3] that authority will also have taken over the functions of the PCC with respect to maintenance and repair.

22.1.2 The applicability of secular legislation

A felling licence[4] is never required for works to trees in a churchyard, regardless of the scale of the operation.[5]

However, local authorities may, and indeed frequently do, make tree preservation orders in respect of trees in churchyards; and churchyards are often included within conservation areas. In such cases, the relevant controls under the Town and Country Planning Act 1990[6] apply exactly as elsewhere – there is no "ecclesiastical exemption" from local authority control over works to trees (as there is in the case of building works to churches which are listed).

Consent is thus generally required from the relevant local planning authority

---

[1] Parochial Church Councils (Powers) Measure 1956, s. 4(1)(ii)(c); Canon F14; Care of Churches and Ecclesiastical Jurisdiction Measure 1991, s. 6(1), as amended by Church of England (Miscellaneous Provisions) Measure 1995, s. 13; see **2.1.7**.

[2] CCEJM 1991, s. 6(5).

[3] 1972 Act, s. 215.

[4] See **Chap. 14**.

[5] FA 1967, s. 9(2)(b).

[6] See **Chaps 15 to 20** (tree preservation orders) and **Chap. 21** (conservation areas).

for the lopping, topping, felling or uprooting of any tree that is subject to a tree preservation order. And notice must generally be given to the authority of any works to trees in a conservation area, which enables the authority, if it wishes, to impose a preservation order on the tree. As has been noted earlier in this Part of this book, both of these requirements are subject to numerous exceptions, but few of those are likely to be of relevance in the context of churchyard trees.

There is, in addition, a specific requirement for the quinquennial inspection of a church to extend to every tree in its churchyard, whether open or closed, that is the subject of a tree preservation order[7] – a practice that might be emulated with advantage by other substantial landowners.

22.1.3 The faculty jurisdiction

The freedom of an incumbent (rector or vicar), priest-in-charge or PCC to carry out any works which affect a church or churchyard is subject to the need to obtain consent from "the ordinary" – that is, in practice, a faculty granted by the archdeacon or, in the case of more major proposals, the consistory court under the chancellor of the diocese. Thus, a faculty will generally be needed for any works of consequence to any existing trees in a churchyard, and for the planting of any new ones; and this will be so whether or not there is a need to obtain consent from, or to notify, the local authority under the Town and Country Planning Act 1990.

The operation of the faculty system in relation to trees is the subject of the remainder of this Chapter. The relevant legislation is principally to be found in the Care of Churches and Ecclesiastical Jurisdiction Measure 1991 ("the 1991 Measure") and the Faculty Jurisdiction Rules 2000 ("the 2000 Rules"),[8] which came into force on January 1, 2001.

There is a broadly similar system operating in Wales in relation to churchyards of the Church in Wales.

22.2 Trees and the faculty jurisdiction

22.2.1 Requirement for a faculty

The extent of control by consistory courts over works to existing churchyard trees and the planting of new ones was in the past the subject of some uncertainty.

Prior to the coming into force of the 1991 Measure, on March 1, 1993, section 20(1) of the Repair of Benefice Buildings Measure 1972 provided that the consent of the parsonages board had to be obtained for:

- the felling, lopping or topping of the trees of a parsonage house which in the opinion of the diocesan surveyor (after taking such expert advice, if any, as he thinks fit) ought to be preserved[9]; and

- the felling of the timber growing in a churchyard.

---

[7]   Inspection of Churches Measure 1955, s. 1A(c), inserted by 1991 Measure, Sched. 3.
[8]   S.I. 2000 No. 2047, replacing the Faculty Jurisdiction Rules 1992 (S.I. 1992 No. 2882).
[9]   Repair of Benefice Buildings Measure 1972, s. 4(3).

It was further provided explicitly that the consent of the ordinary[10] was not necessary for any felling in accordance with section 20[11] – thus avoiding an unhelpful duplication of control.

The need for the consent of the parsonages board for works to churchyard trees was repealed by section 6(4) of the 1991 Measure. It is probably not by chance that it was the 1991 Measure which also explicitly declared (at section 11(1)) that the jurisdiction of the consistory court of a diocese extended to the churchyards appertaining to all parish churches in the diocese. Thus, the effect of the 1991 Measure was (amongst other things) to introduce, or at least to declare the existence of, a single system of control extending to the whole of every churchyard, including not only the graves, funerary monuments, lychgate and other structures, but also the ground itself and the trees and shrubs which are a part of that ground.

It seems probable that in practice many, if not most, works to trees have in the past been carried out without any authorisation from the board (prior to 1993) or a faculty (thereafter). The rationale for that state of affairs, if one were sought, was no doubt that works to trees were considered to be of no particular importance – or, at any rate, of no direct relevance to the life and work of the church as a local centre of worship and mission.

22.2.2 Guidance by diocesan chancellors

The chancellor of each diocese is to give written guidance to all PCCs in the diocese as to the planting, felling, lopping and topping of trees in churchyards, under section 6(3) of the 1991 Measure. This is a slightly strange provision, as the chancellor is not required to give such guidance in relation to any other area of technical expertise. However, it does enable the chancellor to make a list of all the things to do with trees which do not require a faculty – possibly, in some cases, provided that they have been authorised by the archdeacon – and thus to reduce the amount of bureaucracy associated with the faculty system.[12] It also facilitates the dissemination of more general advice as to the planting and care of trees in churchyards.

Such guidance is to be prepared after consultation with the revelvant diocesan advisory committee (DAC); and each DAC should therefore take care to ensure that amongst its members is at least one with arboricultural knowledge and experience. And it may well be sensible for the arboricultural officers of the relevant local authorities to be consulted as well.

The guidance, once prepared, should be generally available; a copy may be obtainable from the secretary of the DAC, or from the diocesan registry.

22.2.3 Works of little significance

It has already been noted that the chancellor's guidance under section 6(3) of the 1991 Measure may provide that certain works can be carried out without a faculty.[13] As an alternative, such provision may be included within the guidance

---

[10] See **22.1.3**.
[11] Repair of Benefice Buildings Measure 1972, s. 20(5).
[12] See the speech of Chancellor Sheila Cameron QC, in the debate on the draft Faculty Jurisdiction Rules, July 10, 2000; General Synod, Report of Proceedings, p. 262.
[13] See **22.2.2**

that every chancellor is to give, under section 11(8) of the 1991 Measure, as to those matters within the jurisdiction of the consistory court which he considers to be of such a minor nature that they may be undertaken without a faculty. These matters are sometimes referred to as the *de minimis* rules (from the Latin phrase *de minimis non curat lex*: the law takes no account of trifles). However, under the guidance currently in force within most dioceses, no works to existing churchyard trees fall within this category.

It would, of course, be possible for a chancellor to direct (under either section 6(3) or section 11(8)) that minor works to trees can be carried out without a faculty, provided that they are done in accordance with the guidance given under section 6(3), and provided that they are not of great significance. The latter proviso could, in turn, be specified by reference to the relevant categories of works exempt from the need for consent under secular legislation, for example:

"(a) in the case of any tree:

   (i)   the carrying out of pruning works, as distinct from lopping or topping[14]; and
   (ii) the carrying out of works required by a notice under paragraph 9 of Schedule 4 of the Electricity Act 1989;

(b) in the case of a tree that is in a conservation area but not subject to a tree preservation order:

   (i)   the cutting down, uprooting, lopping or topping of a tree whose diameter does not exceed 75 millimetres (measured as in regulation 10(2) of the Town and Country Planning (Trees) Regulations 1999); and
   (ii) where carried out for the sole purpose of improving the growth of other trees, the cutting down or uprooting of a tree whose diameter does not exceed 100 mm (as thus measured); and

(c) the lopping or topping of a tree that is neither in a conservation area nor subject to a tree preservation order."

The above list reflects the various exemptions from secular control, so far as relevant, and would, if adopted, minimise the scope for conflict between the church and those other bodies which would like to exercise some measure of control. No doubt other lists of minor operations could be devised.

However, until such a direction is made, any proposal for the carrying out of works to a tree in a churchyard, at least in theory, needs to be authorised by the grant of a faculty. And it is likely that, however the exemptions from control are drafted, many if not all felling operations (as opposed to pruning, lopping and topping) will always come within the scope of those requiring a faculty.

22.2.4 Dangerous trees

Works to a tree are often claimed to be necessary because some or all of it is dangerous. There is no formal exemption from the need for a faculty in such circumstances; but clearly, where a tree is indeed dangerous, steps should be taken as soon as possible to remove the danger – if necessary authorised by the court as a matter of urgency under the procedure in rule 8(3)(a) of the 2000 Rules, or retrospectively under rule 10(1)(a). It is noteworthy that, under the provisions of section 20 of the Repair of Benefice Buildings Measure 1972, already noted,

---

[14] *Unwin v Hanson* [1891] 2 Q.B. 115, CA; see **17.2**.

consent was not required for the felling of timber "necessary to avoid immediate danger to the occupants of . . . [any] building or to the general public".

The advantage of urgent works being authorised by a faculty (if necessary, a confirmatory faculty granted after the event) is, of course, that a condition can be imposed requiring a replacement tree to be planted where appropriate, since there is no automatic requirement to that effect as there is (at least in some cases) under planning legislation.

However, claims as to the supposed urgency of works to trees need to be considered with caution. First, it may be that the condition and location of a tree are such that all or part of it is likely to cause harm to persons or animals (for example, by falling onto them), so that it can indeed properly be said to be dangerous. On the other hand, it may be that the only harm which seems likely is to property – in the form of, for example, a building being damaged by a branch or a whole tree falling onto it, or its foundations being damaged due to the underlying ground subsiding as a result of excessive moisture uptake by nearby tree roots. See the discussion earlier in this book in relation to the need for consent under a tree preservation order.[15]

Secondly, even where a tree is indeed dangerous, it may be appropriate to solve the problem (possibly on a temporary basis) by some means other than works to the tree. Thus, for a danger to exist, there must be both a defective tree and a potential target. Where, for example, it is feared that a tree may fall so as to injure those using a path through a churchyard, it may be sufficient simply to close the path while expert arboricultural advice is obtained as to the best way forward. And where the situation is such as to justify works to the tree, those works should be limited to the part which is the cause of the danger: the existence of a dangerous branch does not justify the felling of an entire tree.

22.2.5 Faculty procedure

A faculty is granted on a petition made to the consistory court of the diocese concerned; the procedure is now to be found in the Faculty Jurisdiction Rules 2000,[16] which came into force on January 1, 2001. These, for the first time, recognised that faculty petitions (applications) relating to proposed works to trees are quite different to those relating to building works, and introduced a special procedure accordingly. The applicants will normally be the incumbent and churchwardens, but where the tree is growing (or is to be planted) in a closed churchyard maintained by a local authority, that authority should be the applicant.[17]

The first step is for the applicants to complete Form 16 in Appendix C to the Rules, which has been designed specifically for petitions relating to trees, and which seeks full details of the proposed works. They should send the form to the DAC,[18] accompanied by a plan of the churchyard concerned (if necessary, just a sketch plan), showing the location of the tree or trees concerned and any planting sites[19]; it would also be helpful to include any relevant photographs. The DAC will consider the proposal, and set out its views on Form 1, which will be sent to

[15] See **17.3.3**.
[16] S.I. 2000 No. 2047.
[17] 2000 Rules, introductory note to Form 16 in Appendix C.
[18] 2000 Rules, r. 3(4).
[19] 2000 Rules, "question" 4 in Form 16.

the applicants. They should then send the completed Form 16, together with the supporting material considered by the DAC, on to the diocesan registry,[20] and give appropriate public notice of the proposal.[21] It is permissible for an applicant to submit a petition without having first sought the views of the DAC, but its views will have to be sought later anyway,[22] so there is no point in not consulting it at the outset – and it will in any event often be able to provide helpful advice.

Perhaps surprisingly, no works to trees fell within the categories of works that could be authorised by an Archdeacon,[23] or fall within those which can be so authorised under the corresponding provisions in the 2000 Rules. Any faculty relating to trees, therefore, has to be granted by the chancellor – even though the guidance prepared under section 6(3) in some dioceses seems to suggest otherwise.

Objections to a proposal may be made by anyone appearing to the chancellor to have sufficient interest in the matter – which includes anyone resident in the parish, and the local planning authority, and may extend to a local amenity group.[24] An unopposed petition may be determined without further ado.[25] An opposed petition may (exceptionally) be determined following an oral hearing if either party or the chancellor requires it[26]; but the vast majority of petitions are determined on the basis of written representations.[27]

22.2.6 Appeal from the consistory court

An appeal lies against the decision of a consistory court on a faculty petition to the Court of Arches (in the Province of Canterbury – roughly the southern two thirds of England) or to the Chancery Court of York (the remainder).[28]

Leave to appeal is required, either from the consistory court concerned or from the relevant appellate court.

22.3 The basis on which control is exercised

22.3.1 General principles

Where works to trees are not urgently necessary to remove a danger, there is no prescribed test as to the approach to be adopted in considering faculty petitions. And there have been very few reported decisions of the consistory courts relating to trees. However, the matter has recently been considered from first principles in *Re St Kenelm, Upton Snodsbury*.[29]

As noted above,[30] the effect of section 6 of the 1991 Measure, and the amendments made by it to the 1955 and 1972 Measures, was to introduce a single

---

[20] FJ Rules 2000, r. 4(3).
[21] The detailed requirements are set out at FJ Rules 2000, r. 6.
[22] FJ Rules 2000, rr. 4(4), 14.
[23] Under the provisions of Appendix A to the Faculty Jurisdiction Rules 1992 (S.I. 1992 No. 2882) or Appendix A to the Faculty Jurisdiction Rules 2000.
[24] FJ Rules 2000, r. 16.
[25] FJ Rules 2000, r. 17.
[26] FJ Rules 2000, rr. 18–21, 23, 25.
[27] FJ Rules 2000, r. 26.
[28] In the provinces of Canterbury and York respectively; see Ecclesiastical Jurisdiction Measure 1963, s. 7, Faculty Jurisdiction (Appeals) Rules 1998 (S.I. No. 1998 1713).
[29] Worcester Consistory Court, November 2001, unreported; noted briefly at (2002) 6 Ecc. L.J. 293.
[30] See **22.2.1**.

system of control extending to the whole of every churchyard, including the trees and shrubs which are a part of it. In relation to the control of works to church buildings, a series of decisions of the consistory courts and the appeal courts have made it clear that a consistory court must have regard both to the role of a church as a local centre of worship and mission, and to its importance (if any) as a building of special architectural or historic interest;[31] and clearly practical considerations such as those relating to maintenance and repairs will also be relevant. In the case of churchyards, by contrast, it will not be often that an issue will arise that will affect the role of a church as a local centre of worship and mission (other than the pastoral concerns that regularly arise in connection with burial and exhumation).

On the other hand, issues may well arise that affect:

- the setting of the church building and thus its character and appearance as a building of special interest;

- the structures within the churchyard, and in particular (but by no means exclusively) those of special interest, and their settings;

- the character and appearance of the churchyard as a whole; and

- the contribution of the churchyard to the character and appearance of the area surrounding it.

And, again, practical considerations, such as those relating to maintenance and repairs, will frequently be very important.

Against that background, the correct approach to be adopted by a consistory court in relation to proposals to carry out works to existing trees would seem to depend on whether or not the tree is subject to a tree preservation order, or is in a conservation area. There are thus several possible scenarios.

22.3.2 Trees subject to a tree preservation order

Where a tree in a churchyard has been made the subject of a tree preservation order, this is a clear statement by the planning authority that it regards the tree to be of especial value; as is reflected by the criminal liability attaching to the carrying out of almost any works without its explicit consent.[32]

It follows that, where the authority or the Secretary of State has decided to granted consent under the order for the carrying out of works to such a tree, it would only be appropriate for the consistory court to reconsider the matter if there was some ground of objection which had not been fully taken into account in that decision – particularly where that ground related to the work and mission of the church.

This approach echoes that of consistory courts deciding cases where planning permission is needed for a proposal as well as a faculty. Thus, for example, in *Re St Mary's, King's Worthy*,[32a] the Winchester Consistory Court (Clark Ch) stated:

". . . there is a strong argument for saying that, once the planning authority has granted permission for a particular proposal, issues [such as traffic flow and parking availability]

---

[31] See, for example, the decision of the Court of Arches in *Re St Luke's, Maidstone* [1995] Fam 1.
[32] See **Chapter 19**.
[32a] (1998) 5 Ecc. L.J. 133.

ought not to be raised for reconsideration by a consistory court. In the exercise of my discretion, however, I have agreed to hear evidence relating to these matters, but only on the basis that the decision whether or not to grant a faculty is unlikely to be affected by it unless the evidence is of a very strong and compelling character. In other words, I shall assume the planning authority made the correct decision in this respect, unless there is convincing evidence to the contrary."

The decision of the Blackburn Consistory Court in *St James, Stalmine*[32b] is to similar effect. The position would seem to be the same in relation to proposals for tree works that require consent under a tree preservation order as well as a faculty.

And, of course, where the planning authority, and the Secretary of State on appeal, have refused to authorise works to a tree protected by a preservation order, only in the most exceptional circumstances is there likely to be any point in the consistory court considering an application for a faculty – since, even were one to be granted, it would still be a breach of the order for the works to be carried out.

22.3.3 Trees in conservation areas

Where a tree is in a conservation area (but not subject to a tree preservation order), the authority must be notified of proposed works to trees under section 211 of the Town and Country Planning Act 1990[33] – here, too, a failure to comply will lead to prosecution. If, following such notification, the authority wishes to prevent the works, it must impose a preservation order on the tree. The position would then be as with any other tree protected by a preservation order.[34]

If the planning authority explicitly approves the works, then, again, it would only be appropriate for the court to reconsider the matter if there was some ground of objection that had not been fully taken into account.

If, on the other hand, the authority declines to make any decision, the consistory court must do so: the position is as with trees outside conservation areas.[35]

22.3.4 Works to trees in other cases

The third scenario is where a tree is neither subject to a tree preservation order nor within a conservation area – or where it is in a conservation area and the authority has declined to make a decision. In such a situation, the court must decide.

In this scenario, the right approach would seem to be to consider, first, in the light of the four factors highlighted above:

- the amenity value of the tree in itself;
- its contribution to the amenity value of the churchyard as a whole; and
- any loss of amenity likely to arise from the carrying out of the works.

It would also be appropriate to consider the value of the tree as a habitat for

---

[32b] (2000) 6 Ecc. L.J. 81.
[33] See **Chapter 21**.
[34] See **22.3.2**.
[35] See **22.3.4**.

wildlife, particularly in the case of a veteran tree; and any historical associations that may exist. Then, if the conclusion is reached that the carrying out of the proposed works would lead to a loss of amenity, it will be necessary to consider the need for the proposed works, as put forward by the petitioners. Here, too, it will be important to pay particular attention to any factors said to affect the role of the church as a centre of worship and mission, and to pastoral concerns, such as the effect of the tree on nearby graves. And, finally, obviously, it will be necessary to consider whether the loss of amenity will be outweighed by the need for the works.[36]

It will also be necessary in some cases to consider the financial consequences of the possible options. The reason for this is because, if remedial action to avoid future problems (for example, the removal of one branch) would cost relatively little, it would clearly be undesirable to lose altogether a tree of significant amenity value (at least until a suitable replacement has had a chance to establish itself). If, on the other hand, such action would cost a great deal (as with underpinning a medieval church), it would equally clearly be more appropriate to fell the tree. In many cases, of course, the true position will be somewhere in the middle.

This approach, unsurprisingly, echoes that advocated by the Secretary of State in his advice to planning authorities on the approach they should adopt in considering applications for consent under tree preservation orders.[37]

22.3.5 Planting proposals

Consent is never needed from the planning authority for the planting of new trees, but a faculty is needed for planting in a churchyard.

In practice, it is likely that planting of one or two trees, provided it is carried out in accordance with the Chancellor's guidelines under section 6(3) of the 1991 Measure,[38] is likely to be considered *de minimis*, but that will depend on the guidance given under section 11(8).[39]

In any event, the principles set out at **Chapter 10** will be relevant here.

22.4 Unauthorised works

Where it appears that unauthorised works are about to be carried out (including works to trees in a churchyard), an injunction may be issued by the consistory court restraining the person responsible from starting or, as the case may be, continuing the works.[40]

Where unauthorised works have already been carried out, so that it is too late to serve an injunction, a restoration order may be issued by the court, requiring the person responsible to take such steps as the court considers necessary to restore the position to that which existed immediately before the works were started.[41] Clearly, it is not possible to replant a tree that has been unlawfully

---

[36] *Re St Kenelm, Upton Snodsbury*, Worcester Consistory Court, November 2001, unreported; noted briefly at (2000) 6 Ecc. L.J. 293.
[37] *Guide to Law and Good Practice* (DETR, 2000). See **18.3.3**.
[38] See **22.2.2**.
[39] See **22.2.3**.
[40] Care of Churches and Ecclesiastical Jurisdiction Measure 1991, s. 13(4).
[41] 1991 Measure, s. 13(5).

felled, but it might well be appropriate for a consistory court to use its powers under these provisions to require a replacement tree or trees to be planted.

Injunctions may be issued and restoration orders made on the application of an archdeacon or any interested party, or by the court of its own motion.[42] It may be noted that the first injunction ever granted under these provisions was apparently at the behest of a local authority seeking to prevent trees in a churchyard being felled without either a faculty or consent under the tree preservation order to which they were subject.[43]

---

[42] CCEJM 1991, s. 13(6). For procedure, see Faculty Jurisdiction (Injunctions and Restoration Orders) Rules 1992 (S.I. 1992 No. 2884).

[43] Re St Michel, Tylers Green, 1992, Oxford Consistory Court, unreported.

Part V

Hedgerows

"There is an unnecessary prejudice against trees and hedges, and if those who dislike them were better informed, they would be more alive to their advantages and less fearful of their disadvantages."

– *Report of the Committee on Hedgerow and Farm Timber* (1955).

"Essentially you have a traditional landscape feature trying to survive in a twentieth-century environment. There used to be hundreds of cows here when I was a boy, but now there are just seven dairy herds in the whole of Cambridgeshire. Once you no longer have animals, you don't need field boundaries. Potatoes, after all, don't wander across the road. In practical terms, hedgerows are an anachronism and an attractive luxury. In 1946, we had thirty-five miles of hedgerows on the farm. Now we have fourteen, but it still costs us £4,000 a year to maintain them."

– Lord de Ramsey, of the Country Landowners' Association.

Chapter 23

Inclosure Act Hedgerows

23.1 Introduction

A significant number of boundary hedges, some of which remain in the countryside, but some of which are now in built-up areas, were planted under the provisions of inclosure Acts and awards from the eighteenth and nineteenth centuries, or even earlier.

This used to be thought to be of only historical interest, until it was (relatively recently) remembered that the awards in some cases required the hedges in question not only to be planted, but also to be maintained "for ever". This requirement, if interpreted literally, might in some cases have the effect of preventing the development of land enclosed by the hedges (particularly where the hedge in question divides the land from a neighbouring highway). As a result, claims were brought in several county courts in the 1990s, initially at least with some degree of success, by concerned environmentalists.[1]

This Chapter accordingly outlines briefly (at **23.2**) the process by which the inclosure process took place, and then considers (at **23.3**) whether the provisions of the Acts and awards are still enforceable.[2]

23.2 The inclosure movement[3]

23.2.1 Historical background

The Romans probably found Britain already a hedged land; and there are many references in Anglo-Saxon charters to hedges. However, the pattern of the

---

[1]   See, in particular, *Seymour v Flamborough Parish Council*, 1996, unreported, considered at **23.3.1**.

[2]   Some of the material in this part of the book originally appeared in a different form in Herbert-Young (ed.) *Law, Policy and Development in the Rural Environment* (University of Wales Press, 1999). The author is grateful to the University Press for permission to reproduce it here.

[3]   The authors of books, articles and other published material on these matters differ, apparently randomly, as to whether this word should be spelt "inclosure" or "enclosure" – or, of course, sometimes one and sometimes the other. For consistency, the spelling "inclosure" has been adopted throughout this book to refer to the widespread process of land tenure reform by Acts and awards in the 17th to 19th centuries – partly to conform with legislation, and partly to distinguish it from "enclosure" of land in general. See the note to the same effect in Harris and Ryan, *Common Land*. And *cf.* the distinction, equally arbitrary, between "inquiries" and "enquiries".

countryside varied. In the central, more crowded area of lowland England, stretching from York and King's Lynn to Weymouth, and characterised by thorn, elders and apples, there were, by the time of the Norman Conquest, few hedges. This area, referred to by Dr Oliver Rackham[4] as the Planned Countryside, was still broadly open when, centuries later, following the Inclosure Acts, it was carved up into hedged fields and straight roads, laid out in a drawing office. Not all the hedges even in this area, however, are recent; and there are within it still some Anglo-Saxon hedges, medieval woods and ancient trees that the inclosure commissioners left intact.

In the peripheral areas, on the other hand – the western part of England from the Fylde down to Exeter, and the south-eastern section up to the New Forest, the Chilterns and Thetford Chase (Rackham's "Ancient Countryside") – there is a hedged and walled landscape dating from any of forty centuries between the Bronze Age and the Stuarts; a landscape of hedgerow oaks, limes, wild pears and birches. The highland zones of England, from the Peak District to the Scottish border, together with West Devon and Cornwall, are different again. And not all hedges were consciously planted; a few are relics of woods, since grubbed out, leaving their edges as field boundaries, and others are hedges that have developed naturally at the edges of fields. Whether a hedge or wall was used as means of enclosing a field largely depended on the availability or otherwise of suitable stone – walls, being of more permanent construction, were generally preferred.

The number of hedges increased during the Middle Ages. In some areas of Ancient Countryside, they were at that period as numerous as they have ever been; and in the Planned Countryside, although less numerous, hedges were present round most villages, and often on parish boundaries. In Tudor and Stuart times, hedges were increasingly valued for the timber in them – penalties for "hedge-stealing" increased to include whipping and the stocks. In the Ancient Countryside, losses of hedgerows were roughly balanced by additions; but in the Planned Countryside, hedges increased as individual fields, and here and there a whole parish, were inclosed.

But, of course, it is true that the Great Inclosures were a time of more new hedging (and walling) than ever before or since. More than 300,000 km of hedges were planted between 1750 and 1850 – approximately equal to (but, note, not more than) all those planted in the previous five hundred years. The hedges themselves, at first quite elaborate, became more commercialised and perfunctory as the inclosure movement advanced. And although many were planted, others were destroyed; in the Ancient Countryside, particularly, existing fields were enlarged. In addition, from 1750 the number of hedgerow trees gradually declined, so that by 1870, after a century of agricultural prosperity, there was a maximum number of hedgerows and a minimum number of hedgerow trees. The mechanisms by which this inclosure was achieved are considered below.

In the eighty years after 1870, which were, in general, times of agricultural depression, very few hedges were destroyed, except those immediately required for urban development or wartime airfields, and the numbers of hedgerow trees increased to a new peak around 1950. Thereafter, the numbers of hedges and hedgerow trees declined dramatically.

The result of this historical evolution is that in the Ancient Countryside the majority of hedges are older, much older, than 1700; and even in the Planned

---

[4] *Trees and Woodlands in the British Landscape*, revised edn (1990). This Chapter owes much to Dr Rackham's authoritative work in this field. See, in particular, Chapter 10.

Countryside, pre-inclosure hedges are not uncommon. Dr Max Hooper has shown that there is a surprisingly close correlation between the number of tree and shrub species in a hedge and its age in centuries – at least in some areas of England. Inclosure Act hedges thus typically have two, for example, hawthorn (often used) and ash; whereas a hedge with ten or more tree species in a thirty-yard stretch is likely to be pre-Conquest. This rule, although handy, should be treated with some caution, as other research suggests that woody plant diversity is only weakly related to age.

23.2.2 The process of inclosure

It has already been noted that a significant proportion of the hedgerows that now exist in lowland England (at least in the Planned Countryside[5]) are the result of the Inclosure Acts. In general, in the early stages of the inclosure movement, land was inclosed by agreement[6]; but this gradually gave way to what is sometimes referred to as parliamentary inclosure – that is, inclosure by award, associated with an Act of Parliament.

The first Inclosure Act was probably 4 Jas 1, c. 11, which authorised the inclosure of nearly one-third of Herefordshire in 1606.[7] Thereafter, it has been estimated, there were in the region of 4,500 or more Acts, almost all of which are still in existence – that is, they have not been repealed. The process by which this all took place has been reviewed over many years by a number of historians, many of whom were motivated by indignation at the perceived injustice of it all.[8] Of those, Marx was perhaps the most famous, but (for once) by no means untypical in his conclusion:

". . . the law itself becomes the instrument of the theft of the people's land . . . The parliamentary form of the robbery is that of Acts for the inclosure of commons, in other words, decrees by which the landlords grant themselves the people's land as private property, decrees of expropriation of the people."[9]

In the seventeenth century, the general pattern was inclosure by agreement, with only a few Acts being passed to confirm prior agreements. Gradually, however, the agreement was abandoned, and the Act became primary. Thus, in the period 1700–1760, 280 inclosure Acts were passed, with a further 4,000 or so between 1760 and 1840.

Inevitably, those Acts were broadly similar, albeit incorporating some features reflecting local conditions. The Act provided for the appointment of commissioners, whose task was to make a survey of the existing pattern of land ownership in the parish concerned, and they, in turn, appointed surveyors to assist them. The

---

[5]   See **23.2.1**.
[6]   An alternative method, used occasionally to inclose common land, was to rely on the Statutes of Merton and Westminster: see Scrutton, *Commons and Commonfields*, (1887), pp. 168ff.
[7]   Other than, possibly, 37 Hen 8, c. 2, which (in 1545) authorised the King to partition Hounslow Heath.
[8]   See two articles in the *Journal of Legal History*: 'An Introduction to the Inclosure Acts', Sharman, (1989) 10(1), at pp. 45–70; and 'Inclosure: Agreements and Acts', Brown and Sharman, (1994) 15(3), at pp. 269–86.
[9]   Karl Marx, *Capital*, quoted in Cain and Hunt, *Marx and Engels on Law*, (Academic Press, 1979), p. 70. In fact, however, it is by no means certain that the process was as unreasonable as has been generally made out; for an alternative view, from the sixteenth century, see Tussier, *A Comparison Between Champion Country and Several*, E E Text Society, p. 140.

commissioners were then to set out new roads and footpaths, and to make specific allotments to particular landowners, and for the poor, and to distribute the remaining land amongst all those with a claim. The distribution by the commissioners, which was set out in an award, was to form the basis of title in future.

There were then passed in the nineteenth century two general Acts, aimed at simplifying the process by lessening the need for a specific Act to be promoted for each parish,[10] and a further Act enabling inclosure by agreement without the need for a specific Act at all.[11] Finally, the General Inclosure Act of 1845 set up a permanent body of paid commissioners who could inclose any land (other than within 15 miles of London or within a specified distance of other large towns[12]). The procedure under that Act was, nevertheless, more or less the same as under the local Acts.

The rate of inclosure slowed dramatically in the last third of the nineteenth century, and the last inclosure award appears to have been in 1914.

As already mentioned, the most complete list available of such Acts and awards appears to be that assembled by W E Tate, in *A Doomsday of English Inclosure Acts and Awards*.[13] The awards themselves may be available in the Public Record Office and individual county record offices.

23.2.3 The contents of inclosure awards

The significance of inclosure in the present context is that every allotment (that is, every parcel of land allotted to the Lord of the Manor, to tithe owners or to other named persons) was to be enclosed with a fence or hedge. The relevant Act might thus require the commissioners themselves to carry out the task of enclosing, hedging, ditching and fencing the several parcels of land, and (of greatest significance for later generations), in their final award, to direct who should repair and maintain such boundaries. In other cases, the owners of the allotments were to be responsible.

The Act would also make transitional provisions for fencing land until the hedges grew, deal with the ownership of trees growing on land allotted to the new owners, and prohibit the planting of trees and hedges within a specified distance of the new roads – to avoid them becoming unusable due to being shaded from the wind and the sun.[14]

23.3 The continuing relevance of the inclosure Acts

23.3.1 Introduction: the Flamborough case

It had been generally supposed, until the 1990s, that the old Inclosure Acts were of no continuing significance. However, they were then resuscitated by environmental campaigners, as a means to prevent development perceived to be

---

[10] 41 Geo 3, c. 109 (1801); 1 & 2 Geo 4, c. 23 (1821).
[11] 6 & 7 Will 4, c. 115 (Lord Worsley's Act of 1836).
[12] Inclosure Act 1845, s. 14.
[13] Reading University Press, 1967. A similar work by John Chapman, *Guide to Parliamentary Enclosures in Wales* was published by the University of Wales Press in 1992 in relation to inclosures in Wales.
[14] See also **6.4.5**.

undesirable, by forcing the owners of Inclosure Acts hedges to maintain them intact. In some instances, the mere threat of litigation was sufficient to lead to the desired result – thus, one industrious activist, Colin Seymour, was involved in two cases where the owners of the hedges in question (the parish councils of Garforth and Methley, both near Leeds) decided to replant them, rather than resist court proceedings.[15]

Then, in June 1996, Seymour brought an action in the Hull County Court, *Seymour v Flamborough Parish Council*,[16] to enforce the terms of an eighteenth century inclosure award, relating to a hedge at Flamborough, in Yorkshire, where he happened to live; and it was held that the award was still enforceable.

The decision in the *Flamborough* case was unsatisfactory for a number of reasons, to which attention is drawn below – and because the plaintiff was representing himself, and the defendant Council (the owner of the hedge) was not represented at all, so that the law was not fully argued. The outcome of the litigation was, nevertheless, widely reported (in the popular press, not the law reports), in terms which suggested that it had established that all Inclosure Acts were fully enforceable.

Unsurprisingly, other cases followed, and some reached the courts.[17] However, in both the cases directly considering the enforceability of awards under inclosure Acts, *Marlton v Turner*[18] (relating to a hedge at Field Dalling, in Norfolk) and *Meddick v Shiplake PC*[19] (in Oxfordshire), the courts explicitly declined to follow the decision in *Flamborough*, and both claims failed. And in *R v Solihull BC, ex p. Berkswell PC*,[20] the High Court carefully avoided the question.[21]

23.3.2 The continuing enforceability of the obligation

In the *Flamborough* case itself, the hedge in question had been planted under the terms of an inclosure award, made in accordance with the relevant Inclosure Act (of 1765), which required the owner of the land on which the hedge was planted to "make and forever maintain a ditch and fence to divide the allotment from the Bempton Road". Further, the award provided that the boundary was to be a live hedge, not a fence (in the modern sense of that term). The land was, by the time of the action, in the ownership of the Parish Council, which wished to remove the hedge, and replace it with a close-boarded fence, to create a better bowling green. The court (HH Judge Cracknell) concluded that the 1765 Act was still in force, so that the Council was required to maintain the hedge "forever".

A different approach was taken in the second case, *Marlton v Turner*,[22] which related to an inclosure award under an Act of 1808, which required the owners of certain land at Field Dalling in Norfolk to "forever keep in good repair and condition" a hedge between it and the adjacent highway. The obligation was laid upon the then owner of the land "and his heirs". The owner of the land now

---

[15] Thirteenth Report of House of Commons Environment, Transport and Regional Affairs Committee, Environment Sub-Committee, Session 1997–98, HC 969–I (above), para. 115.

[16] 1996, unreported.

[17] There must, presumably, be cases other than the two highlighted here; the author would welcome details (or, better, a transcript) of any other relevant decision.

[18] Noted briefly at [1997] C.L.Y. 4233.

[19] December 1999, unreported.

[20] (1998) 77 P. & C.R. 312.

[21] See **23.3.5.**

[22] Noted briefly at [1997] C.L.Y. 4233.

wanted to block up an existing opening in the hedge and replace it with another one nearby, to enable the carrying out of development for which planning permission had been granted; and an action was accordingly brought in the Norwich County Court, in 1997, in an attempt to frustrate this.

The court (HH Judge Langan) in this case followed *The Earl of Cadogan v Armitage*[23] in holding that the phrase "heirs" was equivalent to what are now more usually known as "successors in title". However, he went on to find that an award under an Inclosure Act was similar in character to a normal conveyance, so that the positive obligations imposed within such an award may be enforced only as much as similar obligations imposed in contractual agreements between neighbouring landowners. And, of course, under normal common law principles, such obligations may only be enforced where they are negative in character.[24] It followed that the obligations were no longer enforceable on the present owner.

It must be questionable whether *Marlton* is correct on this point. Even if the substance of an obligation under a statute is similar in character to that of an obligation under private law, the nature of a statute arguably means that its requirements are binding regardless of consequences. In any event, the decision turned upon the wording of the 1808 Act that authorised the inclosures in that case.

By contrast, it may be noted that section 83 of the Inclosure Act 1845 conferred upon the valuer making an inclosure award a power to require the maintenance of the fence for ever by such person as he should direct. In practice, the person so directed was the owner or owners for the time being of the relevant land being inclosed; and that would seem to amount to a statutory obligation binding on such an owner in the absence of any other consideration.

Indeed, it was an award under the 1845 Act, made in 1867, that was the subject of the third of these cases, *Meddick v Shiplake PC*,[25] decided in the Slough County Court in 1999. This concerned an award which, amongst other things, required the owners of certain plots to be make and maintain fences, in relation to certain land specified in a table. Those plots included a field on which planning permission had now been granted for residential development; and, as might be expected, a claim was brought by the owner of nearby land that the Parish Council (now the owner of the field) should be forced to maintain the hedge between it and the road, thus frustrating the development. The court held that "the owner" meant "the owner for the time being" – although that conclusion depended on the precise wording and all the surrounding circumstances, and might not apply in other cases.

In principle, therefore, a provision in an inclosure award requiring a fence or hedge to be maintained "for ever" means just that, and may be still be capable of being enforced centuries later. But that still begs two questions – what is meant by "maintain", and by whom may such an obligation be enforced.

23.3.3 The extent of the obligation to maintain

Even if an award does require the current owner of a piece of land (as in the *Flamborough* case) to "forever maintain" a hedge bounding it, or (as in *Marlton v*

[23] (1823) 2 B. & C. 197, at pp. 213, 214.
[24] *Austerberry v Oldham Corporation* (1885) 29 Ch.D. 750; *Jones v Price* [1965] 2 Q.B. 618, per Willmer L.J. at p. 633.
[25] December 1999, unreported.

Turner) to "forever keep in good repair and condition" such a hedge, what is the physical extent of that obligation?

The point did not arise in *Flamborough*, since the proposal in that case was to remove the hedge altogether, which would on any analysis have constituted a failure to maintain it. It was, however, considered in *Marlton v Turner*. It has already been noted that the court in that case considered that the obligation in the award was not still capable of being enforced; but it nevertheless went on to consider what would be the position if such an obligation were enforceable (for example, where the owner of the land at the time of the award still owned the land). The judge held that such a requirement would not prevent the replacement of one opening in a long hedge with another:

"It seems to me, as a matter of common sense as well as of proper interpretation, that to breach the hedge by an access of the kind proposed is in no way inconsistent with the keeping of the hedge in good repair and condition. The hedge will remain, for by far the greater part of its length, in position after the proposed work just as it has done for the past two centuries and more.

"Obviously, uprooting could be done along such a length of the hedge short of the whole as to involve a breach of the award. The point at which that stage would be reached is a matter of degree, but it is a point of which, in my judgment, the works now proposed fall far short."[26]

That approach, which seems eminently sensible, was followed in *Meddick v Shiplake PC*.[27]

It was, incidentally, pointed out in *Meddick* that the Inclosure Act 1845 used the word "fence" to mean, indifferently, a hedge or wall as well as a fence in the modern sense of the word[28] – but that will not always apply in relation to earlier awards – see, for example, the terms of the award in the *Flamborough* case, noted above.[29]

The conclusion would thus seem to be that, even where a hedge is subject to a requirement in an inclosure award as to its repair or maintenance, that would not of itself prevent the making of one or more openings in it – provided that the hedge essentially remains in existence.

23.3.4 Who may enforce the obligation

Even where the requirements of an award are still enforceable, and even where the landowner or person responsible for carrying them out is carrying out works on a sufficient scale to amount to a breach of them, that does not mean that anyone can necessarily bring an action in the courts to seek redress. Thus, to engage in litigation, a person must have sufficient "standing".[30]

The simplest case is where a hedge is on the line of the boundary between two properties in private ownership. There seems little doubt that in such a case any obligation under an inclosure award to maintain it may only be enforced by the

---

[26] Transcript, pp. 14–15.
[27] December 1999, unreported.
[28] See, in relation to the Inclosure Act 1845, *Ellis v Arnison* (1822) 1 B. & C. 27.
[29] See **23.3.2**.
[30] The term generally used by the courts, in line with CPR, Part 54 (judicial review), in place of the old *locus standi*.

owners of the two properties in question, as a private law matter.[31] It has also been commonly accepted that it is permissible for two adjoining landowners to agree by mutual consent that a fencing obligation in an inclosure award should not be enforced, as happened in, for example, *Garnett v Pratt*[32] (although that decision does not explicitly authorise the practice); but even in that situation it is possible for the award to be later enforced.[33]

The more common, but potentially less straightforward, case is where the hedge in question is on the boundary between a plot of land and the public highway. In *Flamborough*,[34] the action was brought by a private individual, who (as well as being something of an expert in this area of the law) happened to own land elsewhere in the village that had also been the subject of the same award, and by the Yorkshire Wildlife Trust. The court considered that, where the boundary in question adjoined a highway, any aggrieved local resident was entitled to seek the enforcement of the award.

In *Marlton v Turner*, on the other hand, the court held that a private landowner A, albeit a local resident, had no right to challenge the duty of landowner B to maintain a boundary between his (B's) land and the public highway. This was so even if, as was the case in this instance, A and B were neighbours – it was, after all, not the boundary between them that was in dispute. More generally, Langan J. held as follows:

"If an obligation of a public nature is said to have been broken, there are various means of enforcement: by the public authority which is charged with the duty of enforcing the performance of the obligation (that is, direct enforcement against the party allegedly in breach); or (in some cases) by the Attorney-General in the relation of the complainant (which is another form of direct enforcement); or by the complainant's seeking judicial review of the failure of the public authority to secure performance of the obligation (which might be described as a form of direct enforcement).

"What cannot . . . be done is to take proceedings qua individual to enforce public law obligations, for example to restrain an alleged breach of planning control. It is this kind of impermissible marriage which is being attempted in this action."[35]

This passage was adopted by Hague J. in the third of these cases, *Meddick v Shiplake PC*,[36] who considered the issue of "standing" much more thoroughly.[37] He took as his starting point the rule laid down by the House of Lords in *Gouriet v Union of Post Office Workers*,[38] to the effect that:

". . . a private citizen, except as relator in an action by the Attorney General, has no [standing] in private law in a civil action to obtain an injunction to restrain another private citizen . . . from committing a public wrong by breaking the criminal law, or a declaration that his conduct is unlawful, unless the plaintiff [claimant] can show that some legal or

---

[31] *Seymour v Flamborough PC*, June 1997, unreported, transcript, p. 11; *Meddick v Shiplake PC*, December 1999, unreported; transcript, pp. 13-14.
[32] [1926] 1 Ch. 897.
[33] *Garnett v Pratt* [1926] 1 Ch. 897.
[34] June 1996, unreported. See **23.3.2.**
[35] August 1997, unreported; transcript, p. 17.
[36] December 1999, unreported.
[37] With the assistance of very full argument by counsel, to one of whom the present author is indebted for assistance on this point generally.
[38] [1978] A.C. 435.

equitable right of his own has been infringed or that he will sustain some special damage over and above that suffered by the general public."[39]

The judge noted that one exception to that rule would be where inhabitants of a particular community bring an action on behalf of themselves and the other inhabitants, to enforce a proprietary right enjoyed as inhabitants (as opposed to members of the general public). He thus considered that the litigation in the *Flamborough* case should have been brought by the Attorney-General as a relator action on the application of Mr Seymour or the Wildlife Trust, or by either of them as a challenge in judicial review proceedings. And he held that Mr Meddick had no standing to bring an action in the instant case, either as a member of the general public or as a member of the community, or as the owner of nearby land.

23.3.5 *Effect of liability under an inclosure award in the context of proposed development*

It has already been noted that these cases are almost always brought not to preserve the hedge in question, but rather to prevent development that has already been permitted.

However, the conclusion from the above analysis of the litigation would seem to be that, in spite of the success of Mr Seymour in *Flamborough*, it is not likely to be worthwhile for a private landowner to take action in the courts other than with the leave of the Attorney-General. An exception to this would be where it could be shown:

- that an inclosure Act hedge had been, or was to be, removed altogether, rather than simply breached; and

- that special damage had been suffered by the prospective litigant, or that such damage was threatened.

Although the latter might occur in relation to some provisions in an inclosure award,[40] it is difficult to see how it would arise in the context of a boundary hedge fronting a highway.

As to an action brought with the leave of the Attorney-General, it is uncertain what his or her approach would be if there were to be shown a clear breach of an award, but no harm other than that caused by the carrying out of the development that is sought to be frustrated; but if leave were to be refused, it would be impossible to seek any form of review.

Nor is it wise to challenge the effect of a planning permission which has been granted for development solely on the basis that its implementation would inevitably lead to the loss of a hedge that appears to be subject to a maintenance liability under an inclosure award. Thus in *R v Solihull BC, ex p. Berkswell PC*[41] the leave of the High Court was being sought for an application for judicial review to quash a planning permission on the basis that its implementation would lead to

---

[39] As summarised by Lord Diplock in *IRC v National Federation of Self-Employed and Small Businesses* [1982] A.C. 617, at p. 638H.
[40] As with the right to hold a fair on waste land of the parish, in *Wyld v Silver* [1963] Ch. 243, CA; see also *Neaverson v Peterborough RDC* [1902] 1 Ch. 557, CA.
[41] (1998) 77 P. & C.R. 312.

the loss of several hedges which were said to be required to be maintained in perpetuity for ever under the terms of an inclosure Act of 1802.

Sullivan J. carefully avoided the question of what the effect was of the 1802 Act in isolation, and whether its terms were enforceable by a parish council, or simply by the private landowners concerned, or by their successors in title – although he did point out that any application for a declaration on such an issue should be brought promptly.[42] Instead, he dismissed the application on the grounds that, even if the provisions of the Act were enforceable in relation to the hedge concerned, that would only constitute a private law restriction on implementing the permission – in the same way as the existence of a restrictive covenant or a ransom strip might frustrate a development proposal for which permission had been granted.[43]

The environmental consequences of implementing the present proposal, including the loss of the hedge, had been carefully considered by the planning authority, and there was thus no basis on which to impugn the grant of permission merely because it might be incapable of implementation.

23.3.6 Conclusion

County court decisions are, of course, of no binding authority. However, in the light of decisions such as *Marlton v Turner*, which was, incidentally, not cited to the court in *ex p. Berkswell PC*, and *Meddick v Shiplake PC*, it now seems less likely that the argument that was successful in the *Flamborough* case will succeed again. But it may do. And if it does, and particularly if it does so in the higher courts, the result will presumably be that inclosure awards will, in effect, be considered to be generally enforceable, at least in some circumstances.

In that situation, Parliament might act to change the law. After all, it cannot be in the public interest that the intention of planning authorities (and the Secretary of State) can be thwarted by legislation passed many years ago for quite different purposes. It is noteworthy that the hedge in the *Flamborough* case itself was "undistinguished . . . barely maintained, unkempt and straggly" – it would, for a number of reasons, not be within the scope of the Hedgerows Regulations 1997 at all, let alone "important" enough to merit protection. Although the industry of Mr Seymour at Flamborough, and of others who have used the same tactics elsewhere to halt unwanted development proposals, is impressive, the use of eighteenth-century and nineteenth-century Inclosure Acts cannot be a sensible way to provide for the protection of hedges now.

The conclusion of the House of Commons Environment Sub-Committee looking at the whole issue was that "the Government should as a matter of priority investigate the nature and typical incidence of the legal responsibilities for the protection and maintenance of field boundaries in the Inclosure Acts with a view to issuing guidance on the matter".[44] The Government, in its response to the Sub-Committee, accepted that it was reasonable to conclude that obligations under the inclosure Acts and awards, to maintain land boundaries for ever, existed in a large number of cases. But it reasoned as follows:

---

[42] (1998) 77 P. & C.R. 312, at p. 318.
[43] See also *Vasiliou v Secretary of State for Transport* [1991] 2 All E.R. 77, CA, and *British Railways Board v Secretary of State for the Environment* [1993] 3 PLR 125, H.L.
[44] HC 969–I (above), para. 119.

"Given the uncertainties surrounding the judgment in the *Flamborough* case and the fact that neither central nor local government powers of enforcement in relation to the legal responsibilities for the protection and maintenance of field boundaries in the Inclosure Acts, however, the Government does not believe further investigation of the matter would be fruitful. We consider that effort is better directed towards strengthening the current legislative framework."[45]

It is not at all clear how that reasoning followed from the conclusion that preceded it, but it is clear that no amending legislation is likely on this topic for the foreseeable future.

---

[45] The Government's response to the Environment, Transport and Regional Affairs Committee's Report: The Protection of Field Boundaries, para. 16.

Chapter 24

Protection of Important Hedgerows

24.1 Introduction

24.1.1 Loss of hedgerows

The first of the two quotations with which this Part of the book[1] opens represents the view of a government committee reporting over forty years ago, as life returned (more or less) back to normal after the end of the Second World War, and changing farming methods began to make an impact on the rural landscape. However, although the civil servants in Whitehall (largely familiar with towns and suburbs) were able on occasion to promote the virtues of hedgerows, such views were not widely shared by those who mattered – the farmers. They knew perfectly well that hedgerows took up space, required time-consuming and expensive maintenance, harboured pests, and impeded the creation of larger, more sensibly shaped fields suitable for being worked with modern agricultural machinery.

So, in the 1950s and 1960s, hedgerows disappeared at a rate that was alarming to those who valued them as an amenity. Thus the influential Countryside Commission study, *New Agricultural Landscapes*, reported in 1974 that:

". . . since 1945 there have been fundamental changes in the structure and methods of farming which have brought about changes in the landscape almost as extensive as those which have occurred during the 'inclosure movement'. Many mourn the loss of traditional landscapes, and believe that the emerging landscapes will be of poorer quality."[2]

Indeed, it has been alleged that half of the hedgerows that were present in 1946 had been destroyed by the mid-1970s – some through removal, but the majority through neglect. Some were replaced, but replacement hedges were in many ways no substitute for those that were lost. The chairman of the Commission, in his foreword to the 1974 study, noted that "many of the lowland landscapes inherited from earlier generations have been, or soon will be, replaced by new landscapes of greatly reduced scenic and wildlife interest". And government advice four years later was that "losses of trees and hedgerows since the war years represent an

---

[1] At p. 595.
[2] *New Agricultural Landscapes*, a study by Westmacott and Worthington for the Countryside Commission (1974), para. 1.1.

erosion not only of landscape quality, but also of important wildlife habitats".[3]

Again, however, such concerns were those of non-farmers, who therefore had to find apparently practical arguments in favour of retaining hedgerows.[4] It was thus pointed out that hedges can be barriers against soil erosion; but in Britain that is scarcely a problem.[5] They provide shelter to animals; but not as effectively as even the humblest shed. And they control the movement of animals; but to remain stock-proof hedges need attention, and they are not as efficient as barbed wire and electric fences – which of course are readily movable. But sheds, barbed wire and electric fences are not attractive – at least not to the eyes of urban dwellers, who are used to a landscape of small fields bordered by old hedges, rich in wildlife, and laid by hand so as to allow the emergence of trees at intervals. Further, as public awareness of history has grown, hedgerows are valued also as archaeological evidence of past land-use patterns. Concern has thus been widely and continuously expressed over the loss of hedgerows throughout the last 50 years.

It might be thought that, in the light of that concern, the destruction would have slowed down or stopped. However, not only did it continue, but it did so at an accelerating rate. The average net loss of hedgerow each year (destruction less replacement), which was 4,000 km in the period 1947–69, rose to an average of 4,600 km in 1969–80, 6,200 km in 1980–85, and 7,600 km in 1985–90. The reasons for the loss are very simple, and are epitomised in the second of the two opening quotations, from Lord de Ramsey of the Country Landowners' Association, who farms almost 3,000 hectares in East Anglia.[6]

Throughout this post-war period, as the widespread debate continued about landscape change in the countryside, the statistics on which many assertions were loosely based appeared increasingly inadequate. More recently, therefore, the Department of the Environment commissioned two survey reports from the Institute of Terrestrial Ecology (ITE). The first revealed that between 1984 and 1990, the total hedgerow length fell by over 20 per cent in England, and 25 per cent in Wales: in both, 9 per cent of hedgerows were removed or destroyed, and 19 per cent ceased to be classified as hedgerows as a result of neglect or conversion into another form of boundary (23 per cent in Wales). The only good news was that the position improved significantly in the following period, 1990–94: the average annual loss dropped from 9,500 km to 3,600 km.[7]

Against this loss should be set replacement planting of an average of 1,900 km per annum in 1984–90, rising to 4,400 km in 1990–93.[8] The official government line is that this means that "the rate of gains from new planting [were] more than outweighing the losses from removal in numerical terms"[9]; but an official from the Countryside Commission has pointed out that "it is a continuing source of surprise how some commentators have attempted to equate a newly planted hedge

---

[3]   Department of the Environment Circular 36/78 (WO 64/78), Memorandum, para. 30.
[4]   See, for example, Nan Fairbrother, *New Lives, New Landscapes* (Penguin, 1972).
[5]   Except, possibly, on the eastern fringes.
[6]   At p. 595.
[7]   *Changes in Hedgerows in Britain between 1894 and 1990* and *Hedgerow Survey 1993*, contract reports for the Department of the Environment by the Institute of Terrestrial Ecology.
[8]   *ibid.*
[9]   *The Hedgerows Regulations: A Guide to the Law and Good Practice*, Department of the Environment, Ministry of Agriculture Fisheries and Food, and the Welsh Office, 1997, para. 2.5.

with one which has just been lost and may have taken centuries to develop".[10]

24.1.2 Protective mechanisms

Against that background, this Chapter first reviews briefly (at **24.2**) the attempts that have been made to give some measure of protection to the vanishing hedgerows. Until 1997, these took two forms, the classic "carrot and stick" approach: the former in the shape of grants being available for hedgerow retention, and the latter by means of various forms of legislation, largely ineffectual.

The remainder of the Chapter then considers legislation aimed specifically at protecting hedgerows, in particular the Hedgerows Regulations which came into force in mid-1997 (see **24.3**). The purpose of the new system is to protect "important" hedgerows from unnecessary removal. There are two ways in which this could have been achieved. First, it would have been possible to require that "lists" or "schedules" should be drawn up of all-important hedgerows, and then to provide that consent should be obtained to remove a hedgerow thus identified. That is the method that has been used in Britain to protect ancient monuments,[11] historic buildings[12] and trees.[13] It has, however, the disadvantage that it is a very slow process for all the items of value to be identified; and that in the meanwhile many are lost.

The alternative approach, which has been adopted in the 1997 Regulations, is to require that almost all works to almost any hedgerow are to be notified to the appropriate authority, which then has a specified time in which to decide whether the hedgerow is important enough to merit protection and, if it is, whether the works proposed are sufficiently important to justify removing the hedgerow (see **24.4**, **24.5**). The legislation could have required the first of those decisions to be made by an authority, or an officer, as an ad hoc professional judgment (as is done with selecting buildings for listing and trees for "preserving"), but the mechanism that was in fact chosen was for the choice to be made on the basis of theoretically objective criteria, generally set out in Schedule 1 to the Regulations (considered in more detail at **24.6**).

The carrying out of unauthorised works to hedgerows is a criminal offence (**24.7**).

24.2 Protective mechanisms before the Hedgerows Regulations

24.2.1 Grants

Given the various practical benefits accruing from the removal of hedgerows, already noted,[14] it is not surprising that, until 1976, financial assistance was available from central government to assist farmers to "improve" their farms in this way. Thus one farmer in the early 1970s had on his farm of 242 hectares more than three km of hedges, which cost £150 a year for maintenance. He accordingly

---

[10]   Paper delivered by David Gear at seminar in 1997 organised by Reigate and Banstead Borough Council and Arboricultural Association.
[11]   Under the Ancient Monuments and Archaeological Areas Act 1979.
[12]   Under what is now the Planning (Listed Buildings and Conservation Areas) Act 1990.
[13]   Under Part VIII of the Town and Country Planning Act 1990: see **15.6**.
[14]   See **24.1.1**.

grubbed up all the hedges and trees, and piped the drains to fill in the ditches, at a cost of £200 per hectare for the area involved, partly paid for by grants. That land was then worth £1,200, and increased the total farm yield by 900–1,000 kg per hectare. All this was in addition to the more efficient and, therefore, less costly working of the land, which was his original motive.[15]

That has all changed now. The Hedgerow Incentive Scheme, introduced by the government in 1992, was designed to combat the problem of losses through neglect. It is now part of the Countryside Stewardship Scheme, formerly administered in England by the Ministry of Agriculture, Fisheries and Food (MAFF) and now by the Department for Environment, Food and Rural Affairs (DEFRA), which offers grants for the planting and restoration of hedges – although, as noted, new planting may not of itself be of any great benefit for a while. In Wales, the position is similar: Cyngor Cefn Gwlad Cymru (the Countryside Council for Wales) operates an all-Wales whole farm agri-environment scheme, replacing the widely admired Tir Cymen and the Hedgerow Renovation Scheme.[16]

The House of Commons Environment Sub-Committee in 1997–98 considered in detail the whole issue of the funding of incentive schemes, the balance between funding maintenance and restoration, and the design of a fair and effective cross-compliance scheme which places upon farmers a basic duty to care for the field boundaries (both hedgerows and walls) on their holdings. The Sub-Committee's report[17] makes a valuable source of further information.

24.2.2 General legislation prior to 1997

In addition to these limited financial incentives, there was already some legislation giving a small measure of protection to hedgerows, prior to the introduction of the Hedgerows Regulations 1997 – and it should be noted that any requirements arising under earlier legislation have not been superseded by the new provisions.[18] Nor does consent under the 1997 Regulations to remove a hedge override any continuing requirement to maintain it that may arise under an inclosure Act or award.[19]

There is thus at least some control over works to individual trees in the hedgerows. Firstly, a felling licence would be required from the Forestry Commission under section 9 of the Forestry Act 1967, for the felling of any living tree. A licence is not required, however, where only small volumes of trees are felled, or where the trees felled are all small. These provisions have already been considered in detail[20]; but they are not likely to be relevant in many cases, since the amount of trees, as opposed to hedging plants, included in a hedge will often not be sufficient for a licence to be required.

It would also be possible for a local authority to make a tree preservation order to protect a specific tree or group of trees within a hedge, under powers in Part VIII of the Town and Country Planning Act 1990. This procedure, which has been considered in **Part IV** of this book, is not frequently adopted in the case of hedgerow trees, at least in rural areas, although it is by no means unheard of.

---

[15] Fairbrother, *New Lives, New Landscapes* (Penguin, 1972), pp. 67–68.
[16] HC 969-I (above), para. 176.
[17] HC 969-I (above); see particularly paras 163–210.
[18] HR 1997, reg. 6(3); and see *Hedgerows Guide*, paras 5.23 to 5.28.
[19] See **Chapter 23**.
[20] See **Chapter 14**.

Where an order has been made, consent for the carrying out of almost any works to the tree or trees (not just felling) would be required from the authority that made the order – which would probably be difficult to obtain.[21] If a hedgerow is in a conservation area (again, unusual but not unknown), notice of the carrying out of works to any tree will need to be given to the authority.[22]

Hedges may also be important habitats for wildlife.[23] The Conservation (Habitats, etc) Regulations 1994 implement in the United Kingdom the requirements of the EU Habitats Directive, so that it is now an offence to kill, injure, take or disturb the listed animal species, or to destroy their resting places or breeding sites, or to pick, collect, cut or uproot the listed plant species. For details, see relevant Government guidance.[24] In addition, there are specific controls relating to badger setts; any interference with a sett requires a licence from English Nature or the CCW.[25] These controls, which are aimed primarily at protecting the fauna within hedgerows, will obviously provide some limited degree of protection for the hedgerow itself.

Some eight per cent of the land area of Britain is within areas that have been designated as sites of special scientific interest (SSSIs)[26] – which include national nature reserves, special protection areas under the Birds Directive, and special areas of conservation under the Habitats Directive.[27] Where a hedgerow is in an SSSI, the landowner and occupier will have been provided by English Nature or the CCW with a list of operations likely to damage the special interest of the site – which might well include the destruction or pruning of a hedge. Owners and occupiers must then give four months' notice if they intend to carry out any of the operations specified. Further, where an owner undertakes not to carry out the work, he or she may negotiate a management agreement and be paid compensation based on profits foregone, including an element for the costs of the maintenance of the hedge.[28]

Some farms are protected by voluntary schemes within environmentally sensitive areas.[29]

Finally, a hedgerow may occasionally be on the site of an archaeological monument that is of sufficient national importance to have been scheduled by the Secretary of State, under the Ancient Monuments and Archaeological Areas Act 1979; and indeed the hedgerow may itself be scheduled.[30] Any works affecting a monument (which would probably include the grubbing-up of a hedge running across its site) would then require scheduled monument consent to be obtained from the Department of Culture, Media and Sport (or the National Assembly for Wales). For further details, see PPG 16 (in England), and Welsh Office Circular 60/96.

---

[21] TCPA 1990, ss. 198 ff. See **Chapter 18**.
[22] TCPA 1990, ss. 211–214; see **Chapter 21**.
[23] See **9.3**.
[24] See Annex G to PPG 9. In Wales, from Cyngor Cefn Gwlad Cymru (the Countryside Council for Wales); see Technical Advice Note TAN 5.
[25] See Protection of Badgers Act 1992, and Home Office Circular 100/91.
[26] See **9.3.8**.
[27] Wildlife and Countryside Act 1981, s. 28; Conservation (Natural Habitats, etc.) Regulations 1994. See also PPG 9, Annex A.
[28] 1981 Act, s. 15.
[29] Under Agriculture Act 1986, s. 18; see **9.4.4**.
[30] See '**9.4.2**.

24.3 Legislation specifically to protect hedgerows

24.3.1 Legislation promoted prior to 1995

Whilst the alterations in recent years to the regime of grants for hedgerow retention[31] were welcomed by the conservation lobby, they were not enough to save the most important hedgerows in the face of commercial pressures, ignorance and simple neglect. Nor were the existing powers under other legislation (including the Inclosure Acts) described above. There were, therefore, in the 1980s a succession of attempts to protect hedgerows by means of more specific legislation, including three unsuccessful private members' bills.

There was then a proposal by Mr James Batho, in his report to the Secretary of State on tree preservation policies and legislation,[32] that local authorities should be allowed to make hedgerow management orders, subject to the payment to owners of compensation similar to that payable in respect of management agreements under the Wildlife and Countryside Act 1981. That suggestion was taken up in a consultation document on the Batho proposals issued by the Government in 1990.[33] In reliance on that, the Government resisted calls in the House of Lords for the extension of tree preservation legislation to be extended to cover hedgerows, in the debate on what became the Planning and Compensation Act 1991.[34]

Two more private members' bills followed in the early 1990s, supported by the Countryside Commission. They, too, were unsuccessful, but they led directly to Mr Gummer, the then Secretary of State for the Environment, confirming in 1994 that the Environment Bill would include "an enabling power for the preservation of hedgerows of particular value".

24.3.2 EC Habitats Directive

European legislation also required action to be taken, since article 10 of the EC Habitats and Species Directive required Member States to encourage the management of linear boundary features (which would obviously include hedges):

"Member states shall endeavour, where they consider it necessary, in their land use planning and development policies and, in particular, with a view to improving the ecological coherence of the Natura 2000 network, to encourage the management of features of the landscape which are of major importance for wild fauna and flora.

"Such features are those which, by virtue of their linear and continuous structure (such as rivers with their banks or the traditional systems for marking field boundaries) or their function as stepping stones (such as ponds or small woods), are essential for the migration, dispersal and genetic exchange of wild species."[35]

Partly to implement that Directive, the Government of the United Kingdom set targets in the UK Biodiversity Action Plan,[36] pledging itself:

---

[31] See 24.2.1.
[32] See 16.2.7.
[33] *Review of Tree Preservation Policies and Legislation*, Department of the Environment and the Welsh Office, 1999, paras 91 to 105.
[34] Hansard, January 29, 1991, cols 652–656; see also *Hansard*, cols 747–749 (July 25, 1991).
[35] Council Directive of May 21, 1992 on the Conservation of Natural Habitats and of Wild Flora and Fauna (1992/43), art. 10.
[36] *Bio-diversity: The UK Steering Group Report*, HMSO, 1995; and see PPG 9.

- to halt the loss of species-rich hedgerows by neglect or removal by the year 2000, and all loss of hedgerows which are both ancient and species-rich by 2005;

- to achieve the favourable management of 25 per cent (that is, around 47,500 km) of species-rich and ancient hedges by the year 2000, and 50 per cent (95,000 km) by 2005; and

- to maintain overall numbers of hedgerow trees within each county or district, at least at current levels, through ensuring a balanced age structure.

However, if these targets were to be met, far more needed to be done, both through boosting incentive schemes and through raising interest and awareness among land managers. And legislation would be required to prevent the unnecessary removal of important hedgerows.

24.3.3 *The Environment Act 1995*

The Government's 1994 commitment led, in due course, to the enactment of what is now section 97 of the Environment Act 1995. This provision enabled regulations for the protection of important hedgerows (note, not all hedgerows) to be made by the appropriate ministers – in England, the Secretary of State for the Environment and the Minister for Agriculture, Fisheries and Food, and in Wales the Secretary of State for Wales.[37]

Such regulations were not to be made without consultation with all the appropriate bodies (including representatives of those likely to be affected, local authorities and environmental conservation groups), and needed to be approved by a resolution of each House of Parliament.

24.3.4 *The Hedgerows Regulations 1997*

Draft regulations were duly published in the autumn of 1996. Considerable concern was expressed regarding the mechanics of the new control regime and, in particular, over the criteria for evaluating "important" hedgerows. Revised regulations were placed before Parliament in March 1997, which still raised many of the same concerns – in particular, that there should be allowances to mitigate the economic impact of the new controls, and that local authorities should not be allowed to interfere in the countryside. It was also strongly urged on behalf of the farming lobby that there should be a reference to the contribution of hedgerows to the landscape. Some of the defects in the Regulations are highlighted in the remainder of this Chapter.

Recognising that there was an election just around the corner, a move was made to defer the whole matter, to be considered afresh by the next Government. However, it was also recognised that a new administration might have other priorities, and that such a tactic would postpone the whole issue for months, if not years. Overall, it was generally accepted that, whilst the draft regulations were far from perfect, they were only a first attempt, and better than nothing. Accordingly,

---

[37] Environment Act 1995, s. 97(8); as to the identity of the government departments presently responsible, see **24.5.8**.

in the last debate of the last day of that Parliament, the Hedgerows Regulations were approved, to come into force on June 1, 1997.[38]

From that date, important hedgerows have received statutory protection for the first time, so that to remove such a hedge without authorisation is a criminal offence, punishable in some circumstances by an unlimited fine. The Government has also issued a useful publication, *The Hedgerows Regulations: A Guide to the Law and Good Practice*[39] ("the *Hedgerows Guide*"), which explains the working of the new system and provides helpful practical advice.

24.3.5 Review of the Regulations

As noted above, it was always recognised that the 1997 Regulations were but a first step in attempting to protect hedgerows of value. They constitute a complex system of control, and it remains to be seen whether it will be effective in achieving its stated purpose. To obtain an indication of how the Regulations are operating, a questionnaire was circulated in 2002 by DEFRA to all local planning authorities. The 127 authorities that responded with numerical information indicated that, between them, they received some 1,585 removal notices in the first four years of the new system, which led to the issue of 401 retention notices. During the same period, there were some 18 prosecutions for unauthorised works.

The incoming Government recognised the problems, however, and announced on May 29, 1997, the day before the Regulations came into force, the setting up of a review group to see how more effective protection might be given to hedgerows in general, and important hedgerows in particular. The brief of that group focused on whether the time limits within which authorities have to respond to removal notices should be extended, and whether the criteria for defining important hedgerows could be improved and simplified. The group issued its conclusions in June 1998.[40]

But the ambit of the group's review was severely restricted, in that it was directed to consider only the Regulations, rather than the 1995 Act itself. It, nevertheless, did point to the need to consider the amendment of primary legislation – to enable local authorities, as well as ministers, to define important hedgerows, to introduce criteria relating to landscape character, and to expand the definition of hedgerow to include other types of field boundary.

The House of Commons Environment Sub-Committee also concluded in 1997 that the present system (including both primary and secondary legislation) be reformed, in much the same ways.[41]

The Government generally welcomed the recommendations of the Review Group and the Sub-Committee, but, as might have been expected, it was not enthusiastic as to new primary legislation. It instigated research into the effect of possible new criteria for defining "important" hedgerows – the results of which were published in the summer of 1999. A general consultation as to possible changes to the 1997 Regulations is expected in the summer of 2002, with amending Regulations being made thereafter. Possible amendments are noted here as appropriate.

---

[38] Hedgerows Regulations S.I. 1997, No. 1160.
[39] Published by Department of the Environment, Ministry of Agriculture Fisheries and Food, and the Welsh Office, 1997; reprinted 1998, DETR, with slight revisions; references in this Chapter are, except as noted, to the revised editions.
[40] *Review of the Hedgerows Regulations 1997*, DETR, 1998.
[41] HC 969–I (see n. 17 above), paras 75–102.

24.4 Hedgerows subject to the Regulations

24.4.1 The definition of a "hedgerow"

The word "hedgerow" itself is not defined either in the 1995 Act or the 1997 Regulations. The *Hedgerows Guide*[42] suggests that the definition in the *Oxford English Dictionary* may be used as a guide: "a row of bushes forming a hedge, with the trees, etc. growing in it". During the parliamentary debate on the Environment Bill, the Government confirmed that a wall or bank on its own would not qualify for protection – even though in some parts of the country stone walls are every bit as important in historical and landscape terms as living hedges.

Subject to that basic uncertainty, however, all hedgerows are within the scope of the Regulations, unless they are excluded either because of the type of land they border, or because of their length.

24.4.2 Hedgerows within the scope of the Regulations

The Regulations thus apply, by virtue of regulation 3(1), only to hedgerows growing on, or adjacent to, any of the following:

- common land;
- protected land;
- land used for agriculture or forestry; or
- land used for the keeping or breeding of horses, ponies or donkeys.

The first two of these are defined in the regulations.[43] "Common land" means common land or a town or village green within the meaning of the Commons Registration Act 1965. "Common land" is itself defined in that Act as land subject to rights of common and waste land of a manor[44]; and "town or village green" as (in summary) land that has been used by the inhabitants of a locality for exercise and recreation.[45]

"Protected land" means land protected as a local nature reserve[46] or as an SSSI.[47]

"Agriculture" is also defined in the Regulations, and has the same meaning as in the Town and Country Planning Act 1990; that is, it includes:

". . . horticulture, fruit growing, seed growing, dairy farming, the breeding and keeping of livestock (including any creature kept for the production of food, wool, skins or fur, or fore the purpose of its use in the farming of the land), the use of land as grazing land, meadow land, osier land, market gardens and nursery grounds, and the use of land for woodlands where that use is ancillary to the farming of land for other purposes".[48]

---

[42] *Hedgerows Guide*, paras 3.3–3.5.
[43] Hedgerows Regulations ("HR") 1997, reg. 2(1).
[44] Commons Registration Act 1965, s. 22; "rights of common" are there further defined.
[45] 1965 Act, s. 22(1), amended by Countryside and Rights of Way Act 2000, s. 98; and see *New Windsor Corporation v Mellor* [1975] 1 Ch. 380; *R v Oxfordshire County Council, ex p. Sunningwell Parish Council* [2000] 1 A.C. 335, H.L.
[46] Under National Parks and Access to the Countryside Act 1949, s. 21; and see PPG 9, para. A.23.
[47] See **24.3.1**.
[48] TCPA 1990, s. 336(1).

It includes the use of land as allotments[49] or for fox farming.[50] The definition does not itself include the breeding and keeping of horses, but land used for those purposes is included in the Regulations in its own right.

Where a hedgerow falls within the Regulations as a result of the above, any part of it is also a "hedgerow" for the purposes of the Regulations.[51]

A hedgerow on land owned by the Crown is not, for that reason alone, exempt from the Regulations.[52] And a hedgerow owned by a local authority is also subject to the Regulations.[53]

24.4.3 Hedgerows outside the scope of the Regulations

The Regulations do not apply, however, to any hedgerow within or bounding the curtilage of a dwelling-house.[54] A "dwelling-house" is not defined in these Regulations; it is elsewhere defined as not including a building containing one or more flats or a flat within such a building.[55] A "curtilage" is an area about a building; and there need not be a physical enclosure of the land within the curtilage, but the land in question at least needs to be regarded in law as part of one enclosure with the house.[56] The result is that garden hedges are not protected, even if they would otherwise be classified as "important", and even if they form the boundary between the garden of a dwelling-house and one of the relevant types of land (common, etc.). The reason for that exclusion is far from clear.

The other preliminary matter is that a hedgerow is only subject to the Regulations if it is of a reasonable length, that is:

- it has a continuous length of at least twenty metres;

- it meets (by intersection or junction) another hedgerow at both ends; or

- it is part of such a hedgerow.[57]

For the purposes of calculating the length of a hedgerow, it is treated as ending at any point where it meets another hedgerow; and any gap in it (whether or not it is filled) of less than 20 metres is to be considered as part of the hedgerow.[58] The above is a summary of the provisions of regulation 3, but working out whether a hedge is subject to the Regulations can in practice be less than straightforward. The Hedgerows Guide contains a helpful Annex (B) explaining how the definition works in practice, with illustrative diagrams.

The result of these provisions is that, as a broad generality, the Regulations apply to all hedgerows in rural areas that are of a reasonable length, and a few in urban and suburban areas. The main threat to the latter is urban development, and they will thus largely be protected by the normal planning process – since,

[49] Crowborough Parish Council v Secretary of State for the Environment [1981] J.P.L. 281.
[50] North Warwickshire Borough Council v Secretary of State for the Environment [1984] J.P.L. 434.
[51] HR 1997, reg. 3(2).
[52] Environment Act 1995, s. 115(1).
[53] See 24.5.5 as to procedure.
[54] HR 1997, reg. 3(3).
[55] TCP General Permitted Development Order 1995, art. 1(2); although Greater London Council (General Powers) Act 1984, s. 5 provides that a "dwellinghouse" includes a flat.
[56] McAlpine v Secretary of State for the Environment [1995] 1 PLR 15; see also Dyer v Dorset County Council [1988] 3 W.L.R. 213, CA.
[57] HR 1997, reg. 3(1), (2).
[58] HR 1997, reg. 3(4), (5).

presumably, the effect of a proposed development on hedgerows would be a material consideration in the determination of whether or not it should be permitted. Although, if a potentially important hedgerow is removed before the planning authority becomes aware of its existence, there is nothing that can be done to restore it. The 1998 Review group accordingly supported the carrying out of research on threats to urban hedges.[59]

24.5 Proposals for works to hedgerows

24.5.1 Notification to the local authority

If a hedgerow is one to which the Regulations apply (as to which, see above), almost any proposal to remove it or any part of it must be notified to the local planning authority.[60] "Remove" means "uproot or otherwise destroy",[61] which might include any act resulting in the destruction of a hedgerow – whether carried out on the land on which the hedgerow is growing, or on other land nearby.

The *Hedgerows Guide* contains the following advice:

"A judgement on whether the proposed work or activity constitutes 'removal' will have to be made according to the circumstances of the individual case. However, taking out selected individual woody species may, depending on the facts of the particular case, amount to removal of a stretch of hedgerow. On the other hand, it is unlikely that insertion into the hedgerow of a pole to carry overhead electricity distribution or telecommunications lines would involve taking out or destroying a portion of the hedgerow, and so should not be regarded as removal. Nor should earthworks near hedgerows, such as trenching for the installation of underground cables or pipes, usually lead to their removal or destruction – provided that care is taken not to damage roots, especially those with a diameter larger than 20 millimetres and clumps of smaller roots."

It is not clear what is the basis of the figure of 20 mm.

It has been held that a tree is "destroyed" when an act, such as the severing of its root system, is carried out as a result of which it ceases to have any further use as an amenity, that is, it is no longer worth preserving.[62] The same would, presumably, apply to the woody plants comprising a hedge.

The requirement to notify works does not apply in a number of situations, listed in regulation 6(1). These broadly fall into two categories:

- certain relatively minor works; and

- certain cases where works have been approved under other procedures, or are for some other reason considered to justify the removal of a hedgerow.

Each of these is considered in turn.

[59] *The Review of the Hedgerow Regulations 1997*, DETR, 1988, paras 6.4–6.6.
[60] HR 1997, reg. 5.
[61] Environment Act 1995, s. 97(8).
[62] *Barnet London Borough Council v Eastern Electricity Board* [1973] 1 W.L.R. 430.

24.5.2 Minor works that do not need to be notified

A number of relatively minor categories of works do not have to be notified to the authority. These are as follows:

> "(a) for making a new opening in substitution for an existing opening which gives access to land . . .;
> (b) for obtaining temporary access to land in order to give assistance in an emergency;
> (c) for obtaining access to land where another means of access is not available or is available only at disproportionate cost;
> . . . and
> (j) for the proper management of the hedgerow."[63]

The first of these is straightforward, and enables one opening in a hedgerow to be replaced with another. The resulting gap must be filled up with a new hedge within eight months[64]; failure to do so is a summary offence punishable by a fine of up to level 3 (see below for offences generally).[65] The 1998 Review sensibly recommended that this exemption be limited to the creation of a gap of up to 9 metres.[66]

The second exemption is no more than common sense; examples given in the *Hedgerows Guide* include the removal of a stretch of hedgerow in order to allow access for an ambulance, in the event of immediate medical assistance being required; or to enable the restoration of utility services where they have been cut off from a whole village or settlement.[67] The third exemption, too, is self-explanatory. In both cases, it should be remembered that land includes cables or other utility apparatus in or on it, and land covered by water such as ponds and streams.

The last of these exemptions is likely to be the most controversial in practice; the *Guide* comments as follows:

"Cutting back a hedgerow, in a manner that does not result in its destruction, is unlikely to constitute its 'removal' . . .

"However, this provision has been included to make clear that appropriate hedgerow management techniques, which may necessitate the hedgerow being cut back to ground level (such as coppicing) and which may sometimes be viewed by members of the public as removal, are exempt. Repeated coppicing, at too frequent intervals, or the deliberate cutting down of a hedgerow to ground level where such cutting has never formed a traditional technique of hedgerow management in an area, would not be covered under this exemption.

"This provision also allows, if necessary, the removal of dead or diseased shrubs or trees from a hedgerow, or of elder bushes as part of restoration works (*eg.* coppicing and gapping), without prior notification."[68]

The *Guide* also notes that a number of organisations have published booklets and other guidance on proper techniques of hedgerow management.[69]

---

[63] HR 1997, reg. 6(1).
[64] HR 1997, reg. 6(2).
[65] HR 1997, regs 7(2), (5). See **24.7, Appendix C**.
[66] *The Review of the Hedgerow Regulations*, DETR, 1988, paras 6.17–6.19.
[67] *Hedgerows Guide*, para. 4.5.
[68] *Hedgerows Guide*, paras 4.15–4.16.
[69] *Hedgerows Guide*, para. 4.17.

24.5.3 Works authorised under other procedures

A number of other categories of works do not have to be notified to the authority, where they have been approved or authorised under other procedures or legislation.[69a] These are works:

"(d) for the purposes of national defence[70];
(e) for carrying out development for which planning permission has been granted [in response to an application or under Parts 11 or 30 of Schedule 2 to the TCP General Development Order];
(f) for the carrying out [by drainage boards, local authorities and the Environment Agency of] work for the purpose of flood defence or land drainage;
(g) for preventing the spread of, or ensuring the eradication of, [a plant or tree pest][71];
(h) [carried out by the Highways Agency in relation to trunk roads and motorways];
(i) to prevent obstruction of or interference with electric lines and plant or to prevent danger."[72]

Category (e) allows works to hedgerows where necessary to implement development that has been the subject of a specific grant of planning permission – on the basis that the planning authority (or the Secretary of State as appropriate) will have taken into account the importance of the hedgerow in deciding whether or not to grant permission. Indeed, in the light of the general duty of authorities to require the retention of an important hedgerow, unless there is a good reason to justify removal,[73] it would seem to follow that a planning authority should not grant planning permission for any works leading to the loss of such a hedgerow, unless there is a similarly good reason – that is, the effect of a proposal on any important hedgerows will be a material consideration[74] that will carry considerable weight.

However, the removal of a hedgerow must still be notified if it is required for the carrying out of "permitted development" – that is, development permitted by article 3 of, and Schedule 2 to, the TCP (General Permitted Development) Order 1995. The exceptions are development under a private or local Act (Part 11 of Schedule 2) or the provision of a toll road facility (Part 30) – which do not need to be notified, presumably because the effect of the works in question on the hedgerow will (or at least should) have been considered before the Act was passed or the road was authorised. The same is true of Highways Agency proposals (category (h)), which routinely involve the preparation of an environmental statement.

Categories (f) and (i) are justified because the authorities in question are all subject to general duties to protect the environment in carrying out their functions.[75] In addition, the need for such works (and works to eliminate plant and tree disease, category (g)) is likely in most cases to outweigh the desirability of preserving the hedgerow.

[69a] HR 1997, reg. 6(1)(d)–(i).
[70] See The Review of the Hedgerow Regulations, DETR, 1988, paras 6.20–6.21.
[71] See Plant Health (Great Britain) Order 1993, arts. 22, 23; and Plant Health (Forestry) (Great Britain) Order 1993, arts. 21, 22; see **11.5**.
[72] In consequence of an order under paragraph 9 of Schedule 4 to the Electricity Act 1989; see **7.2.1**.
[73] HR 1997, regulation 5(5)(b). See **24.5.6**.
[74] Under TCPA 1990, s. 70(2).
[75] See **15.11**.

24.5.4 Service of a hedgerow removal notice

Where proposed works do not fall within any of the above exceptions, the notification of the works (known as a "hedgerow removal notice") must be served by "an owner" of the hedgerow. Such a person is described by the *Hedgerows Guide* as "the applicant".

This is distinct from the provisions relating to the various permissions required under the planning Acts, for which an application may be made by anyone (such as a contractor or a prospective purchaser); it is not entirely satisfactory, as what matters is that the notice is served, not that anyone in particular serves it. "Owner" is defined as the freeholder or agricultural tenant of the land on which the hedgerow is growing.[76] Where the hedgerow was planted on A's land but has encroached on B's, A is the owner, but where it actually forms the boundary between two areas of land in different ownership, the two owners will be entitled to the hedge as tenants in common[77]. It follows that the requirement for the notice to be served by "an" owner rather than by "the" owner means that, in such a boundary case, it can be served by either of the two owners.

Alternatively, a utility operator may serve a notice where it needs to remove all or part of a hedgerow to carry out its functions – although it may be wise in such case to ensure that the owner is informed.

The planning authority for this purpose will be the district or borough council, where there are two tiers of councils, and the national park authority and the Broads Authority in their areas.[78] Where a hedgerow straddles the boundary between the areas of two or more authorities, the notice should be given to the one whose area contains the majority of the hedge.

The notice must be broadly in the form prescribed in Schedule 4 to the Regulations. That is, it should clearly identify the hedgerow concerned and the part to be removed (preferably by reference to a map of scale 1:2,500), and provide any evidence of its age; the *Hedgerows Guide* suggests items that should normally be acceptable for the purpose.[79] The notice should also make clear the status of the applicant, and state his or her reasons for the proposed works. The 42-day period for the consideration of such a notice[80] only starts once all the information has been received to the satisfaction of the authority.

The authority has no right to insist on the use of any particular form, or to require more information than is specified in Schedule 4. Nor is it entitled to more than one copy of any information supplied.[81]

No fee is required for such an application.

24.5.5 Responses to notification

Once an authority has received a hedgerow removal notice, together with relevant supporting documents, photographs or other evidence, it should check that the information supplied is sufficient to comply with the Regulations.[82] Obviously, if

[76] HR 1997, reg. 2(1).
[77] *Waterman v Soper* (1697) 1 Ld. Raym. 737; *Holder v Coates* (1827) Moo. & M. 112; *Lemmon v Webb* [1895] A.C. 1, H.L., affirming [1894] 3 Ch. 1, CA; see **4.2, 3.2**.
[78] HR 1997, reg. 2(1).
[79] *Hedgerows Guide*, para. 5.11.
[80] See **24.5.5**.
[81] *Hedgerows Guide*, para. 5.10.
[82] See **24.5.4**.

it is not, it should promptly seek from the applicant whatever it considers to be missing.

Once the notice is complete, the authority has 42 days (that is, six calendar weeks, not 42 working days) in which to decide what to do – either to issue a "hedgerow retention notice" or to state that it has no objection to the hedgerow being removed. It should, therefore, as a matter of good practice, acknowledge receipt of the notice and inform the applicant of the dates on which the 42-day period starts and finishes.

The planning authority must consult the parish or community council where one exists (or all of them where the hedgerow straddles the boundary of more than one parish or community); as the *Guide* points out, such councils may have useful local knowledge; and they may have an important role in enforcing the system of control.[83] However, given the tight timescale for responding to the notice, this consultation should be carried out – and responded to – very promptly.[84]

In practice, the authority will no doubt carry out a site visit to ascertain the status of the hedgerow, its length, the number of species in it, and so forth, to decide whether it is an important hedge within the meaning of the Act and the Regulations; the *Guide* includes a useful checklist of information to be collected on such a visit.[85] There is power for the authority to enter any land for this purpose, and to take samples of any hedgerow and any soil – the relevant provisions are broadly equivalent to those applying in connection with consent under tree preservation orders.[86]

The authority is also required to maintain a register of hedgerow removal notices it has received.[87] It may give further publicity to such notices if it considers it appropriate – it might, in particular, consult local groups or individuals who are known to have special knowledge of or interest in local history or botany.

The 6-week period for response may be extended by agreement; but it is unclear why an owner would ever want to agree to an extension. If the owner has not received a retention notice within the 6-week period, the works may proceed perfectly lawfully – just as if a notice had been received formally allowing removal to proceed. If the authority has not obtained within six weeks sufficient evidence to justify the issue of a retention notice, that is its problem; it is not entitled to issue a retention notice after the expiry of the period. Nor can it issue such a notice simply to gain more time.

Because of the limited timescale in which the authority must work, it may be sensible for a procedure to be agreed in advance to enable removal notices to be dealt with promptly. One possibility would be for officers to have delegated powers to decide whether or not particular hedgerows are important, and for elected members to decide whether to allow the removal of those that are considered important.[88] Where the authority is itself the owner of all or part of the hedgerow, the decision-making must be by an officer or committee not responsible for the management of the land on which it is growing.[89]

[83] *Hedgerows Guide*, paras 6.7, 6.8.
[84] HR 1997, reg. 5(3), (4).
[85] *Hedgerows Guide*, paras 6.10–6.15.
[86] HR 1997, regs 12–14; *Hedgerows Guide*, paras 6.16–6.24.
[87] HR 1997, reg. 10(a).
[88] *Hedgerows Guide*, para. 8.4.
[89] HR 1997, reg. 15.

The 1998 Review of the Regulations, unsurprisingly, recommended extending the time limit from six to eight weeks.[90]

Once an authority has made a decision, one way or the other, or has received notice of a decision made by the Secretary of State, that too must be recorded in the register.[91]

24.5.6 Issue of notice that a hedgerow may be removed

In response to a hedgerow removal notice, an authority must issue a notice that the hedgerow in question may be removed if it forms the view that the hedgerow is not important.[92] The question of whether a hedgerow is or is not "important" is crucial, and is considered in more detail below.[93]

The authority may also issue such a notice if it considers that the hedgerow is important, but that the applicant has made out a sufficient case to justify its removal. The Regulations make it clear that such a course will only be appropriate in exceptional cases; but the *Guide* gives examples of where removal might be justified – notably where the alternative would be even less desirable. Reasons stated to be normally insufficient include personal financial circumstances, changes of land ownership and rationalisation of holdings.[94]

Where the applicant has received from the authority a notice stating that the hedgerow may be removed, or where the authority has made no response at all within the 6-week period, the applicant may lawfully remove the hedgerow at any time within two years of serving the original removal notice.[95] Note that there is no obligation on a local planning authority to issue a notice allowing the removal of a hedgerow in the above circumstances – it could simply do nothing. But it is obviously good practice to do so, to put the matter beyond doubt.

There is no statutory right of appeal against the issue of a notice allowing the removal of a hedgerow, or against an authority's failure to issue a retention notice in time; the only route of challenge (for example, by a local amenity group) would be to seek judicial review of the authority's action or inaction.[96]

24.5.7 Issue of hedgerow retention notice

A retention notice may only be issued in relation to an important hedgerow (within the meaning of the Act and the Regulations); but if the hedgerow is important, a notice must be given unless there is a good reason to suggest otherwise.[97]

A retention notice must state in terms that the hedgerow (or a specified part of it) is not to be removed, and the basis on which the authority has decided that the hedgerow in question is important – that is, which of the criteria in Schedule 1 apply.[98] The notice should also make clear that it will remain in force until:

---

[90] *The Review of the Hedgerow Regulations 1997*, DETR, 1998, para. 7.19.
[91] HR 1997, reg. 10(b)–(d).
[92] HR 1997, reg. 5(5)(a).
[93] See **24.6**.
[94] *Hedgerows Guide*, paras 8.16–8.20.
[95] HR 1997, reg. 5(1)(d).
[96] See **18.6.1**, **18.6.2**.
[97] HR 1997, reg. 5(5); see **24.5.6**.
[98] HR 1997, reg. 5(2), (7).

- it is quashed following a successful appeal to the Secretary of State;

- it is withdrawn by the authority; or

- it is superseded by a notice from the authority stating that the hedgerow may be removed, following the service of a new hedgerow removal notice.

The last two courses of action will only occur in practice if new information comes to light suggesting that the hedgerow is not important, or circumstances change so as to justify its removal.[99]

As already noted, a retention notice must be communicated to the applicant within 42 days of the original removal notice, unless a longer time has been agreed – that is, it must be posted (by recorded delivery or registered letter) so as to arrive by the end of the relevant period, or it can be left at the address given on the removal notice, or delivered into the hands of the applicant.[1]

24.5.8 Appeal against retention notice

Finally, if an owner receives a retention notice, an appeal against it may be made to the Secretary of State, within 28 days of the notice being given.[2] There is no prescribed form, but the appellant should serve a copy of the appeal on the local planning authority involved. Nor is there a fee payable.

The "Secretary of State" is in this case the Secretary of State for Environment, Food and Rural Affairs or the National Assembly for Wales. But the appeal is made to the Planning Inspectorate, which handles it through to the eventual decision. No grounds of appeal are given in the Regulations; the *Hedgerows Guide* simply suggests that an appeal may be made "on any reasonable grounds".[3] It is likely that the appellant will seek to argue:

- that the hedgerow is not important; and/or

- that, even if it is, its removal is justified for some reason.

As to the second of these, it would seem that, in the light of regulation 5(5)(b), the burden is very much on the appellant to justify removal, not on the authority to justify retention.

Generally, the provisions relating to appeals against retention notices are much the same as are found in relation to the various types of appeals under the planning Acts: if either party requires it, a hearing must be held, which may take the form of an inquiry (with the potential for an award of costs being made if either party requires it).

Where the appeal results in a retention notice being quashed, it appears that the removal of the hedgerow must still take place within two years of the original removal notice being served. That could cause problems where the matter takes a long time to be resolved at appeal (especially if a further challenge is made in the High Court), but presumably a further removal notice could be served, which would almost inevitably lead to a favourable result.

---

[99] HR 1997, reg. 5(8); *Hedgerows Guide*, paras 8.11, 8.21–8.22.
[1] HR 1997, reg. 16(2), TCPA 1990, s. 329; *Hedgerows Guide*, paras 8.23–8.25.
[2] HR 1997, reg. 9; *Hedgerows Guide*, Chapter 9.
[3] *Hedgerows Guide*, para. 9.4.

24.6 Important hedgerows

24.6.1 Introduction

It has already been noted that the question of whether a hedgerow is or is not important is crucial.

This reflects the terms of the enabling power in the Environment Act, which make it clear that the purpose of any regulations made under the Act is not to protect all hedgerows, but only "important" ones, for which replacement planting is not an adequate substitute. The Act also provides that the question whether a hedgerow is or is not "important" for the purposes of this section is to be determined, not on the basis of an ad hoc on-site judgment by an appropriately qualified professional, but in accordance with prescribed criteria.[4] And the 1997 Regulations do, indeed, prescribe a number of criteria, which are designed to be objective, and thus render unprofitable any argument as to whether a particular hedge merits protection.

The first criterion, in regulation 4(a), is that a hedgerow should be at least 30 years old – presumably as at the date on which notice is given of the intention to remove it. The specimen removal notice makes it clear that anyone seeking to remove a hedgerow relying on a claim that it is less than 30 years old will have to provide suitable evidence to prove it – and the *Guide* makes some suggestions as to the type of evidence that may be relevant.[5]

The other criteria as to the importance of a hedgerow are set out in Schedule 1 to the Regulations. Part II contains the eight criteria themselves – 1 to 5 relating to archaeology and history, and 6 to 8 relating to wildlife and landscape. Relevant definitions are in Part I of Schedule 1. As might be expected, helpful information in relation to each of the criteria is given in the *Hedgerows Guide*.[6]

24.6.2 Criterion 1: parish boundary

Criterion 1 is that a hedgerow marks the boundary of a parish or township existing before 1850[7]; the best evidence in relation to this will be the historical maps mentioned below.[8] The year 1850 was selected so as to pre-date the rationalisation of parish boundaries that created current civil parishes. The effectiveness of this criterion will be limited in heavily populated areas by the exclusion from protection of hedgerows bounding residential curtilages.[9]

24.6.3 Criteria 2 and 3: archaeology

Criterion 2 is that a hedgerow incorporates an archaeological feature that is a scheduled monument at the date of the proposal[10] or that was recorded in an SMR at the relevant date.[11] Criterion 3 is that a hedgerow is wholly or partly on land that is within a site that is a scheduled monument at the date of the proposal

---

[4]   Environment Act 1995, s. 97(2).
[5]   HR 1997, Sched. 4; *Hedgerows Guide*, para. 5.11.
[6]   *Hedgerows Guide*, Chapter 7.
[7]   HR 1997, Sched. 1, Pt II, para. 1.
[8]   See **24.6.4**.
[9]   See **24.4.3** above.
[10] Under s. 1 of the Ancient Monuments and Archaeological Areas Act 1979; see **9.4.2**.
[11] HR 1997, Sched. 1, Pt II, para. 2.

or that was recorded in an SMR at the relevant date, and is associated with any monument or feature on that site.[12] "Archaeological feature" and "incorporates" are not defined.

The schedule of monuments is compiled under the Ancient Monuments and Archaeological Areas Act 1979, and may be inspected at the offices of the Department of Culture, Media and Sport or of English Heritage, or in Wales at Cadw: Welsh Historic Monuments. The boundary of a scheduled monument is the red line on the plan that forms part of the schedule entry.[13]

SMRs are usually maintained by the English county councils outside the metropolitan areas, by groups of metropolitan district councils, and by the six archaeological trusts in Wales. They often include scheduled monuments as well as other items of archaeological interest, and are regularly consulted in the course of the normal development-control process. They are, however, not always up to date, and the "relevant date" approach means that information subsequently recorded in an SMR cannot be taken into account, which is unfortunate. The boundaries of sites in SMRs are not precisely defined.

The results of the field test carried out by ADAS for the Department of the Environment suggests that, in practice, criteria 2, 3 and perhaps 4 will have very little effect.[14]

24.6.4 Criterion 4: evidence of manorial history

Criterion 4 is that a hedgerow marks the boundary of a pre-1600 estate or manor recorded at the relevant date in an SMR or in a document held in a record office, or is visibly related to a building or other feature of such an estate or manor.[15] The record office means the Public Record Office, the British Library (Manuscript Collection) and the National Library of Wales (Department of Manuscripts and Records) and other national and local record offices and libraries. The most fruitful source of information is likely to be the Public Record Office at Kew and the relevant County Record Office.

Relevant documents are likely to be estate maps (from 1580 onwards), tithe maps and awards (usually from the 1840s, and usually where there had been no previous Inclosure Acts), inclosure maps and early Ordnance Survey maps (together with their field books, now in the British Museum). Earlier charters and manorial records will need to be translated into modern English, but this has been done in some cases; and they sometimes provide useful information by their description of estate boundaries in the form of "perambulations", which may mention hedges and other features.

24.6.5 Criterion 5: remnant of pre-inclosure field system

Criterion 5 is that a hedgerow:

(a) is recorded in a document held in a record office as an integral part of a field system pre-dating the Inclosure Acts; or

---

[12] HR 1997, Sched. 1, Pt II, para. 3.
[13] *R v Bovis Construction Ltd* [1994] Crim. L.R. 938, CA (Crim Div).
[14] *The Hedgerows Evaluation System: A System for Identifying Important Hedgerows*, a contract report by ADAS for the Department of the Environment, 1996, para. 4.2.2.
[15] HR 1997, Sched. 1, Pt II, para. 4.

(b) is part of, or visibly related to, any building or other feature associated with such a system which:

(i) is substantially complete; or

(ii) which is identified by the local planning authority in a relevant development control document as a key landscape characteristic.[16]

It is not clear what is meant by "integral" or "substantially complete"; but it is noteworthy that the 1998 edition of the *Hedgerows Guide* (unlike the original, 1997, edition) comments[17] as follows:

". . . the phrase 'pre-dating the Inclosure Acts' should be taken to mean before 1845 (whether or not Inclosure Acts exist for the area in question), that being the earliest of the Acts known by the collective title given by the Short Titles Act 1896.

"Any document used in support of paragraph 5(a) should identify the hedgerow in relation to the wider field pattern. Whether the hedgerow is an 'integral part of the field system' is a matter of judgment, on the basis of what the field pattern now is (rather than that recorded in the document) and whether the pattern would no longer be discernible if the hedgerow was removed."

This suggests that this criterion may be of greater significance than might have been thought.

It is not clear what the scope of "documentation prepared by the planning authority for the purposes of development control" will be. Here, too, it is unfortunate that research subsequent to the relevant date cannot be taken into account.

24.6.6 *Criterion 6: presence of wildlife*

Criterion 6 relates to the presence in the hedgerow of one or more rare species of plant or animal. It thus requires that a hedgerow should now contain species listed in paragraph 6(3), or be recorded as having done so at some date in the period leading up to the relevant date; the period is five years in the case of animals and birds (presumably including insects and other invertebrates), and ten years for plants.[18]

The species in paragraph 6(3) are:

(a) birds listed in Part I of Schedule 1 to the Wildlife and Countryside Act 1981[19];

(b) animals listed in Schedule 5 to the 1981 Act[20];

(c) plants listed in Schedule 8 to the Act[21];

(d) birds classified as "declining breeders" in the Red Data Book *Birds in Britain*;

(e) species classified as "endangered", "extinct", "rare" or "vulnerable" in the

[16] HR 1997, Sched. 1, Pt II, para. 5.
[17] *Hedgerows Guide*, 1998 edn, paras 7.22, 7.23.
[18] HR 1997, Sched. 1, Part II, para. 6(1).
[19] See **9.3.2**.
[20] See **9.3.3**.
[21] See **9.3.4**.

British Red Data Books entitled *Plants*, *Insects* and *Invertebrates other than Insects* and in the Red Data Book of Britain and Ireland on *Stoneworts*.

The Red Data Books were published for the Nature Conservancy Council (the predecessor to English Nature) and the Joint Nature Conservation Committee. The relevant department of DEFRA[22] can supply a single list of all the relevant species.

Once again, it is unfortunate that the picture is effectively frozen at the relevant date; no new information can be taken into account.

24.6.7 Criteria 7 and 8: presence of numerous woody species

Criterion 7 relates to the number of woody species present, which is an indication both as to the richness and interest of the hedge in terms of its biodiversity and as to its age. To be classified as "important" on this count, a hedgerow must be in one of the following groups:

(a) it has at least seven of the woody species listed in Schedule 3 to the Regulations;

(b) it has six woody species, together with three of the features specified in paragraph 7(4);

(c) it has six woody species, including a black poplar, a large-leaved lime, a small-leaved lime or a wild service; or

(d) it has five woody species, together with four of the features specified in paragraph 7(4).[23]

The number of species required is reduced by one for hedgerows in the north of England (north of a line roughly from the Ribble to the Humber).

The number of woody species in a hedgerow is to be calculated as follows:

- where the hedgerow is less than 100 m long, by counting those in the central 30 m stretch;

- where the hedgerow is between 100 m and 200 m long, by counting those in the central 30 m stretch of each half, and taking the average; and

- where the hedgerow is more than 200 m long, by counting those in the central 30 m stretch of each third, and taking the average.[24]

It will be noted that the choice of 30 metres correlates with Hooper's rule, noted earlier,[25] relating to the age of a hedgerow. Indeed the ADAS study[26] suggests that criteria 7 and 8, and particularly 7, will probably protect more historic hedges than the "archaeology and history" criteria.

The features specified in paragraph 7(4) are:

---

[22] See **Appendix D**.
[23] HR 1997, Sched. 1, Part II, para. 7(1).
[24] HR 1997, Sched. 1, Part II, para. 7(3).
[25] See **23.2.1**.
[26] ADAS report (see note 14 above), para. 4.2.2.

(a)   a bank or wall supporting the hedge for half its length;

(b)   gaps which in aggregate do not exceed 10 per cent of the length of the hedgerow;

(c)–(e)   an average of at least one standard tree per 50 m of hedgerow;

(f)   at least three of the woodland species listed in Schedule 2, within 1 m of the outermost edges of the hedgerow;

(g)   a ditch along half the length of the hedgerow;

(h)   links with neighbouring hedgerows, ponds or woodlands; and

(i)   a parallel hedge within 15 m of the hedgerow.

Criterion 8 is similar to criterion 7, but relates to hedges along a public bridleway, byway or footpath. It requires that a hedgerow must have within it at least four woody species[27–28] and at least two of the features listed in paragraph 7(4)(a)–(g). In other words, a hedge that is not quite as interesting in terms of wildlife may still be important if it is more generally visible because it is next to a public right of way.

As will be readily appreciated, these criteria, whilst (relatively) straightforward in theory, will require considerable investigation to work in practice. Further, in spite of the title given to these three criteria, they actually hardly relate to "landscape" at all.

24.6.8 Review of criteria

The 1998 Review of the Regulations put forward a number of suggestions for revising the criteria, and recommended that they should be field-tested.[29] If new or amending Regulations are introduced during the currency of this book, therefore, any new criteria for determining important hedgerows should be carefully checked before deciding whether a particular hedgerow is, or is not, likely to be important.

One more general criticism often made of the existing system is that many of the criteria relate to documents and information at "the relevant date" – that is, March 24, 1997, when the Regulations were made. That is unfortunate, as it means that the position will become gradually more and more detached from the latest state of knowledge as to, for example, whether an archaeological feature is or should be included in a Sites and Monuments Record (SMR), or which birds and insects are of special significance.

Unfortunately, this cannot be avoided, as the 1995 Act requires that it is the relevant Ministers who must prescribe which hedgerows are important.[30] The Regulations can therefore only prescribe criteria for "importance" by reference to documents that have been written at the date on which the Regulations are made – Ministers cannot after all, approve criteria drafted by reference to documents that have not yet been written, as that would be effectively to substitute someone else's opinion for that of Ministers.[31] It is to be hoped that in any future revision

[27–28] Even in the north of England!
[29] *The Review of the Hedgerow Regulations 1997*, DETR, 1998, Chapter 5.
[30] Environment Act 1995, s. 97(2).
[31] *The Review of the Hedgerow Regulations 1997*, DETR, 1998, Annex C, paras C17–C21.

of the Act, a way will be found round this problem, without diluting the advantages of consistency and predictability possessed by the present system.[32]

One other feature which may be introduced is that future Regulations may prescribe certain categories of hedgerow which are considered important in each part of the country, and then allow authorities to decide whether a hedgerow in that area falls within one of the relevant categories.

24.7 Unauthorised removal of hedgerows

24.7.1 Removal of a hedgerow without having notified the authority

It is an offence to remove a hedgerow, either intentionally or recklessly, in contravention of regulation 5(1), or to cause or permit someone else to do so.[33]

The elements of the offence thus created are as follows:

(1) that a hedgerow has been removed;

(2) that it was one to which the Regulations applied;

(3) that the removal had been carried out, caused or permitted by the accused;

(4) that the carrying out, causing or permitting of the removal had been intentional or reckless;

(5) that the removal was in none of the categories in regulation 6 (exemptions from the requirement to notify the authority); and

(6) that the authority had not been notified in accordance with regulation 5(1).

The first four elements must be proved by the prosecuting authority, to the criminal standard (beyond reasonable doubt[34]). As to the second element, this has already been considered fully.[35] Each of the other three will be a matter of fact.

The fifth and sixth elements must be disproved by the accused, to the civil standard (on the balance of probabilities[36]). That is, it is for the accused to prove, if possible, that the removal of the hedgerow in question did come within one of the exempting categories, rather than for the authority to prove that it did not. If that is not possible, the accused must then seek to prove (again, to the civil standard) that the authority had been notified in accordance with regulation 5(1) – that is:

• that a hedgerow removal notice had been given to the authority;

• that the authority had issued a notice stating that the hedgerow may be removed;

• that the removal was carried out in accordance with that notice; and

• that it was carried out within two years of the original notice to the authority.

---

[32] *The Review of the Hedgerow Regulations 1997*, DETR, 1998, paras 3.11–3.20.
[33] HR 1997, regs 7(1), 5(1).
[34] See **19.2.2**.
[35] Environment Act 1995, s. 97(4)(d); HR 1997, regs 3, 7(3); see **24.4**.
[36] See **19.4.2**.

The second of these will not apply where the authority, in fact, made no response at all to the original hedgerow removal notice; indeed, it will by definition be impossible to produce any evidence to prove that. If, however, the accused alleges that no response was made to the notice (or even that the authority indicated that the removal could go ahead), the burden then shifts to the authority to prove that it issued a hedgerow retention notice and communicated it to the owner of the land within 42 days of the original removal notice. These various matters also have been considered fully already.[36a]

The removal of a hedgerow without a removal notice having been given to the authority is an either-way offence punishable by a fine of up to the statutory maximum in the magistrates' court, or an unlimited fine in the Crown Court.[37]

The principles applying to the prosecution of offences in respect of unauthorised works to trees protected by a tree preservation order[38] apply equally to the unauthorised removal of hedgerows. If an authority considers that such an offence is about to be committed, it may apply to either the High Court or the county court for an injunction.[39]

Finally, in deciding whether to instigate a prosecution for this offence, the question of whether the hedgerow was "important" is theoretically irrelevant. However, an authority may consider it inappropriate to prosecute for the removal without notice of a hedgerow that is known (or at least strongly suspected) not to be "important". After all, if notice had been given, there would be nothing that the authority could have done to retain it. The position is thus somewhat analogous to the removal without notice of a tree in a conservation area that would probably not have been suitable to be the subject of a tree preservation order. In either case, an offence would have been committed, but it is difficult to see that a prosecution would be in the public interest.[40-41]

24.7.2 Removal of an important hedgerow in defiance of a retention notice

Where a hedgerow retention notice has been issued, and has not been withdrawn, it is an offence to remove intentionally or recklessly the hedgerow to which it related, or to cause or permit another to do so.[42] The elements of the offence thus created are as follows:

(1) that a hedgerow has been removed;

(2) that it was one which was the subject of a hedgerow retention notice;

(3) that the retention notice had not been withdrawn or cancelled;

(4) that the removal had been carried out, caused or permitted by the accused;

(5) that the carrying out, causing or permitting of the removal had been intentional or reckless.

This is possibly more straightforward than the other offence created by regulation 7(1). All but the third element fall to be proved by the prosecution to the criminal

---

[36a] See **24.5**.
[37] HR 1997, reg. 7(4).
[38] See **Chapter 19**.
[39] HR 1997, reg. 11; *Hedgerows Guide*, Chapter 13.
[40-41] See **21.4.3, 19.5.2**.
[42] HR 1997, regs 7(1), 5(9).

standard. It is up to the defendant to produce evidence that the notice has been withdrawn or cancelled.

The removal of an important hedgerow in breach of a retention notice is an either-way offence punishable by a fine of up to the statutory maximum in the magistrates' court, or an unlimited fine in the Crown Court.[43] In determining the fine to be imposed following a conviction, the court is to have regard to the likely benefit which has accrued or which seems likely to accrue to the person responsible.

Again, if an authority considers that such an offence is about to be committed, it may apply to either the High Court or the county court for an injunction.[44]

24.7.3 Partial removal of a hedgerow

The unauthorised removal of a stretch of hedgerow is, in principle, an offence, since a "hedgerow" is defined by the Regulations to include a part of one. However, the removal of parts of a single hedgerow, so that there is still a hedgerow standing after the works, is not an offence.

The 1998 Review thus urged the introduction of a prohibition on action to convert an important hedgerow into a non-important one – for example, by removing a single woody species – as that was a clear loophole that should be blocked.[45]

24.7.4 Replacement

Where a hedgerow has been removed in contravention of the Regulations by a landowner or utility operator, the authority may require the owner or operator to plant a replacement, of specified species and position.[46]

Once the replacement has been planted, it is for the next 30 years to be regarded as an "important" hedgerow – so that, in effect, it cannot be removed again. It should be noted that a replacement notice could, in theory, be issued where a hedgerow that was not "important" was removed without notice having been given, but it would presumably not be appropriate to take action in those circumstances.

Finally, if an owner or utility operator is required to plant a replacement hedge, an appeal may be made to the Secretary of State against the requirement, within 28 days of the notice being given.[47] Here, too, no grounds of appeal are given; but otherwise the provisions are much as are found in relation to the various appeal mechanisms in other legislation.

---

[43] HR 1997, reg. 7(4).
[44] HR 1997, reg. 11; *Hedgerows Guide*, Chapter 13.
[45] *The Review of the Hedgerow Regulations 1997*, DETR, 1998, para. 6.14.
[46] HR 1997, reg. 8; *Hedgerows Guide*, Chapter 11.
[47] HR 1997, reg. 9; *Hedgerows Guide*, Chapters 9 and 12.

Appendices

"Even if the world wos to end tomorrow, I'd still plant a tree today."
– Anon., graffiti on bridge in Oxford (2001)

Appendices

Appendix A

Sample conditions for use with planning permissions

*These conditions should obviously be used with care and discretion, and adapted as necessary to suit particular circumstances. For further commentary, see **10.4.1** and **15.9**.*

Outline permissions

[A1.] The plans and particulars submitted in accordance with condition [xx] above shall include a plan showing the location of every tree which has any stem with a diameter of over 75 millimetres (measured over the bark at a point 1.5 metres above ground level), and either:

(a) is on the application site; or

(b) is on adjacent or nearby land and is located so that the application site includes any land within the outermost limit of its crown spread or any land at a distance from the tree equal to half its height,

allocating a reference number to each such tree, and showing which of those trees are to be retained following the completion of the development hereby permitted.

[A2.] The plans and particulars submitted in accordance with condition [xx] above shall include, either on the plan submitted in accordance with Condition [A1] or on a separate plan, in relation to each tree indicated on that plan as being retained:

(a) the extent of its crown spread;

(b) its approximate height; and

(c) an area surrounding each tree, the boundary of which is below the outermost limit of its crown spread, or at distance equal to half its height, whichever is the further from the tree.

[A3.] The plans and particulars submitted in accordance with condition [xx] above shall include, either on the plan submitted in accordance with Condition [A1] or on a separate plan or schedule, in relation to each tree indicated on that plan as being retained:

(a) its species, the diameter of its main stem or stems (measured over the bark at a point 1.5 metres above ground level);

(b) an assessment of its general health and stability and of any significant features likely to be relevant to its future health and stability;

(c) an indication of any topping, lopping or other works proposed to be carried out to it during the course of the development; and

(d) details of any proposed changes of ground level or other works to be carried out within the area referred to in paragraph (c) of Condition [A2].

[A4.] The plans and particulars submitted in accordance with condition [xx] above shall include, either on the plan submitted in accordance with Condition [A1] or on a separate plan, details of every tree, shrub and hedge to be planted, including its proposed location, its species, its size at the date of planting, and the approximate date when it is to be planted.

Detailed permissions: approval of details prior to the start of works

[A5.] No works or development shall be carried out until the local planning authority has approved in writing the full details of which trees and shrubs are to be retained [, by reference to a plan showing the location of every tree which has any stem with a diameter of over 75 millimetres (measured over the bark at a point 1.5 metres above ground level), and either:

(a) is on the application site; or

(b) is on adjacent or nearby land and is located so that the application site includes any land within the outermost limit of its crown spread or any land at a distance from the tree equal to half its height].

[A6.] No works or development shall be carried out until the local planning authority has approved in writing [, either by reference to the plan submitted in accordance with Condition [A5] or otherwise,] the full details of every tree, shrub and hedge to be planted, including its proposed location, its species, its size at the date of planting, and the approximate date when it is to be planted.

Protection of trees during the works

[A7.] The protection of any existing tree to be retained in accordance with [the approved plans and particulars] [Condition [A5]] shall achieved as follows:

(a) no equipment, machinery or materials shall be brought onto the site for the purposes of the development until fencing has been erected in accordance with [those plans and particulars] [*or* plans and particulars which shall have been previously approved by the Council in writing];

(b) if that fencing is broken or removed during the course of carrying out the development, it shall be promptly repaired or replaced to the satisfaction of the Council;

(c) the fencing shall be maintained in position to the satisfaction of the Council, until all equipment, machinery and surplus materials have been moved from the site; and

(d) within any area fenced in accordance with this condition, nothing shall be stored, placed or disposed of on above or below the ground, the ground level shall not be altered, no excavations shall be made, nor shall any fires be lit, without the prior written consent of the Council.

Planting of new trees

[A8.] Trees and shrubs shall be planted in accordance with the details approved by the Council under Condition [A6].

Protection of trees after the completion of the development

[A9.] No works shall be carried out, within a period of [two years] from the completion of the development, for the cutting down, felling, uprooting, removal, destruction, lopping or topping of any of the trees or shrubs retained in accordance with Condition [A5] or planted in accordance with Condition [A6], or any tree or shrub planted as a replacement for any of those trees or shrubs, other than as may be approved by the Council in writing.

[A10.] If, within a period of [two years] from the completion of the development, any of the trees or shrubs retained in accordance with Condition [A5] or planted in accordance with Condition [A6], or any tree or shrub planted as a replacement for any of those trees or shrubs, is cut down, felled, uprooted, removed, or destroyed, or dies or becomes, in the opinion of the Council, seriously damaged or defective,

(a) the Council shall be notified as soon as reasonably practicable; and
(b) another tree or shrub of the same species shall be planted at the same location, at a time agreed in writing by the Council,

unless the Council agrees in writing to dispense with or vary the requirement.

Appendix B

Sample conditions for use with consents under tree preservation orders

These conditions should obviously be used with care and discretion, and adapted as necessary to suit particular circumstances.

Scope of consent

[B1.] The works hereby consented shall consist only of those detailed in the application, as qualified by these conditions, and shall be completed in their entirety.

[B2.] The works hereby consented shall consist only of those detailed in the application, [as amended by the letter of [*date*]] [and shown on drawing number [*specify*].

[B3.] This consent does not authorise the works to [*or* felling of] trees [*specify*] which formed part of the application.

[B4.] The pruning works shall consist of the following:

    (a) the cleaning out of any stumps, dead wood, hung up branches and climbers, the removal of sucker growth, plus trunk cleaning to a height of [*specify*] metres above ground level;

    (b) crown lifting to a maximum height above ground level of [*specify*] metres;

    (c) lateral crown reduction by [*specify*] %, including reshaping and balancing;

    (d) crown reduction by a maximum of [*specify*] %;

    (e) crown thinning throughout the crown to a maximum of [*specify*] %, [inclusive of the above work];

    (f) reshaping and balancing.

[B5.] The works shall not include:

    (a) the removal of any branch of which any part is more than [*specify*] millimetres in diameter, measured over the bark;

    (b) any pollarding or topping;

    (c) any reduction in the height of the tree.

Approval of details prior to the start of works

[B6.]   No works to any trees shall be carried out until the local planning authority has approved in writing the full details (including location, species and size at planting) of every tree and shrub and hedge to be planted by way of replacement for those to be felled under the terms of this consent, including its proposed location, its species, its size at the date of planting, and the approximate date when it is to be planted.

Method of carrying out the permitted works

[B7.]   All works shall be carried out by an appropriately experienced and qualified tree surgeon.

[B8.]   All works shall be carried out so as to conform to British Standard 3998:1989, *Recommendations for Tree Works*.

[B9.]   The stumps of the felled tree[s] shall not be chemically treated [and shall be grubbed or ground out and removed at the time of felling].

[B10.] The stumps of the felled tree[s] shall not be grubbed or ground out or removed, but shall be treated with an appropriate herbicide, to prevent regrowth.

[B11.] The works hereby permitted are to be completed within two years of the date of this consent [unless the Council agrees in writing to dispense with this requirement].

Planting of new trees

[B12.] Trees [and shrubs] shall be planted in accordance with the details approved by the Council under Condition [B6].

[B13.] Trees [and shrubs] shall be planted to replace the trees to be felled under the terms of this consent, in accordance with details supplied by the applicant in the letter to the local planning authority of [*date*]] [and shown on drawing number [*specify*]].

[B14.] The replacement trees to be planted in accordance with the above condition[s] are to be planted in the next planting season following felling.

Protection of new trees after the completion of the works

[B15.] No works shall be carried out, within a period of [two years] from the completion of the development, for the cutting down, felling, uprooting, removal, destruction, lopping or topping of any of the trees or shrubs or planted in accordance with Condition [B12] [B13], or any tree or shrub planted as a replacement for any of those trees or shrubs, other than as may be approved by the Council in writing.

[B16.] If, within a period of [two years] from the completion of the development, any of the trees or shrubs or planted in accordance with Condition [B12] [B13], or any tree or shrub planted as a replacement for any of those trees or shrubs, is cut down, felled, uprooted, removed, or destroyed, or dies or becomes, in the opinion of the Council, seriously damaged or defective,

(a) the Council shall be notified as soon as reasonably practicable,
(b) another tree or shrub of the same species shall be planted at the same location, at a time agreed in writing by the Council,

unless the Council agrees in writing to dispense with or vary the requirement.

Appendix C

Penalties for criminal offences

A number of statutes, referred to at various points in this book, provide for certain activities in certain circumstances to be criminal offences. Where such a statute only refers to the maximum penalty on summary conviction – that is, following trial in a magistrates' court – the offence is referred to as a "summary offence". Where a higher maximum penalty is provided in the event of conviction on indictment – that is, following trial in the Crown Court (by a jury) – the offence is referred to as a "triable either way" offence.

In either case, maximum penalties following summary conviction are fixed by reference to the standard scale prescribed by section 37 of the Criminal Justice Act 1982; different amounts may be substituted by order under section 143 of the Magistrates' Courts Act 1980 (as amended by section 48 of the 1982 Act). The current scale, fixed at October 1, 1992 by section 17 of the Criminal Justice Act 1971, is as follows:

Level on the scale	Amount of fine
1	£200
2	£500
3	£1,000
4	£2,500
5	£5,000.

By virtue of section 32 of the Magistrates' Courts Act 1980, where a statutory provision refers to "the statutory maximum", that is equal to the "prescribed sum", which is currently £5,000.

Appendix D

Relevant organisations

GOVERNMENT DEPARTMENTS

Office of the Deputy Prime Minister,

Urban Policy Unit (UPU 2), Eland House, Bressenden Place,
London, SW1E 5DU
Phone: 020-7944-3000 (public enquiry office)
Web-site: www.urban.odpm.gov.uk/greenspace/trees/index.htm
(tree preservation orders, trees generally, and high hedges: see 16.2.8)

Department for Environment, Food and Rural Affairs,

Conservation Management Division, Area 4D, Ergon House, 17 Smith Square,
London SW1P 3JR
Phone: 020-7238-5667
Web-site: www.defra.gov.uk
(hedgerows)

National Assembly for Wales
(Cynulliad Cenedlaethol Cymru)

Planning Division 1A, Welsh Assembly Government, Cathays Park,
Cardiff, CF10 3NQ
Phone: 029-2082-3883
Web-site: www.wales.gov.uk
(tree preservation orders, trees generally, and high hedges)

FORESTRY COMMISSION

(contact the Headquarters or National Offices for details of District Offices and Conservatories)

Headquarters and National Office (Scotland),

231 Corstorphine Road, Edinburgh, EH12 7AT
Phone: 0131-334-0303
Web-site: www.forestry.gov.uk

National Office (England),

Great Eastern House, Tenison Road, Cambridge, CB1 2DU
Phone: 01223-314546

National Office (Wales),

Victoria Terrace, Aberystwyth, Ceredigion, SY23 2DQ
Phone: 01970-625866

OTHER SOURCES OF GENERAL ADVICE

Tree Advice Trust
(formerly Arboricultural Advisory and Information Service)

Alice Holt Lodge, Wrecclesham, Farnham, Surrey GU10 4LH
Phone: 01420-22022
Web-site: www.treeadviceservice.org.uk

The Tree Council

51 Catherine Place, London SW1E 6DY
Phone: 020-7828-9928
Web-site: treecouncil.org.uk

English Nature

Northminster House, Northminster Road, Peterborough,
Cambridgeshire, PE1 1UA
Phone: 01733-455000
Web-site: www.english-nature.org.uk
(contact the national office at Peterborough for details of regional offices)

PROFESSIONAL ORGANISATIONS

Arboricultural Association,

Ampfield House, Ampfield, Romsey, Hampshire, SO51 9PA

Phone: 01794-368717
Web-site: www.trees.org.uk

Institute of Chartered Foresters,

7a St Colme Street, Edinburgh, EH3 6AA
Phone: 0131-225-2705
Web-site: www.charteredforesters.org

International Society of Arboriculture, UK and Ireland Chapter

148 Hydes Road, Wednesbury, West Midlands, WS10 0DR
Phone: 0121-556-8302

National Urban Forestry Unit

The Science Park, Stafford Road, Wolverhampton WV10 9RT
Phone: 01902-828600
Web-site: www.nufu.org.uk

Royal Forestry Society,

102 High Street, Tring, Hertfordshire, HP23 4AF
Phone: 01442-822028
Web-site: www.rfs.org.uk

RELEVANT VOLUNTARY BODIES

Ancient Tree Forum,

c/o Woodland Trust, Autumn Park, Dysart Road, Grantham,
Lincolnshire, NG31 6LL
Phone: 01476-581111
Web-site: www.woodland-trust.org.uk/ancient-tree-forum

Bat Conservation Trust,

15 Cloisters House, 8 Battersea Park Road, London, SW8 4BG
Phone: 0845-130-0228
Web-site: www.bats.org.uk

Garden History Society,

70 Cowcross Street, London, EC1M 6EJ
Phone: 020-7608-2409
Web-site: www.gardenhistorysociety.org

National Trust,

36 Queen Anne's Gate, London, SW1H 9AS
Phone: 020-7222-9251
Web-site: www.nationaltrust.org.uk

Woodland Trust,

Autumn Park, Dysart Road, Grantham, Lincolnshire, NG31 6LL
Phone: 01476-581111
Web-site: www.woodland-trust.org.uk

Index